Violent Crime

Analysts have long noted that some societies have much higher rates of criminal violence than others. They also have observed that the risk of being a victim or a perpetrator of violent crime varies considerably from one individual to another. In societies with ethnically and racially diverse populations, some ethnic and racial groups have been reported to have higher rates of violent offending and victimization than other groups. This exceptional collection of original essays explores the extent and causes of racial and ethnic differences in violent crime in the United States and several other contemporary societies.

Divided into three thematic sections, the volume begins with empirical analyses of homicide for several large urban areas in the United States. Chapters in the second section examine patterns of domestic violence in the United States, youth violence in Canada and New Zealand, and racially motivated violence in England and Wales. The authors conclude their study by taking on the task of explaining racial and ethnic disparity in rates of violent crime. In the final seven chapters, they critically examine the credibility of the evidence of group differences in rates of violent crime and debate the merits of many of the popular theories that have been put forth to explain them.

Darnell F. Hawkins is Professor of African-American Studies, Sociology, and Criminal Justice at the University of Illinois at Chicago. He is the editor of *Homicide among Black Americans* (1986), *Ethnicity, Race, and Crime: Perspectives across Time and Place* (1995), and *Crime Control and Social Justice: The Delicate Balance* (forthcoming), and he has published more than forty articles. He is a founding member of the National Consortium on Violence Research (NCOVR).

Cambridge Studies in Criminology

Editors

Alfred Blumstein, *H. John Heinz School of Public Policy and Management, Carnegie Mellon University*

David Farrington, *Institute of Criminology, University of Cambridge*

Other books in the series:

Violent Crime

Assessing Race and Ethnic Differences

Edited by

Darnell F. Hawkins

University of Illinois at Chicago

CAMBRIDGE
UNIVERSITY PRESS

PUBLISHED BY THE PRESS SYNDICATE OF THE UNIVERSITY OF CAMBRIDGE
The Pitt Building, Trumpington Street, Cambridge, United Kingdom

CAMBRIDGE UNIVERSITY PRESS
The Edinburgh Building, Cambridge CB2 2RU, UK
40 West 20th Street, New York, NY 10011-4211, USA
477 Williamstown Road, Port Melbourne, VIC 3207, Australia
Ruiz de Alarcón 13, 28014 Madrid, Spain
Dock House, The Waterfront, Cape Town 8001, South Africa

http://www.cambridge.org

First published 2003

Printed in the United States of America

Typeface ITC New Baskerville 10/12 pt.   *System* LaTeX 2_ε [TB]

A catalog record for this book is available from the British Library.

Library of Congress Cataloging in Publication Data

Violent crime : assessing race and ethnic differences / edited by Darnell Hawkins.
     p.   cm. – (Cambridge studies in criminology)
    Includes bibliographical references and index.
    ISBN 0-521-62297-2 – ISBN 0-521-62674-9 (pbk.)
    1. Crime and race – United States.   2. Minorities – Crimes against –
United States.   3. Violent crimes – United States.   4. United States – Race
relations.   5. United States – Ethnic relations.   6. Crime and race.
7. Minorities – Crimes against.   8. Violent crimes.   I. Hawkins, Darnell
Felix, 1946–   II. Cambridge studies in criminology (Cambridge University Press)
HV6791 .V558   2003
364.2′56–dc21   2002066515

ISBN 0 521 62297 2 hardback
ISBN 0 521 62674 9 paperback

Contents

Contributors

Frankie Y. Bailey, *University of Albany*
Ben Bowling, *University of Surrey*
Marino A. Bruce, *University of Wisconsin-Madison*
Chanchalat Chanhatasilpa, *University of Maryland*
Jeanette Covington, *Rutgers University*
Kelly R. Damphousse, *University of Oklahoma*
Margaret E. Ensminger, *Johns Hopkins University*
David P. Farrington, *University of Cambridge*
David M. Fergusson, *University of Otago*
John Hagan, *Northwestern University*
Darnell F. Hawkins, *University of Illinois at Chicago*
Robert J. Jagers, *Howard University*
Calvin C. Johnson, *University of Pennsylvania*
Rolf Loeber, *University of Pittsburgh*
Ramiro Martinez, Jr., *Florida International University*
Jacqueline Mattis, *University of Michigan*
Bill McCarthy, *University of California at Davis*
Paula D. McClain, *Duke University*
Joan McCord, *Temple University*
William Oliver, *Indiana University*
Coretta Phillips, *London School of Economics*
Beth E. Richie, *University of Illinois at Chicago*
Marc Riedel, *Southern Illinois University*
Vincent J. Roscigno, *The Ohio State University*
Harold M. Rose, *University of Wisconsin-Milwaukee*

James F. Short, Jr., *Washington State University*
Evan Stark, *Rutgers University-Newark*
Magda Stouthamer-Loeber, *University of Pittsburgh*
Victoria E. Titterington, *Sam Houston State University*
Katrina Walker, *East Carolina University*

Foreword

James F. Short, Jr.

Despite impressive achievements, American criminology continues to suffer from a host of theoretical and methodological weaknesses. Among these, conceptualization and measurement of race and ethnicity, and of racial and ethnic behavioral differences, are major impediments to the advancement of knowledge. This is not unique to criminology, of course, but that neither excuses nor explains our failure to do a better job. Darnell Hawkins's introductory essay explores both the validity and the reliability of biological and social constructions of race – topics too long neglected by criminologists.

Importantly, this volume explores racial and ethnic distinctions beyond the familiar African-American/white, as well as recognizing that ethnic distinctions have achieved global importance in an increasingly mobile world.

The concentration of American criminologists on crime and criminals *in the United States* is a problem of long standing. This somewhat ethnocentric – not to say myopic – practice is not a major focus of the present volume, but research from Canada, New Zealand, and England and Wales adds a great deal to the book.

Ethnocentrism takes many forms and here again Darnell Hawkins and his colleagues are enlightening. Scholars in the social and behavioral sciences are notorious for conducting our research within the boundaries of our disciplines – this, despite the inherently interdisciplinary nature of criminology. Moreover, we tend to restrict our vision within narrowly defined methodological and theoretical preferences. Chapters in this volume approach racial and ethnic contexts of violence from a variety of disciplinary, methodological, and theoretical perspectives.

This book also addresses previously understudied problems, populations, and violence-related phenomena, such as the historical roots of codes of behavior that support or require violence, and of moral development, and the consequences of conceptual ambiguity and "race neutral" theory and research.

Finally, editor Darnell Hawkins issues a clear and unmistakable challenge: ideological biases and simplistic approaches to understanding violent crime have too long hampered both the acquisition of knowledge and efforts to control violence. Moving beyond these limitations requires that the contexts within which behaviors are defined as violent, as well as the contexts in which violence occurs, be understood.

These contributions are consistent with trends in all the social and behavioral sciences, and they are as necessary as they are important. The changing racial and ethnic character of the United States clearly requires a broader focus. In the past, data limitations have limited systematic comparison of races other than black and white, an irony that should escape no one in view of the presence, since European conquest of the continent, of large numbers of native populations and groups.

Part II continues the study of previously understudied populations by comparing native (aboriginal) and other youth in Canada and New Zealand, respectively. The former, by Bill McCarthy and John Hagan, builds on their earlier study of another understudied population – "street youth" (see Hagan and McCarthy, 1997). The international contribution to this rich mix of studies is further enhanced by treatment of "racist victimization" (most commonly referred to as "hate crimes" in the United States; see Jenness and Broad, 1997; Jacobs and Potter, 1998) in England and Wales.

Migrations of many types throughout the world (see Tonry, 1997) virtually ensure that future research will require even more subtle treatment of ethnic and racial distinctions and the contexts within which they exist, as these relate to crime and other behaviors.

In sum, editor Darnell Hawkins here broadens the focus of violence studies in a variety of ways. There is much to be learned in these pages. Readers should be warned, however, not to expect simple or easy answers to the puzzles here addressed. Contributors prudently acknowledge limitations in their data and in their ability to explain observed relationships. Although they break new ground in coverage of racial and ethnic groups, and in recognition of the importance of context, much research and more rigorous theoretical development will be required if knowledge of the important topics here addressed is to be advanced beyond its present relatively underdeveloped state.

Editor's Introduction

Darnell F. Hawkins

I am convinced that in the next century millions will cut each other's throat because of 1 or 2 degrees more or less of cephalic index.

> – Varcher de Lapouge, late 1880s, as quoted by Ruth Benedict, *Race: Science and Politics* (1940)

European expansion overseas, therefore, set the stage for racist dogmas and gave violent early expression to racial antipathies without propounding racism as a philosophy. Racism did not get its currency in modern thought until it was applied to conflicts in Europe – first to class conflicts and then to national. But it is possible to wonder whether the doctrine would have been proposed at all as explaining these latter conflicts – where, as we have seen, the dogma is so inept – if the basis for it had not been laid in the violent experience of racial prejudice on the frontier.

> – Ruth Benedict, *Race: Science and Politics* (1940)

Generally speaking, there has been an ethnic succession in all areas of crime, beginning with the Irish, who were the first identifiable minority to inhabit urban slums. In the 1860s *Harper Magazine* observed that the Irish "have so behaved themselves that nearly 75 percent of our criminals are Irish, that fully 75 percent of the crimes of violence committed among us are the work of Irishmen...." Speculation as to the causes of the alarming rate of crime among the Irish centered on ethnic traits, especially the intemperate disposition of the Irish "race."

> – Stephen Steinberg, *The Ethnic Myth: Race, Ethnicity, and Class in America* (1981, 1989)

Living in a culture of inequality, poverty, discrimination, racism, unemployment, and debasement of values, is humanly demeaning especially for blacks, a culture in which the very condition of being black is in some ways treated as a crime, a crime which leads to crime, because the only outlet for the resulting emotional frustration is its effect, namely, violence. In the culture of racism,

where so many are scarred and criminalized, the victims are euphemistically called "the race problem," implying that the victims are the cause of it. The latest solution to the problem by government is the threatened enlistment of thousands more police, and the building of more overcrowded prisons.
        – Ashley Montagu, *Man's Most Dangerous Myth:*
                The Fallacy of Race (1942, 1997)

Increased use of police power has been justified as necessary to combat civil disorder. But the paradox is that the violence that the police attempt to control is inspired in many instances by the police themselves. And more important, much of the violence in these situations is actually committed by the police.... The state, quite understandably, does not regard its own actions as violence, or if such actions are considered, they are defined at best as "legitimate violence." So it is that the looting of property during race "riots" is defined as violence by the state, but killing of looters is legitimate.
        – Richard Quinney, *The Social Reality of Crime* (1970)

In the U.S., Blacks are less than 13 percent of the population but have 50 percent of all arrests for assault and murder and 67 percent of all arrests for robbery.... On the other hand, Orientals are under-represented in U.S. crime statistics.... The same pattern is found in other countries. In London, England, Blacks make up 13 percent of the population, but account for 50 percent of the crime. A 1996 government commission in Ontario, Canada, reported that Blacks were five times more likely to go to jail than whites, and 10 times more likely than Orientals. In Brazil, there are 1.5 million Orientals, mostly Japanese whose ancestors went there as laborers in the 19th century, and who are the least represented in crime.... Studies find that Blacks are more aggressive and outgoing than Whites, while Whites are more aggressive and outgoing than Orientals.
        – J. Philippe Rushton, *Race, Evolution, and Behavior* (1999)

Contributors to this volume were asked to provide empirical analyses, theoretical essays, or state-of-the-art reviews aimed primarily at answering two major questions:

- Are there racial and ethnic differences in rates of criminal violence?[1]
- To the extent that differences can be shown to exist, what are the causes of the observed disparity?

The result is a collection of essays divided into three major sections. The first part of the volume contains five chapters that explore ethnic and racial

---

[1] Many contemporary analysts of race and ethnicity also question the idea that terms such as "ethnic" and "racial" denote different social constructs. They suggest that the word "ethnic," as used here to imply cultural distinctions *within* racial categories, may be problematic to the extent that it presumes that cultural differences do not also mark the boundaries between races. In their view, the label "ethnic" can be used to denote differences traditionally thought of as "racial."

differences for homicide offending and victimization in several urban areas of the United States. In the second section are two chapters that examine racial differences in rates of domestic violence in the United States. Also included are three very informative essays that explore ethnic and racial differences for both lethal and nonlethal forms of violence in Canada, New Zealand, England, and Wales. The final section contains seven chapters that seek and offer explanations for ethnic and racial differences through the use of data analysis and critiques of extant theory. Much of this discussion is aimed at explaining disproportionate rates of violence among African Americans.

The queries to which the authors respond arise out of a long-standing and often highly politicized research tradition within the social and behavioral sciences. Spanning more than a century, the prophetic and pointed observations at the start of this introduction illustrate for the reader the broader historical, political, and socioeconomic contexts within which the chapters contained in this volume are inevitably and inextricably embedded. They also reveal quite clearly the ideological and epistemological disagreement, lack of resolution, and polemics that have resulted from earlier attempts to probe the questions addressed by the present volume. Reflecting their historical link to the promulgation of racist and ethnocentric social policy within and across nations, scholarly and public discussions of race and ethnicity have always been marked by emotion and contentiousness. Similar tensions related to social class, race, ethnicity, politics, and public policy have also permeated scholarly and public discourse on crime and punishment, both during the past and today. Thus, the question of ethnic and racial difference in rates of involvement in criminal violence, the theme of this volume, brings to the fore a combination of the considerable discord that has permeated these two interrelated and highly contested areas of public and scholarly concern.[2]

---

[2] Many current analysts of race, crime, and justice issues, especially those conducting research in the United States, complain that the contentiousness and political turmoil that often surround this area of research detract from efforts to conduct research that reflects scientific objectivity and an unbridled search for knowledge. Some cite such recent incidents as the cancellation during the early 1990s of a conference on the biology of violence to be convened by an agency of the U.S. federal government after objections from liberal and minority interest groups as evidence of the depths of the current problem. By contrast, even a cursory review of the history of such research in the United States reveals that these tensions are hardly new. Many of the earliest investigators in this area of study, most of whom are now heralded as icons of an objective and politically unbiased research tradition, worked amid the scholarly and public misconceptions of their era. Indeed, their work on this topic arose in response to such misconceptions. Pioneers such as W. E. B. Du Bois, Thorsten Sellin, Edwin Sutherland, Clifford Shaw, and Howard McKay used their work to counter perceptions of the innate criminality of African Americans and southern and eastern Europeans. These perceptions were, of course, an integral part of the social Darwinist and eugenicist movements of the period.

Contexts and Cautions

Although the use of racial categories to distinguish and label various groupings of human beings has been widely accepted in Western and non-Western
societies for many centuries, important questions regarding the validity and
utility of the notion or concept of "race" remain. Challenges to its presumed meaning and relevance can now be found across a wide range of
disciplines, including literary criticism, jurisprudence, and the traditional
social science disciplines of anthropology, psychology, and sociology. Building on the pioneering efforts of Ruth Benedict, Ashley Montagu, and other
early anthropologists, many contemporary social analysts, some referred to
as "critical race theorists," reject what are labeled "essentialist" or "biological determinist" views of race differences. They insist instead that race is a
"social construct," the origins of which reflect less an attempt to *objectively*
classify humankind than an exercise in social control and dominion. Critics
also note that most of the social behaviors that are linked etiologically to
racial difference by some social analysts are very complex phenomena whose
variability across groups cannot be attributed to "race" differences alone.

Beyond these widely cited social scientific challenges and reconceptual-
izations of the notion of race, potential critiques of traditional racial categorizations also have come from the biological sciences. Many contemporary
medical scientists and researchers continue to see some utility in racial labels. Aware of the large racial differences often seen in rates of illness and
death from various diseases, researchers have used clinical trials that take
into account the race or ethnicity of subjects in an attempt to determine if
there are group differences in genetic susceptibility to some diseases. Similar trials have been used to determine the extent to which groups differ
in their responses to medications and treatment protocols. Findings from
some of these studies have proven to be quite promising; but researchers
have been quick to note that global racial categories, such as those based
on skin color or other superficial markers, may prove in the long run to
be of only limited use for such purposes. The ongoing Human Genome
Project is likely to show that racial differences are not entirely a figment of
the "biological imagination," but preliminary findings from this important
scientific breakthrough may have already begun to reveal the inadequacy of
simplistic, global, phenotype-based racial categories.

Within the criminal justice arena, similar challenges to conventional ideas
and beliefs can be noted. Over the last several decades, many criminologists,
often labeled as conflict theorists or critical criminologists, have challenged
the meanings assigned to many of the core concepts employed in this area
of research. For these analysts, "crime" (including criminal violence) does
not represent a phenomenon whose definition is uniformly clear or uncon-
testable. Similarly, the labels "criminal" and "criminality" are said to denote

neither fixed traits nor conceptions that are divorced from the political economy and power differentials found in a given society. In this regard, they have observed that conceptions of what constitutes a "crime" often vary considerably across race, ethnic, and class boundaries, from one nation or society to another, and from one era to another within the same society. Furthermore, even if one accepts the idea that definitions of criminal conduct flow from widely agreed-on norms and values, work conducted within the conflict perspective also reminds us of the considerable bias and exercise of discretion that is frequently observed in law enforcement and in the administration of justice. For researchers in this tradition, questions of whether racial differences in crime and violence exist, and the offering of reasons for any observed differences, often cannot be fully disentangled from questions of bias, power, privilege, and protection of group interest. See Taylor, Walton, and Young (1973) for an excellent review of research in this tradition in the United States and Europe. As Quinney (1970) notes above, whether an act of violence is seen as a crime or not is often in the eye of the (powerful) beholder, or his or her agent.

Other analysts of race, crime, and justice, including those commentators whose observations appear at the beginning of this introduction, offer other necessary cautions to those who would take on the tasks assigned to contributors to this volume. These cautions derive from our knowledge of the history of American and world race relations and its relevance to the topic at hand. The study of racial difference in the tendency to resort to violence is complicated by the fact that acts of violence and aggression, whether at the level of the individual, the crowd, or the nation-state, have routinely marked the presumed boundaries between racial and ethnic groups. Indeed, violence has been used to "define" these groups and, once defined, to enforce public and private adherence to such labeling. Throughout human history, particularly in instances of societal attempts at *ethnic differentiation*, actual social and cultural differences between groups are often trivial at the start of this process. Any profound differences that do emerge appear gradually over time and typically in the aftermath of repeated acts of organized intergroup violence. In addition, although geography and climate have played a major role in shaping over many millennia what are now perceived as racial differences, recent human history has seen numerous instances within multiracial societies where violence has been used to prevent interracial sexual contact and intermarriage. These are, of course, obvious means of reducing what is perceived as racial "difference."

Thus, at first glance to ask whether there are racial and ethnic differences in levels of violent offending and victimization appears to beg the question. Violence has been the tool by which some racial and ethnic groups have conquered others. Violence also has been instrumental in subsequent efforts by such groups to amass the social, economic, and political capital required to maintain dominance, including the power to label individuals as members of one racial or ethnic group as opposed to another. Given the historically grounded link between violence and ethnic or racial differentiation, it is plausible that though perceived racial and ethnic groups may differ in other ways, the resort to violence may not be a behavioral trait that distinguishes them. Critical criminological analysts remind us that the crimes of the powerless are more numerous than those of the privileged only if we fail to remember that "a crime by another name – (is still a crime)" (Reiman, 1984).

Yet, it is also true, as Fanon (1967, 1968) has argued, that under conditions of prolonged and profound subordination, perhaps especially in societies where "race" marks lines of social cleavage, much of the violence of the oppressed tends to turn inward against members of their own group. At the same time, the institutionalization of group oppression and disadvantage may reduce over time the need for ongoing violent, militaristic repression on the part of the dominant group. This observation may have much relevance for our understanding of the comparatively high rates of interpersonal violence that are observed among "minorities" in many industrialized nations and in many developing, postcolonial societies of the world at the turn of the twenty-first century. The problem of within–race and within–ethnic group violence among disadvantaged populations is a theme that is explored in each of the three sections of the present volume. The persisting problem of internecine violence among African Americans is of particular concern for contributors to the volume.

Despite such critiques of traditional conceptions of race, crime, and criminal violence, many researchers have continued to use primarily "essentialist" conceptions of race in an attempt to explain group differences for a wide variety of behaviors and social attributes. These include intelligence, athletic ability, criminal conduct, human aggression, sexual conduct, family formation and functioning, and economic and cultural progress and achievement. In recent years, views of the relationship between race and violence can be found in the work of such researchers as Wilson and Herrnstein (1985), Herrnstein and Murray (1994), and Rushton (1995, 1999). All have suggested that racial differences in rates of violence likely reflect innate predispositions to such behavior. Although considered controversial, their views have found considerable acceptance among some communities of scholars and among members of the general public. Theirs and other, similar investigations published over the last four decades illustrate quite clearly that despite continuing criticisms of traditional conceptions of race and criminality, many continue to believe in the existence of separate and distinct "races" of humankind, whose biological differences are linked to, among other things, varying levels of violent and aggressive behavior. Although many social scientists have chosen to ignore or downplay the importance of these views of race and crime, they remain part of the mix of competing explanations for any differences in rates of violent conduct observed across those groupings said to be the world's "races." The three sets of authors cited above have provided data, research findings, and lines of argument that are neither strikingly original nor without conceptual and methodological flaws. In each instance, however, through their critical and often detailed examinations of alternative hypotheses, they have succeeded in highlighting the very real inadequacies and weaknesses of the assortment of "environmental" theories favored by their critics as explanations for racial and ethnic differences. Therein lies their potential contribution to the literature in this developing area of research.

Coverage and Scope of Volume

In my earlier work on the subject of race and ethnic differences in rates of crime and violence, I have staked out clear ideological stances (Hawkins, 1986, 1991, 1993, 1994, 1995b, 1997). Many of these stances are evident in my commentary in this introduction. However, two major nonideological themes run consistently through all of my own work. One is the proposition that social scientists who conduct research on this topic must first clearly delineate what we know *and do not know* about the extent of such group differences. I have cautioned that much remains unknown about the *true* extent of ethnic racial disparity for the *full range of behaviors* defined as crimes or violence, and across the *multiplicity of racial and ethnic* groups that reside in modern industrial societies such as the United States, and increasingly, Western Europe. A second major theme has been the suggestion that where wide racial and ethnic disparity is shown to exist, as in the United States both during the past and today, social scientists must move beyond mere documentation of such difference to attempt to determine its causes. Whereas these are the avowed goals of all who study race, crime, and justice, numerous observers have noted our failure over the years to accomplish this seemingly straightforward task.

Given my observations in this introduction, some readers may question the omission of chapters that provide data and detailed discussion of each of the multifaceted dimensions of the race-ethnicity-violence nexus that I have sought to describe. Because no single volume can assemble the full array of contributions needed to provide a truly comprehensive view of the interplay among race, ethnicity, and violence, certain decisions regarding coverage had to be made. Both practical considerations and matters of interest guided those decisions. Authors were asked to provide chapters that would explore the problem of *interpersonal criminal* violence, typically those acts referred to as *common law* offenses in the United States and other nations influenced by Anglo-Saxon legal traditions. These are the forms of violent behavior that have been the subject of most past criminological research on racial and ethnic difference, for example, see Hindelang (1978). Increasingly, the study of race differences in interpersonal violence also encompasses work on violence and aggression conducted within the behavioral sciences and in public health. With the exception of the public health arena, researchers within these traditions have tended to focus on racial and ethnic differences among those who *commit* acts of violence, as opposed to *victims*. A more comprehensive examination of racial differences that incorporates greater attention to group-level violence, for example, mob actions, riots, revolts, and also subtler forms of violence committed by the privileged or on their behalf must await future volumes. I do include in the present volume two very insightful chapters by Ben Bowling and Coretta Phillips and Frankie Bailey. They explore important dimensions of intergroup violence in England and the United States. See Kelman and Hamilton (1989) for an informative social psychological study of "crimes of obedience," a category that includes many governmentally sanctioned forms of interpersonal violence.[3]

For many other readers, my discussion of the historical and ideological origins of research and public discourse on race, ethnicity, crime, and violence may seem informative, but its usefulness for improving our understanding of *contemporary* patterns of interpersonal violence may be questioned. In response, I would suggest that the chapters in this volume offer much to show that knowledge of the past always informs our understanding of the present. I also believe that a reflexive analytic approach (Gouldner, 1970) that explores the assumptions and intellectual legacies that underpin our scientific inquiries is extremely valuable. I include in the volume several chapters that explore racial and ethnic differences for both violent offending and victimization in societies other than the United States (e.g., see McCarthy and Hagan, Chapter 6; Fergusson, Chapter 7; and Bowling and Phillips, Chapter 8). These contributions illustrate for the reader the relevance of the cross-national perspectives offered by the commentators whose observations are cited at the start of this introduction. Their inclusion also reflects my view that interpersonal violence, in all its various forms, represents at the dawn of the twenty-first century a problem of global magnitude. Although violence rates have dropped in the United States over the last decade, they remain at levels far exceeding those found in most other industrialized nations. In addition, much evidence suggests that rates of interpersonal, criminal violence are rapidly increasing in many other parts of the globe, including portions of Eastern Europe, South Africa, Brazil, Mexico, and other parts of Latin America.

---

[3] The term "interpersonal violence" does not necessarily exclude all forms of intergroup conflict and aggression. What is currently labeled "hate crime" and many other violent encounters involving small groups of individuals are essentially interpersonal in nature.

The contributors to the present volume have had to overcome several hurdles. My own earlier work (1986) and recent essays by LaFree (1995) and Sampson and Wilson (1995) have noted the reluctance of contemporary criminologists and other social scientists in the United States to engage in discussions of the extent and causes of racial differences in crime and violence. For quite understandable reasons, some of which have been described in this introduction, race and race differences remain emotionally and politically charged and divisive topics in the United States and in many other societies around the world. Reflecting this contentiousness, the scientific study of race, ethnicity, and violence must be conducted in a society in which racial and ethnic stereotyping often leads to perceptions of unequal levels of violence across groups even in the absence of reliable or conclusive data. For example, a 1990 survey of a nationwide sample of Americans revealed that 56 percent of white respondents described African Americans as more prone to violence than whites. Latinos were also described as more violent than whites or Asians (Bobo and Kluegel, 1997). These beliefs may reflect the effects of persisting racial stereotypes on perceptions among the public, an awareness by respondents of the wide racial disparity that exists in rates of criminal violence in the United States, or a combination of both. There is some evidence that due to the nature of media coverage of crime, many Americans believe rates of crime and violence among African Americans to be higher than they actually are. The potential misuse of social scientific research to further foster such stereotypes may be one factor contributing to the disinclination of many contemporary researchers to engage in research and discussion of racial differences in crime.

For researchers who overcome their hesitation and are willing to undertake such studies, significant barriers to the collection of complete and reliable data exist, many of which are described in various chapters of this volume (see also Short, 1997). Race and crime data–gathering efforts reflect the biases and policy concerns of government agencies and the interests that they represent. For example, in the United States today, unlike during the past when "white" immigration was a matter of public debate, there are significant practical and political barriers to the collection by government of data for persons of European heritage. As a result, crime and violence data do not exist for most of the diverse white ethnic groupings found in the nation. For social scientists pondering the questions posed at the start of this introduction, such data would be invaluable, as would data sources that would allow for the calculation of rates of crime and violence for the diverse ethnic groups that comprise Asian Americans, Native Americans, Latinos, and, increasingly, African Americans. Among other uses, such data might help social scientists test various theories that posit the importance of cultural and subcultural differences for explaining group differences in rates of violence. Almost every contribution to the present volume alludes to or explicitly explores the significance of cultural and subcultural differences in explaining racial and ethnic variations in rates of violence.[4]

Despite inadequate data and the very real potential for distortion and misuse of findings, social scientists in the United States, Western Europe, and other parts of the world have begun in recent years to confront head-on the questions surrounding race and ethnic differences in crime and violence. Several notable edited or authored volumes have appeared in just the last few years (e.g., see Hawkins, 1995; Marshall, 1997; McCord, 1997; Short, 1997; and Tonry, 1997). Each volume has shown the need to engage in more and more sophisticated research and to mine alternative and previously overlooked sources of data on race and ethnic differences in crime and violence. The present volume, the first devoted in its entirety to exploring the multiple dimensions of the nexus of race, ethnicity, and *violence*, builds on those earlier efforts with a full awareness of some of the limitations of the present work, as well as the work that preceded it. While marking an excellent start to dialogue in this very important area of criminological and race relations research, contributors to this volume are unanimous in their belief that there is much work to be done. Definitive answers to the questions posed earlier do not come easily, often because of the paucity of data available and partly due to the very complexity of the research designs needed to fully explore racial and ethnic differences and to test rival hypotheses.

Much of that complexity is evident when one takes note of both long-standing and newly emerging findings and facts from this area of research. For example, explanations that are grounded in the view that *either* biological *or* abiding cultural differences across groups explain ethnic and racial disparity in rates of interpersonal violence have long had to contend with a variety of seemingly anomalous findings. Among these are studies that show substantial variation in the rates of violence *within* demarcated racial and ethnic groupings. The arguments of Rushton (1995, 1999) and Herrnstein and Murray (1994) are challenged by studies that show much variation in rates of interpersonal violence among persons of African ancestry in the United States and Africa in the past (Bohannan, 1960) and within the black population of the United States today (Hawkins, 1999). As in the past, within-race analyses pose serious challenges to theories that posit the existence of large and innate race differences in behavior. As shown in the present volume, apart from the example of African Americans, many other within-race and between-race differences in levels of interpersonal violence in the United States also exist and require explanation. Many have not been explored due to an absence of reliable race- and ethnicity-specific crime data and the resulting tendency of American criminologists to focus almost

---

[4] Limited data on both race and ethnicity in Canada and Western Europe also hamper research efforts in those areas of the world.

exclusively on the study of black-white differences (Hawkins, 1999). Within-race and within-ethnic group analyses, such as those conducted in several chapters in the present volume, also raise questions regarding the applicability of many theories and explanations that are based on notions of economic disadvantage or culture.

Explaining change over time has proven to be a problem for most efforts at theory making within the social sciences. Several major temporal shifts in levels of interpersonal violence in Europe and America also may suggest that many of the currently competing theories of ethnic and racial difference may require amendment or revision. For example, a sharp rise and gradual decline in rates of criminal violence in Western European societies and America over the last four to five centuries has been reported by Gurr (1977) and others. Other studies have shown a decline in rates of violence among white ethnics and Asian Americans in the United States during the last two centuries or less (Lane, 1979, 1986, 1997; Gurr, 1989; Monkkonnen, 1995; Steinberg, 1995; Hawkins, 1993, 1999). Without modifications, many widely cited social theories that posit the importance of culture, subculture, economic deprivation, structural disadvantage, or biological difference appear to be inadequate for accounting for such change.

Findings from contemporary Europe and other industrialized nations offer similar etiological challenges. Although much of the work on this topic in these regions has just begun, early studies may suggest that many of the explanations long associated with the study of group differences in the United States may not be applicable. Group differences in rates of crime and violence observed in those areas of the world do not appear to be easily explained by traditional notions of minority versus majority, white versus nonwhite, and possibly economically disadvantaged versus advantaged (Marshall, 1997; Tonry, 1997). My own work and that of Martinez (1999) on homicide trends has suggested that many puzzles remain in terms of explaining the ethnic and racial distribution of lethal violence and its change over time in the United States (Hawkins, 1999).

Further complicating and informing efforts to explain the racial and ethnic patterning of interpersonal violence are two distinct, but increasingly interconnected, streams of research that have examined characteristics *of the individual offender* and the immediate *contexts and environments* in which offenders live and in which acts of violence occur. Studies focusing on the former have examined traditional social and personal correlates of interpersonal offending as well as the neuropsychological and neurochemical bases for differences between individuals. These studies are far more sophisticated (conceptually and methodologically) than the psychological studies of aggression, abnormal behavior, and psycho- and sociopathology that marked an earlier era. Chapters in the present volume by Fergusson (Chapter 7) and Farrington, Loeber, and Stouthamer-Loeber (Chapter 11) are examples of research in this tradition. Studies in the latter tradition have examined local community and neighborhood effects on varying levels of violence. Innovative studies of how community- and neighborhood-level contextual factors impact racial differences in rates of interpersonal violence have also been published in recent years (e.g., see Krivo and Peterson, 1996; Sampson, 1997; and Sampson, Raudenbush, and Earls, 1997). Increasingly, the best work in each of these areas of research combines elements of both modes of analysis.

Together, these research protocols may ultimately take us far toward an understanding of varying levels of violent involvement by individuals living under similar conditions, and individuals living in certain neighborhoods as compared to others. They also may prove to have much to offer discussions of race and ethnic differences. In fact, some progress has already been made toward that end. For example, researchers have observed that *within* racial and ethnic groupings, attention to individual differences (e.g., inherited predispositions, developmental pathways, etc.) and to differences in localized environmental contexts may explain varying levels of interpersonal violence. Still at issue in this research is the question of the extent to which explanatory models based on individual-level and neighborhood-level correlates of violent offending "map" onto models that are based on the presumption of the etiological significance of race and ethnic group membership. That is, can they fully account for ethnic and racial differences?[5] This is a question posed by Farrington, Loeber, and Stouthamer-Loeber in Chapter 11 of the present volume. Much more work remains ahead in this important line of inquiry, partly because many of the samples of subjects used to analyze developmental trajectories for violent offenders have not always been racially or ethnically diverse.

All of the authors contributing to the present volume are cognizant of the long-standing problems in the study of race, ethnicity, and violence that I have described in this introduction, and all have sought to overcome or address them in various ways. My own biases and predilections notwithstanding, my objective when soliciting authors to contribute to this volume was to assemble a very diverse group of scholars who would offer new and innovative approaches to the study of race, ethnicity, and violence. Despite my unsuccessful attempts to solicit chapters on racial and ethnic differences

---

[5] Even in societies marked by ethnic, racial, and social class cleavages that lead to much intergroup conflict, not all individuals (even those of the same age, gender, etc.) are equally likely to engage in the intergroup violence that marks group boundaries. In addition, in times of relative "peace" between groups or under conditions of geographic isolation, some individuals exhibit much higher rates of intragroup aggression and violence than others. The fact that individual differences matter for the etiology of interpersonal violence does not, however, suggest that race and ethnic differences are driven by precisely the same factors that account for differences among individuals.

in the nineteenth century, violence among Native and Asian Americans, and a review of the biogenetic literature, I believe the present collection of essays largely represents substantial progress toward that goal. Although they share a commitment to scientific methods, the use of appropriate data, and the accuracy of data interpretation, these authors hardly speak with one voice. They differ in the conclusions they reach, and often within the same chapter, competing, alternative explanations and interpretations for reported findings are offered. Through their collective effort to engage in such criticism and self-examination, the authors have avoided the tendency to replace a legacy of biological determinism in this area of research with a nonreflexive form of social determinism. The chapters build on the past but offer much to help guide much needed future research efforts in this important area of social inquiry.

Violent Crime

PART I

Homicide Studies

Homicide Risk and Level of Victimization in Two Concentrated Poverty Enclaves: A Black/Hispanic Comparison

Harold M. Rose
Paula D. McClain

Introduction

Regardless of race or ethnic status, victims of homicide in the United States are drawn most often from the lower socioeconomic classes. More recently, however, a growing number of researchers have begun to focus attention on the context and/or environment in which homicide within the lower socioeconomic classes occurs (See Morenoff and Sampson, 1997; Almgren and others, 1998; Krivo and Peterson, 1996). More often than not, this means focusing attention on urban neighborhoods described as economically disadvantaged or as neighborhoods of concentrated poverty (Massey, 1995). The current focus on concentrated poverty neighborhoods as a primary environment of concentrated homicide victimization is partially an outgrowth of interest in the phenomena described as the underclass. Underclass research had its origins in work done in the 1980s (see Glasgow, 1980; Murray, 1984; Wilson, 1987; Auletta, 1981).

The validity of the concept of the existence of an urban underclass in the United States and its various definitions have been severely criticized, and is not universally accepted among academic researchers. In this instance, we focus our attention on two sets of urban neighborhoods that satisfy the definition of extreme poverty neighborhoods, that is, 40 percent poor, in a single large Midwestern urban center. It is in neighborhoods that transcend this poverty threshold that homicide victimization rates are usually highest. It is in neighborhoods like these that researchers have identified a number of critical dimensions that are thought to lead to elevated homicide risk (see Sampson, Raudenbush, and Earls, 1997). Thus, our focus on neighborhoods of concentrated poverty is designed to help us better understand variations in homicide risk levels among two minority populations,

3

blacks and Hispanics, during the 1989–93 interval, residing in a single urban center, Milwaukee, Wisconsin.

The 1989–93 interval generally coincides with the most recent upsurge in urban homicide in the United States. In viewing these two residential clusters as environments of elevated homicide risk, our approach will place primary emphasis on victimization rather than offending. We do look, however, at the offending practices of youth and young adults in these settings. The victimization approach employed in this paper reflects the demographic perspective of the authors.[1]

We also must note the importance of studying homicide as a way of estimating the extent of actual racial and ethnic differences in crime and victimization. Of all violent crime statistics, homicide statistics are the least biased, meaning that they are far more accurate than other violent crime statistics. All of the other crime statistics rely on victim reporting to the police and police agencies reporting to a host of local, state, and federal agencies. If a victim does not report a crime, it is not counted. Or, even if reported, police agencies for a variety of reasons may not report it to the various data collection agencies. Thus, we know that these crime statistics are biased in a number of ways and do not reflect the actual levels of violent crime. Homicide statistics, by contrast, do not rely on self-reported data but result from one source – the discovery of a body. As such, the bias in homicide statistics is minimal. Therefore, homicide studies are a good way to begin a volume on racial and ethnic differences in crime.

Concentrated Poverty Neighborhoods: Environments of Violent Victimization

We assume that the growth of concentrated poverty neighborhoods is a reflection of local level effects of the globalization of the economy, and the social and economic polarization thought to accompany it, such as the loss of limited skill jobs, the growth of low-paying jobs, and, among others, the relocation of jobs from the central city to the suburbs (Wilson, 1987, 1996; Massey and Denton, 1995; Kasarda, 1993). Those most negatively affected by these changes find themselves in close contact with others who also have been negatively affected by economic change. Wilson (1987), in describing the changes taking place in Chicago's black community, suggests that more successful blacks are able to abandon these communities, and, as a result, leave behind a residual population with only limited resources with which to alter its status, at least through employment in the legitimate economy.

[1] In this instance, homicide is primarily viewed as a cause of death rather than a criminal offense. Researchers adopting an offender perspective most often represent a criminological orientation.

The question becomes – Does the growth in the number of extreme poverty neighborhoods lead to an escalation in levels of lethal violence as some writers suggest (see Anderson, 1999)? If so, does the risk of victimization vary across race/ethnicity and gender? Furthermore, does the structure of victimization in extreme poverty neighborhoods differ from that in nonconcentrated poverty neighborhoods? These are the questions that are central to the research presented in this chapter.

Milwaukee, Wisconsin: A Temporary Target of Economic Dislocation

Milwaukee, a midsized American manufacturing belt city with a historical reputation as a prosperous working-class center (Hamilton, 1972), saw that reputation diminish as an outgrowth of the loss of manufacturing jobs between the late 1970s and the mid-1980s. By the end of the 1980s, however, the city had experienced a remarkable economic recovery. Despite the recovery, its black population was left behind as black male joblessness continued at a high level. Neighborhoods of concentrated poverty rapidly expanded in the city's black community. By 1990, more than half of the city's black neighborhoods could be described as extreme poverty neighborhoods. Yet, this pattern was not confined to the city's black community, as concentrated poverty neighborhoods were also prevalent in the city's substantially smaller Hispanic community.

In 1990, Milwaukee had a total population of 628,000, of which 190,000 or 30.2 percent were black, and 40,000 or 6.4 percent were Hispanic. A disproportionate share of both groups was housed in concentrated poverty neighborhoods. These were neighborhoods in which drug and gang activity were most pervasive. Given the vagaries present in the two clusters under review, one might conclude that we should expect them to be among the most violent in the city.

The black population in Milwaukee is almost five times as large as its Hispanic counterpart. Nevertheless, we believe it important to measure the extent to which the two groups have been involved in the upsurge in homicide victimization that began locally in 1989. Milwaukee, like a number of large American cities, experienced a rapid increase in victimization levels beginning in the middle to late 1980s that finally leveled off in the early to mid-1990s. Being classified among the growing number of cities where homicide levels had reached all time highs was a new experience for Milwaukee.

Historically, urban homicide in the United States reached its highest levels in those large American cities that were primary targets of black migration beginning during World War I and ending prior to 1970. A number of those places experienced an upsurge in levels of victimization between

1965 and 1975, an interval that was characterized by an earlier drug epidemic. By 1990, several large American cities, such as New York, Los Angeles, Chicago, and Miami, were the places of residence with growing black and Hispanic populations, a sizable share of whom were poor. These also were places in which new rounds of violence occurred leading to unprecedented levels of homicide. In such centers, drug and/or gang activity was increasing. These activities are often assumed to be associated with the expansion of zones of concentrated poverty. It is in these zones that employment in the mainstream economy is low and employment in the illicit economy is where youth and young adult males frequently turn for economic support (see Wilson, 1996).

The Microspatial Targets of Investigation

Differences in population size between the two populations suggest that they would contribute differentially to the level of observed victimization from 1989 to 1993. In each of the years, blacks accounted for the single largest number of victims. By the end of the period, black victimizations hovered around 80 percent of the total. Yet, Hispanic victimizations were also increasing, but at a much slower rate. What we are primarily concerned with, in this instance however, is how these two populations, residing in a set of similarly situated neighborhoods, were differentially engaged in behaviors leading to fatal victimizations. In effect, we are attempting to isolate indirectly an environmental influence on risk of victimization in two ethnic residential clusters.

   In order to give equal attention to these two populations at risk, we focus on homicides occurring in two sets of eleven neighborhoods. In one set of neighborhoods, blacks represent the predominant population, and in the other, Hispanics represent the predominant or subpredominant population (see Figure 1.1). In both instances, a group of contiguous concentrated poverty neighborhoods have been chosen as target neighborhoods. Thus, we are attempting to detect differences in levels and risk of victimization in two distinct race/ethnic populations. It should be noted, however, that there are more than forty black concentrated poverty neighborhoods in the city and we have chosen to direct our attention to only eleven. By contrast, the eleven target Hispanic neighborhoods represent the only neighborhoods in the city in which the Hispanic population was in the majority or near majority in 1990.

Differences Among the Target Neighborhoods. The neighborhood clusters possess similarities across a number of important social variables, but they differ on a number of dimensions as well. The most obvious differences are in levels of segregation and the presence of persons from abroad.

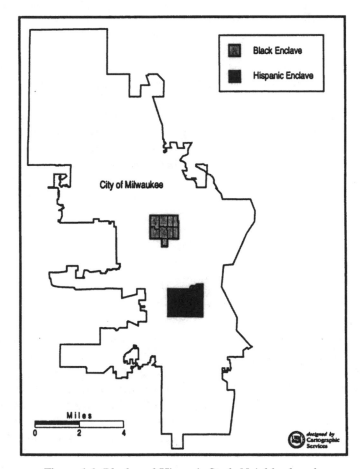

Figure 1.1. Black and Hispanic Study Neighborhoods

Blacks are much more intensely segregated in the study neighborhoods than are Hispanics. In no instance do Hispanics constitute more than two-thirds of the neighborhood population, and in several instances hover around only two-fifths of the population. In none of the observed neighborhoods do blacks constitute less than 90 percent of the total. Massey (1995) has suggested that it is at the intersection of poverty and segregation that the potential for lethal violence reaches its peak.

One final distinction that differentiates these two neighborhood clusters is the prevalence of households headed by females. Among Hispanic households, 26.6 percent are headed by females, whereas in the black neighborhoods more than three-quarters of all households are female-headed. A number of homicide researchers associate high levels of female-headed households with weakened informal social control that results in increases in levels of violence among youth (Sampson, 1987; Ousey, 1999; Phillips, 1999).

During the most recent intervals in which homicides peaked in the United States, 1965–75 and 1985–95, blacks constituted the primary victims and offenders. As a result of the high levels of black involvement in lethal violence nationally, some researchers have described black males as practitioners of a subculture of violence (Wolfgang and Ferracuti, 1967). Nonetheless, not all researchers agree. Some have rejected outright the categorization of black males as practitioners of a subculture of violence as an adequate explanation for the rise and fall of homicide peaking patterns (see Cao, Adams, and Jensen, 1997). That distinction aside, blacks have experienced the highest homicide risk levels of any race/ethnic population in the United States since homicide statistics were first recorded. Even so, after controlling for race, homicide rates vary substantially across place (Peterson and Krivo, 1993).

Why So Few Comparisons of Levels of Black and Hispanic Victimization?

Research on the recent upturn in urban homicide risk levels has focused almost exclusively on killings taking place in the nation's larger black communities. Little attention, until recently, has been focused on Hispanic victimizations, even though they constitute a significant urban population residing in expansive barrios in a growing number of urban centers. One reason, no doubt, for the failure to devote attention to Hispanic victimization is related to data quality and the absence of Hispanic scholars with a professional interest in the subject. Martinez (1997: 18) recently noted that "although the seriousness of the Latino homicide problem is recognized, its study is largely ignored."

Until relatively recently, the ethnic status of victims and offenders was not reported to the FBI. At the national level, Hispanic victims were often identified as white, thereby making it difficult to define national homicide rates for persons of Hispanic origin. This is further complicated by the use of ethnic categories within the Hispanic population that divides the population into ethnic-origin groups, such as Cubans, Mexicans, Puerto Ricans, and other South Americans.

At the national level, the absence of data providing racial identifiers has slowed efforts to compare Hispanic victimization and risk levels with those of blacks and whites. At the local level, however, comparisons have already begun (see Shai and Rosenwaike, 1988). Studies comparing victimization rates among blacks, whites, and Hispanics at the city level show variations in levels of risk among these groups in individual cities. Generally, levels of

Table 1.1. *Mean Homicide Rates Based on Race and Ethnicity for the City of Milwaukee – 1990 Rate per 100,000*

Gender	Black	Hispanic	White
Male	106.0	50.0	11.6
Female	14.5	–	3.8

Source: Computed by the authors based on data provided by the Milwaukee Police Department.

Hispanic risk fall somewhere between those of blacks and whites (Zahn, 1988). The discrepancy in levels of Hispanic variation seemingly depends on the socioeconomic status of the predominant Hispanic group – Mexican, Puerto Rican, or Cuban – in the local population. In Miami, recent work shows that the difference in the mean homicide rate between Latinos and Anglos was nominal (Martinez, 1997). In this instance, the predominant Hispanic population is Cuban, a group that occupies a higher socioeconomic position in that community's economy than do other Hispanic sub-populations. What we generally know the least about, however, is how black and Hispanic populations residing in similarly disadvantaged neighborhoods differ in victimization levels.

Black and Hispanic Levels of Homicide Victimization in Milwaukee. In Milwaukee, homicide victimization rates (1989–93) for blacks, Hispanics, and whites can be seen in Table 1.1. Table 1.1 reveals the relative ranking of prevailing levels of risk, based on both race/ethnicity and gender, among the three populations.[2] As the table illustrates, males are most often involved in interactions leading to homicide. Hispanic victimization levels fall somewhere between that of blacks and whites, but are substantially more elevated than that of white males. Although Hispanic males exhibited an elevated risk level, not a single Hispanic female was killed during the 1989–93 interval. The extremely low rate of Hispanic female victimization may be suggestive of unique features of Hispanic culture that mitigate against female homicide victimization.

As is true nationally, homicide levels, especially urban homicide levels, are driven by conduct engaged in by black males. While national aggregate

[2] The rates displayed in Table 1.1 were derived based on the mean number of homicides occurring over a three-year period involving victims from each of the identified groups divided by the size of its population at the time of the 1990 census multiplied by 100,000, that is, HR = V/P × 100,000.

homicide levels decreased during the early 1980s, shortly thereafter homicide levels in selected urban areas, for example, Washington, DC, New Orleans, Los Angeles, and St. Louis, among others, appear to have climbed. Since 1985, young black males age fifteen to twenty-four years led the upsurge in urban homicides as both victims and offenders (Blumstein, 1995). Ironically, while risk levels for black males age fifteen to twenty-four years old were rising, risk levels for black males forty and over were declining (see Almgren and others, 1998).

Milwaukee: A Newcomer to High Homicide Victimization

Milwaukee, a city without a history of high levels of homicide, began to join the cluster of urban centers experiencing the most recent epidemic of rising homicide in the late 1980s. Among the more frequent explanations given for the most recent cyclical increase in risk levels are growth of crack cocaine markets (Johnson, 1993; Blumstein, 1996), the growth of urban gangs (Klein, Maxson, and Cunningham, 1991; Spergel, 1992), and the easy availability of handguns (Wright and others, 1992; Blumstein, 1995; Zimring, 1996). The attraction of poor urban youth to gang involvement, drug sales, and easy access to guns is thought to constitute the catalyst for the increased homicide levels in Milwaukee and similar places during the early 1990s.

Milwaukee's Black and Hispanic Populations. Blacks and Hispanics now constitute more than 36 percent of the city's population, with the black population alone making up 30 percent of the total population. Both groups experienced substantial growth during the decade of the eighties. For blacks, between 1985 and 1990, sizable numbers of migrants from elsewhere in the United States chose to settle in Milwaukee. As a result, Milwaukee registered a positive net migration gain, unlike the pattern in other larger Midwest urban centers that experienced net migration losses in their black populations. Migration was a substantial contributor to the 30 percent black population increase occurring in the 1980s. The Hispanic population increased even more rapidly, exceeding 50 percent. Much of this growth was from immigration from abroad.

The Identification of Target Black and Hispanic Neighborhoods. The two neighborhood groups selected for comparison are comprised of eleven census tracts each. Both the black and Hispanic neighborhood clusters can be described as zones of high or concentrated poverty, although they exhibit poverty levels that describe them as either high poverty, or extreme poverty neighborhoods, 40 percent poor families. Such neighborhoods are described by some scholars as zones of underclass residence and are thought to support the evolution of an underclass culture (Massey and Denton, 1995; Anderson, 1999). Such labels smack of territorial stigmatization without objectively acknowledging the process that has led to this outcome (see Wacquant, 1996). Jargowski (1996) and Anderson (1999) indicate that even among the poorest of neighborhoods, practitioners of nonmainstream values are likely to constitute the minority. Even within these ecological spaces, broad differences can be observed in particular aspects of their social environment. Nevertheless, the combination of high levels of racial segregation and high levels of poverty appear to stimulate an increase in levels of violent victimization (Peterson and Krivo, 1993; Massey, 1995). The question becomes – How do these differences manifest themselves in ethnic-specific settings? For instance, black majority neighborhoods characterized by extreme poverty are places where homicide levels are generally higher than those in neighborhoods where poverty is less extreme. Can the same pattern be observed in Hispanic neighborhoods?

The north side neighborhood cluster is the place of residence of almost 12 percent of the city's black population, but constituted the place of occurrence of 16 percent of the city's homicides in 1990. At the same time, the south side neighborhood setting was home to just under two-fifths of Milwaukee's Hispanic population. It should be noted, however, that these two neighborhood groups, respectively, were the sites of 16 and 4 percent of all homicides committed in the city in 1990. The north side cluster included in this investigation represents less than one-fourth of the concentrated poverty neighborhoods in the city's black community.

What these data suggest are that homicides, in a single year, are four times more likely to occur in black extreme poverty neighborhoods than in similarly situated Hispanic neighborhoods. As it turns out, the black victimization rate, in this cluster of neighborhoods, exceeded 100 per 100,000 in 1990. The victimization rate in the Hispanic cluster was substantially lower, measuring 20 per 100,000 in the same year. What accounts for the wide gap in victimization rates in two similarly situated concentrated poverty neighborhood clusters?

Krivo and Peterson (1996) recently addressed the problem in racial disparities in crime levels between blacks and whites residing in high and/or extreme poverty neighborhoods using data from Columbus, Ohio. They concluded that disadvantaged environments were more important than race in explaining observed differences. Peeples and Loeber (1994) also addressed a variant of this question by examining differences in delinquency rates between black and white youth residing in underclass (high poverty neighborhoods) and nonunderclass neighborhoods in Pittsburgh, Pennsylvania. They found that black youth residing in neighborhoods similar in status to those of white youth engaged in delinquent acts on a scale similar to that of their white peers.

Ostensibly, these investigations are attempting to separate out race effects from neighborhood effects on rates of criminal and/or delinquent behavior. Our goal is to ascertain differences in risk of victimization among the minority populations residing in neighborhoods with similar levels of neighborhood poverty. Our results will reflect the shortcomings of employing a single measure, such as concentrated poverty, to assess differences in dangerousness across ethnically specific neighborhoods, specifically, black versus Hispanic.

Selecting an outer limit to define extreme poverty neighborhoods to fit the definition used to identify a universe of underclass neighborhoods is not without limitations. This assumes that one neighborhood is very much like any other along those dimensions that influence acts of lethal violence. Noting the shortcoming of projecting an almost universal pattern of social and economic behavior to persons residing in neighborhoods designated as underclass, Jargowsky (1996) states:

> ...there is much more heterogeneity in economic and social indicators within such neighborhoods than is commonly believed. Most residents of high poverty neighborhoods are not nearly as isolated from values as popular stereotypes suggest the mainstream economy and mainstream. (p. 580)

Thus, given the diversity within these neighborhoods, differences in victimizations should be expected.

Acts of Lethal Violence and Differential Neighborhood Stress Levels

In this section, we attempt to account for the discrepancy in the frequency of acts of lethal violence in extreme poverty neighborhoods that might be loosely labeled ghetto and barrio neighborhoods. In order to determine if indicators other than poverty might be at work in influencing the adaptive behavior of the neighborhood population, we utilized a set of stress scores that were devised in earlier work as a measure of environmental stress (Rose and McClain, 1990).

The observed scores were derived through principal components factor analysis. A series of eleven census variables were used in the factor analysis. These include percent families with below poverty income, percent female-headed households, percent females divorced and separated, male labor force participation rates, percent high school graduates, percent recent migrants, percent housing vacancy, percent crowded housing, percent males age fifteen to twenty-four years, median rent, and median family income. Other researchers have employed alternate approaches in an effort to measure environmental stress. Harries and Powell (1994) employed stress scores

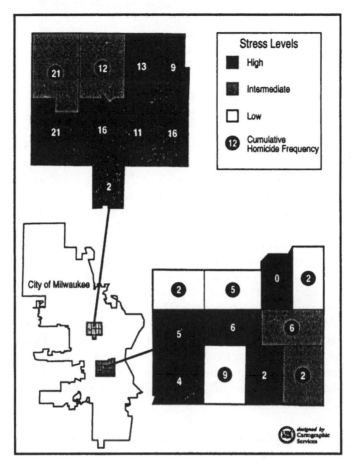

Figure 1.2. Observed Stress Levels and Cumulative Homicide Frequencies in a Sample of Black and Hispanic Neighborhoods

to demonstrate their efficacy in illustrating the spatial pattern of juvenile gun violence in the city of Baltimore.

Three sets of common factors were extracted that were labeled social disorganization, social rank, and economic opportunity. The factor scores on the social disorganization and social rank dimensions were summed in order to derive a stress score for each observation. The stress scores allow us to partition high poverty neighborhoods across a range of variables that are assumed to be important contributors to violence (see Figure 1.2). The small number of observations in the present investigation allows us to use the stress scores in only a descriptive rather than an analytic context.

Differences in the prevalence of high stress at the neighborhood level demonstrate the existence of differences in a contextual effect that could heighten the probability of violence. If stress levels are associated with levels of victimization, as Harries and Powell (1994) suggest, then logically we would assume that neighborhoods registering higher levels of stress would also be neighborhoods in which the frequency of victimization would be elevated.

Black and Hispanic Differences in Levels of Neighborhood Stress. The stress scores demonstrate that the Hispanic high poverty enclave includes fewer high stress neighborhoods than does the black high poverty enclave (see Figure 1.2). Within the black neighborhood group, eight out of the eleven neighborhoods qualify as high stress neighborhoods. By contrast, in the Hispanic neighborhood group, only five of the eleven neighborhoods have stress levels that place them in the high stress group. If stress, as defined here, is less pervasive and less intense in a cluster of Hispanic neighborhoods than in a similar cluster of black neighborhoods, we should anticipate lower homicide risk levels and possibly differences in the circumstances leading to lethal encounters in the two clusters under observation.

However, even in black and Hispanic neighborhoods exhibiting similar stress levels, the number of black victimizations is substantially greater than the number of incidents in Hispanic neighborhoods. Four-fifths of all victimizations took place in the black high poverty neighborhood sample. Yet, even within this cluster, a small group of neighborhoods accounted for the lion's share of all victimizations.

Stress Levels and Homicide Frequency. Variations in intensity of stress and its association with homicide frequency at the neighborhood level differ between the two poverty enclaves. Homicide frequency more often occurs in high stress black neighborhoods than in high stress Hispanic neighborhoods. During the five-year interval (1989–93), 77 percent of all black enclave victims were victimized in high stress neighborhoods. By contrast, fewer than 45 percent of Hispanics were victimized in high stress neighborhoods in the Hispanic enclave. On its face, it appears that stress levels play a weaker role as a contributor to violent victimization in poor Hispanic neighborhoods than is the case in similarly situated black neighborhoods. It might be that the circumstances of death vary within these enclaves in such a way that stress is a poorer predictor of the likelihood of victimization in one setting, but not in the other.

What is apparent, however, is that our black poverty enclave represents a more dangerous environment than does the Hispanic poverty enclave. During the initial year (1989), only a single homicide was recorded in the Hispanic enclave, whereas twenty-two were recorded in the black enclave

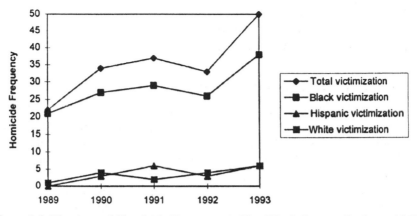

Figure 1.3. The Annual Homicide Frequency in Two Ethnic Poverty Enclaves: 1989–1993

(see Figure 1.3). In subsequent years, the number of victims in the Hispanic enclave increased, and, by the end of the period, the ratio of black victimization to Hispanic victimization was 6 to 1.

As indicated earlier, the Hispanic enclave was less intensely segregated, and, in a number of neighborhoods, whites were still a majority of the neighborhood population. In an environment in which Hispanics and whites shared residential space and responded to similar levels of stress, one might expect occasional interactions that would lead to lethal outcomes, particularly if these interactions involved youth gang conflict. An unexpected finding associated with victimization in the Hispanic enclave is that almost two-fifths of the victims were non-Hispanic whites. Hence, violent interactions in the Hispanic enclave produced a more diverse mix of victims than was the case in the black poverty enclave. Fewer than five percent of the victims in the black poverty enclave were nonblack, a condition, no doubt, that is an outgrowth of higher levels of segregation in the black neighborhood cluster.

It is evident that forces other than sheer differences in population size has led to a substantial gap in the number of victimizations taking place in the two ethnic enclaves. Differences in the intensity of stress are associated with differences in victimization levels, but the association appears to be less strong in the Hispanic enclave than in the black enclave. This suggests that the two communities may differ in terms of the prevalent motivation for violence, as well as the subsequent structure of victimization. Furthermore, the participants in these encounters may differ in terms of gender, age, and relations between victim and offender. Finally, we wish to determine differences between the two enclaves in the extent to which drugs, gangs, and guns serve as motivators in escalating the risk of violence, as these are factors that are often associated with the most recent upsurge in urban violence nationally (Blumstein, 1995).

Homicide in Target Neighborhoods

As is true nationally, males dominate homicide in our study neighborhoods. During the most recent interval of escalating risk levels nationally, in those environments in which homicides more often take place, gender differences have grown. This has led to lowering the annual percentage of female victims. In high-risk urban centers, males often comprise more than 80 percent of all homicide victims (Rose and McClain, 1998). In Milwaukee, males account for more than four-fifths of the total in both enclaves, registering almost 88 percent in the black neighborhood cluster and slightly less than 84 percent in the Hispanic cluster. While the rate of homicide victimization among older males has been declining nationally, the inverse has characterized the victimization of younger males (Blumstein and Rosenfeld, 1998).

The Growing Importance of Young Adults' Propensity for Violence. Males age fifteen to twenty-four represent the primary target population in the most recent upsurge in urban victimization levels (Derber, 1996). Some scholars believed that urban youth residing in high poverty neighborhoods have a weaker attachment to traditional values than do those of an older generation (Zimring, 1996; Blumstein, 1995; Massey, 1995). Black youth in particular, either in an effort to survive or in a rejection of mainstream values, have been described as adopting a code of conduct that is at odds with that of earlier generations (Anderson, 1999). These behaviors have been cited by some scholars as evidence of a growing oppositional culture (Anderson, 1994; Bourgois, 1995; Calmore, 1995; Shihadeh and Flyn, 1996; Heimer, 1997) presumed to be embedded in a desire for peer respect and the need for status often associated with the acquisition of selected consumer items (Nightingale, 1993; Haymes, 1995).

All in all, regardless of motivation, youth, especially juveniles, interact with their peers in ways that have led to an increase in the body count among the young in poor and near poor neighborhoods across America. Now we explore the question of to what extent that conduct has manifested itself in the two enclaves under investigation.

Comparative Young Adult Behavior in Target Neighborhoods. Victims in the city's black enclave were more likely to be fifteen- to twenty-four-year-old males than was true of the Hispanic enclave. More than 35 percent of all victims in the black high poverty neighborhoods were young black males. In the Hispanic neighborhood cluster, just slightly more than one-fifth of the victims fell in the above age category. The discrepancy in the victimization levels between young black and Hispanic males suggests the operation of either a different set of motivating forces or a lesser intensity of the same or similar forces. The forces most frequently cited for the upward movement of young black victimization levels are increasing involvement with gangs, participation in the drug economy, and a propensity to acquire and arm themselves with handguns (Blumstein, 1995; Zimring, 1995). That being the case, we should expect some differences in the structure of victimization in the two neighborhood groups, as well as differences in killings that occur in public spaces, for example, street killings, and those that take place in residential or other private spaces, for example, nonstreet killings (see Tardiff et al., 1995).

In the black neighborhood enclave, we speculate that acts associated with symbolism and predation would be more often associated with the fatal blow than in the Hispanic enclave. Thus, we would expect robbery-related, gang-related, and drug-related victimizations to be more prevalent or commonplace. Interpersonal conflict growing out of arguments associated with close personal bonding is expected to decline in prevalence during the interval.

Victim/Offender Relations

In order to determine the validity of our speculation, we recorded the victim/offender relationships reported by the FBI for the years 1989–93 (see Table 1.2). We combined strangers and unknowns into one category of relationships, and acquaintances and other knowns into a second category. We assume that the category stranger and unknown will be more frequently associated with acts involving predation and symbolism, while acts stemming from interpersonal conflict and/or issues associated with emotional bonding will be associated more often with relations among acquaintances and other knowns. It should be noted, however, that this dichotomous grouping does not fully capture the essence of the behavior described previously. Decker (1996) has demonstrated that a growing number of recent victimizations should be categorized as deviant, as they do not easily fit the dichotomy employed here.

The data in Table 1.2 fail to support our predicted associations between victims and offenders in the two enclaves. Given the greater prevalence of fifteen- to twenty-four-year-old male victims in the black enclave, we assumed that predatory and symbolic actions would transcend all others in importance. The data show that in most years stranger and unknown killings were more prevalent in the Hispanic enclave. We are cautious, however, in our interpretation of this situation as the annual frequency of victimization is much lower in the Hispanic enclave than in the black enclave. Although

Table 1.2. *The Changing Structure of Victimization in a Sample of Milwaukee Black and Hispanic Neighborhoods: 1989–1993*

	1989	1990	1991	1992	1993
Black Enclave					
Percent Stranger/ Unknown Victims	8.0%	63.0%	65.6%	69.6%	45.0%
Percent Acquaintance/ Other Known Victimizations	92.0%	37.0%	34.4%	30.4%	55.0%
Hispanic Enclave					
Percent Stranger/ Unknown Victims	100.0%	85.8%	87.5%	22.0%	59.0%
Percent Acquaintance/ Other Known Victimizations	0.0%	14.2%	12.5%	78.0%	41.0%

stranger and unknown victimizations were more prevalent in the Hispanic enclave, the difference between the two clusters of neighborhoods is seven percentage points. Furthermore, the motives of those involved in unknown circumstances may differ between the two groups. These findings do, however, suggest a growing commonality in the behavior of youthful males in both enclaves.

The Circumstances of Death in Sample Neighborhoods. While victim/ offender relations provide some clues to the range of behaviors that might be involved in fatal interactions, they do not allow us to address directly some of the issues that were raised earlier. That is, to what extent have conflicts around gang, drug, and robbery activities led to increasing the level of victimization in the two neighborhood clusters? Data from the final two years of the interval, 1992 and 1993, permit us to specify the circumstances associated with the fatal acts.[3] A sample of thirty-seven incidents out of a total of seventy-seven is utilized to gain greater insight into those factors leading up to fatal outcomes. After reviewing the court records, we are in a stronger position to establish if, in fact, gangs, drugs, and guns were a force in promoting acts of lethality in the local settings.

Although the sample incidents represent a small number of cases, they do not appear to be out of line with cases representing the city sample. Twenty three cases represented incidents occurring in the black enclave in 1992 and 1993. Fourteen incidents occurred in the Hispanic enclave during the same period. In both samples, victims and offenders tend to be concentrated among youth and/or young adults.

[3] The circumstances of the fatal events were extracted from Milwaukee court records.

Youthful offenders tend to be slightly more prevalent in the black enclave than in the Hispanic enclave. Drug-related victimizations occur more frequently in the black enclave followed by other arguments and gang-related killings tend to dominate the circumstances associated with most fatal interactions. Based on a limited number of cases, it becomes apparent that drug- and gang-related killings are growing in importance in the two Milwaukee neighborhood clusters.

The prevalence of gun use is lower than anticipated, as were killings growing out of other arguments. In those instances in which death involved intimate partners and/or child abuse, body force and knives were more likely to represent the weapon used. Child abuse cases were occurring with greater frequency than anticipated, a factor that led to an increase in child killings.

Court documents provided information describing a broad array of characteristics of both victims and offenders. Two things stand out that are important in the context of this investigation. One is evidence of an increase in multiple offender offenses, such that a substantial share of all offenses falls into this category. Multiple offender victimizations are most frequently associated with gang and drug killings. Second, it was not uncommon to have multiple offenders that represented a mix of race/ethnic populations, for example, black and Hispanic offenders and a black victim, or Hispanic and white offenders and a Hispanic victim. These mixed race/ethnic offenders were observed in both enclaves. It is not our intent to suggest that this is a widespread practice, but it appears that when youth share common social space, the ethnic mix of violent collaborations increases the likelihood of multiethnic involvement.

The Site of Victimization: Street versus Nonstreet. On a final note, the ratio of street killings to nonstreet killings varied within the two enclaves. In the Hispanic enclave, street killings were no more likely to occur than nonstreet killings. Given the higher percentage of killings growing out of conflict between primary relations, such as intimate partners, parents, and children, this should be expected. Within the black enclave, however, street killings tended to predominate. Almost three-fourths of all victimizations recorded occurred outside of residential structures, for example, streets, alleys, vacant lots, and in automobiles, as logically one might expect given the high involvement of drug- and gang-related killings. Street killings were most frequently associated with multiple offender events, the use of a handgun or long gun, and the involvement of youthful offenders. In both enclaves a common trend was underway that involved multiple youths accosting a single victim and assaulting that victim with a handgun. In the final two years, drugs and gangs were of growing importance in contributing to the level of violence observed in our sample neighborhood clusters.

Summary and Conclusion

This chapter has attempted to ascertain if blacks and Hispanics residing in high poverty neighborhoods experience similar levels of homicide risk or if there are substantial differences in frequency of victimization. Nationally, homicide victimization rates show black risk levels exceed those of Hispanics by a ratio of more than 2 to 1. But seldom have studies that compared these groups viewed the differences in level of victimization from the perspective of the residential environment in which the two populations reside.

Because elevated risk among black populations is most pronounced in high poverty neighborhoods, we selected a sample of high poverty neighborhoods in a single city that contained a predominance of black and Hispanic residents in order to determine the extent to which acts of violent victimization varied across such neighborhoods. In these neighborhood clusters the size of the black population was approximately one and one-half times larger than the Hispanic population. Thus, if no differences existed in the demographic structure of the population and/or the levels of poverty, we would expect the frequency of black victimization to exceed that in the Hispanic enclave by a factor of more than 4 to 1 over the five years.

In order to illustrate the prevalence of internal differences within these extreme poverty neighborhoods, we derived a set of stress scores. We found that the internal distribution of stress had an association with frequency, but not a very strong one. Black neighborhoods exhibited higher stress levels than did the Hispanic neighborhoods. Apparently, stress levels in the latter neighborhoods produced a weaker association than in the former. Thus, stress levels alone do not allow us to account for the differential frequency of victimization in the two race/ethnic enclaves.

This investigation demonstrated that a gap exists in homicide victimization levels in black and Hispanic neighborhoods, characterized by high levels of neighborhood disadvantage. Nevertheless, we failed to examine analytically the association of the contribution of levels of disadvantage to homicide victimization levels (see Sampson, Raudenbush, and Earls, 1997). There were other omissions as well. No attempt was made to examine the physical or functional characteristics of individual neighborhoods within the selected clusters for possible clues. For instance, neighborhoods characterized by greater commercial activity may represent a locus of higher victimization levels as they tend to bring people together. Moreover, black and Hispanic residents might possibly respond to similar levels of disadvantage in different ways. Ousey (1999) demonstrated recently that homicide risk is not invariant across race, an indication that groups respond to external forces in unique ways.

There is a need for more neighborhood-based comparative studies if we are to gain a better understanding of what accounts for similarities and differences in black and Hispanic victimization levels. Presently, a number of large urban centers have substantial black and Hispanic populations that could be used for comparative studies. In this way homicide researchers would be in a stronger position to account for differences in level and pattern of victimization based on residence in high poverty neighborhoods and/or on the differential openness of local economies to black and Hispanic youth.

One additional factor that requires attention in future research is differences in risk and frequency of victimization among subgroups within the black and Hispanic populations (see Hawkins, 1999). Increasing immigration has led to more ethnically diverse black, for example, black American, Jamaican, and Haitian, and Hispanic, for example, Mexican, Puerto Rican, and Cuban, populations in many U.S. urban centers. Examining subgroup differences would provide greater insight into the role of culture on victimization risk in poor neighborhoods.

Moving Beyond Black and White Violence: African American, Haitian, and Latino Homicides in Miami[1]

Ramiro Martinez, Jr.

How and why does violent crime vary across racial and ethnic groups? Researchers of American social problems have grappled with this question for more than a century, with most attention being paid to differences between blacks and whites. Black-white comparisons have been the norm since W. E. B. Du Bois completed his pioneering study, *The Philadelphia Negro*, in 1899 (Du Bois, 1899: 235–86; see also Hawkins, 1999; Bobo and Johnson, 2000). Du Bois, like others in his era, observed the impact of crime, including violence, and criminality on conditions within Philadelphia's black community and noted the necessity to incorporate an analysis of crime into his "social study" (for a fuller treatment of the Du Boisian perspective, see Bobo, 2000).

In fact, most early examinations of the relationship between race/ ethnicity and crime during the early twentieth century described the effects of cultural absorption, acculturation, and social adjustment on both black migrants and European immigrants moving into urban areas such as Philadelphia (Lane, 1979; 1986; 1997). Varying levels of criminal involvement were linked to levels of acculturation and assimilation into American society, suggesting that more than a hundred years ago criminologists were

[1] I thank Police Chief Raul Martinez, ex-Assistant Chief John Brooks, Lt. George Cadava, Lt. Bobbie Meeks, and former Lt. John Campbell of the Miami Police Department (MPD). Special thanks to past and present detectives in the MPD Homicide Investigation Unit for permitting continued access over the past several years. I also thank Matthew T. Lee and Raymond Paternoster for assistance and comments. Initial funding was provided in part through the National Science Foundation (SBR-9515235), and in later stages, a Ford Foundation Postdoctoral Minority Fellowship, the Harry Frank Guggenheim Foundation, and the National Consortium on Violence Research (NCOVR). NCOVR is supported under grant # SBR-9513949 from the National Science Foundation. The conclusions presented in this article are mine alone and should not be taken as the view of any official agency. I am, of course, responsible for any omissions, or errors of fact.

fully aware of a possible race-ethnicity-crime linkage. This connection was largely conceptualized as the product of or associated with the geographical movement of large groups of people. Moreover, *racial* differences in crime and violence were seen primarily in terms of black versus white, while *ethnic* differences were described largely in terms of foreign-born versus native-born whites (Martinez and Lee, 2000a).

While contemporary scholars still face and attempt to address the question of what accounts for racial and ethnic differences in crime, both American society and thinking about race, ethnicity, and violent crime have changed considerably over the last century. Indeed, a simple dichotomy of black versus white no longer captures the extent of racial differences within the U.S. population. Furthermore, unlike studies conducted during earlier decades, for the most part immigrant status is not considered a significant variable in most recent studies of urban violence (but see Lee, Martinez, and Rosenfeld, 2001, for exceptions; see also Morenoff, Sampson, and Raudenbush, 2001). During the century since Du Bois's pioneering work focused attention on crime and other urban problems in black Philadelphia, large Latino[2] and Asian communities have emerged in urban areas across the United States. Consider that the first census of the twenty-first century shows the Latino and African-American populations in rough parity (Schmitt, 2001).

Furthermore, the Afro-origin population has grown increasingly diverse. For example, the Haitian population surpasses the size of populations of "native-born" African Americans in many census tracts in Miami, Florida (Dunn, 1997; Elliott and Grotto, 2001). In some large cities of the United States, especially those on the East Coast, persons of Latin-American, Jamaican, or West African ancestry constitute sizable shares of the black population. Together these changes have important implications for the question of what accounts for racial and ethnic differences in violent crime. My primary objective in this chapter is to better inform future analyses by providing a map of the basic contours of changing race and ethnic distinctions (Latino, African-American, and Haitian) and patterns of violent crime in Miami, Florida. Miami is a large, multiethnic[3] U.S. city that has witnessed major demographic changes during the last two to three decades.

---

[2] For purposes of this paper, "Latino" refers to people of Mexican, Puerto Rican, Cuban, or any other Spanish-speaking descent from the Caribbean or Central and South America living in the United States. When appropriate, I will mention specific Latino groups.

[3] Non-Latino whites or Anglos also reside in Miami, but their fraction in the city population and homicide involvement is very small. Rather than compare whites, who mostly reside in the affluent community of Coconut Grove, to ethnic minorities residing in much less affluent areas, I direct attention to the three largest similarly situated nonwhite ethnic groups.

The Present Study

This chapter raises a number of analytical and substantive questions about the need to bring immigration back into the picture after several decades of inattention to its effects on crime. Amid a new era of dramatic demographic transformation, it is necessary to reexamine the nature of racial and ethnic differences in American violent crime (see Martinez and Lee, 2000a). This reexamination also must include greater attention by researchers to the relationship between crime and immigration. Despite the prominent attention given to the study of crime and immigration during the early decades of the twentieth century, the relationship was overlooked during ensuing decades.

As scholars have pointed out, there are several reasons that the link between crime and immigration has been overlooked during the latter part of the twentieth century. First, some social scientists have cautiously avoided the study of subjects such as immigration and crime, because research findings may be misused as they were in the past to fuel stereotypes of crime-prone immigrants (Sampson and Lauritsen, 1997). Second, racially disaggregated data sets on the criminal involvement and victimization of Latinos, "nonnative" black Americans, or subgroups among Asian Americans are rare and generally require time-consuming and expensive data collection efforts (Martinez and Lee, 1999; 2000b). Third, like most rapidly emerging developments, contemporary immigration patterns have not been widely studied by criminologists. This has left basic questions unanswered about issues like selectivity among immigrants (particularly as this relates to "political" versus "economic" or "legal" versus "illegal" immigration patterns), the macrosocial causes and effects of immigration, and the importance of distinctions within immigrant groups when examining crime (Gans, 1992).

Nevertheless, while much research has been conducted on the relationship between race and violent behavior, few studies have explored the nature and extent of this relationship in Latino populations (Valdez, 1993; Alaniz, Cartmill, and Parker, 1998) and even fewer have done so in a Haitian population (Martinez and Lee, 2000b). To address this overlooked issue, the independent effects of recent immigration, net of a host of other factors, on community levels of homicide and ethnic-specific homicide counts are examined. In addition to its unique focus on immigration, this analysis utilizes four strategies in order to generate the most meaningful and valid results. First, data are drawn from Miami, Florida, a city that offers particular advantages for the study of crime, ethnicity, and population change because of its diverse population. During the last decade, the city has seen the inflow of large numbers of Latino and Haitian immigrants (Stepick, 1998). Prior to their arrival the city's population consisted of large concentrations of native whites, African Americans, and Cuban Latinos. Miami's current population allows for useful comparisons between foreign-born and natives and between various racial and ethnic groups found in the city.

Second, since the "neighborhood" is considered one of the most significant levels of analysis for social comparisons, particularly those involving crime, we explore these dimensions at the census tract level, a commonly used proxy for communities or neighborhoods (Messner and Tardiff, 1986; Lee, Martinez, and Rosenfeld, 2001). Third, because the forces influencing homicide vary across racial/ethnic groups (Ousey, 1999), I assembled a racially disaggregated homicide data set using data collected directly from the city of Miami Homicide Investigations Unit.[4] This allows linking ethnic/race-specific homicides (African-American, Haitian, and Latino) to the tract level with population characteristics gathered from the 1990 Census. Finally, this study employs Poisson regression, the most appropriate multivariate statistical technique (see Long, 1997) for modeling rare homicide events at the tract level. This method represents an advance over previous research that has relied heavily on ordinary least squares regression models. Prior to exploring this relationship, I review an influential perspective on immigration and review the contemporary literature (see Martinez and Lee, 1999).

Significance and Background

The proposed research study is embedded in two distinct but overlapping lines of inquiries, each of which tends to emphasize certain variables or processes. The first line of exploration has a foundation in the body of ecological research on poverty, social disorganization, and violent crime dating back to the early work of Shaw and McKay (1931; 1942). The second is more contemporary and focuses on documenting the incidence of violent crime within Latino groups. This type of investigation (as best as I can determine) had its inception in the 1930s with the pioneering work of Taylor and his colleagues (1931; see also Bowler, 1931).

Ecological Research. This scholarly tradition emerged in the 1930s with the influential studies conducted by Shaw and McKay (1931). The primary focus of this research was to document the role that poverty and other social conditions play in the criminal behavior of European immigrants and black migrants in Chicago's urban neighborhoods (Martinez, 1997). The results

---

[4] Homicide and other types of violent crime are concentrated in the city of Miami, not in Miami-Dade County. The much larger and unincorporated surrounding area is serviced by the Miami-Dade County Police Department, which encompasses a heavily rural and suburban population. Consider that in 1996 the number of homicides in Miami and Miami-Dade County were roughly similar. But the population size is over three times larger in the county than the city.

from this line of study suggest that, among other factors, the likelihood of violence is shaped by poverty and influenced by the relatively large numbers of recent immigrants living in the urban neighborhoods that were studied. This perspective is relevant to the contemporary experiences of Latinos in the United States, and particularly those in Miami. Recent reports indicate that higher proportions of Latino than black households in the United States have incomes that place them below the poverty level, and that Miami leads major cities in proportion of residents living in impoverished conditions (Holmes, 1996; Goldberg, 1997).

Furthermore, consider that Miami serves as a major import site into the United States and has had record levels of homicide (McBride et al., 1986; Martinez, 1997). Both of these factors have contributed to widespread stereotypes that most of the local criminal activities (e.g., drug lords) are linked to the Latino, that is primarily immigrant, population (Inciardi, 1992). For example, Martinez and Lee (2000b) reported that the popular media singled out the Mariel Cubans as responsible for the rise in violent youth crime associated with drug trafficking in the early 1980s. Yet, evidence emerged that the "Marielitos" were not overrepresented in drug homicides across that entire time period (Martinez and Lee, 2000b).

For Latinos and Haitians, however, immigration is an opportunity to re-visit the association between violence and integration, a key component of the social disorganization school of social theory. While violence is un-doubtedly influenced by economic deprivation, the distribution of immi-grants across neighborhoods and year of entry also influence violent victim rates, net of the impact of economic stress (Grenier and Stepick, 1992). The central issue has been the long-term concern over whether Haitian and Latino communities are decimated by corresponding violence, or if violent events between individuals are exacerbated by conditions influenced, di-rectly or indirectly, by the presence of immigrants. For instance, research on San Antonio homicides between 1940 and 1980 discovered that Mexican-origin male homicide rates fell in between those of whites and blacks, and that homicide remained concentrated in poor areas of the city, regardless of residents' ethnicity (Bradshaw, Johnson, Cheatwood, and Blanchard, 1998). Another study found that alcohol availability, not percent foreign-born, was an important influence on youth male violence in three California cities with sizable Latino populations (Alaniz, Cartmill, and Parker, 1998). Finally, an investigation of Puerto Rican newcomers discovered that those living out-side of New York City had homicide rates comparable to native whites, while Puerto Ricans living in the boroughs of the city had high rates of homicide (Rosenwaike and Hempstead, 1990).

Several scholars have carefully thought about homicide among several distinct ethnic groups in Miami, Florida. Even though the media often depicted Mariel refugees as crime-prone, the empirical evidence confirmed that they were rarely overrepresented as either homicide victims or offenders. In fact, after a short time period, they were much *less* likely to offend than Miami's established Cubans, most of whom arrived in earlier decades with greater amounts of social and human capital (Martinez, 1997a). In addition, despite a steady flow of Latino immigrants in the 1980s, Miami's homicide rates continued to decline (Martinez, 1997b). Finally, Martinez and Lee (1998) found that while African Americans were overrepresented in homicide incidents relative to group size, Miami's Haitians and Latinos were underrepresented, and in some cases the rate of homicide among the two immigrant groups was *lower* than that of non-Latino whites (Anglos).

In line with prior investigations, the criminal participation of immigrant groups varies considerably in different cities. A good illustration of this feature is provided in a study of Latino homicide among El Paso's Mexicans and Miami's Cubans (Lee, Martinez, and Rodriguez, 2000). Despite the two cities' similar employment and poverty rates (and other economic characteristics), El Paso's Latino homicide rate was almost three times lower than that in Miami. In addition to city-specific characteristics like Miami's greater income inequality (see Martinez, 1996, for a discussion of absolute versus relative deprivation among Latinos) and possibly older tradition of gun use, other local conditions shaped the comparatively high and heavily Cuban homicide rate. For example, Cubans (and later Central Americans) settled in a more violent area of the country (south Florida) than Mexicans (El Paso and the Southwest), and regional contexts may shape each group's involvement in homicide. Wilbanks (1984) demonstrated that Miami's homicide trends mirror those for south Florida generally, and that this area experienced a sharp rise in homicides *preceding* the arrival of thousands of Cuban refugees in the Mariel boatlift of 1980 (see also Epstein and Greene, 1993). Thus, Miami's Latinos lived in a location experiencing higher levels of violence than El Paso's Mexican-origin Latinos (Lee, Martinez, and Rodriguez, 2000).

While important differences were revealed by the experiences of Cuban and Mexican-origin, investigated in the research described earlier, other studies also have considered within-group differences among ethnic groups (see Hawkins, 1999, for a similar strategy). In one of the few studies comparing and contrasting the incidence of violence (as measured by homicide) among foreign-born blacks, Martinez and Lee (2000b) found that Mariel Cuban, Haitian, and Jamaican immigrants were generally less involved in homicide than natives. Comparing the early 1980s, when these groups first began arriving in Miami in large numbers, to the late 1980s, the authors discovered a strong pattern of declining violence, especially for Jamaicans and Mariels, while Haitians continuously maintained a low overall rate. As these immigrant groups grew in size, and had a higher proportion of adult males, homicide rates rapidly declined. This finding suggests that rapid immigration may not create disorganized communities, but may instead stabilize neighborhoods through the creation of new social and economic institutions (see also Portes and Stepick, 1993).

In sum, the small number of studies providing empirical evidence finds that immigrants in the United States are generally *less* involved in crime than other ethnic groups, in spite of the standard perception about the *immigration-generates-crime and criminals* connection. These findings are at odds with expectations derived from the social science literature. These include the belief that settling in extremely poor neighborhoods and adaptation difficulties should foster high rates of criminal involvement (see Hagan and Palloni, 1999; Martinez and Lee, 2000a). Furthermore, these findings suggest that immigrant experiences are heavily shaped by local conditions, and it is likely that these circumstances influence criminal involvement to a larger degree than the cultural traditions of the groups themselves.

Ethnicity-specific Studies. Another substantive topic, which has long received attention in the literature, has been the ethnicity and crime connection. As elaborated below, this chapter not only builds on this research tradition but also moves beyond it to address the concerns mentioned earlier in this narrative. It focuses in particular on how Latinos and Haitians are influenced by violence, and more important, if this influence is similar at the community level, net of traditional characteristics of violent crime.

Even though investigations on race and violence that move beyond black and white comparisons as the main analytic framework to include Latinos are rare, and studies that include non-Mexican Latino victims are even rarer, some research literature does exist. In an early analysis of Mexican-origin crime in several cities as part of the 1931 Wickersham Commission, Taylor (1931) concluded that Mexican crime rates seemed to be in line with population size. But, most important, patterns of criminal involvement varied considerably across cities and were shaped by a host of social factors including poverty and the age and sex distributions of the immigrant population. Furthermore, Taylor (1931: 235) also discovered that Mexican criminal involvement displayed "interesting diversity within the same locality," suggesting the need to examine structural factors differentially affecting immigrants in socially meaningful areas like neighborhoods, rather than larger political divisions like cities and states. In short, there was no single conclusion that could be drawn about "Mexican crime rates" independent of the local community context.

Even with this early work in mind, subsequent Latino crime research was scarce (see Martinez and Lee, 1998, for review of the literature). In spite of the fact that the Latino population is substantial in some areas of the country (e.g., the Southwest), and predominantly of Mexican origin, historically their small numbers in most localities have made it difficult to study ethnic distinctions (U.S. Bureau of the Census, 1993). With Latinos now projected to become the largest ethnic minority group in the United States, this failure to examine ethnic distinctions appears to be at odds with media images that expound on the dangers they pose to society and to Anglo demographic dominance. Since researchers are driven in part by media images, their failure to more carefully examine Latino crime and violence is somewhat surprising (Martinez, Lee, and Nielsen, 2001).

The most prominent image of Latino threat appeared in the 1980 Mariel boatlift when most Cuban refugees landed in Miami. Writers fueled a crime-prone image by proclaiming that Mariel-related crime was spreading across the United States without presenting *any* systematic evidence to support this notion (Tanton and Lutton, 1993). Nevertheless, the violent Mariel image flourished as politicians, commentators, and others posing as social scientists (cf. Lamm and Imhoff, 1985; Tanton and Lutton, 1993) continued to promote the notion of the crime-prone immigrant.

Current research contradicts this popular notion. For example, by examining in a multivariate context whether there are differences in victim-violator relationships or crime incidents involving family members, intimates, strangers, and acquaintances, net of other predictors, we can better determine whether immigrants (e.g., Mariels, Haitians) were overrepresented in particular types of violent crime. This enables a test of whether the perception of Mariels as disproportionately involved in crime and violence is in fact accurate or is a misleading stereotype. In a recent article, Martinez, Lee, and Nielsen (2001) examine these differences in homicide victim-offender relationships across racial/ethnic groups (e.g., whites, African Americans, Afro-Caribbeans, Mariel Cubans, and non-Mariel Latinos) in Miami for the years 1980 through 1990. Controlling for ethnicity and the relationship between victims and perpetrators, and a host of other important explanatory and control variables, the authors discovered that Mariels were rarely overrepresented in homicide types and in the rare instance (e.g., acquaintance killings) when they were overinvolved the effect soon dissipated.

In summary, the research on the ethnicity and crime connection seems to suggest that the emergence of Latino and Afro-Caribbean violence has been due primarily to poor social conditions. Among these are high poverty, poor housing, few health and educational services, and other deleterious circumstances that dominate Latino communities in places like Miami. Before exploring these issues in greater detail, I move from the literature review to the current study beginning with a brief description of the research site.

Research Setting

The city of Miami is ideally suited for this study. First, data from the FBI's Uniform Crime Report (UCR) demonstrates how Miami led the nation in homicide rates throughout the 1980s and had homicide rates higher than comparably sized cities over this same period (see annual editions of *Crime in the United States*, 1980–95). Second, data from the 1990 U.S. Census indicates that the city of Miami area has one of the highest concentrations of non-Mexican-origin Latinos (U.S. Bureau of the Census, 1990; 1993). In 1990, most of the Latino residents living in Miami were of Cuban, Dominican, Puerto Rican, Honduran, and Nicaraguan origin (see U.S. Bureau of the Census, 1990). Furthermore, the 1990 U.S. Census Bureau data also indicates that about 10 percent of all persons living in the city of Miami were French Creole speakers, presumably of Haitian origin, and that the city of Miami holds the second largest Haitian population in the United States (Dunn, 1997; see Stepick, 1992).

Moreover, poverty data from the U.S. Census Bureau indicates that almost 50 percent of Latinos in the city of Miami were living below the U.S. poverty level, a level much higher than the national rate of 11.2 percent for non-Latino whites but lower than that of Haitians (U.S. Census, 1990). The numbers of immigrants moving to Miami are likely to increase (as are their poverty rates), since southern Florida continues to be one of the most popular destination points for young and poor immigrants from South America, Central America, and the Caribbean Basin. The latest census bureau population report estimates that Miami-Dade County now has the highest percentage of Latinos of any large county in the nation (Driscoll and Henderson, 2001). Other sources predict that the number of Haitians will soon surpass that of African Americans, making Miami the first city in the United States with a larger foreign- than native-born black population (Dunn, 1997).

Since Latino and Haitians dominate the social and economic landscape of Miami, any sign of high crime is likely to generate stereotypes of crime/drug-prone immigrants. Even though it is located in a region of the United States with historically high rates of violent crime, and had the highest criminal homicide rate for large cities from 1948 to 1952 – a period predating recent immigration – this image has endured beyond what would be expected from the long-term effects of disorganization (see Sampson and Lauritsen, 1997; Wolfgang, 1958: 25). Thus, accommodating the demands of population growth reminds us that immigration has consequences for certain community characteristics, such as poverty, and consequences for the perception of violent crime when the presence of newcomers overshadows the number of established residents. These images are not always in line with contemporary research findings, but reflect stereotypes that immigration facilitates crime, a notion not always grounded in reality (Lee, Martinez, and Rosenfeld, 2001).

Data and Method

My purpose in this section is threefold. First, the mechanisms by which recent immigration might generate violence will be explored. This is done by examining the proportion of recent immigrants in a given tract, over and above traditional predictors of violence. Second, this link should have a separate impact on disaggregated homicide levels, requiring moving beyond overall total counts. Exploring the implications of this process on group-specific killings (African-American, Haitian, Latino homicides) accomplishes this goal. Third, an assessment is made of the effects of economic deprivation and census tract characteristics in the city of Miami.

To address these issues, data on homicides during the 1988 through 1993 period was collected directly from files in the Homicide Investigations Unit of the city of Miami Police Department (MPD) and the Miami-Dade Medical Examiner Office (ME). Each individual homicide and supplemental homicide case was manually drawn from stored MPD and ME files, copied, read, and coded by a trained research assistant. The address of the homicide incident is also contained in these files, allowing linkage to data from the 1990 decennial census at the tract level. Furthermore, direct access to detailed internal files was necessary to distinguish white or African Americans from Latinos and Haitians, since the latter two ethnic groups are not typically, or at least consistently, coded in the FBI's Uniform Crime Reports or Supplemental Homicide Reports.[5] Although some researchers question the accuracy of official police data and maintain it portrays an inaccurate impression of crime in the United States, nearly all acknowledge that homicide is the most reliably recorded index crime (Lane, 1997).

The primary unit of observation in the following analysis is the census tract, or the seventy census tracts with more than five hundred residents in Miami. Census tracts are used because they are commonly used as neighborhood proxies in ecological level research (Messner and Tardiff, 1986; Alba et al., 1994; Morenoff and Sampson, 1997). Furthermore, factors such

---

[5] Multiple sources of information were used to assess the race and ethnicity category reported by Miami homicide investigators, most of whom were of Cuban or Puerto Rican origin. For example, a few "Latinos" were coded by skin color as "white" or "black" in the ME files but "Latin" in MPD documents or vice versa. Both data sources provide other information such as their surnames, country of birth, or narratives translated from Spanish to English. In those rare instances when skin color, instead of ethnicity, I recoded as "Latino" not as "White" or "Black" victims. Similar efforts were taken for "Haitian" victims. Most were coded as "BH" for black Haitian, but in a handful of cases a French Creole surname (e.g., Pierre, Dorvil, Jacques, etc.) provided clues that the victim was not African American. When all else failed, I asked the detective in charge of a specific case to verify ethnicity.

as income, poverty, and other valuable information are available from 1990 census reports, allowing detailed examination of areas where killings occured in the city of Miami.

There are two features of this approach and data that must be accounted for in the analysis: the counts of homicide are rare and include values of zero, and these events are dispersed across ecological units such as census tracts in a highly skewed manner. The use of ordinary least squares regression is inappropriate, since it assumes normal distributions and logarithmic transformations of the dependent variable do not induce normality. However, to compensate for the nonnormal distribution of homicides, a maximum likelihood estimator is employed to deal with *counts*, not rates. In Poisson regression, parameters are estimated through a maximum likelihood procedure, which has a number of desirable properties, including an asymptotic distribution, consistency, and efficiency (Feinberg, 1984). More specifically, homicides are conceptualized as counts of events per unit, a description suggesting that use of a Poisson random component or the related negative binomial specification is most suitable (Osgood, 2000). The general analytic strategy is to assess the independent effect of immigration on the frequency of ethnic-specific homicide counts across census tracts, controlling for a host of variables described below.

Although scholars are not in complete agreement on what set of variables should be used in homicide research, I have included a number of commonly used measures. First, a measure of population size is included to control for the fact that highly populated tracts will have greater numbers of persons at risk. Next, the percentage of persons living below the poverty line is an indicator of economic deprivation and that is used as well. I also include two control variables: (1) the percentage of the tract population that is young (aged fifteen to twenty-four years) and male; and (2) the percentage of the population that is non-Latino black. Both measures control for the population in each tract that is most at risk of homicide victimization, at least at the national level. Also included is a social control measure of the potential for intact families, percent divorced, in each Miami census tract. This measure is a proxy for family supervision and used by other scholars as well.

Following the tenets of social disorganization theory, I have included a measure of the percent of "new" immigrants.[6] In this case, the fraction of residents who arrived in the United States between the years 1987 through 1990 (regardless of legality) is included in the analysis. Social disorganization theory suggests that the presence of recent immigrants will weaken community organization and institutions, thus affecting criminal activity by contributing

---

[6] There is not an attempt to assess legality. Undocumented persons are not distinguished from others in any tract. Instead, this variable looks at the effect of new residents in census tracts.

Table 2.1. *Variables and Descriptive Statistics (N = 70)*

Variables	Values	Mean	S.D.
African-American Homicides	Number of African-American homicides in each tract	6.57	10.36
Haitian Homicides	Number of Haitian homicides in each tract	0.60	1.52
Latino Homicides	Number of Latino homicides in each tract	4.86	3.99
Population Size	Number of persons in each census tract	5215	2004
Percent Poor	Percent of families below the federal poverty line	32.50	14.26
Percent Divorced	Percent of population older than 15 years that is currently divorced or separated	22.48	7.04
Percent Young Male	Percent of the population male and aged 15 to 24 years	6.59	1.22
Percent Black	Percent of the population that is non-Latino black	29.72	37.69
Percent New Immigrant	Percent of the population foreign-born and arrived since 1987	9.46	6.49

to population turnover and ethnic heterogeneity. In Miami, this could have implications for both Latino and heavily Haitian areas, some of which are close to older, more established African-American communities. I turn to the findings in the next section.

Results

The descriptive statistics exhibit both similarities and differences with regard to the variables appearing in Table 2.1. The dependent variables for the three race-specific models used in this study are displayed first: the average number of African-American, Haitian, and Latino homicide counts in each tract. Miami has a much higher number of homicides per tract for African Americans than for Haitians and Latinos. Since our dependent variable is a *count* rather than a *rate*, a measure of the population size or group-specific population (logged in the Poisson model) is included to control for the fact that highly populated tracts might have greater numbers of homicide events.

Next, since tracts with high levels of poverty are commonly thought of as particularly crime-prone, percent poverty is included. Miami has a higher percentage of people in poverty than the total U.S. population; however, it is necessary to remember that this factor could also vary across neighborhoods and by ethnicity. The standard deviations associated with poverty are substantial and, therefore, highlight the wide variation of persons living in impoverished conditions across the tracts (which range from 11 to 68 percent in poverty). Still, this variable could influence ethnic-specific homicide in each city, regardless of this dispersal.

The table also highlights the tract level fractions of the percent of the population that is divorced, percent young and male, and percent black. Nearly 20 percent of the "legal-age" population is divorced. The percentage of the population that is male and between the ages of eighteen and twenty-four years is around 6 percent, and one-third of the population is non-Latino black. Moreover, the average number of persons in each neighborhood (census tract) is over five thousand residents and considerable variation is apparent in each tract. Some areas have as few as six hundred residents and others spiral up to eleven thousand persons with most leaning toward the high end.

But these variables alone do not adequately illustrate the complexity of demographic controls, disorganization, or deprivation. Finally, we have included a measure of the percentage of "new" immigrants (in this case, those who arrived in the United States between the years 1987 and 1990, as measured by the 1990 census). Social disorganization theory suggests that the presence of recent immigrants will weaken community organization and institutions, thus affecting criminal activity by contributing to population turnover and ethnic heterogeneity. Furthermore, as we have mentioned, politicians and pundits have suggested that the newest immigrants are a crime-prone group, a claim seized on by the media especially with regard to the 1980 Mariel boatlift in Miami (see Martinez, 1997). Unfortunately, there has been little empirical research at the tract level to address these allegations. The current study is therefore one of the first to assess the impact of recent immigration, independent of variables like poverty and age structure, on homicide events.

Overall, these descriptive findings portray the relatively harsh conditions in many Miami neighborhoods. All of the ingredients for disorganization and deprivation apparently exist and a host of deleterious conditions could potentially shape tract level homicide. The question is whether these circumstances influence homicide and, if so, whether there are racial and ethnic differences in their effect on the risk of homicide offending and victimization.

To explore the crime and immigrant link, I begin by presenting maps of the spatial distribution across tracts of total homicide rates and percentages of new immigrants (using quartiles for both). Miami has a high

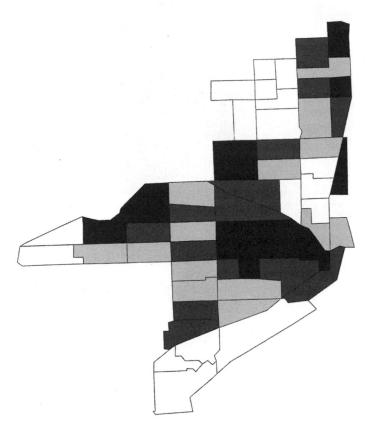

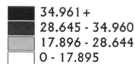

34.961+
28.645 - 34.960
17.896 - 28.644
0 - 17.895

Figure 2.1. Miami Tracts by Percent of New Immigrants

percentage of new immigrants, but, as the maps in Figures 2.1 and 2.2 show, "high immigrant" tracts do not correspond well with "high homicide" tracts. In fact, only *two* of the high homicide tracts (over 57 homicides per 100,000 total population) in northeast Miami overlap with high immigrant tracts (over 35 percent new immigrants). Many Miami tracts with *no* or *few* homicides have high levels of new immigrant residents. Most high homicide tracts are centered in areas with very few immigrants (e.g., Liberty City, Overtown) or in the downtown area. While the maps give some sense of the spatial concentration of homicide incidents, the important question is to what extent immigration influences homicide independent of the effect

57.071+
30.176 - 57.070
14.827 - 30.175
0 - 14.826

Figure 2.2. Miami Tracts by Total Homicide Rate

of other variables – a question that is answered in the multivariate analysis that follows.

Poisson Results

Table 2.2 presents the Poisson regression coefficients estimating the independent effects of all variables for African-American-, Haitian-, and Latino-specific homicide counts, without the new immigration variable. According to the results, percent poverty and non-Latino black are the only two significant predictors of *all* dependent variables. Tracts with high poverty rates

Table 2.2. *Poisson Regression Effects of Independent Variables on Race-Specific Homicide Counts (N = 70)*

	African American	Haitian	Latino
Intercept	−2.63*	1.54	−0.054
	(.043)	(.529)	(.483)
Population size (ln)[a]	.121**	.018	.123**
	(.033)	(.012)	(.288)
% Divorced	−.040	−.048	−.011
	(.081)	(.034)	(.098)
% Poverty	.248**	.279*	.403**
	(.045)	(.158)	(.055)
% Young and Male	.187**	−.719**	.029
	(.055)	(.222)	(.048)
% Non-Latino Black	.315**	.315**	−.141**
	(.019)	(.068)	(.021)
Log Likelihood	−498.288**	−89.114**	−158.082**

Note: Standard Errors are in parentheses.
[a]Group-Specific Data
*$p < .05$ (one-tailed)
**$p < .01$ (one-tailed)

are also areas with high homicides, suggesting that impoverished conditions give rise to *all* ethnic homicides. Despite this similarity, the results also reveal that this effect is stronger for Latinos than for African Americans and Haitians. The impact of poverty is similar among foreign- and native-born blacks.

Despite this important parallel between poverty and homicide, some differences also exist in the findings. Although the increased percent of non-Latino black is related to higher African-American and Haitian homicides, as would be expected, the direction on Latino killings is negative. There is at least one important reason for this effect and it is understandable in the context of neighborhood segregation in Miami. Latino-dominant areas have relatively small African-American populations, if any, and in fact, percent black and percent Latino were negatively and highly correlated with each other ($r = −.80$). The chances for outside group interaction are relatively small even in ethnically diverse Miami neighborhoods.

Results for some of the control variables conform to expectations but exceptions arise. For young males, the impact attains significance in two instances but in different directions. The increased African-American killings correspond to a greater young male population, but Haitian homicides are higher in areas with fewer young males. There probably is a substantial difference in the age distribution for both Afro-origin populations (see Dunn, 1997). Teenaged males were not disproportionately represented among the recent Haitian influx, which was fueled by political despair and widespread poverty in the nation of Haiti. Rather, Haitian adults, older males, and some intact families populated the first large 1980 boat waves. A high proportion of young males, by contrast, significantly increases the number of African-American homicides.

In sum, all three ethnic group homicides are positively affected by impoverished conditions. But, again, important similarities and differences exist. The levels of African-American and Latino homicides are both shaped by the number of residents in each tract. Haitian and African-American homicides are influenced by group size, but the percent of the neighborhood that is young and male is also an important factor for immigrant and native-born black homicides, but in different directions. The primary implication for all of these findings is that in the absence of a control for recent immigration, the results may change.

In fact, the theoretical foundation built by the early Chicago School implies a direct influence of immigration on local crime. Therefore, to examine this relationship, I explore the association between recent immigration and crime in Table 2.3. The findings reveal that the results are largely consistent with those of the previous model. Like before, the poverty variable has the highest influence on Latino homicides and one of the leading effects on black homicides, but for Haitian killings the magnitude of the effect of poverty has dampened considerably. An increase in immigration has attenuated the role of poverty in Haitian homicides but not to the same extent that it does for African-American or Latino killings. Rather, recent immigration and poverty might have a higher degree of interaction in areas where Haitian homicides occur than in areas where they are infrequent or absent. Regardless, immigration does shape Haitian homicides but to an extent lower than that of any other variable.

The other results still reinforce the view that economic deprivation is more directly associated with African-American and Latino homicides. An increase in poverty is consistently linked to violence in many areas; however, the magnitude is somewhat higher for Latino than African-American killings. The results again show that areas with higher percentages of young males are significantly related to decreased Haitian and increased African-American homicides. Most Haitian homicide victims in Miami are over twenty-four years of age, reflecting the preponderance of Haitian adults in the local population (Lee, Martinez, and Rodriguez, 2000). Again, as shown across all columns, immigration is not significantly related to homicides; thus, the most recent wave of immigration has not had a *direct* impact on homicide.

Table 2.3. *Poisson Regression Effects of Independent Variables and Recent Immigrants on Race-Specific Homicide Counts (N = 70)*

	African American	Haitian	Latino
Intercept	−2.20*	1.54	−0.646
	(.043)	(.529)	(.408)
Population size(ln)^a	.126**	.133	.118**
	(.033)	(.126)	(.029)
% Divorced	−.067	−.049	−.095
	(.083)	(.035)	(.099)
% Poverty	.256**	.019	.362**
	(.045)	(.018)	(.068)
% Young and Male	.173**	−.582**	.025
	(.057)	(.230)	(.048)
% Non-Latino Black	.285**	.413**	−.115**
	(.029)	(.093)	(.032)
% New Immigrants	−.024	.089	.130
	(.017)	(.049)	(.123)
Log Likelihood	−498.288**	−89.114**	−157.521**

Note: Standard Errors are in parentheses.
^{a}Group-Specific Data
*p < .05 (one-tailed)
**p < .01 (one-tailed)

Discussion and Conclusion

By incorporating the impact of immigration on crime (a focal concern among the founders of American sociology and criminology), this chapter is the first to examine the influence of deprivation and disorganization on African-American, Haitian, and Latino homicide in a city with a predominant immigrant population. These findings reveal that an increase in poverty is associated with increased homicides, and this holds in most cases, *regardless* of homicide victim ethnic composition. In turn, other neighborhood characteristics have a varying level of significance on homicide counts. Several implications can be drawn from these findings.

First, the bulk of neighborhood-level homicide research, much of it extended from the work of Shaw and McKay (1931, 1942), describes how deprivation or disorganization shapes local crime. However, crime is also a reflection of larger social, political, and economic processes within neighborhoods, cities, and beyond. This chapter demonstrates how one element of social change – varying numbers and characteristics of newcomers – transforms communities, exacerbates local conditions, and explores why attention to this process is necessary to advance community-level crime research. However, the direct link to violent crime as measured by homicide is not necessarily evident, at least in Miami.

Second, this chapter demonstrates the utility and shortcomings of examining the group-specific level of homicides. An exploration of racially disaggregated homicides reminds us that the range of factors shaping the number of killings might vary by racial/ethnic group, thereby increasing the potential scope of research applied to violent crime. The impact of deprivation and disorganization, however, appears to transcend immigration and ethnicity. An increase in neighborhood poverty has detrimental consequences for African-American, Haitian, and Latino homicides. This influence is less than expected for Haitians when immigration is incorporated, but the implication is that an influx of newcomers might have an *indirect* effect on homicide. This analysis suggests this might be the case in immigrant black killings, but at least for the factors used in this model, there are many similarities between African Americans and Latinos as well. Nevertheless, the basic links among deprivation, disorganization, and homicide are similar for all three ethnic groups.

There is an important caveat. Homicide is a rare event; thus, disaggregating homicide across subpopulations raises the possibility that the data are being strained into small categories and pushed to their limits. The sources and causes of any group differences may extend beyond the analytic capabilities of the data presented and, therefore, these findings should be interpreted with caution. However, rather than accounting for all aspects of immigrant and native-born homicides, I have produced a plausible account of how three distinct ethnic groups are influenced by social and economic factors in a unique immigrant city. Clearly, there are other distinct forces shaping homicide in African-American, Haitian, and Latino communities, but those processes are beyond the scope of traditional census tract variables (i.e., social and human capital, level of gun access, etc.). I have, however, attempted to yield a reasonable set of findings to encourage others to undertake efforts similar to this one in the future.

Still, even with these concerns in mind, this chapter did find that recent immigration does *not* increase community counts of Miami homicide, especially among those ethnic groups likely to be influenced by the deleterious consequences of a massive influx of newcomers, that is, African Americans, Haitians, and Latinos. These findings offer little support for accusations that immigration facilitates criminal violence in a multiethnic city (see Lee, Martinez, and Rosenfeld, 2001). Instead, native- and foreign-born groups could profit greatly from counterclaims that immigration stabilizes communities and buffers impoverished areas from criminal violence (Martinez and Lee, 2000b). The recent growth of diverse groups of ethnic minorities has complicated the relationship among race, ethnicity, and crime, even while scholars ignore this complexity, and place Latino and Afro-Caribbean groups with other "nonwhite" ethnic groups, or, at best, treat them as one of a series of control variables in a statistical analysis. Instead, this chapter places Latinos and Haitians at the center of criminological research.

Future Directions

Like others, I close by stating the obvious: much more research needs to be conducted on ethnic minorities and crime, both in the United States and in other settings. In the United States, we need inquiries that move beyond the black or white dichotomy and explore differences found in the increasingly multiethnic cities of the nation. Such studies will advance our knowledge beyond the conclusions drawn by this chapter. We need more studies on nonlethal violence (e.g., stranger robbery, intimate violence, acquaintance arguments, etc.) to determine whether these activities vary over time or across locales and ethnicity. Some Haitians and Latinos might be at elevated risk of robbery, while others are possibly involved in domestic violence situations, with both being linked to poor economic status and the stress associated with adaptation to a new life. Furthermore, at some point, immigrants and nonimmigrants alike become Americanized in terms of their criminal involvement. The question then is at what degree of integration (e.g., first-, second-, or even third- generation) are Haitians and Latinos engaging in violence like others and when does that take place? Does assimilation suppress or encourage violence?

A related issue is how economic and political refugees from abroad influence local crime (Waters, 1999). Many Haitians and Latinos left wartorn countries and totalitarian regimes throughout the 1980s and settled in the United States. Some were persecuted for political reasons, especially for membership in opposing political groups, and were in many cases the victims of official violence themselves. Others left for economic reasons in search of jobs and better wages. The majority of both refugee groups, however, had to enter the United States without the benefits of legality. This meant planning a long trip, gathering resources to carry it out, crossing at least one border (and in many instances two or three), amassing and carrying relatively large sums of money, and, of course, exposure to enormous personal dangers during the journey to the United States (Menjivar, 2000: 222). As Cecilia Menjivar (2000: 233) eloquently points out:

> When refugee immigrants make use of social webs similar to those used by *regular* immigrants to reach their destinations, it becomes difficult to disentangle whether they are *political* or *economic* migrants. [my emphasis]

Thus, immigration, as it affects other aspects of an individual's experiences and community conditions, is probably not influenced by immigrant status *in and of itself.* The key variable is the effect of conditions in the receiving local context, including an individual's social capital, as well as discrimination, punitive government reactions, and so on, since the circumstances driving them from home have more similarities than is commonly recognized.

Another important topic that warrants attention concerns the growth and effects of immigrants in rural (and suburban) areas. Many Latinos are entering small towns and rural settings in North Carolina, Arkansas, Georgia, Tennessee, Nevada, and Iowa. These areas have experienced phenomenal Latino growth and the consequences of this process remain to be seen. For instance, will rural Latinos be more or less assimilated, subject to discrimination, and singled out than urban Latinos? Will these practices shape violence victimization, criminal involvement, and criminal justice decision-making processes? There obviously is a need for more criminological research on rural and, of course, suburban areas that include Latinos.

Finally, other important issues deserve attention. What happens when the first-generation immigrants have children raised in the United States? After many years of weakened connections, conceptions of poverty "relative to" the old country become less salient and the impact of the persistence of social ties on criminality could diminish. Will Haitian and Latino crime then approach those of other ethnic minority groups? Historical research leads us to expect an increase in violence. But will Haitian and Latino communities provide an exception to expectations? What about Asian (e.g., Vietnamese, Korean, etc.) and Afro-Caribbean (Jamaican, Bahamian) ethnic group differences vis-à-vis crime? Will immigration status and timing of arrival, again, explain potential ethnic differences?

Although these issues are important to examine in the future, my main point bears repeating: scholars of violence research can no longer write seriously about the study of crime and violence as entirely a matter of "black" versus "white" crime. The reality of everyday life in America is too complex to view race/ethnicity and crime research in strict racial dichotomies of black or white. Studying the future, not the past, of violent crime research in urban America requires thinking about ethnicity and acknowledging that ethnic diversity matters, even when easy generalizations no longer exist. There is no doubt that much more research remains to be done in this area and that the findings in this chapter requires others to move forward.

The work of Du Bois (1899) serves as a reminder that race and crime has long been a central concern of American sociology. Having moved away from the issues raised at the turn of the century and ignored since World War II, researchers are now encouraged to bring immigration back in to the study of group differences in rates of crime and to reconsider the importance of work written a hundred years ago. Future research should be open to the idea that immigration can be a positive influence on communities that suppresses crime, and not necessarily a negative influence that encourage criminality or its impact on the level of social disorganization. A significant number of recent immigrants in Miami reside in areas with little or no homicide. This is likely true of other large cities that have experienced a recent influx of immigrants. Concentrating on the mechanisms that differentiate these places from those hit hard by deprivation, poverty, and high rates of crime is an important task. The incorporation of Latinos and Haitians into criminological research will inevitably intensify, and when it does, my hope is that this chapter will provide a foundation on which others can build studies that effectively capture meaningful group differences in violent crime research, as well as a rationale for moving beyond black and white comparisons.

Homicide in Los Angeles County: A Study of Latino Victimization[1]

Marc Riedel

Most people are aware of two facts about homicide and violence. First, poverty and economic disadvantage are related to violence and, second, the majority of minorities are found in urban areas of poverty, economic disadvantage, and high rates of violence. These two views are cobbled together in the view that poverty and economic disadvantage affect all minorities in the same way to produce violent behavior.

In part, this perspective has the consequence of believing that the large amount of research on African-American violence can be readily generalized to other groups. Thus, as Martinez (1996; 1997a; 1997b; 1999) notes, there is little research on Latino crime and few studies comparing Latino violence to violence among whites and other minorities.

It is becoming increasingly apparent that Latinos cannot be indiscriminately grouped with other minorities in studying crime. In the last few decades, a social construction of Latino gangs and Latino violence has appeared (Spector and Kitsuse, 1987; Klein, Maxson, and Miller, 1995). The view of Latinos in terms of a "social problem" of gangs and violence has probably been spurred on by the increase of immigration in Florida, Texas, and California. Finally, the Uniform Crime Reporting Program and National Center for Health Statistics began in the 1980s to collect information on Latino homicides and other crimes. The availability of this data has been an important stimulus to research exploring differences between Latino crime and crimes of other minorities.

---

[1] There is an array of terms without much consensus as to preference used to refer to the race/ethnic groups. "Blacks" or "African Americans" are frequently used terms to refer to people of African descent. I use the term "whites" to mean non-Hispanic whites or Anglos; "Latinos" refer to different Latino groups; and "Asians" are Asians/Pacific Islanders.

The view that economic determinants in the form of social class acts uniformly on all minorities finds expression in structural theories. Hagan (1985) developed a structural theory drawing on the writings of Willem Bonger (1916), who believed class position had to be taken into account to understand the relationships between gender and crime. To take one example, Bonger and Hagan argued that as economic circumstances declined, differences in crime rates between males and females would also decline. In other words, the ratio of white male-to-female rates would be larger than the ratios of either black male-to-female rates or Latino male-to-female rates. Hagan found support for this hypothesis using Canadian data. Riedel (1989) calculated ratios for previous research studies as well as ratios on Cook County (Chicago) and urban counties in Illinois. While there was support for the hypotheses for African American versus whites, there was no support for the limited data on Latinos available from Wilbanks (1984).

Because the ratios of differences for white and minority sex ratios was stronger for data prior to 1975, we calculated ratios for Los Angeles County for 1987 through 1995. There was no support for any of the hypotheses. The mean ratio of white male rates to female rates for the nine-year period was 2.5. Instead of being smaller, as hypothesized, the mean black male-to-female ratio was 5.9 and the mean Latino ratio was 8.5. This is not to suggest economic factors are unimportant; it is to suggest that economic factors have different consequences for different minorities because of cultural factors.

Latinos in the United States

In recent decades, however, Latinos have become a very large segment of the population, particularly in the western and southwestern parts of the United States. Kennedy (1996: 68) points out that the Latino population increased from 14.6 million in 1980 to 21.4 million in 1990. Most of the immigrants have been from Mexico and they are concentrated in two states, California and Texas. Latinos are 28 percent of the population in Texas and 31 percent of the California population. California alone has nearly half of the Latino population and over half of the country's Mexican-origin population.

California is the largest state with an estimated 1999 population of 34,036,000 and Los Angeles is the largest California county (9,790,000) (State of California, 1998). During the 1980s, Los Angeles became a major growth center in the United States and the U.S. capital of the Pacific Rim. Chinchilla, Hamilton, and Loucky (1993) characterize the subsequent economic restructuring of Los Angeles County in the 1990s as the juxtaposition of first world capital (United States, Europe, and Japan) and third world labor composed largely of Latino and Asian immigrants.

The projected year 2000 nonwhite population for Los Angeles County makes the nonwhite population a clear majority (67.2 percent). The Latino population is the largest (45.6 percent) followed by Asians (12.6 percent), African Americans (9.4 percent), and Native Americans (0.3 percent). Population projections for 2010 make Latinos a majority (51.0 percent) with whites declining from 32.1 percent in 2000 to 26.7 percent (State of California, 1998).

It has been noted that explanations that rely on social class variables do not suffice to explain violence among minorities. What further complicates the problem of explanation is that major metropolitan areas underwent a process of economic restructuring in the 1980s and 1990s, which has had an impact on violent crime. Wilson (1987) provides a contemporary interpretation of poverty in his description, mostly of Chicago, of an underclass or ghetto poor and the growth of African-American crime, female-headed families, teenage pregnancies, and welfare dependency. While Wilson's writing had a major impact on thinking about poverty and African Americans, Moore and Pinderhughes (1993) show that economic and social forces have a different impact outside Chicago and on Latinos.

Latinos in Los Angeles

Economic Restructuring. Wilson's book, *The Truly Disadvantaged*, provides a different view from earlier writings of the effects of poverty. Dramatic increases in joblessness and long-term poverty were the outcome of major economic shifts – economic restructuring – that led to a loss and relocation of jobs from industrial centers such as Chicago. Such restructuring also led to a loss of middle-level jobs and a polarization of the labor market. The jobs that remained required either technical skills or education unavailable to inner-city poor or were low-paying jobs with little room for job mobility.

Economic restructuring also has had a major impact outside the "rustbelt." In the Los Angeles barrios examined by Moore and Vigil (1993), Latinos found work in traditional manufacturing: auto assembly, tire, auto parts, and steel factories. However, the 1970s brought about an expansion of high-tech companies and an increase in financial and managerial services associated with the region's "Pacific Rim" orientation. Traditional manufacturing jobs declined rapidly, while very low-wage manufacturing and service jobs expanded.

However, Wilson's analysis of the importance of immigration falls short when applied to Latinos. Immigration from Mexico and Central America to Los Angeles County increased dramatically in the 1970s and 1980s. In an area containing El Hoya Maravilla, a barrio studied by Moore and Vigil, the Latino population was about two-thirds in 1964; by 1980, it was 94 percent. The negative side of this immigration was that all the low-wage jobs were filled by immigrants. In addition, these immigrants were not eligible for public assistance. These circumstances created "perhaps the largest pool of cheap, manipulable, and easily dischargeable labor of any advanced capitalist city" (Soja, 1987) (Cited in Moore and Vigil, 1993: 34). This also meant that Mexican immigrants were more likely to get jobs than Mexican Americans who lived in the same community for a long period of time.

Concentration Effects. One of the most important features of Wilson's (1987) analysis of African-American poverty in Chicago was the increase in the number of poor neighborhoods and proportion of poor people in these neighborhoods between 1970 and 1980. Besides high unemployment, Wilson saw the movement of middle- and working-class African Americans out of these communities to areas with better housing, leading to a loss of achieving role models, weakened marriage market, and less useful job networks. For those left behind, poverty becomes more concentrated.

While jobs have vanished in Latino communities, immigration and a historically lower level of housing discrimination distinguish African-Americans from Latinos (Moore and Pinderhughes, 1993). Extensive immigration has meant many traditional family networks, particularly extended families. The concern about the rise in female-headed households resulting from poverty is also somewhat misplaced. In two of the barrios studied by Moore and Vigil (1993: 36), almost 80 percent of the families with children under eighteen in 1980 were headed by a married couple.

While extensive immigration has contributed to a highly exploitable labor pool, it has also had positive effects. While economic factors lead to families moving in and out of poor neighborhoods, in some cities, there are considerable cross-class linkages that provide resources to the poor who were left behind. Furthermore, the arrival of Mexicans and Central Americans from more traditional cultures has contributed to a strengthening of traditional social controls and networks, a revival of their native language, and the emergence of new community institutions.

Moore and Vigil (1993) also suggest that the reduction in federal resources and subsequent elimination of local agencies may have contributed more to deterioration of barrio communities than demographic shifts. Beginning in the late 1970s, funding was reduced or eliminated for grassroots agencies that provided job training, legal advice to immigrants, and health and social services, and provided programs to help gang youths, heroin addicts, and ex-offenders become reintegrated into the community.

The different consequences of economic restructuring for Latinos in comparison to African Americans suggest that different patterns of homicide may exist. Developing a theory or a modification of a theory to explain differences between these two race/ethnic groups may be premature in view of what little is known about Latino homicide patterns. This is not to say that we cannot trace a theoretical link from the writings of Wilson (1987) and Moore and Pinderhughes (1993) to testable hypotheses about similarities and differences in homicides among the three race/ethnic groups.

There are, however, a few components of economic restructuring among Latinos, such as the impact of immigration, that have implications for violent victimizations. There are other differences between Latino, African-American, and white homicides in which the effect of interaction of racial/ethnic components of culture and economic restructuring are not understood. Combining the preceding with the paucity of research on Latinos, the strategy pursued here is to describe general patterns of homicide victimization and examine differences with respect to gender. Gender is emphasized not only because it is a central status characteristic of most societies, but also because what research exists suggests interesting differences between Latinas, black, and white females.

Research Issues

Total Rates and Trends. While immigration has had negative effects, it also has had the mitigating effect of reducing the amount of social disorganization in Latino communities. Immigration has meant the preservation and extension of a single language, extended families, and cross-class linkages. In addition, the high proportion of intact families are factors that should reduce the devastating effect of poverty.

Previous research indicates that Latino homicide victimization rates are between white and African-American rates. In five southwestern states (Arizona, California, Colorado, New Mexico, Texas) during the years 1977–82, whites had a victimization rate of 7.9 per 100,000, Latinos followed with a rate of 21.6, while African Americans had the highest at 46.0 (Centers for Disease Control, 1986). In Chicago, Block (1993: 284) reports that in 1989 whites and other males had a rate of 10.3, followed by 43.9 for Latino males, and 74.2 per 100,000 for African-American males. Finally, Martinez (1997a: 25) notes that while whites comprised only 10 percent of the population in Miami from 1990 through 1995, they committed 7 percent of the homicides. Latinos were almost 63 percent of the population, and committed 38 percent of the homicides. African Americans were 27 percent of the population and committed 56 percent of the homicides.

> HYPOTHESIS 1: Latinos in Los Angeles County will have total homicide victimization rates that are smaller than African-American and larger than white rates.

Race/Ethnicity and Female Rates. One effect of economic restructuring is the creation of many low-level service jobs that require little training or education and that are readily filled by immigrants. The immigrants also carry with them their cultural values with respect to family and the role of women. Among poor Latinos, two-parent families are not unusual. In examining research on Latinos, Moore and Pinderhughes (1993: xvi) note, "The evidence on familism was skimpy, but there was good reason to believe that in many areas Latino families still operate to support and control their members."

It is also possible that Latino cultural patterns operate to make women less vulnerable as targets of violence. Horowitz (1983: 136), in her study of a Latino community in New York, points to the importance of virginity, motherhood, and submission to men for young women. "Violence," she suggests, "is the antithesis of femininity. Most of what is considered masculine – violence, aggressiveness, domination, and the uncontrolled expression of passion – is the opposite of femininity – submissiveness and controlled passion."

Not overemphasizing this view is important. Submissiveness and passivity may be an invitation to violent exploitation and rates of violence are much greater among Latino than among non-Latino white families (Straus, 1988). Furthermore, both Horowitz (1983) and Vigil (1988) describe the existence of female Latino or Latina gangs. However, Moore and Vigil (1993) indicate that, while there are many "traditional" family networks in Los Angeles barrios, more egalitarian patterns are appearing.

The available research does show a smaller amount of Latina victimization. For the southwestern states mentioned earlier, African-American females have the highest homicide rates, while the Latina rates were only slightly greater than white female rates (Centers for Disease Control, 1986). Block (1993) also found Latina homicide rates to be similar to white female rates in Chicago.

Vigil (1988) also notes that in interbarrio fighting between gangs, there was an understanding that women, children, and elders were not to be targeted. Sanders (1994) pointed out that, while members of these three groups were sometimes killed in drive-by shootings, they were regarded as accidental victims who happened to be in the line of fire.

HYPOTHESIS 2: Latina homicide victimization rates will be more similar to white female victimization rates than to African-American female victimization rates.

Intimate Partner Homicides. If the Latina victimization rates are substantially different from African-American and white rates, an obvious area of exploration is the relationship of Latina victimization to intimate partner homicides. It is "obvious" because a large number of female homicide victims are killed in intimate partner settings (Cardarelli, 1997).

The pattern in previous research indicates that Latina victimization tends to be highest in intimate partner relationships, while African-American females tend to be lowest. Using data from the entire state of California for 1987 through 1996, Riedel and Best (1998) examined sex ratios of killing among husbands and wives, commonlaw relationships, and boyfriends/ girlfriends for whites, Latinos, and African Americans. Using computed percentages rather than ratios for whites, Latinos, and African Americans, 81.5 percent of Latino intimate partner homicides were females. Both white (79.8 percent) and African-American (59 percent) intimate partner relationships had lower percentages of female victims.

Among Chicago homicides originating in assaults, there was little difference between Latinas (46.9 percent), black (45.9 percent), and white (49.5 percent) female victimizations with respect to intimate partner homicides. Latinas (7.6 percent) were similar to black (9.6 percent) females and different from white (13.6 percent) females in the category of other family victimizations.

For the most socially distant relationships of offenders known to the victim, such as friends, acquaintances, and work relationships, Latina victimizations (26.6 percent) were more similar to white (28.6 percent) females and least similar to black (37.6 percent) female victimizations. Finally, in Chicago assault homicides, Latinas were more frequently victimized by strangers (19.0 percent) than either black females (6.7 percent) or white females (8.4 percent) (Block, 1988: 50).

It is evident that Latina homicides in relation to victim/offender relationships is a variegated picture of results depending on the city. Part of the reason may be that Latinos is a broad category including Mexicans, Cubans, and other Latin American countries. Hence, given the distribution of different Latino groups in U.S. cities, there may be different cultural patterns that account for differences in the violent victimization of Latinas (Martinez and Lee, 1999).

While the previous research supports a hypothesis of low Latina victimization, it is unclear how Latina victimization contributes to intimate partner and other victim/offender homicide relationships. Rather than stating a hypothesis, we will examine Latina rates and their contribution to different types of victim/offender relationships.

Race/Ethnic Differences in Ages Among Females. Research indicates that females, like males, are homicide victims primarily in the fifteen to thirty-four age range. Rodriguez (1988: 78) found that homicide rates for females peaked in the ages sixteen to twenty-four. A more detailed analysis indicated race/ethnic-age-specific homicides were highest (10.1 per 100,000) for white females in the sixteen to twenty age group. Latinas (18.9) and black females (30.8) had the highest rate in the twenty-one to twenty-four age group.

Valdez and Nourjah (1988: 98) used data derived from death certificates to study homicide in southern California. Homicide rates were highest for the twenty-five to thirty-four age group of females with white females having the lowest rate (5.5) followed by Latinas (8.5) and black females (28.4).

However, race/ethnic-age-specific rates among the very oldest groups are very different. For the sixty-five to seventy-four age group, all three groups were very similar. Latinas had a rate of 4.0, whites a rate of 3.9, and black females a rate of 3.0. By contrast, in the seventy-five year and older group, black females had a rate of 31.1 per 100,000, a rate of 6.8 for white females, and a rate of 3.3 for Latinas. It does appear that Latinas share with other race/ethnic groups a high risk for homicide victimization in the young ages. The evidence with respect to older females only partially supports Vigil's (1988) claim that older Latinas were not targeted.

> HYPOTHESIS 3: The highest homicide victimization rates for Latinas will be in the fifteen to thirty-four age range.
> HYPOTHESIS 4: Homicide victimization rates for Latinas at all ages will be larger than white female rates and smaller than black female rates.

Gangs, Race/Ethnicity, and Male Rates

We will not examine gang involvement among the three race/ethnic groups, because the present data on gang-related homicides suggests that these homicides are underreported to the Criminal Justice Statistics Center (CJSC). Based on gang definitions used by Maxson and Klein (1995), they report about 25 percent more gang related homicides than are found in this data. It is not known why data reported to the CJSC contains a smaller number of gang homicide than was obtained from the gang control units used by Maxson and Klein.

Male Victimization and Victim/Offender Relationships. Whereas gang-related homicides cannot be distinguished from other types of homicides in this study, those homicides remain in the data set. It is likely that many homicides are the result of gang shootings, because gangs are a common characteristic of urban areas where Latinos reside. Indeed, as Sanders (1994) indicates, gang membership may be passed on from father to son.

Although it is difficult to determine its prevalence among Latino males, the cult of *machismo* is one that will increase the probability of violent conflicts with intimate partners and family members as well as other males (Martinez-Garcia, 1988). Its contemporary expression is found in the subculture of violence where one man insulting another is cause for a response that can range all the way from a counterinsult to lethal violence (Wolfgang and Ferracuti, 1967; Luckenbill, 1977). Hence, *from the perspective of victims,* we should find that Latino males should have the lowest involvement in intimate partner homicides and higher involvement in homicides outside the family.

Block's (1988: 50) study of assault homicides in Chicago gives partial support to the preceding. Male Latinos had the smallest percent of intimate partner victimization (2.5 percent), followed by white males (7.5 percent) and black males (13.4 percent). Likewise, Latino males also had the lowest (4.1 percent) involvement in other family homicides in comparison to white males (8.2 percent) and black males (7.4 percent).

For the more socially distant relationships of friend, acquaintance, employer, co-worker, and so on, black males (65.0 percent) were more heavily involved in these types of homicides, while Latino males (59.4 percent) and white males (56.3 percent) were very similar. While homicides in relationships outside the family did not favor high involvement by Latino males, homicides involving strangers were higher among Latino males. Thirty-four percent of Latino males were victimized in stranger relationships, while 14.0 percent of black males and 26.6 percent of white males were killed by strangers.

> HYPOTHESIS 5: The percent of Latino males involved in intimate partner and family killings will be smaller than the percent of white and black males.
>
> HYPOTHESIS 6: In cases of other relationships known to the victim, but outside the family, Latino male victimization rates are between white and black male rates. Latino males are most frequently victimized in stranger relationships.

Race/Ethnic Differences in Ages Among Males. There is a widespread consensus that homicide is a young man's offense and we should expect that to be true of Latino males as well. Although rates vary among the three race/ethnic groups, most homicide victims were males between ages fifteen and thirty-four (Centers for Disease Control, 1986; Leyba, 1988; Rodriguez, 1988; Block, 1993). For example, Valdez and Nourjah (1988: 98) studied homicides in southern California in 1985 and found that black males (fifteen to twenty-four) had a rate of 108.9 per 100,000, followed by Latino males (44.7) and white males (13.3). For the ages of twenty-five to thirty-four, the rates were 139.1 for black males, 56.4 for Latino males, and 15.1 for white males.

For ages sixty-five to seventy-four, Valdez and Nourjah found Latino male rates (14.4) were between white male (8.1) and black male (46.8) rates. However, in the seventy-five years and older group, as with females, black male rates were 19.8 while Latino male (6.6) and white male (5.2) rates were very similar.

HYPOTHESIS 7: The highest homicide victimization rates for Latino males will be in the fifteen to thirty-four age range.

HYPOTHESIS 8: Homicide victimization rates for Latino males will be larger than white male rates and smaller than black male rates at all ages.

Weapon

Based on a study of 6,956 homicides in New York City, Rodriguez (1988: 84) found that Latinos were more likely to be killed by firearms than blacks or whites. Among Latino victims, 62.6 percent were killed by handguns, while 48.3 percent of white victims and 56.9 percent of black victims were killed by handguns. There was less than a 3 percent difference among the three groups in the use of cutting instruments. Puerto Ricans are the largest single group of Latinos in New York; results may be different in Los Angeles County, where Latinos of Mexican descent are the largest group.

In Chicago, Block (1993: 319) found that among race/ethnicity groups, Latino male victims were most frequently killed by automatic firearms. Fifty percent of street gang-related homicides and about 70 percent of "other expressive" or confrontational homicides of Latino victims involved automatic firearms. In an earlier analysis of homicides that began with assaults, Block (1988: 54) found that Latinos had the highest percent of victimizations with firearms and whites the lowest. For males, 73.1 percent of Latino male homicides were by firearms; this compares with 65.8 percent of blacks and 52.5 percent of whites. For females, Latinas likewise had the highest percent (59.5 percent) of victimizations with firearms, followed by black females (53.2 percent) and white females (43.9 percent). Despite the differences among the three race/ethnic groups, it is still abundantly clear that firearms are the favored weapon in homicides.

While there are stereotypes that Latinos favor knives in violent encounters, there is no evidence in Chicago assault homicide victimizations. Latinos, both males (19.1 percent) and females (15.2 percent), had the lowest percentage of knife killings. Knives were used in black male killing in 24.3 percent of the cases and 19.1 percent of the black female killings. For whites, 24.3 percent of males and 19.1 percent of females were killed by knives.

Other weapons such as hands, feet, clubs, poison, vehicles, suffocation, and so on were used most frequently against women. Among Latinos, 25.4 percent of Latinas, 24.1 percent of black females, and 36.9 percent of white females were killed by other weapons. Among males, other weapons were found most frequently in white male victimizations (23.2 percent) and infrequently among black (8.8 percent) and Latino (7.8 percent) males. The finding that more women were killed by other weapons highlights Browne's (1997) observation that, while women can be as aggressive as men in domestic conflicts, the superior physical strength of males in using such weapons as hands, feet, and clubs is substantially more lethal.

> HYPOTHESIS 9: The most frequent homicide weapon for whites, Latinos, and African Americans of both genders is firearms.

Precipitating Event

Leyba (1988: 115) found in her study of homicides in Bernalillo County (Albuquerque, NM) that among Latinos, 82 percent did not involve a felony. Among whites, 72 percent were nonfelony, and among African Americans, all eighteen cases were nonfelony homicides.

Block (1988: 48) found that 69.0 percent of Latino males and 72.5 percent of Latinas were killed in a fight, brawl, or argument. This contrasts with 54.2 percent of white males, 62.4 percent of white females, 72.0 percent of black males, and 73.7 percent of black females killed in nonfelony encounters.

Latinos are unlikely to be lower in nonfelony homicides than whites when compared to felony homicides. The reason is that white males and females are more frequently working at jobs where they are targets for robberies as well as moving in public spaces, such as going to and from jobs on public transportation, where they are also likely to be robbery or rape targets.

> HYPOTHESIS 10: The percent of Latinos victimized in felony homicides will be lower than the percent of whites victimized in felony homicides.

Method

The source of data for this study are all homicides reported to the California Criminal Justice Statistics Center (CJSC) from 1987 through 1998.[2] Of the 42,093 homicides reported to the police during that period, we selected all homicides ($N = 19,808$) reported as occurring in Los Angeles County.

From this file, we excluded justifiable homicides ($N = 1,011$) and manslaughters ($N = 111$). The analysis file contained 18,686 wilful homicides or murder cases or 94.3 percent of all homicides reported in Los Angeles County from 1987 through 1998. During that period, there were 8,949 Latino, 6,430 black, 2,403 white, 509 Asian, and 335 homicide victims of "other" race/ethnic groups. There were sixty cases where race/ethnic

[2] We are grateful to Tricia Clark and Linda Nance, Criminal Justice Statistics Center, for their help. The data was reformatted for SPSS with KEDIT and a macro generously provided by Kent A. Downs of the Mansfield Software Group.

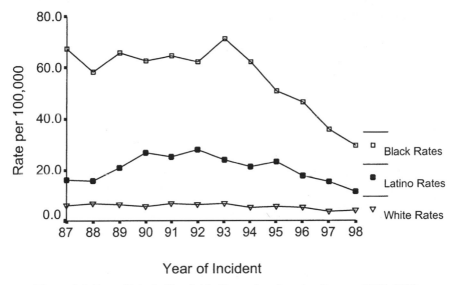

Figure 3.1. Race/Ethnic Homicide Rates: Los Angeles County, 1987–1998

identification was missing. Race/ethnic groups other than whites, blacks, and Latinos were excluded from the analysis.

The *number of homicides* or homicide *counts*, as opposed to *rates per 100,000* persons at risk, give very little indication of the actual risk of victimization for these race/ethnic groups. While there are more Latino than African-American homicide victims, the risk of homicide among Latinos is actually substantially lower than for blacks, because Latinos are a larger proportion of the general population in Los Angeles County. Conversely, blacks, who comprise a smaller proportion of the county's population, are at greater risk because of a substantially higher population-based rate of homicide.

Results

Rates and Trends by Race/Ethnic Group. Figure 3.1 indicates that the first hypothesis was supported. Consistent with previous research, Latino homicide rates were higher than white rates and substantially lower than African-American rates per 100,000.

Figure 3.1 indicates substantially different trends for the three groups using race/ethnic-specific rates. The risk of black victimization was the highest, showing a peak rate of 71.2 in 1993, which was later than occurs for the other two groups. Black rates varied between 1987 through 1992, peaked in 1993 (71.2), then declined to 29.7 per 100,000 by 1998.

Latino rates increased to a peak of 28.1 per 100,000 by 1992, then declined to 11.6 by 1995. Like black rates, white rates peaked in 1993 (6.9), then declined to 3.9 per 100,000 by 1998.

Table 3.1. *Race/Ethnic-Gender Specific Homicide Rates: 1987–1998*

	Blacks		Latinos		Whites	
Year	Males	Females	Males	Females	Males	Females
87	116.3	24.0	28.0	4.0	8.2	4.0
88	99.0	21.8	27.6	3.3	9.4	4.4
89	115.7	21.4	35.8	4.7	8.7	4.3
90	111.8	18.7	46.4	5.9	8.1	3.1
91	118.1	16.9	44.7	4.9	10.3	3.2
92	110.8	18.9	49.5	5.5	8.7	3.8
93	122.8	25.5	42.2	5.2	10.2	3.6
94	116.3	14.1	38.6	3.2	7.4	2.9
95	91.4	14.7	40.3	5.1	8.4	2.8
96	81.7	15.2	31.4	3.6	7.1	3.1
97	65.6	9.8	27.1	3.1	5.1	2.2
98	54.3	8.0	19.8	3.0	5.0	2.9

There are two observations to be made about the three race/ethnic rates in Figure 3.1. First, while the three rates were distinct, Latino rates were closer to white than to African-American rates. Given the effects of restructuring and immigration, it can be suggested that Latino communities have not become as socially and culturally disorganized as African-American communities.

Second, all three groups participate in the declining homicide rates that are a fixture of national rates as well. Each race/ethnic group has shown lower rates since 1993. There is little agreement on the causes of the decline in homicide rates although there have been thoughtful attempts to explain it (Blumstein and Rosenfeld, 1998). The causes, whatever they are, seem to be having an impact on all three race/ethnic groups, albeit with the greatest impact on black rates. On the one hand, the greater change in black rates may be a statistical artifact: given the relative size of the rates for the three groups, black rates have a greater possible range of change than Latino or white rates. On the other hand, changes in the level of the causal variables may be having a greater effect on African-American than Latino and white rates.

Race/Ethnicity and Gender Rates

Table 3.1 gives the race/ethnic-gender-specific homicide rates for the twelve-year period for males and females.

Table 3.1 shows that black male victimization rates consistently had the highest rates for the twelve-year period. Black male rates were over four times as high as Latino male rates and between ten and twenty times higher than

Table 3.2. *Victim/Offender Relationships by Race/Ethnicity of Female Victims*

	Female Race/Ethnicity			
Relationship	Blacks	Latinas	Whites	Total
Intimate Partners	171	235	209	615
	(22.2)	(33.9)	(36.8)	(30.5)
Other Family	93	93	89	275
	(12.1)	(13.4)	(15.7)	(13.5)
Other Known	306	193	152	651
	(39.8)	(27.8)	(26.8)	(32.1)
Strangers	199	173	118	490
	(25.9)	(24.9)	(20.8)	(24.1)
Total	769	694	568	2031
	(100.0)	(100.0)	(100.0)	(100.0)

white male rates. While there were large differences among the different male and female race/ethnic groups, the three groups had peak rates in the early nineties then declined.

Table 3.1 indicates support for the second hypothesis, namely, Latina rates are more similar to white female than African-American female rates. Black female victimization was between four and five times higher than the victimization rates for Latina and white females. The mean intragender ratio for African-American females/Latina was 4.1; for African-American females/white females, it was 5.1 while for Latinas/white females, it was 1.3.

Female Victimization and Victim/Offender Relationships. To explore the similarities and differences among Latina, black, and white females further, we examined female victimization by victim/offender relationships.

Table 3.2 suggests that Latinas, while their rate of victimization was low, tend to be victimized by a greater variety of victim/offender relationships than either white or African-American females. With respect to intimate partner victimizations, Latinas (33.9 percent) resembled white female victims (36.8 percent) more than black female victims (22.2 percent). While the three race/ethnic groups were similar with respect to victimization among other family members, Latinas presented different patterns with respect to the other two more socially distant relationships.

Among "Other Known" relationships between victim and offender, Latinas (27.8 percent) resembled white females (26.8 percent). However, among stranger victimizations, Latinas (24.9 percent) were more similar to black females (25.9 percent).

In the absence of more detailed data, results about Latinas suggest a group of women in economically disadvantaged settings who are both harmed

Age of Female Victims

Figure 3.2. Mean Female Race/Ethnic-Age-Specific Rates of Victimization, 1987–1998

and benefit from intimate partner relationships. On the one hand, their violent victimization in intimate partner relationships may be the outcome of patriarchal relationships in which they are perceived as not behaving correctly in their subordinate status. This interpretation is consistent with Straus's (1988) results, mentioned earlier, that Latino families are more violent than non-Latino families.

On the other hand, it has to be recognized that in male-dominated societies, women receive a measure of protection by falling under the protective mantle of some male, either a family member or intimate partner (Baumgartner, 1993). In those instances, we would expect their homicide victimizations for the "Other Known" category to be much lower than black females, which Table 3.2 indicates is the case.

Finally, of course, family cohesion cannot completely override the effects of poverty and social disorganization. Even assuming that Latinas have somewhat of a protected status, they cannot avoid being a target in a high crime area. In this instance, we would expect violent victimization by strangers to be similar to that of the other disadvantaged group – black females.

Female Victimization at Different Ages. To explore Latina victimization a final step, we calculated the mean of twelve years of rates for each of five age groups. These mean values are plotted in Figure 3.2.

Figure 3.2 shows that mean black female rates were highest in the fifteen to thirty-four age group (27.2 per 100,000), which supports the fourth hypothesis. The age range of fifteen to thirty-four was the only one where Latina killings (6.8) are higher than white females (4.5). The mean rates between the white females and Latinas were nearly identical in the two age ranges, thirty-five to forty-four and forty-five to sixty-four. In the age range sixty-five to one hundred, the mean Latina rate (1.5) was less than the white female rate (3.3).

African-American female rates declined from the fifteen to thirty-four age high to 8.3 at ages forty-five to sixty-four, but then increased to 9.9 in the sixty-five to one hundred age group. Like male victimization rates, which will be seen in the next section, African-American female victimization rates remain high throughout their life span.

The result comparing Latina to white females gives limited support to the fourth hypothesis, which stated Latina rates will be higher than white female and lower than black female rates. It is true that Latina rates are substantially lower than black female rates. However, from ages thirty-five to sixty-four, Latina rates were almost identical with white female rates and in the sixty-five to one hundred category, Latina rates were lower.

The increase in homicide victimization among Latinas, relative to white females, in the fifteen to thirty-four age range is consistent with what was suggested in previous research. The ages from fifteen through thirty-four are those where women are getting married and victimized for the first time. This is also the age range where women are more likely to be unaccompanied in public settings and susceptible to attacks by strangers. The decline in homicide victimization among aged sixty-five to one hundred Latinas is consistent with Vigil's (1988) finding that in gang warfare, old people should not be targeted.

Race/Ethnicity, Males, and Victim/Offender Relationships. Table 3.3 is a cross tabulation of type of victim/offender relationship by three race/ethnic male groups. A general view of the table shows that males were seldom homicide victims in intimate partner or family murders. Males were victimized most frequently in relationships in which the offender was known but outside the family.

The fifth hypothesis stated that Latino males would show the smallest involvement in intimate partner and other family homicides; this is supported in Table 3.3. Latino males were 0.9 percent of intimate partner homicides compared to 3.0 percent of black and 5.4 percent of white males. For other family homicides, only 3.4 percent of Latino males were victims compared to 4.7 percent of black males and 9.2 percent of white males.

The sixth hypothesis stated that Latino male percentage of "Other Known" to the victim homicides would be between black and white percentages is supported. The percent of Latino males killed in "Other Known" relationships (52.9 percent) was less than the percent of black males

Table 3.3. *Victim/Offender Relationship by Race/Ethnicity of Male Victims*

Relationship	Male Race/Ethnicity			
	Blacks	Latinos	Whites	Total
Intimate Partners	114	48	70	232
	(3.0)	(0.9)	(5.4)	(2.2)
Other Family	177	189	118	484
	(4.7)	(3.4)	(9.2)	(4.5)
Other Known	2135	2984	594	5713
	(56.1)	(52.9)	(46.1)	(53.2)
Strangers	1379	2420	506	4305
	(36.2)	(42.9)	(39.3)	(40.1)
Total	3805	54641	1288	10734
	(100.0)	(100.0)	(100.0)	(100.0)

(56.1 percent), but more than the percentage of white males (46.1 percent). By contrast, consistent with the second part of the sixth hypothesis, Latino males were killed more frequently by strangers (42.9 percent) than either black males (36.2 percent) or white males (39.3 percent).

If Martinez-Garcia (1988) is correct in her analysis of *machismo*, then we should expect fewer Latino male intimate partner and other family victims. Latino male involvement in stranger homicides is high as predicted, but it is unclear why it is not also higher in other known relationships than African-American male victimization.

Male Victimization at Different Ages. The seventh hypothesis states that Latino male rates will be highest in the fifteen to thirty-four age range. The eighth hypothesis states that Latino male victimization rates will be lower at every age than African-American rates and higher than white male rates. We calculated the mean of twelve years rates for each of five age groups. Figure 3.3 shows that both hypotheses are supported.

While rates were low for the three groups before the fifteen to thirty-four age category, they were extremely high for fifteen to thirty-four black males ($\bar{X} = 210.1$). Black males in this age group were over seventeen times more likely to die of homicide than white males ($X = 11.9$) and over three times more likely than Latino males ($\bar{X} = 68.2$).

Among older age groups, Latino homicide victimization rates were similar to white rates. While there was a substantial difference between Latino and white males in the forty-five to sixty-four age group (19.8 vs. 9.0), the mean rates were very similar in the sixty-five and older groups, which is consistent with Vigil's (1988) claim, mentioned in the previous section, that

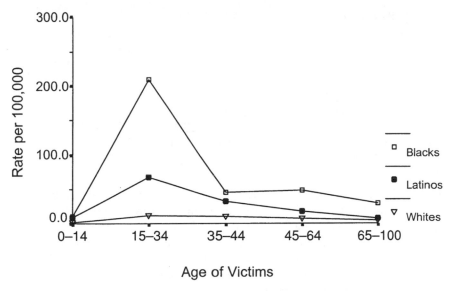

Figure 3.3. Mean Male Race/Ethnic-Age-Specific Homicide Rates, 1987–1998

the elderly are not targeted in interbarrio conflicts. Black males, on the other hand, were consistently higher: at ages sixty-five and older, the black male victimization rate ($\bar{X} = 29.6$) was still over six times higher than the white male rate ($\bar{X} = 4.8$). Thus, while the risk of homicide victimization is extremely high for young African-American males, it is very high for black males of *all* ages (Reiss and Roth, 1993).

Weapons

Weapons are classified into firearms (handguns and other firearms), knives, and other weapons. Percentages for each weapon classification, race/ethnic group, and gender are given in Table 3.4.

Table 3.4 presents ample confirmation of the ninth hypothesis, that is, that firearms are the most frequently used weapon among all three race/ethnic groups. Almost 80 percent of male victimizations and 56.1 percent of female victimizations were by firearms. The highest use of firearms in homicides occurred for black males (83.4 percent), followed closely by Latino males (81.7 percent), and white males (59.3 percent). Among females, by contrast, the greatest occurrence of firearms occurred for Latinas (63.6 percent), followed by black females (58.9 percent) and white females (42.8 percent).

Knives were used slightly more frequently to kill females (13.8 percent) than males (11.2 percent). Knives were used to kill white males (18.5 percent) most frequently and black males least frequently (9.2 percent). Latinas

Table 3.4. *Weapons by Race/Ethnic Group by Gender*

Weapon	Males				Females			
	Black	Latino	White	Total	Black	Latina	White	Total
Firearms	83.4	81.7	59.3	79.9	58.9	63.6	42.8	56.1
Knives	9.2	11.1	18.5	11.2	13.4	12.4	16.1	13.8
Other	7.4	7.2	22.3	8.9	27.7	24.1	41.1	30.1
Total	5364	8024	1662	15050	1028	889	708	2625

were killed least frequently by knives (12.4 percent), while white females were killed most often (16.1 percent). Generally, the differences among the six groups was relatively small with respect to knives as a weapon.

Other types of weapons were used far more frequently on women (30.1 percent) than men (8.9 percent). Other weapons account for about 7 percent of black and Latino male homicides. However, 22.3 percent of white males were killed by other weapons.

In examining female use of weapons other than knives and firearms, all three groups of females were killed more often by other weapons than males. What is unusual about Table 3.4 is the high percentage of white males (22.3 percent) and white females (41.1 percent) victimized by other weapons.

A large part of the reason white females are killed more often by other weapons may be because a large proportion are killed in intimate partner conflicts. It is reasonable to suppose that knives and other weapons might be the nearest available weapon in a domestic conflict and, therefore, used more frequently. But how can the high percentage of white males victimized by other weapons be explained? While they are a larger percent of victims in intimate partner homicides, the difference between black and white males is very small (see Table 3.3).

It is not clear what accounts for this concentration of other weapons among white males. It does appear to be a configuration that distinguishes white homicides, but the reasons for it are unknown.

Precipitating Events

The Los Angeles data were classified into two categories to examine the effect of "motives" or precipitating events. The felony category included killings associated with such offenses as robbery, rape, burglary, and motor vehicle theft. Nonfelony homicides included those associated with such offenses as lover's triangle, brawls, and arguments. Table 3.5 gives the relationships between precipitating events, race/ethnic group, and gender.

Table 3.5. *Felony-Nonfelony Circumstances by Race/Ethnic Group by Gender*

Circumstance	Males				Females			
	Black	Latino	White	Total	Black	Latino	White	Total
Felony	24.0	20.6	38.8	23.8	27.8	20.5	34.0	27.0
Nonfelony	76.0	79.4	61.2	76.2	72.2	79.5	66.0	73.0
Total	4679	7045	1467	13191	900	792	632	2324

Consistent with the tenth hypothesis, Latino males and females were victimized in felony murders less frequently than either African-American or white females and males. White males and females are most frequently victimized in felony homicides because, as noted earlier, whites are more likely to be engaged in economic activities that make them attractive targets for such offenses as robberies.

About three-fourths of homicides in Los Angeles were not committed with a contemporaneous offense; that is, they were nonfelony homicides. Both Latino males and females were most frequently involved in nonfelony homicides. Put another way, Latinos were more frequently involved in homicides that originate in conflicts. These kinds of homicides fall within aggressive actions that "seek to compel and deter others, to achieve a favorable social identity, and to obtain justice, as defined by the actor" (Felson, 1993: 104). Sanders (1994), in his study of southern California gangs, notes how frequently drive-by shootings and other types of lethal violence occur because of threats to turf or imagined insults which offend the individual and collective identity of gang members. Insults to ego or "face attacks" also may figure prominently in the motivation of nongang homicide.

Conclusions

From an examination of the research literature as well as an analysis of Latino homicide in Los Angeles County, the following generalizations are warranted. First, it seems abundantly clear from studies in other parts of the United States as well as research in Los Angeles County that there are a large number of Latino homicides. However, when the amount of homicides are examined in relation to the size of an increasingly large population, that is, using rates, Latino homicides consistently fall between African-American homicide rates and white rates with a pronounced tendency to be more like white than black rates.

On the basis of available evidence, it is difficult to attribute causal relationships either in terms of economic restructuring or cultural patterns brought from a mother country. Too little is known about either set of causes. While economic restructuring is insightfully discussed by Moore and Pinderhughes (1993), much more needs to be done to explain its impact on violence. By contrast, to attribute patterns of homicide to general cultural traits among Latinos is to assume a cultural homogeneity that does not exist in very cultural diverse groups.

Female Victimization. Latina homicide victimization is probably the most distinctive pattern of comparisons with other race/ethnic groups. Because of social and economic disadvantages endured by African Americans and high female victimization rates, there is a tendency to expect similar rates from Latinas, another socially and economically disadvantaged group.

This is far from the case. Consistent with other research, Latina victimizations are very low and comparable to homicide victimizations of white females. While Latinas are above white females in the fifteen to thirty-four age group, they decline until the sixty-five to one hundred age group, when their victimization rate is less than that of white females.

We have speculated that Latinas may suffer homicide victimizations comparable to white females because they are intimate partners in relationships in which males are dominant and females are expected to be submissive, compliant, and at risk of domestic violence. However, it is consistent with a *machismo* view of women for men to provide protection to her among others who may know both her and family members. Hence, the percentage of cases in which the offender is known to the victim but outside the family is comparable to white females. However, because they do live in high-risk areas of a city, Latinas suffer about the same level of stranger victimization as black females.

In short, Latina victimization is very similar to a picture of women in traditional relationships in which intimate partners offer them a measure of protection outside the family while being possible victimizers themselves. At the same time, because of external circumstances, male protection cannot extend to protection from stranger attacks.

Male Victimization. Because most homicides are committed by young males, it is no surprise that homicide rates for Latino males should be similar to total homicide rates. The mean age rates based on a twelve-year period indicate that, like blacks and whites, the victimization rates peak in the fifteen to thirty-four age group; in later ages, all three groups show a decline. Like total rates, Latino male rates are between white and black rates at every age. Latinas and Latino males have very similar patterns of homicide victimization in the oldest age category (sixty-five to one hundred): their rates are either lower than whites or the same.

When Latino male victimization patterns are examined in relation to victim/offender relationships, it is a mixed pattern. With regard to intimate partner relationships, Latinas are frequently victimized, while Latino males seldom are. There is little difference among Latinas between the three groups with respect to victimization by other family members, while Latino male victimization is similar to black males.

Latinas are infrequently victimized by other known offenders (27.8 percent), while Latino males are victimized over half the time (52.9 percent). Both Latinas and Latino males experience a high amount of victimization by strangers.

While the concept of *machismo* encourages male role expectations that may serve to explain male homicide patterns as well as female victimizations, more evidence is needed before the concept is more than merely suggestive with respect to one Latino group. What the research literature, as well as this study, suggests is that there are very distinct differences in homicide patterns between males and females. These differences lack a comprehensive explanation.

Weapons and Precipitating Circumstances

Perhaps the least surprising finding because of its repeated appearance in prior studies is the popularity of firearms as a homicide weapon. Except for white female victims, over half of the victims of every other race/ethnic group, male and female, were killed by firearms.

There were very few differences between and among genders of the three groups with respect to weapons. The one finding that was unusual was the high percentage of other types of weapons among white males. The victimization of white females occurs disproportionately in intimate partner relationships in which physical assaults and the use of household items as weapons is not unusual. But the same cannot be said of white males, where intimate partner homicides are relatively small.

There are few large differences in comparing felony and nonfelony homicides among the three race/ethnic groups. White male and female victims are disproportionately involved in felony homicides because they, more frequently than blacks or Latinos, hold jobs that are economic targets for robberies and robbery homicides. While previous research also suggests that Latinos will have a lower involvement in felony homicides, there is no persuasive explanation for this pattern.

This study has been more successful at finding differences and similarities among African-American, Latino, and white homicides than explaining them. It is clear that Latinos in Los Angeles County share many characteristics with Latinos elsewhere, but there also are differences that probably reflect the fact that Latino is a label that covers a variety of groups with quite different cultural backgrounds.

A theory that attempts to explain violence will have to take account of this diversity as well as distinguish Latinos from African Americans and whites. What complicates the latter task even more is that African Americans are not a homogenous group either, a fact that is only now becoming part of the problem to be explained (Georges-Abeyie, 1981; Hawkins, 1999).

Economic Correlates of Racial and Ethnic Disparity in Homicide: Houston, 1945–1994[1]

Victoria E. Titterington, Ph.D.
Kelly R. Damphousse, Ph.D.

Introduction

An understanding of the diverse social factors that influence urban homicide has been sought since the pioneering work of Wolfgang (1958). Beginning with his analysis of 588 homicide victims and 621 offenders in Philadelphia during the years 1948–52, Wolfgang provided a detailed analysis of offenders and victims by race, sex, age, victim-offender relationships, and previous criminal records of either party. He also analyzed methods of killing, the degree of violence, the contribution of alcohol, and the motives of offenders for these homicidal incidents. Wolfgang's documentation of the marked differences by race and ethnicity of homicide victims and offenders has spawned an ongoing investigation into the question of what contributes to minorities' overrepresentation in urban killing.

This chapter begins with a review of findings from earlier studies of racial and ethnic differences in homicide at the city level. We then discuss racial and ethnic representation among Houston's homicides over the past fifty years and the role of the economy during each period. The chapter concludes with a discussion of questions that remain unanswered that may generate future research into the urban phenomenon of lethal violence.

[1] Funding for this research was provided by the National Institute of Justice #7-7004-TX-IJ, the College of Criminal Justice, Sam Houston State University, and the Office of Research and Sponsored Programs, Sam Houston State University. The authors express their appreciation to William G. Edison, Jr. and to the officials of the Houston Police Department, particularly Captain Richard Holland, for their assistance with this project. Address all correspondence to: Victoria E. Titterington; College of Criminal Justice, Sam Houston State University; Huntsville, Texas 77341-2296; (Voice) 409-294-1662; (Fax) 409-294-1653;(Internet) icc_veb@shsu.edu.

Previous City-Level Homicide Research

There have been numerous city-level studies of homicide, both before and since Wolfgang's (1958) exemplary analysis of lethal violence in Philadelphia. Almost all of these studies, including that of Wolfgang, have reported considerable ethnic and racial disparity in rates of homicide in the United States (Bullock, 1955; Pokorny, 1965; Block, 1985, 1993; Martinez, 1996a). In the case of Philadelphia from 1948 to 1952, Wolfgang (1958) found that blacks accounted for 63 percent of both homicide victims and offenders, although they were a minority of the overall population. Similarly, in Houston in the late 1940s and from 1958 to 1961, blacks were overrepresented as both homicide victims and offenders (Bullock, 1955; Pokorny, 1965).

The recent, large-scale effort of the National Institute of Justice (1997) to study a decade of homicide in eight U.S. cities has given us a view of lethal violence in urban America as the twentieth century ended. This project focused on a combination of cities showing recent significant increasing, decreasing, or unchanging trends in homicide. These included Atlanta, Detroit, Indianapolis, Miami, New Orleans, Richmond, Tampa, and Washington. In all eight of these cities, despite their disparate geographic locations and socioeconomic experiences of the last decade of the twentieth century, blacks (specifically those young and male) incurred homicide victimization risk five to twenty-five times their representation in the population.

The studies just cited and others (Wilbanks, 1984; Zahn and Sagi, 1987) make it clear that racial and ethnic minorities have consistently been disproportionately represented among homicide victims and offenders in urban America. Yet, most of these studies have been efforts to compare non-Latino blacks and non-Latino whites. In the past decade, the Latino population has increased in most major U.S. cities. Some cities in particular – Chicago, Miami, Houston – have seen rather major increases in the size of their Latino populations. The major influx of Latinos to Chicago and Miami, as well as major increases in the proportions of Latinos and Asians in Houston, leads to the question of how such demographic changes have affected the profile of homicide in cities with long-standing high rates of lethal violence. More to the point, has the emergence of more than one "minority" within a city altered the homicide victimization risk to blacks, chronically overrepresented among homicide victims and offenders, relative to the risk of newer racial/ethnic minority subgroups?

As the third largest ethnic group within the United States, the representation of Latinos among homicide victims and offenders is of particular concern. Interestingly, one of the first researchers to acknowledge the importance of including the percent of Hispanics in a given community as a predictor of homicide rates was Bullock (1955) in his analysis of Houston homicide from 1945 through 1949. In Pokorny's (1965) analysis of Houston homicide, he determined that Latinos were indeed overrepresented in lethal violence, with a homicide victimization rate of 12.1 per 100,000, compared to a black victimization rate of 32.3 and a non-Latino white rate of 5.3.

With Block's (1985) work in analyzing homicide patterns and trends in Chicago, the inclusion of Hispanics in homicide analyses gained new attention. She found that homicides among Latinos, relative to changes in their proportion of the overall population, increased faster than those of Anglos and blacks. In addition, in an analysis of Latino homicide across 111 U.S. cities as of 1980, Martinez (1996a: 142) determined that the average Latino homicide rate (almost 20 per 100,000 Latinos) was twice the overall 1980 U.S. homicide rate.

Block (1993) has continued her analysis of changes over time in Chicago in the rates of Latino and black homicide victimization – relative to one another and to non-Latino whites – racial and ethnic disparities continue to be apparent. In 1970, the Latino male homicide victimization rate was 38 per 100,000 population. Almost thirty years later, in 1989, this rate was 44 per 100,000. For black males in Chicago, the victimization rate peaked at 105 per 100,000 in 1974 and had declined to 74 per 100,000 in 1989. In contrast to this experience of minority males, white male homicide victimization rates were relatively stable, and dramatically lower, over the same time period, at 11 per 100,000 in 1970 and 10 in 1989. For females in Chicago during this same thirty-year period, rates of homicide victimization were comparable for Latino and non-Latino whites, fluctuating around 3 to 5 per 100,000. Yet, the black female rate over this same period ranged from a peak of 21 per 100,000 in 1974 to 17 per 100,000 in 1989 (Block, 1993).

In a related vein, Martinez (1996b) analyzed homicide offending and victimization among Latinos, blacks, and Anglos for the period 1990 through 1995 in Miami. One of his more intriguing findings was that, while urban Latinos are typically overrepresented as homicide victims and offenders, they – especially Cubans – are not in Miami. Martinez's analysis further revealed that Latinos were killed at a rate half their population size, typically falling between black and Anglo percentages. Results of these studies, coupled with the continual Latino immigration into the United States, suggest the importance of analyzing lethal violence within increasingly disaggregated racial and ethnic subgroups.

Including some of the city-level analyses of homicide just cited are a number of studies of lethal violence in Houston covering much of the past century. These will now be described, as a backdrop to what we may learn about this phenomenon from the mid-1980s to mid-1990s.

Houston and Twentieth-Century Homicide

Despite the city's notable role as a center for advanced science, technology and medicine, Houston has a long-standing distinction as one of the most violent cities of the United States. For most of the twentieth century, Houston has had a homicide rate triple that of the rest of the country. The city's homicide rate averaged 22.7 per 100,000 during the postwar forties (1945–9), in contrast to a national average rate of 7.3. Although Houston's murder rate dropped considerably, to 11.9, between 1958 and 1961, it was still well above the national rate of 7.2. Through most of the period from the early 1970s to the mid-1990s, Houston's homicide rate stood at three times the national average. Even within Texas, one of the more violent states in the country, the city of Houston has had the highest number of murders per 100,000 residents since 1981 (taking over from Dallas and Fort Worth). As compared to other major urban areas in the United States, Houston was among the twenty deadliest for the period 1985 to 1994, with a mean homicide rate of 26.59 (National Institute of Justice, 1996).

The high rates of violence just described seem surprising, given Houston's relative prosperity during the past three decades and its notable role as a center for advanced science, technology, and medicine. Yet, a number of factors during the past three decades in Houston have contributed to this level of lethality and lead to our present interest in comparing the racial/ethnic and socioeconomic dynamics of contemporary homicide in the city with those patterns described by previous researchers. These include the South's development (particularly in the 1970s) into an economically thriving and increasingly urbanized region, followed by a severe economic downturn for the region during the late 1970s and much of the 1980s. Also, whereas Houston's minority population in the 1960s was primarily African American, it is now comprised of large proportions of Hispanic and Asian residents as well. Additionally, in the 1980s, illegal drugs and gang-related violence became major dynamics in American violence as both situational and motivational factors in many homicides. Given these and other economic, political, and demographic variations within Houston over the past half century, we are interested in what, if any, effect these changes have had on poor, minority representation among homicide statistics for the city.

Previous analyses of the sociodemographic characteristics of Houston homicide reveal, not surprisingly, that racial and ethnic minorities have been disproportionately represented among both the city's poor and its homicide victims over the last half of the century. Bullock's (1955) analysis of 489 Houston homicide cases from 1945 to 1949, for example, indicated that the highest murder rates were found in census tracts clustering around the city's central business district, areas primarily populated by the city's black residents. The areas of highest homicide concentration included eighteen of the city's sixty census tracts. While these tracts contained only one-third of the Houston adult population, almost three-quarters of the homicide cases were located here. These eighteen tracts possessed a disproportionate amount of old homes (built before 1919), dwellings in need of major repairs, and low rental properties. Two-thirds of Houston's African Americans lived within these tracts. In turn, African Americans comprised 67 percent of both victim and suspect populations and Hispanics accounted for approximately 9 percent of all persons involved in these lethal incidents. Just as revealing were the economic characteristics of this murder-prone portion of Houston. Half of Houston's gainfully employed citizens lived in these high murder tracts, yet over two-thirds of the workers were laborers and domestic servants. And over half of Houston's unemployed citizens lived in this same area. As for educational status, 39 percent of the city's population twenty-five years of age or older lived within these boundaries, yet accounted for 63 percent of the city's residents with less than a fifth-grade education.

Pokorny's (1965) major study of Houston homicide examined records from 1958 to 1961. As in Bullock's (1955) analysis of Houston homicide for the late 1940s, African Americans again comprised a disproportionate number of both homicide victims and offenders, representing roughly 63 percent of each, while comprising only 23 percent of Houston's 1960 population. Pokorny found that the homicide victimization rate of blacks was 32.3 per 100,000, compared to 12.1 for Hispanics and 5.3 for whites. Pokorny also noted that, as in the earlier period, 94 percent of the homicide incidents were intraracial. He observed, however, a drop in the percentage of intraracial/ethnic incidents for Hispanics, from 97.7 percent during 1945–9, to 81.3 percent during 1958–61. Pokorny speculated that this was an indication that Hispanic whites might have become more assimilated into the general white group during the interim; that is, Hispanics were interacting more with whites, resulting in greater opportunity for interracial killing.

Compared to other studies of Houston homicide (Beasley and Antunes, 1974; Cloninger and Sartorius, 1979; Rose and McClain, 1990), a somewhat unique perspective of lethal violence in this technologically sophisticated city was offered by Lundsgaarde (1977). He first ascertained that census tracts with the heaviest concentration of African Americans had the largest number of homicides, which he attributed to the low socioeconomic status of blacks in those areas. Like Pokorny, he found that 94 percent of cases were intraracial, that blacks were much more likely than whites to become homicide victims and, in the tradition of Wolfgang (1958), that males were more likely than females to experience lethal violence. Lundsgaarde also paid particular attention to victim-offender relationships and to the theoretical concept of "victim-precipitated homicides." Quite similar to Wolfgang's findings regarding homicide in Philadelphia, Lundsgaarde found that killings in Houston were most frequently the result of altercations or disputes over relatively trivial matters, involved killers and victims who knew each other, were often victim-precipitated and usually occurred in a residence or bar.

Lundsgaarde (1977) then took the work of his predecessors a step further by examining the legal disposition of a subsample of two hundred cases of homicide that occurred in Houston in 1969. He offered detailed evidence in support of the hypothesis that, in the commonlaw tradition, the state's interests are best served by punishing "public crimes" most severely, whereas it may view itself as powerless to prevent crimes of passion that occur in more "private" settings. Specifically, Lundsgaarde found an inverse relationship between the level of legal sanctioning and the degree of prior intimacy between homicide victim and offender. He suggested that, as a culture, Texas, in general, and Houston, in particular, treated life quite callously. This was reflected in the large number of homicides occurring in 1969 that were deemed justifiable ("no bill") by the grand jury. Specifically, homicides between family members or friends, or for which no private property was being defended, were not as likely to be prosecuted as stranger and/or felony homicides.

In tandem with the critical role that race/ethnicity generally plays in homicide is that of economics. Likewise, the economic experience over time of specific racial and ethnic subgroups in Houston is well documented. Before combining these factors in our description of Houston homicide for the past half century, we highlight some of the evidence regarding the correspondence of socioeconomic disadvantage and homicide rates of racial and ethnic minorities.

Economic Indicators of Homicide Risk

For both Latinos and blacks, strong evidence exists that economic forces seem to determine their elevated risks for homicide. Some of this research has focused on the adverse role of economic inequality on the status of minority groups (Blau and Blau, 1982; Shihadeh and Steffensmeier, 1994). The thesis of this research is that the economic inequality of minority groups leads to feelings of frustration that may be manifested in nonlethal and lethal violence. In turn, the work of Bailey (1984), Sampson (1987), and Parker (1989) indicates that minority members are particularly impacted by social and economic deprivation that occur alongside levels of education and income.

The seminal work of Land, McCall, and Cohen (1990) offers arguably the most convincing evidence of this connection between socioeconomic inequality and high homicide rates. These researchers synthesized the results of twenty-one extant studies of homicide, covering three decennials (1960, 1970, 1980) and three units of analysis (states, SMSAs, cities). Among the eleven structural covariates used in their model to estimate homicide rates, two of the significant predictors of homicide to emerge from this analysis were a composite measure of resource deprivation (that included income inequality and the percentage of the population that was African American) and unemployment.

Rose and McClain (1990), in their major study of predominantly African-American neighborhoods of five large U.S. cities, drew increased attention to the role of economics in urban areas. In their analysis of homicide in Atlanta, St. Louis, Detroit, Houston, Pittsburgh, and Los Angeles, these researchers presented persuasive evidence of the need to address the requisite education/skills of a postindustrial labor market and the preparedness for such noncriminal occupations of young black males.

In the first national-level analysis of the role of poverty and inequality in Latino homicide, Martinez examined these and other sociodemographic predictors of Latino homicide in 111 U.S. cities during 1980. His analysis revealed that, while larger Latino poverty rates were associated with lower homicide rates, a leading predictor of homicide was Latino income inequality. In turn, he found that educational attainment was the strongest predictor of homicide for this subgroup.

The correlation of various measures of socioeconomic disadvantage (disproportionately affecting minorities) and homicide risk consistently emerge in the research literature. For this reason, the following section of this chapter provides an overview of the Houston economy during the twentieth century as a foundation from which to examine the sociodemographic characteristics of homicide more closely.

Houston Yesterday and Today

Much of the residential and commercial transformation of the South during the first half of the twentieth century was reflected in the experience of the city of Houston. Between 1950 and 1990, for example, Houston's population grew by 174 percent. It now exceeds 1.7 million, rendering it the fourth largest U.S. city. In the mid-1970s, over five thousand people each month migrated to the city, drawn by its low cost of living, unprecedented growth in housing units, and seeming surplus of jobs and potentially high wages (Bullard, 1987). This has left Houston with the unofficial label as the place where everyone is from somewhere else. At the same time, Houston is among those southern cities that attract more low-income migrants than they lose. Yet, from the standpoint of the city's image-management campaigns, its ethnic and racial diversity is decidedly underplayed, resulting in the creation of an "invisible" community composed primarily of minorities (Bullard, 1987). This is despite the fact that, by 1990, blacks and Hispanics each accounted for approximately 28 percent of the city's populace.

Figure 4.1 illustrates the primary race and ethnic composition of Houston throughout the twentieth century (Bureau of the Census, 1993). The figure shows how the city experienced a demographic shift over the 1900s similar to the South as a whole. A large proportion of the population was made up of African Americans at the turn of the century, followed by a substantial

74

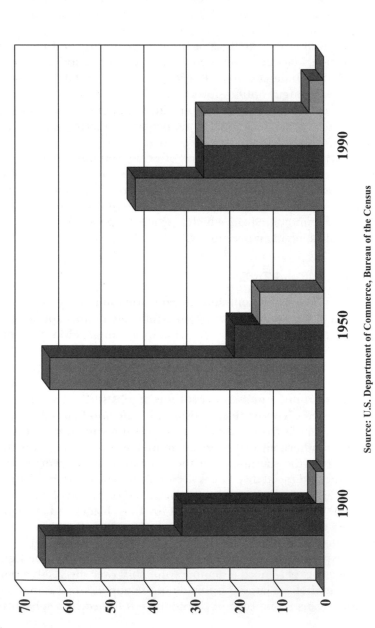

Source: U.S. Department of Commerce, Bureau of the Census

Figure 4.1. Changes in Race and Ethnic Distribution Among Houston Residents, 1900–1990

decline at the mid-century point. This mid-century dip in the black population was reversed at the end of the century as the percentage of the black
population in Houston approached the numbers exhibited in 1900. The
figure also suggests that while Houston's minority population for most of
the century has been primarily African American, it is now comprised of a
large proportion of Hispanics as well. The percentage of Houston's population that is black has ranged from a high of 32.7 percent in 1900 to 21.0 in
1950, and increasing to 28 percent in 1990. By contrast, whereas Hispanics
represented between 2 and 5 percent of Houston's residents into the late
1940s, starting after World War II, this proportion has steadily risen, to over
one-quarter of the city's population in 1990.

With its heavy dependence on the oil and petrochemical industry,
Houston was among the cities hardest hit by the worldwide oil glut and
plunging oil prices in the 1980s. Unemployment skyrocketed from 4.6 percent in January 1981 to 9.6 in January 1993. This new economic downturn
was not experienced equally among racial groups in Houston. The unemployment rate for blacks, for example, was 2.9 percentage points higher than
it was for whites in 1982. Later in the decade, as the full impact of the reces-
sion was taking effect, black unemployment exceeded white unemployment
by seven percentage points (Bullard, 1987).

Because the city of Houston is now comprised of large proportions of
both blacks and Hispanics, along with a small but growing percentage of
Asians, we think it is important to look at the relative representation of all
of these groups, along with non-Hispanic whites, among the city's poor, its
educated, its labor force, and its income earners. Figures 4.2 through 4.6
provide this comparison.

Figures 4.2 and 4.3 illustrate the strong connection between racial and
ethnic educational attainment and occupational experience. Although
black and Hispanic educational levels have increased, they clearly lag behind those of whites (Bureau of the Census, 1993). Those blacks and
Hispanics who have achieved more education represent increasing percentages of "managerial and professional specialty" employees in Houston's
labor force. Yet, they are disproportionately represented among the city's
poorly educated and low-skilled, low-paid occupational groups. The fact
that a larger percentage of blacks than Hispanics now occupy high-skill,
high-wage positions may in part be attributable to their having been a sizable number of Houston's citizens for much longer than Hispanics. In
other words, as a group, blacks have had much longer to assimilate than
Hispanics.

Although the per capita income of the Houston Primary Metropolitan
Statistical Area (PMSA) increased slightly from 1980 to 1990, this is due to
increases in the number of people working rather than increases in the earnings of those employed. Median household income is unevenly distributed

76

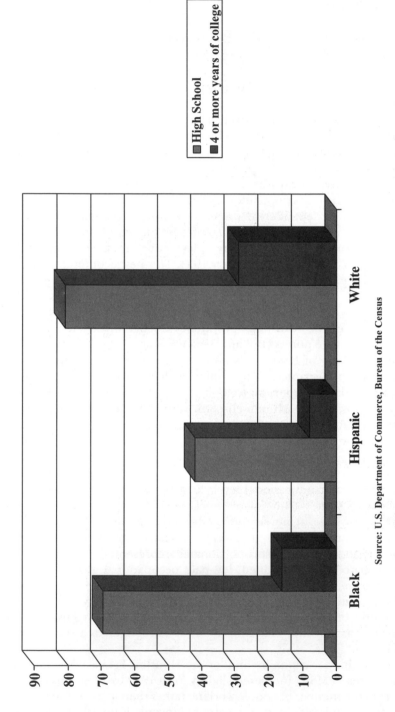

Source: U.S. Department of Commerce, Bureau of the Census

Figure 4.2. Comparative Percentages of High School and College Graduates, by Race/Ethnicity, 1990

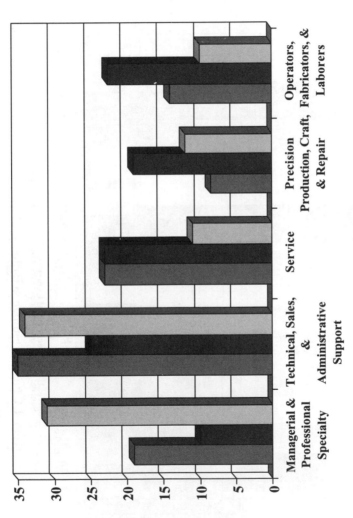

Source: U.S. Department of Commerce, Bureau of the Census

Figure 4.3. Occupational Distribution by Race/Ethnicity, Houston PMSA, 1991

78

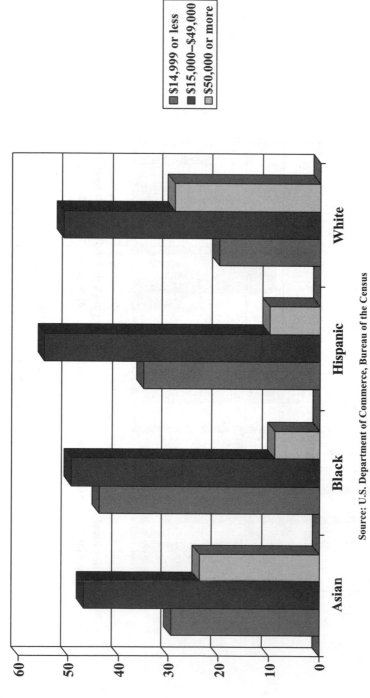

Source: U.S. Department of Commerce, Bureau of the Census

Figure 4.4. Income Distribution for Race/Ethnic Groups, Houston, 1990 (percentages)

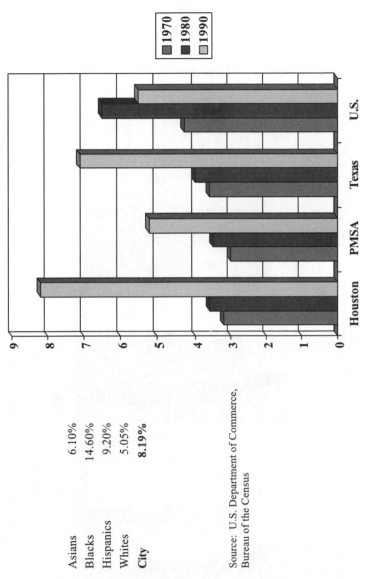

Figure 4.5. Comparative Unemployment Rates, 1970, 1980, 1990

Asians	6.10%
Blacks	14.60%
Hispanics	9.20%
Whites	5.05%
City	**8.19%**

Source: U.S. Department of Commerce,
Bureau of the Census

79

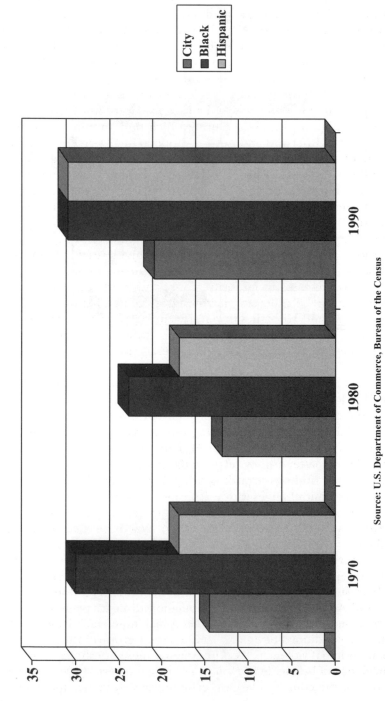

Source: U.S. Department of Commerce, Bureau of the Census

Figure 4.6. Comparative Percentages of Persons in Poverty, by Race/Ethnicity, 1990

among racial and ethnic groups, as shown in Figure 4.4 (Bureau of the Census, 1993). It is noteworthy that the percent of Asians with household incomes of $50,000 or more is much closer to whites than to the other major racial/ethnic minorities of blacks and Hispanics, despite the fact that they are the newest major subgroup of Houston's citizens.

The economy of Houston and the region surrounding it has had a large effect on the economic well-being of its citizens. Houston thrived during the economic boom of the 1970s, during which time the unemployment rate was as low as 3.1 percent and poverty dropped to 13 percent. Yet, both unemployment and poverty increased dramatically during the economic bust of the 1980s. As seen in Figure 4.5, not only was Houston's 1990 overall unemployment rate considerably higher than that of the state or nation, but also the unemployment rate of blacks exceeded that of the city overall by 78 percent (Bureau of the Census, 1993).

In contrast to a national poverty level of approximately 14 percent in 1990, Houston's poverty rate stood at 21 percent. This increase in Houston's poverty rate is a result of increases in unemployment and low-wage employment, as well as increases in minority groups with traditionally low-wage occupations. Figure 4.6 reflects a narrowing of the gap between the percentages of blacks and Hispanics in poverty compared to the city's overall population. Yet, each of these groups still has 10 percent more of its respective members in poverty than the city overall (Bureau of the Census, 1993).

Just as blacks, and more recently Hispanics, have been disproportionately represented among the homicide offenders and victims within Houston, we see that the educational, occupational, and income levels of these two groups are striking. Despite some intragroup gains over time, these two groups continue to lag well behind non-Hispanic whites in social-structural ways that we know matter as they relate to the risk of lethal violence.

Coupling earlier findings regarding urban homicide with recent demographic and economic changes within Houston, as well as other U.S. cities, results in a number of questions. This study examines the particular experience of Houston by answering the following: How have changes in the racial and ethnic composition of this city affected the representation of its respective minority groups among homicide victims and offenders? Has the historical overrepresentation of blacks among those at risk of homicide in Houston been superceded by the risk for its newer minority groups, namely Hispanics and Asians. Has increased population diversity been accompanied by increased levels of *inter-* versus *intragroup* homicide? How do the socioeconomic conditions of emergent immigrant groups influence their involvement in lethal violence? We will examine these questions by analyzing the incidence of homicide in Houston during the period 1985 through 1994. As one of the country's largest, economically dynamic, and racially and ethnically heterogenous cities, it offers an important window through which to view urban homicide as we enter the twenty-first century. What follows is a description of the process by which we analyze the economic and racial/ethnic disparity in Houston homicide over the past half century.

Steps in the Analysis

To assess the intersection of race, ethnicity, and homicide in Houston in the 1900s, we use data collected in two separate enterprises. First, we rely on the information found in the data analyses presented in three of the previously cited studies of homicide in Houston (Bullock, 1955; Pokorny, 1965; Lundsgaarde, 1977). These investigators each obtained data directly from the homicide division of the Houston Police Department for 1945–9, 1958–61, and 1969, respectively. Likewise, we use homicide data provided by the Department for the 4,944 incidents of homicide that occurred during the period 1985 through 1994. Information extracted from these 1985–94 files includes homicide motive, relationship between victim and offender, location and type of premise where the offense took place, type of weapon used, and the race, gender, and age of the victim and offender. These data were then supplemented by cross-referencing cases by date with all published homicide accounts within the *Houston Chronicle*. These newspaper accounts helped provide otherwise missing data in some cases and more details on motives and the situational contexts of homicide in others.

We first report the relative percentage of the population for each of the four primary racial/ethnic groups at five points in time between 1945 and 1994. We then calculate their respective homicide victimization rates, as measured by the number of deaths per 100,000 of that subgroup within Houston's population. The time periods selected for our analysis include years covered by previous studies: 1945–9 (Bullock, 1955), 1958–61 (Pokorny, 1965), and 1969 (Lundsgaarde, 1977). We divide the most recent data, collected by us, into five-year increments, 1985–9 and 1990–4. Given the substantial fluctuations in homicide overall during this ten-year period (in Houston and nationally), as well as changes in the population proportions of each racial/ethnic group within Houston, we gain an improved understanding of recent trends in homicide risk for each group.

We also compare the characteristics of homicide incidents and rates, to the extent possible, across the three previous studies just noted and the present one. This is done to ascertain both consistencies and deviations in the ethnicity or race of homicide victims and offenders as well as the characteristics of areas in which the majority of these killings took place. We are particularly interested in how the city's tremendous economic, geographic, and population growth over this period may have altered homicide risk for its residents. As well, we look at the distribution of methods used, incident location, and victim-offender relationships.

Characteristics of Houston Homicide over Time

Table 4.1 is offered as a means of comparison among four of the numerous studies, including the present one, of lethal violence in Houston. We first display the percentages of homicide victims and offenders (where known) by race and ethnicity. The biggest change over time in the racial and ethnic distribution of homicide victims is that Hispanics now account for a larger percentage of all victims than non-Hispanic whites, although blacks continue to far exceed the numbers of any other group. As expected, the relative percentages of offenders, by race and ethnicity, are very similar to those of victims.

In 3,856 (78 percent) of the homicide incidents that occurred between 1985 and 1994, the race/ethnicity of both the victim and offender are known. Although the vast majority of homicides in Houston continue to be intraracial, it is noteworthy that 17 percent of these incidents were interracial. Closer inspection of this 17 percent of cases revealed that just over 42 percent of the offenders were black, 23 percent were Hispanic, 20 percent were non-Hispanic white, and 3 percent were Asian. As for victims in these interracial incidents, 40 percent were non-Hispanic whites, 28 percent were Hispanic, 40 percent were black, and 6 percent were Asian. Among the largest interracial victim-offender combinations, 23 percent were black-on-white, and 14 percent each were Hispanic-on-white and black-on-Hispanic. Martinez (1996b) also found, as had Wilbanks (1984) for earlier years in Miami, that Latinos were more likely to be victims of intergroup homicide in the 1990s than in earlier periods. Based on the variety of ways the profiles of Latino and non-Latino killing varied, Martinez suggests that the victim-offender relationship and type of homicide are likely a reflection of unique racial/ethnic group dynamics.

Whether the analysis of the sociodemographic characteristics of high homicide areas pertains to census tracts, as in previous studies, or to police districts, as in this study, we note the similarities therein. Bullock (1955) and Lundsgaarde (1977) were each describing the census tracts in which the majority of homicides occurred, whereas our present analysis of homicide for 1985–94 pertains to the two police districts in which 38 percent of all such incidents occurred. As expected, for each of these four time periods, these high homicide areas are characterized by almost exclusively racial and ethnic minorities (the majority of whom are poorly educated) and high levels of unemployment. While avoiding overgeneralizations about the connection among these factors and homicide, one thing that is illustrated by these findings is that the existence of almost equal numbers of two minority groups

Table 4.1. *Selected Characteristics of Homicide in Houston, 1945–1994 (Percentages)*[1]

	1945–9 (Bullock) $N = 489$	1958–61 (Pokorny) $N = 425$	1969 (Lundsgaarde) $N = 268$	1985–94[2] $N = 4,944$
Victims by Race/Ethnicity				
Non-Hispanic White	23%	38%	22%	20%
Black	67	63	70	48
Hispanic	9	7	6	30
Asian	–	–	1	3
Offenders by Race/Ethnicity				
Non-Hispanic White	24%	29%	26%	15%
Black	67	63	66	53
Hispanic	9	8	7	28
Asian	–	n/a	–	2
Other	–	–	–	2
Interracial Incidents	4%	7%	6%	17%
Young Offenders (−18 years)	–	n/a	3%	7%
Sociodemographics of High Homicide Areas				
Black Population	42%	n/a	94%	> or = 75%
Hispanic Population	24	n/a	1	> or = 25
Less than High School	(<5th grade)			
Education	19	n/a	73	>51
Unemployed	11	n/a	5	9–15
Homicide Method				
Firearm	n/a	64%	86%	70%
Knife	n/a	25	11	23
Other	n/a	11	3	7
Incident Location				
House/Apartment	42%	42%	40%	41%
Bar	29	14	20	2
Parking Lot/Street/Alley	21	26	17	39
Other	8	18	23	18
Victim-Offender Relationship				
Intimates	n/a	7%	26%	10%
Family	n/a	23	15	7
Friend/Acquaintance	n/a	44	43	38
Strangers/Unknown	13%	26	16	45

[1] Numbers may not equal 100 due to rounding.
[2] Offender's race/ethnicity known for 78% of cases.

somewhat displaces homicide risk for the "first" of these two groups. In the case of Houston, as the relative proportion and representation in homicide of blacks have decreased, these same two factors have increased for Latinos. In fact, these two groups are near parity in several unfortunate ways – education levels, occupational and income levels, and percentages in poverty.

At least two other important observations may be drawn from Table 4.1. Those in streets and alleys, as well as "other" locations, have now vastly superseded the incidence of homicide in bars. At least 25 percent of the approximately five thousand homicides for the decade of 1985–94 were felony-related incidents, including robbery-homicides, as well as those involving gangs and drug transactions. The nature of each of these types of killing would explain the incident locations we now observe. We also note a substantial increase in the percentage of incidents in which the victim and offender were strangers or their relationship was unknown. We recognize that collapsing these two categories into one is arbitrary, yet the fact that in only 55 percent of cases were the victim and offender clearly prior acquaintances (if not friends or family) represents a noteworthy deviation in homicide of the past decade to that of earlier periods.

Table 4.2 provides a delineation of the proportions of Houston's population represented by each of the four major racial/ethnic subgroups – non-Hispanic whites, blacks, Hispanics, and Asians. We recognize that these categorizations are arbitrary, with numerous subgroups of Latinos included in the Hispanic category, for example. Yet, these categories provide for general comparisons across race and ethnicity over this fifty-year time period. As seen in Table 4.2, Houston's overall homicide rate has been chronically high, despite fluctuations over the five time periods. In fact, throughout most of the twentieth century, Houston's murder rate has been two to three times the national average. More telling however is the dramatic difference in relative risk based on the race and ethnicity of victims and offenders.

The extent of "white flight" from Houston's city proper is clear in Table 4.2. There has been a 45 percent decrease in the proportion of Houston's population made up of non-Hispanic whites. Yet, despite the fact that the relative risk of homicide victimization for whites has remained the lowest of all groups over this fifty-year period, the risk in 1990–4 was twice that of 1945–9. This suggests that for those whites without the means to "seek refuge in suburbia," the lethality of the central city has increased.

Table 4.2 also reveals that the percentage of blacks has remained more constant than any other racial/ethnic subgroup, comprising roughly one-fifth of the city's population throughout this fifty-year period. Their numbers were somewhat lower at the end of the 1960s, as apparent economic opportunities lured many of the South's blacks to northern cities. However, for each of these five time periods, their homicide victimization rate has been two to

Table 4.2. *Numbers and Mean Rates[1] per 100,000 Population of Victims in Criminal Homicide, Houston, by Race and Ethnicity*

	Overall		Non-Hispanic Whites		Blacks		Hispanics		Asians	
	Pop.	Hom. Rate	% Pop.	Hom. Rate	% Pop.	Hom. Rate	% Pop.	Hom. Rate	% Pop.	Hom. Rate
1945–9 (Bullock) (n = 489)	490,339	23	74	7	21	64	5	35	n/a	n/a
1958–61 (Pokorny) (n = 425)	938,219	12	67	6	18	32	15	12	n/a	n/a
1969 (Lundsgaarde) (n = 268)[2]	1,232,802	23	59	9	25	45	16	8	1	6
1985–9[3] (n = 2,234)	1,809,013	28	47	10	27	47	23	48	3.5	31
1990–4[4] (n = 2,710)	1,630,553	33	41	15	27	58	28	33	4	24

[1] Rates are rounded.
[2] Estimates based on the 216 of 268 homicide incidents for which victim race/ethnicity was identified.
[3] Based on 1985 population estimates, U.S. Bureau of the Census.
[4] Based on 1990 population estimates, U.S. Bureau of the Census.

two and one-half times the city's overall rate and the highest among minority groups, with the exception of 1985–9, in which the homicide rates of blacks and Hispanics were virtually the same.

Our findings for Hispanic homicide risk echo those of Zahn (1987) and Martinez (1996a). In both Zahn's analysis of a nine-city sample and Martinez's study of 111 U.S. cities, overall Latino homicide rates fell between those of blacks and non-Latino whites. In Houston, for three of these five points in time, the homicide victimization rate for Hispanics has occupied an intermediate position between those of non-Hispanic whites and blacks. Only during the period 1985–9 did their relative risk exceed that of blacks. We believe this is partially explained by the fact that Hispanics' labor force participation in the region increased from 9 percent in 1970 to 20 percent in 1990, now exceeding that of blacks. Also, until 1990, 5 to 10 percent fewer Hispanics than blacks were in poverty (Bureau of the Census, 1993).

The homicide victimization risk for Asians was extremely high for the period 1985–9, with a homicide rate ten times their proportion of Houston's population. By 1990–4, this risk decreased to six times their percentage of the population. We believe this rapid decrease may reflect a more rapid assimilation into mainstream society, based on their labor force participation and income as earlier discussed. If this continues to be the case, their rates may continue to fall substantially.

Summary

At this writing, Houston is eight times larger geographically than it was fifty years ago, increasing from seventy-four to over six hundred square miles. It is also over three times larger in population, having grown from approximately 490,000 residents in 1945 to over 1.6 million today. This chapter has attempted to show how violence (as exemplified by acts legally declared to be homicides) intersects with race and ethnicity in a large, southern American city. We have shown that this relationship between violence and race/ethnicity is not a new phenomenon but one that has had varying dimensions over the past century. Demographic dynamics (migration patterns) have impacted this relationship as Houston has experienced first a decrease in the black population in the early part of the century and then an increase in the last half of the century. This recent increase in the black population has been accompanied by a 10 percent increase (from 18 percent to 28 percent) between 1980 and 1990 in the Hispanic population. During this same period, Houston experienced a huge economic downturn, from which it is just now beginning to recover. Throughout all this, the white homicide rate has maintained a relatively steady rate. Thus, what was predominantly a dichotomous picture of race and ethnic composition of homicide victims until the 1980s is now one of two major minority groups sharing in this social misfortune.

As elsewhere, many of Houston's projected labor force demands for the future are in low-skilled, low-paying service jobs and in high-skilled, technologically advanced occupations. Given the city's slow progress in addressing the educational, occupational, and income deficits of its most disadvantaged citizens, we may expect that these minority groups – particularly blacks and Hispanics – will continue to share in the perennial tragedy of lethal violence.

The Race/Ethnicity and Poverty Nexus of Violent Crime: Reconciling Differences in Chicago's Community Area Homicide Rates

Calvin C. Johnson
Chanchalat Chanhatasilpa

Introduction

Research on the relationship among race, poverty, and violent crime has a long tradition that is grounded in theoretical and empirical sociological literatures aimed largely at explaining the geographic and spatial distribution of violence (Wolfgang and Ferracuti, 1967; Beasley and Antunes, 1974; Loftin and Hill, 1974; Mlandenka and Hill, 1976; Anderson, 1999). One of the earliest theoretical perspectives suggested that the highest rates of violence are found in poor communities in which oppositional subcultures promote public displays of toughness and fatalism among residents (Wolfgang, 1967). These communities are typically described as neighborhoods with large ethnic or racial minority populations and places where residents are resentful and frustrated by their lack of economic opportunity and social isolation (Blau and Blau, 1982; Messner, 1983; Logan and Messner, 1987; Peterson and Krivo, 1993). Violence is considered a manifestation of feelings of diffused anger, resentment, and frustration, all of which are closely associated with economic disadvantage (Phillips, 1997). When the anger and frustration is not well managed, violence is just one of many outcomes (e.g., see Messner, 1983, for a similar discussion on hostility and aggression; Harer and Steffensmeier, 1992; Hsieh and Pugh, 1993). Proponents of this perspective posit that the association between racial/ethnic composition and criminal violence attenuates as stressors like resource deprivation and inequality are alleviated (Block, 1979; Messner, 1982; Williams, 1984; Sampson, 1985; 1986; Messner and Tardiff, 1986). Thus, resource deprivation and inequality are considered important determinants of violent conduct in racial/ethnic minority communities, or at least as important as racial/ethnic composition (Loftin and Hill, 1974; Blau and Blau, 1982; Messner and Tardiff, 1986).

Researchers have also reported that the association between racial/ethnic composition and criminal violence reflects the geographic concentration of high-risk populations (Sampson and Lauritsen, 1994). Short (1997) posits that communities have become noticeably segregated by race/ethnicity with most poor blacks living in poor black communities and most poor whites living in nonpoor white communities – a finding that Wilson (1987) and Massey and his associates (1994) have observed in Chicago. Because poor blacks are geographically concentrated, the relationship(s) among race, ethnicity, class, and violent crime at the macro-level could possibly reflect the segregation and concentration of high-risk populations (Wilson, 1987; Krivo and Peterson, 1996). When communities are saturated with high-risk populations, a "tipping" effect may be observed that results in rising homicide rates (Sampson and Lauritsen, 1994). Surprisingly, this discussion focuses on what Sampson and Wilson (1995) described as the artificial distinction between the basic tenets of structural and subcultural perspectives.

Additional sociological studies published during recent years have proposed a link between violence and the capacity of communities to "self-regulate" local social processes that occur within their boundaries. It is said that healthy and functioning communities collectively develop a consensus around notions of what are acceptable and unacceptable social interactions within the community and with persons from outside its boundaries. Thus, almost by definition, a community is characterized as an area of effective social control and regulated space. Self-regulation and other regulatory capacities constitute a form of social inoculation that reduces the likelihood that crime and disorder will develop from within or infiltrate community boundaries from without.

These concepts derived from the study of community may have relevance for understanding how race, economic disadvantage, and violent crime are linked. For example, proponents of these views have suggested that, while economic deprivation is perhaps sufficient to motivate individuals to participate in crime, especially in the presence of opportunities for wrongdoing, much of the documented association between violence and deprivation is perhaps accounted for by community self-regulation, community [social] control, or collective efficacy (Kornhauser, 1978; Bursik and Grasmick, 1993; Johnson, 1997; Sampson, Raudenbush, and Earls, 1997). A community that shows collective and reciprocal willingness to combat crime and disorder ("you watch my back and I'll watch yours") will be far less likely than its spatial counterparts to experience crime (Wilson, 1987; Sampson, Raudenbush, and Earls, 1997; Sampson and Raudenbush, 1999). Furthermore, scholars have suggested that social networks are the foundation of informal controls because they facilitate collective action through networks of friendship and kinship ties (Karsada and Janowitz, 1974; Bursik and Grasmick, 1993;

Bellair, 1997). Residents in communities with effective social networks are likely to have more interaction with one another and express, either passively or actively, their commitment to the basic principle of a community consensus. Because of residents' involvement in the social network, a community is able to wield informal controls to oppose practices that are not aligned with basic community principles (Bellair, 1997; Sampson, Raudenbush, and Earls, 1997).

Despite the insights provided by recent empirical investigations that have explored these possible links between community and crime, we believe that they do not provide a complete understanding of the roles played by poverty and economic inequality in explaining racial and ethnic differences in violent crime rates across communities. This critique forms the basis for the discussion and data we present in this chapter. We believe that past research on the effects of poverty on racially disaggregated *homicide* rates in the U.S. cities is perhaps the closest we have come to a sustained effort at successfully disentangling the relationship among poverty, race, ethnicity, and violent behavior (e.g., see Harer and Steffensmeier, 1992; Smith, 1992; Parker and McCall, 1997; and Parker and McCall, 1999; Ousey, 1999; Peterson, Krivo, and Harris, 2000). Although valuable, these studies have tended to be largely examinations of violent crime within the context of large urban centers with large numbers of poor nonwhite residents. Often, this has led to the perception of violent crime as largely an urban, minority problem. We believe this perception partly reflects a social science research agenda that has emphasized the accumulation of knowledge about crime in urban, minority America while underemphasizing crime and violence found in suburban and rural communities where whites live. Because of these limitations recent scholars have suggested the need for a closer examination of structural differences among more widely varied and diverse communities as a basis for providing better community-level explanations of variations in the distribution of homicide and nonlethal violence (Short, 1997; Ousey, 1999).

In pursuit of that objective, we argue in this chapter that economic deprivation and other structural disadvantages increase homicide rates in communities through their deleterious impact on community control regardless of the racial composition of the community. In this context, we suggest that poor white communities are no more immune to high levels of homicide than black communities. For example, in 1990, roughly 25 percent of the white residents in Miami, Detroit, and San Antonio lived below the poverty level, and these cities were among those in the United States with the highest homicide rates, between 16 and 20 per 100,000 residents, respectively (Glickman, Lahr, Wyly, and Elvin, 1998). Three smaller cities with relatively large concentrations of poor white residents (Little Rock, AR; Louisville, KY; Oklahoma City, OK) had homicide rates (approximately 5 to 7 per

100,000 residents) comparable to overall rates for New York City, Houston, and Los Angeles – larger cities with concentrated black poverty (Federal Bureau of Investigation, 1999; U.S. Bureau of the Census, 2000).

In this chapter, we attempt to expand, through conceptual and theoretical elaboration, some of the current discussion about the race, poverty, and homicide nexus. We propose that:

1. A community's racial composition is associated with its homicide rate but not independently of its economic status.

That is, minority communities with high levels of homicide are places with high levels of structural poverty and other social disadvantages that erode the ability of these communities to collectively combat crime and other social ills. In our analyses, we use a series of ordinary least squares models to show the complexity of the relationships and to offer support for our perspective. We focus on the net effects of racial/ethnic composition, economic deprivation, and their nexus on homicide rates. We are particularly interested in these relationships in terms of community violence. Our analysis investigates these relationships in a stepwise manner to highlight various beliefs about the race/ethnicity, poverty, and violence nexus that have emerged from the literature on this topic. Specifically, we begin with an investigation of one of the most common models estimated with city-level data – homicide rate regressed on racial composition. These results will give us an understanding of racial/ethnic composition as a determinant of community homicide rates assuming that racial/ethnic composition is variable and other structural factors are invariant across areas. However, we believe this model is an inadequate representation of the social structure and therefore proceed by reconciling the previous findings with two predictions.

As discussed by Sampson and Lauritsen (1994) and Short (1997), the association between the racial/ethnic composition of a community and homicide rates is expected to diminish or disappear once factors like socioeconomic status, social control, or poverty are statistically controlled. Thus, in the second stage of our investigation, we add economic deprivation and community control variables as well as other structural factors. The last stage of the investigation focuses on a prediction that has been offered by Wilson (1987) and later by Krivo and Peterson (1996). Following their lead, we further propose that:

2. The relationship between racial/ethnic composition and homicide rates is partially accounted for by structural disadvantage *and* levels of social control.

Although it is plausible that the proportion of racial/ethnic minority residents and poverty is independently associated with its homicide rates, we posit that poor black communities will tend to have higher homicide rates than nonpoor black areas. Indeed, we believe that this pattern exists between poor and nonpoor communities of any racial/ethnic composition. Poverty is expected to be deleterious in areas of any racial/ethnic compositions. The study below describes how the association between racial/ethnic composition and homicide rates is partially contingent on economic deprivation and its effect on community social control.

Data Sources

Data for this analysis come from two sources. The Community Area demographic, social, and economic data are from *The Local Community Fact Book* (Chicago Fact Book Consortium, 1983, 1996). The city of Chicago was selected because its population is very diverse along lines of race, ethnicity, and socioeconomic status; its distinct communities often are divided along these dimensions, and there exists an abundance of accessible information about the city and its residents. *Community Fact Book* data have been collected for the seventy-five historically recognized communities of Chicago for more than sixty years. A Community Area is a geographically linked collection of census tracts that share historical patterns of growth and settlement. Historically, these areas have had a distinct set of inhabitants with collective interests and business and organizational participation that set them apart from their neighbors (Chicago Fact Book Consortium, 1996). Although we compromise somewhat the concepts "community" and "neighborhood" by using Community Areas, the data collected for each area provide many opportunities to study changes in the composition and structure of the smaller, "true" communities contained therein. In our study, the concepts "community" and Community Area are not coterminous.

The homicide data we use in our Community Area analysis come from the *Chicago Homicide Dataset* (1996), which contains data on all homicides, except police shootings and justifiable deaths, occurring in the city of Chicago between 1965 and 1994. The data were collected and analyzed by Carolyn Rebecca Block and Richard Block.[1] It contains more than twenty-three thousand records and one hundred variables related to victim, offender, and incident characteristics.[2]

We merged the two datasets to combine the structural data (the *Chicago Community Fact Book*) with the homicide data (the *Chicago Homicide Dataset*). To link the two datasets, the homicide data was aggregated to the Community Area. We assigned each homicide record a Community Area; thus, we

---

[1] Richard Block geocoded the entire dataset, linked addresses to census tracts, and supplied this information to the archived version of the *Chicago Homicide Dataset*. A Community Area variable, created by aggregating tracts, is also included in the archived data.

[2] For an excellent review of the *Chicago Homicide Dataset*, see Block and Block (1994).

summarized the homicide counts for each Community Area and year. The final dataset contains 1970, 1980, and 1990 structural data and corresponding homicide data for each Community Area.[3]

Community Area data collected between 1970 and 1990 provide a reasonable picture of the structural disadvantage facing communities shortly after a period of major economic displacement. While urban poverty had been concentrated in ethnic communities before 1970, severe poverty became more pronounced during the 1970s – especially toward the end of the 1970s – when urban America finally realized the end of an economy dominated by manufacturing to one characterized by the near dominance of service industries. This shift produced a skill mismatch that resulted in a surplus of low-skilled workers who were not well suited for the labor force (Wilson, 1987, 1997; Wacquant and Wilson, 1989; Massey, 1990; Massey et al., 1994).[4] Besides the development of severe economic deprivation within Community Areas, we also observed a decrease in Chicago's white population by one-third and an increase in the Hispanic and black populations by 70 percent and 9 percent respectively. This structural shift occurred during a time when the homicide rates for whites increased, the homicide rates for Hispanics outpaced that group's population growth, and the homicide rates for blacks decreased (Block and Block, 1992; Block, 1993). Although Chicago does not contain large populations of economically deprived white residents heavily concentrated in any one Community Area, it does allow us to preliminarily investigate how structural poverty impacts communities that are more or less nonblack.

Measures

The Community Area homicide rate represents a three-year mean rate – the three years surrounding and including the decennial census year.[5] Unlike many nonfatal crimes, using homicide as a dependent variable reduces the likelihood of reporting biases. Homicides rarely go unnoticed or unreported.

[3] We only discuss the findings for 1980 and 1990. The findings for 1970 are not discussed because one of the variables used to weight the community capacity scale has a sign in the opposite direction and thus challenges our conceptual argument for using this measure in 1970. Although the results are consistent across all three study years, the findings for 1970 appear in the Appendix (Table A-1).

[4] Remember that large industries, especially those in the Midwest and Northeast, set in motion a migration of unskilled to semiskilled workers whose subsistence depended on the continued existence of large industries (Lieberson, 1980).

[5] Despite the advantages of using Community Area as the unit of analysis, preliminary analyses of univariate and bivariate data plots indicated that two community areas (The Loop and O'Hare) were different from the others. Both communities were dropped from the analysis because their high transient activities inflated the person time at risk of homicide victimization and the opportunity for would-be offenders.

Table 5.1. *Chicago Community Area Characteristics, 1980 and 1990 (N = 75)*

	Min	Q_1	Q_2	Q_3	Max
Average Homicide Rate, 1980	.00	17.12	53.65	114.64	276.13
Average Homicide Rate, 1990	.00	21.21	49.82	129.39	395.58
% Below Poverty, 1980	1.50	5.10	11.50	23.40	60.90
% Below Poverty, 1990	.00	7.00	14.00	28.00	70.00
Unemployment Rate, 1980	3.60	6.00	8.30	13.60	29.50
Unemployment Rate, 1990	3.00	7.00	11.00	18.00	45.00
Rate of Public Aid, 1980	.11	2.39	7.48	18.09	68.08
Rate of Public Aid, 1990	.15	3.04	9.16	19.64	49.30
Proportion Black, 1980	.00	.00	.13	.94	.99
Proportion Black, 1990	.00	.01	.23	.96	.99
Proportion Hispanic, 1980	.00	.01	.04	.13	.78
Proportion Hispanic, 1990	.00	.01	.07	.25	.88
Proportion Non-Hispanic White, 1980	.00	.04	.62	.88	.99
Proportion Non-Hispanic White, 1990	.00	.02	.45	.79	.98
% Owner Occupancy, 1980	.50	22.40	38.10	67.60	90.60
% Owner Occupancy, 1990	2.00	27.00	43.00	71.00	91.00
Residential Stability, 1980	33.20	52.10	63.20	70.90	79.20
Residential Stability, 1990	36.00	55.00	63.00	71.00	79.00
% Children in Husband-Wife Household, 1980	21.50	54.80	72.50	85.20	92.10
% Children in Husband-Wife Household, 1990	23.00	57.00	75.00	83.00	90.00
Persons per Household, 1980	1.70	2.50	2.80	3.30	4.90
Persons per Household, 1990	1.70	2.50	2.80	3.20	4.40
% Age 14–20, 1980	6.10	10.60	12.50	14.80	19.30
% Age 14–20, 1990	4.00	8.00	10.00	12.00	15.00

The homicide rates are positively skewed as indicated by the quartile distribution in Table 5.1. The median homicide rates are closer to the 25th percentile than to the 75th percentile. This pattern was present in each study year and indicated that only a few communities had high homicide rates.

Our measure of racial/ethnic composition is the proportion each racial/ethnic group composes of the Community Area.[6] The value for any one group ranges between 0 (no representation) and 1 (complete representation). Because we hypothesized that a community's racial/ethnic minority composition is associated with homicide rates, we created a

---

[6] Race and ethnic groups other than black and Hispanic were combined with the numbers for white residents in a community.

Table 5.2. *Factor Loadings of Indicators for Economic Deprivation and Community Control, 1980 and 1990 (N = 75)*

Indicator	1980	1990
	Economic Deprivation	
% Below Poverty	.971	.969
Unemployment Rate	.952	.977
Rate of Public Aid	.963	.989
	Community Control	
% Owner Occupancy	.977	.985
Residential Stability	.690	.670
% Children in H-W	.770	.670

separate variable for each race/ethnic group: (1) white, (2) black, and (3) Hispanic.

Economic deprivation (DEP) – our measure of poverty – is a weighted factor score composed of three indicators: (1) the percentage of families with combined incomes below the poverty level; (2) the unemployment rate for civilians sixteen years and older; and (3) the rate of public assistance per one hundred residents. Together these indicators provide a refined measure of severe poverty at the Community Area, for example, see Bursik and Grasmick (1993). We chose the weighted scale approach to avoid the potential of multicollinearity of our independent variables and because we believe it is unlikely that each variable contributes equally to the construct. The regression factor score is the sum of each variable weighted by its factor score. Perhaps surprisingly, the indicators of economic deprivation have similar associations with the construct. As shown in Table 5.2, the economic deprivation variable captures three poverty-related indicators that have consistent high factor loadings above .95.

Community control (CC) – a proxy measure of the capacity of communities to wield social control – is a weighted factor score composed of three indicators: (1) the percentage of owner occupied housing units; (2) the rate of residential stability; and (3) the percentage of children living in husband-wife households. We intended to measure the degree to which a community has the collective capacity to control local activities (see Elliott et al., 1996; Sampson, Raudenbush, and Earls, 1997). Based on the literature, we hypothesize that in communities with high levels of capacity to control, residents are more likely to take steps to prevent the occurrence of disorder and to take other necessary steps to inhibit personal violence. These effects might include greater participation in local initiatives to prevent and control crime and delinquency, especially violent crimes. Although the indicators of this measure have only moderate factor loadings (see Table 5.2), we believe that it measures the degree to which communities can assemble collectives to combat undesirable activities because it has face validity.[7]

As with any spatial analysis of violence, the percentage of residents between the age of fourteen and twenty is a factor worth exploring. Empirical studies continue to show that teenagers and young adults commit crime and are victims of crimes more often than individuals from other age categories (Hindelang, Gottfredson, and Garofalo, 1978; Land, McCall, and Cohen, 1990). Conceptually, the percentage of young residents is interesting because young people participate in lifestyle activities that place them at greater risk of being victims and offenders. Therefore, we expect communities with high percentages of young people to have higher rates of violent crimes than communities with lower percentages of young people. Table 5.1 shows a relatively stable distribution of teenage population across the study years.

Population density – measured as population per household – is another factor that is important to our investigation (see Table 5.1). Literature has indicated that population density (especially within the context of urbanization and crowding) can be important in explaining violent crime. More specifically, population density destroys the community organization by increasing the level of anonymity among residents (Fischer, 1976; Roncek, 1981; Sampson, 1985; Wilson, 1987; Block, 1993; Sampson et al., 1997). As highlighted in this literature, reciprocal guardianship behaviors in which residents are familiar and concerned with one another are more difficult to maintain in densely populated communities due to increased anonymity among neighbors. Once these relationships and behaviors become ineffective, the community is less capable of regulating and controlling interpersonal violence.

Analysis Plan

We are primarily interested in the association between race/ethnicity and community homicide rates that is net of economic deprivation and vice

---

[7] Residential stability had a negative loading in 1970 and positive loadings in 1980 and 1990. After analyzing the descriptive statistics for residential stability, we recognized the historical significance of migration patterns in and out of Chicago Community Areas. By 1970, racial/ethnic minorities began experimenting with new housing opportunities made possible by the passing of the Fair Housing Act. As a result, many racial/ethnic Community Areas, even European ethnic areas, were experiencing a great deal of residential instability. However, by 1980 and certainly by 1990, residential stability was the rule. Community Areas of all racial/ethnic makeups had become residentially stable. We believe the negative loading for residential stability in 1970 was picking up this historical trend. Therefore, this loading does not compromise the validity of Community Control.

versa. Assuming the association between racial/ethnic composition and homicide rates to be significant, a general interpretation of this finding is that racial/ethnic composition is associated with differences in homicide rates net of the potential association with economic deprivation and vice versa. Because we know that community economic deprivation and racial/ethnic composition are not independent structural phenomena, the use of modes of data analysis and statistical tests that assume such independence would be misleading. The observation by Wilson (1987) and Massey and his associates (1990 and 1994) that 70 percent of poor whites live in nonpoor neighborhoods compared with 15 percent of poor blacks provides support for investigating the interdependent association of economic deprivation and racial/ethnic composition and the subsequent association with homicide rates. Short (1997) also suggests that the intersection between poverty and racial/ethnic composition might very well explain differences in the patterns of violence in black and white communities. Unfortunately, Short also notes that analyses of these relationships are complicated and rarely conducted.[8] Perhaps a more appropriate analysis within the framework outlined by Wilson and Short would involve a test of the interaction between economic deprivation and racial/ethnic composition and its association with community homicide rates. This is a general test of the association between a community's racial/ethnic composition and homicide rates, assuming *constant* levels of economic deprivation. It seeks to determine whether the race/ethnicity associations are comparable at each level of economic deprivation.

We conducted three analyses to investigate the relationships among race/ethnicity, economic deprivation, and homicide rates. We designed the first set of analyses to establish a community's racial/ethnic composition as a significant predictor of Community Area homicide rates. To investigate this relationship, we regressed community homicide rates on racial/ethnic composition (the proportion of black and Hispanic residents). This analysis provides a first approximation of the association between racial/ethnic composition and community homicide rates independent of other structural factors. Next, we added control variables assumed to be associated with community homicide rates – economic deprivation, capacity to control, percent age fourteen to twenty, and the number of persons per household. (We

---

[8] The rareness of this sort of research may be due to the complexity involved in designing the models as well as the difficulty in interpreting the results. Although we estimated a simple version of the intersection between race/ethnicity and economic deprivation, we found the interpretation of our findings quite challenging. The challenge was not necessarily in the interpretation of the parameter estimates. Instead, we were more concerned about making the interpretation as intuitive as possible. Perhaps this may provide at least part of the reason for Short's (1997) observation of the rareness and/or inadequate attention to this issue.

Table 5.3. *OLS Coefficients for the Bivariate Regression of Community Area Mean Homicide Rates (Square-root) on Community Structural Characteristics, 1980 and 1990 (N = 75)*

	HOM 1980	HOM 1990
Economic Deprivation (DEP)	3.674	4.749
	(.238)	(.225)
	15.463	21.146
Community Control (CC)	−3.354	−3.600
	(.289)	(.426)
	−11.624	−8.443
% Age 14–20	.595	1.234
	(.159)	(.178)
	3.736	6.928
Population Density	1.849	3.535
	(.921)	(1.100)
	2.008	3.213
Proportion Hispanic	3.393	−3.223
	(2.972)	(2.933)
	1.142	−1.099
Proportion Black	6.859	9.626
	(.812)	(.840)
	8.447	11.456
Proportion White	−8.392	−11.546
	(.724)	(.859)
	−11.595	−13.448

Note: The Downtown Loop and O'Hare were omitted from the estimation. Numbers in parentheses are standard errors followed by t-ratios. A t-value of 1.645 is significant at the .05 level for a one-tailed test.

note that each of the control variables had significant bivariate coefficients across the study periods, as shown in Table 5.3). This analysis allows us to determine the strength of the racial/ethnic composition variables' association with community homicide rates. In addition, we can determine the degree to which the control variables – specifically economic deprivation – account for a large part of the association between racial/ethnic composition and community homicide rates. Here, we should observe a sizable decrease in the magnitude (size) of each racial/ethnic composition coefficient.

The third set of analyses investigated the effect of the proportion of black, Hispanic, and white residents on community homicide rates across constant levels of economic deprivation. To investigate these relationships, we added

Table 5.4. *OLS Coefficients for the Regression of Community Area Mean Homicide Rates (Square-root) on Community Structural Characteristics, 1980 and 1990 (N = 75)*

Model 1	HOM 1980	HOM 1990
Proportion Hispanic	11.144	8.403
	(1.882)	(1.770)
	5.922	4.748
Proportion Black	8.358	11.539
	(.717)	(.841)
	11.662	13.720
Constant	3.281	2.206
Adjusted R Square	.650	.720

Note: The Downtown Loop and O'Hare were omitted from the estimation. Numbers in parentheses are standard errors followed by t-ratios. A t-value of 1.645 is significant at the .05 level for a one-tailed test.

(to the previous model) the interaction effects of the proportion of black residents and the proportion of Hispanic residents with economic deprivation. This model also allows us to investigate the effect of economic deprivation on homicide rates in communities with different racial/ethnic compositions and show in another way that economic deprivation accounts at least partially for the race/ethnicity-homicide relationship. Each model is part of an exercise to highlight the complicated nature of the race, ethnicity, and class nexus. What follows is a discussion of the findings from the analyses.

Results

As shown in Table 5.3, the bivariate coefficients indicate that each predictor variable, including those used to construct the factor composites, are associated with Community Area homicide rates. Thus, our initial assumptions about model specifications with the chosen predictors do not appear to have been made in error.

Tables 5.4 to 5.6 provide nested specifications of the racial/ethnic composition and economic deprivation relationships with community homicide rates. To reiterate, Model 1 tests the initial hypothesis that racial/ethnic composition is associated with community homicide rates (the "Race/Ethnicity Model"); Model 2 tests a more general hypothesis that economic deprivation and other relevant control variables account for a substantial portion of the

Table 5.5. *OLS Coefficients for the Regression of Community Area Mean Homicide Rates (Square-root) on Community Structural Characteristics, 1980 and 1990 (N = 75)*

Model 2	HOM 1980	HOM 1990
Economic Deprivation (DEP)	2.190	2.814
	(.493)	(.433)
	4.440	6.495
Community Control (CC)	−.754	−.931
	(.423)	(.395)
	−1.783	−2.360
% Age 14–20	−.087	−.254
	(.210)	(.180)
	−.416	−1.413
Population Density	1.335	.669
	(1.106)	(.979)
	−1.207	.684
Proportion Hispanic	7.541	4.277
	(1.641)	(1.725)
	4.596	2.480
Proportion Black	4.406	5.416
	(.807)	(.930)
	5.455	5.826
Constant	9.013	4.446
Adjusted R Square	.890	.912

Note: The Downtown Loop and O'Hare were omitted from the estimation. Numbers in parentheses are standard errors followed by t-ratios. A t-value of 1.645 is significant at the .05 level for a one-tailed test.

association between racial/ethnic composition and community homicide rates (the "Structural Partitioning Model"); Model 3 tests another general hypothesis that the association between economic deprivation and community homicide rates is consistently deleterious whatever the racial/ethnic composition of the areas (the "Structural Disadvantage Model").

As shown in Model 1, racial/ethnic composition was consistently associated with community homicide rates at each study year. Black and Hispanic communities had higher homicide rates than their white counterparts.

Our examination of Model 2 – the "Structural Partitioning Model," which includes measures of deprivation and demographic controls – shows that the coefficients for racial/ethnic compositions were reduced by nearly half though they remained statistically significant. In this model, economic

Table 5.6. *OLS Coefficients for the Regression of Community Area Mean Homicide Rates (Square-root) on Community Structural Characteristics, 1980 and 1990 (N = 75)*

Model 3	HOM 1980	HOM 1990
Economic Deprivation (DEP)	3.600	3.144
	(1.289)	(1.440)
	2.793	2.183
Community Control (CC)	−.716	−.920
	(.431)	(.400)
	−1.660	−2.300
% Age 14–20	−.093	−.311
	(.201)	(.185)
	−.466	−1.686
Population Density	−1.330	.749
	(1.052)	(.977)
	−1.264	.767
Proportion Hispanic	−3.005	−.851
	(4.122)	(3.136)
	−.729	−.271
Proportion Black	4.608	5.408
	(.834)	(1.101)
	5.526	4.912
DEP*Hispanic	5.901	3.974
	(3.022)	(2.622)
	1.953	1.515
DEP*Black	−1.632	−.414
	(1.120)	(1.346)
	−1.458	−.308
Constant	9.089	4.907
Adjusted R Square	.901	.914

Note: The Downtown Loop and O'Hare were omitted from the estimation. Numbers in parentheses are standard errors followed by t-ratios. A t-value of 1.645 is significant at the .05 level for a one-tailed test.

deprivation was consistently associated with community homicide rates at each study year. Furthermore, the coefficient for economic deprivation increased over the two study years – a clear indication that economic deprivation became more deleterious over time. This association corresponds to the period associated with the formation of the urban underclass (Wilson, 1987; Massey, 1990; Massey et al., 1994). Capacity for control was consistently associated with decreases in community homicide rates. All else equal, communities with high capacity for control experienced fewer homicides than those communities with low capacity for control.

The relationship between economic deprivation, community control, and community homicide rates was net of the relationship between racial/ethnic composition and community homicide rates. Because we chose to use racial/ethnic composition as a series of proportions, the interpretation of the coefficients speaks to the differences in communities we could hypothetically classify as white, black, or Hispanic.[9] Using whites as the reference group, we observed patterns of homicide rates that were higher in black and Hispanic communities than in white areas (see Table 5.5). Specifically, we notice that the intercept for the model at each period was significantly large. In the general sense, we can interpret these findings to mean that (all else being equal) communities with no (0) whites – those communities with the largest proportions blacks and Hispanics – had high homicide rates.[10] However, this model fails to take into account the extant literature about the concentration of black and Hispanic poor in inner-city America. Also, black and Hispanic poor communities are more densely populated with poor residents and more likely to be adjacent to one another or in close proximity. Their white counterparts are more likely to live among nonpoor residents or in less densely poor areas.

The coefficients for the percentage of the population that are teenagers (sixteen to twenty) and population density (persons per household) were not associated with community homicide rates as specified in our models (as indicated by the nonsignificant coefficients during the study years despite significant bivariate coefficients). Similar findings have been reported in other studies of homicide (see Land, McCall, and Cohen, 1990). We omitted both variables from the remaining discussion.

Model 3 provides the best illustration of the way we understand the intersection between racial/ethnic composition and economic deprivation to work with community homicide.[11] Examination of the models allows us to make comparisons between racial/ethnic composition and homicide rates in economically deprived (poor) and nondeprived (nonpoor)

---

[9] We do not attempt to provide a classification scheme that identifies Community Areas along race/ethnicity lines. However, the variables were constructed to allow us to more or less make testable hypothetical statements about the relationship between a Community Area's racial/ethnic composition and homicide rates. In the general sense, the race/ethnicity variable is a measure of effects due to a particular racial/ethnic group.

[10] This is the interpretation of the intercept in this model. It is the effect of the proportion white at level zero.

[11] The constant is the base homicide rate in white Community Areas and the coefficient for economic deprivation is what is added to the constant to determine the rate in poor white areas. To determine the comparable rates in black and Hispanic Community Areas, the main effect coefficients for racial/ethnic composition are used to compare rates in nonpoor areas and the interaction effect coefficients are used to compare rates in poor community areas.

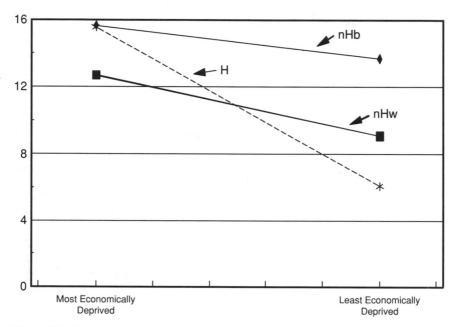

Figure 5.1. Community Area Homicide Rates across Level of Economic Deprivation, 1980

communities. Figures 5.1 and 5.2 illustrate the effect given the complexity of interpreting models specified with interaction terms. As observed in each figure, the relationship between economic deprivation and community homicide rates is most glaring at the lowest levels of economic deprivation (nonpoor areas). At this level, the rates for black communities are much higher than the rates in white and Hispanic areas. However, as communities become more economically deprived (poorer) – whatever the racial/ethnic composition – the rates start to converge. Each figure shows that the differences between homicide rates for each race-specific community is greatest in the least economically deprived areas (nonpoor) than in the most economically deprived areas (poor). Moreover, the significant and marginally significant interactions indicate that the difference between homicide rates in nonpoor and poor communities is greatest for Hispanic areas. Although the rates are lowest in areas with low levels of poverty, the rates soar and are highest in areas with high levels of poverty. Thus, this analysis indicates that the most economically deprived (poorest) areas have the worst patterns of homicide rates whatever the racial/ethnic composition.

Discussion and Conclusion

What do we make of the association between racial/ethnic composition and community homicide rates seen in this analysis? Whatever the

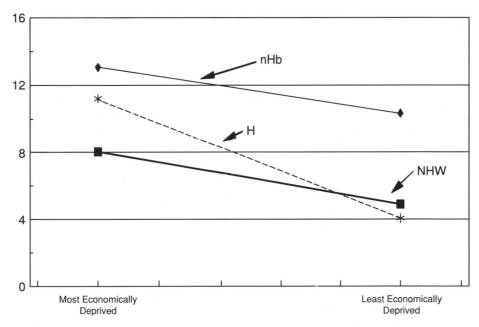

Figure 5.2. Community Area Homicide Rates across Level of Economic Deprivation, 1990

interpretations, and there are many, they may have major policy implications. For example, if the relationship is a matter of "pure" economics, then we could suggest policy directives that focus on economic revitalization within communities with histories of high unemployment and underemployment rates, especially in those communities considered most likely to present opportunities for illegitimate and risky financially rewarding opportunities associated with violence. However, if the relationship is a matter of racial/ethnic composition, then a couple of logical policy directives might be: (1) to target communities populated by high-risk groups for special attention by law enforcement agencies and other agencies responsible for crime prevention; or (2) to use housing policy to reduce the concentration of poor, minority residents in the inner cities and disperse them across the urban landscape. These are policy directives that have already begun in the form of crackdown and zero tolerance policing practices that have recently received a great deal of attention in the Bronx area of New York City, in Los Angeles, Chicago, and other smaller cities across the country. Disperse Housing Program (DHA) initiatives can be found in Chicago, Denver, and Baltimore.

Our analyses provide support for the general hypothesis that the association between racial/ethnic composition and homicide rates is contingent partially upon the level of economic deprivation within the community.

To understand how we reached this conclusion, we turn to a discussion of Tables 5.4, 5.5, and 5.6. As observed in Table 5.4, the coefficients for the proportion Hispanic and black were large compared with the level for the proportion white. Notice that the magnitude (size) differences for each of the racial/ethnic composition variables persist across each study year. Thus, at this point we could have concluded, albeit erroneously, that racial/ethnic minority community had high homicide rates of extreme magnitude. However, this model failed to consider the association that community homicide rates may have with other structural factors. Once we controlled for structural factors assumed to have an association with community homicide rates (specifically economic deprivation), the coefficients for racial/ethnic composition reduced in magnitude by roughly 50 percent. That is, the size of the coefficients for the proportion Hispanic residents and the proportion black residents decreased by one-half when we considered the area's level of economic deprivation, community control, population density, and percentage teenage population.

Clearly, over half the association between community homicide rate and race/ethnicity is attributable to factors other than race/ethnicity. As such, the net effect of minority racial/ethnic composition is sensitive to other structural factors. Is community-level homicide really associated with racial/ethnic composition or other factors like economic deprivation and community control? This question arises from the contemporary context of racial/ethnic segregation, concentrated poverty, and decreasing homicide rates in our inner cities. These cities are poorer and have greater concentrations of racial/ethnic minorities than in any of the preceding decennial census years, but they are also experiencing decreases of 10 to 15 percent in homicide victimizations. Given these patterns, more research is needed to determine how minority racial/ethnic composition and community homicide rates are associated.

At another point in the analysis, we investigated whether homicide rates in poor white communities were different from those in poor racial/ethnic minority areas. Indeed, we notice in Figures 5.1 and 5.2 that racial/ethnic differences in homicide rates are less pronounced when communities are poor and more pronounced when communities are nonpoor. We interpret the patterns observed in Table 5.6 in terms of homicide rates for racial/ethnic groups at various levels of poverty. More specifically, the poorest Hispanic and black communities have homicide rates that are similar to the poorest white Community Areas. In contrast, nonpoor communities of similar distinctive racial/ethnic compositions are not as similar. To understand why this may be the case, we offer the following explanations. The poorest communities will have similarly deleterious homicide rates, not because of the racial/ethnic composition of the Community Area, but because poverty creates ripe opportunities for negative life circumstances to flourish and attack the collective properties of the community. As Robert Sampson and his associates noted in studies conducted during the 1980s and early 1990s, poverty operates to disrupt protective community controls, for example, see Sampson and Lauritsen (1994). These elements are necessary to combat crime and delinquency at the community level. Therefore, it does not surprise us that poor communities of all racial/ethnic compositions would have higher homicide rates than those found in the respective nonpoor communities. Indeed, structural poverty is consistently shown to be associated with homicide.

In contrast, we expect the nonpoor communities to have noticeably lower homicide rates. As observed in Figures 5.1 and 5.2, nonpoor black communities had higher homicide rates than those found in nonpoor Hispanic and white areas. We understand the disparate rate to be a function of migration and post facto segregation. Recall for a moment that poor white residents are less likely to live in poor communities than poor black residents. Thus, the concentration of poor whites is a less common occurrence than the concentration of poor black residents. When we do find high concentrations of poor whites, they tend to be found in rural areas of the United States. Some of these areas have high homicide rates, especially in Appalachia. In addition, middle-class black communities are more likely to be found near poor communities, especially those that are poor and black. As a result, the homicide rates for middle-class black communities might be high because the physical boundaries between these communities and the poorest areas "fade out" and make social boundaries less distinctive. Conversely, the physical boundaries between black and nonblack communities are more obvious and transcend social environments, thus creating social boundaries that closely resemble the physical boundaries. These findings also address another wrinkle in the race/ethnicity, class, and interpersonal violence nexus. Particularly, we gave special attention to racial/ethnic composition and its association with Community Area homicide rates before and after controlling for poverty. Although the association between race/ethnicity and community homicide rates seemed significant independent of other structural factors, when we introduced structural poverty to our model specification, the typical association between race/ethnicity and Community Area homicide rates became less apparent. Rather than draw definitive conclusions about these findings, we would like to offer three suggestions to researchers and policy makers concerned about the associations among race/ethnicity, poverty, and homicide.

First, we should study no one component of the race/ethnicity, poverty, and homicide nexus in a vacuum. To continue to study in a cursory fashion the association between racial/ethnic composition and homicide is unsatisfying, does not provide an understanding about how and why race/ethnicity is important, and potentially could lead to erroneous conclusions about the relationships. The research in this area has often used the racial composition in geographic locations (particularly black residents) synonymously with the economic conditions of the same location. As we have shown, other structural factors (especially economic deprivation, our measure of structural poverty) accounted for half the initial relationship between racial/ethnic composition and homicide. Furthermore, homicide rates in the poorest Community Areas were deleterious whatever the racial/ethnic composition. Therefore, any attempt to use race/ethnicity should take into account the potential intersections with other structural factors, especially when strong conceptual support exists for such analyses (Sampson, 1986). To continue developing our understanding of the race/ethnicity, poverty, and homicide nexus, the research community will need to explore the impact of structural measures independently of race and ethnicity. We have attempted to explore such a relationship using Chicago Community Area data (see also recent studies by Krivo and Peterson, 1996; and their associates).

We also encourage further development of more obvious intersections between the nexus. Particularly, we must examine the individual and situational circumstances surrounding homicide events (to include spatial and temporal) with more detail. As outlined throughout the National Research Council report, *Understanding and Preventing Violence* (Reiss and Roth, 1994), and *Poverty, Ethnicity, and Violent Crime* (Short, 1997), the determinants of violence flow from the individual, macro-structural, and situational levels of analyses. Thus, before we can begin to understand the causes of violent crimes, we must unravel the associations at each level and bring findings from these levels together to provide meaningful interpretation of our data.

Second, the fact that structural poverty is associated with community homicide rates in inner-city Chicago does not mean that Chicago's community structures typify other large metropolitan cities. Policy makers often find themselves making misguided recommendations because they overextend the generalizability and applicability of study findings. Therefore, global policy recommendations about how to combat the effect of structural poverty on community homicide rates should proceed with extreme caution until examinations of the race, poverty, and crime relationship(s) have been investigated in other cities using other units of analyses (e.g., census tracts, blocks, and other spatially meaningful units). Our presentation of the findings addresses community-level determinants of homicide for a Midwestern city (namely Chicago) in 1980 and 1990.

Finally, these findings may point to the potential "shock effect" that might occur when programs intended to improve the economic position of the long-term poor err and cause a greater downward spiral in their economic position. Specifically, we need to be mindful of the unintended consequences of policies that, while based on good intentions, may actually cause more harm than good. For example, poor communities are more likely than nonpoor communities to experience disproportionately high levels of homicide victimization, for reasons explained above. Welfare reform policies that are intended to improve the economic circumstances of poor families also must attend to unintended consequences that might make their communities more vulnerable to abnormally high levels of homicide victimization. Research has not yet addressed the potential effect of these types of policies on crime, especially criminal violence. When such research begins to develop, we should give careful attention to national variations in local responses to reform and the association between these responses and homicide rates. Furthermore, researchers should pay close attention to the fiscal and social capacities of localities and their ability to control crime, especially in areas that have large concentrations of poor or racial/ethnic minorities. We would hypothesize that localities with low fiscal capacity or community control capacity are less able to bear the burden of specific economic reforms, and therefore are more susceptible to the deleterious effect of poverty on crime. Likewise, many other communities will become susceptible as they struggle with the new fiscal strain and the inability to collectively build community control capacities.

Appendix

Table A1. *Chicago Community Area Characteristics, 1970 (N = 75)*

	Min	Q_1	Q_2	Q_3	Max
Average Homicide Rate	.00	7.23	29.60	90.50	231.87
% Below Poverty	2.10	4.00	6.40	15.50	44.40
Unemployment Rate	1.90	2.80	3.70	4.90	13.40
Rate of Public Aid	.21	.45	.96	1.96	6.91
Proportion Black	.00	.00	.04	.69	.99
Proportion Hispanic	.00	.01	.02	.06	.55
Proportion White	.00	.30	.81	.97	1.00
% Owner Occupancy	.60	15.9	35.8	68.4	89.7
Residential Stability	25.10	35.00	44.10	52.20	70.80
% Children in Husband-Wife Household	51.70	80.30	85.70	88.70	92.20
Persons per Household	2.00	2.80	3.10	3.40	4.40
% Age 14–20	8.00	10.40	12.10	13.20	18.60

Table A2. *OLS Coefficients for the Bivariate Regression of Community Area Mean Homicide Rates (Square-root) on Community Structural Characteristics, 1970 (N = 75)*

	HOM
Economic Deprivation (DEP)	4.005
	(.258)
	15.528
Community Control (CC)	−3.708
	(.313)
	−11.854
% Age 14–20	.804
	(.241)
	3.329
Population Density	2.604
	(1.096)
	2.376
Proportion Hispanic	2.911
	(5.812)
	.501
Proportion Black	9.938
	(.755)
	13.170
Proportion White	−10.863
	(.671)
	−16.186

Note: The Downtown Loop and O'Hare were omitted from the estimation. Numbers in parentheses are standard errors followed by t-ratios. A t-value of 1.645 is significant at the .05 level for a one-tailed test.

Table A3. *OLS Coefficients for the Regression of Community Area Mean Homicide Rates (Square-root) on Community Structural Characteristics, 1970 (N = 75)*

Model 1	HOM
Proportion Hispanic	15.073
	(2.792)
	5.398
Proportion Black	10.893
	(.665)
	16.380
Constant	1.989
Adjusted R Square	.783

Note: The Downtown Loop and O'Hare were omitted from the estimation. Numbers in parentheses are standard errors followed by t-ratios. A t-value of 1.645 is significant at the .05 level for a one-tailed test.

Table A4. *OLS Coefficients for the Regression of Community Area Mean Homicide Rates (Square-root) on Community Structural Characteristics, 1970 (N = 75)*

Model 2	HOM
Economic Deprivation (DEP)	2.047
	(.529)
	3.867
Community Control (CC)	−.881
	(.533)
	−1.653
% Age 14–20	−.508
	(.212)
	−2.398
Population Density	1.332
	(1.019)
	1.307
Proportion Hispanic	7.863
	(2.533)
	3.103
Proportion Black	5.340
	(1.080)
	4.942
Constant	6.380
Adjusted R Square	.880

Note: The Downtown Loop and O'Hare were omitted from the estimation. Numbers in parentheses are standard errors followed by t-ratios. A t-value of 1.645 is significant at the .05 level for a one-tailed test.

Table A5. *OLS Coefficients for the Regression of Community Area Mean Homicide Rates (Square-root) on Community Structural Characteristics, 1970 (N = 75)*

Model 3	HOM
Economic Deprivation (DEP)	4.552
	(1.293)
	3.520
Community Control (CC)	−.572
	(.551)
	−1.038
% Age 14–20	−.529
	(.205)
	−2.583
Population Density	1.395
	(.986)
	1.415
Proportion Hispanic	1.266
	(6.279)
	.202
Proportion Black	6.339
	(1.136)
	5.582
DEP*Hispanic	1.460
	(5.627)
	.259
DEP*Black	−2.647
	(1.140)
	−2.321
Constant	4.960
Adjusted R Square	.888

Note: The Downtown Loop and O'Hare were omitted from the estimation. Numbers in parentheses are standard errors followed by t-ratios. A t-value of 1.645 is significant at the .05 level for a one-tailed test.

Other Contexts, Settings, and Forms of Violence

Sanction Effects, Violence, and Native North American Street Youth

Bill McCarthy
John Hagan

In the last three decades, researchers of the relationship between race and crime in North America have broadened their focus beyond differences between blacks and whites to include other groups: for example, studies of Hispanics and Asians are increasingly common. However, one group is continually underrepresented in studies of crime and, particularly, studies of violence: American Indians, or, as they are known in Canada, Aboriginals.[1] In the preamble to her groundbreaking study of violence among American Indians, Bachman (1992) notes that prior to her work, multivariate studies of causes of Aboriginal violence were virtually nonexistent. Four years later, Nielsen and Silverman (1996: xii) found little had changed since Bachman's research. They remark that,

> [i]n putting together this volume, we discovered that empirical research on Native peoples was relatively scarce in the crime and criminal justice literature. . . . In fact it is reasonable to say that Native issues of crime and justice have been neglected in U.S. research.

This oversight is surprising. Although Native peoples represent a small proportion of American and Canadian populations, they are consistently overrepresented in these nations' arrest and incarceration statistics. For example, Silverman (1996) estimates that in the period between 1987 and 1992, less than 1 percent of the U.S. population was American Indian; however, in these years the arrest rate for violent crime among American Indians was approximately 50 percent higher than for white Americans; for homicide, it was about 70 percent larger (see also Bachman, 1992; LaFree, 1995;

---

[1] The terms Natives, First Nations, Indigenous Peoples, and Indians are also used to refer to Aboriginal peoples; as well, distinctions are often made between Treaty/Non-Treaty, Status/Non-Status, Metis, Inuit, and specific tribal groups. In this work, we use the term Aboriginals to refer to individuals with Native North American ancestry.

Snyder-Joy, 1995).[2] According to U.S. Department of Justice figures, the rate
of imprisonment for American Indians in 1997 was 38 percent higher than
the national average; in that year, 47 percent of the American Indian correctional population was in jails or prisons, compared to 32 percent of the
national correctional population (Greenfeld and Smith, 1999).

In Canada, estimates indicate that in the early 1990s, approximately
4 percent of the population was Aboriginal (Statistics Canada, 1993).
Statistics Canada does not collect data on the race or ethnic origin of arrested or convicted persons; however, data from earlier years and provincial
and municipal records suggest that, in the late 1980s, the violent crime
rate for Aboriginals was approximately four times the national average,
and that 22 percent of all homicide suspects were Aboriginal (Roberts
and Doob, 1997: 488). In 1997-8, about 17 percent of the Canadian federal prison population was Aboriginal (Statistics Canada, 1999a). At the
provincial level, this overrepresentation was even more dramatic: in five of
the ten Canadian provinces, Aboriginals represented at least 15 percent
of the inmate population; in three provincial jails, they constituted more
than 45 percent of all incarcerations (Nielsen, 1992; Roberts and Doob,
1997; Statistics Canada, 1999a). In his summary of cross-national studies of
racial disparities in offending and incarceration, Tonry (1997: 12) concludes
that:

> [i]n Australia and Canada, arrest and imprisonment disparities affecting
> Aborigines and natives are even greater than black/white disparities in other
> English-speaking countries.

Adults commit more violent crimes than youth. In 1996, only about
19 percent of Americans charged with a violent crime were under the age of
18 (Maguire and Pastore, 1997) and in Canada approximately 20 percent
of violent crime arrests involved a youth (Statistics Canada, 1999b); yet, in
the United States, the percentage of youth charged with a violent offense
rose 60 percent from 1987 to 1996 (Maguire and Pastore, 1997) and in
Canada, the violent youth crime rate was 77 percent higher in 1998 than in
1989 (after taking into consideration the small declines since 1994; Statistics
Canada, 1999b).

Specific data on Aboriginal youth offending and incarcerations are less
readily available; however, in their summary of the existing literature,

---

[2] Silverman (1996) demonstrates that complications with some U.S. censuses (e.g., 1950 and
1960) and crime rate data probably inflated prior reports of disproportionate American Aboriginal involvement. More recent data indicate that for many crimes Aboriginal involvement
is considerably less than that of black Americans; however, it is higher than that of white
Americans. Tonry (1997) provides a more general discussion of these issues and points to
several problems that arise when trying to measure racial (or ethnic) disparities within and
between nations.

Armstrong et al. (1996) conclude that, compared to other youth (both blacks and whites) reservation youth have higher levels of criminal involvement. They (1996: 79) report that in the "most detailed description of national [U.S.] rates of delinquency among juvenile offenders on reservations, . . . the rate of arrest was greater, at 60.0 per 100,000 juveniles, than for either black (52.6) or white youth (33.9) in 1979." Armstrong and colleagues add that although the offenses committed by American Indian youth were disproportionately minor and substance-abuse related, involvement in serious crimes against persons has escalated in recent years. They note that by the middle of the 1980s, rates of serious crimes for American-Indian youth were three times higher than the general U.S. youth population. Similar trends in offending exist in Canada, and as Nielsen (1992: 4) notes, Aboriginal youth also experience disproportionate involvement with the criminal justice system: "Considering that about 80 percent of Native youth drop out of school before completion . . . a young Native boy has a much better chance of being arrested before he turns 18 than he does of graduating from high school."

Criminologists offer several explanations for higher levels of minority offending – violent and otherwise – and criminal justice contact; these include individual-level theories based on biopsychological factors, family socialization, subcultures of violence or poverty, and economic strain. As well, theorists point to macro-level explanations that focus on social disorganization (Sampson and Lauritsen, 1997). Those who study Aboriginal violence also introduce concerns associated with cultural conflict, alienation, and historical mistreatment (Bachman, 1992; Beauvais, 1996; Nielsen and Silverman, 1996). We discuss some of these ideas in greater detail in our subsequent discussion; however, our primary interest reflects a different tradition. Specifically, we explore ideas first emphasized by writers in the labeling tradition and more recently revived and revised by sanction and cumulative disadvantages theorists. We use these insights to explore relationships between race, police arrests, and involvement in violent crime.[3] Our analysis focuses on a specific group of Aboriginal youth: those who voluntarily leave or who are expelled from their homes and live on the street. We collected data from Aboriginal youth as part of a larger study of youth who live on the streets of two large Canadian cities: Toronto and Vancouver. Those who study violence often note that high school or institutional populations often provide limited variation on measures of violence or theoretically important independent variables (Short, 1997: 20–1); neither of

---

[3] As noted by Roberts and Doob (1997: 481), several Canadian government inquiries and commissions have documented the disproportionately high levels of Aboriginal offending and incarceration and the direct and indirect contributions of criminal justice discrimination; however, they note that there are only a few detailed, scholarly studies of these issues and that "little has been done to alleviate the problem" (518).

these conditions apply to street youth, so they provide an excellent opportunity to explore ideas about the causes of violence.

We begin our chapter with a brief overview of the classical labeling approach. We extend this discussion and introduce some of the recent and most notable theoretical developments drawing on this perspective; collectively these explanations focus renewed attention on the role of disadvantages and sanctions in encouraging subsequent offending. We then describe our previous use of these theoretical insights to understand the relationships between sanctioning and involvement in a variety of offenses. We argue that these theories are particularly valuable for explaining the experiences of Aboriginal street youth. After describing our data and measures, we present results from an analysis of police sanctions and violence among Aboriginal street youth. We conclude our work with a discussion of the broader implications of police sanctions for minority youth violence.

Origins and Elaborations of the Labeling Approach

As Becker (1973) notes, there is no labeling theory per se; instead, labeling represents a theoretical approach or sensibility to understanding crime. Thus, several writers – from varied traditions – have developed key ideas commonly associated with the labeling perspective. Rather than reviewing the individual works of each theorist, we simply summarize the most salient features of this approach (see Paternoster and Iovanni, 1989, for a more detailed review). Unlike most theories of crime, the labeling approach argues that the causes of offending vary dramatically over time. It maintains that initial offenses – acts of "primary deviance" – reflect a diverse and unsystematic array of causes. These early crimes encourage subsequent offending (i.e., "secondary deviance") when offenders have both been negatively labeled by others and have internalized or accepted these definitions.

Labeling operates at several levels: labelers may generalize the negative behavior to a master status, defining and treating labeled people exclusively on the basis of this identification; and labeled individuals may internalize their negative label, incorporate it into their self-identity, and use it to guide their subsequent actions. At the structural level, labeling individuals may limit their ability to associate with nonlabeled others, thus encouraging the development of and entrenchment in an identification with a deviant group. At the same time, labeled individuals may be shunned by nondeviant individuals, denied membership by nondeviant groups, and excluded from normative activities (e.g., employment).

Although family, friends, and a host of people (e.g., employers and teachers) can participate in the labeling process, justice officials are essential in affixing criminal labels. This process begins with police interactions and typically involves "status degradation ceremonies." Guided by stereotypical conceptions of offenders, police actions often deny individuals' nondeviant and unique personality characteristics and thus reinforce an exclusive criminal identity. As a result, criminal justice actions may encourage, rather than discourage, subsequent offending.

Until recently, the traditional labeling approach received little empirical support; in most studies labeling effects were nonexistent or in the direction opposite than predicted (Gove, 1980; Paternoster and Iovanni, 1989). However, in the past decade several criminologists have revisited labeling's central themes and found evidence consistent with some of its hypotheses (e.g., Hagan and Palloni, 1990). The most promising developments involve recent reformulations by several writers; frequently referred to as "sanction" theories, these works offer important insights into the labeling process.

In works closely paralleling each other, Braithwaite (1989) and Scheff and Retzinger (1991; see also Scheff, 1988) focus on the emotional repercussions of labeling. Braithwaite argues that in many non-Western cultures, criminal justice responses to offenders reflect a reintegrative philosophy of behavior-specific punishment, rituals of shaming, and reacceptance by and reconnections with one's community. This approach is common to a diverse set of cultures that includes modern Japan, Australian Aborigines, and many North American Native groups. In contrast, the "Western" justice systems of the United States and Canada typically involve a stigmatizing approach that punishes the person more than the behavior, carries a long-term and highly visible label, and alienates offenders from their communities. In non-Western societies, shame diminishes with culturally and structurally patterned reintegration into the community; in Western ones, there are few mechanisms for reintegration and shame is often unremitting and increases over time. Scheff and Retzinger (1991) argue that if unresolved, feelings associated with stigmatization and shaming may lead to explosions of rage and anger. These outbursts may be violent and indiscriminately directed at targets other than the source of the feelings.

Sherman (1993) extends these ideas in his theory of defiance. He notes that criminal sanctions – and the labels accompanying them – have varying effects and are influenced by social settings and by types of offenders and offenses. In some cases, sanctioning has little if any effect, in other situations it promotes deterrence and in others, defiance. According to Sherman, five factors encourage defiant responses to sanctioning: (1) the perception that the punishment is illegitimate and unfair; (2) the absence of strong bonds to the sanctioning agent and community; (3) the definition of the sanction as stigmatizing; (4) denial of the feelings of shame the sanctions cause; and (5) the development of pride in isolation from the sanctioning community. Referring to the first of these conditions, Sherman maintains that sanctions are typically seen as unjust when sanctioning agents are disrespectful to offenders or when offenders interpret sanctions as arbitrary, discriminatory, excessive, or undeserved. Thus, Sherman connects the emotional focus of Braithwaite's and Scheff and Retzinger's work with classical labeling theories' concerns about the actions of sanctioning agents.

Sampson and Laub (1995) offer a further extension of the above ideas in their "life-course theory of cumulative disadvantage." They note that many criminologists have recognized the advantages of a life-course, or developmental approach to crime (e.g., Farrington, 1986; Thornberry, 1987; Hagan and Palloni, 1988; Sampson and Laub, 1993), and some have suggested that labeling theory is consistent with this approach (e.g., Loeber and LeBlanc, 1990). In the present context, the value of a life-course approach lies in locating the interplay between backgrounds, sanctioning, and offending as part of "chains of adversity" (Rutter, 1989). Life-course analysis reminds us that life experiences are located in individual trajectories and that these trajectories may be redirected by events or "turning points" (Elder, 1994). Rutter extends the traditional notion that single events operate as turning points, arguing that in addition to their immediate effects, individual life experiences may form part of or initiate a chain reaction in which one negative event leads to others. Thus, the effect of these experiences may be exacerbated by the occurrence of additional negative events.

Sampson and Laub (1995) argue that chains of adversity represent cumulative continuities of disadvantage that are linked to four key institutions of social control: families, schools, peers, and state sanctions. They suggest that disadvantages arising in the first three institutions increase the likelihood of involvement in crime and of state sanctioning. Offending and labeling "knife off" further life chances by reducing possibilities for building human and social capital: the offender label often prohibits participation in occupations; it discourages others from starting or continuing in relationships with the labeled person; and its exclusionary consequences encourage associations with other labeled people. In general, Sampson and Laub's work ties the focus on labels and sanctions into sequences that include earlier family- and community-based life-course experiences. These experiences represent ecological contexts from which disadvantages originate, lead to formal sanctions, and cumulate across the life-course (Sampson and Lauritsen, 1997).

Together, the works reviewed above suggest an approach to sanctioning that attributes postsanction crime to the following: (1) an accumulation of negative experiences that weaken people's ties to their community and encourage involvement in acts of primary deviance; (2) sanctioning of these behaviors in ways that are disrespectful to offenders; (3) offenders' beliefs that the sanctions are stigmatizing, capricious, prejudicial, or unwarranted and thus unfair; (4) the absence of social process involving rituals of shaming, reacceptance and reconnections with community; (5) the offenders' failure to address their feelings of shame associated with the sanctions; and (6) offenders' further isolation from their communities because of the application of sanctions and the negative labels that accompany them. We suggest that these processes likely influence street youth's involvement in violent crimes, and are particularly relevant for minority youth such as Aboriginals.

Labeling, Street Youth, and Aboriginal Involvement in Crime

In an earlier paper (Hagan and McCarthy, 1997b), we draw on classical labeling theory to explore various ways in which state sanctioning practices are related to street crime. Using data from a sample of homeless youth, we investigate the possibility of an intergenerational sanction sequence. Following the lead of Hagan and Palloni (1990), we explore ways in which the actions of crime-control agents reproduce criminal behavior through their treatment of the children of criminal parents. Our analysis reveals that youth who were arrested after leaving home and whose parents had been arrested for a criminal offense were disproportionately involved in offending subsequent to their arrest. This pattern appears regardless of which parent was arrested and is evident among both males and females.

In a further analysis, we explore connections between parental use of force, arrest, and subsequent involvement in crime (Hagan and McCarthy, 1997a). Drawing on the extensions of labeling theory described above, we argue that youth who are abused by their parents may interpret their victimization as a type of negative stigmatization; this view may inspire feelings of shame, which if unresolved, may result in spirals of anger, rage, and behavioral outbursts. Negative interactions with police and other agents of the state may intensify these spirals, culminating in explosive, defiant criminal acts. Our data are consistent with these ideas and reveal that familial violence interacts with police sanctions and amplifies involvement in a variety of street crime. Thus, for abused youth, police sanctions more often result in criminal acts of defiance than in deterrence.

The present analysis builds on the above findings. We suggest that like other homeless youth, Aboriginal youth may endure several life experiences that can form "chains of adversity"; leaving home or being asked to leave extends these chains, as do street experiences common among the homeless. Negative interactions with police and police sanctions may add further links to these chains, intensifying Aboriginal youth's feelings of shame, humiliation, and rage, and encouraging violent outbursts.

Several studies suggest that Aboriginals are disproportionately exposed to an array of negative life experiences that resonate with the image of chains of adversity discussed above. In her review of the European settlement of North America and the internal colonialism that accompanied it, Bachman (1992) describes several dire consequences for Aboriginals: Aboriginal societies were disrupted and the ensuing geographical displacement intensified cultural conflicts, social disorganization, economic strain, and people's perceived powerlessness; these decreased the influence of existing norms and the social control of family and community. In their review of studies of Aboriginal delinquency, Armstrong et al. (1996) also emphasize the negative effects of macro, structural forces of unemployment, poverty, and economic dependence; structural conditions that place many Aboriginal families and communities in the "marginal underclass." This class position has several deleterious consequences including family breakdown, parental neglect, parental and youth substance abuse, troubled educational experiences, and familial abuse (Lujan et al., 1989). Bachman (1992) adds that many Aboriginal reservation communities support a subculture that tolerates both external and internal violence (e.g., physical abuse and suicide) and exacerbates problems arising from the social disorganization characteristic of reservation life.

The difficulties experienced by many Aboriginals are intensified when they leave reservations and rural communities. According to Nielsen (1996) and Roberts and Doob (1997), current estimates suggest that more than 50 percent of North American Aboriginals live "off-reserve," predominantly in large urban centers. Although city living can provide greater educational and employment opportunities, the opposite often occurs and for many transplanted Aboriginals, city life intensifies their economic strain (Dumont, 1993; La Prarie, 1994). Aboriginal youth who leave their families (or are expelled from them) face additional sources of strain. Studies reveal that inadequate food, shelter, and employment are common features of street life and that criminal opportunities abound (see Hagan and McCarthy, 1997a); alone or in concert, these structural conditions forge additional links in the chains of adversity some minority youth experience.

Aboriginal youth also face more unique problems, particularly those arising from their membership in two distinct and often incompatible cultures. In terms of police encounters, many Aboriginal cultures stress nonconfrontational approaches that encourage offenders to acquiesce to authorities, take responsibility for their actions and feel shame for inappropriate behaviors (Dumont, 1993; La Prairie, 1994); however, youth culture, particularly street youth culture, promotes an opposite, confrontational, and defiant style when interacting with authorities (Baron, 1989; Neugebauer-Visano, 1996). These contradictory forces may increase the stress Aboriginal youth experience on the street.

In addition, Aboriginal youth may be subject to prejudicial police action. Survey data suggests that youth often interpret police behavior as discriminatory and based on negative stereotypes. Neugebauer-Visano (1996) found that Toronto youth typically interpret their interactions with police as evidence of police harassment and bias. She notes that regardless of their racial background, youth agreed that minority males were the most frequent targets of police harassment. Using data from non-Aboriginal and Aboriginal high school students, Cockerham and Forslund (1975) found that compared to the former, the latter were significantly less likely to agree that they liked the police; indeed, less than 20 percent of Aboriginal youth agreed that, in general, the police treat teenagers with respect. Other studies suggest that these views are consistent with police practices. For example, Depew (1992) cites several Canadian studies that relate disproportionately high Aboriginal arrest rates to police oversurveillance of minority communities.

According to Tonry (1997), several factors stimulate police attention to minorities. One of the most salient causes is that greater minority arrest rates heighten police suspiciousness of minorities. As a result, police frequently stop and investigate minority nonoffenders who have patterns of speech, dress, and recreation similar to offenders. Tonry also notes that for a variety of reasons (e.g., self-esteem, self-assertion), some members of minority groups, particularly youth, act in ways that police define as strange, threatening, or disrespectful. He concludes that these factors, police stereotypes, and minority behaviors that evoke these stereotypes, contribute to well-documented police practices of stopping minority youth, and the latter's often defiant, hostile response. In his review of the literature on police-minority contact, Sherman (1993: 464) emphasizes the deleterious effect of arrest on subsequent offending:

> The fact is that young males, especially the poor and minorities, are much more exposed than lower crime groups to police disrespect and brutality, both vicariously and in person, *prior* to their peak years of arrest and initial involvements in crime.

Bachman (1992) proposes that a similar process occurs for Aboriginal adults, arguing that the hostility and defiance that result from negative contact with police and other justice officials frequently erupt in acts of interpersonal violence. In part, Bachman bases her argument on Williams's (1979) research on arrests and dispositions in Seattle. Williams concludes that neither minority status nor low socioeconomic status sufficiently explains Aboriginal and non-Aboriginal differences in arrest rates. Instead, Williams hypothesizes that

> [a] potentially valid explanation for the alarming arrest rate for Indians may be as basic as anti-Indian bias. Whether correctly or incorrectly, the contemporary Indian often feels that he is the recipient of prejudice and discrimination.... And it is this very climate which can so easily foster an insidious brand of resentment, humiliation, frustration, and anger which may manifest itself in high rates of social deviance. (1979; in Bachman, 1992: 82)

Griffiths and Verdun-Jones (1994: 641) reach a comparable conclusion in their summary of inquiries into Canadian Aboriginal-police relations:

> A consistent finding of many commissions of inquiry and research studies is that the relations between the police and Aboriginals are often characterized

by mutual hostility and distrust, increasing the likelihood of conflict and high arrest rates.

Thus, prejudicial police action may compound earlier adverse experiences and further entrench Aboriginals in criminal trajectories. As Sherman (1993: 464) notes, for many youth the temporal priority of police contact "suggests a powerful role of police disrespect in sanction effects." Our research indicates that street youth are disproportionately subject to negative police attention and that many of these youth respond with hostility and defiance (Hagan and McCarthy, 1997a); we argue that this pattern may be exacerbated for Aboriginals. Indeed, for Aboriginal youth who leave already problematic native communities and take to the streets, police encounters may create a new kind of ecological context in which violence becomes more common.

Studying Sanctioning Effects Among Aboriginal Youth

In this section, we offer an exploratory test of the effects of police sanctions on Aboriginal youth and their involvement in violent street crime. The data for this study were collected in a panel study of 482 youth living on the streets of Toronto (330) and Vancouver (152) during the summer of 1992. We define street youth as people between the ages of sixteen and twenty-four who do not have a permanent place to live. As we noted earlier, previous research suggests that these youth form a population that is at high risk of conflict with the law (e.g., Hagan and McCarthy, 1997a). More than half of the youth in our sample were picked up and charged by the police since leaving home, a level of criminal sanctioning far higher than in school samples (e.g., although they do not provide data on arrests, Hindelang, Hirschi, and Weiss [1981] report that approximately 18 percent of their sample had been held by the police).

A team of fourteen interviewers (including two Aboriginal interviewers) met the research participants in twenty-one social-service agencies for the homeless, as well as in several nonagency locations (e.g., parks, street corners, and shopping malls). Youth completed a structured interview and a self-report survey and were paid $20 for participating in the study. We recontacted these youth for a second and third interview; however, there was considerable attrition by the third wave. In this analysis, we avoid concerns related to differential attrition by using a cross-sectional approach and analyzing data for the entire sample. We recognize that this strategy cannot provide a rigorous test of the causal sequences described above; thus our work is preliminary and its findings suggestive. We also are aware that street youth represent a small part of the youth population; however, like other high-risk youth (e.g., those in gangs), street youth are one of the few populations that provide sufficient variation on both violence and its correlates. In earlier analyses, we demonstrate that sample-selection biases that influence the composition of street samples have little effect on the causal process associated with street crime (McCarthy and Hagan, 1992); thus, we are confident that our analysis has wider applicability.[4]

Definitions and Measures. We measure our dependent variable, violence, with a scale based on three self-report items: assault, assault with a weapon, and assault with intent to seriously injure (see Table 6.1). Our first of two primary independent variables of interest is the respondent's Aboriginal status. Scholars recognize difficulties associated with constructing an operational definition of Aboriginal status and accept that designations by self or by others will undoubtedly undercount individuals of Aboriginal ancestry (Bachman, 1992; Silverman, 1996). We use interviewer designations and acknowledge the restrictive nature of our categorization.

Our second key independent variable measures police contact on the street; this item refers exclusively to instances in which youth believe they were arrested for "*being on the street*," rather than for committing a specific criminal offense. Although neither vagrancy nor homelessness is an offense in Canada, street youth report that they are often arrested for activities unrelated to criminal activities; these include arrests for living on the street without parental consent (before the ages of sixteen in Toronto, nineteen in Vancouver), loitering, the consumption of alcohol in public places, suspicion, "disorderly conduct," and in response to complaints made by business owners and other citizens (nonstreet youth are also vulnerable to these and other types of "unfair" arrest, see Sherman, 1993).

We introduce several additional independent variables in our analysis. These variables serve two functions: they may highlight processes by which other factors intervene between Aboriginal status and offending, and they test the spuriousness of any association between police sanctions and involvement in violent crimes.

At a broad level, variables central to theories of crime and particularly violence can be divided on the basis of their *sociogenic, ontogenetic,* or *situational* origins (Sampson and Laub, 1995; also see Dannefer, 1984). Sociogenic phenomena include social structures, motivations or processes (e.g., class, strain, or learned behavior); ontogenetic factors highlight individuals' genetic, psychological, or personality features (e.g., criminal propensity); and situational variables refer to contextual features of environments and the people who live in them (e.g., routine-activities or character-contests).

---

[4] Most of our data come from structured interviews, although some material was gathered from interview observations and self-reports (see Hagan and McCarthy, 1997a, for a discussion of the reliability and validity of these data).

Table 6.1. *Concepts and Indicators*

Variable Name	Indicator
Aboriginal	Aboriginal = 1*
Age	In years
Gender	Male = 1*
Disrupted Family	Absence of 1 or more biological parent = 1*
Parental Neglect	Scale (α = .729) of 10 items measuring how often the respondent's mother and father did the following while the respondent lived at home: knew the respondent's whereabouts and who s/he was with when the respondent went out; talked or did things with the respondent; and how much the respondent wanted to be like them: 1 = Always, 2 = Usually, 3 = Sometimes, 4 = Rarely, 5 = Never
Parental Substance Abuse	Alcohol or drug abuse by either parent = 1*
Parental Unemployment	Unemployed parent (not a homemaker) = 1*
Family Criminality	A family member (includes siblings, step-relations) charged with a criminal offense = 1*
Parental Physical Abuse	Scale (α = .827) of 10 items measuring how often mothers and fathers were the first to do the following when they had differences with the respondent: threaten to hit; throw something; slap, kick, bit or hit with a fist; hit with an object; beat: 0 = Never, 1 = Rarely, 2 = Sometimes, 3 = Often, 4 = Always
Violent Toward Parents	Respondent first to use violence against a parent when s/he had differences (before the age of 8) = 1*
School Problems	Scale (α = .638) of 3 items measuring the respondent's average grade in the last year of school: 0 = 81 to 100, 1 = 71 to 80, 2 = 61 to 70, 3 = 51 to 60, 4 = 41 to 50, 5 = 0 to 40; and (1) how often s/he had trouble understanding material or (2) problems with teachers: 0 = Never, 1 = Rarely, 2 = Sometimes, 3 = Often, 4 = Always
Drug Use at Home	Scale (α = .630) of 3 items measuring how often the respondent used marijuana, hallucinogens, or cocaine products at home: 0 = Never, 1 = 1, 2 = 2, 3 = 3–4, 4 = 5–9, 5 = 10–19, 6 = 20–29, 7 = 30–59, 8 = 60+
Home Violence	Scale (α = .758) of 3 items measuring how often the respondent did the following before leaving home: beat someone so badly the victim needed medical attention; used a weapon in a fight; attacked someone with the intent to seriously injure: 0 = Never, 1 = 1, 2 = 2, 3 = 3–4, 4 = 5–9, 5 = 10–19, 6 = 20–29, 7 = 30–59, 8 = 60+

Table 6.1. *(cont.)*

Variable Name	Indicator
Arrested at Home	Scale (r = .300) of 2 items measuring how often the respondent was arrested for any reason: 0 = Never, 1 = 1, 2 = 2, 3 = 3–4, 4 = 5–9, 5 = 10–19, 6 = 20–29, 7 = 30–59, 8 = 60+
Street Adversity	Scale (α = .805) of 5 items measuring how often the respondent went without food, spent nights walking the streets, slept in bus stations, stayed all night in a restaurant, and slept in a park: 0 = Never, 1 = Rarely, 2 = Sometimes, 3 = Often, 4 = Always
Criminal Opportunities	How often the respondent had a chance to make money illegally when living on the street: 0 = Never, 1 = Rarely, 2 = A few times a month, 3 = A few times a week, 4 = A few times a day
Deviant Beliefs	Scale (α = .626) of 5 items measuring how strongly the respondent agreed or disagreed with the following statements: Unless in self-defense, it is always wrong to hit others; It is always wrong to take other's property; It is always better to be honest; It should be illegal to take drugs; It is wrong to break the law: 0 = Strongly Agree, 1 = Agree, 2 = Uncertain, 3 = Disagree, 4 = Strongly Disagree
Arrested for Being on the Street	How often, since leaving home, the respondent had been picked up by the police for *being on the street*: 0 = Never, 1 = 1, 2 = 2, 3 = 3–4, 4 = 5–9, 5 = 10–19, 6 = 20–29, 7 = 30–59, 8 = 60+
Street Violence	Scale (α = .764) of 3 items measuring how often the respondent did the following since leaving home: beat someone so badly the victim needed medical attention; used a weapon in a fight; attacked someone with the intent to seriously injure: 0 = Never, 1 = 1, 2 = 2, 3 = 3–4, 4 = 5–9, 5 = 10–19, 6 = 20–29, 7 = 30–59, 8 = 60+

* Dummy-coded variable.

Other works in this volume offer summaries of the theoretical orientations that emphasize these various phenomena so we do not review them here; instead, we accept that all three types of variables may play important roles in the initiation and continuation of violent offending and we introduce measures of each type in our analysis.

We introduce indicators of age and gender, given their influence on offending in most research. To these variables, we add several measures of family characteristics and dynamics that reflect concerns emphasized in a variety of sociogenic theories. We include several variables central to theories of social control and strain: parental neglect, parental substance abuse (alcohol and drug), marital breakdown, parental unemployment, physical abuse, and problems in school. Depending on one's theoretical orientation, these factors are either the source of weak social bonds that free people from social constraints and thus encourage crime (Gottfredson and Hirschi, 1989) or they represent sources of strain that motivate offending (Agnew, 1992). We also control for processes emphasized in differential association theory with measures of deviant beliefs and family members' involvement in crime.[5] Many of these variables are of further interest because, as noted above, they reflect several of the conditions assumed to be common among troubled Aboriginal families (e.g., neglect, substance abuse, and violence).

Our analysis also includes a measure of ontogenetic concerns about biological predispositions and proclivities established early in the life-course, particularly those manifested in the use of violence against parents. In a previous analysis (Hagan and McCarthy, 1997a), we found that youth who were the first to use force in their interactions with their parents, and did so before reaching the age of eight, were more likely to commit violent street crime. We use the same measure here. We control for any remaining sources of criminal propensity with measures of drug use and involvement in violent crime while living at home. We include a scale measure of police arrest at home (for any reason) in order to separate the effects of home and street sanctioning.

We use two variables to control for the influences of situational variables connected to street life: street adversity (i.e., hunger and lack of shelter) and criminal opportunities. These variables capture experiences that change relatively frequently over short periods of time and whose effects may be short-lived. All told, we include eighteen independent variables in our analysis; although a sizable number, collinearity diagnostics suggest minimal distortion due to multicollinearity (Fox, 1991): the square-roots of the variance inflation factors scores are less than 1.3 and only two tolerance scores are above .65 (the exceptions – violent crime at home and home arrests – have scores of .75).

Results

Approximately 15 percent ($N = 70$) of our sample are Aboriginal youth, a percentage considerably higher than the proportion of Aboriginals in the overall youth population of Canada. According to Census data, there were

---

[5] We recognize that some of these variables – family criminality, for instance – may be measuring ontogenetic as well as sociogenic influences and that these are not easily separated.

Table 6.2. *Descriptive Statistics for Aboriginal and Non-Aboriginal Street Youth*

	Aboriginal (n = 70)		Non-Aboriginal (n = 412)	
	X	SD	X	SD
Age	19.690	2.850	19.820	2.450
Gender	.610	.490	.690	.460
Disrupted Family	.914	.282	.672*	.470
Parental Neglect	33.071	7.175	33.434	7.417
Parental Substance Abuse	.671	.473	.444	.497
Parental Unemployment	.500	.504	.439	.498
Family Criminality	.700	.460	.500*	.500
Parental Physical Abuse	9.129	8.110	10.165	8.491
Violent Toward Parents	.114	.321	.155	.363
School Problems	6.671	3.678	6.041	3.144
Drug Use at Home	5.629	5.935	6.485	6.074
Home Violence	1.643	3.575	1.718	3.542
Arrested at Home	1.914	3.082	1.379	2.477
Street Adversity	7.357	3.818	7.461	4.606
Criminal Opportunities	3.000	1.360	2.760	1.500
Deviant Beliefs	7.729	1.202	6.733	3.612
Arrested for Being on the Street	1.930	.231	1.380*	.219
Street Violence	4.857	5.251	3.539*	4.880

$*p < .05$

approximately 2.9 million youth aged fifteen to twenty-four in Canada in 1991; of these, ninety-seven thousand, or approximately 3 percent, were Aboriginal (Statistics Canada, 1992; 1993).

In Table 6.2, we compare Aboriginal street youth with their non-Aboriginal counterparts. Our comparisons reveal that both groups of youth are disproportionately male and have an average age of approximately 19.7 years. In contrast to suggestions that Aboriginal youth and their families are unique in the type and extent of their social disadvantages, we found that both groups of youth typically left families that had some experience with parental unemployment and that scored high on scales of neglect, substance abuse, and physical violence. Aboriginal and non-Aboriginal street youth also encountered similarly high levels of school problems, expressed comparable ambivalence toward social norms regarding law, crime, and honesty, and reported similar involvement with drugs. Compared to non-Aboriginal youth, Aboriginals report lower mean levels of involvement in violent crime at home – both against parents and others – and higher levels of police contact; however, none of these differences are significant.

Once on the street, both groups of youth describe high levels of street adversity and exposure to criminal opportunities.

Nonetheless, there are important differences between the two groups. For example, Aboriginal youth disproportionately left families characterized by marital breakdown and family criminality. Furthermore, in contrast to both non-Aboriginal street youth and their own involvement in home violence, Aboriginals report significantly higher levels of violent street crime. In terms of prevalence, 57 percent of non-Aboriginal street youth had committed one assault on the street and 43 percent had committed three or more; in comparison, 70 percent of Aboriginals had used violence, and 59 percent had used it more than twice. Incidence figures suggest a comparable pattern: Aboriginal and non-Aboriginal street youth report similar levels of violent offending at home (mean scores of 1.64 and 1.72 respectively), but the former report significantly more involvement in street violence than do the latter (4.86 versus 3.54). Aboriginal youth also report significantly greater police contact: 38 percent of non-Aboriginal youth had been picked up on the street by the police, compared to 53 percent of Aboriginal youth; moreover, 25 percent of the former had been arrested three or more times compared to 36 percent of the latter. Incidence data indicate that the mean average of street arrests for Aboriginals (4.857) is also significantly greater than that for non-Aboriginals (3.539). These differences are consistent with our thesis that police contacts are a source of change in the context and consequences of life on the street for Aboriginal youth.

Table 6.3 summarizes the correlations between our independent variables and two measures of involvement in violent crime. As anticipated by the findings in Table 6.2, correlations for violent crime at home reveal that offending is negatively related to variables central to a variety of perspectives. Consistent with ontogenetic explanations, violence is negatively related to age and positively associated with the respondent's drug use and childhood use of violence against parents. As predicted by sociogenic theories, it is associated with family criminality, parental unemployment, parental physical abuse, school problems, and deviant beliefs. As well, there is a sizable correlation between home offending and arrest. Note, however, that home violence is unrelated to Aboriginal status. The remaining coefficients indicate that involvement in violent crimes at home has several effects on street life: it increases adversity, criminal opportunities, arrest, and further violent offending.

The results in Table 6.3 also reveal that, in contrast to violent offending at home, Aboriginal status is positively and significantly related to street violence. In addition, the following ontogenetic and sociogenic variables have significant, positive effects on street violence: parental neglect and physical abuse; childhood violence against parents; school problems; and drug use. Consistent with the labeling approach, arrest at home also correlates

Table 6.3. *Correlates of Involvement in Home and Street Violence (N = 482)*

	Home Violence	Street Violence
Aboriginal	−.005	.094*
Age	−.144*	−.046
Gender	.040	.081
Disrupted Family	−.002	.057
Parental Neglect	.062	.143*
Parental Substance Abuse	−.021	.028
Parental Unemployment	.125*	.026
Family Criminality	.092*	.078
Parental Physical Abuse	.160*	.157*
Violent Toward Parents	.163*	.136*
School Problems	.118*	.210*
Drug Use at Home	.342*	.260*
Arrested at Home	.517*	.300*
Street Adversity	.118*	.274*
Criminal Opportunities	.146*	.293*
Deviant Beliefs	.104*	.254*
Street Violence	.529*	–
Arrested for Being on the Street	.209*	.326*

*$p < .05$

with street violence. The final coefficients indicate that violent crime is associated with several of our street or situational measures: adversity, criminal opportunities, and arrest.

The relationships suggested by our mean and correlational data are also evident in the OLS results we present in Table 6.4. This table contains estimates for three equations of street violence: the first introduces background sociogenic and ontogenetic variables, the second adds situational indicators of street experiences, and the third includes our measure of police contact on the street.[6] As expected, the first equation indicates that Aboriginal status has a positive and significant effect on street violence even when controlling for background correlates. This equation indicates that, at the multivariate level, involvement in violent street crime is also positively and significantly associated with school problems and involvement in violent offending while living at home. Alone and in concert, these factors represent important initial links in the chains of adversity associated with involvement in street violence.

[6] We enter deviant beliefs in our third equation, because we assume that although beliefs are informed by earlier experiences, they are also influenced by street life and reflect the respondents' views at the time of the survey.

Table 6.4. *OLS Regression of Involvement in Street Violence (N = 482)*

	Street Violence		Street Violence		Street Violence	
	b	se	b	se	b	se
Aboriginal	1.365*	.551	1.095*	.534	.969	.529
Age	.055	.081	.052	.079	.081	.079
Gender	.817	.437	.461	.424	.379	.419
Disrupted Family	.497	.424	.472	.408	.455	.403
Parental Neglect	.049	.027	.019	.026	.027	.026
Parental Substance Abuse	−.100	.426	.329	.656	.244	.649
Parental Unemployment	−.617	.391	−.677	.372	−.670	.368
Family Criminality	−.119	.398	−.112	.377	−.107	.372
Parental Physical Abuse	.024	.025	.013	.024	.009	.023
Violent Toward Parents	.677	.555	.466	.529	.361	.524
School Problems	.198*	.060	.102	.060	.087	.059
Drug Use	.064	.035	.014	.044	.016	.034
Home Violence	.676*	.065	.670*	.063	.660*	.062
Arrested at Home	−.022	.090	−.037	.086	−.080	.086
Street Adversity			.141*	.045	.103*	.045
Criminal Opportunities			.446*	.131	.392*	.130
Deviant Beliefs			.160*	.053	.154*	.053
Arrested for Being on the Street					.319*	.089
Constant	−2.893		−4.075		−4.543	
Adjusted R^2	.318		.371		.386	

*$p < .05$

The results for our second equation reveal that the effect of Aboriginal status is mediated by two situational measures of street life, each of which has a large and significant effect on violence: that is, violence increases with street adversity and exposure to criminal opportunities. These effects suggest that street experiences make substantial contributions to the cumulative disadvantages that characterize the lives of street youth. As well, deviant beliefs further augment involvement in violent crime. Notwithstanding the influence of these variables, the effect of Aboriginal status remains significant.

In the third equation we add our measure of street arrest. Unlike police contact at home, this variable has a sizable and significant relationship with violent street crime, net of the other variables in the equation (including prior offending); moreover, it diminishes the effect of Aboriginal status, reducing it to nonsignificance. Police sanctions' intervening role between Aboriginal status and involvement in street violence indicates that

Aboriginal youth are more likely to be arrested for being on the street and suggests that these encounters contribute to their involvement in crime.[7] In additional analyses we explored first-order interactions involving Aboriginal status and several variables: parental criminality, physical abuse, and sanctioning; however, none of these effects are significant.

Discussion

In his essay on sanctioning, Sherman (1993: 445) recasts the classical question, "Does punishment control crime?" and asks a more provocative one: "Under what conditions does each type of criminal sanction reduce, increase, or have no effect on future crimes?" Our preliminary research affirms the significance of the latter question. Our analysis indicates that, on average, Aboriginal youth are arrested more frequently than their non-Aboriginal counterparts before they leave home, but that this difference is neither substantial nor significant; moreover, when prior offending is controlled for, this sanctioning appears to have minimal consequences for subsequent involvement in violence. However, Aboriginal youth report considerably higher levels of negative police contact on the street – as measured by arrests for noncriminal activities – and these street arrests mediate the effect of Aboriginal status on street violence. The intervening effect of street arrests suggests that Aboriginal street youth are disproportionately exposed to negative police interactions and that this later increases their involvement in violent crime. The varying effects of police sanctions also resonate with studies of other aspects of the criminal justice system. Research suggests that Aboriginal status sometimes tempers criminal justice outcomes, whereas in other situations it intensifies their severity (e.g., see Hagan, 1974; 1975; Bynum and Paternoster, 1984; Snyder-Joy, 1995).

The different effects of arrests are consistent with Sherman's hypothesis about the importance of the setting and context in which sanctioning occurs. It is conceivable that the effect of police sanctioning may operate differently for Aboriginal youth when they live at home – often on reservations and in small communities – as compared to the street. The former settings are far from problem-free; nonetheless, levels of social control and support may be higher and levels of strain lower than on the street. The variation in sanctioning effects also suggests that the consequences of a sanction may depend on its location within an individual's life-course trajectory. Sanctioning may introduce a turning point directing youth away from subsequent

---

[7] A comparable analysis that uses street arrests as the dependent variable reveals that the bivariate effect of Aboriginal status is *not* reduced to nonsignificance in models *limited to background variables*; moreover, adding a measure of street violence introduces only minor changes to the size of the Aboriginal effect. These results suggest that greater contact with police is not simply a result of greater involvement in violent street crime.

crime; however, it can also add additional links to rather lengthy chains of adversity. In our research, street arrests appear to have the latter effect.

Our research suggests that the families of Aboriginal street youth resemble those of other street youth in their high levels of many problems (e.g., economic strain, family breakdown, substance abuse). Negative interactions with police may compound these difficulties, encouraging subsequent offending and further entrenching street youth in dysfunctional lifestyles. These possibilities have broader implications for Aboriginal youth. Aboriginal populations are disproportionately young. According to 1991 Census data, approximately 36 percent of Canadian Aboriginals were under the age of fifteen compared to about 21 percent of the total population (Statistics Canada, 1992; 1993). U.S. data point to a similar but less extreme trend: as of the 1990 census, 30 percent of American Indians were younger than fifteen compared to 20 percent of whites (U.S. Bureau of the Census, 1992). Negative police contact, particularly involving young Aboriginals, may increase the probability that, in the near future, North America may witness increasing numbers of angry, young Native youth whose response to sanctioning may include explosive outbursts of criminal violence.

As noted earlier, our cross-sectional analysis is a preliminary step in exploring the differing effects of sanctioning. Thus, our work neglects several key elements of the processes specified by the sanctioning theories we discussed. For example, we do not have any direct measures of the feelings of shame and rage central to Braithwaite's and Scheff and Retzinger's approaches and that we assume accompany police sanctions. Furthermore, our analysis focuses exclusively on main and first-order interaction effects and ignores the possibility of higher-order interactions involving Aboriginal status, sanctioning, and home and street experiences; thus, we neglect one of Sherman's key points.

We also fail to explore any indirect effects of sanctions, associations that figure prominently in Sherman and Scheff's work. As well, our investigation considers a relatively brief period of time in our respondents' lives and does not address Sampson and Laub's concern with the lifelong consequences of events and experiences. Subsequent analyses must explore these issues if we are to improve our understanding of the role of sanctions in offending.

Notwithstanding these limitations, our study does address and elaborate on several crucial aspects of racial disparities in crime and justice. In a recent review of this literature, Sampson and Lauritscn (1997: 363–4) urge that we give greater attention to ecological contexts, cumulative disadvantages, and understudied groups. We suggest that the ecology of the street represents a high risk context that intensifies the disadvantages experienced by particular youth, including those from various ethnic, cultural, and racial groups. We see our work as a step in developing a street criminology that is more broadly sensitive to the causal processes that affect these youth.

A criminology of the street builds on the contributions of studies of school youth who live in more protected environments; yet, it directs attention to structures and processes that are of less importance in the more conventional lives of school youth. Background variables – those that typically concern school criminologists – clearly have important consequences for criminal involvement; however, these are dwarfed by the problems that youth encounter on the street, whether they are homeless or have homes but spend most of their time on the street. Moreover, characteristics of the street condition the effects of many background variables. For example, although many nonminority youth are exposed to family problems, economic strain, community disorganization, and exposure to street life, a disproportionate number of minority youth experience these disadvantages. Studies have demonstrated that a large number of these youth respond to their cumulative disadvantages by increasing their involvement in street life (e.g., Sullivan, 1989; Anderson, 1990; Freeman, 1996); some hang out on the street, some live there, and others join gangs. Regardless of the paths they choose, these youth increase the likelihood that they will be without adequate economic resources, have limited access to employment or schooling, and have greater exposure to crime, police contact, and sanctions.

Race or minority status can exacerbate the effects of these disadvantages, when, for example, minority youth are discriminated against by people on the street, employers, service providers, and, as our research suggests, police and other criminal justice agents. In an earlier study, Hagan et al. (1978) find that police proactively target areas that they view as "offensible space," that is, parts of the city where they believe offenders congregate. When asked why police presence was greater in these areas, police department members referred to problems arising from low-cost housing, unemployment, and the greater number of "blacks," "immigrants," and other minorities (1978: 396). Our research demonstrates that these police encounters do not discourage offending; instead, arrests add to cumulative disadvantages, contributing to a street ecology that further elevates the risk of intensified criminal involvement (Raudenbush and Sampson, 1999). As a result, street life, crime, police contact, and criminal justice sanctions become increasingly intertwined, feeding into each other and making it difficult for minority youth to break this cycle. For many minority youth, arrests add further links in the chains of adversity they have experienced, increasing their use of violence and further entrenching them in a criminal justice system that cannot address the cumulative disadvantages that characterize their lives.

Ethnicity and Interpersonal Violence in a New Zealand Birth Cohort

D. M. Fergusson[1]

Historical Prologue

Present-day New Zealand society was formed as a result of an agreement (The Treaty of Waitangi) signed in 1840 between the British Crown and representatives of the indigenous Maori people. In essence with this agreement, Maori agreed to accept the sovereignty of the Crown in return for full rights of British citizenship, while the Crown undertook to preserve the traditional rights and ownership of the Maori people. Following the signing of the Treaty of Waitangi, the indigenous Maori people were exposed to a progressive process of colonization, which led to an increasing alienation of Maori from their traditional lands, waters, and resources, an increasing urbanization of Maori, and a general decline of Maori culture and language in New Zealand.

Introduction

It has been well documented that individuals of Maori descent and/or cultural identification are at higher risk of a range of disadvantageous outcomes including poorer educational achievement, higher rates of poverty and housing difficulties, higher risks of health problems, greater involvement in criminal offending, and higher rates of psychiatric disorder. These persistent and consistent linkages between ethnicity and individual or social well-being have led to a search for explanations of the origins of social

[1] This research was funded by grants from the Health Research Council of New Zealand, the National Child Health Research Foundation, the Canterbury Medical Research Foundation, and the New Zealand Lottery Grants Board. I would also like to acknowledge Dr. John Broughton and Christine Rimene of the Ngai Tahu Research Unit for their assistance in the preparation of this paper.

disadvantage among Maori. One aspect of this concern has focused on the issue of interpersonal violence among Maori. These issues were highlighted both locally and internationally by the graphic scenes of family and interpersonal violence portrayed in the New Zealand film *Once We Were Warriors*, which portrayed the lifestyle of a contemporary dysfunctional Maori family. At a more abstract level, official statistics recording rates of interpersonal violence clearly suggest that Maori are at greater risk of involvement in violent behaviors, including physical child abuse (Fergusson, Fleming, and O'Neill, 1972; Kotch, Chalmers, Fanslow, Marshall, and Langley, 1993) and violent offending (Lovell and Norris, 1990). These comparisons suggest that officially reported rates of violent behaviors among Maori are between two to four times higher than the corresponding rates among Europeans (Pakeha).

At the same time, both fictional portrayals and official statistics may provide a misleading perspective on the linkages between interpersonal violence and ethnicity. Clearly, in fictional portrayals the demands of plot may highlight issues in an attempt to produce an interesting story. Similarly, official statistics may be biased as a result of the social and legal processes by which individuals come to official attention (Duncan, 1970; Hampton, 1974; Jackson, 1988a, 1988b; Newbold, 1992; Pratt, 1990; Sutherland, Hippolite, Smith, and Galbreath, 1973). There is, therefore, clearly a need to examine the extent to which rates of interpersonal violence among Maori differ from rates among Europeans (Pakeha) in a way that avoids the potential biases of fictional portrayal or official statistics.

In addition, the observation that a particular ethnic group has a higher or lower rate of interpersonal violence by itself does not provide an explanation of why rates of violent behaviors differ across cultures. While there have been few analyses of the origins of ethnic differences in interpersonal violence in New Zealand, there has been continued analysis and debates about the more general tendency for ethnicity to be related to rates of crime in New Zealand. Broadly speaking, there have been three perspectives on the linkages between ethnicity and antisocial or criminal behaviors.

The Labeling/Conflict Perspective. One explanation of the differentials in rates of offending is that these differences are due to biases in the ways in which offending behaviors are measured. In most studies, comparisons of offending rates by Maori and non-Maori have been based on rates of officially recorded offending. However, official offending statistics measure not only the rate at which offenses occur but also the legal and other processes that lead children and young persons to be classified as offenders. It has been suggested by a number of authors that the apparently higher rates of offending among Maori are due to a bias in the way in which offending is measured (Duncan, 1970; Jackson, 1988a, 1988b; Hampton, 1974; Newbold, 1992; Pratt, 1990; Sutherland, Hippolite, Smith, and Galbreath, 1973). In particular, it has been suggested that Maori offenders are more likely to be detected and classified as offenders by New Zealand's justice system (Duncan, 1970; Sutherland et al., 1973; Jackson, 1988a, 1988b).

While there have been attempts to explain differences in offending from a labeling theory perspective, the evidence on the extent to which Maori and non-Maori differences in offending rates can be attributed to biases in the ways in which offending has been measured is very limited and, furthermore, it has been pointed out that any bias in official statistics is unlikely to be large enough to explain the large differentials in rates of offending between Maori and non-Maori (Fifield and Donnell, 1980). Thus, while it is possible that the use of official offending statistics inflates the differences in rates of Maori and non-Maori offending, it is unlikely that all of these differences can be explained as an artifact of the way in which offending has been measured and classified.

The Socioeconomic Disadvantage Perspective. An alternative explanation is that differences in rates of offending reflect socioeconomic differences between the Maori and non-Maori populations. This explanation is based on two sets of observations. First, it has been well established that on a range of indicators including educational achievement (Benton, 1988; New Zealand Council for Educational Research, 1988), unemployment (Hill and Brosnan, 1984), income (Brosnan, 1982), socioeconomic status (Davies, 1982), housing (Bathgate, 1988), and health (Pomare and de Boer, 1988), Maori children tend to be reared in home environments subject to relative social and economic disadvantage. It also has been well established that such disadvantages are associated with an increased vulnerability to young offending (Thornberry and Farnworth, 1982; Van Dussen, Mednick, Gabrielli, and Hutchings, 1983; Wadsworth, 1979; West and Farrington, 1973). Therefore, it may be argued that the higher rate of offending among Maori is a reflection of the differences in the socioeconomic and related distributions of Maori and non-Maori in New Zealand. The socioeconomic hypothesis predicts that when due allowance is made for socioeconomic factors, Maori children are at no greater risk of offending than non-Maori.

This explanation was studied by Fergusson, Donnell, and Slater (1975), who examined the extent to which apparent differences in Maori and non-Maori rates of offending could be explained by the effects of socioeconomic factors. Their analysis suggested that adjustment for socioeconomic status was sufficient to explain some component of the apparent correlation between ethnicity and offending, but even after adjustment there were still tendencies for Maori to offend at higher rates than non-Maori. Before adjustment, Maori children offended at 3.1 times the rate of non-Maori, whereas after adjustment this difference reduced to 2.4 times.

There are, however, a number of limitations in the analysis reported by Fergusson et al. (1975). First, offending was measured on the basis of official offending statistics and, as noted previously, it is possible that these statistics lead to an inflated estimate of the difference in rates of offending by Maori and non-Maori. Second, control for social factors was limited to the use of a single measure of socioeconomic status based on parental occupation. It is possible that this measure was not sufficiently sensitive to measure all of the variation in the social and economic differences between the Maori and non-Maori populations. As a result of both of the above factors, the adjusted rates reported by Fergusson et al. (1975) are likely to produce an overestimate of the true differences in rates of offending between Maori and non-Maori after adjustment for socioeconomic factors.

More recently, Fergusson and his associates have examined the relationships between both self-reported and officially recorded offending in a birth cohort of New Zealand children studied into adolescence (Fergusson, Horwood, and Lynskey, 1993a; 1993b). These studies have produced two general conclusions about the origins of linkages between ethnicity and crime in New Zealand. First, the associations between self-reported crime and ethnicity were adequately explained by a range of social and familial disadvantages that were more prevalent in Maori families (Fergusson et al., 1993a). However, linkages between ethnicity and officially recorded offending could not be explained entirely in these terms and Maori children were found to be at increased risks of arrest even when due allowance was made for offense severity and social factors (Fergusson et al., 1993b). These results clearly suggest that officially recorded statistics may be influenced by labeling biases in which Maori children are more likely to come to official attention than non-Maori children with a similar offending history and social background.

The Maori Perspective (He Whaipaanga Hou). In recent years, an alternative perspective on Maori offending and other Maori disadvantages has been emerging. This perspective emphasizes the role of cultural factors rather than social or economic factors as determinants of rates of offending among Maori and has been most clearly articulated by Jackson (1988a; 1988b). Jackson (1988) proposed both a theory of Maori crime and a methodology for testing this theory. The kernel of this theory is that the higher rates of offending among Maori are due to factors that are unique to Maori and place Maori at greater risk of both offending and being classified as offenders. These factors can be divided into system-based factors, such as the police, courts, and Justice Department; and offender-based factors. Jackson (1988a; 1988b) identifies a series of offender-related factors that he suggests are unique to Maori. These include cultural factors, family factors, community factors, and individual factors relating to the disadvantaged status of the Maori community that conspire to place young Maori at greater risk of involvement in criminal behavior. He argues that these factors are unique to Maori and place young Maori at greater risk.

To test and develop this theory, Jackson (1988a; 1988b) proposed a research methodology based on a Maori perspective. In this methodology, explanation of the sources of offending among Maori is based on the experiences of Maori people rather than on the comparative analysis of statistical data. To implement this methodology, Jackson (1988a; 1988b) attended hui (meetings) with over six thousand Maori participants throughout New Zealand and, on the basis of these hui, a consensual account of the perceived sources of Maori offending was constructed. Jackson (1988a; 1988b) emphasizes that this methodology is consistent with traditional Maori culture and values, which emphasize the role of consensual decision making and problem solving.

Against this general background, this chapter reports on a study of the relationships between ethnicity and interpersonal violence in a cohort of New Zealand–born children that has been studied from birth to young adulthood. In general terms, the aims of this analysis are to address the following issues.

First, the analysis aims to document ethnic differences in rates of both self-reported and officially recorded involvement in interpersonal violence at the age of eighteen. The central question addressed in this analysis is: To what extent are young Maori at greater risk of being both victims of and perpetrators of violent offenses?

Second, the analysis aims to provide a profile of social and family differences between Maori and non-Maori during childhood and adolescence to examine the extent to which there were ethnic differences in a series of social, economic, and family factors that may have contributed to later patterns of interpersonal violence in young adulthood.

Finally, the analysis examines the extent to which ethnic differences in interpersonal violence can be explained by ethnic differences in social, economic, and family factors. More generally, the analysis seeks to answer the question: To what extent are Maori at higher risk of involvement in interpersonal violence and to what extent can ethnic differences in involvement in violent behaviors be explained by ethnic differences in social, economic, and family conditions?

Method

The analysis reported here is based on data gathered over the course of the Christchurch Health and Development Study (CHDS). The CHDS is a longitudinal study of a birth cohort of 1,265 children born in all maternity units in the Christchurch (New Zealand) urban region during a four-month period during mid-1977. The cohort has now been studied at birth, four months, one year, and annual intervals to the age of sixteen and again at age eighteen, using a combination of methods including interviews with parents, testing and interviewing of children and young people, teacher questionnaires, and data from official records. In general terms, the aims of the study have been to build up a running record of the life history, social circumstances, health, and well-being of a relatively large cohort of New Zealand children growing up over the period from 1977 to the present time. The analysis reported here examines the following measures gathered over the course of the study.

Measures of Involvement in Interpersonal Violence at the Age of 18 Years. Data on involvement in interpersonal violence at around the age of eighteen was gathered from two sources:
Self-report. At age eighteen, cohort members were interviewed by trained and experienced survey interviewers using an extensive personal and mental health questionnaire that took approximately 1.5 hours to administer. Part of this questionnaire included questioning on the individual's involvement in interpersonal violence. In the present analysis, three self-report measures of involvement in interpersonal violence are reported.

i. Whether the individual reported committing at least one violent offense during the period from seventeen to eighteen years. This questioning was based on items from the Self-Report Delinquency Inventory (Elliott and Huizinga, 1989).
ii. Whether the individual reported committing recurrent (three or more) violent offenses over the period from the age of seventeen to eighteen.
iii. Whether the individual reported being the victim of a violent assault over the period from sixteen to eighteen years.

Police record data. On the basis of signed consent provided by the cohort members and their parents, it was possible for the research group to obtain official record data from the records held by the Youth Aid section of the New Zealand Police. These records showed that just over 3 percent of the cohort had come to police attention for violent offenses by the age of eighteen years.

The Measurement of Ethnic Identification. There are three different ways by which individuals may be classified as being of Maori descent. First, individuals may be classified as Maori on the basis of descent with individuals having some Maori ancestry being classed as Maori. Second, ethnicity may be defined on the basis of self-identification with those individuals reporting identification with Maori culture being classified as Maori. Finally, in recent years Maori have frequently stressed the view that ethnic identification should be defined on the basis of whakapapa (lineage). In contrast to definitions based on descent that requires that the individual have at least one Maori ancestor, definition on the basis of whakapapa requires that the individual can trace his lineage back to specific Maori ancestors and can identify the tribal affiliation of these ancestors.

In this study, two bases for defining ethnicity were available:

i. Descent. Of the cohort of 1,265 children entering the Christchurch Health and Development Study, 11.2 percent were of some Maori descent. In 80 percent of cases, children of Maori descent came from bi-ethnic families in which one parent was of Pakeha (European) ethnicity and the other of Maori ethnicity.

ii. Parental definition. At age fourteen years, parents were asked to describe the young person's ethnic status.

In practice, analyses using definitions of ethnicity based on descent or parental definition of ethnicity yielded very similar conclusions. In the present analysis, the definition used is based on parental report of the young person's ethnic identification. Of the 1,025 young people studied at the age of eighteen years, 96 (9.4 percent) were classified as Maori using this definition.

Social and Family Background. Over the course of the CHDS, extensive information has been collected on the social, childhood, family, and parental characteristics of the cohort. A number of these measures are included in the analysis to characterize the differences between Maori and non-Maori in terms of these factors. The measures considered included:

i. *Measures of socioeconomic background:* These included measures of socio-economic status based on the Elley/Irving Scale of Socio-Economic Status for New Zealand (Elley and Irving, 1976); measures of parental educational achievement and measures of self-reported family income.

ii. *Measures of childhood family circumstances:* These included measures of exposure to parental separation and/or divorce (Fergusson, Horwood, and Lynskey, 1994a); measures of exposure to family conflict (Fergusson, Horwood, and Lynskey, 1992); measures of the extent of parental use of physical punishment (Fergusson and Lynskey, 1997); and measures of parental bonding based on the parental bonding instrument (PBI) developed by Parker and his associates (Parker, Tupling, and Brown, 1979). In addition, the analysis included a global index of family problem behaviors based on the measures described by Fergusson, Horwood, and Lynskey (1994b). This index provides a simple account of the number of family disadvantages and difficulties that each cohort member was exposed to over the period from birth to the age of fifteen years.

iii. *Measures of parental characteristics:* Measures of sociodemographic background and family circumstances were supplemented by a number of measures of self-reported parental difficulties including: (a) problems with alcohol; (b) usage of illicit drugs; and (c) involvement in criminal offending.

Sample Sizes and Sample Attrition. The analysis reported below is based on a sample of 1,025 young people for whom data on involvement in interpersonal violence at the age of eighteen years was available. This sample represented 81 percent of the original cohort and 92.3 percent of all cohort members who were alive and residing in New Zealand at the age of eighteen. The sources of sample loss arose from out-migration from New Zealand (56.3 percent of sample loss), refusal to participate in the research by age eighteen (35.4 percent of sample loss), and death (8.3 percent of sample loss). Comparisons of the 1,025 participants in the research with the 240 of nonparticipants suggested that these groups were similar with respect to a number of sociodemographic variables including maternal age, family size, child ethnicity, and gender. There were, however, small but detectable tendencies ($p < .01$) for the sample to underrepresent children from families of lower socioeconomic status, children whose parents lacked formal educational qualifications, and children who entered single-parent families at birth. However, these biases were small and previous analyses in which corrections have been made for selective sample losses have suggested that the effects of nonrandom losses on the validity of the analysis are negligible (Fergusson, Fergusson, Horwood, and Kinzett, 1988; Fergusson and Lloyd, 1991).

While there is good reason to believe that internal validity was not influenced adversely by selective sample losses, there were, however, other sources of sample selection that place constraints on the conclusions that may be drawn from this analysis. In particular, the sample was drawn from a regional sample in the South Island of New Zealand. Since the Maori population is not uniformly distributed throughout New Zealand and has greater representation in the North Island, it is possible that a sample derived from the South Island may not be fully representative of Maori within New Zealand. Given this sample limitation, the results are likely to provide an adequate account of the linkages between ethnicity and interpersonal violence within a South Island–based sample of Maori but should be applied cautiously in making inferences about North Island Maori populations. Nonetheless, it is not unreasonable to assume that the trends evident within a South Island–based sample will broadly reflect those present within a North Island population.

Table 7.1. *Rates (%) of Violent Offending and Involvement in Violence among Maori and non-Maori Participants in the Christchurch Health and Development Study at Age Eighteen*

Measure	Maori (N = 96)	Non-Maori (N = 929)	Relative Risk (95% CI)	p
Any violent offense (17–18 years)	33.3	17.6	1.9 (1.4, 2.6)	<.001
Repeated (3+) violent offenses (17–18 years)	19.8	8.4	2.4 (1.5, 3.7)	<.001
Police record for violence (ever)	7.9	2.8	2.9 (1.1, 7.4)	<.05
Victim of assault (16–18 years)	28.4	17.3	1.6 (1.2, 2.3)	<.01

Results

Rates of Interpersonal Violence Among Maori and Non-Maori.
Table 7.1 compares the rates of self-reported violent offending; recurrent self-reported violent offending; officially recorded police contact for crimes of violence; and reports of being a victim of violent assault among Maori and non-Maori participants in the Christchurch Health and Development Study at the age of eighteen. Each comparison is tested for statistical significance using the chi-squared test of independence and the strength of the association between ethnicity and rates of interpersonal violence is described by the relative risk statistic.

The table shows pervasive evidence to suggest greater involvement in interpersonal violence by Maori. At age eighteen, young Maori were more likely to report involvement in any violent offenses and to report repeated violent offending over the past year, they were more likely to have an official police record for violent offending, and reported higher rates of being a victim of assault over the period from age sixteen to eighteen years. The relative risk estimates suggest that young Maori were approximately 1.5 to 3 times more likely to be involved in violent offending or to report being a victim of violence than non-Maori.

Childhood and Family Antecedents of Violent Behaviors. The results in Table 7.1 clearly suggest that young people of Maori ethnicity are at greater risk of being both perpetrators and victims of violent crimes. Furthermore, since these results use both self-report and official record data, it seems likely that the ethnic differences in violent behaviors in Table 7.1 are unlikely to reflect reporting biases or artifacts that may be present in official

Table 7.2. *Comparison of Social, Family, and Related Characteristics of Maori and non-Maori Participants*

Measure	Maori %	Non-Maori %	p
Sociodemographic Factors			
Mother lacked formal educational qualifications	68.8	49.2	<.0001
Family of semiskilled/unskilled socioeconomic status	42.4	25.4	<.0001
Family income in lowest quartile of income distribution	43.8	23.3	<.0001
Childhood Experiences			
Parents regularly used physical punishment during childhood	22.9	10.3	<.001
In highest quartile on parental conflict scale	41.8	21.7	<.0001
Experienced 3+ changes of parents during childhood	37.8	16.3	<.0001
In lowest quartile of maternal care score	40.5	24.0	<.001
In lowest quartile of paternal care score	34.5	23.7	<.05
In highest quartile of maternal overprotection score	34.8	25.5	<.10
In highest quartile of paternal overprotection score	33.3	23.2	<.05
Parent/Family Characteristics			
Parental history of alcohol problems	24.5	10.8	<.0001
Parental history of illicit drug use	41.8	23.2	<.0001
Family history of criminal offending	21.3	9.4	<.001
In highest decile on family problems scale	23.6	7.8	<.0001

record data. However, the presence of a correlation between ethnic status and reported involvement in violence does not provide an explanation of why young Maori are at greater risk of involvement in violent behaviors. As has been noted earlier, one explanation of this tendency may be that young Maori are exposed to different social, economic, and childhood factors that may place them at greater risk of later involvement in interpersonal violence. This issue is examined in Table 7.2, which compares Maori and non-Maori on a number of prospectively measured descriptors of childhood family, economic, and related circumstances. For ease of presentation, these measures have been expressed in dichotomous form and the association between ethnicity and the dichotomously scored social, economic, and family factors is tested for statistical significance using the chi-squared test of independence.

Inspection of the table shows the presence of pervasive differences in the social, economic, and family circumstances encountered by Maori and non-Maori cohort members. In general, children of Maori ethnicity tended to come from less socially and economically advantaged homes characterized by lower levels of parental educational achievement; lower family socio-economic status, and lower family income levels. During childhood, they had greater exposure to a series of potentially disadvantageous features including more frequent use of physical punishment by parents, greater levels of parental conflict, more frequent changes of parents, and experienced lower levels of parental care and higher parental overprotection than non-Maori. In addition, there were higher rates of personal problems among Maori parents including alcohol abuse, illicit drug use, and criminal offending.

The social profile that emerges of the Maori sample is clearly of a group of young people who were more frequently reared in home environments that were characterized by sources of material disadvantage, family dysfunction, and parental difficulties that were likely to contribute to future problems of adjustment. To place this matter in perspective, it is important to note that not all children in Maori families were reared in conditions of disadvantage or family dysfunction and that not all non-Maori avoided these conditions. Rather, there were often small but nonetheless consistent tendencies for the rates of family disadvantage and dysfunction to be higher among Maori.

The Role of Social, Economic, and Family Factors in Ethnic Differences in Interpersonal Violence. Consideration of the results in Table 7.2 clearly leads to the conjecture that the higher rates of involvement in interpersonal violence by young Maori may reflect their general social background and childhood circumstances. It was possible to test this hypothesis by examining the relationships between ethnicity and involvement in interpersonal violence when due allowance was made for the differences in the family and social background characteristics shown in Table 7.2. To achieve this, risks of violent behaviors were modeled using logistic regression methods by fitting the model:

$$\text{Logit } \Pr(Y_i = 1) = \beta_0 + \beta_1 X_1 + \Sigma \beta_j Z_j$$

where $\text{Logit } \Pr(Y_i = 1)$ was the log odds that a given individual would display a given form of interpersonal violence, X_1 was the dichotomous variable representing the individual's ethnicity and Z_j were the set of family social and related factors described in Table 7.2. The critical test provided by this model involves estimation of the association between ethnicity and violence when the main effects of the confounding factors Z_j are taken into account. In

Table 7.3. *Log Likelihood Ratio (LR) Chi-Square Tests of Effect of Ethnicity on Outcome Measures after Adjustment for Covariates*

Outcome	LR Chi-Square for Ethnicity (1 d.f.)	p
Any violent offense (17–18 years)	1.48	>.20
Repeated (3+) violent offenses (17–18 years)	1.97	>.15
Police record for violence (ever)	1.37	>.20
Victim of assault (16–18 years)	2.63	>.10

Table 7.4. *Rates (%) of Violent Offending or Involvement in Violence among Maori and non-Maori after Adjustment for Covariates*

Outcome	Maori	Non-Maori	Adjusted Relative Risk	Significant Covariates[a]
Any violent offense (17–18 years)	23.6	18.4	1.3	1, 2, 4, 5
Repeated (3+) violent offenses (17–18 years)	13.0	8.6	1.5	5
Police record for violence (ever)	5.3	2.9	1.8	5
Victim of assault (16–18 years)	24.5	17.8	1.4	1, 3, 4

[a] Covariates: 1 = parental use of physical punishment; 2 = maternal care score; 3 = parental history of alcohol problems; 4 = family history of offending; 5 = multiple family problems score.

particular, if the confounding factors Z_j explain the association between ethnicity and risks of interpersonal violence, it would follow that the regression coefficient β_1 would be not significantly different from zero. By contrast, evidence of a significant nonzero coefficient β_1 would imply that, independently of family social and related factors, ethnicity was associated with risks of involvement in interpersonal violence.

The results of the logistic regression analysis are summarized in Tables 7.3 and 7.4. Table 7.3 shows log likelihood ratio chi-square test of the null hypothesis $\beta_1 = 0$ from the regression model for each outcome. This analysis shows that in all cases ethnicity was not significantly related to risks of interpersonal violence when due allowance was made for social, family, and related factors. These hypothesis tests are elaborated in Table 7.4, which shows estimates of the associations between ethnicity and measures of violent offending, adjusted for family, social, and related circumstances. These estimates may be interpreted as being the rates of interpersonal violence that would have been observed among Maori and non-Maori, had both populations been exposed to a similar mix of childhood family and economic factors. The table also shows for each comparison the covariate factors that were significant in the regression equation.

The results in Table 7.4 elaborate and clarify the conclusions drawn from Table 7.3. It may be seen that when ethnic differences in violent offending and involvement in violence were adjusted for social, economic, and family factors, all differences in rates of interpersonal violence among Maori and non-Maori were small and statistically nonsignificant. The key variables that explained associations between ethnicity and risks of violence span a series of measures relating to family circumstances and parenting behaviors including: parental use of physical punishment, the level of parental care, parental history of alcohol problems, family history of offending, and multiple family problems. More generally, the results in both Tables 7.3 and 7.4 conveyed the clear impression that the higher rates of interpersonal violence among young Maori were largely a reflection of the greater exposure of this population to family and social conditions that encouraged the development of violent behaviors and that once due allowance was made for the contextual variables, there was little evidence to suggest that young Maori were any more, or any less, prone to involvement in interpersonal violence than children of non-Maori descent.

Discussion

The preceding analysis has examined linkages between ethnicity and interpersonal violence in a New Zealand sample. The major findings and their implications are reviewed below.

First, it is clear that by the age of eighteen years, young Maori in this birth cohort were at greater risk of involvement in interpersonal violence. This increased risk of involvement in interpersonal violence was manifest in higher rates of self-reported violent behaviors, increased rates of police contact for violence, and higher rates of reports of being a victim of violent assault. To the extent that these measures spanned self-report and official record data, there can be little doubt that Maori in this cohort had higher rates of involvement in, and exposure to, interpersonal violence as young adults.

Subsequent analysis suggested that the higher rate of involvement in interpersonal violence among young Maori could be predicted from, and explained by, prospectively measured childhood and family circumstances. In particular, examination of the social, economic, and family profiles of Maori and non-Maori showed that during childhood, Maori had greater exposure to a series of disadvantageous conditions including socioeconomic disadvantage, higher rates of exposure of adversity during childhood, and higher rates of parental problems and difficulties. When these childhood factors were taken into account, the associations between ethnicity and interpersonal violence became statistically nonsignificant. The principal factors that explained the correlations between ethnicity and interpersonal violence centered around a series of measures describing childhood and parenting variables. Young Maori had higher rates of exposure to physical punishment during childhood, reported lower maternal care scores, more often came from families characterized by parental alcohol problems and criminal offending, and more often came from families facing multiple social and related problems. It would appear to be this configuration of family related factors that largely explained the higher rates of involvement in interpersonal violence among young Maori. The results of this study suggest that when due allowance was made for these family-related factors, rates of involvement in interpersonal violence were not significantly higher than among non-Maori reared in similar childhood environments.

The explanation of the origins of higher rates of interpersonal violence among young Maori that emerges from this analysis appears to reflect an account that is a hybrid of socioeconomic and cultural explanations of the origins of ethnic differences in interpersonal violence. At first sight, the finding that measures of family disadvantage and family functioning largely explain the higher involvement of young Maori in interpersonal violence appears to be consistent with a socioeconomic explanation of the origins of ethnic differences. However, while measures of family functioning and disadvantage overlap with socioeconomic factors, it is quite clear that these factors are not simply a reflection of social and economic disadvantage but relate more to intrafamily behaviors and practices. What the results clearly suggest is that within Maori families in this cohort, levels of family functioning and parenting practices were such that young Maori were exposed to home environments more likely to encourage future involvement in interpersonal violence. The major question that requires resolution concerns the factors and processes that have led to higher levels of family dysfunction and difficulties in contemporary Maori families. It is likely that a precise answer to this question will be difficult to obtain, since such an answer requires adequate historical data characterizing the ways in which Maori social and family disadvantage has developed in New Zealand. However, in broad outline, it seems likely that the difficulties and disadvantages faced by contemporary Maori families are likely to represent the end point of a long-term historical process that has involved many components, including: the pressures faced by and change in Maori culture and language following colonization; the loss of land and economic power base experienced by Maori; increasing urbanization of Maori; and the general reduction of status and prestige (mana) of Maori people within the context of New Zealand society (Duff, 1993; Jackson, 1988a; 1988b; Kelsey, 1984; Walker, 1996). It is likely that each of these changes has conspired to increase the likelihood that present-day Maori families are faced with stresses, pressures, and a history that increases the likelihood of family difficulties and dysfunctions that in turn are reflected in a large number of statistics showing relative Maori disadvantage in New Zealand.

At the same time it is important to place such findings in a clear statistical context. Findings showing ethnic differences in rates of violence and other forms of personal difficulty often become transformed in social debates to imply that these problems are the exclusive domain of one ethnic group. This stereotype is often highly misleading, since elevated rates of difficulties in one social group may obscure the fact that most members of this group are not involved in the difficulty. One useful way of looking at the role of ethnicity in rates of interpersonal violence is to examine the population attributable risk (PAR) for ethnicity. The population attributable risk gives an estimate of the percentage reduction in interpersonal violence that would occur if rates of this involvement were the same in Maori as they are in non-Maori. This estimate suggests that even before adjustment for family factors, ethnicity played only a relatively modest role in involvement in interpersonal violence in this cohort. Estimates of the PAR suggest that if Maori had the same rate of interpersonal violence as non-Maori, rates of involvement in interpersonal violence within this cohort would have been reduced by only 9 percent to 25 percent depending on the outcome assessed. The modest contribution of ethnicity to rates of interpersonal violence highlights the fact that while Maori were at higher relative risk of involvement in interpersonal violence, the majority of those involved in violent behaviors were non-Maori owing to the large number of non-Maori within the cohort.

In recent years, New Zealand has been involved in a painful reanalysis of the role of Maori within New Zealand society and a search for solutions for both past injustices and present-day inequities between Maori and non-Maori (Spoonley, 1990; Duff, 1993; Walker, 1996). In the course of this debate, considerable emphasis has been placed on providing Maori with increased power and control over their social, personal, and economic destinies (Jackson, 1988a; 1988b; Duff, 1993; Walker, 1996). The present analysis highlights two issues that are relevant to this debate. First, the comparisons on interpersonal violence and, indeed, of Maori/non-Maori comparisons in general, highlight the need for greater social equity and particularly the need for a society in which ethnicity is unrelated to individual life opportunities and life risks. Second, the findings suggest that within the area of interpersonal violence and, probably, many other areas of personal functioning, the major priority is that of developing social, economic, and related policies that strengthen Maori family functioning and empower

Maori families in ways that reduce the number of young Maori who are exposed to the mix of family disadvantage and family dysfunction that appears to be associated with increased risks of psychosocial problems during childhood and into later life.

There are two important caveats that should be placed on this analysis. First, the analysis has been based on a particular birth cohort of New Zealand children studied in a particular region in New Zealand. The extent to which the findings for this cohort hold for other contemporary cohorts or other parts of New Zealand is open to debate. In particular, as noted previously, because of the South Island base of the study, the cohort underrepresents children of Maori descent, and it may be that the factors influencing involvement in interpersonal violence may differ regionally and may vary across different birth cohorts. Thus, while the present analysis provides an account of the prevalence of interpersonal violence and potential origins of ethnic differences in this birth cohort, further research is needed to examine the extent to which these trends and conclusions apply to cohorts in different regions of New Zealand and from those born subsequent to this cohort.

Second, the results have been based on a combination of self-report and official record data to provide a profile of ethnic differences in interpersonal violence in the CHDS cohort. It is likely that both sources of measurement will be subject to errors of measurement and this could influence findings. In general, the validity of the analysis above rests on the assumption that errors of measurement in the reporting of interpersonal violence for Maori and non-Maori are statistically independent of the individual's ethnic status.

A further issue relating to measurement concerns the extent to which it is realistic to use survey-based measures to describe rates of interpersonal violence among Maori. In particular, in recent years there have been claims that research into Maori should be conducted by Maori researchers using a Maori methodology (Jackson, 1988a; 1988b; Rolleston, 1989; Pomare et al., 1995). It may be argued from this perspective that the present interview-based study using a standardized questionnaire that was applied to both Maori and non-Maori could produce misleading results. At the same time, the findings of this study generally support claims made by Maori researchers about the disadvantages and difficulties faced by young Maori (Jackson, 1988a; 1988b; Duff, 1993; Pomare et al., 1995). To the extent that there is a convergence of conclusions reached by different methodologies, this suggests that the results of the present study are likely to be robust and are unlikely to simply reflect bias arising from the choice of a particular research methodology.

Racist Victimization in England and Wales

Ben Bowling

Coretta Phillips

Introduction

Students of "race," class, ethnicity, and violent crime in Europe and North America have been preoccupied by the reportedly higher rates of violence committed by ethnic minorities. Although it has been observed that, on both sides of the Atlantic, most crime is committed – unsurprisingly – by the white majority community, popular concern and scholarly attention have focused on the disproportionate rates of arrest and imprisonment among minority communities. As Russell (1998) suggests, a preoccupation with concepts such as "black criminality" and "black-on-black crime" have tended to obscure or ignore the extent of "white-on-white crime" or "white-on-minority" violence, to the extent that the very terms seem odd. A further consequence of the narrow focus of the "race and crime debate" is that, until recently at least, criminologists and others have tended to ignore racist violence; that is, violence specifically targeted against ethnic minority communities and incidents that are aggravated by racism and racial prejudice.

In recent years, this situation has started to change significantly. In the 1980s, public concern about racist violence increased in North America (Hamm, 1993), continental Europe (Bjorgo and Witte, 1993), and Britain (Bowling, 1999), which led to the development of new directions in research and public policy. During the 1990s, a number of well-publicized incidents heightened this concern about racist violence in numerous places. In the early 1990s in Germany, for example, there was a spate of arson attacks against asylum seekers' hostels and the homes of people from ethnic minorities. Of these crimes, the most atrocious was an arson attack on November 23, 1992, in Molln by two neo-Nazi skinheads, in which three members of the Arslan family, of Turkish origin, were burned to death (Hamm, 1993).

Of the recent cases in the United States, the murder of James Byrd stands out as the epitome of a racist crime. On June 7, 1998, John William King, Shawn Berry, and Lawrence Brewer, three roommates, were out driving when they encountered James Byrd hitchhiking. After offering him a lift, the three then beat Byrd unconscious, stripped him, and chained him to the back of their pickup truck and dragged him for two and a half miles until his head and right arm were ripped from his body. At the subsequent trial, it was found that King had been involved, for some years, in racist extremism and was tattooed with Nazi SS symbols and a depiction of a black man being lynched. All three men were found guilty. King and Brewer were sentenced to death by lethal injection, while Berry – who had no history of racist activities – was sentenced to life in prison without the possibility of parole for forty years.

On April 22, 1993, while waiting with a friend for a bus in Eltham, southeast London, England, Stephen Lawrence, an eighteen-year-old black man, was stabbed to death. Stephen's friend Duwayne Brooks later reported that Stephen, who had been looking out for the bus further up the street, had been engulfed by a group of five or six white youths, one of whom shouted "what, what, nigger!." Stephen Lawrence was stabbed twice with a long knife; both stab wounds severed major arteries, and after running some distance he bled to death on the pavement. In February 1997, an inquest jury returned a unanimous verdict that "Stephen Lawrence was unlawfully killed in a completely unprovoked racist attack by five white youths."

The police investigation following Stephen's death failed to lead to the conviction of the killers and was condemned as "palpably flawed" and incompetent. In July 1997, after more than four years of campaigning by Neville and Doreen Lawrence, Stephen's parents, the Home Secretary Jack Straw announced a public inquiry into the murder, chaired by Sir William Macpherson.[1] The Lawrence Inquiry took evidence from eighty-eight witnesses and received 148 written submissions amounting to more than one hundred thousand pages of evidence. The report concluded that there was a series of fundamental flaws in the conduct of the investigation by the Metropolitan Police Service and that this was the result of "professional incompetence, institutional racism and a failure of leadership by senior officers" (Macpherson, 1999: 317). It documented the denial of the racist motive for the murder among at least five police officers, and the racist stereotyping of Duwayne Brooks at the scene, where he was wrongly assumed to be one of the protagonists in a fight between youths rather than a victim of an unprovoked attack. It goes on to criticize the use of inappropriate and

---

[1] See Macpherson (1999), Cathcart (1999), Norton Taylor (1999), Bowling (1999).

offensive language and the insensitive and patronizing handling of Mr. and Mrs. Lawrence throughout the investigation.

The murder of Stephen Lawrence and the subsequent flawed police investigation echoes the experience of many victims of racist violence in Britain. Rather than being an isolated case, it epitomizes the extensive empirical and documentary evidence gathered over the last four decades. The remainder of this chapter reviews this literature on the British experience of racist violence and points tentatively toward some explanations for the patterns that emerge. We also examine some of the individual, community, and statutory responses to victimization, raising questions about the effectiveness of policing and law enforcement. While the focus is on the British experience of violent racism, the parallels in other European and North American countries point to the international nature of white-on-minority violence.

The Extent and Nature of Racist Victimization

The history of racist violence in Britain is a long but discontinuous one (see Panayi, 1996; Bowling, 1999). There is evidence of attempts at forced removal of people of color since the time of Elizabeth I and examples of attacks against Jews in Britain stretching back to the twelfth century (Fryer, 1984; Panayi, 1996). The violence targeting black and Asian sailors in British ports immediately after World War I and World War II (in 1948) is well documented (Jenkinson, 1996; Panayi, 1996). The late 1950s saw several antiblack riots in London, Nottingham, and elsewhere (Panayi, 1996). During the 1970s, the emergence of the "skinhead" youth culture, its link with the rise in popularity of extreme right political activism, was accompanied by an apparent increase in racist incidents. These developments led to an increase in official concern, and eventually in the 1980s the police and Home Office began to keep records of "racial incidents" (Bowling, 1999). These have shown steady increases since the 1980s, to stand at just fewer than fourteen thousand incidents recorded in 1998 (see Figure 8.1).

Recent Home Office research has shed some light on patterns of racially motivated incidents recorded by the police (Maynard and Read, 1997). Based on a survey of all police forces in England and Wales, the authors found that there was wide variation in what was actually recorded and counted as racially motivated (see also Sibbitt, 1997; Bowling, 1999). Where the type of crime was known, 38 percent of incidents comprised verbal abuse, 21 percent assault, and 20 percent damage to property. Only 2 percent were recorded as serious crime. However, where racially motivated incidents are recorded as serious crime – such as "Grievous Bodily Harm" or murder – they are frequently not recorded as racial incidents. Their categorization as a specific type of serious crime overrides and negates their definition by the

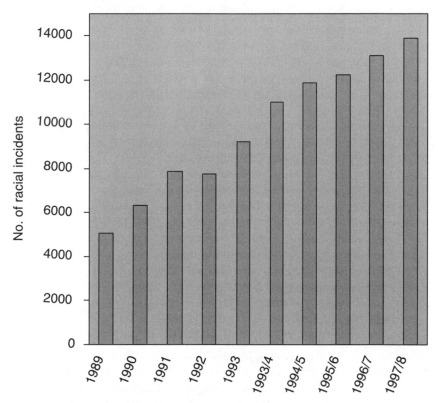

Figure 8.1. Racial Incidents Recorded by the Police in England and Wales, 1989–1997/8

police as "racial" (see also Bowling, 1999: 151–4). To some extent this was what happened in the Stephen Lawrence murder.

The police forces that record the largest number of racially motivated incidents tend to be in metropolitan areas where there are significant ethnic minority communities. After calculating the number of racially motivated incidents per one thousand ethnic minority population, however, Maynard and Read (1997) found that three provincial forces in the north of England had the highest victimization rates of 14 or more per 1,000 black or Asian population. Differences in reporting and recording practices dog attempts to make comparisons of the extent and nature of racist violence across time and space. Nonetheless, this finding supports earlier research showing that where people from ethnic minorities make up only a small proportion of the local population, they are at greater risk of victimization than their "inner-city" counterparts (see Smith, 1989; Hesse et al., 1993; Sampson and Phillips, 1992, 1996; Bowling, 1999).

Survey Estimates of Racist Violence. Like any other form of crime, racial "incidents" recorded by the police reflect only a small proportion of all those that occur – thus concealing the so-called dark figure. In order to overcome the inadequacies of police records, a number of local crime surveys since the early 1980s have attempted to make quantitative estimates of racist violence. Each of these has identified low levels of reporting to the police (see, for example, Brown, 1984; Jones et al., 1986). In Bowling's study in the London borough of Newham, 21 percent of black women, 19 percent of Asian men, 18 percent of Asian women, and 17 percent of black men had experienced some form of racist victimization (1999: 196). A small proportion of white people – 8 percent of men and 7 percent of women – also said that they had been racially victimized. In this locality, Bowling estimated that no more than 5 percent of racial incidents were recorded by the police (see also Saulsbury and Bowling, 1991).

Every sweep of the British Crime Survey (1988 to 1996) has found that more than one-third of assaults directed against Asians and blacks were thought by respondents to be racially motivated, as were about half of the incidents involving threats. The use of racist language was the main reason given by both black and Asian respondents for thinking that the incident was racially motivated. Using British Crime Survey data for 1988 and 1992 combined, Fitzgerald and Hale (1996) found that of a national sample, 4 percent of blacks, 5 percent of Indians, and around 8 percent of Pakistanis and Bangladeshis had been the victims of racially motivated offenses in the previous year. Grossed-up estimates using BCS victimization rates suggested that there were about 143,000 incidents of crime and threats against black and Asian people, which were thought to have been motivated by racism, in 1997 (Percy, 1998). This represented 15 percent of the estimated total of 984,000 incidents against them altogether. Around forty-one thousand of these incidents were *reported* to the police, compared with the 12,222 *recorded* by the police that year. Expressed as a proportion, 29 percent of the incidents are *reported to* the police, and about 8 percent are *recorded by* the police.

The Process of Racist Victimization and Its Impact. Estimating the "real" extent of violent racism is an exercise fraught with conceptual and method-ological problems (Hesse et al., 1992; Bowling, 1993a; 1999: 150–68). Not only is the attempt to count so many complex events occurring across time and place difficult, but it is in some ways misconceived. Considering the pat-terns of intimidation and harassment that provide part of the context for serious violence, it becomes clear that the issues of safety and perceptions of safety cannot realistically be "measured." Feminist research on violence against women also has observed that the experience of sexual assault or domestic violence can be better understood as a continuum, connecting "everyday" abuse with extreme acts of violence (e.g., Kelly, 1987; Stanko,

1988). Similarly, conceiving of violent racism as a process allows connections to be made between the racist abuse at one end of the spectrum and murder at the other. Studies have confirmed the pattern of repeat victimization among victims of racist violence (e.g., Sampson and Phillips, 1992; Phillips and Sampson, 1998).

This context also helps to explain ethnic minorities' elevated fear of crime (Genn, 1988; Pearson et al., 1989; Feagin and Sikes, 1994; Bowling, 1999). On a number of dimensions, people from ethnic minority communities are more fearful than those from white communities, and this is particularly the case in relation to fear of violent racism. The BCS probes further to attempt to measure people's perceptions of safety and unsafety. Percy (1998) shows that on the street, and especially at home alone at night, people from ethnic minorities feel less safe than white people and it seems likely that feelings of "unsafety" affect individual freedom of movement. For example, people from ethnic minorities (Pakistanis and Bangladeshis in particular) avoid going out at night through fear of crime, avoid walking near certain types of people, and are always accompanied when walking out after dark. More detailed analysis showed that while 13 percent of white respondents said they avoided certain places or events (such as football matches, night clubs, theaters, or pubs) because they fear crime or violence, this was true of 29 percent of blacks, 27 percent of Indians, and 22 percent of Pakistani and Bangladeshis (Percy, 1998: 33). Although the relationship between fear, crime, and victimization is a complex one, fear of "ordinary crime" among people from ethnic minority communities is fundamentally shaped by their *fear of racist victimization*. Although this is not a frequent occurrence for most people, pernicious racist abuse does sometimes precede extreme acts of violence, as exemplified in the case of Stephen Lawrence. This experience provides a backdrop to the lives of many people from ethnic minorities in Britain today.

Police records and victimization surveys, already referred to, are the two most common methods of quantifying the extent of violent racism. Although this measurement has its value, alternative sources often enable richer and more meaningful information to be collected. Among these alternative sources are qualitative techniques (e.g., Chahal, 1999); case studies employing mixed methods (e.g., Bowling, 1999); journalistic accounts (e.g., Bufford, 1993; Rose, 1996); records of local monitoring groups (e.g., Newham Monitoring Project, 1991); and public inquiries, such as that carried out by Macpherson into the events surrounding the murder of Stephen Lawrence (see also Hesse et al., 1993). Indeed, like sexual harassment and domestic violence against women, the issue of racist violence emerged onto the public agenda only as a result of the work of activists campaigning for victims' rights who drew, for their evidence, on case studies and documentary methods.

There are, of course, some methodological limitations to using these sources. Journalistic accounts may be unrepresentative, while reports of monitoring groups are typically partisan in nature. Nonetheless, both are often richer and more contextualized than academic sources that rely on interviews with someone once or, at most, on only a few occasions. Similarly, public inquiries provide the opportunity to learn about the way in which individuals and organizations think about problems. By documenting the collective experience of thousands of people who have experienced such violence, a greater degree of insight has been gained regarding the victims' perspective.

We can now say with some confidence that racist violence affects a considerable proportion of the ethnic minority communities on an enduring basis, and that serious and mundane incidents are interwoven to create a threatening environment, which undermines their personal safety and freedom of movement. What is now required is a shift away from the victimological perspective to an analysis of the characteristics of offenders, the social milieu in which violence is fostered, and the process by which it becomes directed against ethnic minorities.

Racist Offending: from Profiling to Explanation

The focus on victims has tended to obscure the importance of researching racist offenders. Moreover, there has been a reluctance to examine racist offenders partly, perhaps, because it risks appearing to "understand" racist behavior rather than simply to "condemn" it (Bowling, 1999: 306). Racist offenders have no allies in the political mainstream; they are doubly condemned because of their violence and their racist expressions. Police and politicians rarely get beyond epithets – "yobs," "louts," and "thugs" – to describe such offenders. Even criminologists have frequently opted for shallow "theoreotyping," constructing academic theories out of common stereotypes (Pitts, 1995; Bowling, 1999: 305). There has been a renaissance in research on offending and offenders in recent years, but there are still few studies that seek to explore racist offenders' backgrounds, experiences, and motives.[2] And yet, examining the offender's perspective is critical for developing ways of responding to violent racism.

Until recently, our knowledge of racist offenders relied principally on information from the victim. We know from victims' accounts that most of the people committing acts of violent racism are men and are young adults – aged between sixteen and twenty-five – though young children and older adults have been reported (Mayhew et al., 1989; Aye Maung and Mirrlees-Black, 1994; Sibbitt, 1997; Bowling, 1999). Aye Maung and Mirrlees-Black

---

[2] See, for example, Bufford (1993) and Webster (1997).

(1994), using 1992 BCS data, found that three-quarters of Asian victims of violent incidents (wounding, common assault, and robbery) and threats involved more than one offender and two-fifths involved four or more. Nine out of ten Asian council tenants interviewed in Bowling (1999) who had been victimized were attacked by more than one offender. In instances of violence or threats reported to the British Crime Survey, which were thought to be racially motivated, victims nearly always cited white offenders.

Sibbitt's (1997) qualitative study of the perpetrators of racist harassment adds the socioeconomic dimension to this profile, using police records, case studies, and interviews. Sibbitt found that the perpetrators' racist views were shared by the communities to which they belonged, and offenders saw this as legitimating their action. Thus, wider communities not only "spawn" perpetrators but they reinforce their behavior by not condemning it. Although Sibbitt's typology of racist offenders identifies three types (*"the pensioners," the "people next door," and the "problem family"*), they are all united by their attitudes toward ethnic minorities, which serve to focus individuals' grievances and sense of injustice on an external scapegoat. Frequently, racist offenders react to what they see as preferential treatment or access to scarce social and economic resources, such as housing, employment, and education. This is epitomized in the comment made by a woman cited by Sibbitt (1997: 102): "They refuse to learn English – the kids have to get a special teacher in. *My son could do with a special teacher, but he won't get it, will he?*"

The evidence that violent racism is concentrated in areas of multiple deprivation points to the relevance of economic and social factors. However, *per capita* rates of victimization suggest that racist violence also afflicts rural, suburban, and relatively prosperous areas as well as blighted inner-city locales.[3] Moreover, the evidence for a relationship between economic changes and violent crime in general is mixed. Field (1990) found that violent crime increases during periods of *increased* consumption and declines during periods of economic downturn. The economic scapegoating of ethnic minorities is one of five main theoretical approaches to explaining why ethnic minorities are the targets of violence directed against individuals, their homes, places of worship or entertainment, and at other aspects of social and cultural life.

A second popular explanation contends that levels of hostility and violence are related to the size of minority population, or increases in its size over a short period of time (Bjorgo and Witte, 1993). In 1958, for example, riots in Nottingham and Notting Hill were said by Labour and Conservative politicians to have been caused by the arrival of "too many" black people, which had caused resentment among the "indigenous" white population, resulting in a violent backlash. The "upsurge" in racist violence in Germany

---

[3] See also Husbands (1993).

in the early 1990s was blamed directly by many commentators on the arrival of a "flood" of asylum seekers. In our view, this reasoning is flawed for
several reasons. Historically, minority populations have come under attack
in Britain even when their numbers were tiny – in the thousands or even
mere hundreds, as was the case in the riots in 1919 (Jenkinson, 1996). In
Britain today, racist violence is also prevalent where black and Asian people
make up only a small minority – sometimes only 1 or 2 percent – of local populations. The "numbers thesis" also fails to explain violence against Jewish
people, their property, and places of worship and burial, who comprise
0.5 percent of the U.K. population. Although actual numbers, or even increases in numbers, may not provide an explanation for violent racism, it
may be that the *meaning* attached to these changes does. Research has indicated that racist violence is common in neighborhoods where black and
Asian people make up a small but *increasing* minority of a neighborhood
and where community sentiment defines this as problematic. Authors including Husbands (1982), Smith (1989), and Hesse et al. (1992) point to
the relationship between racist victimization and white territorialism and exclusionism. White neighborhoods may be maintained as "[t]he prospect of
violent intimidation is a strong disincentive to black households who might
otherwise wish to move away from the poor properties in which they are
overrepresented" (Smith, 1989: 161–2).

The attempt to explain the extent of violent racism as a reaction to "the
numbers" is consistent with the assumption that policies to reduce the number of immigrants would reduce the extent of violence targeted against
them. In contrast to this view, however, the empirical evidence from several contexts suggests that racist violence has increased dramatically *after*
governments have advocated or implemented measures to restrict immigration and asylum. Among the periods of most ferocious racist violence in the
United Kingdom was 1981 in the immediate aftermath of the 1980 Nationality Act, which ended "primary immigration" from former colonies in the
Caribbean and Africa, and also severely restricted the rights of dependents
to join families settled in Britain. In Sweden, a wave of racist violence started
in May 1990, five months after the government tightened its liberal asylum
policy (Bjorgo, 1993; Bjorgo and Witte, 1993: 7). In Germany, racist attacks
and riots intensified dramatically after the government initiated a debate on
reducing the numbers of asylum seekers coming into Germany (Atkinson,
1993; Bjorgo and Witte, 1993: 7–8).

Theories of culture include a third approach to explaining racist violence.
Common in media representations of racist violence are depictions of racism
as an aspect of "national character." Goldhagen argues that the holocaust
in Germany must be seen as a specifically German phenomenon, rooted in
the pursuit of "German national political goals" (1996: 7). His approach is
to "explain the culture's constitution, its idiosyncratic patterns of practice,

and its collective projects and products" (1996: 15). England's history of racism is very different from Germany's. However, the history of chattel slavery, colonialism, and support for South African apartheid, as well as the configuration of contemporary racism, might suggest that racist violence has a specifically English cultural variant.

A fourth approach draws on the evidence that racist violence is associated with the consumption of alcohol, either as a direct result of intoxication (by lowering inhibitions) or in the social context of drinking, such as crowd behavior after bars have closed (Tuck, 1989; Field, 1990: 8). Although it seems likely that alcohol can be seen as a contributory factor, the "drunken pranks" explanation is frequently used to suggest that incidents are unconnected with racism. Some practitioners have gone to ridiculous lengths to redefine racist incidents as merely drunken hooliganism (see Graeff, 1989: 131; Pearson et al., 1989: 128). Heavy consumption of alcohol is a typical trait in diverse forms of violent racism. Anti-Jewish pogroms in Russia at the turn of the century (Klier, 1993: 133–5), riots against Italian immigrants in France in the 1890s, numerous instances of racist violence in Britain, fire bombings of asylum centers in Scandinavia and Germany in the 1990s; all appear to have alcohol as a contributory factor (Bjorgo, 1993: 35–6, 41–2). However, the finding that offenders are often found to be under the influence of alcohol can be misinterpreted to mean that no further explanation is necessary. Alcohol should be seen as only one means for overcoming inhibitions once a situation arises. As Bjorgo and Witte (1993: 10) put it, "even if an act of violence is perpetrated under the influence of alcohol, this certainly does not mean that it may not also be influenced by racist motives."

Although the activities of extreme right-wing organizations[4] and their links to ordinary communities are well documented in numerous contexts, this fifth theoretical approach has rarely been used to analyze the experiences of ethnic minority victims in the United Kingdom. It is evident that many aspects of the ideology, language, and practices of explicitly racist or extreme right-wing groupings are shared in common across Europe and the United States. Lööw (1993), for example, interviewed members of the Swedish "white power networks," and found that the rhetoric of these networks is a mixture of national socialist terminology of the 1930s and the contemporary code of the Ku Klux Klan and other American white supremacist groups. Themes identified by Lööw in Sweden – including a belief in "ZOG – Zionist Occupational Government," denial of the holocaust, defense of the "white race" against its "enemies" (communists, homosexuals, Jews, immigrants, and antiracists) – appear to be common to similar organizations in

---

[4] There are numerous such groups including National Front, Column 88, British National Party, Combat 18, the Ku Klux Klan, White Aryan Resistance, and so on; Choice; English Solidarity; International Third Position (see Searchlight; CARF; etc.).

other Scandinavian countries, Germany, the United States, and Britain. The similarity between these materials is uncanny, and at their center is a notion of a specifically *European* superiority and supremacy (see Bjorgo and Kaplan, 1998).

In several different national contexts, there appears to be a relationship between the most extreme forms of racist politics and the manifestation of both explicitly racist attacks and apparently *apolitical* acts of violence directed at ethnic minorities. It seems that politically motivated racists are able to influence – directly and indirectly – groups of young people who hold "anti-immigration" views or are in some other way sympathetic to racist ideology. Although international neo-Nazi groups appear to have little centralized leadership or hierarchy, they do cooperate in a number of ways (Jensen, 1993). The British National Party, for example, has participated with German neo-Nazi groups in paramilitary training. One crucial medium for spreading racist ideas and inciting violence is "Oi-music," with extremely brutal, racist, and violent lyrics and its associated youth culture. A recent development is the use of computer networks by neo-Nazi organizations and looser networks of racist supremacists. Internet newsgroups exist where racist ideology can be disseminated, Nazi memorabilia purchased and distributed, and information on bomb-making, "hit-lists," and hate campaigning circulated.

One final approach to explaining racist violence that deserves mention is a theory proposed by Beck and Tolnay (1995), which integrates some of the elements set out above. Their thesis is based on an analysis of violence toward African Americans in the era of the white lynch mob and can be expressed as a formula. Beck and Tolnay argue that the potential for racist violence is the product of the extent of racist ideology, the permissiveness of the state response to racist violence, and competition for scarce resources (such as economic wealth, political power, and social status). If each of these necessary factors are present, all that remains is some form of "triggering event" to lead to an outbreak of antiblack violence.

Responses to Racist Violence

Individual and Community Self-Defense. Although survey research has focused on fear of crime, the most commonly reported reaction to crime is anger. Bowling's survey in East London, for example, found that 70 percent of the victims of racist violence felt angry, compared with shocked (44 percent), while comparatively few – 27 percent – felt fearful (1999: 216). The personal experiences of racist violence are so diverse, however, that it would be difficult to describe the ways in which individual people, families, and communities have sought to shield themselves from victimization. At the most personal, measures have included moving away from more spacious or well-maintained property in localities where racist violence is prevalent to safer areas, and other strategies to avoid situations where "trouble" may be found such as particular pubs, or a particular area on soccer match days. Individuals also put in place situational crime prevention measures such as shatterproof glass and fireproof mailboxes to reduce the impact of violent racist victimization (Bowling, 1999: 222).

In response to a collective experience of victimization, communities have also acted together in self-defense. In the 1958 racist riots, black transport workers provided escorts to and from places of employment. In response to racist assault in the 1970s and 1980s, youth movements were formed to oppose racist organizations such as the National Front, who were staging provocative marches through areas of ethnic minority settlement. These grew in the 1980s into a strong self-defense movement, focusing on racist attacks and racism in policing, and were linked politically to the antiracist movement (Newham Monitoring Project, 1991).

The State Response. Witte (1996) has noted that the state response to racist violence has been very similar in France, the Netherlands, and Britain. At first, governments ignored the problem entirely or denied the racist nature of the violence. When this was no longer possible because of the extent of demands among ethnic minority communities for protection, racism became linked with questions of "immigration" and "integration" of victimized communities while racial prejudice and violence are seen as "side effects." Because migration was seen as the dominant topic, state responses largely consisted of migration-*restricting* policies (such as the Nationality and Immigration Acts [Solomos, 1993]) – what Witte refers to as "excluding recognition" – and simultaneous antidiscrimination policies (such as the Race Relations Acts, 1965, 1968, and 1976). The resulting "two-faced" state response is a result of being caught between "pressures from racist sentiments, parties and ideologies and pressures from anti-racism movements and ideologies" (Witte, 1996: 201–3).

The moment that the British state officially recognized racist violence as a specific social problem was November 1981, with the publication of the Home Office report *Racial Attacks* (Home Office, 1981). Until 1981, as racially motivated attacks and harassment did not officially exist, there was no publicly stated police or government policy to deal with it. Two years later, this situation had changed dramatically. A range of governmental agencies – among them the House of Commons, Home Office, Metropolitan Police, Association of Chief Police Officers, and the Greater London Council – each elevated racist violence to the status of "urgent priority" (see Bowling, 1999, Chapter 3). The subsequent years have seen a rapidly increasing policy debate about ways of tackling racially motivated crime. This has focused on policing, the "multiagency approach," and new legislation.

The Police Response. Findings from the BCS suggest that satisfaction with the police response is significantly worse in dealing with reported racial incidents than with incidents in general. In Bowling's (1999) study of an area with a high rate of victimization, just under one in ten people who reported to the police said they were very satisfied with the way in which the police handled the matter, while only 44 percent were very or fairly satisfied. This contrasted sharply with comparable 1988 BCS figures of 22 percent and 60 percent, respectively. This suggests that victims of racial incidents are much less likely to be satisfied with police service than victims of crime in general. The most common complaint among those who are dissatisfied with the police response was that the police did not "do enough," that they failed to keep the victim informed, and that they seemed not to be interested (Bowling, 1999: 235–8). Some respondents were very critical of the police response, pointing specifically to what they saw as police prejudice against blacks and Asians. One commented, "They don't get the offenders. And if they catch them they don't charge them. If I was to offend someone like this the police would harass me instead of turning a blind eye which is what I feel they do in case of white offenders. And the offenders feel they can do anything they like as they are always let off" (Bowling, 1999: 237). The same study found that only a very small minority – as few as 5 percent – felt generally very satisfied with the way in which racist harassment was dealt with in their area and less than one-third were at all satisfied. This picture res-onates with the documented experience of minority communities. A long string of reports on the police response to ethnic minorities in general and to the victims of violent racism have been highly critical of their treatment (see Bowling, 1999, for a review). Early studies indicated that "the police do not do enough to detect the everyday crimes that affect ordinary people" and went further to say that reporting crime sometimes invited police harass-ment such as rough treatment, inappropriate questioning, and immigration checks (Institute of Race Relations, 1987). Such allegations continue to be made against the police today.

It is clear that the police continue to deny that racist violence is a problem and are, in practice, frequently unwilling to acknowledge the possibility of racist motives for many attacks in the face of strong evidence. This can, in part, be explained by racist stereotyping by individual officers who define ethnic minorities as potential offenders rather than as potential victims. This was the experience of Duwayne Brooks in the aftermath of the murder of his friend Stephen Lawrence. There is evidence of widespread racist assump-tions, prejudice, and stereotyping in the culture of the police organization, too. As Bowling (1999: 248–56) documents, many police officers are not only *not opposed* to racism but actually share the values of the racists who are vic-timizing ethnic minority communities. Some police officers empathize with the white man who "resents having *his* area taken over," or sympathize with white "yobs" who feel that "the system" that should be working for *them* is working also for black and Asian communities. Some think it is "despicable" when Asian people speak their mother tongue, and believe that "failing to adapt" to English customs (wearing traditional clothes, for example) renders them both "threatening" and "vulnerable." These racist attitudes and prejudices are clearly reflected in the behavior toward black and Asian victims, witnesses, suspects, employees, and the general public. Compounding the effects of individual and cultural racism is the *institutional racism* that is built into the policies and practices of the organization. This is the systemic discrimination against people from ethnic minorities irrespective of the intent of individuals. It is to be found in the stereotyping of people from ethnic minorities as shifty, untrustworthy, and devious. And it can be seen in such outcomes as black and Asian victims being left dissatisfied with how the police handled their cases, about how well informed they were, and what action (or lack of it) is taken. The ultimate consequence of individual, cultural, and institutional racism is a failure to deliver either a *quality service* or *equality* of service and protection.

The Multiagency Response. One of the central planks of government policy on racist victimization throughout the 1980s and 1990s was the "multiagency," or "partnership approach." The origins of this approach lie in the history of postwar British rational scientific management and grew partly from the belief, which strengthened during the 1970s and 1980s, that the police alone could not be expected to reduce crime (Weatheritt, 1986; Bowling, 1999: 101–49). Since complex social problems such as racism and violence are rooted in contextual factors such as housing, education, and the consumption of alcohol (and its licensing), a multifaceted approach involving the police, local government, community organizations, schools, and other social institutions was called for. Against the logic of this idea, however, the research on the effectiveness of the multiagency approach has been equivocal at best, and damning at worst (see, for example, Rein, 1983; Weatheritt, 1986; Bowling, 1999: 140–5). A multitude of problems beset attempts to develop a multiagency approach to racist violence. Two Home Office–funded projects set up to develop the approach both fell short of their stated goals (Saulsbury and Bowling, 1991; Bowling and Saulsbury, 1993; Sampson and Phillips, 1995; Phillips and Sampson, 1998). Both studies identified major differences in the way in which organizations defined and understood the problem, a denial of the extent and nature of the problem, blaming victims for failing to "integrate," and a reluctance to investigate or take action against perpetrators for fear of a white backlash. In fact, ethnic minorities who experienced violent racist victimization were not defined as victims, were blamed for their own victimization, or informed that inaction against offenders was the most appropriate statutory response, *all at* *the same time.* Duwayne Brooks and Neville and Doreen Lawrence were all victims of this doublespeak following the murder of Stephen Lawrence, suffering what can certainly be described as "institutional racism" and perhaps as "statutory victimization."

Racist Violence in England and Wales after the Lawrence Inquiry

The inquiry into the murder of Stephen Lawrence brought to light many of the issues central to this chapter. It demonstrated that black and Asian people in Britain are specifically targeted for "everyday" and politically organized racist violence and that this enduring experience of being under attack fundamentally affects how ethnic minority communities think, feel, and act. The inquiry demonstrated that racist violence undermines their *sense* of security as well as their actual safety; it curtails their freedom of movement including their ability to visit certain localities; it affects fundamental life choices such as where to live and work. Calls for protection by black and Asian communities have typically been met with denial either that a problem existed, that it bore any connection with racism, or that there were weaknesses in the subsequent police response. The Lawrence inquiry brought to light evidence that police are "racism-blind," or have a worldview that favors racist offenders over black and Asian communities. Ultimately, it demonstrated the failure to meet the requirement to do justice, be fair, and ensure community safety.

The murder of Stephen Lawrence seemed to demonstrate the emptiness of the claim that the police and criminal justice system offered equal protection irrespective of race or ethnic origin. The main suspects – who had a history of extreme violence – committed a brutal murder and were then able to get away with it with impunity. Despite the exertion of a great amount of effort, police investigators were unable to collect sufficient evidence to put a case before the court. The Lawrence Inquiry's acknowledgment that the initial investigation was "marred by a combination of professional incompetence, institutional racism, and a failure of leadership by senior officers" was symbolically important (Macpherson, 1999: 46.1). Even more significant was the empirical and documentary evidence that the Lawrence Inquiry unearthed and exposed to public view. As Jack Straw, the Home Secretary, commented in presenting the Inquiry report to the House of Commons, it had "opened all our eyes to what it is to be black or Asian in Britain today." A renewed commitment to tackling racist crime, to ensuring that ethnic minority communities are properly served and protected, and to a new era of "antiracist policing" are grounds for optimism about the future. Stephen Lawrence will be remembered as one of at least ninety victims of racist murder over the past four decades in Britain. But if his death is to mean more than this, police protection and their use of coercive powers must now be fair, accountable, transparent, and respect the fundamental human rights to life, liberty, and security of the person.

Conclusion

The explicitly racist murders that have occurred in recent years in Britain, continental Europe, and North America have extended the spectrum of topics in the "race and crime debate" and have focused public attention on "white-on-minority" violence in its most extreme form. What seems clear from the research evidence from England and Wales, however, is that explicitly racist murder is the most extreme tip of an iceberg comprised of less serious instances of violence, and instances in which the presence and relevance of racism may be less clear-cut. This research evidence suggests a range of future directions for scholarship in this area.

First, some analytical groundwork is required to establish the boundaries of the problem of racist violence. There are some cases in which both the extreme levels of violence and the explicitness of racist ideology render categorization unproblematic. However, there also are many thousands of instances of such conduct as intimidation, verbal abuse, and vandalism, which may terrorize individuals and communities, which are not so readily recognized by law enforcement agencies or commentators as "violence" (Jacobs and Potter, 1998; cf. Bowling, 1993a). Similarly, there are instances in which questions of racist motivation or causation are troubled by the existence of other motives or explanations. It is perhaps too much to expect these conceptual issues to be resolved with any great finality, but they do require continued examination and exploration.

Second, there is a clear need to develop quantitative and qualitative techniques to estimate the extent and nature of racist violence at local and regional levels. This chapter has shown, in common with other work in this sphere, that officially recorded instances of racist crime have some limitations, partly the result of the definitional issues mentioned earlier, but compounded by weaknesses in local police and federal recording systems. Alternative methods – using survey technology, secondary analysis of police records, and case studies – offer opportunities to shed light on this problem at both local and national levels. Third, there is a need to develop theories to explain the manifestation of racist violence in specific localities, as well as its extent at a national level. Some theories have been set out above (many of which have been found wanting), but there are surely further lines of inquiry that can be developed.

Finally, there is a need to know more about what works in practice to reduce racist violence. Laws enhancing penalties for hate crimes in the United States and for "racially aggravated offences" in the United Kingdom have been introduced and their use and impact requires close monitoring, especially in the light of the skeptical appraisal of their likely effectiveness (Jacobs and Potter, 1998; Malik, 1999). Alternative sentencing approaches – including those designed to rehabilitate offenders – require close monitoring and evaluation. There also are a range of community-based crime prevention initiatives springing up in a variety of different jurisdictions, including antiracist youth work, educational programs, and the like. It must be hoped that scholars working within the field of "race," ethnicity, and crime will take on this research agenda.

Race, Gender, and Woman Battering

Evan Stark[1]

Introduction

This chapter contributes to an exploration of the themes that drive this volume by analyzing the racial dimensions of woman battering. Part I introduces the problem, defines its scope, differentiates common domestic violence from the pattern of coercive control, and provides an overview of its significance. Drawing on population surveys primarily, Part II summarizes racial differences in the rates of domestic violence as well as in trends, demographics, dynamics, consequences, and in the response to interventions. Part III focuses on explanations for the unique configuration of battering in black couples, contrasting accounts that emphasize family pathology to cultural, historical, and political explanations. The conclusion considers possible sources of resilience and prevention in the black community.

The Scope of the Problem

Defining the Problem. In common parlance, domestic violence, family violence, spouse abuse, and woman battering are used interchangeably to refer to physical assaults in a family setting. Domestic violence statutes differ from state to state in which types of relationships and which types of violence they cover, although they universally focus on discrete acts of harm.[2] In fact,

---

[1] Evan Stark, MSW, Ph.D. is Associate Professor, Graduate Department of Public Administration, Rutgers University-Newark and Director of the school's Masters in Public Health program.

[2] Legal definitions of violence may include acts intended to cause physical pain or injury, threats (Connecticut's Domestic Violence Response Act), or acts against property (Seattle's Municipal Code), and may focus on the age of cohabitants (Connecticut) and on the fact, status, and length of cohabitation and range from present cohabitants only (Municipal Code, Richmond, VA) through all persons who are "social partners" (Seattle).

Please send comments to: 11 Forest Trail, Woodbridge, CT 06525, e-mail: EDS203@juno.com

in most relationships domestic violence is ongoing, not episodic, and is not literally "domestic," because most victims are not married to and/or living with the persons who are hurting them. More important, the most devastating context of domestic violence involves a pattern of coercion and control where the physical assaults prohibited by law may be relatively minor.

National Family Violence Surveys reveal that battered wives are assaulted an average of three times annually (Straus et al., 1980), although abuse of black victims may be somewhat less frequent (Lockhart, 1987). Between 25 percent and 30 percent of all abused women suffer "serial victimization," many are beaten at least once a week (Klaus and Rand, 1984), and 10 percent of batterers attack their partner an average of sixty times per year (Straus, 1996). In my forensic practice, I regularly encounter women who have been assaulted hundreds of times. Men who abuse one partner, meanwhile, often abuse others as well (Buzawa et al., 1999).

Once considered a "family" problem, it is now clear that domestic violence affects separated women much more often than married or divorced women (Bachman and Salzman, 1995) and that domestic violence is common in "dating" relationships (West, 1995) and among same-sex as well as heterosexual couples (Ricks et al., 2000).[3] Survey data also indicate that women as well as men assault their partners, although women are much more frequently injured by domestic assaults and are more likely to consider partner assault a "crime" (Straus et al., 1980; Straus and Gelles, 1986; Bachman and Salzman, 1995).

If the focus on discrete episodes and on "families" is misleading, so is the emphasis on violence. Many relationships are characterized by simple domestic assault, where one or both partners use varying degrees of physical force to settle disagreements; in many other situations, abuse occurs as part of a general pattern of violence and criminality (Buzawa et al., 1999). Women may be hurt more frequently than men in these situations, but they may also see fighting as a positive means to resolve power differences.[4] Importantly, however, there is mounting evidence that a large proportion of domestic violence cases involve what feminists call *woman battering*,[5] where

---

[3] Confusion arose about whether battering was limited to families or to violence and whether women and men were equally assaultive because the dominant research model identified the family as the major source of tension, only measured force used in intact couples, limited itself to physical abuse used to resolve conflicts, and equated assaults with defensive acts (Straus et al., 1980; Gelles, 1997).

[4] In inner-city neighborhoods, females learn that "fighting" is a preferred means to resolve tensions, even if you "lose," because the alternative may involve being exploited or "dissed."

[5] In contrast to the *family violence model*, the *feminist model* views sexual inequalities as the source of tension; domestic violence is said to exemplify "violence against women" (along with rape or sexual harassment, for example); and physical abuse is paired with nonviolent forms of male domination rather than with violence by other family members (Breines and Gordon, 1983; Browne, 1987; Stark and Flitcraft, 1996; Dobash and Dobash, 1979; 1992; Jones and Schecter, 1992).

frequent or routine but generally low-level physical abuse is supplemented by a broad spectrum of strategies to dominate partners and deprive them of basic liberties (Stark and Flitcraft, 1986; Jones and Schecter, 1992; Jones, 1994). In addition to physical and sexual assault, this pattern of "coercive control" typically includes some combination of sexual assault or coercion, threats, psychological degradation, the destruction of property, child abuse or neglect, stalking, isolation from friends and family, and a pattern of control over key aspects of the victim's life, including money, food, sexuality, physical appearance, social life, transportation, work, religion, and access to help (Stark, 1996). For example, in a sample of victims ($N = 118$) whose partners were arrested for domestic violence, 38 percent reported they were not free to come and go as they pleased, 45.8 percent were denied access to social support, 58.5 percent were denied access to money, and 46 percent experienced between three and fifteen other restrictions in their daily routines (Buzawa et al., 1999). Conversely, abused women in a representative sample of 734 AFDC recipients in Massachusetts were eight times more likely than nonabused women to report that a current or former boyfriend would not let them go to school or work (16 percent versus 2 percent) (Allard et al., 1997). Where common couple violence is often sporadic and may occur in response to particular family stressors, the type of battering that involves coercive control is an *ongoing* process of subjugation, unilaterally initiated by males without the provocation of situational conflicts or external stressors.[6]

Although strategies of coercive control violate rights that are critical to freedom, personal development, and citizenship, this pattern has no legal standing and has yet to be empirically differentiated from its less dramatic counterparts. As a result, evidence on racial dimensions of domestic violence subsumes situations in which couples "fight" – and may view their use of force as legitimate – where one partner uses violence primarily to hurt his partner physically, and the pattern of domination known as coercive control.

The Domestic Violence Revolution. Evidence about partner abuse has been accumulating since the late 1960s, when Parnas (1967) reported that Chicago police received more calls regarding "domestics" than were received for murder, aggravated assault, and all other serious crimes combined. These were typically treated as "nuisance" calls, however, and little was done to remedy the problem (Buzawa and Buzawa, 1990). Noninterference was a particular problem in communities of color, where, according to

---

[6] In one sample 77 percent of assaults were not preceded by verbal disputes (Gayford, 1975). Indeed, 10 percent of battered women are beaten in their sleep (Eisenberg and Micklow, cited in Okun, 1986).

Hawkins (1987), police viewed blacks as "normal primitives" who accepted violence and were indifferent to its consequences.

The true significance of woman battering only became clear in the 1970s, after Erin Pizzey (1974) and immigrant women of color living in the Chiswick section of London opened the first modern battered woman's shelter. The years since have witnessed a virtual revolution in how society deals with the problem, prompted largely by the battered women's movement and its supporters (Dobash and Dobash, 1992). Whether or how significantly the resulting changes have reduced partner violence is a matter of debate. Nevertheless, appreciation of this conspicuous form of subjugating women has helped to demystify conventional gender roles and given new poignancy to the critique of sexual inequality.

As Alice Walker dramatized in *The Color Purple*, just yesterday, historically speaking, the use of force to "discipline" female partners was widely considered a male prerogative. Today, this same behavior constitutes a "domestic violence" crime for which more than one million persons are arrested annually. In the past, even when it was censored by community leaders or extended family members, abusive behavior was "just life." Today, millions of women and children utilize community-based shelters or seek court orders to protect themselves from abusive men. Over $1 billion have been invested to research domestic violence and ensure that this formerly "private trouble" is treated appropriately. The numbers justify this investment. With an estimated prevalence of somewhere between 20 and 30 percent of the female population, domestic violence is the major cause of injury for which women seek medical attention (Stark and Flitcraft, 1996); and a significant contributor to child abuse, divorce, and a broad range of additional health, behavioral, and mental health problems (Jaffe, Wolfe, and Wilson, 1990; Stark and Flitcraft, 1996; Buzawa and Buzawa, 1990; Waits, 1990; Levinger, 1965).

The Importance of Domestic Violence for Blacks. Battering would significantly affect black Americans even if they were not overrepresented among the most vulnerable populations. In fact, battering by a partner is the leading cause of death among black women under age forty-five and a major cause of their physical injury, disability, homelessness, unemployment, suicidality, unwanted pregnancy, substance abuse, and AIDS (Stark, 1990; Stark and Flitcraft, 1996). The lives of black men are also threatened by their uncritical participation in battering. Approximately 20 percent of black male deaths due to homicide originate in partner assault (Stark, 1990) and hundreds of thousands of black men are arrested each year for domestic violence crimes. Among children exposed to domestic violence, a significant proportion – estimates range of 30 percent to 90 percent – may suffer physical, psychological, and developmental problems (Stark and Flitcraft, 1990; Randolf and Conkle, 1993; Jaffe, Wolffe, and Wilson, 1990). Battering is the precipitant of half of all child maltreatment and an even higher percentage of child homicides (Stark and Flitcraft, 1988; 1996). Thousands of black women and teens are arrested each year because they have retaliated violently to battering. Indeed, Crenshaw (1994) reports that 63 percent of all young men between the ages of eleven and twenty who are imprisoned for homicide have killed their mothers' batterers. Many of these young men are black. Countless numbers of black women have been compelled to crime in an abusive relationship (Richie, 1996).

Black men assault or kill other men more frequently than they do their partners. But battering may be even more devastating than stranger assaults, AIDS, or comparable health or criminal justice problems. Although there are no racial comparisons reported, rates of injury for female victims were greater for violence by an intimate (52 percent) than by a stranger (20 percent), an acquaintance or friend (26 percent), or another relative (38 percent) (Bachman and Salzman, 1995; Sanchez-Hucles and Dutton, 1999). The economic consequences of domestic violence are estimated to be 15 percent of the total crime costs (Miller, Cohen, and Wiersema, 1996), far greater than the proportion of total crime attributed to domestic violence (Bachman, 1994; Perkins and Klaus, 1996; Sanchez-Hucles and Dutton, 1999). Controversy surrounds whether woman battering is more common among blacks than whites, whether it is primarily a lower-class phenomenon, or whether psychological, cultural, or sociopolitical factors best explain why men batter women or why women become trapped with abusive men. But one thing is starkly clear. Alongside its health consequences and the economic burden battering places on the service system, there is another profound cost. Because of its coercive elements, the battering of black women severely curtails their liberty to develop and autonomously employ their capacities on their own behalf or on behalf of their families, communities and the economy.

Given the "news" about domestic violence, black leaders have been surprisingly silent (Asbury, 1987; Sanchez-Hucles and Dutton, 1999). Black-on-black violence and "broken" ghetto families have been recurrent themes in public dialogue about race in America, particularly in debates about welfare reform and criminal justice policy (Wilson, 1987; Wilson and Wicquant, 1989). Yet, this discussion concerns males attacking other males and the associated reform proposals, such as those for job or school programs, are designed to uplift males almost exclusively (Wilson, 1987). Black feminists are a marked exception to the neglect of domestic violence. Maya Angelou, Frances Beale, Flo Kennedy, Audre Lorde, Haki Madabutti, Toni Morrison, Barbara Smith, Angela Davis, Barbara Omalde, Jill Nelson, Alice Walker, and particularly bell hooks provide incisive critiques of sexual violence by black men. Still, Beth Richie's pathbreaking study *Compelled to Crime* (1996) is the only major work on black battered women based on primary research.

To victims of battering, neglect of the problem in discussions of violence is tantamount to denying its significance.

Complimenting the relative silence among black leaders is the neglect of racial issues by domestic violence specialists (Report of the Task Force, 1996).[7] Evidence about domestic violence comes primarily from student samples, convenience samples of volunteer subjects, and random population surveys. But blacks have been historically underrepresented at the major universities where domestic violence research is conducted, are often not present in sufficient numbers to include in population studies, and are reluctant to volunteer for research experiments, in part because of a history of misuse as research subjects (Cannon et al., 1988). Even where members of nonmajority groups are included in research samples, however, their proportion in the study group or the size of the study group may be too small to support comparisons. Other studies fail to analyze race and ethnicity separately or to report the racial composition of the study population (Report of the Task Force, 1993). In these instances, "color blindness" works to conceal the unique constellation of culture and psychology that defines the experiences of black victims.[8] By contrast, official statistics elevate domestic violence in communities of color to "near mythic proportions" because blacks utilize public agencies more frequently than whites (Root, 1996). The sexist norms at the root of battering transcend race. Still, generalizations about battering based on nonblack or service populations fail to capture the unique contribution of racial dynamics. One result is that interventions based on these generalizations are often insensitive to the needs of black battered women or their partners as well as to the unique cultural strains that could mobilize blacks behind norms of just and equal partnerships. An even more nuanced account is needed once differences in social class, ethnicity, or family experiences among blacks are considered alongside race.

Part Two: Racial Dimensions of Battering

Evidence on Racial Differences. The studies summarized in this section have reached varying and in some cases contradictory conclusions about such basic questions as how common domestic violence is among blacks, whether it is more common among blacks than whites, whether domestic violence is more common in middle- or lower-class relationships, whether

---

[7] The literature on sexual assault is similarly biased. For example, Neville and Pugh (1997) found that fewer than 3 percent ($N = 7$) of the 277 psychological research articles published between 1987 and 1994 included an analysis of African-American women.

[8] Publicity given to affluent and well-known victims to whom politicians and the media are likely to pay attention can obscure the special problems faced by low-income and minority women.

domestic violence among blacks is increasing or decreasing, whether injury or psychosocial problems are its most significant consequence, and whether criminal justice intervention has been effective in reducing domestic violence among blacks.

Racial Comparisons. Using a well-established instrument called the Conflict Tactics Scale (CTS), a National Family Violence Survey in 1976 asked couples what tactics they used when they had arguments. Relatively few black families were included ($n = 147$), but the results were nonetheless surprising. African Americans reported that they used violence to resolve conflicts nearly four times as often as did whites (Hampton and Gelles, 1994). Using a more representative sample of 580 nonwhite families, a second National Family Violence Survey (1985) reported less dramatic racial differences. Approximately 8 percent of black women had been severely assaulted at least once during the year, more than twice the percentage of white women, and black women suffered 1.23 times as much "minor" violence. These findings echoed results of a Harris Poll of Kentucky Housewives (Schulman, 1979; Hampton and Gelles, 1994).[9] Similarly, a Bureau of Justice Statistics Report found that, on average, for each year between 1992 and 1996, about 12 per 1,000 black women experienced violence by an intimate compared to about 8 per 1,000 white women (Greenfeld et al., 1998).[10] But the National Crime Victims Survey (NCVS), designed to measure only violent acts considered criminal by their victims, found no significant differences in domestic violence among non-Hispanic whites, Hispanics, and African Americans (Bachman, 1994).

Significant racial differences were also reported for violence committed *by* black women. Where white women had the lowest rates of violence against their husbands (115 per 1,000), black women had the highest rates (207 per 1,000), with Hispanic women falling in the middle (Hampton and Gelles, 1994; Campbell, Masake, and Torres, 1997). The same surveys also showed that a third of all couples experienced one or more episodes of partner violence during their marriage, although the results for blacks were not reported separately. In sum, domestic violence appears to be 1.5 to 2 times more common among blacks than whites and affects a third or more of all black couples.[11]

[9] Interestingly, the national population survey found there were no differences in reported rates of child abuse, although blacks are overrepresented in child abuse reports.

[10] Because the NCVS interviews focus on crimes and are conducted in victim's homes, they exclude both the most serious cases (which women may be reluctant to describe in front of their partners) and the vast majority of nonserious assaults that may not be considered "crimes" by victims.

[11] Because the surveys measure violent acts committed during the year of the interview as well as whether family members have "ever" been abused, it is impossible to estimate either the

The Role of Social Class. What accounts for the apparent racial disparities in domestic violence? Undoubtedly, greater economic disadvantage among blacks is an important factor. The Kentucky Harris Poll (Schulman, 1979) reported relatively small class differences in domestic violence. By contrast, the Bureau of Justice Statistics Report (Greenfeld et al., 1998) found that women in households with incomes below $7,500 reported nonlethal domestic violence ten times more often than those with incomes of $75,000 or more. Since blacks are disproportionately poor and lower-income families are more prone to report domestic violence, their higher rates may reflect class rather than racial differences.[12] Indeed, where social class has been held constant, racial disparities in domestic violence victimization have diminished, disappeared, or actually been reversed (Bachman, 1994; Bachman and Salzman, 1995; Kantor, Jasinski, and Aldarando, 1994), although they persist for perpetrators (Perkins and Klaus, 1996). Several studies specifically designed to weigh the influence of social class have found virtually identical rates of violence against wives in black and white couples in similar social classes (Lockhart and White, 1991; Cambell, Masake, and Torres, 1997). Meanwhile, among a representative sample of AFDC recipients in Massachusetts, black women were significantly less likely than white women to report they had been abused (Allard, Colten, Albelda, and Cosenza, 1997).

An intriguing if counterintuitive finding is that interpersonal violence may be more common among middle-class rather than low-income black families. A survey of marital violence experienced by 307 black and white women across three social class positions reported that there were no racial differences in the overall proportion of abused women, but that black middle-class women experienced more violence than either their white counterparts or lower-class and upper-class black women. Although more middle-class black than white women reported abuse, white couples reported more frequent assaults than blacks (Lockhart, 1987; Lockhart and White, 1989). By contrast, Casenave and Straus (1979) found that wife abuse was less common among middle-income African Americans than middle-income European Americans.[13]

incidence (new cases annually) or the prevalence (couples currently at risk) of domestic violence, statistics that are key to evaluating interventions.

[12] Even so, race remains important, since racial discrimination is an important source of low wages and unequal job opportunities experienced by blacks.

[13] While self-reported class differences among blacks may be important, class comparisons involving blacks and whites should be interpreted cautiously. Social class in the United States is typically measured by income alone rather than by a composite of occupation, social status, and, perhaps most important, "wealth" (e.g., property, stock, savings, inheritance, etc.). Thus, blacks and whites with similar incomes may nonetheless differ dramatically in their overall social position.

Domestic Violence Trends Among Blacks. Richard Gelles (1997) reports that there have been significant declines in both family homicides and in "wife-beating" over the past two decades, largely due to effective intervention. For example, U.S. Department of Justice (1994) data indicate an 18 percent decline in the rate of spousal homicides by husbands between 1976 and 1992. During this same period, according to Gelles (1997), "wife-beating" decreased from 38 per 1,000 women (in 1976) to 19 per 1000 (in 1992), a 48 percent decline. If Gelles is right, an estimated six hundred thousand fewer women were victimized by their partners in 1992 than in 1976, when the domestic violence revolution began.

Closer examination reveals that a dramatic decline in the spousal homicide rate among blacks largely accounts for the overall decrease in spousal homicide (which actually began in 1980). Blacks account for 43.7 percent of the homicides committed by family members and for 45.6 percent of all spousal homicide victims, a far higher ratio of homicide to proportion of the population than among whites (Mercy and Saltzman, 1989). According to FBI statistics, between 1976 and 1985, spousal homicide rates among whites remained virtually unchanged. By contrast, the homicide rate for black husbands declined 52.0 percent (from 12.7 to 6.1 per 100,000) and for black wives declined by 45.8 percent (from 9.6 to 5.2 per 100,000). Since a high proportion of spousal homicide is the culmination of ongoing domestic violence, these changes reflect a significant decline in the most severe acts of domestic violence by blacks. Indeed, by the second Family Violence Survey, the severest forms of husband-wife violence had declined more sharply among black than white couples (Gelles and Straus, 1988; Hampton et al., 1989; Gelles, 1997).

Optimism based on these statistics may be premature, however. To start, the 18 percent decline in homicides by husbands since 1976 seems unimpressive compared to the much greater decline in all homicides during the same period, as much as 50 percent in the major cities (Morgenthau, 1995) where blacks live in large numbers.[14] Moreover, setting domestic homicides against the background of overall homicide rates reveals a seeming paradox: although the proportion of male murder victims killed by their wives declined during the domestic violence revolution (i.e., between 1977 and 1992), the proportion of female murder victims killed by husbands actually increased from 54 percent to 70 percent (Valente, 1995). This suggests that interventions introduced during this period protected black males far more than they did females. This might be true, for example, if making shelters

---

[14] For example, between 1992 and 1997, homicides declined 64.3 percent in New York City, 47.5 percent in Los Angeles, 47.5 percent in Houston, and 49.6 percent in San Francisco (cited in Massing, M., "The Blue Revolution," *New York Review of Books*, V. XLV, No. 18, Nov. 19, 1998, p. 33).

or other protections available to black battered women gave them a viable alternative to violent retaliation.

The claim that nonfatal domestic violence is declining is suspect as well. The survey researchers based this conclusion only on "severe abuse," such as repeat punching with a fist, kicking, biting, beatings, and attacks with knives and guns. When so-called minor violent acts are included, such as throwing something at a partner, pushing, grabbing, shoving, and slapping, for instance, there is a statistically insignificant decline in domestic violence between 1976 and 1985 and a dramatic increase afterward. In fact, by 1992, overall domestic violence committed by husbands against wives had returned to the level in 1976. These trends were not calculated separately for blacks. But, it is likely that, *while the severest forms of domestic violence declined significantly among blacks after 1976, overall levels have changed little if at all.*

These trends may reflect the fact that interventions target severe domestic violence, but do little to regulate minor acts of abuse. The law prohibits *all* domestic violence. But as a practical matter, the severity of assault guides decisions to arrest or prosecute domestic violence offenders, provide protection for victims, or admit women to shelters (Loseke, 1992; Stark and Flitcraft, 1986; Buzawa and Buzawa, 1996). The unfortunate fact is that, while the types of domestic violence that have increased are unlikely to cause serious injury, when they become routine, they provide the substructure of coercive control, the most serious form of battering.

Racial Dynamics of Battering. What little research there is on dynamics suggests important racial differences in the pattern of coercive control. When they enter abusive relationships, white women are already more isolated than black women, less likely to be employed, and are more likely to expect their partner will take care of them (Richie, 1996). White offenders exploit this situation by eliciting loyalty and exacerbating isolation and material and personal dependence. They forbid partners to work, deny them money, and control how they cook, clean, or care for children (Asbury, 1987). The black batterer is more likely to exploit the woman's role as economic "provider," particularly in "middle-class" relationships. Black batterers are more flexible about housework and children than whites, even assuming certain "homemaking" functions (Hampton, 1987). Instead of preventing his partner from working, the black batterer is more likely to police her work outside the home and restrict her activities inside. White victims often experience their extended family as a trap from which they want to escape (Richie, 1996). But multigenerational, extended family and friendship networks are particularly important for low-income black women (McAdoo, 1979). As a result, family boundary issues are a common source of combat in black couples (Hampton, 1987) and isolation from family and extended kin networks is a major point of humiliation.[15] My black clients have been forbidden to attend church, attend family functions, or to socialize at or after work. They have been forced to wear beepers, to ask permission to make phone calls or send holiday cards and had their phone calls monitored. Obsessive jealousy, or disagreements about drugs or money frequently complement isolation in these relationships. The abusive husband of a Jamaican woman, one of the most feared "dreds" in Hartford, hid in a tree outside her house after they separated and jumped down when she tried to leave. Black women who are the sole source of income for their families receive public assistance and those who supplement their income off the books are particularly vulnerable to the intimidation tactics used by batterers. But so are middle-class black women who can exhaust their psychic resources trying to keep their chaotic personal life a secret. Because of the greater importance of family supports for black women, they are more likely than whites to respond dramatically to social isolation, with suicide attempts for example, and are less likely to medicate their stress with substances that jeopardize their children, family ties, and/or their employability. Conversely, both work and religion are common realms of autonomy for black women, "safety zones" whose invasion frequently precipitates a lethal crisis in battering relationships.

What Are the Major Consequences of Domestic Violence for Blacks?
Following from the near-universal emphasis on physical assault in abusive relationships, the most commonly cited outcome of domestic violence is physical injury. Black women are more likely than whites to seek assistance for injuries related to domestic violence. A randomized review of over thirty-five hundred medical records at Yale-New Haven Hospital concluded that almost one woman in five (18.7 percent) who visited the emergency room with an injury had been assaulted by a partner, making domestic violence the leading cause of injury for which women sought medical attention. Black women comprised 21 percent of the subjects in this study, but constituted over half (51 percent) of the women with injuries that resulted from battering (Stark and Flitcraft, 1996).

Injury is an important outcome of domestic violence throughout the life-course for black women. Young married women in their twenties and early thirties are at highest risk. But, injuries caused by domestic violence are significant among young girls as well as older women. For example, in a Philadelphia emergency department comprised largely of black patients, domestic violence caused 34 percent of the injuries to girls aged sixteen to eighteen and 18 percent of the injuries to women over age sixty-one

---

[15] Family structures also may become the context for entrapping a partner. In my caseload, it is common for a young black woman to move to her boyfriend's house and for him to enlist his family, including his mother, in surveillance and control.

(McLeer and Anwar, 1989). These populations fall between the cracks of existing services.

Sexual assault is another common experience in battering relationships. Battering is the context for a third of all rapes and for half of the rapes to women over thirty, a group in which black women are disproportionately represented (Stark and Flitcraft, 1996). Both the pattern of domestic violence injuries – their concentration on the face, breast, and abdomen, for instance – and their disproportionate occurrence during pregnancy – suggest the sexual origin of much abuse (Stark and Flitcraft, 1996). For black women, sexual exploitation by an intimate has particular significance, evoking the shame of subjugation to a white master (Richie, 1996).

Despite its association with injury, studies show that life-threatening acts of male violence are the exception rather than the rule in battering relationships (Straus and Gelles, 1986; Stark and Flitcraft, 1996). Victims of domestic violence are more likely to be injured than victims of other crimes reported to the National Crime Victim's Survey (Lentzer and DeBarry, 1980). Even among battered women who came to an emergency room complaining of injury, however, only 2 percent required hospitalization, the same rate as women who fall in the home (Stark and Flitcraft, 1996). What is distinctive about battering is the frequency of assault and the cumulative terror induced by chronic physical intimidation.

The Yale hospital studies revealed that, subsequent to abuse, an inner-city population of battered women were five times more likely to attempt suicide than nonbattered women; fifteen times more likely to abuse alcohol; nine times more likely to abuse drugs; six times more likely to report child abuse; and three times more likely to be diagnosed as "depressed" or psychotic. These outcomes were so common that Stark and Flitcraft (1996) estimated that 45 percent of drug and alcohol use among women resulted from domestic violence as well as 45 percent of child abuse, almost a third of all female suicide attempts, and significant percentages of female ("family") homelessness, HIV disease, and mental illness (Stark and Flitcraft, 1996). Among a nationally representative probability sample of HIV-infected adults, for instance, 18.5 percent of black non-Hispanic women, 18.1 percent of the Hispanic women, and 26 percent of the white, non-Hispanic women were abused (Zierler et al., 2000). The fact that black women in the general population have lower rates of these problems than white women underlines the importance of abuse in their lives. Moreover, it is now clear that the chronic stress associated with coercion and control elicits many of these problems rather than the "trauma" of physical abuse.

Psychological Consequences: Battered Woman's Syndrome. The most widely cited psychological outcome of domestic violence is "battered woman's syndrome," a nearly disabling depressive condition closely related to the posttraumatic stress disorders (PTSD) found among combat veterans and victims of stranger rape (Herman, 1992). According to Lenore Walker (1979, 1984, 1989), battered woman's syndrome is elicited by "cycles of violence" consisting of tension buildup, an explosive episode of severe assault, and a "honeymoon" phase when the batterer apologizes. Women who stay with the abusive partner because they mistakenly believe he will change are revictimized until they learn that escape is futile, concentrate on survival, fail to seek help or accept it when offered, and suffer a range of cognitive, emotional, and behavioral deficits called "learned helplessness" (Walker, 1989).

Battered woman's syndrome is both a significant consequence of domestic violence and a potent explanation for why some women get entrapped in abusive relationships, develop complex psychosocial problems, fail to report battering, and strike out violently in situations in which an outsider sees viable options. Some courts require evidence of the syndrome to prove battering has occurred and expert testimony on the syndrome has been widely used to mitigate criminal charges of homicide or other crimes (Downs, 1996).

Nevertheless, battered woman's syndrome affords limited insight into the causes, dynamics, or consequences of battering among blacks. Focusing on the offender as the source of a victim's problems counteracts a cultural tendency to hold women accountable when things go wrong in black families.[16] Still, battered woman's syndrome is probably uncommon among black women, offers a poor explanation for why they "stay" with abusive men, and can actually damage their prospects in criminal proceedings.

Initially developed from a study of largely white, middle-class volunteers, Walker's model has never been validated in a random population sample or in a sample of women of color. Research suggests the "cycle of violence" characterizes only 14 percent of abusive relationships (Dobash and Dobash, 1984) and that "learned helplessness" is equally atypical. Most battered women *do* separate from abusive partners, often multiple times, *do* seek help aggressively (as hospital data and shelter utilization indicate), and are active problem solvers, exhibiting "heightened reason" (Blackman, 1989) rather than cognitive deficits. Compared to victims of assault by strangers or acquaintances, for instance, battered women are as likely to report assaults that cause injury to police and more likely to report assaults where no injury occurred (Bachman and Salzman, 1995).

In court settings, Walker's model reduces an extremely complex interpersonal dynamic to a one-dimensional and stigmatizing psychological formula

---

[16] By contrast, Thompson and West (cited by Neville and Pugh, 1997) found that African-American men and women were sensitive to rape-related issues and placed minimal blame for the assault on victims/survivors.

of victimization. Adapting battered woman's syndrome as the standard for abuse is particularly harmful because black females are more likely than white women to fall outside its purview (Allard, 1991; Ammons, 1995). Courts have denied the battered woman's defense to victims who have not suffered the severe violence associated with "traumatic" reactions.[17] Moreover, application of the syndrome privileges victims who are unassertive, passive, and dependent in the face of oppression, discounting the experiences of women who work outside the home, have a criminal history, respond violently to abuse, or who are otherwise assertive or independent.[18] Although black women are disproportionately represented in the latter group, because of prevailing stereotypes, they are more likely to be perceived as aggressive even when they present a dependent profile.

Why do Battering Relationships Endure? Black women generally seek help aggressively. But they may be less likely than white women to leave abusive partners or to report assaults where the assailant is an acquaintance or intimate (Neville and Pugh, 1997). A compelling explanation of "why women stay" highlights some combination of economic disadvantage, religious prescriptions, emotional ambivalence, and sexist cultural beliefs holding that a woman is "nothing" without a man. Still, millions of black women facing these same constraints successfully end bad relationships. Many black women rationalize partner violence by pointing to the special stressors faced by black men. The black battered women Richie (1996) interviewed at Riker's Island often felt sorry for the men in their lives, as their mothers had for their abusive fathers, even to the point of tolerating their violence. Other black women accept abusive partners because they cherish nonabusive facets of the relationship. Still others hesitate to call police because they feel responsible for the abuse, are involved in criminal activity themselves, because they interpret calling police as a betrayal of community values, because they believe that calling will be ineffective, as it has been historically, or because they fear police will overrespond, leading to consequences for their partner that are far more severe than they believe his acts warrant. Important, too, is a deeply ingrained conservative belief in the

---

[17] bell hooks (1989) argues that, in setting apart a distinct class of women who have been repeatedly abused, the term "battered woman" simultaneously stigmatizes a class of victims and discounts the significance of being hit a single time, as she was by a male partner. We share hooks's view that a calculus of physical harms is an inappropriate measure of abuse, but juxtapose this to a model where basic liberties are denied, not to a model in which abuse is less frequent.

[18] In a study of predominantly African-American women charged with homicide, Mann (1996) argues that their history of prior arrests for violence excludes them from a defense based on battered woman's syndrome and "belies a suggestion that they were either helpless or afraid of their victims" (1996: 171). She admits, however, that in 84 percent of the cases, the victim's actions precipitated his death.

black community, reinforced by the church, that the integrity of the family unit comes before personal health and safety.

Ultimately, however, it is the batterer's continued access to his partner that determines whether abuse will continue, not a woman's decisions to leave or stay. This is why fewer than half (42.8 percent) of domestic violence arrests involve currently married or living together partners (Buzawa et al., 1996).

Black Female Suicidality: An Illustration of Coercive Control

Black women frequently react to coercive control by developing somatic complaints, depression, low self-esteem, or other indirect ways to express fear and rage, feelings that could be life-threatening if expressed directly. When these defense mechanisms fail, suicidality is a common result, a situation I call "control in the context of no control."[19]

Reviewing the complete medical records of women identified at an inner-city hospital as having attempted suicide in a single year ($N = 176$), Stark and Flitcraft (1995) reported that 29.5 percent ($N = 52$) of the women were battered. But, while 22 percent of the white women who attempted suicide ($N = 28$) were battered, 48.8 percent of the black women ($N = 22$) in the sample were battered ($p < .001$). In other words, half of all black women who attempted suicide did so in the context of ongoing abuse, making abuse the single most important cause of suicidality among black women. The contribution of institutional neglect to this pattern is illustrated by another dramatic finding: 36.5 percent ($N = 19$) of the battered women who attempted suicide had visited the hospital with a complaint attributable to abuse on the same day as their attempt.

The Response to Services. Rooted in an extensive network of criminal justice, legal, and community-based services, the societal response to domestic violence highlights *safety* for victims and *accountability* for perpetrators. The battered women's movement also emphasizes *empowerment*, that is, enhancing a victim's autonomy and her capacity to resist abuse in the future, although this aim is not universally shared (Fagan, 1996).

Arrest and prosecution are the primary mechanisms for ensuring offender accountability. Despite a dearth of resources to implement these reforms, police in most jurisdictions are mandated to arrest domestic violence offenders and numerous cities now host prosecutorial and court

---

[19] Black females have *relatively low* rates of suicide (Earls et al., 1991; Thompson and Peebles-Wilkins, 1992). Paradoxically, the rate of *suicide attempts* has been rising sharply among young black women (Garrison et al., 1993), possibly in response to battering.

units specializing in domestic violence (Buzawa et al., 1999). Because of mandatory arrest policies, black men and women are now proportionally more likely than whites to be arrested for domestic violence crimes (Bachman and Coker, 1995) and more likely to be charged with aggravated battery versus a less serious crime (Bourg and Stock, 1994). Whether these racial differences reflect continued police bias or the greater prevalence and seriousness of domestic violence among blacks is unclear. Arrest may have a paradoxical effect for some blacks, however, leading to debate about whether the policy should be continued. Arrest initially appeared to significantly reduce the reoccurrence of abuse (Sherman and Berk, 1984). But, in replicating this research, one study indicated that unemployed minority offenders actually increased their violence following arrest, apparently because arrest had little significance for a population with extensive police involvement for other problems and because only 5 percent of these cases were ever prosecuted (Buzawa and Buzawa, 1996; Schmidt and Sherman, 1996; Buzawa et al., 1999).

Given the focus of the law on discrete criminal episodes and the typically low level of domestic violence incidents, the vast majority of domestic violence offenses are charged as misdemeanors and few offenders go to jail. Instead, courts rely heavily on administrative interventions to establish accountability and safety, including batterer's counseling programs lasting anywhere from twelve weeks (in Connecticut) to fifty-two weeks (in California). In the absence of established links between abuse and psychopathology, such programs rely on behavior modification and psychoeducation to convince men to assume responsibility for the violence, monitor their feelings, and to select nonviolent means of expression. Williams (1994) argues that black men are underrepresented in these programs because they fail to take ethnically sensitive approaches. At best, however, weak sanctions and widespread normative support for key facets of controlling women mean that only a small number of batterers stop their abuse as the result of counseling (Davis and Taylor, 1999).

How black battered women perceive criminal justice is unclear. Formerly married black women are more likely to report domestic violence than any other group. And, when violence causes injury, black battered women are also more likely than white women to call police (Bachman and Coker, 1995), often as a negotiating strategy to maintain the relationship. At the same time, if she is married at the time of the assault, the black woman is also most likely to employ retaliatory violence (Neff et al., 1995) and, in turn, is actually more likely than her partner to be charged with aggravated assault (Bourg and Stock, 1994). Given the extent to which black women support their partners, they may interpret repeat abuse as a profound form of betrayal, a posture that echoes the sentiments of Bessie Smith and other classic blues singers (Davis, 1998). Still, while black women resort to domestic violence more frequently than white or Hispanic women, there is no evidence that they employ coercive control.

The Battered Woman's Shelter

Black women played a range of roles in the development of shelters and in their national organizations, although domestic violence was not a priority for traditional black women's organizations, clubs, and church groups. Coley and Beckett (1988) reported that black battered women were more likely than white women to use medical services and less likely to use shelters or other human services. But a well-designed survey of shelter residents in Texas suggested that marital status and income were more important predictors of shelter use by blacks and whites than racial differences in help-seeking (Gondolf, Fisher, and McFerron, Jr., 1988). Black women have less access to shelters than white women. Given the general dearth of services in the South and disinvestment in metropolitan areas where blacks are concentrated, with the marked exception of Washington, DC, states with the highest percentage of blacks have a more severe shortage of domestic violence programs than other areas (Coley and Beckett, 1988).

The early laissez-faire approach in many shelters allowed open expression of racist sentiments by residents. Shelter rules limiting outside contact also placed undue hardships on black women who depended for support on extended family and kin networks (McAdoo, 1979) or who worked outside the home, even if only in the informal economy. But black women were attracted to the early shelter movement by its broad notion of women's empowerment and because the philosophy of collective self-management permitted them to seek safety without assuming the demeaning victim role associated with other human services. Given their tendency to view battering as the combined result of discrimination and individual malevolence, black women strongly identified with the change-oriented model of advocacy. Their social understanding of battering meant that black battered women retained their self-confidence and satisfaction with their lives even though their situation appeared to change little after a shelter stay (Sullivan, 1994; O'Brien, 1995).

As shelters evolved into mainstream service providers, however, many programs shifted their emphasis from advocacy to counseling, adapted a traditional organizational structure, and introduced gatekeeping mechanisms that excluded women who didn't fit the stereotypic victim profile (Loseke, 1992). These changes have negatively affected black battered women. Black women are often resistant to counseling services because their families are unsupportive, they don't understand the benefits of counseling, feel uncomfortable discussing family relationships with strangers, and because they fear that counseling will damage their self-image of being able to cope with their problems (Bingham and Guinyard, 1982; Coley and Becket, 1988). As importantly, black women are skeptical about an approach to service that separates individual from social change, because they recognize how injustice and discrimination frustrate even the best-intentioned problem solving in black communities. Moreover, black battered women may be more committed than white women to making their relationships "work" (Richie, 1996), an attitude that is strongly discouraged in shelters. Conversely, racial stereotypes discourage shelter staff from addressing psychological dimensions of the black woman's experience. This tendency is exacerbated because black women often disclose traumatic incidents without revealing the magnitude of the injury or of their pain, a phenomenon the historian Darlene Clark Hine (1989) views as part of a "culture of dissemblance."

PART III. Explaining the Dynamics of Woman Battering Among Blacks

This section turns from the victims of domestic violence to analyze why black men batter their partners. Apart from unrepresentative clinical samples (Dutton, 1995) and behavioral typologies (Hamberger et al., 1997), there is little research that bears on the immediate causes of abusive behavior, let alone its specific etiology in the black community (but cf. Sanchez-Hucles and Dutton, 1999). Alcohol and a history of violence in childhood correlate with abusive behavior, as they do with violence generally, but neither factor is predictive or causal (Stark and Flitcraft, 1988).[20] Sadly, the only individual factor that consistently predicts battering is whether a partner has already been abusive (O'Leary, 1993).

General explanations of why men batter their partners alternately emphasize the evolutionary role of male dominance (Buss, 1999), psychopathology (Dutton, 1995), cultural and familial supports for violence (Gelles, 1997), patriarchal institutions (Dobash and Dobash, 1979; Stark and Flitcraft, 1996), or these factors in combination (Harway and O'Neil, 1999). Whatever motivates individual abusers, battering became widespread because it was reinforced by a combination of mainstream values that demeaned women and legitimated male control, institutional complicity with offenders, and persistent barriers to sexual equality. As the historian Linda Gordon puts it, "One assault does not make a battered woman. She becomes that because of her socially determined inability to resist or escape" (1990: 258).

The Myth of Black Violence. While not specifically focused on domestic violence, a vast literature speculates about the origin of black-on-black

---

[20] So, for example, at least 70 percent of those exposed to violence in childhood do *not* become abusive adults (Kaufman and Zigler, 1987) and the vast majority of current batterers were not exposed to abuse as children (Stark and Flitcraft, 1984).

violence in general, presumably because young inner-city black males use criminal violence more readily than whites. This supposed "fact" has been linked to unemployment (Wilson, 1987), deficits in culture and character (Kardiner and Ovesy, 1962; Poissaint, 1972), and to a "tangle of pathology" allegedly endemic in families headed by black mothers (Frazier, 1939; Moynihan, 1965). Can these accounts also illuminate woman battering?

Over the years, a range of white writers have advanced the racist stereotype that their "primitive" character, lack of cultural connection, and "supermasculinity" leads black males to excessive criminality and violence, what Hoberman (1997) calls the King Kong principle. Examples of this argument extend from popular literature (e.g., the turn-of-the-century novels by Thomas Dixon) to academic tracks such as *Crime and the Man* (1939) by the physical anthropologist Earnest Albert Hooton and the recent *Crime and Human Nature* (1985) by James Q. Wilson and Richard J. Hernnstein. Such beliefs remain widespread. Thus, in a recent telephone survey, 52 percent of 3,678 whites responded that the words "aggressive or violent" accurately described "most blacks" (Sniderman and Carmines, 1997).

A similar association of black manhood with violence, particularly against women, criminality, and an insatiable sexual virility is also part of the black vernacular (Abraham, cited in Wiggins, 1973; Strong, cited in Wiggins, 1973) and is illustrated today in "gangsta" rap.[21] A sophisticated variant of this argument is the portrait of an "underclass" comprised of black families headed by women, unwed teen moms, and of unemployed young men who use hard drugs and commit violent crimes more frequently than whites (Wilson, 1988). Alvin Poussaint (1972) and Cornell West (1994) claim that self-hatred drives these youth to form a "subculture of violence" that embodies their "walking nihilism." Implicit is a huge characterological divide between middle-class and ghetto males. Thus, for Henry Louis Gates (PBS interview, 1998), street life among black youth is "like a foreign country with which I have nothing in common."

A subtheme in the argument about underclass violence is the responsibility of black mothers for the "tangle of pathology" at its roots (Hernton, 1965; Grier and Cobbs, 1968). E. Franklin Frazier's (1939) description of a "harmful matriarchy"[22] is echoed in Wilson (1988) and Wilson and Wacquant's (1989) claim that the decision by black mothers to remain single deprives their sons of "strong" male models and so contributes to their violence. When the resulting arrests shrink the "marriageable pool" of available men,

---

[21] An interesting counter to this gendering of violence is the New York–based gangsta rap group Bytches with Problems (*The Bytches*, Def Jam, 1991).

[22] To his credit and unlike Moynihan, Frazier (1939) did not define the "matriarchy" as the dominant family form among blacks.

underclass violence and female-headed households are perpetuated across generations.[23]

The prevalence of battering among middle-class blacks discounts its origins in underclass violence. Moreover, even if some ghetto youth are "nihilistic," this impulse is unlikely to motivate the calculating pattern of control evident in battering. In fact, the belief that young black males are more violent or lawless than whites relies on a single source of notoriously biased evidence, the number and relative proportions of black males arrested, convicted, and imprisoned for violent and drug-related crimes (Miller, 1997; Tonry, 1997). Less biased sources of information, interviews with victims of serious crimes and self-report studies for instance, provide an entirely different picture of black violence than arrests (Stark, 1993). For example, the National Crime Victim Surveys (NCVS) revealed that the disproportion between assaults by blacks and whites was much smaller than believed, while the National Youth Survey (NYS) found no racial differences in acts of violence (Elliott et al., 1983; U.S. Department of Justice, 1986). Meanwhile, surveys consistently show a greater proportion of whites than blacks use hard drugs and that whites use hard drugs more frequently (Krisberg et al., 1986; but cf. Brunswick, 1988). Additionally, no major longitudinal study supports the connection between female-headed households and violence or drug abuse by sons. In sum, the myth of black violence cannot explain why black men are more likely than whites to abuse their partners.

Black mothers may certainly help instill sexist attitudes. In their psychoanalytic account of how the caste system shaped gender identity among blacks, Kardiner and Ovesey (1962) described cases in which male violence against partners arose either because black mothers overemphasized the importance of "being a man" or so dominated their households that sons displaced their frustrated dependency and hostility onto other women. The negative influence of abusive husbands/fathers on their sons may be even greater, however. Kardiner and Ovesey (1962) also described families in which a father's cruelty against his wife led the son to distrust his own masculinity, fear his capacity, and to become nonassertive or, conversely, to become hypermasculine (our term) through excessive domination of women. Conversely, black women who witness their fathers abuse their mothers are more likely to be battered as adults (Lockhart and White, 1989) or to idealize white family life (Richie, 1996). Black family structure may also be implicated in the distortion of male identity. Some scholars argue that the extended structure typical of black family life in the South, so important in

[23] Earlier versions of the "marriageable pool" argument emphasized skewed sex ratios due solely to demographic factors such as birth rates, migration, intermarriage, and sex differences in life expectancy (Cox, 1940; Jackson, 1973).

other respects, denied black males "a discourse with which to express pain" (hooks, 1992), a problem commonly associated with battering.

If the myth of black violence cannot explain the origins of battering by black males, its dissemination may make service providers less receptive to black victims. The myth also may aggravate sexual tensions in the black community by reinforcing stereotypes that black men and women hold of themselves and of one another and by legitimating these stereotypes in popular media. To some critics, even the most misogynist examples of male blues, hip hop, or gangsta rap represent what Rose (1994) calls an "oppositional practice." As Robin Kelly (1994) puts it, "In a world where male public powerlessness is often turned inward on women and children, misogyny and stories of sexual conflict are very old examples of the 'price' of being 'baaad'" (1994: 187). Even so, whether put to music or embedded in sociological jargon, the image of black males as nihilistic gunslingers whose only real choice is where to direct their rage feeds hopelessness and cynicism back to the younger generation, and reinforces the lore of the streets – which neither originates among blacks nor is limited to the lower class – that a fast buck, protecting our rears, and dominating women is the bottom line.

Domestic Violence and Racism. A more relevant explanation of battering by black men emphasizes how racial and economic discrimination in the larger society shape sexual politics among blacks. In this view, domestic violence is a maladaptive but compensatory response to social and economic pressures (Hampton and Yung, 1996) that deny black males the opportunities accorded to their white counterparts and breed self-contempt. In short, racism causes battering.

The provider role has simultaneously been esteemed and denied to many black men due to racism, leading to "disrespect" of black males as "idle." In response, some blacks have turned to sexual dominance as an alternative route to manhood. If black women become scapegoats for black frustration and anger at sociocultural barriers, this is because their low social status relative to members of the oppressive majority and the relatively few resources they have to protect themselves make it permissible (and "safe") to hurt them (Burns, 1986; Koss et al., 1994). Thus, according to Sanchez-Hucles and Dutton, "practices of cultural violence and control that have been perpetuated against people of color become internalized and acted out within these communities" (1999: 202). This reaffirmation of male authority helps resolve what is widely believed to be a chronic crisis in black masculinity (Harper, 1996). For black men, gender becomes the modality through which race (and class) are lived (Gilroy, 1993).

The combination of racial oppression and economic exploitation unquestionably gave a peculiar caste to how gender was defined and practiced in the United States, inextricably linking racial, sexual, and economic identities in historically specific constellations that privileged certain expressions of manhood or womanhood and subordinated others. For example, the duality between homemaker and provider that dominated the sex role socialization of Euro-American families for two centuries is not indigenous to black families in the United States. While black families living under slavery or afterward were no less violent than whites, the absence of deeply rooted cultural and institutional supports for male authority in the slave and farm families of the South permitted more egalitarian relationships. The slave economy had no place for a singular "family provider" (Davis, 1973), while black working-class families living under Jim Crow carved out a "social space" that emphasized "collectivist values, mutuality and fellowship" (Kelly, 1994: 36). In this world, black families assumed a level of female socialization to paid employment and male socialization to domesticity and service that afforded males (and females) a range of positive identities that were independent of the subordinate status imposed by racism, class pretensions (including the moralizing of the black middle-class), and wage work.

After World War I, however, as black families became fully "integrated" into an urban, capitalist Euro-American economy, their traditional sex-role flexibility was replaced by a rigid patriarchal pattern supported by the privileged access to industrial jobs, wages, and salaries afforded males. Many black male wage earners reproduced the same internal conflicts evident in white families by peaceably exploiting the domestic labor of women and children. But many of the black males excluded from the mainstream economy chose to fulfill the patriarchal ideal by becoming dominators/controllers. Behind the critique of white economic supremacy as "emasculation," many black women as well as men recognized power over women as a proxy for otherwise unattainable male status (hooks, 1992). A side effect of interpreting economic failure as a loss in masculinity, that is, as femininity, was the hypermasculinity evident in the vernacular, sustained in gangsta rap, and associated with the suppression of so-called female impulses among black males. What started as a compensatory reflex to obstructed opportunity evolved until, regardless of social class, black manhood declared itself through the domination of black women.

Situational Ethics. In a classic article on biracial adoption, Chestang (1972) described another facet of this process, the attempt to ward off the inevitable social inconsistencies that arose from the unrealistic expectation that blacks would be just and fair in the face of systemic injustice, unfairness, and a sense of personal impotence. To buffer the negative consequences of living with these inconsistencies, they developed a "relativistic" morality and situational ethics. But it had the opposite effect, simultaneously reducing the influence of "the transcendent" morality of indigenous cultural institutions such as the church, and rationalizing adaptation to the pragmatics of male dominance. The struggle to maintain a sense of intrinsic worthiness in the face of extrinsically imposed devaluation elicited what Chestang terms a "depreciated character" in which "pride in victory" was replaced by "victory in its pride," "making it" with its defensive inversion, not "being had" or, more immediately, having one's way with others, particularly women.

Recognizing the importance of racial and economic injustice must not mitigate individual responsibility for abuse. As black feminists remind us, blaming sexism on racist victimization supports a worldview wherein black men can deflect attention from the sexual power and privileges accorded to them solely by maleness. In addition, in emphasizing the compensatory dynamics of male domination, the argument minimizes the extent to which battering garners immediate material, sexual, and social benefits for men. From the batterer's vantage, it is women's independence that elicits his abusive behavior, not his social impotence.

It is easy to exaggerate the relative economic advantage of women in the black community (Malveaux, 1988), particularly given the "obligation" they assumed to financially support black men, even if this meant working two or even three paying jobs. Still, the relative material basis for female independence was greater among black women than among white and bolstered their capacity to resist stereotypic family norms, including those enforced through domestic abuse. Nowhere was this more apparent than among the working-class black women who formed the club audience for Bessie Smith and Ma Rainey in the 1920s. As Davis (1999) points out, these performances created a cultural space in which a community of black women regularly transgressed the barriers separating the private and public spheres, owned their sexual desire and their capacity to respond to mistreatment, and thought openly about the ambiguities that attended efforts to achieve self-determination within family and community institutions controlled (if only by proxy) by the puritanical/patriarchal black middle class depicted so beautifully in Toni Morrison's *Paradise*.[24]

The Dialectics of Gender Entrapment. Ironically, the greater independence of black females could also increase their vulnerability to battering, a process brilliantly depicted in Beth Richie's *Compelled to Crime* (1996). Based on the life histories she collected, Richie discovered that, compared to their white and nonbattered black counterparts, African-American battered women shared privileges and values idealized by the black middle class

---

[24] While the classic female blues artists frequently sang about domestic violence by black men, they rarely sang about rape. Apart from the politics surrounding the rape discourse in the 1920s – the rape of black women was identified by middle-class black women in the club movement with white men – Davis (1998) suggests this reflected the reluctance to be seen as helpless or passive victims.

as the foundation of "stable" (presumably nonviolent) families. Contrary to stereotype, the black battered women had been "stars" in their families of origin, critical family members on whom others depended. They had enjoyed high self-esteem, and exhibited identities as competent, resourceful, and potential-filled girls who aspired to "success."

As these "stars" "bumped up against the limits" set by gender and race discrimination at school or at work, however, their extraordinary capacities were displaced into their opposites: modifying their social expectations, they returned to the private sphere and reduced "success" to "making things work" at home, even if this meant supporting abusive partners financially as well as emotionally.[25] Race pride also acted as a trap: the women's sense of cultural solidarity and racial awareness combined with their understanding of how African-American families had been historically discredited to produce an exaggerated sense of loyalty to their abusive partners and a tendency to blame external factors – substance use, racial discrimination, or unemployment, for example – for the violence. What Richie calls "gender entrapment" often included criminal activity at the command of abusive partners, to support their partners, or to express their inexpressible rage at being abused. But there were even worse psychological effects. As Richie observes, "their desperate attempts to make their violent marriages 'work,' lest their identities be completely shattered, led to profoundly immobilizing feelings of failure and self-blame, which resulted in increased vulnerability" (1996: 75).[26]

Richie's unique contribution is to show how women were trapped in abusive relationships by cultural traditions, family patterns, and social psychology in the black mainstream. By contrast, the black women who had avoided abuse were relative "outsiders" who lacked privileges, modeled themselves after mothers who fought back against abusive husbands, and went it alone, holding to a view of femininity and family life that contrasted markedly with the alternately demeaning and idealized images promoted by religion, education, and the media. In sum, even at the level of interpersonal dynamics, the unfortunate truth is that the persistence of battering among blacks owes far less to a distortion of character or family structure, to "nihilistic" violence by males or their living in households from which fathers are absent, than to the opposite tendency to take what Gilroy (1993) calls "the trope of family" as the only site of redemption. Here, the roots of woman battering are sought in such mainstream norms as the tradition of marrying

[25] By contrast, the white women hoped to be taken care of by their partners and so, for them, isolation and dependence were points of vulnerability rather than the consequence of battering.

[26] Richie wisely distinguishes the reality of street and interpersonal violence that *all* of the women in her sample experienced from the ongoing coercion and abuse depicted in the gender entrapment model.

for life and other correlates of religious conservatism, a high tolerance for suffering, the expectation that troubles are inevitable, a propensity to separate without dissolving a relationship or to stay together for the children, and to "understand" rather than to hold husbands accountable for violent behavior.[27]

Conclusions

Domestic violence is more common among blacks than whites, affecting one of every three black women and children in the United States and countless black men. Despite a marked decline in the severest forms of partner violence, a sharp increase in so-called minor acts of abuse may indicate a simultaneous rise in "coercive control," a particularly harmful form of battering that jeopardizes personal freedom. The distinctive pattern of coercive control among blacks includes economic exploitation, isolation from family and friends, and rigid control in the domestic sphere. Love for liberty and equality is difficult to sustain in the next generation when children witness their mothers deprived of both. When the ordinary liberties of so many black women and children are denied, the effectiveness of the whole is impaired.

Battering accounts for a range of health, behavioral, and mental health problems among black women. For example, isolation from sources of support helps account for the higher rates of injury black victims suffer and for their greater propensity to turn their rage against themselves or their partners. A secondary outcome is that black men and women are arrested for domestic violence more often than whites and face more serious charges. The dominant portrait of woman battering, the battered woman's syndrome, and the dominant pattern of intervention with men, perfunctory arrest with few sanctions beyond assignment to counseling, fail to explain abuse among black couples or its outcomes.

Attention to woman battering threatens to further pathologize black families. However, because it originates in the illegitimate power black men choose to exercise over women and causes a range of problems now ascribed to individual deficits or the intrinsic weakness of black families, focusing on battering can actually depathologize black families and improve their overall well-being. Ironically, according to Chestang and Richie, the threat battering poses to black families may reflect the exaggerated importance families take on to men and women denied social fulfillment on the basis of their race. For many black men, like the black battered women Richie

---

[27] While the black church has served historically to provide women with a mechanism for coping with oppression, interviews with African-American women in the Christian Methodist Episcopal Church reveal it is also another structure of dependence, reporting pervasive sexism, an ideology of gender domination as well as sexual harassment (Whitson, 1997).

(1996) interviewed at Riker's Island, the family – or heterosexual relations in general – become what Gilroy (1993) terms a "site of redemption" for the wrongs suffered in society at large. When this happens, black women are defined as "safe" targets for frustrated rage even as they rationalize trying to "make things work" at all costs.

Criminal justice interventions have contributed to the sharp drop in serious spousal violence among blacks. Battering among blacks can be further reduced by ensuring the racial consistency of these interventions while broadening sanctions and court protections to liberty-denying forms of coercive control. Prevention ultimately entails eliminating the race, sex, and class inequalities at its roots. Because current rehabilitative efforts are often demeaning to blacks, short-run prevention initiatives should be linked with affirmative traditions in black culture. One example is the "conversion parable" that has been successfully incorporated into twelve-step recovery programs with blacks and work with black ex-convicts (Brisbane and Womble, 1990). As illustrated by *The Autobiography of Malcolm X* and the oaths sworn at "The Million Man March," redemption is offered to males who repudiate drugs, sexual predation, and violence against women, and embrace a commitment to protect and provide. Similarly powerful is the association between the rights violated by coercive control and the humiliations blacks were made to suffer under slavery and afterward.

Prevention initiatives also can exploit suppressed themes in the black experience, particularly those that challenge the hegemonic equation of masculinity with domination (Connell, 1987). The equation of masculinity with social justice is one such alternative theme. A complimentary tradition, as illustrated by writers from William Wells Brown, Fredrick Douglass, and Martin Delaney through W. E. B. Du Bois, equates masculinity with defensive violence against the white oppressor, particularly in defense of black womanhood (Takaki, 1972), and suggests a moral choreography in which force is employed selectively to suppress abusive behavior and as an affirmation of community and family. Black men who abuse rather than protect black women betray this tradition.

To apply to woman battering, these themes must be "degendered." In the more stolid models of conversion – like those offered by The Million Man March, for instance – the man's commitment to the provider role is predicated on an obedient family/coterie/audience of devoted female "followers." Meanwhile, as illustrated in "The Coming of John" from *The Souls of Black Folk* (Du Bois, 1982), the equation of male respect with the defense of black womanhood presumes that men are responsible for (and therefore ultimately control) black women's sexuality. This view holds male authority over women as legitimate, even as it condemns abuse. One logical consequence of this approach is dramatized in Toni Morrison's *Paradise* (1996), when the puritanical black male cultural elite in "Ruby" demonizes the sexually independent black women at the "Convent," then savages them. The evolution of male protectiveness to coercive control becomes more likely when men interpret the "defilement" of black women (e.g., by other men) as a primeval betrayal, which inhibits the "full flowering of their manhood" (Carby, 1998).

Appropriately reframed, each of these approaches – the conversion parable, identifying woman battering as a civil rights issue, and associating the struggle against abuse with social justice – offers a strategic opportunity to prevent battering by drawing on the tradition of self-recovery. A key to this process entails explicating the "gender entrapment" of abusive males that occurs when masculinity is identified with untenable levels of control, women are selected as objects of this control, and domination is pursued through choices that put the lives, liberties, and chances for intimacy of men as well as women at risk. Men must be helped to understand how futile is the quest to recover what has been lost to injustice by disabling women. Undeniably, a man may gain tangible rewards by imposing servitude on a partner. But these are as nothing compared to the benefits that would accrue from extending the civil rights agenda so that equality, self-determination, safety, and dignity are assured for black women in personal life. Doing so would liberate the capacities currently suppressed through coercive control to support personal achievement, the development of strong black families, and social justice in economic, political, and cultural life.

Gender Entrapment and African-American Women: An Analysis of Race, Ethnicity, Gender, and Intimate Violence

Beth E. Richie, Ph.D.

Introduction

In other chapters of this volume and elsewhere, researchers have reviewed national and local data, which reveal the serious and complex societal problems, which result from high rates of interpersonal violence. They also have documented the extent of racial and ethnic disparity for both victimization and offending. Among the varied forms of interpersonal aggression, intimate violence, particularly violence against women, has now clearly been shown to be a significant and persistent social problem that may result in death and has serious consequences for individuals, their families, and society as a whole (Dobash, 1992; Crowell and Burgess, 1996; U.S. Department of Justice, 1997; FBI, 1995; Stark and Flitcraft, 1996).

According to the Bureau of Justice Statistics and the FBI, between 1992 and 1996, there were more than 960,000 documented violent victimizations of women by an intimate partner. This figure includes aggravated and simple assaults, rape and sexual abuse, murder, and robbery (Bureau of Justice Statistics, 1996, 1997a). The average rate for this period was eight violent victimizations per one thousand women, which represents a decline from 10 per 1,000 in 1993 to 7.5 in 1996. An assessment of lethal violence for 1996 indicates that 1,800 murders (approximately 9 percent of the total) were attributable to intimates, and in nearly three out of four of these crimes, the victim was female. In fact, research has consistently shown that when compared to men, women are five to eight times more likely to experience intimate violence firmly establishing gender as the most predictive variable in the intimate offending and victimization patterns (Bureau of Justice Statistics, 1998).

Other research explores the relevancy of additional sociodemographic variables in the rates of interpersonal violence. For example, when age of the victim is considered, younger women appear to be at greatest risk: women between the ages of sixteen and twenty-four had the highest per capita rate of intimate violence of any age group. Research on male perpetrators confirmed this age profile. Data from the 1985 Family Violence Survey indicated, for example, that young men are most likely to abuse their spouses and that the rate declines with age (Fagan and Browne, 1994).

> Over 20 percent of men between ages 18 and 25 and 16.9 percent of men between 26 and 35 committed at least one act of domestic violence in the past year. Violence was reported by 7.2 percent of men ages 36 to 50 and 4.5 percent of those are over 50. Youth has not been found to be a risk factor for elder abuse perpetration, although the rate of elder abuse is lower than the rate of other forms of family violence. (Crowell and Burgess, 1996)

A strong relationship is also found between income level and intimate violence. In a comprehensive review article, Hotaling and Sugarman (1990) report that in those studies that measure income, wife assault is more common and more severe in families with lower socioeconomic status. Important new research is underway that looks beyond family income to explore the relationship between violence among intimates and conditions associated with persistent poverty and receipt of public assistance (Raphael, 1996). Preliminary analysis of this data confirms the link between socioeconomic status and violence against women.

Researchers in the field of intimate victimization have explored a number of other situational and environmental factors ranging from stress (Hotaling and Sugarman, 1990), personality characteristics (Gondolf, 1988; Dutton et al., 1994, 1995; Warshaw, 1997), social isolation, alcohol and drug abuse (Leonard and Blane, 1992), and intergenerational transmission of violence (U.S. General Accounting Office, 1996). The picture that emerges from this research suggests that each of these factors influence the rates of intimate violence to some degree.

Race and ethnicity are also central variables in the most recent analyses of the problem of intimate violence. According to the Bureau of Justice Statistics, black women experience a higher rate of nonlethal violence than other groups; 12 per 1,000 compared to 8 per 1,000 for white women and 9 per 1,000 for Hispanic women. The differences by race and ethnicity become even more pronounced when lethal violence is considered. The Second National Family Violence Survey found a strong relationship between race/ethnicity and domestic violence, even when accounting for income (Gelles and Straus, 1988).

The extent or significance of the influence is inconclusive, complicated by the fact that many of the aforementioned variables are highly correlated with one another. Of particular importance is the link between racial or ethnic disparity in rates of intimate violence and socioeconomic status.

It may well be that most, if not all, of the racial and ethnic differences relate to levels of socioeconomic well-being. Yet, even with the imprecision, a compelling aggregate picture emerges that points clearly to the saliency of both race/ethnicity and gender as independent variables in the pattern of intimate violence and victimization. In fact, no other two variables emerge as consistently as race/ethnicity and gender in the current research; serious intimate violence is more likely to be perpetrated by males than by females.

While descriptively convincing on some accounts, there are still conceptual problems in the literature on intimate violence with regard to race/ethnicity and gender. For example, neither the presence of covariance among the aforementioned variables, nor the influence of other (nonindividual) factors, are adequately considered in descriptions of the rates, trends, and lethal consequences of violence against women. This is especially problematic in violence research with regard to women from racial/ethnic minority groups. The lack of rigor in the treatment of race/ethnicity as an analytical category limits the ability of policy makers and advocates to respond effectively to the problem of gender violence in communities of color.

More precisely, the problems with the research for those scholars concerned about women of color who experience intimate violence are both methodological and theoretical. In some ways, these gaps reflect two broad problems with the overall approach to research on victimization, but they pose particular dilemmas for those interested in the relationship between violence, race/ethnicity, and gender. Together they call for a different analysis, one that questions the fundamental epistemological assumptions on which the aforementioned research is based in order to establish a more critical framework for understanding the current state of the knowledge about violence against women. In this chapter, I argue that what is needed is rigorous qualitative research on women of color for whom differences in rates of intimate victimization explain only one dimension of the problem, ignoring critical nuanced differences in experience, class variations in communities of color, and need for culturally specific programs.

Methodological Concerns. The first set of problems is methodological. These concerns emerge when the understanding of demographic difference in rates of violence against women remains at the level of quantitative or statistical analysis. They begin with the problem of definition. According to the NRC and other review articles, the definition of violence against women varies from study to study.

> Some studies of sexual assault were limited to rape (e.g., Essock-Vitale and McGuire, 1985); others included physical contact in addition to rape (e.g., Wyatt, 1992); and still others used a very broad definition that included

non-contact abuse (e.g., Sorenson et al., 1987). Given the discrepancy in definitions used to assess the phenomenon, differences in prevalence rates are to be expected. (Crowell and Burgess, 1996)

This problem results in a significant level of imprecision in the incidence rate data when comparisons between different studies are attempted.

When cross-cultural or multicultural samples are used, a different problem arises. As noted in the NRC and elsewhere, most measures of violence against women are developed by Anglo researchers and not tested for meaning on different ethnic groups (Crowell and Burgess, 1996). They therefore miss the important and unique ways that culture influences the findings drawn from subjects' interpretations of events and how one's language may be used to project particular meaning. Unreliable measures may skew data collected on marginalized social groups resulting in inaccurate conclusions about intimate victimization. In addition, when the research findings are reviewed, wide variation in sample size, content, and approach is noted (Crowell and Burgess, 1996). With a few exceptions, most studies still focus on white populations, threatening their potential to generalize to communities of color.

The third related methodological issue concerns the question of causation. As previously noted, rates of violence against women vary by race/ethnicity, socioeconomic status, age, and other variables. Conclusions drawn from analyses of these differences often imply a unidimensional covariance. In so doing, they skew more complex interaction between multiple variables. So, for example, while national studies suggest that African Americans are more likely to report abuse than whites, the variance may actually be explained by the interaction of race and other variables such as socioeconomic status (Crowell and Burgess, 1996), reporting behavior, police surveillance, and/or differential use of weapons, in which cases a report is automatically made (Crowell and Burgess, 1996).

Theoretical Concerns. The second problematic issue, which requires careful analysis, is linked to both the practical application of data on violence against women and, more important, the development of theory. To fully grasp the importance of this issue, and the methodological concerns earlier observed, the historical context from which research on violence against women emerged must be noted. Academic interest in intimate victimization followed years of grassroots activism by women's advocates who sought to convince a hesitant public that the intimate sphere of social life was, in fact, a dangerous place for some women (Schechter, 1982). In effect this early work was undertaken to make problematic that which was either ignored or unquestioned (Kanuha, 1997). The literature that characterized this time argued that what was once understood to be an isolated circumstance in some families was actually a more commonplace experience. It was a pattern of intimate victimization that was neither isolated nor insignificant. Furthermore, in the analysis put forward by authors Martin (1976), Dobash and Dobash (1992), Walker (1989), and Browne (1992), a link was established between the individual (private) experience of victimization and various social factors; most prominently gender inequality. They and others argued that this inequality in the intimate sphere reflects the generalized subordinate position of women in public life. A key feature of the theoretical arguments that were emerging at the time was that they were race-neutral; they did not focus on the particular vulnerabilities among different races of women, emphasizing instead the more general situation of women as a social category.

Another important dimension of this emerging literature was its multidisciplinary nature. The perspectives of psychologists, sociologists, and historians were advanced; all centered on the salient role that gender inequality assumed in the analysis of violence against women. In addition, the accepted body of literature was unusual in that scholars did not solely produce it nor was it only geared toward academic audiences. Contributors to the growing literature included authors who do not typically occupy a place in knowledge-generating agencies like universities (Yllo, 1988), and much of the texts were equally informed by a commitment to authentically reflecting the experiences of survivors of intimate violence and a conscious interest in making the problem a general (rather than an individual or personal) one. Again, survivors of intimate violence were understood to share a set of common experiences without regard for difference by race or ethnicity.

There are a number of important advantages to this original formulation of the analysis of intimate victimization, not the least of which is the persistent analysis of the public, social, and institutional macro-processes that exacerbate intimate violence toward women. By contrast, there are a number of conceptual and political problems. Most prominent is that despite critiques from women of color who were involved in both the activist movement and the development of literature that emerged from it, a race-neutral or "regardless of race" argument became a major tenant of the antimovement literature that now is in conflict with the mainstream research presented in the early parts of this chapter (Kanuha, 1997).

As a result, in this early body of literature that focused on gender inequality, it was suggested that violence against women – unlike most other criminal justice concerns – was not significantly affected by variables of race/ethnicity, socioeconomic position, and age. That is, the prevailing analyses of domestic violence understood the problem to be more or less universal in its ability to affect the lives of women, unlike other forms of social malaise that were often seen to differentially affect persons based on their social standing. So unlike most analyses of crime that reflect a higher rate of victimization and offending among socially and economically disenfranchised people of color, the patterns of violence against women were understood to be different, not concentrated in the most vulnerable groups in society.

This gender-inequality but race-neutral framework has continued to influence social policy, intervention, and public perception about intimate violence (and advanced an understanding of the problem of domestic violence as both extensive and universal in important ways). It allowed for the infusion of considerable resources into prevention programs and victim services. In fact, it could be argued that recognition that violence had a potential impact on any/all families (including those with economic, social, and political capital) legitimized the topic as an important public concern. Without overstating mainstream acceptance, some very powerful (mostly male) stakeholders took a position that argued for legal and legislative changes that would respond to violence within families, including their own (Richie, 2000). The lack of significance, in the ethnic variation, in the experience of intimate violence has led to persistent epistemological problems with the data and subsequent intervention strategies. This race-neutral theoretical perspective has resulted in monolithic responses to the problem, lack of culturally specific programming, and policies that have differential impact on different ethnic communities. Take, for example, mandatory arrest policies that have been shown to have a disproportionate impact on minority communities who are overrepresented in arrest statistics or counseling programs that assume all intimate violence victims respond positively to psychosocial intervention.

Against the aforementioned race-neutral analytical frame, research that identifies different rates of intimate violence in different ethnic groups has been met with some intellectual resistance, leaving some criminal justice scholars, feminist activists, and domestic violence researchers in the unusual place of arguing *against* a racially neutral approach to understanding violence against women. We now have data that supports the existence of racial and ethnic differences in rates but a theoretical orientation and public policy that can't accommodate or make sense of this new understanding. The analysis of the data regarding racial and ethnic differences remained at the level of descriptive or comparative analysis rather than offering a more complex consideration that looks at interactive effects, broader contextual issues, or structural dimensions of the differences (Hall, Tessero, and Earp, 1995).

A Different Approach

These methodological and conceptual problems both skew the data and, paradoxically, conceal the extent of differences that even quantitative

analyses of intimate violence in different populations show. Advocates who
work with groups of battered women who are immigrants, adolescents, les-
bians, or otherwise marginalized, concur, arguing for a reconceptualization
of the problem, more community-based research programs, and more contextualized analyses. These calls would uncover, for example, the embedded
nature of violence against women, the multiple effects of various forms of
violence and poverty, the reasons for variations in help-seeking behavior
of different ethnic groups vulnerable to social stigma, and the subsequent
limitations of existing approaches to violent intimate victimization.

Such an approach would require qualitative research that could go beyond the single dimension of the problem that earlier quantitative studies
captured. These studies would explore the aggregate or the intersection of
the various forms of abuse, based on the evidence that there may be overlap.
In addition, they would avoid the predetermined (researcher-driven) categories that are unable to capture the nuanced pattern of experiences or the
nature of violence that different groups of women experience (Crenshaw,
1994). Last, while there is now a solid body of literature that documents violence against women in dominant groups in society, a different approach
would reveal the particular experiences of some women are not at all represented in the prevailing body of domestic violence research.

This chapter argues for such an approach; one that utilizes a different
research method and samples of groups of women who are not well represented in the dominant body of literature. I will attempt to show how a
more complex analytical view of intimate violence provides a deeper and
more nuanced picture of the causes and consequences of the problem, one
that challenges the policy and intervention approaches that are currently
assumed to be "best practices." Such a revised approach is important, for
while the past twenty years have yielded important legal and legislative reform, tremendous growth in services for victims and offenders, and shifts in
public consciousness about domestic violence, there are groups of women
who are only minimally impacted by these advances. Shelters for battered
women, crisis intervention programs, legal services, and public awareness
campaigns have only had so much effect, for, while national trends indicate
that the overall rate of intimate victimization is declining, there is other evidence to suggest that for some groups of women, domestic violence, sexual
assault, and partner homicide are persistent problems. This includes those
women who are involved in illegal activities, and women who may be reluctant to call the police, use mainstream social services, or report incidences
of abuse to agencies because of their marginalized social position and their
precarious legal status (Richie, 1996). Research on workplace violence, for
example, does not include places where illegal drug transactions are taking
place. Similarly, women involved in prostitution or otherwise working in the
sex industry are less likely to report having been raped by a customer or

stalked by a pimp. Young women who are truant do not appear in the large datasets collected at school, and if a woman is hurt by her crime partner during a robbery or sexually harassed in a place where stolen goods are collected, there is little likelihood that her experience of violence will appear in official reports or research findings.

In this chapter, I use African-American women from low-income communities who are involved as defendants in the criminal justice system as a case in point to show how differences can be empirically evaluated. The chapter will describe both how they differ from other samples and how the difference constitutes the basis of a new theoretical paradigm, which I call "gender entrapment." This theoretical approach potentially contributes to the overall understanding of intimate violence, as well as offers a new epistemological approach to the study of other problems facing low-income African-American and other marginalized communities. It will suggest that to understand causation, and the public policies they derive from such knowledge, a contextualized approach that allows for the introduction of multiple variables must be used.

Toward that end, following a description of the sample used for this study, I will describe the social processes that surround domestic violence in the above-mentioned population, highlighting the issues that are particularly salient in terms of race/ethnicity and class. To isolate the variable race from class, I will introduce findings from a subsample of white battered women from the same socioeconomic group in the comparative analysis section of this chapter. This methodological strategy will serve to defend against one of the central criticisms others and I have made regarding the collapsing of these two variables. Next I will explain how "gender entrapment" provides an explanation of the causes of and responses to domestic violence in the lives of some African-American women. In the conclusion, I suggest ways that this theoretical model could serve as a more general approach to the study of criminological issues in the African-American community.

The Sample. The theory of gender entrapment is based on qualitative research conducted by the author in a large urban jail, which detains women awaiting trial. While smaller in pure numbers than their male counterpart, when considered by rate, women represent the fastest growing cohort of incarcerated people in the United States (BJS, 1994). In 1995, I conducted a series of life-history interviews with twenty-five African-American battered women detained at Riker's Island Correctional Facility, one of the largest jails in the United States. The goals of the project were to uncover the relationship between violence against women and their involvement in illegal activities. I undertook this study in the midst of the following intellectual and academic trends: (1) interest in new scholarship on race, class, and gender; (2) concern about the growing prison-industrial complex; and (3) the new research on violence against women of color in low-income urban communities. I was particularly interested in learning about the lives of women whose circumstances and identities leave them at the intersection of these trends: low-income African-American battered women who commit crimes.

I used the life-history interview method and a grounded theory approach to data analysis. The findings indicate a complicated pattern that some African-American women face when they experience domestic violence. The pattern is influenced by a multiplicity of factors, including their early childhood experiences as girls in their households, the construction of a cultural/racial identity, and critical events in the public spheres of their lives as members of a marginalized ethnic and gender group. A pattern emerged from the stories that showed how these factors varied by race/ ethnicity and experiences of abuse, thereby distinguishing the backgrounds of the African-American battered women from other groups of women described in the dominant literature.

The Social Process. For the overwhelming majority of the African-American battered women, a central factor in their gender entrapment was the series of shifts in their identities in response to conditions in the private sphere and experiences in the public domain. The African-American battered women grew up as relatively privileged children in their households of origin. Despite social and economic limitations and compared to other children in their household, the women in the subgroup received more attention, a greater proportion of material resources, and emotional interest from the adults around them. They developed an optimistic sense of their future, and felt the expectations of social success generated by their privileged status.

While their early childhood was characterized by a sense of being competent and desirable African-American girls, when they entered the public sphere, they felt the limitations of their gender, race/ethnicity, and class status. They felt unable to actualize their dreams for social success when educational and occupational opportunities were unavailable or withheld, and they felt the stigma of discrimination based on hierarchical institutional arrangements. The gender entrapment process began here, when the African-American battered women's identities developed in their households of origin were contradicted by their experiences and treatment in the public sphere. The contradiction has a particularly gendered and racial aspect, which turned out to be an important finding from this study.

While the African-American battered women's public identities became more fragile, they continued to feel that a "successful" family life, as defined by dominant ideology, was within their reach. The more they became socially disenfranchised, the more they longed for the respect and sense of accomplishment that they had come to believe was possible from their childhood experiences. The African-American battered women held firmly to their interest in establishing traditional nuclear families and hegemonic intimate relationships with men; however, the African-American men with whom they were involved were also marginalized, and thus unable to assume the traditional patriarchal roles as "heads of household."

Subsequently, the African-American battered women described feeling compelled to provide opportunities for the African-American men to feel powerful in the domestic sphere by relinquishing some of their status and authority. The discrepancy between the women's reality and their socially constructed ideals required them to work hard to manage the contradictions they felt, and left them vulnerable to gender entrapment.

The nature of the trauma associated with the onset of abuse in their intimate relationships caused another shift in the African-American battered women's identities. Violence from their intimate partners effectively destroyed their sense of themselves as "successful" women and eroded their hopes for an ideologically "normal" private life. They felt betrayed, abandoned, and disoriented, and yet ironically loyal to the African-American men who were abusing them. Few reached out directly for assistance, attempting instead to manage the violent episodes and conceal the signs of abuse. Their avoidance of criminal justice intervention, in particular, was noteworthy and consistent with the general sense of the hostile relationship between communities of color and the police in cities like New York.

Typically, the violence escalated over time, reaching extreme levels. The subjects were threatened with constant emotional, physical, and sexual abuse or seriously injured; some were permanently disfigured, and fearful that their batterers would eventually kill them. The shifts in their identities – as powerless fearful women at serious risk of losing their lives – once again cemented their vulnerability to gender entrapment, leading them to participate in illegal activities for which they were eventually arrested and detained in jail as criminals rather than offered services as victims of crimes.

Comparative Analysis. A comparison of the gender-identity development in the samples of African-American battered women and African-American women who were not battered, found that both groups were influenced in significant ways by the organization of their households of origin. However, the African-American nonbattered women described feelings less affected by the dominant ideology, their families were more isolated from institutions in the dominant social structure, and they had looser networks of social support in their communities. The African-American women who were not battered were less likely to be influenced by hegemonic values, they expressed less sensitivity to the social and economic position of African-American men, and they identified more strongly as members of an oppressed group. They understood that some African-American men used their experiences of racial discrimination as an excuse to subordinate African-American women, which led the women in this subgroup to establish a more oppositional stance towards the men in their lives. The African-American nonbattered women grew up expecting to be treated badly by men, and were therefore less likely to do the emotional work necessary to tolerate or excuse physical abuse.

The one area in which African-American nonbattered women did express solidarity with African-American men was in their distrust of the criminal justice system. However, since the women were not victimized by the men, they did not need to depend on law enforcement for protection. Ironically, the African-American nonbattered women identified themselves as "victims of the system" more than "criminals" or "offenders," whereas the African-American battered women had a more complex analysis of their multiple identities that shifted over time.

Further refinement of the gender entrapment model developed in this study was gained from a comparison between the black battered women and the white women interviewed in this study. For the white battered women, gender-identity was also constructed in their families of origin. Their household arrangements most closely mirrored the ideological norm in structure: typically they were patriarchal, rigidly organized by gender and generation, and in most cases they were oppressive environments. As such, the white battered women's attempts to attain the ideologically normative family structure were characterized by less failure, and therefore created less internal tension and less ambivalence about their roles, responsibilities, and privileges as women.

Another significant difference between the white battered women and the African-American battered women was the absence of a culturally constructed sensitivity to men's needs. From a very early age, the white women interviewed for this study felt inferior to the men in their lives. Unlike the African-American battered women, they did not feel that they had the means, strength, or interest in protecting the men in their lives. When they were battered, they felt less ambivalent and confused, they understood their risks immediately, and they were more likely to reach out for help. Without overstating the availability of services for white battered women, documentation and public recognition of the abuse was both symbolic and practical in decreasing their sense of isolation and shame. In terms of the relationship to the legal system, the white battered women developed mistrust of the criminal justice system *after* being arrested, in contrast to either group of black women who felt mistrustful even *before* their involvement in it as criminals and/or victims.

The Theory of Gender Entrapment. The term "gender entrapment" is borrowed from the legal notion of entrapment, which implies circumstances whereby an individual is lured into a compromising act. From the study described in this chapter, the gender entrapment theoretical paradigm is conceptualized as an alternative to race-neutral theoretical constructs. It explains the dynamic process of cumulative experiences, which begins with the organization of the women's cultural and gender-identity development in her family of origin, leading to the experiences of violence in their intimate relationships, and, in this case, culminating in forced involvement in illegal activities. I argue that gender entrapment results in some black battered women being penalized for activities they engage in and emotions they express even when those behaviors are a logical extension of the gender identities, productive strategies that enhance their safety, reflections of their particular culturally constructed gender roles, and a response to the violence they experience in their intimate relationships.

The theory of gender entrapment developed in this chapter assumes that social relationships and institutional practices are organized in such a way as to regulate the behavior of social actors according to their gender. It also assumes that cultural influences are profound, creating a dynamic interaction between the public and private sphere of human life. From this conceptual point of view, historical patterns and cultural practices influence and are influenced by internal psychological processes. Emotional expression, identity development, and the meaning social actors have in family life play an important role in gender entrapment by influencing the ways in which women establish and maintain intimate, social, and institutional relationships. The experiences of women of color and the meanings attached to them are unique: the violence experienced by women of color must be evaluated from the perspective of race/ethnicity as well as gender. Gender, race/ethnicity, and violence interact with social stigma and deviance to negatively affect some social actors. Understanding the experience of being battered within the context of black women's life-course events and the broader social structure is critical to prevention and intervention strategies, so descriptive, quantitative analyses of violence must be expanded to include attention to culturally specific forms of gender inequality, institutionalized racism, and community norms and expectations.

Conclusion

For the past decade, researchers in the area of intimate violence, with persistent pressure from the advocacy community, have been developing a body of literature that exposes troubling high rates of intimate violence against women in this country. More recently, studies have concluded that women who are members of racial/ethnic minority communities are particularly vulnerable, thereby positioning the variable "race/ethnicity" as centrally as the variable "gender" when considering significant risk factors. The extent to which the emergence of this qualitative data on intimate violence posed difficult theoretical questions for the community of scholars and activists who were, for various reasons, invested in a race-neutral approach has been noted, as have been the problems posed for violence prevention policy makers and service providers in the field. Most important, this chapter has described the increased risk faced by women of color who experience intimate violence, using the case of African-American battered women while arguing that some of them have been ill served by race-neutral research (Richie, 1996).

The specific theory of gender entrapment, and the more general methodological decisions regarding qualitative approaches to victimization research, were presented as attempts to begin to remedy these problems. The study described in this chapter attempted to fill the empirical gaps in the research on domestic violence in the lives of black women and women's criminality by looking beyond the superficial, unidirectional explanations that prevail in the dominant research on violence against women. It attempted a deeper level of analysis; where the intersectionality of gender-identity, emotional attachments, race/ethnicity, and violence creates a subtle, yet profoundly effective system of organizing women's behavior into patterns that leave them vulnerable to private and public subordination, to violence in their intimate relationships, and, in turn, to incarceration for the illegal activities in which they subsequently engage. I argue race/ethnicity is key here. As such, the gender entrapment theory helps to explain how some black women who participate in illegal activity do so in response to ultimate violence, the threat of violence, and other forms of coercion by their male partners. The study showed how these black battered women were invisible to dominant researchers, mainstream social service programs, legal advocacy groups, and feminist antiviolence projects because the nature of their abuse resulted in their being labeled "criminals" rather than "victims" of crimes, which is more consistent with the "race-neutral" theoretical approach.

The gender entrapment theory presents only one conceptual case. However, its conclusions regarding the value of a different approach to racial and ethnic variations in causes and consequences of intimate violence may be generalized to support the need for other case examinations (other ethnicities, other socioeconomic groups of black women, settings other than correctional facilities). In the end, its promise is to broaden and deepen the literature on intimate violence so that race and ethnicity appear as central, complex, nuanced variables and, ultimately, so that women of color are less affected by the devastation of intimate violence.

Explaining Racial and Ethnic Differences

How Can the Relationship between Race and Violence be Explained?

David P. Farrington
Rolf Loeber
Magda Stouthamer-Loeber

Racial Differences in Violence

There is no doubt that African-American juveniles are more likely than Caucasian juveniles to be arrested for serious (index) violent offenses in the United States (homicide, forcible rape, robbery, and aggravated assault). In 1992, for example, there were sixteen arrests for index violence per 1,000 African-American juveniles, compared with 3 per 1,000 Caucasian juveniles (Snyder and Sickmund, 1995). There were 7 arrests per 1,000 African-American juveniles for robbery, compared with 0.8 for Caucasians; 8 arrests per 1,000 African-American juveniles for aggravated assault, compared with two for Caucasians; 48 arrests per 100,000 African-American juveniles for homicide, compared with six for Caucasians; and 68 arrests per 100,000 African-American juveniles for forcible rape, compared with fifteen for Caucasians (Snyder and Sickmund, 1995).

African-American:Caucasian ratios in violence are less when violence is measured by self-reports. For example, in the National Youth Survey, Elliott (1994) found that, at the peak age of seventeen, 36 percent of African-American males, 25 percent of Caucasian males, 18 percent of African-American females, and 10 percent of Caucasian females admitted to committing a serious violent offense (robbery, rape, or aggravated assault involving injury or a weapon) in the previous year. Weis (1986: 4) concluded that "among the major sociodemographic and etiological correlates of crime, only one is clearly discrepant in its correlations with self-reports and official records – race" (the present chapter focuses only on African Americans and Caucasians, not on other ethnic groups).

Why do official records and self-reports differ in their conclusions about racial differences in offending, and which is more accurate? The two methods of measurement have somewhat different advantages and problems. An advantage of official records is that they include the worst offenders and offenses and that (at least in the case of convictions) they establish unambiguously that an offense has been committed according to legal criteria such as *mens rea* and rules of evidence. By contrast, some innocent people may be convicted, or plea bargaining may cause differences between types of offenses and types of convictions. The problems of official records are that only the tip of the iceberg of offenders and offenses are recorded and that those offenders who are recorded may be unrepresentative of all offenders because of bias in official processing (e.g., against African Americans or those living in high-crime areas where there is more police patrolling). Official records underrepresent offenses more than offenders. For example, West and Farrington (1977: 28) found that, while only 13 percent of self-reported burglaries led to a conviction for burglary, 62 percent of self-reported burglars were convicted for burglary.

The main advantage of self-reports is that (to the extent that they are accurate) they can provide complete information about offenders and offenses. One of their problems, however, is that exaggeration, concealment, and forgetting by respondents make them inaccurate, especially since low literacy and low verbal skills are associated both with offending and with invalid responding. Another problem is that it is sometimes unclear whether acts reported would really have led to convictions in court; for example, would involvement in a gang fight really lead to a conviction for aggravated assault? Self-reported acts often cover rather trivial offenses; for example, 36 percent of self-reported "serious violent offenses" were too trivial to be charged, according to Elliott and Huizinga (1989). Another problem is that the worst offenders may be missing from samples interviewed, for example, because they are more elusive or uncooperative or because they are in institutions (Cernkovich, Giordano, and Pugh, 1985).

For many reasons, perfect correspondence between official records and self-reports would not be expected. Nevertheless, the validity of self-reports is usually tested by comparing them with official records, on the assumption that recorded offenses are "true" offenses. Most commonly, the incidence of offending (or number of offenses) is measured in official records, and the prevalence of offending (or number of offenders) is measured in self-reports. Consequently, an African-American:Caucasian ratio of 2:1 in self-reports could be compatible with a 6:1 ratio in official records if the average African-American offender committed three times as many offenses (or three times as many serious offenses) as the average Caucasian offender.

The most direct test of the concurrent validity of self-reports is to investigate what percentage of those with an official record admit the offense leading to that record. Hindelang, Hirschi, and Weis (1981) found that Caucasian boys (aged fifteen to eighteen in Seattle) failed to report 10 percent of offenses in arrest records, compared with 15 percent for

Caucasian girls, 33 percent for African-American boys, and 27 percent for African-American girls. Similarly, in the National Youth Survey, Huizinga and Elliott (1986) found that Caucasian boys failed to report 16 percent of offenses leading to arrests, while African-American boys failed to report 39 percent (on a broad matching criterion). Hindelang et al. (1981) concluded that the African-American:Caucasian ratio was higher in official records than in self-reports because self-reports were more valid for Caucasians than for African Americans. However, another possibility is that African-American boys are more likely to be arrested unjustifiably than Caucasian boys.

Another test of the concurrent validity of self-reports is to investigate what percentage of those who have been arrested admit that they have been arrested. Again, Hindelang et al. (1981) found considerable racial and gender differences in this: 76 percent of Caucasian male delinquents reported that they had been picked up by the police, compared with 52 percent of Caucasian females, 50 percent of African-American males, and only 30 percent of African-American females. However, the figures in Hirschi (1969: 77) indicate no difference between Caucasian and African-American male delinquents in admitting being picked up by the police (about 60 percent of Caucasians and 61 percent of African Americans admitting this). Furthermore, Farrington, Loeber, Stouthamer-Loeber, van Kammen, and Schmidt (1996) found that 53 percent of Caucasian boys who had been petitioned to the juvenile court for an index offense admitted being arrested by the police, compared with 65 percent of African-American boys.

Farrington et al. (1996) also investigated the validity of self-reports in predicting future court petitions. They found that African-American boys admitted more serious offenses than Caucasian boys; in the Pittsburgh Youth Study, 33 percent of African-American boys in the oldest sample were serious delinquents up to assessment A (explained later in this chapter), compared with 18 percent of Caucasian boys. Self-reports had similar predictive validity for African-American and Caucasian boys, but African-American boys were more likely to be petitioned to court at all levels of delinquency seriousness. For example, 12 percent of Caucasian boys and 30 percent of African-American boys committing minor offenses were subsequently petitioned to court for delinquency: 36 percent of Caucasian boys and 63 percent of African-American boys committing serious offenses were subsequently petitioned to court for delinquency.

The most plausible conclusion from all this research is that African-American boys do indeed commit more violent offenses than Caucasian boys. However, true racial differences in offending are amplified in official records, perhaps because of biases in police or court processing, differences in police patrolling in African-American versus Caucasian neighborhoods, differences in demeanor by African-American versus Caucasian youth when apprehended by the police, or other variables correlated with both race and the probability of arrest.

Explaining Racial Differences

There are many possible explanations of racial differences in violent behavior. This chapter follows a developmental criminology approach, focusing on risk factors for violent behavior by individuals. It is beyond the scope of our chapter to review more macro-social explanations based on community structures or ecological conditions, racial discrimination or segregation, differences in economic or political power, or other types of sociostructural inequalities (see Hawkins, Laub, and Lauritsen, 1998; Covington, 1999). While the social and developmental life-courses of African Americans and Caucasians in the United States are products not only of their individual experiences but also of their membership in historically disadvantaged and unequal social and economic groupings, our focus is on individuals, and more particularly on boys.

A risk factor for violence is defined as a factor that predicts a relatively high probability of violence. High impulsiveness, low intelligence and school attainment, poor parental supervision, harsh parental discipline, large family size, a young mother, a broken family, low socioeconomic status, and living in a high-crime neighborhood are some of the most important risk factors for male youth violence (Farrington, 1998; Hawkins et al., 1998). It is possible that there are racial differences in violence because African-American boys are more likely than Caucasian boys to possess these risk factors. For example, African-American boys may have relatively lower school attainment and may be more likely to come from broken families, live in high-crime neighborhoods, and so on. Another possibility is that these risk factors may be more strongly related to violence for African-American boys. For example, poor parental supervision may be a better predictor of violence for African-American boys than for Caucasian boys.

Rowe, Vazsonyi, and Flannery (1994) tested these two alternative hypotheses in explaining racial differences in intelligence, attainment, and social adjustment. They contrasted racial differences in developmental processes (measured by differences in correlations between risk factors and outcomes) with racial differences in levels of predictor variables. They concluded that developmental processes were the same for different racial groups, and that racial differences in outcomes were attributable to racial differences in average levels of their exposure to predictor variables. Similarly, Vazsonyi and Flannery (1997) found that family and school correlates of self-reported delinquency were very similar for Caucasians and Hispanics.

Other researchers have reached different conclusions. McLeod, Kruttschnitt, and Dornfeld (1994) analyzed data from the National

Longitudinal Survey of Youth-Children. In agreement with the conclusions of Rowe and his colleagues (1994), they found many significant differences between African-American and Caucasian children in risk factors. For example, African-American children were more likely to be living in poverty, with young, never-married mothers, and a large number of siblings, and they were more likely to experience physical discipline (spanking). However, there also were differences between African-American and Caucasian children in the independent predictors of antisocial behavior. Poverty, the mother's lack of education, and the mother's unemployment were predictive for Caucasians but not for African-Americans, whereas the number of siblings was predictive for African-Americans but not Caucasians, and spanking was predictive for both.

Deater-Deckard, Dodge, Bates, and Pettit (1996) reached different conclusions about relationships between physical discipline and antisocial behavior (externalizing problems) among African-American and Caucasian children. As noted by other researchers, African-American children were more likely to experience physical discipline and to be living in low socioeconomic status (SES), single-parent families. However, physical discipline was associated with antisocial behavior only for Caucasian children; the race × discipline interaction was significant. Deater-Deckard and colleagues speculated that physical discipline may have a different meaning in African-American and Caucasian families; specifically, in African-American families, physical discipline may not indicate any lack of warmth, and may indeed indicate concern for the child. Based on a study of low-income African-American mothers, Kelley, Power, and Wimbush (1992) put forward a similar argument.

In further analyses of the same sample, Deater-Deckard, Dodge, Bates, and Pettit (1998) found that the number of risk factors correlated with the level of antisocial behavior for Caucasian children but not for African-American children. Gottfredson and Koper (1996) reached similar conclusions for drug use. It is possible that risk factors are more prevalent among African-American children but (as a consequence?) less powerful in their effects on antisocial outcomes. This idea is reminiscent of the "gender paradox" discussed by Loeber and Keenan (1994): girls are less likely than boys to show conduct disorder, but conduct-disordered girls are more seriously affected (in the sense of having more comorbid conditions such as hyperactivity, anxiety, and substance use) than conduct-disordered boys. Against this hypothesis, however, Matsueda and Heimer (1987) found that broken homes had a larger impact on delinquency for African Americans than for Caucasians.

Paschall, Ennett, and Flewelling (1996) obtained similar results to McLeod and her colleagues (1994). Compared to Caucasian males, African-American males were exposed to more risk factors for violence, and the predictors of violence differed for the two groups. Living in a single-parent family predicted fighting for African Americans, but low attachment to parents and family conflict predicted fighting for Caucasians. In further analyses of young adults, Paschall, Flewelling, and Ennett (1998) found that the race × SES interaction was significant in predicting violence; African Americans were more violent than Caucasians only among the low-SES part of the sample. (SES included poverty and the number of years of schooling of subjects and their parents.) Finally, Cernkovich and Giordano (1987, 1992) concluded that family variables were more strongly related to delinquency for Caucasians than for African Americans, whereas school bonding variables were equally strongly related for both.

Following the risk factor/developmental criminology approach, the key questions addressed in the present study are as follows:

1. Are African-American boys more violent than Caucasian boys, according to reports by the boys, mothers and teachers, and according to court petitions for index violence?
2. What are the most important risk factors for violence?
3. Can the relationship between race and violence be explained by risk factors such as ADHD (Attention Deficit Hyperactivity Disorder), low achievement, poor parental supervision, physical discipline, low SES (socioeconomic status), broken families, bad neighborhoods, and young mothers?
4. Are African-American boys exposed to more risk factors for violence than Caucasian boys?
5. Do risk factors predict violence differently for African-American and Caucasian boys?
6. Is the cumulative effect of the number of risk factors different for African-American and Caucasian boys?

The present analyses are based on the middle sample of the Pittsburgh Youth Study.

The Pittsburgh Youth Study

The Pittsburgh Youth Study is a prospective longitudinal survey of the development of offending and antisocial behavior in three samples of about five hundred Pittsburgh boys, totalling 1,517 boys (Loeber, Farrington, Stouthamer-Loeber, and van Kammen, 1998). At the time they were first contacted in 1987–8, random samples of first-, fourth-, and seventh-grade boys enrolled in the City of Pittsburgh public schools were selected. At that time, 72 percent of all children resident in the City of Pittsburgh attended public schools. The City of Pittsburgh covers the inner-city population of about 370,000 (in 1990) out of the Pittsburgh-Beaver Valley Metropolitan

Statistical Area of about 2,243,000 (Hoffman, 1991). Many of the assessments in the Pittsburgh Youth Study were designed to be comparable to those used in two other contemporaneous longitudinal surveys conducted in Denver, Colorado (Huizinga, Esbensen, and Weiher, 1991) and Rochester, New York (Thornberry, Lizotte, Krohn, Farnworth, and Jang, 1991).

Out of about one thousand boys in each grade selected at random for a screening assessment, about 850 boys (85 percent) were actually assessed. The boys completed a self-report questionnaire about antisocial behavior and delinquency (Loeber, Stouthamer-Loeber, van Kammen, and Farrington, 1989), while their primary caretakers completed an extended Child Behavior Checklist (Achenbach and Edelbrock, 1983), and their teachers completed an extended Teacher Report Form (Edelbrock and Achenbach, 1984). We will refer to the primary caretaker as the mother because this was true in 94 percent of cases. Participants did not differ significantly from the comparable male student population in their scores on the California Achievement Test (CAT) and in their racial composition (African American or Caucasian). This chapter focuses only on African Americans and Caucasians because there are very few other sizable racial or ethnic groups in Pittsburgh.

From the screening assessment, a risk score was calculated for each boy indicating how many of twenty-one serious antisocial acts he had ever committed (including types of stealing, running away, firesetting, truancy, vandalism, robbery, gang fighting, attacking with a weapon, joyriding, burglary, liquor use, and marijuana use). Information from the boy, mother, and teacher was taken into account. The risk score was used to select the sample for follow-up, which consisted of approximately the 250 most antisocial boys in each grade and about 250 boys randomly selected from the remaining 600. Hence, the screening sample of about 850 per grade was reduced to a follow-up sample of about 500 per grade.

The five hundred boys in each grade were then assessed every six months for three years, with data collection from the boy, mother, and teacher on each occasion. Regular data collection from the middle sample then ceased, but the oldest and youngest sample are still (in 2000) being followed up at yearly intervals. Rolf Loeber and Magda Stouthamer-Loeber are the principal investigators of the Pittsburgh Youth Study, with David P. Farrington as co-investigator. The study has mainly been funded by the U.S. Office of Juvenile Justice and Delinquency Prevention and the U.S. National Institute of Mental Health.

The present analyses are based only on the middle sample of boys, who were aged about ten when they were first assessed. Explanatory variables measured in the screening assessment and first follow-up six months later (assessment A) are compared with violence reported by the boys, mothers, and teachers, and with petitions to the juvenile court for index violence up to 1994. The middle follow-up sample comprises 508 boys, 259 of whom were high risk and 249 of whom were randomly chosen from the remainder who were screened. Of the sample, 56 percent were African American, 92 percent were living with their natural mother, and 41 percent were living with their natural father at assessment A. At this time, their median age was 10.6 years, and they were then followed up in court records for 5.8 years up to a median age of 16.4 years (for more information about the middle sample, see Farrington and Loeber, 1999).

A major aim in the Pittsburgh Youth Study was to measure as many factors as possible that were alleged to be causes or correlates of offending. The first follow-up (assessment A) was much more extensive than the screening assessment. The boys completed the Self-Reported Delinquency scale of Elliott, Huizinga, and Ageton (1985), while the mothers again completed the extended Child Behavior Checklist and the teachers again completed the extended Teacher Report Form. These questionnaires yielded data not only on antisocial and violent behavior but also on individual factors such as hyperactivity and shyness. In addition, the mothers completed a demographic questionnaire yielding information about adults and children living with the boy, and the Revised Diagnostic Interview Schedule for Children (DISC-P; Costello, Edelbrock, and Costello, 1985) that yielded child psychiatric diagnoses such as ADHD. The boys completed the Recent Mood and Feelings Questionnaire (Costello and Angold, 1988) as a measure of depressed mood. Also, CAT results on reading, language, and mathematics were obtained from the schools.

Various questionnaires were used to assess parental discipline and supervision, parent-child communication, parental disharmony (where two parents were present), parental stress, parental anxiety, and parental substance use. Socioeconomic status was assessed using the Hollingshead (1975) index, based on parental occupational prestige and educational level. Where two parents were present, the highest score was recorded. Housing quality (based on such features as the structural conduction of the house and visible signs of peeling paint) was assessed by the interviewer. Neighborhood quality was rated by the mother and also assessed from census data.

In order to maximize the validity of all variables, information from different sources was combined as far as possible, as was information from screening and assessment A. The combined measure of delinquency seriousness based on mothers, boys, and teachers was a better predictor of court petitions than self-reported delinquency alone (Farrington et al., 1996). Hence, the combined reports of violence are used in this chapter in preference to self-reports alone. Only brief descriptions of variables are included in this chapter; more extensive descriptions can be found in the book by Loeber and his colleagues (1998).

Court records were obtained from Allegheny County Juvenile Court (paper files). The City of Pittsburgh is included in and surrounded by Allegheny

County, which had a population of about 1,336,000 in 1990 (Hoffman, 1991). Six boys who moved outside Allegheny County during the two years after assessment A were excluded from the court analyses, as were seven boys with no consent forms or incomplete records. In order to carry out a genuinely predictive analysis, two boys with court records for index violence before assessment A were excluded, leaving 493 boys in the court analysis who had no official record at age ten.

Detected juvenile offenders in Allegheny County may be referred to the Juvenile Court by the police or other agencies (e.g., the school board). The intake officer (in the probation department) reviews all cases and almost always meets with the alleged offender, the family, and the victim. The intake officer may dismiss or withdraw cases because of doubts about whether the offender is in fact guilty, doubts about whether there is sufficient evidence to prove that the offender is guilty, or for procedural reasons such as the victim not turning up. The intake officer may divert the offender (e.g., by giving a warning or requiring informal probation) if the case is minor or the offender is young and criminally inexperienced. If the intake officer believes that there is sufficient evidence that the juvenile is guilty, and that the case is too serious for diversion, the case will be petitioned to the Juvenile Court. We have only counted petitioned cases. Therefore, our recorded juvenile offenders are relatively serious cases where there is convincing evidence of guilt.

The Pittsburgh Youth Study has a unique combination of features:

a. It is a multiple-cohort accelerated longitudinal design (Bell, 1954; Farrington, 1991), although only the middle cohort is studied in this chapter;
b. It contains a high-risk sample and a representative sample, thus maximizing the yield of antisocial boys while still permitting conclusions about the general population;
c. Information from the boys, mothers, and teachers was obtained every six months on seven occasions for the middle sample, and data collection is continuing annually for the youngest and oldest samples;
d. The main focus of interest is on offending, violence, and child psychiatric disorders;
e. The sample size of about five hundred per cohort is relatively large;
f. The multiple-cohort design means that results obtained with one sample can be tested for replication with others;
g. There has been a very low attrition rate from the first follow-up onward; 94 percent of the follow-up sample of boys in the middle cohort were interviewed in the seventh assessment;
h. Information has been obtained about a wide variety of theoretical constructs, including individual, family, socioeconomic, peer, and neighborhood measures.

Explanatory Variables

There was a great deal of data reduction to try to produce distinct measures of a relatively small number of key theoretical constructs. The aim was to eliminate redundancy without significant loss of information. Only clearly explanatory variables were included as predictive factors. For example, peer delinquency was excluded, since it could merely be measuring the boy's own delinquency (since 76 percent of seriously delinquent acts in the middle sample were committed with others). Correlates of delinquency were excluded. Amdur (1989) pointed out that a common fault in much delinquency research is to include measures of the outcome variable as predictors. If two variables basically measure the same underlying construct, using one as a predictor of the other will artifactually increase the percentage of variance explained, but this is of little practical significance for the explanation or prevention of delinquency.

In order to avoid collinearity problems in regression analyses, we deleted variables that were highly correlated (phi > .40) with other, conceptually similar variables. For example, the age of the mother at her first birth was retained in preference to the age of the mother at the birth of the boy (phi = .45), and a broken family (not living with two biological parents) was retained in preference to living in a single-parent, female-headed household (phi = .59). However, African-American race and bad neighborhood (according to census data) were both retained in the analysis (phi = .52), as were African-American race and living on welfare (phi = .42) and broken family and living on welfare (phi = .43), because these were judged to be important and distinctly different variables.

Eventually, the information collected in the screening and A assessments was reduced to forty key explanatory variables or risk factors (see Loeber et al., 1998; Farrington and Loeber, 1999), divided into four categories: child, child-rearing, socioeconomic, and parental. In general, variables were only included if between 15 percent and 35 percent of boys could be identified as a risk group. However, exceptions were made for some variables because of their importance (e.g., family on welfare, broken family, African-American race). The Pittsburgh data could have been reweighted back to the screening sample (but not to the original target population) by appropriate multiplication. However, reweighting was not done because, while it changed prevalence estimates, it did not change measures of association, which are the focus of this chapter.

For many analyses, explanatory variables were dichotomized, as far as possible, into the "worst" quarter of males (e.g., the quarter with the lowest income or lowest intelligence) versus the remainder. The one-quarter/three-quarters split was chosen to match the prior expectation that about one-quarter of the sample would be referred to court as juveniles. There are many advantages of dichotomized variables (Farrington and Loeber, 2000). First, they permit a "risk factor" approach, and also make it possible to study the cumulative effects of several risk factors. Second, they make it easy to investigate interactions between variables (which are often neglected with continuous variables because of the difficulty of studying them). Third, they make it possible to compare all variables directly by equating sensitivity of measurement. Some variables are inherently dichotomous (e.g., broken family, family on welfare). In many studies, it is difficult to know whether one variable is more closely related to an outcome than another because of differential sensitivity of measurement rather than differential causal influence.

Fourth, dichotomous data permit the use of the odds ratio as a measure of strength of relationship, which has many attractions (Fleiss, 1981). The odds ratio is easily understandable as the increase in risk associated with a risk factor. It is a more realistic measure of predictive efficiency than the percentage of variance explained (Rosenthal and Rubin, 1982). For example, an odds ratio of 2, doubling the risk of violence, might correspond to a correlation of about .12, which translates into 1.4 percent of the variance explained. The percentage of variance explained gives a misleading impression of weak relationships and low predictability. Unlike correlation-based measures, the odds ratio is independent of the prevalence of explanatory and outcome variables and independent of the study design (retrospective or prospective). Nevertheless, because of the mathematical relationship between the logarithm of the odds ratio and the product-moment (phi) correlation (Agresti, 1990: 54), conclusions about relative strengths of associations based on odds ratios and phi correlations are similar. Also, the odds ratio emerges in logistic regression analyses as a key measure of strength of effect while controlling for other variables.

Fifth, using dichotomous data and the odds ratio encourages the study of the worst affected individuals. In delinquency research, there is often more interest in predicting extreme cases (e.g., "chronic" offenders) than the whole range of variation. Some variables are nonlinearly related to delinquency, with a large increase in delinquency in the most extreme category compared with the remainder. For example, in the Pittsburgh study, the percentage of boys petitioned to the juvenile court was 40 percent of those with three or more siblings, compared with 25 percent of those with two siblings, 25 percent of those with one sibling, and 22 percent of those with no siblings. Some variables (e.g., self-reported delinquency) often have a highly skewed distribution, causing the product-moment correlation to have a theoretical maximum value considerably below 1 and hence again to give a misleadingly low impression of the strength of a relationship.

While dichotomization is a way of dealing with these various problems, it is often criticized because of loss of information and lower measures of association (Cohen, 1983). However, loss of information is also involved in other commonly used analytic techniques, for example combining several different aspects of parenting into one composite variable, or including only a small subset of measured variables in an analysis. Our assessment is that, for many purposes, the advantages of dichotomization outweigh its disadvantages.

Official and Reported Violence

An advantage of using the middle sample is that only two boys had a court petition for index violence before the explanatory variables were measured (up to assessment A). After excluding these two boys from the analysis, the explanatory variables were genuinely predictive of court violence. After assessment A, fifty-nine boys had a court petition for index violence: 56 (21 percent) of 273 African-American boys, compared with only 3 (1 percent) of 220 Caucasian boys, an amazing difference (odds ratio or OR = 18.7).

A second measure of violence was based on reports by boys, mothers, and teachers about the boy (a) attacking someone with the intention of seriously hurting or killing them, (b) using force to get money or possessions from someone, or (c) hurting or forcing someone to have sex. Thus, the reported violence was based on multiple reports of aggravated assault, robbery, or forcible rape. Gang fights and carrying a weapon were not included in reported violence.

Up to assessment A, 110 (22 percent) of the 508 boys had committed index violence, according to themselves, their mothers, or their teachers. This was true of 83 (29 percent) of the 284 African-American boys, and 27 (12 percent) of the 224 Caucasian boys (OR = 3.0). After assessment A, information about violence was available from five waves of data collection, up to age thirteen. After assessment A, 149 (30 percent) of the 494 boys (excluding fourteen who were missing on at least three of the five assessments and were not violent) were reported to have committed index violence, including 109 (40 percent) of the 275 African-American boys and 40 (18 percent) of the 219 Caucasian boys (OR = 2.9).

Reported violence up to assessment A significantly predicted reported violence after A. For African-American boys, 65 percent of those who were violent up to A were also violent after A, compared with 29 percent of those not violent up to A (OR = 4.5). For Caucasian boys, 41 percent of those who were violent up to A were also violent after A, compared with 15 percent of those not violent up to A (OR = 3.9). Therefore, the degree of continuity in violence was similar for African-American and Caucasian boys. Reported violence up to A also significantly predicted court violence after A for each ethnic group. For African-American boys, 31 percent of those who were violent up to A were referred to court after A, compared with 16 percent of those not violent up to A (OR = 2.3). For Caucasian boys, 4 percent of those who were violent up to A were referred to court after A, compared with 1 percent of those not violent up to A (OR = 3.7). Reported violence after A was also related to court violence after A for both African-American boys (OR = 3.0) and Caucasian boys (OR = 9.8).

Predictors of Violence

In Table 11.1, explanatory variables are divided into child, child-rearing, socioeconomic, and parental factors, all measured up to assessment A (at about age ten). The odds ratios measure the strength of relationships between explanatory variables and violence.

Of the forty explanatory variables, twenty-two were significantly related to reported violence up to assessment A: child variables such as lack of guilt, high ADHD, and low achievement (boy, mother, teacher rating); child-rearing variables such as poor parental supervision, poor parent-child communication, and the mother's physical punishment; socioeconomic variables such as a broken family (not living with both biological parents), low SES, and the family on welfare; and parental variables such as a poorly educated father, a young mother (under age eighteen at the time of her first birth), and parental anxiety/depression. The previously mentioned relationship between African-American race and reported violence up to A (OR = 3.0) was the second strongest relationship, after lack of guilt (OR = 4.1).

Twenty-four of the forty explanatory variables significantly predicted reported violence after assessment A: child variables such as lack of guilt, low achievement on the CAT, and being old for the grade (which indicates being held back because of low achievement); child-rearing variables such as parental disagreement on discipline, unhappy (disharmonious) parents, and poor parent-child communication; socioeconomic variables such as living in a broken family, living in a bad neighborhood according to the mother, and low SES; and parental variables such as behavior problems of the father, parental substance use, and a young mother. Not surprisingly, reported violence up to A was the strongest predictor of reported violence after A (OR = 5.0). African-American race (OR = 2.9) was a slightly weaker predictor than lack of guilt (OR = 3.3), low achievement on the CAT (OR = 3.2), a broken family (OR = 3.1), and being old for the grade (OR = 3.0).

Only fifteen of the forty explanatory variables significantly predicted court violence after assessment A. African-American race was by far the strongest predictor (OR = 18.7). Of the four categories of variables, the strongest predictors were socioeconomic: the family on welfare (OR = 3.7) and living in a broken family (OR = 3.4). Other strong predictors of court violence were low achievement on the CAT (OR = 2.7), a young mother

Table 11.1. *Predictors of Violence (Odds Ratios)*

	Violence		
Variable	Reported Up to A	Reported After A	Court After A
Child			
Lack of guilt (PT)	4.1*	3.3*	2.5*
Old for grade (P)	2.1*	3.0*	2.6*
HIA problems (PT)	2.5*	2.6*	1.0*
High ADHD score (P)	2.6*	2.1*	1.1
Low achievement (PBT)	2.6*	2.0*	1.9*
Low achievement (CAT)	2.3*	3.2*	2.7*
Depressed mood (B)	1.3	1.9*	0.8
Shy/withdrawn (PT)	1.6*	1.6*	1.2
Child-rearing			
Poor supervision (PB)	1.6*	1.1	1.3
Poor communication (PB)	1.8*	1.9*	0.9
Physical punishment (PB)	1.7*	1.6*	1.1
Low reinforcement (PB)	0.9	1.1	1.8*
Disagree on discipline (PB)	1.7	2.7*	1.5
Unhappy parents (P)	1.5	2.0*	1.8
Socioeconomic			
Low SES (P)	2.0*	2.2*	2.0*
Family on welfare (P)	2.1*	2.0*	3.7*
Unemployed father (P)	1.9	1.8*	1.0
Unemployed mother (P)	1.4	1.2	2.1*
Small house (P)	1.7*	2.1*	1.4
Broken family (P)	2.6*	3.1*	3.4*
Bad neighborhood (P)	1.9*	2.3*	2.6*
Bad neighborhood (C)	1.6*	2.0*	2.2*
Parental			
Father behavior problems (P)	2.0*	2.2*	1.3
Parent substance use (P)	1.4	2.2*	1.1
Parent anxiety/depression (P)	2.1*	1.3	0.9
High parental stress (P)	1.8*	1.7*	0.8
Young mother (P)	2.1*	2.0*	2.7*
Poorly educated mother (P)	1.5	1.4	2.4*
Poorly educated father (P)	2.2*	1.8	1.6
Large family (P)	1.3	1.4	2.4*
Other			
African American (P)	3.0*	2.9*	18.7*
Reported up to A	–	5.0*	3.4*
Reported after A	–	–	4.6*

Note: B = Boy, C = Census, P = Parent, T = Teacher. CAT = California Achievement Test, HIA = Hyperactivity-impulsivity-attention deficit, *p < .05 (one-tailed, based on confidence interval). No significant relationship: Low religiosity, anxiety, few friends, low organizational participation, low jobs/chores involvement, boy not involved, boy not close to mother, no set time home, poor housing.

(OR = 2.7), being old for the grade (OR = 2.6), living in a bad neighborhood according to the mother (OR = 2.6), and lack of guilt (OR = 2.5). Reported violence before A (OR = 3.4) and after A (OR = 4.6) were both significantly related to court violence.

There were fewer significant predictors of court violence than of reported violence, but to a large extent the predictors of court violence were a subset of the predictors of reported violence. The unique predictors of court violence were low parental reinforcement (approval for good behavior), an unemployed mother, a poorly educated mother, and large family size (three or more siblings). These family-related factors may possibly be associated with the decision to petition a case rather than to choose informal processing.

Multivariate Analyses

Regression analyses were carried out to investigate how far the relationship between race and violence might be mediated or explained by other risk factors. For example, were African-American boys more likely to be violent purely because they were more likely to be living in broken families or in bad neighborhoods?

Strictly speaking, logistic regression analysis should be carried out with dichotomous data. However, the major problem with logistic regression is that a case that is missing on any one variable has to be deleted from the whole analysis, often causing a considerable loss of data. Fortunately, with dichotomous data, ordinary least squares (OLS) regression produces very similar results to logistic regression (Cleary and Angel, 1984), and indeed the results obtained by the two methods are mathematically related (Schlesselman, 1982: 245). Missing data are not such a problem with OLS regression, because missing cases can be deleted variable by variable, thereby using as much of the data as possible. Both OLS and logistic regression analyses were carried out, on the assumption that most confidence can be placed in results that are replicated in the two analyses.

Hierarchical regression analyses were carried out. Generally, it was expected that child-rearing factors (e.g., poor supervision) would cause child factors (e.g., lack of guilt) rather than the reverse, that socioeconomic factors (e.g., low SES) would cause child-rearing factors (e.g., poor supervision) rather than the reverse, and that parental factors (e.g., a young mother) would cause socioeconomic factors (e.g., the family on welfare) rather than the reverse. There is a surprising degree of consensus among longitudinal researchers (e.g., Rutter, 1981; Larzelere and Patterson, 1990) and contextual researchers (e.g., Simcha-Fagan and Schwartz, 1986; Gottfredson, McNeil, and Gottfredson, 1991) that neighborhood and socioeconomic factors have indirect effects on delinquency via their effects on child-rearing and individual factors. African-American race was entered last in all regression analyses, because it could not be caused (changed) by any other factor, and because the aim of the analyses was to identify risk factors that explained the relationship between race and violence. Other causal orders are of course possible; for example, socioeconomic factors could influence parental factors rather than the reverse. The present ordering was justified empirically by Farrington and Loeber (1999), who also showed that similar results were obtained with alternative hierarchies of influence.

In predicting violence, the block of child factors was entered first, then the block of child-rearing factors, then the block of socioeconomic factors, then the block of parental factors, and finally race. Because we wanted to investigate independent effects of explanatory variables, forward stepwise regression was used. Table 11.2 shows F changes and LRCS (Likelihood Ratio Chi-Squared) changes rather than weights (beta weights or partial ORs) because the weights are so sensitive to the intercorrelations between the particular variables included in the model (Gordon, 1968). F changes and LRCS changes show how far one variable predicts violence independently of others.

Table 11.2 shows that lack of guilt and low achievement (rated by the boy, mother, and teacher) were the only significant independent factors for reported violence up to assessment A in both the OLS and logistic regression analyses. African-American race was still a significant risk factor in both analyses after controlling for all other independent risk factors. However, the strength of the relationship between African-American race and violence was considerably reduced after controlling for independent risk factors. The F change decreased from 22.65 ($p < .0001$) for race alone to 8.69 ($p = .002$) after controlling for independent risk factors, and the LRCS change decreased from 22.83 ($p < .0001$) for race alone to 13.30 ($p = .0002$) after controlling for independent risk factors.

It might be expected that the strength of the relationship between race and reported violence up to A would decrease even more after controlling for all twenty-one significant risk factors. This was true. However, African-American race was still a significant risk factor for violence in both the OLS (F change $= 5.67$, $p = .009$) and logistic (LRCS change $= 6.23$, $p = .006$) regression analyses, after first entering all twenty-one significant risk factors in the equation.

Unfortunately, with twenty-one risk factors, the logistic regression analysis was severely affected by missing data, and in fact was only based on 199 cases with complete data out of the 508 boys in the middle sample. In order to avoid this problem of missing data, a risk score was derived for each boy, specifying the percentage of risk factors out of twenty-one that he possessed. (Where a boy was not known on a risk factor, the percentage was based on fewer than twenty-one risk factors, so no boy was missing on the risk score.) The risk score was first entered into the equation, and then race. The

Table 11.2. *Hierarchical Multiple Regression Analyses*

	OLS		Logistic	
Variable	F change	p	LRCS change	p
Reported Violence up to A				
Lack of guilt	39.09	.0001	33.23	.0001
Low achievement (PBT)	9.13	.001	6.60	.005
High ADHD score	3.09	.040	–	–
Physical punishment	–	–	4.65	.016
Bad neighborhood (P)	2.82	.047	–	–
Broken family	–	–	4.89	.014
Young mother	3.58	.030	–	–
Parent anxiety/depression	2.61	.050	–	–
African American	8.69	.002	13.30	.0002
African American (All)	5.67	.009	6.23	.006
African American (Risk)	4.07	.022	5.13	.012
Reported Violence After A				
Reported up to A	52.55	.0001	49.17	.0001
Low achievement (CAT)	19.30	.0001	19.38	.0001
Lack of guilt	12.43	.0003	8.19	.002
Old for grade	9.22	.001	3.44	.032
Depressed mood	2.66	.052	–	–
HIA problems	–	–	4.26	.020
Disagree on discipline	4.89	.014	3.81	.025
Bad neighborhood (P)	3.62	.029	–	–
African American	2.85	.046	3.00	.042
African American (All)	–	–	–	–
African American (Risk)	3.91	.024	4.42	.018
Court Violence After A				
Reported after A	33.58	.0001	28.65	.0001
Reported up to A	7.43	.003	5.63	.009
Old for grade	4.03	.023	3.80	.026
Family on welfare	9.53	.001	8.86	.001
Unemployed mother	–	–	3.87	.025
Bad neighborhood (P)	–	–	3.55	.030
Large family	4.99	.013	4.16	.021
African American	16.99	.0001	19.71	.0001
African American (All)	8.99	.002	4.75	.015
African American (Risk)	16.22	.0001	23.76	.0001

Note: p values one-tailed because of directional predictions. B = Boy, P = Parent, T = Teacher, CAT = California Achievement Test, HIA = Hyperactivity-Impulsivity-Attention Deficit, OLS = Ordinary Least Squares, LRCS = Likelihood Ratio Chi-Squared. (All) = Controlling for all significant predictors. (Risk) = Controlling for risk score based on all significant predictors.

results showed that African-American race was still a significant risk factor for violence in both the OLS (F change = 4.07, $p = .022$) and logistic (LRCS change = 5.13, $p = .012$) regression analyses, but again the relationship between race and violence was reduced.

The significant relationship between race and reported violence up to assessment A did not disappear after controlling for all key explanatory variables measured in the Pittsburgh Youth Study. Could this be because the explanatory variables were dichotomized? In order to investigate this, continuous explanatory variables were used in the analysis as far as possible. Controlling for twenty-one key explanatory variables, race was still a significant risk factor for violence in the OLS regression analysis (F change = 8.38, $p = .002$). The logistic regression analysis also showed this (LRCS change = 2.79, $p = .047$) but, as explained above, was severely affected by missing data.

The OLS and logistic regression analyses were repeated for the prediction of reported violence after assessment A. In this analysis, reported violence up to A was entered first in the equation, then the four blocks of risk factors, and then race. Table 11.2 shows that low achievement on the CAT, lack of guilt, being old for the grade, and the parents disagreeing on discipline all predicted reported violence after A independently of reported violence up to A and independently of each other. African-American race was still a significant predictor (F change = 2.85, $p = .046$ in the OLS analysis; LRCS change = 3.00, $p = .042$ in the logistic analysis).

Controlling for twenty-four significant risk factors (including reported violence up to A), race did not significantly predict reported violence after A in either the OLS or logistic regression analyses. Controlling for a twenty-four-item risk score, race was still a significant predictor (F change = 3.91, $p = .024$ in the OLS analysis; LRCS change = 4.42, $p = .018$ in the logistic analysis). However, there were clear signs in this analysis that the relationship between race and violence was being largely eliminated after controlling for other significant predictors.

In the final regression analysis predicting court violence after assessment A, reported violence up to A and reported violence after A were entered first in the equation, then the four blocks of risk factors, and then race. Being old for the grade, the family on welfare, and large family size were the most important independent predictors of court violence. African-American race was still a significant predictor in all analyses. In light of the strength of the relationship (OR = 18.7) between race and court violence, it seems unlikely that this relationship could be eliminated by controlling for other, unmeasured risk factors.

The independent predictors of reported violence up to A were largely different from the independent predictors of reported violence after A. This could be because reported violence up to A was included as a predictor of reported violence after A, and hence the predictors of reported violence up to A had already had their effects. Similarly, the independent predictors of court violence were largely different from the independent predictors of reported violence after A. This could be because reported violence after A was included as a predictor of court violence, which meant that predictors of court violence could be predicting why boys are referred to court rather than why boys are violent.

Ethnicity and Risk Factors

In attempting to explain the link between race and violence, we focus on reported violence up to assessment A, which could not be fully explained by the risk factors measured in the Pittsburgh Youth Study. This is our best measure of violent behavior, although it is not without problems. For example, mothers and teachers may not have much opportunity to observe violence by boys, and the types of acts reported (e.g., attacking to hurt) may vary considerably in seriousness and may be less serious than acts leading to a court petition for violence. There was continuity between violence up to and after A, and there were twenty-one significant risk factors for reported violence up to A. Were African-American boys more likely than Caucasian boys to experience these risk factors?

Table 11.3 shows the relationships between these twenty-one risk factors and race. For eleven risk factors, the significant OR indicates that more African-American boys experienced the risk factor. The largest OR (92.2) was for living in a bad neighborhood according to the 1980 Census. This was a combined variable based on median family income, percentage of persons unemployed, percentage of families below the poverty level, percentage of persons between ages ten and fourteen, percentage of single-parent female-headed households, and percentage separated or divorced (Loeber et al., 1998: 71). Nearly half (47 percent) of African-American boys lived in bad neighborhoods, compared with virtually no (1 percent) Caucasian boys.

African-American boys were also far more likely than Caucasian boys to live in families on welfare (62 percent as opposed to 20 percent), bad neighborhoods according to mothers (36 percent as opposed to 9 percent), and broken families (77 percent as opposed to 40 percent). Not surprisingly, African-American boys experienced significantly more risk factors than Caucasian boys (7.3 out of 21 on average, compared with 4.4; F = 83.43, $p < .0001$). However, the correlation between the number of risk factors and reported violence was remarkably similar for African-American boys ($r = .295$) and Caucasian boys ($r = .294$). This suggests that more African-American than Caucasian boys might have been violent because African-American boys experienced more risk factors.

Table 11.3. *Ethnicity and Risk Factors for Reported Violence Up to A (Odds Ratios)*

Variable	Versus Ethnicity	For Caucasians	For African Americans
Child			
Lack of guilt	2.0*	3.7*	3.6*
Old for grade	1.4	1.7	2.0*
HIA problems	1.5	2.2	2.5*
High ADHD score	1.1	3.1*	2.5*
Low achievement (PBT)	1.1	1.8	3.1*
Low achievement (CAT)	2.7*	1.4	2.0*
Shy/withdrawn	1.0	1.4	1.7*
Child-Rearing			
Poor supervision	2.3*	1.6	1.2
Poor communication	1.3	2.0	1.6
Physical punishment	1.7*	2.9*	1.2
Socioeconomic			
Low SES	1.8*	3.1*	1.4
Family on welfare	6.5*	1.7*	1.2
Small house	3.8*	2.4	1.1
Broken family	5.0*	2.4*	1.6
Bad neighborhood (P)	5.3*	0.7	1.5
Bad neighborhood (C)	92.2*	0.9	0.9
Parental			
Father behavior problems	1.3	2.7*	1.6
Parent anxiety/depression	0.7	2.9*	2.2*
High parental stress	1.1	1.9	1.8*
Young mother	2.7*	2.8*	1.4
Poorly educated father	1.2	2.3	2.1

Note: B = Boy, C = Census, P = Parent, T = Teacher. CAT = California Achievement Test, HIA = Hyperactivity-Impulsivity-Attention Deficit
*$p < .05$ (one-tailed, based on confidence interval).

In order to investigate this more directly, the risk score was related to violence separately for African-American and Caucasian boys. Figure 11.1 shows that, at almost all levels of risk (holding risk constant), African-American boys were more likely to be violent than Caucasian boys. Therefore, while the strength of the relationship between risk scores and violence was the same for African-American and Caucasian boys, levels of violence were higher for African-American boys.

It is still possible that the relationship between some risk factors and reported violence is different for African-American and Caucasian boys. Table 11.3 shows the relationship between all twenty-one risk factors and

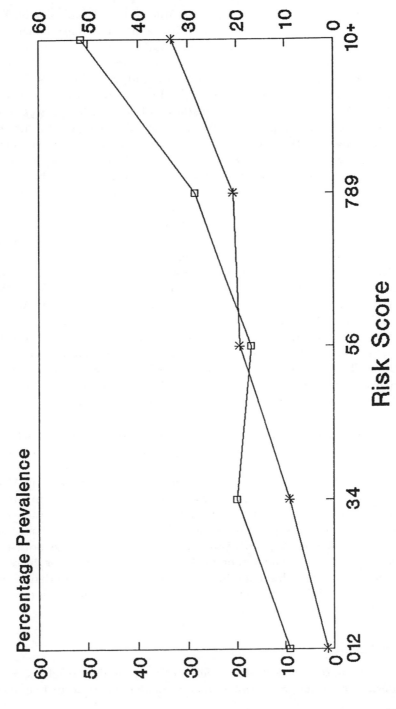

Figure 11.1. Prevalence of Reported Violence

reported violence separately for African-American and Caucasian boys. The mother's physical punishment, low SES, the family on welfare, a small house, a broken family, behavior problems of the father, and a young mother were more strongly related to violence for Caucasian boys. Only low achievement was more strongly related to violence for African-American boys. The interaction term was significant (on a one-tailed test) for a or the mother's physical punishment ($p = .037$), and nearly significant for low SES ($p = .070$) and the family on welfare ($p = .064$). Lack of guilt, being old for the grade, HIA problems, ADHD, parental anxiety/depression, high parental stress, and a poorly educated father were comparably related to violence for African-American and Caucasian boys. There was no relationship between living in a bad neighborhood (according to the Census) and violence for African-American boys; 32 percent of those in good neighborhoods were violent, compared with 29 percent of those in bad neighborhoods. In contrast, 12 percent of Caucasian boys in good neighborhoods were violent, and only two Caucasian boys were living in bad neighborhoods.

Even where the strength of the relationship between a risk factor and violence was similar for African-American and Caucasian boys, levels of violence were higher for African-American boys. For example, for African-American boys, 50 percent of those lacking guilt were violent, compared with 22 percent of those feeling guilt (OR = 3.6); for Caucasian boys, 26 percent of those lacking guilt were violent, compared with 8 percent of those feeling guilt (OR = 3.7). Where the relationship between a risk factor and violence was stronger for Caucasian boys, levels of violence were still higher for African-American boys. For example, for African-American boys, 32 percent of those physically punished (slapped or spanked) by their mothers were violent, compared with 28 percent of those not punished (OR = 1.2); for Caucasian boys, 21 percent of those physically punished by their mothers were violent, compared with 8 percent of those not punished (OR = 2.9).

It is possible that, where risk factors are more prevalent among African-American boys than among Caucasian boys, their relationship with violence might be weaker among African-American boys. This was true for the mother's physical punishment, low SES, the family on welfare, a small house, a broken family, and a young mother. However, it was not true for lack of guilt, low achievement on the CAT, poor supervision, or the two bad neighborhood variables. Therefore, using a measure of strength of relationship that is not inherently confounded with prevalence (the odds ratio), this hypothesis was not confirmed.

Conclusions

According to reports by the boys, their mothers, and their teachers, African-American boys were more violent than Caucasian boys. According to court petitions for index violence, the differential between African-American and Caucasian boys was much greater; 21 percent of African-American boys had a court petition, compared with only 1 percent of Caucasian boys. Reported violence up to assessment A predicted reported violence after assessment A similarly for African-American and Caucasian boys.

The most important risk factors for reported violence up to assessment A were lack of guilt, low achievement, high ADHD, the mother's physical punishment, a bad neighborhood, a broken family, a young mother, and parental anxiety/depression. After controlling for important risk factors, the significant relationship between race and reported violence up to A was reduced but not eliminated, showing that it could not be fully explained by risk factors measured in the Pittsburgh Youth Study. However, the relationship between race and reported violence after A was eliminated after controlling for reported violence before A and important risk factors, suggesting that race differences in reported violence after A might be explained by referring to continuity from reported violence before A.

The strong relationship between race and court violence was reduced but not eliminated after controlling for reported violence (the best available measure of violent behavior) and important risk factors. There are three major explanations for the discrepancies between reported and court violence:

a. There is discrimination against African-American boys at the arrest or court referral stages, possibly based on variables not included in this analysis. For example, Caucasians may be processed informally (rather than petitioned) because they and/or their parents are perceived as more cooperative or less criminal or because their school reports (e.g., of truancy or suspensions) are more favorable. Earlier, we found that certain family-related factors (such as an unemployed or poorly educated mother) were related to court violence but not to reported violence after assessment A, suggesting that they might be associated with the decision to petition.
b. The violent acts of African-American boys are perceived as more serious, perhaps because they are more likely to involve gangs, drugs, weapons, and injuries.
c. The reported violence only covers the time period up to age thirteen, whereas the court violence covers the time period up to age sixteen. Possibly, differences in violence between African-American and Caucasian boys are greater after age 13.

We could not investigate these hypotheses within the scope of this chapter.

In attempting to explain the link between race and reported violence up to assessment A, it was clear that African-American boys were more likely than Caucasian boys to experience important risk factors such as a bad neighborhood, the family on welfare, a broken family, a young mother, and physical punishment. Also, African-American boys experienced more risk factors: an average of 7.3 each, compared with 4.4 for Caucasian boys. Virtually no Caucasian boys lived in bad neighborhoods according to Census variables. It might perhaps be argued that Caucasian boys in Pittsburgh are an inadequate comparison group for African-American boys in Pittsburgh. For example, in order to find a sample of Caucasian boys who suffer similar structural conditions to African-American boys in Pittsburgh, it may be necessary to go to rural areas of the American South, where impoverished Caucasians reside, such as Appalachia. Interestingly, Peeples and Loeber (1994) found that, in nonunderclass neighborhoods of Pittsburgh, African-American and Caucasian boys had similar delinquency rates.

While the correlation between the number of risk factors and reported violence was remarkably similar for African-American and Caucasian boys, the prevalence of violence was greater for African-American boys at almost all levels of risk. This may possibly be because risk factors may be more serious for African-American boys: bad neighborhoods may be worse, physical punishment may be more severe, young mothers may be younger, and the poverty indicated by welfare dependency may be more desperate. Risk factors may have different meanings for different races. Also, risk factors may have a longer duration for African-American boys, or may have interactive (multiplicative) effects. Thus, four risk factors for an African-American boy may indicate objectively worse circumstances than four risk factors for a Caucasian boy. Another possibility is that protective factors (which were not studied in this analysis) might be less common among African-American boys.

Interestingly, some risk factors were differentially related to reported violence according to race. In particular, the mother's physical punishment, low SES, the family on welfare, a small house, a broken family, behavior problems of the father, and a young mother were more strongly related to violence for Caucasian boys and not related to violence for African-American boys. Why this should be so is not clear, although (as pointed out earlier) other researchers have reported comparable findings (McLeod et al., 1994; Deater-Deckard et al., 1996; Paschall et al., 1998). We find it surprising that important risk factors such as physical punishment do not have bad effects for African-American boys. Possibly, these bad effects might be masked by the large number of risk factors experienced by African-American boys. There was no consistent tendency for risk factors that were more prevalent among African-American boys to be less strongly related to violence.

There are a number of important priorities for future research. First, while it is abundantly clear that African Americans are more likely to experience risk factors than Caucasians, it is not clear whether different developmental processes or theories are involved for African Americans and Caucasians. More research is especially needed on the link betwen parental physical punishment and violence, to establish if there really are racially different processes or whether the risk factor has different meanings for African Americans and Caucasians. If there are racially different processes, one implication is that racially different interventions might be needed to reduce violence. Second, future researchers should make special efforts to assemble comparable samples of African Americans and Caucasians, and preferably other racial groups as well. Third, future researchers should measure the quality of the violence in more detail, and should measure violence over longer time periods. Particularly relevant is the study of the types of conflict (and antecedent conditions) that eventually culminate in violence.

We are left with the conundrum of why African-American boys are more violent. We began with the belief that this relationship had to be mediated and explained by variables such as living in a bad neighborhood, a broken family, a young mother, living on welfare, physical punishment, and low achievement. However, while these variables explained most of the relationship between African-American race and violence in the present analysis, they did not explain it all. The challenge for future researchers is twofold: to explain the remainder of the racial difference in behavior, and to explain the even greater disproportionality in official violence.

"Race Effects" and Conceptual Ambiguity in Violence Research: Bringing Inequality Back In

Marino A. Bruce
Vincent J. Roscigno

The United States is a dangerous place to live for racial/ethnic minority citizens. Research on this topic tends to deal primarily with the group with the highest level of violent activity, African Americans. However, recent research suggests that interpersonal violence represents a serious morbidity and mortality concern for other disadvantaged groups as well (Levine and Rosich, 1996). For instance, Martinez (1996) shows that urban Latinos have homicide rates that are considerably higher than the national average. Moreover, Yung and Hammond (1994) show that Native Americans also have violence rates that exceed their European counterparts. Typically, efforts to explain these higher levels of violence direct attention to group attributes or emphasize the social environment in which the group resides. While these approaches have generated some important findings, they are plagued by narrow conceptions of race and racial inequality and, thus, are limited in addressing disparate group patterns of violence.

In this chapter, we attempt to facilitate the reconceptualization process by first critically examining existing research and highlighting conceptual inadequacies. We then draw from stratification research and its explicit discussion of inequality and group outcomes to illustrate that the "effects" of race on violence are linked to very tangible macro-structural, normative, and interactional dynamics; ones sensitive to the local and historical dynamics associated with the social environment in which African Americans, and most race/ethnic minorities, tend to reside. It is our hope that the conceptual tools we introduce, and questions we generate, contribute to a new and more explicit discourse on race and violence as well as systematic empirical efforts to examine the processes outlined.

Dominant Perspectives on Race/Ethnicity and Violence

Research on violence and race falls into three categories. Biocriminal perspectives argue that nonsocial (biological) factors influence levels of interpersonal violence among social groups. Some recent work, in fact, has argued that biological factors have just as much or more to do with the etiology of violent behavior as do social factors (Wilson and Herrnstein, 1985; Ellis, 1990; Herrnstein and Murray, 1994). Cultural perspectives, by contrast, tend to concentrate on normative attributes allegedly specific to a given racial or ethnic group. Violence is seen as resulting from a culture where criminality in general, and violence in particular, are more acceptable forms of behavior (Elkins, 1959; Wolfgang and Ferracuti, 1967; Curtis, 1975). Finally, structural perspectives argue that violence among the poor and/or minority groups stems primarily from the disadvantaged material conditions they face, such as high levels of poverty and unemployment (Blau and Blau, 1982; Brownfield, 1986; Hagan and Peterson, 1995; Hawkins, 1983, 1986; Sampson, 1987).

Biocriminal Perspectives. Of the prevailing ideas about the connection between race and violence, none are more controversial than those falling into the biocriminal camp. Biocriminal theorists argue that violence, like other behavior, is a consequence of physiological attributes. The basic idea is that groups with high levels of violence function physiologically (e.g., enzyme or hormone production) in a manner that predisposes them toward interpersonal violence (Ellis, 1990; Ellis and Walsh, 1997; Herrnstein and Murray, 1994; Wilson and Herrnstein, 1985).

Biocriminal work at the turn of the century did not explicitly focus on race because of the prevailing notions about racial or ethnic superiority and inferiority. "Inferior" groups (e.g., Irish, Italians, and African Americans) were presumed to be physiologically deficient and violence was considered to be a by-product of heritage. Contemporary biocriminal perspectives, in contrast, depart from a strictly biological approach and acknowledge the importance of social environment (Wilson and Herrnstein, 1985; Ellis, 1990; Herrnstein and Murray, 1994). A closer inspection of these ideas, however, reveals that contemporary biocriminal theorists are considerably more forthcoming about racial differences in violence and crime. *Crime and Human Nature* (1985) is an excellent example. In a chapter on black crime, Wilson and Herrnstein argue that differences in black and white crime rates can be attributed to "constitutional differences" between the two groups. The examples of such differences they give are body type, personality, and IQ scores. Although personality and IQ scores can be the product of one's social environment, it is clear that the authors do not depart very far from the classic biocriminal account. They assert that constitutional differences are present during the initial stages of life, suggesting that body type, personality, and IQ are essentially physiologically determined.

During their long tenure in the literature, biocriminal perspectives have generated controversy, especially with the occurrence of monumental political events such as the rise of Nazi Germany and the Civil Rights Movement. As a result, biology-oriented explanations of racial differences in any social phenomena, including violence, have been relegated to the margins of social scientific discourse but remain popular among some segments of the general public. This is not to suggest, however, that such approaches have disappeared from the research literature altogether. To the contrary, modified versions continue to appear in books (e.g., Wilson and Herrnstein, 1985; Herrnstein and Murray, 1994) and scholarly journals (e.g., Ellis, 1990; Ellis and Walsh, 1997; Moffit, 1990; Rowe and Osgood, 1984).

In addition to their political implications, biocriminal perspectives have come under fire for a lack of empirical support (see Jencks, 1994; Shoemaker, 1984; Sutherland and Cressy, 1974). In fact, many of their key hypotheses have yet to be tested, making it nearly impossible to assess the empirical validity of the idea that genetic material or enzyme production, for instance, influences violence (Jencks, 1994). We see criticisms leveled against biocriminal perspectives as quite valid and appropriate. We take these critiques a step further, however, and suggest that biocriminal conceptions of the race-violence linkage are based on flawed assumptions.

The argument that groups exhibiting higher levels of violence are genetically or biologically different, for instance, fails to recognize the fact that race is itself a social construction. Race and ethnicity have and continue to be classification schemes designed for, and that indeed reinforce, unequal distributions of economic, political, and social resources in this society (Lieberson, 1980). By overlooking the dynamic nature of race itself, racial classificatory schemes, and their uses historically, biological and biosocial perspectives are flawed and, indeed, not only reify race but reinforce their own theoretical positions. The result is an overly simplistic theoretical understanding; one that oversimplifies across and with-group biological variation and that is insensitive to the historical and social dynamics of group subordination.

Cultural and Subcultural Approaches. In response to biocriminal ideas, researchers moved to explain racial differences in levels of violence and other forms of criminality along more social scientific lines (Hawkins, 1995). One result was the development of the cultural difference paradigm. Its basic premise is that value systems for particular groups, including African Americans and other ethnic minorities, are qualitatively different from that of the larger society (for instance, see Sutherland, 1934; Sellin, 1938). The disintegration and workings of minority group institutions (e.g., family,

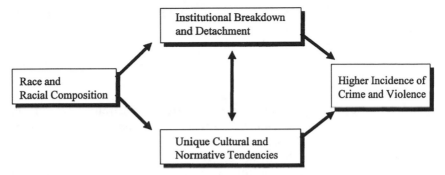

Figure 12.1. Cultural Deprivation Framework for Understanding Varying Levels of Crime and Violence Across Populations

religion, education, etc.) are, at least in part, to blame as group members are denied the opportunity to learn conventional norms and values, including those condemning illegitimate forms of violence (Moynihan, 1965; Wolfgang and Ferracuti, 1967; Auletta, 1982). Instead, a subculture of violence has developed and exists as part of an alternative normative structure for disadvantaged group members.

The result of these processes, it is argued, is that African Americans are more likely to use violence in their day-to-day encounters. They are thought to resolve disputes through violence rather than through more "legitimate" means, such as verbal negotiation (Gibbs, 1988). Thus, whether historically based in their social practices or in their institutional setup, the argument is that violence is rooted in counternormative attributes of the African-American community itself. Figure 12.1 is a visual depiction of these ideas.

In the decade following its introduction, the cultural difference paradigm was the primary explanation for the race-violence connection. Despite its popularity, this school of thought has been criticized on the grounds that they assume a unique subculture based in and adhered to by members of a particular societal subgroup. A number of researchers have disputed this claim, arguing that what are often thought of as unique cultural tendencies are, in fact, emergent phenomena – manifestations of local structural conditions and general levels of opportunity (Taylor, 1979; Wilson, 1987; Anderson, 1990). Structurally oriented researchers have noted the lack of community structural context in cultural interpretations of race, criminal activity, and violence (Hawkins, 1987; 1985; Sampson, 1987; Staples, 1986). Ignoring the structural features of a given community, as Sampson and Wilson (1995) suggest, has the effect of directing attention to alleged problems with and within poor, nonwhite communities while, at the same time, ignoring more macro-societal processes at work. Fundamental structural attributes of a given locality, such as poverty and unemployment, have consequences for the disproportionate breakdown of local institutions like families, churches, and schools (Hawkins, 1985; Staples, 1986). Yet, the cultural frameworks tend to overlook or neglect altogether the interrelation between normative process/institutional deterioration and the structural features of a given place.

Social Structural Approaches. Rather than concentrating on alleged pathological or cultural deficiencies associated with disadvantaged groups, structural criminological approaches explore relationships between material conditions in a given locality and levels of violence. These perspectives suggest that harsh economic conditions facing a population, coupled with very high levels of residential segregation, account for the disparate rates of within-group violence. Here the focus moves us beyond characteristics internal to a given group and instead highlights a group's status and material reality in a class and race-stratified society.

While quite similar, there are at least two strands within the structural camp, each of which varies theoretically on the question of why structure is crucial to the patterning of criminological outcomes. Strain theory posits that crime results from a disjuncture between aspirations espoused by the dominant culture and the "legitimate" resources to obtain them. It is argued that the absence of legitimate avenues of opportunity, such as education and employment, can motivate disadvantaged individuals or groups to pursue alternative and illegitimate routes, including those that tend to be more violent, in order to obtain societally desired ends (Merton, 1938; Agnew, 1992).

The other strand of the structural camp, the social disorganization approach, argues that crime is linked to the disintegration of social bonds between residents and the larger community. Specifically, limited structures of opportunity within a given locality hinder the formation of, or tear down, institutional social control structures, thus reducing a given community's ability to guard against crime (Shaw and McKay, 1945; Bursik, 1988; Bursik and Grasmick, 1993).

Independently, strain and social disorganization perspectives propose different mediating pathways between local structures of opportunity and criminological outcomes. Regardless of these differences, both have influenced the direction of research by suggesting that the key causal forces behind violence are the material conditions and opportunities within a given locality, rather than biological attributes or normative systems. These ideas are displayed in Figure 12.2.

An Empirical Critique of the Three Dominant Perspectives. Most of the empirical research investigating violence among African Americans, regardless of conceptual foundation, uses racial composition, commonly known

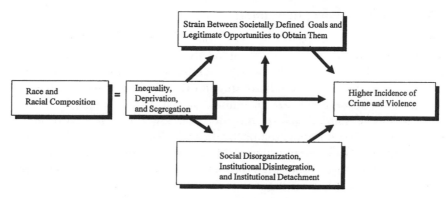

Figure 12.2. Structural Criminological Framework for Understanding Varying Levels of Crime and Violence Across Populations

as %Black, as a proxy for race or culture. Although popular, using racial composition in this manner carries with it some problematic assumptions. The size of the African-American population is presumed to be equivalent to the size of a subpopulation with differing normative characteristics and/or institutional tendencies. Consequently, and given these theoretical operationalizations, one might conclude that the primary source of violence lies within African-American individuals and communities themselves.

Racial composition has also been used with poverty measures to capture structural disadvantage. Using racial composition in this manner avoids derogatory assumptions about African Americans, but the results from structural research have done little to offer a clear picture of how material conditions factor into high levels of violence among this group. Recent studies focusing on methodological problems associated with this line of research conclude that such inconsistency is the result of misspecified empirical models (Messner and Golden, 1987; Land, McCall, and Cohen, 1990). Given the conceptual problems highlighted earlier, model misspecification may be as much the outcome of theoretical limitations as it is the result of methodological shortcomings.

Racial composition in the structural literature denotes material disadvantage; however, this measure does not specify why African Americans are disadvantaged at the outset. This is not to suggest that research has altogether ignored racial inequality as an important factor in the race-violence or race-crime relationship. To the contrary, embedded within some classic (e.g., Du Bois, 1899; Shaw and McKay, 1945) and contemporary (e.g., Peterson and Krivo, 1993; Shihadeh and Steffensmier, 1994) criminological work is the idea that inequality increases the likelihood that individuals or groups may engage in behaviors that can be harmful to themselves and/or others. The problem has to do with clarity and theoretical specification.

Theoretical Reconceptualization

Gaining a better understanding of the race-violence relationship requires a dynamic framework; one that puts at the center processes that reproduce material disparities and even what is typically seen as cultural variation across groups. In the remainder of this chapter, we draw from stratification research and pose a conceptual framework that is more explicit with regard to how certain groups are introduced to and concentrated in places characterized by economic, political, and social disadvantages. We link our stratification process-based understanding with existing cultural and structural work and pose a more comprehensive model. This integration and development, focusing on inequality processes in particular, carries with it clear consequences for empirical measurement, modeling, and interpretation of what race and racial composition actually mean.

Inequality Processes and Resultant Structures of Opportunity. Structural factors and social processes relating to class and racial inequality are an integral part of African-American life, and are central to understanding the patterns of violence we find. The level of inequality facing African Americans in a given locality depends, in large part, on this group's presence and relative size. Stratification research clearly suggests that a large or growing minority group population represents perceived (or real) threats to the economic and political well-being of majority group members (Blalock, 1967). In order to maintain their advantaged position, dominant group members develop practices that discriminate against African Americans and other minority groups (Wilson, 1978; Lieberson, 1980; Olzak, 1992). In the following paragraphs, competition and exploitation accounts of these processes will be discussed. Each lays out the development of racial antagonism and the consequences of that antagonism for historical and current disadvantages faced by African Americans.

Competition theorists (e.g., Blalock, 1967; Olzak, 1992) focus largely on the manifestation of racial antagonism and its consequences for discriminatory action by working-class European Americans. Race relations, it is suggested, remain relatively stable until a significant amount of African-American (or other racial/ethnic minority) labor becomes available for use by capital. Under these circumstances, European-American workers perceive increasing numbers of African-American workers as a threat to their economic status, since employers can easily replace them at a lower cost. When this has occurred historically, European-American workers have set up exclusionary rules and practices, such as denying access to unions or guilds, to fortify their advantaged status (Bonacich, 1976; Lieberson, 1980). The outcome is a wage differential, or split-labor market, between European- and African-American workers even when efficiency and productivity are held constant (Bonacich, 1972; Brown and Boswell, 1995; Semyonov and Cohen, 1990; Tienda and Lii, 1987; Tomaskovic-Devey, 1993). These tendencies also have been observed to lead to higher historical and contemporary levels of residential segregation, poverty, unemployment, and violence (Corzine, Creech, and Huff-Corzine, 1983; Corzine, Huff-Corzine, and Creech, 1988; Falk and Rankin, 1992; Massey and Denton, 1987; Massey and Gross, 1991; Olzak, 1990; Phillips, 1987; Turk, 1982). Thus, material deprivation of African Americans is partially a product of, and may vary spatially as a function of, racial composition and its historical and contemporary relation to economic competition with dominant racial group members. European-American action in defense of racial privilege along with its consequences, rather than simply racial composition, becomes the central focus.

The competition viewpoint has been critiqued for its neglect of class processes in general and of the influence of elite dynamics on racial group well-being (Tomaskovic-Devey and Roscigno, 1996). Exploitation theorists offer an alternative, more class-sensitive approach to understanding racial disadvantage. Basically, the argument has been that elites threaten the material interests of working-class European Americans by proposing to replace them with African-American workers who will work for lower wages (Szymanski, 1976; Reich, 1981). The upper class takes an active role in spurring racial antagonism by pitting groups of workers against each other for material gain. Here the story is not about pure racial competition per se but, rather, has to do with elite exploitation of racial fear and class division. Some have argued that the relative success of elites on such a front is all but certain. Elite success at promoting racial division and therefore race and class exploitation may vary spatially and may require both elite cohesion and a nonwhite population sizable enough to generate fear and antagonism (Roscigno and Tomaskovic-Devey, 1994; Tomaskovic-Devey and Roscigno, 1996).

Both competition and exploitation theories assert that racial antagonism exists because African Americans represent a threat, perceived or real, to the material well-being of working-class European Americans and that this group is prompted to take steps to secure their own economic and political stability (Wilson, 1978; Lieberson, 1980). The discriminatory and exploitive methods employed secure the material interest of dominant racial group members or a certain class faction while intensifying economic, political, and social disadvantages for African Americans and other racial/ethnic minority groups. One way in which this racial inequality is manifested is through job and labor market discrimination, exclusion, and/or concentration in the form of discriminatory pay and hiring as well as from the relegation of African Americans to less prestigious and, therefore, lower-paying jobs (Tomaskovic-Devey, 1993). Kirshenman and Neckerman (1990), in their research on hiring practices in Chicago, show how employers continue to discriminate against nonwhites despite federal guidelines making race-based discrimination illegal. Specifically, they find that European-American employers make decisions about the hiring and placement of minorities based on the unfounded notion that African Americans lack commitment to work and exhibit low levels of productivity.

Coupled with disadvantages at the job level are those deficits having to do with the disproportionate concentration of African Americans and other nonwhite groups into poorer labor market areas (Wacquant and Wilson, 1989; Wilson, 1987; 1996; Lichter, 1989; Tomaskovic-Devey and Roscigno, 1997). Some explain this concentration in terms of general historical and ecological trends. Wilson (1978; 1987; 1996), for instance, suggests that the changing economic structure of major urban areas of the United States, coupled with the rising cost of production, has forced business to either shut down or relocate outside of central cities, especially in localities that are predominately African-American. Because many of the former employees of these transplanted industries lack the human capital or monetary resources to relocate to areas with better employment opportunities, many are compelled to seek employment in the local, low-paying service sector or abandon the labor market completely (Wilson, 1987; Kassarda, 1989). This scenario presents a situation where limited opportunities for African Americans stem from a changing economy as opposed to intentional exclusionary or discriminatory practices.

There are other, more recent lines of theoretical and empirical work that focus on the influence of elite and corporate investment/disinvestment dynamics on local class- and race-based struggles. Given the centrality of elite activity in the reproduction of racial disadvantage, this research should be seen as an extension of classical exploitation theory. New urban theorizing is explicit with regard to the influence of elite activity and human agency on the crises facing many urban areas (Gottdiener and Feagin, 1989). Recent evidence, for instance, suggests that elite investment/disinvestment patterns and local growth machine politics systematically bypass localities with large minority populations, thereby shaping economic development and creating societal racial inequality through spatial patterns of investment (Logan and Molotch, 1987; Molotch, 1988; Wilson, 1992). Redlining of disproportionately African-American areas by banks and insurance companies most assuredly plays a role in reproducing patterns of depressed economic development and racial concentration by both limiting the formation of new businesses and by contributing to the speed at which an area physically declines and is deemed undesirable by potential investors (Squires, DeWolfe, and DeWolfe, 1979; Squires, Valez, and Taeuber, 1991). Finally, the concentration of African Americans into poorer labor areas may be a function of the distorting consequences of racial antagonism, exclusion, and discrimination for long-term economic development or of the dependence of

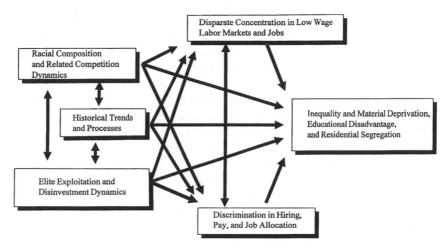

Figure 12.3. Stratification Processual Understanding of Varying Levels of Absolute and Relative Disadvantage Across Populations

local elites on the persistence of a low-wage, labor-intensive labor market (Tomaskovic-Devey and Roscigno, 1996).

These patterns have resulted in and reinforced levels of residential segregation, which itself has consequences for structures of available opportunity. Even though federal law prohibits the intentional separation of the races, residential "steering" by realtors, federally sponsored public housing, and European-American attitudes have kept urban areas segregated (Farley and Frey, 1994; Massey, 1990; Massey and Denton, 1987; 1993; Massey and Gross, 1991; Peterson and Krivo, 1993). This form of discrimination is found to have far-reaching consequences because it adversely affects the next generation of African Americans through the institution of education (Roscigno, 1995). Coupled with manufacturing disinvestment and suburbanization, residentially segregated nonwhite communities contain schools that have poor facilities and an environment that is anything but conducive to learning (Jaynes and Williams, 1988; Roscigno, 1995; 1998). Ramifications of these processes are clear. First, young people in these areas become discouraged and, as a result, drop out of school at much higher rates. Second, those who do make it through school in these localities and graduate are less likely to have the educational or vocational training necessary for college or for a skilled labor market (Wilson, 1987; 1996). As with economic disinvestment, the life chances of African Americans diminish because educational disadvantages cause the window of economic and political opportunity to shrink even further.

Figure 12.3 depicts competition and exploitation processes and their consequences for group disadvantage. Racial composition and inequality are no longer nebulous constructs with little depth. Rather, they are linked with competition and exploitation dynamics, continued concentration in poor labor markets, and processes of institutional inequality and exclusion. By incorporating these dynamics, violence researchers can be more conceptually specific when referring to race and/or racial inequality in their models. Better yet, research should attempt to flesh out and measure these processes rather than merely blending them with the ambiguous use of racial composition – a measure that could be taken to mean one of a variety of things.

The processes discussed above have serious implications for the social structural contexts in which African Americans are disproportionately embedded. In the past, it has been argued that poor life chances resulting from the processes described generate a greater likelihood of violence. Some suggest that individuals in such a situation become angry about their material position and lash out violently at those around them (Grier and Cobbs, 1968; Gibbs, 1994). Portraying African Americans as "dupes," driven to violence by overwhelming structural conditions, is objectionable. Perhaps violence emerges from shifts in normative/cultural patterns that occur as a consequence of a group's embeddedness in a particular structural situation. Bringing in a normative or "cultural" dimension can help make sense of how material disadvantages and inequalities translate into day-to-day interaction and behavior.

Structural Conditions and Normative Boundaries. Unlike traditional cultural approaches, we do not see normative pressures, tendencies, and changes as necessarily an attribute of a population or particular racial group. Rather, they are a manifestation of societal processes (e.g., racial competition, elite activity, etc.) and the consequences of these processes for structural conditions. Extending a social structural understanding in this manner turns attention from the environment itself to social action within a given structural context. Shifting emphasis in this way also guards against losing sight of the individual or of human agency. Human actors are cognizant and rational beings that engage in purposive behavior in accordance with social structure (Giddens, 1984; Messerschmidt, 1993).

A context-sensitive approach to understanding "culture" or normative tendencies can be linked to the work of cultural theorists such as Swidler (1986). In dealing with social strategies and actions, she conceives of "culture" as a set of tools that guide how individuals interpret their circumstances and generate methods for dealing with them. Such an understanding of "culture" can be applied to disadvantaged groups. There is, in fact, evidence supportive of this stance that deals with class- and race-based educational disadvantages, ethnicity and racial separation, and the seemingly antagonistic character of adolescent peer groups located in areas of limited opportunity. With regard to peer group attachments and antagonism in particular, evidence suggests that they are more likely to emerge in places where class- and race-based opportunities and the socioeconomic return to education are more severely limited (Fordham and Ogbu, 1986; Hargreaves, 1967; MacLeod, 1995; Ogbu, 1978; Willis, 1981). Not coincidentally, such areas in the United States tend to be disproportionately nonwhite and highly residentially segregated. This suggests a reflexive process whereby normative responses and boundaries are shaped by what adolescents see as their own opportunities in life. Given that perfect information regarding future opportunities is virtually impossible to acquire, it is likely to be the case that adolescents acquire this information by observing the current economic and occupational status of adults they know (Anderson, 1990; Majors and Billson, 1992; MacLeod, 1995; Roscigno, 1995).

Arguments pertaining to the emergent character of culture can similarly be found in research examining the ethnic character of particular groups within the United States (see especially Burr and Mutchler, 1993; Taylor, 1979; Tomaskovic-Devey and Tomaskovic-Devey, 1988; Yancey et al., 1976). This research suggests that what is often interpreted to be ethnicity or group cultural attributes is, in fact, a subordinate group response to or a normative manifestation of harsh structural conditions (i.e., poverty, discrimination, and residential segregation). Taylor (1979), in an analysis of African-American identity, comes to a similar conclusion. He finds that group identity and related normative attributes, often perceived of as ethnicity, are profoundly shaped by the character of the locality in which the group is embedded and, most important, the extent to which the group is structurally segregated.

Ethnographic research reveals that the permanency associated with the plight of many African Americans in these areas has lead to emergent phenomena, including violence, that further limit life chances (Anderson, 1978; 1990; Keiser, 1979; Liebow, 1967). In an analysis of inner-city youth and sex codes, Anderson (1990) notes that norms for conduct among poorer inner-city youth, while arguably destructive, are "nothing less than the cultural manifestation of persistent urban poverty" (1990: 112).

The lesson here is that what is often perceived of as the unique and preexistent cultural characteristics of a given subordinate group may actually be more a function and outcome of a group's recent and current structural location (Tomaskovic-Devey and Tomaskovic-Devey, 1988). This point is highlighted in a recent piece of research by Alex-Assensoh (1995), who finds that "underclass behaviors" typically thought of as a reflection of African-American culture are, in fact, a reflection of the poverty stricken neighborhoods in which the group exists. She compares the behavior of whites and blacks who are embedded in a similar structural situation and finds that the level of "underclass behavior" is virtually indistinguishable across

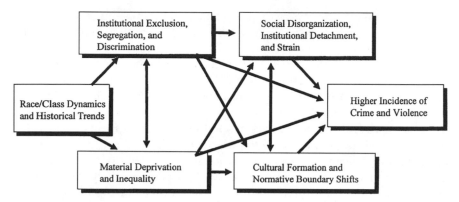

Figure 12.4. Integration of Stratification Process Considerations With Structural and Cultural Criminological Approaches to Crime and Violence

groups, both statistically and substantively. Thus, practices often thought to be associated with culture may have just as much or perhaps even more to do with the material conditions in which a given group is embedded. In Figure 12.4, we offer a broad theoretical overview of the relations discussed previously and their interrelation with normative structures/boundary shifts.

The acknowledgment of local class and race stratification dynamics broadens our understanding and, indeed, informs current violence research. As is evidenced in the figure above, a cultural understanding and especially a focus on normative constraint and boundaries remains important, but only when understood within the context of local opportunity. The emphases of strain and social disorganization perspectives on material deprivation and its consequences for institutional deterioration, detachment, and disjuncture between societally desired ends and legitimate means to achieve those ends is preserved as well. Here, however, we specify why and how material deprivation is created and reproduced in the first place, and possible actors involved. The reader should note that directing attention to mechanisms implicated in the reproduction of racial disadvantage is more than merely a theoretical extension or integration. Rather, it holds with it implications for future research, not to mention policy efforts aimed at stemming current trends pertaining to crime and violence. We conclude by discussing each of these in turn.

Conclusion

Criminological views of racial concentration and racial inequality are problematic. Some assume general biological dispositions or cultural and normative proclivity differences across racial and ethnic groups. Others tie racial composition to levels of material deprivation. Bringing inequality processes back into the discussion clarifies some of the ambiguity and offers a clearer understanding of the mechanisms at work. Beyond linking these violence outcomes to broader social processes, the framework we offer also affords researchers the theoretical tools to systematically tie violence to contemporary and historical specifics of place (see also Hawkins, 1987; Hagan, 1992).

Whether one is speaking of racial competition models for understanding racial disadvantage or variations of a more class-sensitive approach, one thing is clear – theoretical modeling must be sensitive to historical and contemporary dynamics that may make one locality different in process and outcome than another. Rarely are such variations in process made explicit, theoretically or empirically, in violence research. This is unfortunate as predictions themselves regarding black-white differences in violent activity will differ, and may even be opposite, depending on the local dynamics that are being played out. Racial competition points of view, for instance, would suggest increased racial disparity in both material deprivation, crime, and violence in areas of heightened competition since working-class whites benefit from racial struggle relative to their black counterparts. Most class-based approaches, in contrast, would predict a diminished racial gap in such outcomes, as both working-class whites and nonwhites are affected in a similar direction by the historical and contemporary playing out of class struggle, elite economic projects, and their consequences for opportunity. Certainly, these race and class dynamics may and do interact in varying ways. The point, however, is that in order to make clear predictions, one must supplement general theorizing with the historical particulars of place (for instance, see Roscigno and Bruce, 1995; Tomaskovic-Devey and Roscigno, 1996; Bruce et al., 1997). At the very least, it is incumbent on researchers to make explicit their rationale and expectations when using race and/or racial composition in predicting crime and violence outcomes. This includes the conceptual and/or operational specification of not only the direction of the relationship, but the process as well.

Our discussion and theoretical framework imply the need for a multimethod approach to the analysis of violent outcomes. Ethnographic, community, and/or qualitative research endeavors, for example, are quite successful in pointing out both more proximate causal mechanisms in the (re)production of social action and also the importance of experiential knowledge. That is, the experiences of subjects are crucial in making sense of social processes, including those having to do with violence (Wardell and Zajicek, 1995). Historical treatments, moreover, have uncovered macro-level societal changes that have clear ramifications for the phenomena we investigate and whether we should expect the problems we research to be perpetuated or even intensified. Coupled with social structural and aggregate analyses, this multimethod approach lends itself to generalizability and to a clearer understanding of the spatial character of these processes. We believe all of the above are crucial to sound social scientific analysis (in this regard, see Mills, 1959; 1963; Wardell and Zajicek, 1995). Whether at the level of literature review and theory or at the level of an actual research project, a multimethod undertaking will lead to the acknowledgment of multiple contexts at varying levels and will clarify conceptualization and modeling of violence and other criminological outcomes.

The ideas presented and a stratification process-oriented approach more generally hold relevance not only for academicians but also for current policy aimed at curbing crime and violence. By broadening the discourse and focusing on more fundamental societal processes at work, we are pushed to more holistic solutions. Current efforts regarding increased policing of "dangerous" areas, the mentoring of vulnerable adolescent populations, helping gangs come to truces, and creating safe zones for those who feel threatened are indeed all important. However, such remedies, often the product of political partisanship and rhetoric, only address proximate causes and therefore are only a temporary and, at best, minimal fix. They are analogous to taking an aspirin for a headache – covering some of the pain without addressing its cause.

Serious efforts to deal with disparate violence and crime within certain communities must be broader. Along with current policy efforts dealing with offenders and/or potential victims, the focus must be extended to the places in which they live and the social causes of their participation. Discussion and policy on economic development and growth should be central as it has clear consequences for family stability and well-being, the availability and quality of educational resources, and ultimately a sense of attachment and responsibility to community. Just as important should be the strengthening of legal efforts to curb discrimination in housing, education, and on the job. Finally, greater investigative and legal effort should be placed on the uncovering of corporate redlining practices and corporate avoidance of certain areas and populations.

Current political discourse and legislation on violence and crime is far from incorporating such issues into the dialogue. Perhaps this is because of our tendency to see the world in individualistic terms and, thus, believe that the cause lies in bad individuals. Maybe it is because of the fact that it would require a greater political and social commitment, more resources, and an acknowledgment that some people and groups are not getting a fair shake in our allegedly meritocratic system. Then again, broadening the dialogue with regard to causes and solutions may be too threatening a task for political leaders, as some of the blame and cost is shifted away from politically weak and vulnerable groups in our society and toward the more politically and economically powerful. Whichever is the case, remedies will remain limited in their effect until policy efforts are extended to account for the mechanisms that reproduce poor neighborhoods and disadvantaged groups in the first place.

The Violent Black Male: Conceptions of Race in Criminological Theories

Jeanette Covington

Violent crime has been a major problem in African-American communities for many years.[1] Indeed, Uniform Crime Report (arrest) data indicate that African-American males have had significantly higher homicide rates than white males since at least 1930 (Reiss and Roth, 1993). Moreover, these differences have proven to be lasting, as recent arrest statistics indicate that African Americans, who make up 12 percent of the U.S. population, account for 57 percent of all homicide arrests (FBI, 1998; Harris and Shaw, 2000). And while the level of racial disproportionality is more modest for aggravated assaults, blacks still account for as many as 37 percent of aggravated assault arrests (FBI, 1998). Indeed, when blacks and whites are compared in terms of rates per 100,000, African Americans have homicide rates that are 8.8 times as high as those of whites and aggravated assault rates that are 3.9 times as high as white rates (FBI, 1998; Harris and Shaw, 2000).

Yet, violent crime rates do not simply vary by race. They also vary by the size and population density of a community. Hence, when violent crime rates are compared across cities, suburbs, and rural areas, large cities tend to have higher violent crime rates per capita than smaller cities, suburbs, or rural areas (Reiss and Roth, 1993). This has led a number of researchers to analyze the impact of race and urban residence simultaneously. And, when

---

[1] Violent crimes typically refer to the index offenses of homicide, rape, aggravated assault, and robbery. However, many of the theories that will be reviewed in this chapter will be geared toward explaining homicide and assault only – especially homicides and assaults involving male offenders and male victims. Thus, in this paper, violent crime will refer only to these two crimes. Homicide is typically paired with assault because many homicides are the end product of assaults. However, because there are so few homicides, murder rates are taken to be only the tip of the iceberg when considering levels of violence in a population. Hence, murder rates and assault rates are often discussed jointly in studies that compare violent predispositions across groups.

variations in violent crime rates are compared across neighborhoods within a single city, rates of violent crime are typically highest in the city's poorest African-American neighborhoods (Covington, 1999; Covington and Taylor, 1989; Taylor and Covington, 1988; Peterson and Krivio, 1993; Messner and Golden, 1992; Wolfgang and Ferracuti, 1967; Sampson and Wilson, 1995; Sampson, 1985; Curtis, 1975; Shihadeh and Flynn, 1996; Rose and McClain, 1990; Blau and Blau, 1982).

Statistics like these have produced a very lively debate regarding just what accounts for the racial difference in violent crime and the high levels of urban black male involvement in homicides and assaults. One interpretation of these data suggests that black males are more violent because they are more likely to be "members" of highly disputatious neighborhood-based *subcultures*, where a wide variety of trivial insults and gestures are deemed sufficient to provoke violence (Wolfgang and Ferracuti, 1967; Luckenbill and Doyle, 1989).

Others argue that a history of racial oppression and/or contemporary structural constraints have led to the development of distinct *personality traits* that motivate black males to erupt in violent outbursts (Curtis, 1975; Poussaint, 1983; Comer, 1985; Kardiner and Ovesey, 1962; Oliver, 1994; Bernard, 1990; Majors and Mancini-Billson, 1992; Grier and Cobbs, 1992).

In accounting for the origins of violent black (sub)cultures or for black personality traits that lend themselves to violence, these researchers typically reject any notion that African-American motives for violence are a product of the larger American cultural experience. Rather, motivations for black violence are traced back to social, historical, economic, and/or cultural conditions that are *peculiar* to African Americans or African-American communities.

Clearly, then, the twin concepts of a violent black culture or black personality traits that predispose to violence were developed to explain the relationship between race and violent crime that regularly shows up in national- and city-level statistics. Yet, while these macro-level statistics indicate that a strong and consistent relationship exists between race and violence, ethnographic research is typically required for a more detailed understanding of just how and why race is linked to violence. Therefore, research, based on direct observation of violent black individuals or violent black subcultures, has frequently been used to provide such detailed understandings (Hannerz, 1969; Anderson, 1990; Oliver, 1994).

Problems arise because theories that suggest there is a more disputatious black subculture of violence or African-American personality traits that lend themselves to violence are extremely difficult to prove using national- or city-level arrest statistics. In fact, macro-level arrest data lend themselves to other more plausible interpretations of race differences in violence that do not require stretching these statistics to define the subcultures or personalities of an entire race or an entire community of males. Moreover, the twin concepts of a black subculture of violence or of African-American personality traits that predispose to violence are also difficult to prove using ethnographic research.

Yet, even though the concepts of a violent black subculture or violent personality traits among African Americans are not always supported by the data, they continue to guide explanations of race differences in violence. They also operate in the reverse. By suggesting that there is something specific to the subcultures or the personality characteristics of black males that prompts them to turn violent, these explanations are not simply using race differences in violence to explain the causes of violence. These explanations also use the race/violence relationship to *tell us something about the nature of black male character and how it differs from that of the rest of us.* This is because concepts like a violent black subculture or violent African-American personality traits are typically so broadly defined that they diffuse a predilection for violence beyond those black males who are actually violent to many who are nonviolent.[2] These theories, then, have the effect of fostering the notion that there is a vast social and psychological divide between black males and the larger society.

This chapter will address these issues, beginning with a review of various explanations that have been used to account for observed race differences in violence. This will be followed by a critique of these explanations that examines whether they have been (or even can be) supported by macro-level research or ethnographic data. Some consideration also will be given to how these explanations have the effect of diffusing violent predispositions to a wide swath of the black male population and thereby depicting the black male population as socially and psychologically distant from the larger society. Finally, there will be some discussion of how these questionable depictions of black male character could have negative policy implications.

---

[2] This problem with diffusion stems from a tendency to focus on differences between broad categories of people like "blacks" and "whites." The focus on these over-broad categories is, in part, an artifact of the data. The categories of "black" and "white" are easily counted and routinely measured in large-scale datasets like the UCR, NCVS, and studies of arrest data conducted at the state, county, city, or neighborhood level. This has led to the development of theories that are geared toward interpreting the meaning of differences between these easily countable categories of "black" and "white." In developing these theories, there is a tendency to look for social conditions that liken all blacks and separate blacks from whites. Hence, notions about black predispositions to violence are often developed based on across-race comparisons while within-race comparisons are ignored because they cannot be measured with these data. This means that these theorists can successfully distinguish the motives of violent blacks from whites, but they are typically incapable of making distinctions between violent blacks and nonviolent blacks (Covington, 1995; 1999).

Literature Review: Explaining Race Differences in Violence

Disputatiousness and the Subculture of Violence. The notion that certain groups could be subculturally predisposed to turn to violence was originally based on research indicating that violent crime rates tended to be highest in a city's poorest neighborhoods (Thrasher, 1927; Shaw and McKay, 1942). Over the years, a number of theorists attempted to explain these socioeconomic differences in crime by asserting the existence of a lower-class culture that encouraged crime and violence (Miller, 1958; Cloward and Ohlin, 1960; Banfield, 1970). Certainly, all these theorists alluded to race differences in crime as well, yet the class difference in crime was the central focus of their analysis.

Using arrest data from research conducted in Philadelphia's neighborhoods, Marvin Wolfgang and Franco Ferracuti (1967) likewise found that crime rates were highest in the city's poorest neighborhoods. And, consistent with the earlier cultural tradition, they argued that the communities with the highest crime rates had a subculture of violence. By this, they meant that residents of these low-income communities were more inclined to resort to violence to defend their status, honor, or reputation.

However, unlike earlier theorists, their claim that violence was more frequently deemed an appropriate response to insults was not meant to apply to all situations. Rather, the use of violence, for them, tended to be situation-specific. Hence, they argued that what distinguished community-based violent subcultures from the mainstream was their tendency to develop their own cultural rules or norms regarding how to act in specific social situations. So, for example, violence was defined as a legitimate response to insults that were made in situations such as when men were arguing in a bar or on a streetcorner, but not necessarily in other contexts. Those who used violence when honor was threatened were often rewarded by the respect of friends, acquaintances, and bystanders, who as members of the violent subculture tended to approve of violence to resolve disputes and address insults. Wolfgang and Ferracuti also claimed that inflicting grave injuries on those who had meted out insults did not induce feelings of guilt or remorse among members of the subculture. In fact, those who failed to answer various insults with violence could be subjected to ostracism, ridicule, and future bullying.

After reviewing much of the literature on situations that seemed to spark homicides and assaults, David Luckenbill and Daniel Doyle (1989) specified the steps in the violence process initially identified by Wolfgang and Ferracuti (1967). For Luckenbill and Doyle, members of a subculture of violence were more disputatious because they were more likely to see stares, gestures, jostles, and insults as an injury to self and so tended to *"name"* them. Once these affronts had been "named" as the basis for a grievance, disputatious persons were also more likely to demand reparations for the grievance – demands that Luckenbill and Doyle defined as *"claiming."* The harmdoers who leveled the initial insults were often unwilling to back down and defuse the situation because of their own membership in the disputatious subculture. Hence, disputes over minor matters often escalated into violence after grievances had been "named" and reparations "claimed" with no effort to defuse the situation on the part of the harmdoer.

While members of the subculture of violence were likely to hold the same values as persons in the mainstream on other matters, they clearly differed in terms of their disputatiousness. In other words, they were distinguished by their greater willingness to name a wide assortment of gestures, stares, jostles, and facial expressions as violence-worthy and to demand reparations. Persons who were not members of the subculture of violence did not share this definition of the situation and thus likely regarded many of the affronts that subcultural members took seriously as too trivial to merit violent retaliation.

Disputatious subcultures were understandably seen as groups of people who shared a willingness to name, claim, and aggress over minor matters and these subcultural norms were supposedly transmitted from one generation of males to another in violent communities (Wolfgang and Ferracuti, 1967; Luckenbill and Doyle, 1989). While the subculture of violence was used to explain assaults and homicides in low-income white communities, it was argued that a separate and substantially more disputatious subculture of violence was to be found among blacks (Wolfgang and Ferracuti, 1967; Luckenbill and Doyle, 1989). Supposedly, blacks held a definition of the situation that was different from whites and thus were more likely to "claim" reparations for even minor affronts. Wolfgang and Ferracuti (1967) describe these race differences in the following statement:

> ... the significance of a jostle, a slightly derogatory remark or the appearance of a weapon in the hands of an adversary are *stimuli differentially perceived and interpreted by Negroes and whites....* A male is usually expected to defend the name and honor of his mother, the virtue of womanhood ... and to accept no derogation about his race (even from a member of his own race), his age or his masculinity.... The upper-middle and upper social class ... considers many of the social and personal stimuli that evoke a combative reaction in the lower classes as "trivial." (italics mine)

Yet, while both the theories of Wolfgang and Ferracuti (1967) and Luckenbill and Doyle (1989) specify that there is a more disputatious subculture of violence to be found among blacks, they fail to explain how this black subculture of violence came to be more combative than the white subculture of violence. However, this task has been taken up by a number of other theorists.

Violent Predispositions: The Self-Hating Black Male. Alvin Poussaint (1983) offers one explanation for the origins of this subculture by locating it in the unique psychology of the black experience. For Poussaint, institutional racism and the negative images that it projects of blackness have caused African Americans to internalize feelings of self-hatred for themselves because they are black and to hate and degrade other blacks for similar reasons (Poussaint, 1983; Comer, 1985). Institutional racism likewise causes blacks to grapple with chronic feelings of rage and frustration. It is these persistent and uncontrollable feelings of rage and self-hatred that are at the root of many self-destructive behaviors among blacks, largely because these turbulent emotions lower their threshold for violence. Poussaint uses this notion of a lowered threshold for violence to explain why African Americans are given to responding to even the most trivial of slights with violent retaliation. In other words, because institutional racism has caused black males to experience a loss of self-respect, even minor provocations are taken seriously. The intense violent reaction to seemingly trivial affronts is the black perpetrator's way of restoring his fragile and frustrated ego.

Moreover, institutional racism and the degraded images of blackness cause black perpetrators to have little respect for their black victims. Indeed, violence enables them to project their own self-hatred onto their black victims. Their blind rage and their feelings of self-hatred thus allow perpetrators to strike out at black victims without experiencing any feelings of guilt; indeed, their disdain for all things black enables many African-American perpetrators to feel that their victimization of fellow blacks is justified. Hence, for Poussaint, the high rates of black-on-black violence are a natural outcome of widespread feelings of self- and group hatred.

With this self-hatred hypothesis, Poussaint appears to be able to explain many of Wolfgang and Ferracuti's observations regarding the black subculture of violence. After all, black self-hatred and rage can account for both the tendency of blacks to respond with violence to even the most trivial of insults as well as the guilt-free ease with which they are said to injure others.

Yet, while Poussaint acknowledges that Wolfgang and Ferracuti's subculture of violence does explain some black-on-black violence, he faults them for ignoring the psychological underpinnings of this subculture. He likewise parts company with Wolfgang and Ferracuti in respect to their view that the use of violence represents a normal and acceptable behavior within black communities. For Wolfgang and Ferracuti, the cultural transmission of values, meanings, and understandings favorable to violence from one generation to the next makes it possible for a normal low-income black teen growing up in a community with a thriving subculture of violence to come to see violence as appropriate behavior. By contrast, Poussaint concludes that violent perpetrators are psychologically impaired and then goes on to explain how racism has created a psychologically scarred black male who is predisposed to violence.

Poussaint is only one of many researchers who has struggled with the question of the extent to which violence within the black subculture should be viewed as "normal" or as "pathological." Many researchers who have read and attempted to interpret the meaning of the observations made by Wolfgang and Ferracuti (1967) appear to describe an absence of individual pathology in the *transmission* of proviolence values within the black sub-culture. However, much like Poussaint, they often appear to describe the *consequences* of involvement in this violent subculture for both the individual and the group as suggestive and deserving of the label "pathological." Perhaps that is why many who have attempted to explain the *origins* of this violent subculture have, much like Poussaint, described it in terms that explain how a race-specific history of racial oppression and/or race-specific structural conditions can lead to the development of a fundamentally different collective psychology among blacks.

By pointing to historical and structural conditions peculiar to blacks as the foundation for the self- and group-hating psyche of violent black males, Poussaint's work falls into a tradition that rejects any notion that violence among blacks is the product of historical, structural, or cultural experiences that affect all Americans – black and white alike. He thereby moves away from any race-neutral interpretation of black violence and places himself firmly within a tradition that suggests the violent behavior of blacks is evidence of race-specific pathology. Hence, Poussaint's brand of race-specific thinking lends itself to the notion that the race difference in violence, recorded in national statistics, reflects a difference-in-kind rather than a difference-in-degree.

Violent Predispositions: The Brittlely Defensive Black Male. Writing in this vein, Lynn Curtis (1975) identifies both historical and contemporary structural conditions as crucial in the formation of a black violent contra-culture. In accounting for the race-specific historical conditions that led to the formation of this subculture, he suggests that many black males developed a variety of strategies to maintain their personal autonomy during slavery. Hence, *heightened sensitivity* to any threats to their *personal autonomy* early became a part of the black subculture. Blacks were likewise exposed to the southern subculture of violence with its exaggerated sense of honor, its strong weapons-carrying tradition, and its acceptance of vigilantism. When blacks migrated northward, they carried these long-standing southern and slave cultural predilections for violence with them. Indeed, they found their violent predispositions were still relevant in the urban ghettos largely because of structural constraints that they encountered in these neighborhoods.

Immediately on arriving in the urban North, black migrants experienced limited opportunities for social mobility as only the most menial of jobs were available to them. While some of the new migrants resigned themselves to working at low-status, low-wage jobs, for others this compromise was too reminiscent of the docility required in slavery. Indeed their only outlet for acting in terms of a masculine role was to engage in violent masculine expressions at home, in neighborhood bars, in pool halls, and on local streetcorners (Hannerz, 1969; Curtis, 1975). On the face of it, individual blacks who made this adjustment must have looked a lot like white males coping with similar economic marginality.[3] Hence, Curtis seems to be proposing a difference-in-degree as race differences in violence would simply mean that higher unemployment levels among blacks forced more of them to adjust to these structural constraints.

However, he goes on to argue that violent masculine displays typically take on a more exaggerated quality among blacks because they have no other outlets for acting out acceptable male roles. Because of their limited outlets for masculine expression, they develop a "brittle defensiveness" that makes them less willing to walk away from trivial slights than even their economically marginalized white counterparts. Moreover, because so many blacks are forced to make these adjustments, what starts out as separate individual adaptations is transformed into a thriving contraculture for subsequent generations of ghetto blacks as each successive cohort emulates tough guys in the earlier cohorts. As violent masculine roles come to be shared by more ghetto males, others project these images more to avoid ostracism and ridicule.

The fact that more blacks are forced to make these adjustments coupled with their increasing concentration in urban ghettos also means that they typically have the critical mass of individuals needed for a subculture of violence to take off and be sustained over several generations. Indeed, Curtis suggests that the sheer size of the black population concentrated in these large urban ghettos makes for a more intense and exaggerated subculture of violence than in smaller communities; hence, collecting the "brittle sensitivities" of racially scarred individuals in a large urban ghetto creates a cultural milieu that is different in kind.[4]

For Curtis, then, the race-specific combination of historical and contemporary structural constraints and the concentration of blacks in urban ghettos are all *additive*, resulting in a black subculture of violence that is

---

[3] In research on Philadelphia, Roger Lane (1979; 1986) finds that, in the past at least, white males from minority ethnic groups such as the Italians and the Irish had high rates of violent crime. In fact, their rates of violent crime were not all that different from similarly situated African-American males.

[4] Research conducted by Sampson (1985) raises questions as to whether the sheer size of a black population is a good predictor of levels of violent crime.

fundamentally different from that found among low-income whites. He describes this difference in the following manner:

> A central argument for *more frequent and intense* contracultural patterns by the blacks is that they have *adapted to racial as well as class barriers* and unlike the European immigrant groups, they have inherited the unique experience of Southern slavery and violence.... When adhered to by one or more of the parties involved, violent contracultural values and behaviors can facilitate homicide and assault outcomes among young poor black males to a considerable extent, by increasing the probability that conflicts will begin and the likelihood that they will then escalate in physical intensity. The first probability reflects a *brittle defensiveness* and a reiteration of expressive physical manliness in word and action that can generate heated standoffs in situations that persons not accepting contraculture might find trivial. Once an altercation or other conflict has been initiated, the second probability is raised by the precedent of violent conflict resolution learned through past socialization experience. Much of this also applies to husband-wife and other male-female homicides and assaults among poor blacks. (Curtis, 1975: 45, 97; italics mine)

Curtis's depiction of a black contraculture is consistent with similar conjecture and conclusions found in the work of Wolfgang and Ferracuti (1967). Furthermore, in terms reminiscent of Poussaint, Curtis's contraculture represents a psychological adjustment in the form of a distinct personality type derived from historical and contemporary constraints on masculine roles within the black community. In other words, the exaggerated sense of honor and the brittle defensiveness in the face of slights constitute emotional predispositions that make black males more prone to violent conflict resolution than even economically marginalized white males. Indeed, the very fact that current cohorts of black males grow up in an environment in which such violent displays are seen as normal leads Curtis to hypothesize that violent blacks, socialized in the black contraculture, are fundamentally different from violent whites:

> Hypothesis 1 that black killers, assaulters and rapists . . . are *more* violent and explosive in their behavior before and after the crime, are *more* hostile towards parents, are *more* cruel in the commission of their crimes, . . . show *less* guilt and anxiety over their crime and are rejected less by their parents *than white killers, assaulters and rapists as a group*. The same statement is made about black versus white robbers. (1975: 107–8, italics mine)

Hence, through his notions of brittle sensitivities that have their origin in historical experiences unique to blacks, Curtis separates the roots of black violence from the larger American experience. It is clear, then, that Curtis's theory is not meant to be a race-neutral one that looks for similarities between black and white violent behavior. In a manner akin to

Poussaint, Curtis sets forth a race-specific theory that depicts black violence as different-in-kind from white violence.

Both Curtis and Poussaint developed their theories in order to interpret aggregate statistics that show a strong and consistent link between race and violence. However, theories explaining the race-violence link also have been derived from ethnographic research in which violent black individuals and small groups of violent black males are directly observed (Hannerz, 1969; Anderson, 1990; Anderson, 1994). William Oliver's (1994) research on compulsively violent black males represents this type of work in which a theory of race and violence is derived from direct observation of a violent black subculture. Indeed, after observing black males in a violent bar setting, Oliver makes many assertions about the nature of black violence that are quite similar to those of Curtis.

Violent Predisposition: The Compulsively Masculine Black Male. William Oliver (1994) is in agreement with Curtis (1975) that black conceptions of masculinity have been altered by race-specific historical and structural constraints. For him, the race-specific emotional mind-set that primes blacks for violent behavior is tied to the concept of compulsive masculinity. Compulsive masculinity refers to a cluster of behaviors that are meant to demonstrate commitment to norms like toughness, autonomy, sexual conquest, manipulation, and thrill-seeking – norms included in violent subcultures described by Curtis (1975) and Miller (1958).

In accounting for the origins of compulsive masculinity among blacks, Oliver likewise points to race-specific historical conditions like slavery in which black males become overly concerned with being free from any external controls. Their exaggerated tendency to equate autonomy with masculinity continues to find its expression in violent transactions among blacks who equate trivial insults and efforts to provoke them with being ordered around. Violent retaliation then becomes an assertion of their autonomy and manhood as it constitutes a refusal to be ordered about like a child (1994: 51).

However, for Oliver, contemporary structural constraints like high levels of unemployment are far more important in accounting for the development of a ghetto-based compulsive masculinity. High unemployment means that blacks have only limited opportunities to express mainstream masculine roles that require stable jobs and the capacity to support a family. Therefore, in order to fend off any feelings of low self-esteem, they have come to focus on alternative definitions of masculinity – as defined by compulsive masculinity – as a means of compensating for their failure to meet mainstream concepts of appropriate male roles. Hence, the high rates of homicides and assaults among black males can be understood in terms of their compulsive efforts to demonstrate a masculinity that is available to them – a masculinity defined in terms of toughness and autonomy.

Oliver notes that even the most violent of ghetto males are not constantly involved in assaults and murder. However, commitment to compulsive masculinity norms is routinely demonstrated through symbolic displays that take the form of race-specific talk and gestures. For example, ghetto males can display their toughness through a "cool pose" that announces that they are aloof, emotionally detached, and in control, even in risky situations (Majors and Mancini-Billson, 1992). This cool pose is typically communicated via facial gestures, a certain posture, and a style of walking, all of which convey fearlessness to would-be opponents. Symbolic displays of commitment to compulsive masculinity norms also take the form of "tough talking" or woofing to both demonstrate one's own masculinity credentials and to test those of potential opponents. Oliver is well aware that these symbolic displays do not take place in all situations; hence, he focuses on urban "hot spots" – like bars and bar settings (after-hours joints, greasy spoon restaurants, gambling parlors, streetcorners, parking lots of bars) – where these race-specific symbolic displays are likely to occur.[5]

Clearly, bars and bar settings are also hot spots for white male symbolic displays that regularly end in violence (Katz, 1988; Felson et al., 1986; Campbell and Gibbs, 1986; Roncek and Maier, 1991). Indeed, macro-level analyses of neighborhoods indicate that the presence of a tavern in a block significantly increases the number of violent crimes in those blocks relative to blocks that do not have a bar (Roncek and Maier, 1991). Hence, after reviewing this literature, Oliver might have been well on the way to developing a race-neutral theory that pointed out the similarities between black and white violent transactions in hot spots. In this way, high rates of homicides and assaults as a form of violent conflict resolution in urban hot spots might have been explained in terms of factors that stressed a difference-in-degree, like the fact that a larger percentage of black males are likely to be unemployed than white males or a possible greater tendency among low-income, unemployed blacks to patronize these places or the presence of more bars in urban black communities (Crutchfield, 1989; Reiss and Roth, 1993).

While Oliver acknowledges some of these influences, he is still insistent on transforming the violent transactions of African Americans in ghetto bars and bar settings into a difference-in-kind. In fact, he questions whether his observations of violent transactions in a black bar can be generalized to violent confrontations among whites (1994: 54). For Oliver, what makes violent transactions in black bars race-specific behavior has to do with the

---

[5] Oliver might well have included other violent places in his list of hot spots, such as crack-houses, shooting galleries, schools, schoolyards, and local streets (Roncek and Faggiani, 1985; Goldstein, 1989; Anderson, 1990).

fact that blacks are more inclined to take their symbolic displays of commitment to compulsive masculinity norms more seriously than white males in comparable settings. Presumably, African Americans take the talk and the gestures in a leisure time setting like a bar a lot more seriously than whites because they lack alternative settings or institutions (family, job) in which to express masculine roles. For Oliver, the interactions that occur in black bars therefore have more *reputational implications* for African Americans as the bar is practically the only place where masculine reputations in the ghetto can be won, sustained, or lost.

What happens in the urban black bar, then, is likely to affect how other males perceive a man outside the bar and, hence, the jockeying for masculine status in ghetto taverns is likely to be more intense. Even very young black males are aware of the immense significance of appropriate behavior in local bars and their own efforts to prepare themselves for proper bar behavior constitute one of the few ghetto-specific rites of passage. That learning the suitable symbolic displays in bars assumes such significance in the socialization of adolescent ghetto males has to do with the fact that this is apparently one of the few places where they can learn the only accessible masculine role (i.e., compulsive masculinity).

Oliver describes the race-specific importance of symbolic displays in ghetto bars in the following terms:

> Implicit in . . . [the] characterization of bars as unserious social settings is the assumption that the typical white bar patron possesses a personal biography that encompasses one or more serious and socially respected roles. Thus white bar patrons who engage in outrageous or deviant behavior in bars are generally shielded from negative labeling as a result of their successful participation in serious social settings like school, family life, the workplace and civic organizations. . . . [H]owever ethnographic studies suggest that unlike white bars, black bars tend to be regarded as serious social settings and the behavior engaged in while frequenting black bars often has *personal and social consequences* for black bar patrons *in their lives outside the bar setting.* . . . I am suggesting that lower class blacks perceive the bars that they frequent as both unserious and serious social settings. The unserious dimension is the frequenting of bars to engage in time-out activities, including socializing with friends, drinking, dancing and interacting with members of the opposite sex. However, because they are aware of the *reputational implications* that their peers attach to how they engage in time-out activities, lower class blacks are sensitive to the fact that frequenting black bars and bar settings may lead others in the setting to evaluate their conduct either positively or negatively relative to subculturally relevant normative standards. . . . During adolescence, many lower class black boys learn that an important step toward recognition and acceptance as a man is developing the ability to successfully interact in bars and bar settings. . . . [F]requenting bars is akin to a manhood rite of passage for many lower class black males. (1994: 20–3 passim, italics mine)

Obviously much of Oliver's argument turns on his ability to demonstrate the greater significance that black bars have for their patrons relative to white bars. Hence, he lists the functions that black bars serve for ghetto residents. Many of these functions – dancing, meeting women, talking about sports, family problems, and controversial issues – can hardly be said to distinguish black bars from white bars. Other functions such as interacting with others in a bar as a cathartic release from the tensions of being poor and unemployed could reasonably be applied to bars patronized by economically marginal whites. Indeed, the only race-specific functions served by black bars that Oliver lists are their use as places for patrons to unburden themselves of race-specific social stressors such as unemployment, because of racial discrimination, and the stigma of being black in America. Yet, his sample of African-American participants in violent transactions report that many of their fights seem to have been precipitated for non-race-specific reasons that apply equally well to violent whites (see Campbell and Gibbs, 1986; Katz, 1988; Luckenbill and Doyle, 1989). The fact that his respondents do not typically describe their acts as precipitated for race-specific historical or structural reasons makes it harder for Oliver to demonstrate the theorized impact of a history and structure unique to blacks on violent behaviors committed by black individuals.

Violent Predispositions: The Angrily Aggressive Underclass Black Male.
Finally, like many of the other theorists, Thomas Bernard (1990) makes use of a race-specific collective psychology to explain race differences in violence. The psychic state that distinguishes black males from their fellows, for him, is an angry aggression fueled by their suspension in a nearly chronic state of physiological arousal. Bernard identifies structural conditions like living in an urban environment and low social position as two of the forces capable of inducing heightened physiological arousal. Among other things, the crowding, noise, and limited recreational space associated with urban living coupled with the limited money and power associated with low social position combine to induce high levels of stress or physiological arousal in urban poor populations. It is this physiological arousal that leads to angry aggression in the urban poor.

On these grounds alone, there is little to distinguish the levels of physiological arousal and angry aggression that are supposedly experienced by urban poor blacks from those experienced by urban poor whites.[6] However, Bernard argues that arousal states among blacks are further heightened

---

[6] Of course, today very few whites live in the kind of social isolation and concentrated poverty that characterizes the black urban poor (Massey and Denton, 1993; Peterson and Krivio, 1993; Sampson and Wilson, 1995). To some degree, Bernard takes this into account and goes on to speculate about the likely effect of this isolation and concentrated poverty on the collective underclass black psyche.

by the added pressures of living in a society in which they are exposed to the constant stressors of intentional harms associated with racial discrimination. Understandably, individual blacks living in this heightened state of arousal are more likely to aggress and to then develop rules of aggression that both justify their feelings of anger and their aggression toward their victims. These rules typically take the form of demonstrating the blameworthiness of the victim. While much of their anger may be directed at whites, it is easier for them to displace much of their anger onto other blacks that are more accessible and more vulnerable. Hence, the rules for blameworthiness can be modified to justify transferring anger at whites to proximate black victims who can then be victimized with fewer repercussions.

As highly aroused black individuals endlessly expand the rules for assigning blameworthiness, Bernard claims that the number of situations and persons deemed deserving of violent retaliation and the levels of harm required to satisfy those so aroused increases. Because urban poor blacks often live in a state of social isolation where they are surrounded by others who are similarly stirred up, it is possible for these expanded rules for violence to take on a life of their own as they are transmitted from one agitated person to another. For Bernard, these expanded rules for initiating violence can then be generalized into a subculture of angry aggression that can be passed on from one generation of males to another through vicarious learning and reinforcement.

Once a subculture with broadly defined rules for violence emerges, it can then feed back on itself. For example, Bernard argues that already tense social environments are likely to become even more charged with the development of broadened subcultural rules for violence. Additional feedback occurs as black individuals see their already perilously high personal levels of arousal further aggravated just by dint of living in these unsettled and dangerous milieus. Finally, Bernard claims that because blacks are exposed to a unique set of circumstances that place them in a chronic state of high arousal – urban environment, low socioeconomic status, isolation in a more highly charged and dangerous milieu with expanded rules for violence – they gradually become less competent at coping with being on the edge. Their inability to cope with their constant arousal only makes matters worse because it means that their animated emotional states will persist unrelieved.

For Bernard, the fact that urban poor blacks experience a more intense and persistent state of arousal than that experienced by even urban poor whites is thus not simply a matter of the added structural effects of racial discrimination. Rather, it is a product of the interaction between these structural forces and the feedback effects from conditions that grow out of the concentration of many individuals living in a state of heightened arousal.

Bernard describes the interaction between these structural forces and the feedback effects in the following manner:

> First angry aggression in this group (urban black underclass) would be an *additive* effect of each of the social factors: urban environment, low social position and racial and ethnic discrimination. The social isolation of this group would concentrate the aggressive effects of the above factors, resulting in a highly aggressive environment.... Second, in such an environment, each individual's... *rules for anger would tend to expand, so that people would become angry in a greater range of situations and respond with more violence when angry....* Third, *the social isolation* of the group would mean that the... *rules for anger would tend to become subcultural* through interpersonal transmission, becoming *independent* of the structural conditions that gave rise to them.... These *subcultural rules,* thus, would increase the overall aggressiveness of the environment, which would then *feed back* on itself through vicarious and instrumental learning and reasonable expectations of dangerousness. Fourth, social isolation would result in a tendency to transfer arousal to visible and vulnerable people in the immediate environment, especially because the true sources of the arousal [whites responsible for racial discrimination] are largely invisible and invulnerable. (Bernard, 1990: 87; italics mine)

Hence, the combined forces of racial discrimination, social isolation in a more dangerous environment governed by expanded rules for engaging in violence, and the absence of coping styles to reduce arousal levels all interact to create a unique black temperament which is radically different. The constancy and intensity of physiological arousal among blacks once again defines an emotional predisposition to violence that is different-in-kind. (See Table 13.1 for a summary of the theories reviewed in this section.)

Critique

Many of the theories reviewed here rely on the assumption that the relationship between involvement in crime and violence and the macro-level historical and structural forces, uniquely affecting the lives of African Americans, are mediated by collective psychological states. These psychological states can be described in terms of at least three characteristics. First, the collective psychological states that predispose blacks to violence are treated as if they are fixed personality traits, and the subcultures in which these violent predispositions are reinforced and reproduced are depicted as stable. Second, these violent predispositions are described in ways that suggest that they apply to a very broad segment of the black male population. And, finally, the structural and historical forces that give rise to these violent psychological states among blacks are seemingly so powerful that individual blacks are unable to act back on them; in short, the black males discussed in these theories are treated as if they are "determined" by these larger social forces.

That these theorists make these assumptions about the psychological state of African-American males gives rise to a number of problems. These problems will be the subject of discussion in the following sections.

The Problem with Violent Predispositions: Are They Stable or Transient?

Each of the theories reviewed here present black males (or low-income black males) as different "types of people," who are differentially predisposed to violent behavior, because of distinct psychological states (angry aggression, self-hatred/group hatred, brittle defensiveness, compulsive masculinity, etc.), or because these distinct psychological states have induced them to form highly disputatious subcultures (Curtis, 1975; Bernard, 1990; Oliver, 1994). Hence, the violent psychological predilections discussed in this body of work are described as *abiding* parts of the violent black self; their disputatious subcultures are similarly *fixed*, inducing them to differentially "name" a wider array of gestures and behaviors as injurious and "claim" reparations for this expanded list of injuries (Wolfgang and Ferracuti, 1967; Luckenbill and Doyle, 1989). The twin notions of a stable violent self or a perpetually disputatious subculture are useful for theorizing precisely because they are described as fixed. In fact, it is their enduring quality that gives these concepts their predictive power. Put differently, knowing a person is consistently more prone to violence or lives in a community where the local subculture defines more situations as violence-worthy enables one to both explain and predict high rates of violent crime in African-American communities.

However, research from small-scale ethnographies in which violent actors and violent situations are directly observed does not always fit with these notions about a stable violent self or subcultural settings where violence is consistently required (Campbell, 1986; Birkbeck and LaFree, 1993; Oliver, 1994). For one thing, the base rates for violent confrontations, among even the most violent of actors, are often so low that it is apparent that they go for long stretches without aggressive behavior (Campbell, 1986). This means that counts of violent acts – as measured by arrest statistics or victimization rates – may not be a good basis for theorizing about a stable violent self.

This is illustrated in a study conducted by Oliver (1994), who draws on descriptions of eighty-six violent confrontations and thirty additional potentially violent arguments from forty-one African-American male respondents. By almost any measure, these forty-one males would qualify as psychologically predisposed to violence and/or as members of a disputatious subculture. After all, they seemed inclined to "name" and "claim" what many would regard as minor affronts as sufficient grounds to carry on heated arguments and engage in violent retaliation.

Yet, even though most had been involved in anywhere from one to six violent confrontations (many with serious injuries), they also described

Table 13.1. *Summary of Race-Specific Theories*

	Macro-level Historical & Structural Forces	Mediating Psych. Predisposition	Mediating Subcultural Predisposition	Dependent Variable
Wolfgang and Ferracuti, 1967			Black subculture of violence defines more stimuli as deserving of violent retaliation	Explains race difference in violence
Luckenbill and Doyle, 1989			Blacks have a more disputatious subculture of violence with a greater tendency to name and claim	Explains race difference in violence
Poussaint, 1983	1) institutional racism 2) negative images of blackness	Blacks adapt by experiencing: 1) rage and self-hatred 2) self-hatred projected onto other blacks 3) lowered threshold for violence	Blacks form more violent subcultures with a lowered threshold for violence	Individual blacks are more likely to be violent Explains race differences in violence and black-on-black violence

Curtis, 1975	1) slavery 2) southern subculture of violence 3) unemployed/limited access to masculine roles 4) critical mass in urban ghettos	Blacks adapt with: 1) greater sensitivity to threats to personal autonomy 2) brittle defensiveness	Blacks develop a more intensely violent contraculture	Explains race differences in violent crime
Oliver, 1994	1) slavery 2) unemp/limited access to masculine roles	Blacks adapt with: 1) greater concerns for threats to personal autonomy 2) compulsive masculinity	Violence in leisure settings has more reputational implications for blacks	Explains race differences in violence and why blacks are more violent in bars
Bernard, 1990	1) residence in urban environment 2) low social position 3) racial discrimination	Structural conditions induce: 1) heightened physiological arousal 2) transfer of anger at whites onto blacks 3) loss of capacity to cope by reducing arousal levels	Blacks form a subculture of angry aggression Subculture expands rules justifying aggression against others	Explains race differences in violence Explains black-on-black violence

instances in which they had walked away from or smoothed over similar incidents, thereby avoiding violence. Given their varied responses to what passes as violence-provoking situations, one would have to ask if even the most violent among them could be described in terms suggestive of a *stable violent self* (Campbell, 1986). In other words, their erratic use of violence to resolve conflicts makes explanations that speculate on enduring psychological predispositions to violence (self-hatred, angry aggression, compulsive masculinity, brittle defensiveness, etc.) seem inappropriate. Indeed, a skeptical reader might well ask why they weren't unfailingly disputatious when provoked. Or, alternatively, why didn't the rage and undue concern with masculine reputations manifest itself more consistently in this compulsively masculine, angrily aggressive, or brittlely defensive population? The fact that they failed to regularly use violence in response to trivial insults also raises questions about how they maintained their honor and managed their reputations in those instances when they did not respond with violence.

The variable responses of these black informants also raise questions about the notion of a *black subculture of violence* that is more disputatious. In other words, while these males seem to have expanded the rules to define many insults and gestures as deserving of violent retaliation, their variable response to violent situations raises questions about how consistently their acts are governed by these cultural rules. Indeed, these violent informants describe many of the fights, which they observe in and around the bar, as conflicts over trivial matters. They likewise describe some insults and grievances aimed at them as too unimportant to warrant violence and thus they walk away, even though these same grievances are the grounds for violence in other situations. Moreover, when they do fight, they are likely to condemn their opponents as so immature, insecure, or resentful of them as to initiate violent conflicts over insignificant events.

The fact that even violent actors refuse to "name" and "claim" in all situations thus makes it more difficult to define who and when one is a member of this black subculture of violence. Second, the fact that their responses to provocations seem to change over time makes it hard to argue that they have their own singular definition of the situation that demands violence. And the fact that even black males with a history of violent acts can describe the participants in many barroom brawls as immature or insecure raises questions about whether a reputation for toughness necessarily assures one of respect and prestige even among members of the ghetto subculture.

Even in instances where both parties seem willing to name, claim, and aggress, third parties often successfully mediate these disputes by defusing any tensions. The mediators are often friends and relatives of one of the warring parties. The presence of mediators also suggests that there may be no single definition of the situation determining when violent retaliation is appropriate. Indeed, the fact that third-party mediators are capable of defusing some escalating disputes, coupled with the fact that many of these males have themselves walked away from provocations, because they view violent retaliation as immature or as evidence of insecurity, at least points to the possibility that the refusal to fight does not necessarily condemn these men to ostracism from the subculture or subject them to bullying in the future. At the very least, findings like these suggest that it would be useful to try to determine what elements of a situation allow one party to back down with few reputational implications and compare them to situations where backing down has devastating consequences.

Finally, the claim that stressed ghetto males must constantly maneuver through a highly charged hostile environment and thereby are limited in their capacity to cope with these overpowering emotions also must come in for additional scrutiny (Bernard, 1990). After all, the presence of third-party mediators and the tendency of even violent males to walk away from at least some provocations suggest that these males are at least occasionally capable of coping with the stresses in their lives without resort to violence.

The mismatch between many of these theories and the data points to problems with a structural determinism that plagues these explanations. The notion that structural determinants such as race-specific historical and current social conditions are so overpowering that they virtually dictate these collective psychological and subcultural maladjustments gives these theories immense predictive power. However, it is often difficult to know how the constraints dictated by these large-scale, anonymous social forces find their way into the thoughts and perceptions or day-to-day activities of individual actors. It is even more difficult to measure the effects of these aggregate forces on individual perceptions and motivations.

Yet, it is just such structurally deterministic notions that allow many theorists to assert a race difference in violent criminality. Knowing someone's race or where they reside (low-income black community) is sufficient grounds for predicting *stable* race differences in the propensity of individuals to commit crime. Yet, even though these correlations hold at the aggregate level, they fall apart when individual actors are observed in actual interactions. This raises questions about whether "top-down" analyses, which show race differences across communities in violence, actually offer much empirical support for race-specific theories.

Obviously, one problem with this type of top-down analysis has to do with the use of gross indicators such as a person's residence in a high-crime neighborhood as a measure of their membership in a subculture of violence. This tendency to assume a propensity for violence based on a person's community of residence is an artifact of the data. After all, we have data on race differences in violent arrests at *the neighborhood level*. With this kind of data, "membership" in the subculture almost has to be equated with mere residence in the neighborhood. Yet, to do so has the unfortunate effect of confusing a subsociety with a subculture (Fine and Kleinman, 1979; Hawkins, 1983; Covington, 1997). This is because membership in a subsociety is confined to those persons who share exposure to the same structural forces – for example, high unemployment, racial discrimination, and low social position (Curtis, 1975; Bernard, 1990; Oliver, 1994). This means that mere residence in a neighborhood, where all are exposed to the same structural forces, *is* sufficient grounds for establishing membership in a subsociety. However, it is *not* sufficient for establishing membership in a subculture. If membership in a subculture of violence means defining an expanded number of encounters as sufficient grounds to "name" injuries and "claim" reparations (Wolfgang and Ferracuti, 1967; Luckenbill and Doyle, 1989), then neighborhood data on arrests for violent crime cannot help us understand who is or is not a member of the disputatious subculture.

A "bottom-up" analysis in which violent individuals are asked to report on their motivations also may provide little information on race differences in violent criminality. After all, if we were to compare the most violent black bar patrons in Oliver's study (1994) to the most violent white regulars at a white bar (Campbell and Gibbs, 1986; Katz, 1988), it might be difficult to discern any differences in their propensity for violence. More important, it would be hard to know if the violent black actors were motivated by antecedent black-specific macro-level conditions like self- or group hatred, angry aggression, brittle defensiveness, or compulsive masculinity and thereby distinguish them from the violent white actors (see critique of Oliver earlier in this chapter).

Arguments that suggest that blacks have developed a distinctive subculture or definition of the situation fare no better, because if we were to compare Oliver's violent black bars to violent white bars, it would be difficult to determine which bars had a more disputatious culture. Certainly, clear-cut across-race differences could readily be discerned if most individuals in each bar culture had similar definitions of the situation. However, there seem to be varied commitments to naming and claiming among different bar patrons in the same bar culture over time. Moreover, even if such cultural differences could be measured, it might be difficult to link them to their supposed antecedent race-specific historical and structural forces. Finally, because these ethnographic studies make use of small unrepresentative samples of violent actors, they can tell us nothing about the extent or prevalence of violence in a particular neighborhood. Therefore, they offer us no way of making across-race (across-neighborhood) comparisons.

The Problem with Diffusion. The problems associated with race-specific theories are not simply because of the disconnect between macro-level historical and structural forces and the day-to-day situations in which violence occurs. Problems also arise because theoretical devices such as a black subculture or black collective psychological states enable researchers to *diffuse* violent propensities beyond those black males who actually engage in violent acts to nonviolent black males who also must adjust to race-specific conditions. For example, if institutional racism has indeed induced collective psychological maladjustments among blacks such that they experience racewide feelings of black rage, self-hatred, and hatred of other blacks, then one might expect that this psychological scarring would extend to most black males – violent and nonviolent alike. This would apply to black males at all socioeconomic levels and to those living in urban, suburban, or rural communities. Because self- and group hatred are the very emotions that differentially predispose blacks to violence, all blacks who experienced these emotions – violent and nonviolent alike – could then be seen as high risk for violent behaviors. However, there is evidence that black overrepresentation in violence only applies to low-income blacks living in urban poor communities. Blacks in rural and suburban settings have crime rates proportionate to their representation in the population, and at higher socioeconomic levels, the black/white difference in homicides actually disappears (Hawkins, 1983; Reiss and Roth, 1993). Yet, if all that is required to induce previolent emotions like rage and self-hatred in black men is exposure to institutional racism, then black males in all types of communities and at all class levels should be high risk for violence. That they are not means that these explanations of black-specific violence needlessly diffuse violent predispositions to many nonviolent black males.

Certainly some theorists identify conditions that effectively limit violent predispositions to urban poor blacks by arguing that slavery, southern heritage, *and* living in urban communities in which unemployment is high have all added up to produce a black male who is more concerned than nonblacks with threats to personal autonomy or who is more compulsively masculine. In this case, violent predispositions are merely diffused from violent urban poor blacks to nonviolent urban poor blacks rather than all blacks. This means that all blacks subjected to this confluence of social forces – violent and nonviolent alike – are depicted as at greater risk for violent confrontation than whites.

No data have been marshaled to support these assertions about race differences more frequently than homicide rates in which black disproportionality is far greater than for aggravated assaults. In 1997, black males, who accounted for 12 percent of the male population, made up 57 percent of those arrested for homicide (FBI, 1998). This means that approximately 12,539 black males committed homicides in 1997.[7] There are 7,710,000 black males between ages fifteen and forty-four and 5,294,000 in the

---

[7] The figure of 12,539 black males having committed murder is only an estimate and an estimate on the high side. It does not take into account black females who killed in 1997.

murder-prone years of ages fifteen to thirty-four. This means that 5,281,461 black males – ages fifteen to thirty-four – did not kill anyone in 1997 (FBI, 1996; U.S. Bureau of the Census, 1996). While a number of these race-specific theorists note that most blacks are not violent, the race-specific conditions that they argue put blacks at risk – past and current racial in-equalities, high unemployment, underclass isolation – are so inclusive that they seem to implicate all black males or at least all underclass black males. Yet, despite very high murder rates, the actual numbers suggest that very few blacks are driven to make this adjustment in any given year. Clearly, then, the race-specific criminality that they have constructed based on high black murder rates – rather than actual numbers – has been so crudely drawn that it needlessly *diffuses* violent predispositions to millions of black males (Covington, 1995). However, rather than refining these risk factors so as to better identify which blacks who live under adverse circumstances are predisposed to turn violent, most theorists seem to content themselves with the rather obvious caveat that not all blacks or not all underclass blacks are violence prone. Yet, despite this warning, most proceed to paint race-specific violent predispositions with such a broad brush that they place millions of black males in the at-risk population.

This dilemma is caused in no small part by the need to make racial com-parisons in the first place. In fact, a racial comparison requires that condi-tions be identified that *liken all blacks to each other while distinguishing them from whites* (see Covington, 1999, for further discussion of this issue). Yet, in identifying race-specific risk factors (e.g., history of oppression, institutional racism, negative images of blacks, etc.) that distinguish blacks from whites, these theorists construct crude categories that *liken a handful of black killers to millions of black nonkillers.* The unnecessary diffusion of violent predispo-sitions to many nonviolent blacks seems to be an unfortunate consequence of such racial comparisons.

The obvious solution to the problem of diffusion is a more refined con-ception of race-specific predispositions. For example, for those arguing that socialization into a disputatious black subculture of violence causes blacks to "name" more acts as injurious and "claim" reparations, there needs to be some specification of which blacks are members of this subculture and which blacks are not. Moreover, it might be useful to know how long people remain members and to identify the circumstances that indicate that they have ceased to be members. Most important, it might be useful to know which blacks are least likely to adjust to adverse historical and structural conditions by joining a subculture of violence and to then distinguish them from those blacks who are most likely to adjust by seeking to express their masculinity through violence.

For those arguing that blacks develop psychological states that predis-pose them to violence, it would be helpful to specify which blacks adapt to current and past racial inequalities by turning to violence and which blacks do not. Comparisons between these two groups might then clarify why some individuals adapt in violent ways, while others do not.

However, by refining both cultural and collective psychological measures to take variations in individual adaptations to adverse social circumstances into account, we cease to talk about race differences in propensity for crime. Put differently, when more care is taken to subdivide the black population into its violently and nonviolently predisposed parts, it becomes more difficult to talk in terms of race differences in violent propensities because there is no longer a single response unique to blacks. And if within-group differences turn out to be larger than between-group differences, the predisposition to violence would cease to be a trait that could be conceived of as being shared by a racial group. Refined measures that consider within-group differences in adaptations to historical and current conditions, then, might have the effect of deracializing criminality.

The Problem with Determinism and Distancing. The fact that the race-specific theoretical literature focuses on between-group differences while ignoring within-group differences means that we may actually know very little about black crime after reviewing these studies. Instead, what we come away with is a sense of how black communities and black history are different from that of whites and a number of speculations – many unproven or unprovable – on how these differences *might* play a role in explaining high rates of black violence. By confining ourselves to black versus white comparisons and then developing mediating conceptions of black criminal predispositions based only on these across-group comparisons, we ultimately learn little about why some blacks living under these adverse conditions become violent, while most do not. Unfortunately, because our analyses have focused on these between-group differences, we have come away with a representation of black males, which suggests that they are fundamentally different from white males and different in ways that predispose them to violence.

Specifically, black males are depicted as different-in-kind, because they have been so scarred by current and historic racial oppression that they have become a people lacking in humanity. In other words, black males, psychologically conditioned by past and current oppression, are described as so insecure as to be incapable of experiencing compassion for their fellow men. They are driven only by a racewide urge to reassert a masculinity that can be threatened with a mere stare or a minor insult (Anderson, 1990). This, of course, has dire consequences for the social organization of their communities as they seem incapable of maintaining normal social sentiments toward their neighbors and fellows. This expresses itself in their tendency to create a group culture that demands violence and the tendency for psychologically scarred individuals to be drawn to and reproduce this violent group culture generation after generation.

Because the lack of humanity is a feature that is shared racewide, black males seem different and because these theories construct vast social distances between black males and the rest of us, they have implications for policy. After all, while we can acknowledge that historical and structural inequalities have transformed black males in ways so that they have acquired violent predilections, altering current structural inequalities that have caused these unfortunate transformations in the black male psyche would not seem to be enough to reduce crime. Widespread psychological testing and treatment would seem to be in order first to help black males grapple with their self- or group hatred and cope with a rage at whites that displaces itself onto black targets. In addition, counseling also might be needed to help them to resign themselves to their limited employment opportunities in light of current economic realities. Hence, the fundamentally different black psychological predispositions identified in these theories suggest that the change in those pathologized by racial oppression should take priority over changes in structural inequalities.

In suggesting that large-scale, anonymous social forces have so altered the black male psyche, these theories all fall prey to a kind of historical, structural, or cultural determinism that assumes that historical (slavery, southern culture), structural (unemployment, social isolation), or cultural constraints (preexisting definitions of the situation that require violence) are located "out there" somewhere independent of human actors. As independent forces, these historical, structural, or cultural forces are capable of shaping and directing human thoughts and behaviors (Giddens, 1984; Archer, 1994). As such, they afford the black actors, who are controlled by these forces, little freedom of action. Indeed, the very fact that blacks seemingly have little choice but to turn to violence in the face of these historical, structural, and/or cultural conditions is what gives these theories their predictive power and makes them appear more "scientific" (Agnew, 1995).

However, the relationship between structure and behavior is not simply one way. Obviously, many violent actors walk away from conflicts and ghetto males, exposed to supposed criminogenic historical, structural, and cultural conditions, are capable of acting back on presumed historical, cultural, and structural constraints. The fact that they create and recreate new adjustments to these constraints over the course of their lives points to the limits of arguments that present these anonymous macro-level forces as independent of human actors with the capacity to condition, shape, and direct human thought (Giddens, 1984; Archer, 1994; Agnew, 1995).

Conclusions

The theorists reviewed in this chapter explain race differences in violence by trying to identify an elusive fixed, race-specific (or ghetto-specific) predisposition to violence. In many ways, their notions about the nature of black male temperament are not too different from images of black males that are widely accepted by the general public. Hence, whether intentional or not, these theories encourage or reinforce widely held beliefs that black males are to blame for their violent criminality. They encourage these perceptions by trying to persuade us that wide swaths of the black male (or the ghetto male) population have been pathologized by past and present oppression. They also claim that this scarring has produced a black male population that can all too easily be driven to violence by subcultural rules or by overpowering emotions like rage, self-/group hatred, angry aggression, compulsive masculinity, or brittle sensitivity. Hence, it is easy to conclude from their explanations that racism has created a social and psychological divide between black males and the rest of us.

The fact that the images of black males, depicted in these theories, are already so widely accepted may explain why there has been so little outrage expressed over recent increases in the number of black males placed under criminal justice supervision. Nationwide, nearly 30 percent of black males in their twenties are on probation, parole, or in prison and estimates suggest that 28.5 percent of black males have a lifelong likelihood of experiencing some period of incarceration (Bonczar and Beck, 1997; Beck, 1999). Yet, to the extent that these theorists convince us that a truly dangerous class of black males has materialized in the face of racial oppression, the public's reflex reaction to the males described in these theories is likely to be fear coupled with a demand for *more* control and *more* incarceration. Furthermore, because these theorists have attempted to persuade us that these violent predispositions characterize a large segment of the black male population, one could almost be convinced that most black males are high risk for violence. Those influenced by this type of thinking are, therefore, likely to express little public concern when black males are subjected to indiscriminant sweeps and heightened surveillance, whether they have been involved in crime or not. Indeed, because these images of a violent black male temperament can be used to justify additional crackdowns on this population, it is important that we continue to examine these theories carefully to determine the extent to which there is evidence to support their depictions of black male character.

The Structural-Cultural Perspective: A Theory of Black Male Violence

William Oliver, Ph.D.

Introduction

One of the most significant challenges confronting America is the disproportionately high rate of homicide and nonfatal violence occurring among black males. There exists very little consensus among criminologists and other crime scholars regarding "the causes" of black male violence. Numerous explanations have been offered, including acquired biological causes (e.g., head injuries) (Bell, 1987); social disorganization and inadequate socialization (Shaw and McKay, 1942); poverty and economic inequality (Blau and Blau, 1982); racial oppression and displaced aggression (Johnson, 1941; Poussaint, 1983); adherence to the norms of a subculture of violence (Wolfgang and Ferracuti, 1967); joblessness and family disruption (Sampson, 1987); the cheapening of black life as a result of the imposition of lenient sentences against blacks who assault or murder blacks (Hawkins, 1983); and involvement in self-destructive lifestyles centered around heavy drinking (Harper, 1976; Gary, 1986), drug abuse and drug trafficking (Goldstein et al., 1989), and street gangs (Block and Block, 1993; Decker and VanWinkle, 1996). Theoretical explanations of black male violence have generally emphasized the significance of structural factors (Staples, 1974; Hawkins, 1983) or cultural factors (Frazier, 1939; Wolfgang and Ferracuti, 1967).

Although they represent a minority viewpoint, some criminologists maintain that racial differences in violent crime offending may stem from genetic/nonacquired biological factors (Hirschi and Hindelang, 1977; Ellis and Walsh, 1997). For example, proponents of cheater theory suggest that there exists a population of men who possess genes that incline them toward extremely low parental involvement. These men are described as being sexually aggressive and are skilled at the use of devious means to gain sexual success. Consequently, they produce children with low IQ scores, aggressive personalities, and inadequate socialization (Ellis and Walsh, 1997). Hirschi and Hindelang (1977) also have suggested that there is an association between racial disparities in IQ scores and the racial gap in violent offending. They argue, for example, that low IQ increases the likelihood of criminal behavior through its effect on school performance. That is, youth with low IQ scores do poorly in school and school failure is related to delinquency and adult criminal behavior.

Among those scholars who have attempted to provide theory-based explanations for the high rates of black male violence, some have emphasized the causal significance of structural factors (Bailey, 1984; Blau and Blau, 1992; Hawkins, 1983; Messner and Rosenfeld, 1994; Sampson 1985, 1987), while another group has stressed the importance of cultural and subcultural factors (Miller, 1958; Wolfgang and Ferracuti, 1967; Gastil, 1971). Frequently, these have been offered as competing or opposing points of view (Messner and Rosenfeld, 1999). The primary goal of this chapter is to offer a structural-cultural perspective aimed specifically at examining the causes of high rates of interpersonal violence found among African-American males, particularly adolescents and young adults. As its labeling suggests, a major assumption of the perspective is that both structural and cultural factors contribute to the high rates of black male violence in the United States. I also argue that other more micro-level forces (e.g., ghetto-related manhood roles), many of which are derived from structural and cultural forces that shape American society, can be identified as contributors to racial differences in patterns of male violence. In the following section, the prevalence of black male violence is discussed.

The Problem

The disproportionate rates of violent crime found among African Americans have been described in numerous studies and reports. For example, the FBI reports that in 1998, African Americans, who constitute 13 percent of the general population, were overrepresented among persons arrested for murder (53 percent), robbery (55 percent), aggravated assault (30 percent), and assault (34 percent) (U.S. Department of Justice, 1998). A significant characteristic of violent crime in the United States is that most violent incidents tend to involve an intraracial victim-offender relationship pattern. That is, individuals who commit acts of violence generally commit these acts against members of their own racial group. For example, in 1998, 94 percent of black murder victims were slain by black offenders. Similarly, in 1998, 87 percent of white murder victims were slain by white offenders (U.S. Department of Justice, 1998).

Serious violent crime also reflects gender variations in patterns of offending and victimization. For example, in 1998, males accounted for 83 percent of persons arrested for serious violent crimes, including murder, forcible rape, robbery, and aggravated assault. In contrast, females were significantly underrepresented (17 percent) among persons arrested for serious violent crimes (U.S. Department of Justice, 1998). The disproportionate overrepresentation among males as offenders and victims of violent crime also has been consistently reported in the annual National Crime Victims Survey (Bureau of Justice Statistics, 1999).

The most revealing data regarding the disproportionate impact that violent crime is having on African Americans, particularly black males, is the data on homicide victimization. According to the FBI, in 1998, black males represented 38 percent of known homicide victims, followed in descending order by white males (35 percent), white females (14 percent), and black females (9 percent) (U.S. Department of Justice, 1998). High rates of homicide among African Americans also have been reported in compilations of health statistics. According to data compiled by the National Center for Health Statistics (1998), black males had a homicide death rate of 52.6 per 100,000 in 1996, whereas white males had a homicide death rate of 4.7 per 100,000 (National Center for Health Statistics, 1998).

As a group, violence researchers generally regard individuals in the age range between fifteen and twenty-four as the most murder prone. However, there are significant differences between black and white males of this age range in terms of their homicide risk (National Center for Health Statistics, 1998). For example, white males fifteen to twenty-four years of age had a homicide death rate of 6.4 per 100,000 in 1996, whereas black males of this age range had a homicide death rate of 123 per 100,000, nearly twenty times greater than similarly aged white males (National Center for Health Statistics, 1998). Moreover, for every age range, black males have higher rates of homicide death than their white male counterparts of the same ages (National Center for Health Statistics, 1998).

A significant trend in homicide patterns involves the increasing youthfulness of homicide offenders and victims. Young black males experienced dramatic increases in both homicide victimization and offending rates in the late 1980s and early 1990s (Fox and Zawitz, 1998). For example, the number of homicide victims in the fifteen to twenty-four age group increased nearly 50 percent between 1975 and 1992. Moreover, in 1987, homicide accounted for 42 percent of all deaths among young black males. Persons between the ages of fifteen and nineteen experienced the greatest increases in the rate of death due to homicide in this period (Fingerhut et al., 1992). Since 1991, homicide rates have been declining among all race-sex subgroups in the United States. However, it is important to note that in spite of the declining homicide rates among black males, homicide remains the leading cause of death among black males between fifteen and twenty-four years of age (National Center for Health Statistics, 1998).

The Scholarly Heritage of Structural and Cultural Perspectives on Race and Violence

While there is a distinct tendency among criminologists and other scholars who study crime to categorize criminological theories as being structural *or* cultural explanations (Sampson and Lauritsen, 1994), references to both structural *and* cultural factors are evident in several major theories of crime (Merton, 1938; Shaw and McKay, 1942; Sampson and Lauritsen, 1994). Thus, the primary purpose of this section of the chapter is to describe theories and research that have influenced the structural-cultural perspective that I present in latter sections of this discussion.

In his original construction of strain theory, Merton (1938) developed a typology to describe modes of adaptation to structural strain said to be caused by restricted access to the legitimate means designated to achieve culturally defined success goals. Explicit in Merton's structural strain (anomie) theory is his claim that lower-class individuals are most likely to engage in deviant criminal behavior as a form of adaptation to the existing opportunity structure.

In a more recent formulation of strain theory, in what Messner and Rosenfeld (1994) label "institutional anomie" theory, they describe a criminogenic process in which macro-level factors and cultural factors converge in the social production of violent crime. Moreover, Messner and Rosenfeld (1994) describe how culture functions as both a macro-level and micro-level factor in the social production of criminal behavior. As a macro-level factor, culture is manifested in the American Dream mythology that encourages overt emphasis on achieving status through material consumption. Consequently, Messner and Rosenfeld (1994) suggest that the dominance of materialistic concerns weakens the informal social control of the family, church, and school. In contrast, culture also may contribute to micro-level processes. For example, Messner and Rosenfeld (1994) suggest that families, communities, and local civic institutions have a direct influence on the attitudes and behavior leading individuals to engage in criminal behavior as a result of their exposure to cultural practices and processes that encourage economic success by any means.

The importance of structural and cultural factors was also recognized by Shaw and McKay (1942) in their seminal work on social disorganization theory. For example, Shaw and McKay (1942) suggested that there is a relationship between structural forces and cultural adaptations. That is, they argued that structurally disorganized communities (e.g., low economic status, ethnic heterogeneity, and residential mobility) lack adequate formal and informal control mechanisms to inhibit criminal behavior. Furthermore, the lack of community social control leads to the formation of subcultures conducive to illegal activity.

Recently, some contemporary scholars have extended the ecological emphasis of social disorganization theory (Peterson and Krivo, 1993; Sampson and Wilson, 1995). The work of William Julius Wilson (1987, 1996), which describes the emergence of the black urban underclass, has had a major influence on contemporary constructions of social disorganization theory. Wilson (1996) has suggested that ghetto-related behaviors as well as the high rates of violence among the black inner-city poor have been precipitated by structural factors that have lead to social isolation and the breakdown of social control. According to Wilson (1987, 1996), structural factors including racial segregation, de-de-industrialization of the economy and the subsequent loss of high-wage manufacturing jobs, high rates of black male joblessness, and the exodus of advantaged middle-class and skilled black workers from inner-city neighborhoods have contributed to the concentration of poverty and the emergence of a black urban underclass.

Advocates of this approach acknowledge the importance of relying on both structural and cultural factors to explain the high rates of violent crime offending among African Americans. As Sampson and Wilson explain, "Macro social patterns of residential inequality give rise to the social isolation and ecological concentration of the truly disadvantaged, which in turn leads to structural barriers and cultural adaptations that undermine social organization and hence the control of crime" (1995: 53).

The importance of the work of Sampson and Wilson (1995) and other advocates of the more ecologically oriented reformulations of social disorganization theory is that they have sought to explicitly define both the community structural factors *and* the cultural practices that mediate between macro-social forces (e.g., racial inequality, de-industrialization) and the occurrence of criminal behavior in poor black communities. For example, criminogenic social conditions that are characteristic of the community social structure include the lack of interdependent social networks, high rates of family disruption, and high rates of joblessness among black males (Sampson and Wilson, 1995; Wilson, 1996). The specific cultural practices that are said to be associated with the high rates of violence among poor blacks include the lack of collective supervision of youth in public places, overt emphasis on sexual conquest, lifestyles organized around joblessness rather than work, and reliance on illegitimate sources of income (Wilson, 1996).

Urban ethnographers, particularly Liebow (1967), Hannerz (1969), and Rainwater (1970), were among the first scholars to suggest that there was a positive association between exposure to adverse macro-level conditions and the social construction or adaptation of ghetto-related manhood roles.

Based on his participant observation of black males and females who resided in a poor neighborhood in Washington, DC, Hannerz (1969) observed: "Many men are prevented by macrostructural conditions from performing satisfactorily in the mainstream male role and therefore take on a ghetto-specific alternative." What is significant about the classic ethnographic accounts of Liebow (1967), Hannerz (1969), and Rainwater (1970) is that on the basis of independent participant observation field studies, they each concluded that there are many of norms and behaviors that have been situationally adapted by urban poor black males as a means of coping with race-specific structural pressures. While it was not the intent of these scholars to construct theories to explain the racial gap in black and white rates of interpersonal violence, those who seek to construct structural-cultural theories of black male violence cannot ignore their work. This is evident in Curtis's contraculture theory in which he has substantially drawn from the urban ethnographic research. According to Curtis (1975), the disproportionate rates of violence among poor urban blacks is the outcome of the interrelatedness of economic-racial determinism (i.e., macro-level forces) and subcultural adaptations (i.e., micro-level forces), in which some poor young black males exaggerate certain expressions of manliness.

New Theoretical Directions: Combining Structure and Culture

The review presented above clearly indicates that the use of both structural and cultural factors to explain criminal behavior is not a new endeavor among criminologists. Indeed, many structural arguments presuppose cultural dynamics, but these dynamics are simply left implicit (Messner and Rosenfeld, 1999). For example, structural theorists have more than adequately described the motive for violence among poor blacks in terms of racial inequality, relative deprivation, and frustration (Merton, 1938; Blau and Blau, 1983; Messner and Rosenfeld, 1994). Yet, these explanations do not adequately advance understanding of why serious violent offending and victimization is concentrated among young black males. As Hawkins (1999) has pointedly observed, we know very little about within-group variations among African Americans who are at risk for committing acts of violence or becoming a victim of interpersonal violence.

The structural-cultural perspective that I present below seeks to extend the work of Sampson and Wilson (1995). While they acknowledge the existence of a pattern of values and normative adaptations to macro-level forces and disorganizing community conditions, what they have not done is provide a more narrowly constructed description of the *process* in which lower-class black males express ghetto-related values and norms through the enactment of specific manhood roles (Anderson, 1976, 1999; Hannerz, 1969; Majors and Mancini-Billson, 1992) and the relationship between the enactment of such roles and acts of interpersonal violence. Given this particular concern, one of the advantages of the perspective that I have developed involves the expansion of Sampson and Wilson's (1995) discussion of social isolation by describing how black males assume ghetto-related manhood roles. This perspective may potentially enhance understanding of the linkages between structural pressures (i.e., macro-level factors), social isolation, the social construction of particular criminogenic ghetto-related manhood roles (i.e., "the tough guy," "the player," and "the hustler"), routine activities, and definitions of the meaning of conflict situations leading to acts of interpersonal violence, and violent confrontations.

The Importance of Structural Pressures. The primary claim of the structural-cultural perspective is that the disproportionately high rates of homicide and nonfatal violence among black males are directly related to the convergence of structural pressures *and* dysfunctional cultural adaptations to those pressures. The term "structural pressures" is used here to refer to various macro-level institutions (e.g., the political system, the educational system, and the economic system) and society-wide social forces (e.g., racial prejudice and institutional racism) that have been used by the white majority to promote their political and economic dominance and to hinder the capacity of African Americans to have equal access to the legitimate opportunity structure and its resources (Blauner, 1972; Feagin and Vera, 1995; Knowles and Pruitt, 1968).

In prior theoretical and empirical work, criminologists have generally been reluctant to link black violence to racism. Instead, they have relied on vague depictions of racism operationalized in concepts or variables labeled as racial inequality (Blau and Blau, 1982), ascriptive inequalities (Messner and Rosenfeld, 1994), economic inequality (Sampson, 1985; Balkwell, 1990) blocked access to opportunity (Cloward and Ohlin, 1960), and poverty (Bailey, 1984). In contrast, what is significant about my contribution to this discussion is that I make a conscious link between America's overall social structure and racism.

Institutional Racism. In this theoretical model, institutional racism is considered to be a substantial structural pressure for African Americans. The term "institutional racism" is generally used to refer to the systematic deprivation of equal access to the legitimate opportunity structure (e.g., education, employment, and the political process, etc.) based on race (Knowles and Pruitt, 1968). Racial prejudice is often the catalyst leading to institutional racism (Allport, 1979; Feagin and Vera, 1995).

A variety of indicators illustrates the adverse impact American society has had on the capacity of black males to survive and progress. For example, institutional racism in the form of slavery constituted a significant source of stress and traumatization for African Americans (Blassingame, 1975; Akbar, 1984). For 246 years, most African Americans were slaves and were legally the property of their owners (Stampp, 1956). The end of slavery in 1865 was followed by nearly one hundred years of state-sponsored racial discrimination in which African Americans were routinely denied civil rights and equal access to public accommodations, education, employment, credit, and housing (Franklin, 1956). Since the mid-1960s, African Americans have made substantial political, educational, and economic gains as a result of the civil rights movement and the passage of various civil rights acts enacted to dismantle the overt manifestations of institutional racism. However, the legacy of 246 years of slavery, nearly one hundred years of Jim Crow segregation following Emancipation, and contemporary patterns of racial prejudice and discrimination have contributed to the persistence of racial inequality in contemporary America (Wilson, 1978, 1987).

Racial disparity among persons who have incomes below the official poverty level are a significant indicator of racial and economic inequality in contemporary America. For example, in 1996, African Americans had a poverty rate (28.4 percent) two and a half times greater than white Americans (11.2 percent). Moreover, in 1996, 40 percent of black children under age eighteen lived in families that were poor, compared to 15.5 percent of white children (U.S. Bureau of the Census, 1998). The proportion of poor people who reside in ghetto neighborhoods (i.e., census tracts in which at least 40 percent of the residents live in poverty) varies by race. For example, in 1980, only 2 percent of the white poor lived in ghettos, whereas 65 percent of the black poor lived in ghettos (Jargowsky and Bane, 1991). Racial inequality is also evident in racial variations in household income. In 1997, white households had a median income of $44,756, whereas black household income was $26,552, that is, a median income 41 percent greater than that of black households (U.S. Bureau of the Census, 1998).

A commonly held view regarding the persistence of the high rates of poverty among low-income inner-city blacks is that poverty is related to the high rates of joblessness among black males (Kasarda, 1989; Wilson, 1987, 1996). In 1994, black males were two times more likely than white males to be unemployed, 10.6 percent and 4.9 percent respectively (U.S. Bureau of the Census, 1996). Also, it has been estimated that 46 percent of black males between sixteen and sixty-two years of age are not active participants in the labor force (Joe and Yu, 1991). The high rates of black male joblessness have been attributed to a variety of factors, including: employers deliberately screening out black male job applicants based on negative attitudes regarding their potential lack of productivity (Kirshenman and Neckerman, 1991); the loss of jobs because of transformation in the economy involving a shift from low-skill, high-wage, heavy industrial manufacturing jobs to a dual sector economy characterized by an expansion of low-wage service sector jobs and skilled, high-wage technology and information processing jobs (Kasarda, 1989; Wilson, 1987; 1996); the geographical shift in the concentration of jobs from the inner cities to the suburbs (Kasarda, 1989); and a tendency for some inner-city black males to reside in neighborhoods or become involved in social networks or behavioral patterns that weaken attachment to the conventional labor force (Van Haistma, 1989; Wilson, 1996).

Restructuring of the Economy. The restructuring of the American economy is another significant structural pressure that contributes to violent behavior among black males (Wilson, 1987). In research conducted by Sampson (1987), it was established that there exists a strong relationship between black male joblessness, family disruption, and high rates of violence among black males. For example, Sampson's (1987) empirical findings and theoretical explanations (Sampson and Wilson, 1995) suggest that black male joblessness leads to family disruption (e.g., female-headed families and poverty) and that family disruption increases patterns of community disorganization that subsequently increase the likelihood and concentration of high rates of violence in poor inner-city neighborhoods.

According to Wilson (1996), the decline in high-wage manufacturing jobs, the decreasing availability of low-skilled blue collar jobs, and the increasing importance of training and education in the growth industries has had an adverse effect on the employment rates and earnings of low-skilled black workers. Thus, relying on Wilson (1987; 1996), I regard the restructuring of the American economy as a race-neutral phenomenon. That is, the transformation of the economy has emerged as a direct result of technological advances and innovations in the production and distribution of goods and services (Kasarda, 1989). Thus, the restructuring of the economy constitutes a significant structural pressure for all Americans. All Americans, regardless of race, sex, or class, must adapt to shifts in the economy to facilitate their economic survival. For black males, however, the adverse effects of the restructuring of the economy are mediated through historical and contemporary patterns of racial discrimination. Therefore, differential patterns of access to quality education and vocational training enhance social isolation and other adverse effects generally associated with the restructuring of the economy (Kasarda, 1989; Wilson, 1978; 1987; 1996).

Cultural Racism. Some definitional variation or measure of institutional racism (e.g., racial discrimination, racial inequality, economic inequality, etc.) has been used in several theoretical explanations of black male violence and criminology (Bernard, 1990; Davis, 1976; Harvey, 1986; Hawkins, 1983; Johnson, 1941; Poussaint, 1983; Staples, 1974). I also regard institutional racism as a major source of structural pressure for African Americans. However, I extend the emphasis on racism to include cultural racism.

Earlier researchers, especially in the disciplines of education (Ben-Jochannan, 1991), race relations (Allport, 1979; Schaefer, 1993), and psychology (Jones, 1972; Baldwin, 1980), have alluded to the importance of cultural racism; however, most have not fully described it and very few have examined how it affects racial differences in violence.

The term "cultural racism" is used here to refer to the systematic manner in which the white majority has established its primary cultural institutions (e.g., education, mass media, religion, etc.) to elevate and glorify European physical characteristics, character, and achievement and to denigrate and put down the physical characteristics, character, and achievement of nonwhite people. While a primary goal of institutional racism is to block African Americans from having equal access to the legitimate opportunity structure, the primary goal of cultural racism is to diminish the cultural image and integrity of African Americans (Akbar, 1984; Welsing, 1991).

A significant example of cultural racism as a social practice is the conspicuous absence in most elementary and high school social studies curricula of a substantive discussion of the contributions of Africans and African Americans to the development of human civilization (Ben-Jochannan, 1991). The conspicuous absence of African Americans in history textbooks reinforces and promotes racial stereotypes (Schaefer, 1993). It also distorts the history and cultural image of African Americans (Akbar, 1984). Cultural racism also has been promoted in the mass media. In his interpretive history of blacks in American films, Bogle (1973) found that in the first fifty years of American films, African Americans were primarily portrayed as Toms, coons, tragic mulattoes, mammies, and brutal bucks. In later years, these characters were replaced by images of servants, clowns, militants, and criminals (Bogle, 1973). The primary purpose of stereotypical characterizations of African Americans in films was to entertain by stressing their innate inferiority. According to Bogle (1973: 4), "Fun was poked at the American Negro by presenting him as either a nitwit or a childlike lacky."

Negative images of African Americans are also promoted on television programs. For example, the overwhelming majority of black actors on television are employed in comedic roles (Schaefer, 1993). Moreover, Lichter and Lichter (1988) found that almost a third of high school students feel that television entertainment is an accurate representation of real life of African Americans.

Exposure to cultural racism has contributed to the emergence of a cultural crisis among African Americans. There are three factors that have led to this crisis, including: (1) the loss of historical memory, (2) lack of appreciation of the physical characteristics and cultural practices unique to African Americans, and (3) the lack of cultural confidence leading to a lack of cultural competence (Karenga, 1988a) among African Americans. Consequently, in the academic specialty area referred to as black psychology, there is a broad body of literature that suggests that long-term exposure to overt institutional and cultural racism has distorted the personality and mental health of African Americans (Azibo, 1989; Baldwin, 1984; Clark, 1965; Grier and Cobbs, 1968; Welsing, 1978). For example, many black psychologists support Baldwin's (1984) observation that "psychological misorientation" is the most fundamental state of disorder in the black personality (Azibo, 1989). The term "psychological misorientation" was introduced by Baldwin (1984) to describe a black personality disorder characterized by misorientation toward reality. More specifically, "psychological misorientation" is a personality disorder that exists among African Americans resulting from their exposure to social processes and social institutions (e.g., the educational system, mass media, and religion) that promote and disseminate antiblack ideologies, socialization messages, and images (Azibo, 1989; Baldwin, 1980).

Some specific mental health disorders emerging from the general condition of "psychological misorientation" include: (1) antiself disorder, (2) alien-self destructive disorder, and (3) self-destructive disorder (Akbar, 1981). Antiself disorder is a mental disorder in which an African American not only identifies with the dominant group but also identifies with the dominant majority's projected hostility toward African Americans. Alien-self destructive disorder is a condition characterized by an obsession with material accumulation as a means of establishing self-worth and overt denial that racism has threatened the collective survival of African Americans. Finally, self-destructive disorder is a condition that involves self-defeating attempts to survive in a society, which frustrates normal efforts for human growth and development.

The significance of cultural racism as a structural factor associated with black male violence is its persistent and long-term effects related to promoting cultural disorganization among African Americans (Karenga, 1988a; Madhubuti, 1990). That is, as a source of structural pressure, cultural racism has led to the emergence of a cultural orientation and adaptive styles that promote, accept, and tolerate a broad range of deviant and disruptive behaviors within the African-American community, especially among those who are concentrated in inner-city ghettos (Akbar, 1984; Karenga, 1988a; Azibo, 1989; Welsing, 1991; Wilson, 1996).

Summary. While I regard institutional and cultural racism as powerful structural pressures that have had an adverse effect on the capacity of African Americans to survive and achieve the American Dream, these pressures alone are not sufficient to explain the high rates of interpersonal violence involving black males. Indeed, institutional racism has been useful, especially when it has been defined in terms of racial or economic inequality, in predicting or describing the ecological distribution and demographic characteristics of neighborhoods and population groups experiencing the highest rates of homicide and assault (Blau and Blau, 1982; Rose and McClain, 1990). However, violent confrontations are ultimately interpersonal transactions, that is, they are micro-level encounters (Toch, 1969; Luckenbill, 1977; Polk, 1994). To focus solely on structural pressures as "the cause" of the high rates of interpersonal violence among black males fails to consider how various cultural, situational, interpersonal, and intrapersonal factors converge in conflict-ridden *situations* that culminate in violence.

Dysfunctional Cultural Adaptations

Within this theoretical perspective, structural pressures (e.g., institutional and cultural racism and the restructuring of the economy) constitute the independent variable, while various dysfunctional cultural adaptations are operationalized as a set of *intervening* or *mediating* variables that facilitate specific conditions, behaviors, and rationalizations that lead to violent confrontations involving black males.

The concept "dysfunctional cultural adaptation" is incorporated here to refer to culture-related practices and behavior that do not serve a useful purpose relative to facilitating social stability, progress, and development among African Americans. Moreover, dysfunctional cultural adaptations are believed to be linked to various patterns of individual and social instability among African Americans (Akbar, 1981; 1984; Azibo, 1989; Welsing, 1991). The structural-cultural perspective proposes the existence of two dysfunctional cultural adaptations that contribute to the high rates of violent offending and victimization prevalent among black males. The two dysfunctional cultural adaptations are: (1) the lack of an affirming cultural agenda and (2) dysfunctional definitions of manhood. Furthermore, I believe that these adaptations do not represent a unique cultural tradition among African Americans, rather they are *situationally* centered adaptations to a range of adverse macro-level pressures, including racial segregation, blocked access to educational and employment opportunities, de-industrialization, and increased joblessness among black males (Feagin and Vera, 1995; Wilson, 1987; 1996). In addition, the disorganized community structure of many poor black communities offers a fertile local social context conducive for the emergence of dysfunctional cultural adaptations that are more immediately related to the occurrence of acts of violence. As Wilson (1996) has reported, the community structure of black neighborhoods experiencing the highest rates of violence are characterized by social isolation, high rates of black male joblessness, the concentration of poverty, and ineffective management of youth and young adults in public places.

Lack of an Affirming Cultural Agenda. Some researchers have observed that the failure of African Americans to establish a cultural agenda, cultural practices, and cultural institutions to counteract and remedy the negative consequences associated with exposure to cultural racism represents a dysfunctional cultural adaptation (Karenga, 1986; 1988a, 1988b; Madhubuti, 1990). In contrast, for example, the civil rights movement was a mass movement in which African Americans strove to dismantle institutional racism (Franklin and Moss, 1988). There have been brief periods when a segment of the national African American community has sought to initiate a cultural development agenda in the form of self-help, separatism, black cultural nationalism, black consciousness, and more recently Afrocentricism (Asante, 1987; Carmichael and Hamilton, 1967; Garvey, 1923; Karenga, 1988b). However, these movements have tended to be short-lived largely because of the lack of support from the masses of black people (Perkins, 1986). The failure of African Americans to adequately respond to cultural racism has several implications related to the prevalence of violent behavior among black males.

First, the cultural crisis (e.g., the loss of historical memory, the lack of appreciation for black people and their heritage, the lack of cultural confidence, and cultural competence that exist among African Americans) adds to the stress associated with exposure to institutional racism (Azibo, 1989). Bernard (1990) has suggested that the high rates of interpersonal violence among inner-city blacks emanate from the prevalence of physiological arousal that is precipitated by exposure to living in a crowded urban environment, low social position, and racial discrimination. I have extended this view to suggest that exposure to cultural racism enhances physiological arousal and agitation emanating from the exposure to institutional racism. That is, cultural racism, as a result of the psychocultural distortions it promotes in terms of low self-esteem (Clark and Clark, 1947, 1980), self-hate, and hate for other blacks (Akbar, 1981; Baldwin, 1987; Azibo, 1989) increases physiological arousal that increases the likelihood of aggression in conflict situations involving black males (Akbar, 1981; Bernard, 1990). Second, the failure to establish an affirming cultural agenda increases the likelihood that dysfunctional manhood role orientations will emerge and be tolerated by many of those who reside in poor black communities given the adverse consequences and challenges associated with exposure to institutional racism and race-neutral shifts in the economy (Anderson, 1990; Wilson, 1996). Finally, exposure to cultural racism may compel black males to engage in risk-taking behavior (e.g., heavy public drinking, using drugs, selling drugs, gambling, being sexually promiscuous, joining gangs, etc.) as a means of demonstrating their significance as men in spite of being black or because they are black. Thus, efforts to live up to or transcend black male stereotypes may encourage risk-taking behavior that increases the likelihood of violence participation (Majors and Mancini-Billson, 1992; Wilson and Daly, 1993).

Dysfunctional Definitions of Manhood. In recent years, an evolving literature that examines masculinity and manhood has emerged (Brod, 1987; Franklin, 1984; Staples, 1982). In his review of the literature on masculinity, Doyle (1989) concluded that there are five themes that encompass the male role: (1) antifeminity, (2) success, (3) aggression, (4) sexuality, and (5) self-reliance. These five themes are representative of the characteristics and concerns generally associated with the traditional male role. Indeed, there has been criticism of the traditional male role regarding its emphasis on sexism, the sexual objectification of females, emotional aloofness, the glorification of aggression and violence, and the priorities placed on occupational and monetary success at the expense of establishing nurturing relationships (Pleck, 1987). For example, Jourard (1971) has suggested that men should reconsider their commitment to the traditional male role given that there are considerable lethal social and health consequences associated with efforts to live up to its role expectations. However, the view that males are to function as protectors and providers continues to dominate the definition of manhood in American society (Pleck, 1987). There is considerable research that strongly suggests that black men are just as likely as white men to define manhood in terms of being a good provider (Cazanave, 1979; Taylor et al., 1988; Hunter and Davis, 1994).

Historically, however, black males have been the primary target of the overt racial oppression directed toward all African Americans (Ginzburg, 1969; Franklin, 1984, 1987; Madhubuti, 1990). In America, a patriarchal, white male-dominated society, black males as subordinated men have been and continue to be perceived as a threat to the political, economic, and cultural dominance of white men (Madhubuti, 1990; Welsing, 1991). Consequently, the systematic deprivation of equal access to political rights and educational and employment opportunities has frustrated the attempts of many black males to achieve traditional manhood ideals and roles (Hare, 1966; Staples, 1982; Franklin, 1984). Welsing (1991: 87) has suggested that "... the resultant frustration of black manhood potential forces behavior into dysfunctional and obsessive compulsive patterns in areas of people activity in which greater degrees of maleness are permitted to be expressed, (i.e., sex, sports, and entertainment)." Thus, exposure to racial oppression has led some black men to redefine manhood in terms of ideals and roles that they perceive as being *achievable for them given their status and social environment* (Clark, 1965; Liebow, 1967; Majors and Mancini-Billson, 1992).

Hannerz (1969) uses the term "compulsive masculinity alternative" to describe a gender-specific compensatory adaptation that many lower-class black males adopt to cover up their inability to meet the standards of the traditional male role. However, rather than being an effective and functional strategy to cope with environmental stress (e.g., racial discrimination, joblessness, poverty, and low self-esteem), the "black compulsive masculinity alternative," as a compensatory strategy, is a dysfunctional compensatory adaptation. Instead of solving problems in the environment, it generates additional ones.

There are four factors that contribute to the compulsive masculinity alternative being perceived as an acceptable alternative to those aspects of the traditional male role that emphasize independence, responsibility, and providing for one's family. First, each generation of black males must confront the realities of negotiating an economic system that proactively practices racial discrimination against black males and subsequently hinders their efforts to achieve economic stability (Liebow, 1967; Kirshenman and Neckerman, 1991). Second, many black males who adopt the compulsive masculinity alternative do so as a strategy to mitigate negative feelings and stigma associated with their inability to successfully enact accepted and expected aspects of the traditional male role (Hannerz, 1969; Staples, 1982). Third, the persistence of the compulsive masculinity alternative among many poor, urban black males results from male-to-male cultural transmission of manhood ideals, roles, and norms that place overt emphasis on defining manhood in terms of toughness, sexual conquest, manipulation, and thrill-seeking behavior (Franklin, 1984; Anderson, 1990; 1994; 1999). And, fourth, in many ghetto neighborhoods there exists a generalized acceptance and tolerance of exaggerated expressions of manhood (Anderson, 1990; 1994; 1999; Sampson and Wilson, 1995; Wilson, 1996).

Ethnographic studies of blacks residing in poor urban neighborhoods have described several ghetto-related manhood role orientations (Anderson, 1976; 1990; Hannerz, 1969; Liebow, 1967; Milner and Milner, 1972; Rainwater, 1972; Schulz, 1966). Given the similarities of the roles described in various typologies, the manhood roles that involve the greatest risk for violence participation tend to fit into one of the following categories: (1) the tough guy, (2) the player of women, or (3) the hustler.

The Tough Guy. The tough guy is a manhood role orientation in which manhood tends to be defined in terms of demonstrating a willingness to resort to violence as a means of resolving interpersonal conflict (Hannerz, 1969; Oliver, 1984; Canada, 1994). A central feature of the tough guy role involves a concern with projecting an image of aggression and unyielding autonomy. Tough guys are primarily interested in avoiding attempts by others to violate their desire to be free from external interference (Oliver, 1998; Anderson, 1999).

Among black males who adhere to the tough guy role, violent confrontations tend to occur in situations in which a male is either attempting to impose his definition of a situation on his antagonist or he is attempting to avoid his antagonist imposing his definition of the situation on him (Oliver, 1998). Thus, in those encounters that culminate in violence, insults and other acts that are defined as disrespectful are also perceived as autonomy transgressions. Given the importance that black males attribute to autonomy as a measure of manhood, resorting to violence is often a means to gain compliance from an antagonist, a means of retaliating against an antagonist, and/or a means of engaging in symbolic communication with one's antagonist (Oliver, 1998).

The Player of Women. The inability of many young black males to achieve the traditional male role has enhanced their attraction to the "player of women" role as an alternative means of achieving a sense of personal and social significance (Hannerz, 1969; Majors and Mancini-Billson, 1992). Consequently, overt emphasis on sexual conquest and promiscuity is a major aspect of how many lower-class black males define manhood (Anderson, 1990; 1994; Clark, 1965; Hannerz, 1969; Liebow, 1967; Wilson, 1996). Within the black male subculture, especially in streetcorner peer groups, there exists substantial support and respect for those males who successfully demonstrate their commitment to the "player of women" role. In his ethnographic study of inner-city blacks, Anderson (1990: 136) concluded that: "Casual sex with as many women as possible, impregnating one or more, and getting them to have your baby brings a boy the ultimate esteem from his peers and makes him feel like a man."

Efforts to live up to normative expectations related to the "player of women" role increases an individual's risk of becoming involved in a violent confrontation. There are several interpersonal contexts in which black males adherence to the "player of women" role may motivate individuals to engage in violence. These specific interpersonal contexts include: (1) romantic competition between two males who are competing for sexual access and dominance over a particular female; (2) encounters in which a male becomes involved in a violent confrontation as a result of coming to the defense of a female relative or friend who has been sexually exploited and/or emotionally or physically abused; and, (3) encounters in which a woman who has been emotionally and/or physically abused resorts to violence against a male as a means of retaliation (McClain, 1981; Mann, 1996; Oliver, 1998).

The Hustler. The hustler role is a manhood role orientation in which manhood is defined in terms of using one's wits to aggressively manipulate the limited resources of the ghetto to improve one's economic condition and social status (Glasgow, 1981). Attraction to the hustler role results from a subculturally supported belief that it is difficult for black males to achieve economic security through legitimate societal paths (Anderson, 1990; Glasgow, 1981; Hudson, 1972). A central feature of the hustler philosophy emphasizes acquiring money and status without working a legitimate job (Hudson, 1972). There are several types of hustles or "games" that men who define themselves as hustlers use to "make it" or "get over," including: (1) manipulating women, (2) selling drugs, (3) gambling, (4) theft, (5) selling stolen merchandise, and (6) promoting prostitution (Hudson, 1972; Milner and Milner, 1972; Anderson, 1990; Wilson, 1996).

Exploitation of others is a central feature of the hustler philosophy (Hudson, 1972). According to Gouldner (1960), a reciprocal interpersonal transaction is a social interaction in which a primary feature of the encounter involves mutual giving and receiving. Thus, reciprocity contributes to stability and harmony in interpersonal relations. The hustler role, however, involves a significant lack of reciprocity in interpersonal relations. Consequently, the deliberate acts of nonreciprocal behavior associated with the enactment of the hustler role lead to conflict and tension and therefore increases the likelihood that violent confrontations will occur.

Regardless of the type of hustle or "game" that precipitates interpersonal conflict, there are three situational contexts that are most likely to lead to violence as a result of black males' adherence to the hustler role. First are situations in which an individual who believes that he or she has been manipulated or exploited by a hustler initiates an encounter – as a means of seeking justice – that culminates in violence (Oliver, 1998). Second are situations in which a hustler responds with violence to criticism, threats, or acts of violence directed against him by a con game victim. And, finally, there are situations in which the hustler initiates violence against an individual who he believes is interfering with the hustler's efforts to make money or achieve a valued social identity and reputation (Milner and Milner, 1972; Oliver, 1998).

The tough guy, the player of women, and the hustler are manhood role orientations that are a common feature of the manner in which many lower-class black males adapt to the social circumstances in which they find themselves. These specific role orientations function as a catalyst for a wide variety of routine activities and lifestyles (Hannerz, 1969; Anderson, 1990; Majors and Mancini-Billson, 1992).

Routine Activities in the Streets

Advocates of the routine activities approach have suggested that an individual's lifestyle may increase or decrease his risk of experiencing criminal victimization (Hindelang, 1978). According to Hindelang (1978) and his colleagues, individuals who are most at risk for experiencing criminal victimization are more likely than others to frequent public places at night, to share demographic characteristics with personal crime offenders, and to be engaged in behaviors that lead offenders to perceive them to be desirable as crime victims. Violent confrontations among black males tend to occur in public settings (e.g., streetcorners, bars, parking lots) or semipublic settings (e.g., drug houses, illegal gambling houses, pool halls, etc.) (Curtis, 1974; Wilkinson and Fagan, 1996). In the vernacular of the ghetto, these settings are generally referred to as "the streets."

Given the variety of social activities that occur in "the streets," in many ways "the streets" is a significant ghetto institution (Perkins, 1975). For example, it is in "the streets" that ghetto-related manhood roles are learned and enacted (Liebow, 1967; Perkins, 1975; Anderson, 1990; 1994; 1999). A significant aspect of the lifestyle of black males who are most at risk for violence participation is that they tend to spend an inordinate amount of time hanging out in "the streets." In extensive interviews conducted with black males who had a history of fighting in "the streets," those respondents reported four primary reasons for hanging out in "the streets": (1) to socialize; (2) to sell, purchase, or use drugs; (3) to meet women; and (4) to manipulate and exploit others (Oliver, 1998). The activities that attract individuals to "the streets" are attractive because they are the means that black males who adhere to the tough guy, the player of women, and the hustler roles use to demonstrate their commitment to these manhood ideals. Thus, the lifestyle and routine activities of black males who adhere to the compulsive masculinity alternative brings them into regular contact with other men who subscribe to similar values and norms. Given the emphasis that these men place on exploiting others and demonstrating toughness, their routine interaction with one another functions to increase their risk of interpersonal conflict and violence.

Definition of the Situation

While routine activities associated with the enactment of dysfunctional manhood roles unite black males in conflict situations with each other and others, it is how they define these encounters that leads to intrapersonal decisions to engage in violent actions against an antagonist (Oliver, 1998). According to Stokes and Hewitt (1976), the definition and reaction to problematic situations occurs in a situational context in which "participants in interaction interpret one another's acts within a cultural framework." "The code of the streets" is the cultural framework that many lower-class black males use to interpret the intentions and behavior of others (Anderson, 1994; 1999). That is, in the course of social interaction, "the code of the streets" is used to determine whether or not an individual has violated the code and whether or not one should resort to violence as a specific means of maintaining one's autonomy and respect (Anderson, 1994; Oliver, 1998).

"The code of the streets" is a body of beliefs and social expectations that regulate the enactment of street-oriented manhood roles. Beliefs associated with the code assume and promote the idea that a man should be autonomous, sexually promiscuous, dominant in the male-female relationship, and willing to resort to violence to protect his personal interests or personal safety (Anderson, 1994; Hannerz, 1969; Liebow, 1967). A major requirement of "the code of the streets" is that a man should not accept being disrespected by others (Anderson, 1994). Moreover, acts that are defined as disrespectful (e.g., insults, identity attacks, stealing from someone, threats, and acts of violence) are typically regarded as violations of the code (Oliver, 1998). The significance of "the code of the streets" is that it is frequently used as a culture-related standard in which black males attribute blameworthiness to an antagonist. It also provides a rationale that allows an individual to resort to violence against his antagonist if he chooses to do so (Anderson, 1994; Oliver, 1998).

Overview and Conclusions

The importance of the structural-cultural perspective is the emphasis placed on examining how various structural factors (e.g., institutional racism, restructuring of the economy, and cultural racism) and cultural factors (e.g., lack of an affirming cultural agenda and dysfunctional manhood roles) converge to produce high rates of interpersonal violence among black males. A major feature of the perspective is its description of a macro-micro *contextual* reductionism. That is, it attempts to describe how structural and cultural factors converge and lead to conflict-ridden *situations* in which an individual may feel justified in resorting to violence as a means of resolving a dispute.

In the causal chain that has been developed (see Figure 14.1), there are three feedback loops in which a particular factor has an additive effect on a factor that it does not immediately proceed in the sequential ordering and description of the general causal relationship. First, in this theoretical explanation, dysfunctional definitions of manhood are described as dysfunctional cultural adaptations that lead to manhood roles and routine activities that increase the likelihood of conflict and violence. In addition, I argue that dysfunctional manhood roles and the routine activities associated with these roles have an additive effect on the adverse effects related to the restructuring of the economy. That is, commitment to dysfunctional manhood roles and involvement in routine activities associated with these roles weaken black males' attachment to the conventional labor force (Wilson, 1996; Van Haitsma, 1989). Involvement in the social roles and activities

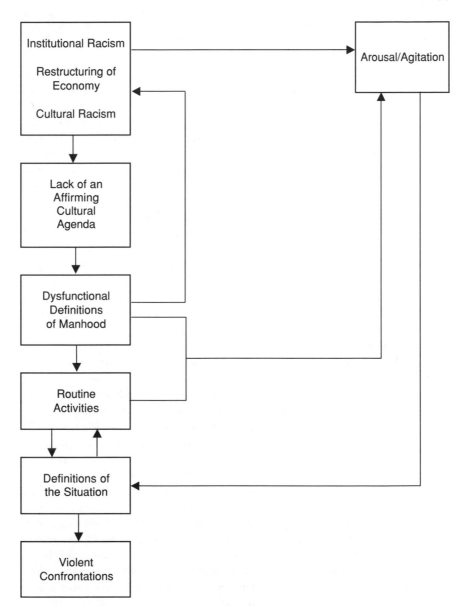

Figure 14.1. Overall Causal Chain of the Structural-Cultural Perspective

of "the streets" reduce the likelihood that lower-class black males will have access to social networks, information and training, and employment opportunities that would encourage a positive adaptation to a changing economic marketplace (Wilson, 1996). Thus, the restructuring of the economy as a source of structural pressure is enhanced as a result of lower-class black males' commitment to dysfunctional manhood roles that reinforce their economic marginality.

Second, the dysfunctional manhood roles and related routine activities combine to enhance a generalized state of arousal in the social world of black men. That is, awareness of how lower-class black males define manhood and the exploitative activities they are prone to engage in has an additive effect on arousal and frustration precipitated by various structural pressures (e.g., institutional racism, restructuring of the economy, and cultural racism). Thus, while these males participate in street activities as a means of establishing their manhood, they are overtly sensitive to the dangers associated with street life. Danger in the streets is typically defined in terms of its potential threats to one's public image and physical safety (Oliver, 1998).

Finally, there is an interactive effect or feedback loop that exists between routine activities and how conflict-ridden situations are defined by black males who witness violent confrontations that occur in the streets. Cohen and Felson (1979) have suggested that before a direct contact predatory crime (i.e., assault, robbery, murder) can occur, the situation must include a motivated offender, a suitable target, and an absence of capable guardians. The processes related to how motivated offenders and suitable targets encounter one another in conflict-ridden situations leading to violence have been explained above. Here, I consider how black males who witness violent confrontations that occur in the streets define routine activities.

The absence of capable guardians who are against predatory violations is a major feature of the situational context in which interpersonal conflict involving lower-class black males escalate into violent confrontations (Canada, 1994; Oliver, 1998). Given the salience of the tough guy, the "player of women," and the hustler in the social world of the streets, the occurrence of interpersonal conflict and violence are defined by many males who witness these encounters as a routine and expected outcome related to hanging out in the streets. In addition, attempts at guardianship as a means of preventing the escalation of conflict to a violent confrontation are less likely to occur in situations involving black males given the general awareness of the known potential lethality of such encounters (Anderson, 1999). Moreover, in extensive interviews with violent black men, Oliver (1998) found that third parties who were unrelated to or who did not maintain a friendship with either of the combatants in a conflict situation were generally perceived as members of an "instigating audience" who actively encouraged the combatants to escalate the interaction from verbal conflict to physical violence.

The structural-cultural perspective of black male violence primarily explains the macro-micro processes contributing to violent confrontations involving black males who maintain a commitment to ghetto-related manhood roles (i.e., the tough guy, the "player of women," and the hustler). Moreover, emphasis has been placed on explaining mostly expressive acts of violence in which black males are motivated to engage in violence as a result of various face-saving concerns, including: self-image defending, self-image promoting, reputation building, and norm enforcing (Toch, 1969). Thus, a major limitation of this perspective is the lack of attention devoted to explaining instrumentally motivated acts of violence (e.g., robbery and drug-related violence) or violent acts committed as a consequence of gang membership (Goldstein et al., 1985; Decker and VanWinkle, 1996; Wright and Decker, 1997).

The prevention implications of the structural-cultural perspective suggest the need for a variety of structural reforms as well as community-based prevention and intervention strategies. The most important structural reform that is necessary to reduce black male violence are proactive strategies implemented by federal and state government in collaboration with the educational system and the business community to establish a national labor market strategy in which job training programs are designed to enhance the adaptability of black males to changing employment opportunities (Wilson, 1987; 1996). Employment in well-paying jobs will substantially reduce the pool of black males inclined to adopt as their primary gender identity dysfunctional manhood role orientations.

Increased rates of employment of black males in jobs that provide income above the poverty level will have a positive effect on community organization within black urban poor and working-class neighborhoods. For example, reducing joblessness among black males will lead to an increase in two-parent families (Wilson, 1996). Consequently, reducing joblessness will lead to a reduction in the overall rate of poverty among African Americans. Also, increased levels of employment among black males will serve as a catalyst for enhancing the capacity of families, friendship networks, and local community organizations to supervise and control teenage peer groups.

Finally, in response to the social problems precipitated by African-American exposure to institutional and cultural racism, there are several prevention strategies that should be implemented. First, on the macro-cultural level, Americans must be encouraged to commit themselves to achieving racial harmony and a society in which racial and ethnic diversity are valued within the context of striving to become one America. A reduction in black-white racial animosity will have positive consequences for black males, especially as it relates to mitigating racial prejudice and discriminatory practices that block them from having full access to well-paying employment opportunities (Kirshenman and Neckerman, 1991). Second, on the micro-cultural level, African Americans must take the initiative to restructure the community-based institutions that they control (e.g., churches, community centers, civic organizations, etc.) to establish programs, social events, and rituals that disseminate historical and cultural information that strengthens the self and social-esteem of African Americans. Moreover, emphasis should be placed on establishing mentoring programs in which young black males who are at risk of involvement in problematic behavior are matched with well-functioning adult male role models (Hill, 1992). Ultimately, the reduction of high rates of interpersonal violence among black males is dependent on the African-American community developing the capacity to socialize at-risk black males to define manhood in terms of values, norms, and roles that lead to conventional patterns of behavior.

A Cultural Psychology Framework for the Study
of African-American Morality and Violence

Robert J. Jagers
Jacqueline Mattis
Katrina Walker

Despite an overall decline in youth violence, urban African-American children and adolescents continue to be disproportionately represented among
both perpetrators and victims of violence (e.g., Snyder and Sickmund,
1999). Although African Americans comprise a mere 15 percent of the U.S.
youth population, they account for over half the arrests for homicide nationwide (Snyder and Sickmund, 1999). Incidents of nonfatal assaults are also
higher among African-American youth compared to youth of other ethnic
backgrounds (e.g., Sanders-Phillips, 1997). The rate of suicide for African-
American males has doubled since 1980 (Snyder and Sickmund, 1999), and
sizable numbers of African-American youth have participated in the violent
activities associated with many of the major urban rebellions (Gale, 1996;
Harris, 1998; Bush, 1999).

The trend toward same-race assaultive violence has made homicide a leading cause of death among African-American adolescents (Coie and Dodge,
1998; Snyder and Sickmund, 1999). In addition, African-American children and youth experience high rates of nonlethal injury (Sanders-Phillips,
1997), and frequently witness acts of violence against others, including murders (e.g., Shakoor and Chalmers, 1991; Jenkins and Bell, 1997). These children and youth are also increasingly exposed to hate crimes, police brutality,
and more subtle forms of structural violence such as substandard housing,
poor education, and high unemployment (Sparks, 1994). The prevalence
of violence in the lives of African-American youth, especially young men, is
so great that the notion of genocide has been offered to accurately describe
their life circumstances (Johnson and Leighton, 1995).

Violence is one of the more pressing problems facing urban African-
American children and adolescents. The frequency and intensity of the interpersonal and structural violence that occurs in urban African-American communities has raised concerns about the moral development of the children

and youth who reside there (Anderson, 1997; 1999; Astor, 1994; Sparks, 1994; Ward, 1988; 1995). Some scholars have argued that these young people are being raised in a cultural context characterized by moral values that are inconsistent with those prescribed by the prevailing American social order. Much of the available literature linking African-American culture, morality, and violence is informed by this "subculture of violence" perspective (Wolfgang and Ferracuti, 1967; Curtis, 1975), which holds that many African Americans participate in a self-perpetuating subculture that rejects mainstream American civility in favor of a so-called street code, characterized by the threat or use of violence to establish dominance and resolve conflicts (Anderson, 1997; 1999; Massey and Denton, 1993; Naison, 1992; Ogbu, 1985; Taylor, 1991; Wilson, 1996). This view has also served to reinforce negative stereotypes and legitimize the overrepresentation of African Americans in the prison-industrial complex (Platt, 1995; Texeira, 1995).

One critique of the subculture of violence thesis is that it reflects and reinforces Eurocentric biases. For example, the assumption that European-American culture fosters decency ignores the ubiquity of violence within mainstream U.S. society (McCord, 1997), especially that which has been perpetrated against African Americans. It further obscures for its adherents the common cultural and moral underpinnings shared by European-American society and black urban street life (Bulhan, 1985; Hagedorn, 1997; Jagers, 1996; Messner and Rosenfeld, 1997; Sparks, 1994).

An alternative perspective emerging in the literature highlights African-American cultural resources that promote resilience and healthy development. Proponents of this perspective have asserted that African-American communal values prescribe a morality of care that limits violent behaviors and fosters collective well-being (Oliver, 1989; Hammond and Yung, 1993; Ward, 1995). Research studies have provided some support for this contention (Jagers, 1997; Stevenson, 1997; Humphries, Parker, and Jagers, 2000); however, the existing literature has not yet adequately developed the connections among communal values, race-related coping strategies, and morality in interpersonal, community, and societal contexts. Further specifying these relationships could stimulate and guide basic and applied research efforts concerned with violence prevention and wellness promotion for African-American children and youth.

This chapter attempts such a project by integrating diverse perspectives on the contributions of culture and morality to African-American violence in order to derive a framework for psychological study in this area. One of its principal assumptions is that the complex intersection of culture, class, and race yields multiple moral communities among urban African Americans. Thus, it proposes four racialized cultural identities (Lamont, 1999), each representing moral cognitions and emotions that prompt or inhibit violence involvement by members of the distinct identity groups. Before doing so, however, working definitions of morality and of relevant forms of individual and collective violence are outlined. The chapter concludes with a brief discussion of the implications of its findings for basic and applied research on youth violence in African-American communities.

Morality, Culture, and Violence. Morality refers to an array of cognitions, emotions, and behaviors relevant to principles of caring and justice (Turiel, 1998). For some theorists, the presence of violence within this order indicates that these relational principles and practices have somehow been compromised (Bandura, 1991; Bandura, Barbanelli, Capara, and Pastorelli, 1996), for example, has coined the term "*moral disengagement*" to capture the psychological mechanisms associated with violence. He used the term to refer to the deactivation of the self-sanctioning processes that lead otherwise moral individuals to commit acts of violence. Bandura (1991) delineated several interrelated deactivation processes, including efforts to reconstruct the violent conduct, obscure personal causal agency, dehumanize or vilify the victims of violence, and/or blame the victims for the violence enacted on them.

This chapter contends, however, that psychological arguments that represent violence as the consequence of personal amorality or moral decay are overly simplistic. Violent behaviors and their related psychological processes are more appropriately understood as outgrowths of complex social arrangements and moral systems. Given that cultures reflect moral orders that define and are defined by relationships among and between individuals and social institutions (Wuthnow, 1987; Shweder, Much, Muhapatra, and Park, 1997), a cultural psychology approach would seem useful for inquiry into the moral underpinnings of various forms of violence.

Generally speaking, violence refers to "any relation, process, or condition by which an individual or group violates the physical, social and/or psychological integrity of another person or group" (Bulhan, 1985: 135). This chapter is concerned primarily with community violence, which encompasses both street-level violence and processes resulting in systemic inequities in the distribution of resources (Sparks, 1994). Bell (1997) elaborates the concept of community violence by distinguishing between its individual and collective forms. He offers that individual forms of community violence include serial killings, predatory or instrumental violence, and interpersonal or expressive violence. (This chapter includes within this category self-destructive acts such as substance abuse and suicide.) Bell further contends that spontaneous mob violence or riots, hate crimes, and systematic violence such as war, institutional racism, and sexism are among collective forms of violence. He places gang- and drug-related violence in independent categories, with the former being construed as both predatory (individual) and systematic (collective) and the latter being construed as including the systematic violence committed by drug dealers to enhance their market share, the economic drug-related predatory violence of drug users, and drug-related violence prompted by pharmacological drug effects.

The Confluence of Culture and Race. The concept of culture has been prominent among contemporary African-American psychologists since the 1970s (Valentine, 1971; Boykin, 1983; Nobles, 1991). Stimulated in part by prevailing notions of African-American deficiency and pathology, scholars argued for analyses that reflected an appreciation of the cultural integrity of blacks. Recently, this approach to issues of culture has gained currency and popularity in mainstream American psychology (e.g., Betancourt and Lopez, 1993; Cooper and Denner, 1998; Greenfield and Cocking, 1994; Shweder, 1991). Cultural psychologists tend to conceive of cultures as shared systems of meaning that are transmitted within and across generations. These meaning systems contain an array of fundamental themes to which individuals orient themselves. Cultural orientations imply repertoires or scripts of personhood and collective identity that define the preferred functional psychology (e.g., cognitive, emotional, and behavioral inclinations) of individuals, groups, and institutions.

This chapter uses Boykin's (1983) triple quandary theory to organize and interrogate competing views of African-American culture and its connections to morality and violence. Boykin's paradigm conceives of African Americans as having to negotiate simultaneously three intersecting social realms of experience: mainstream American (Anglocultural) culture, their African cultural (Afrocultural) legacy, and racial minority status. The pervasiveness of racism in the United States makes the racial minority realm the most relevant for inquiry into the moral implications of community violence as it pertains to African Americans. The experiences of racialized oppression dictate that African Americans evolve an understanding of what being black implies insofar as their relationships with other members of their race and with European Americans are concerned. However, explorations of the Anglocultural theme of acquisitive individualism and the Afrocultural theme of communalism are likewise critical for understanding the moral implications of African-American community violence. These themes are foundational to the understanding and conduct of social relationships between and among African Americans and others.

Acquisitive individualism refers to an orientation in which the effective control and accumulation of people, material objects, knowledge, and influence is seen as a primary indicator of self-worth and social standing (Boykin, 1983; Jagers, 1996). By contrast, communalism connotes an orientation in which the fulfillment of social duties and responsibilities reflects a premium on the fundamental interconnectedness, interdependence, and well-being of one's group (Boykin, Jagers, Ellison, and Albury, 1997; Jagers, 1997; Mattis and Jagers, in press). It seems reasonable then to assume that preference for an acquisitive or a communal orientation would be an important determinant of racial ideology.

Drawing on Sellers, Smith, Shelton, Rowley, and Chavous's (1998) racial identity model, four racialized cultural identities are proposed that extend acquisitive individualistic and communal orientations to the sociopolitical domain of race. An acquisitive orientation can be likened to an assimilationist ideology because it similarly promotes the desire to integrate fully into European-American society. Acquisitiveness also can be paired with an oppressed-minority ideology reflective of disenfranchisement and self-depreciation. By contrast, a communal orientation coincides with a humanist ideology that highlights the commonality of all people. It also shares much in common with a nationalist ideology that emphasizes the uniqueness and centrality of the African-American experience. The implications of the four resulting identity orientations – acquisitive-assimilationist, acquisitive-oppressed, communal-humanist, and communal-nationalist – for understanding African-American morality and community violence are examined in the following sections.

The Acquisitive-Assimilationist Identity. Many theorists have maintained that individualism is the cornerstone of American mainstream culture (Bellah, Madsen, Sullivan, Swidler, and Tipton, 1985; Du Bois, 1972; Etzioni, 1996; Sampson, 1988; Spence, 1985). As Shweder et al. (1997) contend, the priority placed on individual rights, protections, and choices in the United States reflects an ethic of autonomy. However, it is more precise to say that U.S. consumer capitalism demands a cultural emphasis on acquisitive individualism, which focuses on the personal accumulation of wealth, status, and power and represents the interface between material well-being, interpersonal competition, and person-object relations. Acquisitive individualism further implies a "bourgeois morality" characterized by utilitarianism and instrumentality in social relations (Scheler, 1994).

African-American assimilationists abide by American social conventions that mandate cordiality and a nonthreatening persona in the public arena. This gives the impression that U.S. society is based on decency and moral uprightness. However, this veneer of civility masks a moral outlook that allows for the dispassionate, calculated manipulation and exploitation of others while promoting the pursuit of an illusive sense of material well-being. Obscuring personal causal agency and blaming the victim are the moral disengagement processes most relevant for the characterization of black acquisitive assimilationists. Typically, these individuals buy into the notion that self-promotion through the exploitation of others is encouraged within the U.S. social order. They also tend to believe that those who are abused within that order somehow deserve it, and that, if given the opportunity, the exploited would readily exchange places with their exploiters.

The rhetoric of equal opportunity and the reality of differential access to wealth and power make the affective states of anger and envy prominent in the bourgeois morality system of acquisitive assimilationists. Whereas their anger is anchored in racial shame or negative regard (Sellers et al., 1998), their envy is a self-focused emotional state that typically yields a sense of public worthlessness (Tangney, Wagner, Hill-Barlow, Marschall, and Gramzow, 1996). Assimilationists overwhelmingly want to view themselves as different from underachieving blacks; however, despite their best efforts, they cannot escape the social stigmas associated with being black. This version of internalized racism typically prompts within them anger, contempt, and moral outrage at members of their race who do not, cannot, or simply will not find their niche in the white-dominated U.S. social order. They subsequently come to blame less-assimilated or less materially successful blacks (or both) for the negative racial stereotypes embraced by many European Americans (Cose, 1993).

Because their social analysis fails to link circumstantial occurrences such as African-American underachievement and street violence to structural oppression, acquisitive assimilationists typically feel no moral compunction about engaging in efforts aimed at collective uplift. Indeed, they may be some of the harshest and most vocal critics of such efforts. Most concentrate on distancing themselves psychologically from other African Americans, content that the racial segregation prominent in most U.S. urban centers will preclude their physical separation from same-race others from poor backgrounds (Pattillo-McCoy, 1999).

However, limiting community activities and social interactions with other blacks also helps these assimilationists to minimize the probability that they will become victims of predatory violence. Should such an incident occur, these individuals readily turn to and rely on sources of authority sanctioned by the mainstream social order (e.g., police and the judicial system). This is done more out of prudence than moral restraint, because they fear that if they retaliate, they, too, may be subjected to the scrutiny and punishments of these socially sanctioned authorities.

For African-American acquisitive assimilationists, the most immediate social comparisons are their upwardly mobile African-American neighbors, although their ultimate aspiration is to emulate and experience for themselves the privilege enjoyed by affluent European Americans. Failure to possess the valued objects or statuses of whites may prompt within the acquisitive assimilationist feelings of envy and relative deprivation (Merton, 1968), which may lead to disdain and ill-will toward those who have acquired the desired objects or privileges (Salovey, 1991). Although they know that white privilege is sustained through discrimination and exploitation, acquisitive assimilationists resist outward expressions of hostility toward European Americans and their surrogates. Unwilling to challenge the hegemonic system in which they find themselves, they begrudgingly endure inequities such as underemployment, glass ceilings, tokenism, and microaggressions to avoid compromising access to the much-coveted goods and services (Pierce, 1974).

Although the bourgeois morality of African-American acquisitive assimilationists provides them with ample opportunities for manipulation and exploitation, it typically does not stimulate them to commit physical violence against others. By contrast, the resentment and social isolation associated with these assimilationists' frustrated social strivings can sometimes manifest in self-destructive behaviors. For example, Anderson (1991) has argued that the assimilation process may contribute to the high incidence of stress-related illnesses found among African Americans. Related contentions are that the press to assimilate may heighten substance abuse among African Americans (Akbar, 1991; Anderson, 1991), or that it may help explain the dramatic rise in African-American suicide, especially among young men (Snyder and Sickmund, 1999).

The Acquisitive-Oppressed Identity. Acquisitive individualism also can be linked to the oppressed-minority identity. The acquisitive-oppressed African-American identity has been the focus of much of the literature on inner-city social life. Many scholars have suggested that this identity reflects an oppositional cultural agenda that is at odds with that of mainstream white America (Anderson, 1997, 1999; Massey and Denton, 1993; Wilson, 1996). Nonetheless, acquisitive-oppressed African Americans share with their acquisitive-assimilationist peers a priority on possessing goods and services and its related bourgeois morality. They likewise manifest similar types of moral disengagement and related emotions of envy and anger. Unlike the assimilationists, however, poor academic and social skill preparation limit conventional employment opportunities for the acquisitive oppressed, a circumstance that further exacerbates their sense of relative deprivation and intense commodity worship (Nightingale, 1993).

Acquisitive-oppressed African Americans are typically involved in the street economy, a loosely organized system of markets that are a source of legal and illegal goods and services. These individuals tend to be most closely aligned with the illegal sector of this economy and thus are at elevated risk of violence involvement. In this sector, predation in the form of armed theft of urban status items such as gym shoes, sports team paraphernalia, bicycles, jewelry, and cars is motivated to a large extent by envy. However, the crack cocaine trade has dominated the street economy since the 1980s and has stimulated much of the violence within poor, urban African-American communities (Baumer, Lauritsen, Rosenfeld, and Wright, 1998).

A large percentage of the violence associated with the crack trade has been attributed to the youth groups, gangs, cliques, or posses that either sell the drugs themselves or supply drugs and protection to independent peddlers.

For most African-American gang members, selling drugs offers the most viable means of providing for themselves and their families (Whitehead, Peterson, and Kaljee, 1994). These individuals understand that drugs are harmful to others and view their drug dealing as immoral, yet they justify their actions by emphasizing the imperative for economic survival. The moral disengagement process of restructuring conduct leads them to reason that drug dealing is a victimless crime. They further deem selling drugs as far less harmful than other types of criminal activities in which they could engage (Hagedorn, 1997). Restructuring the violent conduct associated with their involvement in the drug trade allows the acquisitive-oppressed to ignore the connection between dealing drugs and the dramatic upsurge in drug-related violence (Baumer et al., 1998). In turn, the addicts they create tend to morally disengage from the acts of predatory violence to which they resort to expedite their drug purchasing and consumption. The addicts' subsequent distortion of consequence and tendency to dehumanize their victims are exacerbated further by the physical and psychological effects of their drug addiction.

Although most are not inclined toward instrumental violence, the gang affiliations of many acquisitive-oppressed African-American drug dealers position them for involvement in systematic gang violence. Appeals to gang loyalty and challenges to members' manhood or womanhood are frequently used to incite violence between rival gangs. Whereas being enmeshed in a gang allows these individuals to obscure their personal responsibility for such acts of collective violence, only a handful of gang members have been found to actually relish the use of violence (Hagedorn, 1994; 1998; Jah and Shah' Keyah, 1995). Hagedorn (1998), for example, concluded that most drug-related street violence is perpetrated by "new jacks," who, like real-life crime bosses (e.g., Al Capone, John Gotti) and movie gangsters (e.g., Al Pacino in *Scarface*, Wesley Snipes in *New Jack City*), embrace the American Dream of power and material success but are highly cynical about the prospect of conventional employment allowing them to realize their status goals. New Jacks view their assimilationist peers as naive people who avail themselves to exploitation by those who, like the New Jacks themselves, have a singular focus on effectively manipulating individuals and events to their material advantage.

The New Jack version of bourgeois morality allows adherents to peddle drugs indiscriminately and employ proactive, instrumental violence to establish, maintain, and expand their drug markets. It further allows them to easily suspend self-sanctioning processes, disregarding or restructuring the consequences of their actions, by placing an extreme emphasis on self-gain rather than on harm done to others. New Jack morality also rationalizes violence by devaluing or dehumanizing the victims of the violence its proponents create. This dehumanization is made easier because the majority of the New Jacks' customers and rivals are other African Americans. Moreover, these gang members' internalized racism or low racial regard lessens any potential guilt or remorse they might feel over the violence they either themselves commit or indirectly sponsor against same-race others.

The violence of the acquisitive-oppressed feeds the cycle of violence occurring in many inner-city communities. Chronic exposure to such violence can contribute to the development of a "victim complex" among some members of poor, urban African-American communities (Bulhan, 1985: 126). This complex frequently entails generalized fear, suspicion, anger, and a heightened sensitivity to personal slights or disrespect (Anderson, 1997; 1999). For some, it manifests as posttraumatic stress disorder (PTSD), with symptoms such as sleeplessness, anxiety, and depression, each of which negatively affect intellectual and social functioning (Osofsky, 1995). Others self-medicate with drugs and alcohol as a means of numbing themselves against street violence, while still others resort to violence themselves (Fitzpatrick and Boldizar, 1993).

Indeed, violent responses to personal victimization are made more likely in black urban poor communities because of the perception that failure to respond in kind may invite further victimization (Anderson, 1997; 1999). Astor (1994) has reasoned that a history of violence exposure prompts youth to key in on the immorality of intentional (or unintentional) provocation (e.g., hitting, name calling, lying, and stealing) and construe physical retaliation as a form of reciprocal justice. Rather than relying on sanctioned authority figures to intervene on their behalf, many of these youth elect to take revenge on those who transgress against them. They practice what has been variously termed "street justice" (Ward, 1988), concrete reciprocity (Piaget, 1965), or the talion ("eye for an eye") principle (Boesak, 1995).

The need or desire of the African-American acquisitive oppressed to resort to street justice prompts these individuals, especially New Jacks, to accept and even glamorize the prospects of incarceration and violent confrontations with competitors or police. Involvement in the illegal sector of the street economy increases the likelihood that acquisitive-oppressed persons will have frequent interactions with police, the judicial system, and the penal system. Indeed, many of them reify the stereotype of the dangerous black male youth and thereby help sustain the momentum of the burgeoning prison-industrial complex in this country (Platt, 1995; Texeira, 1995). However, their symbiotic relationship with law enforcement places them and other African Americans at serious risk of heightened police brutality, wrongful imprisonment, and victimization.

The Communal-Humanist Identity. The notion of communalism is fairly ubiquitous in the literature concerned with the persistence of African cultural vestiges among African Americans (Boykin et al., 1997; Kambon, 1992; Nobles, 1991; Sudarkasa, 1997; Ward, 1995). Communalism offers an alternative framing of self-other relations to that represented by acquisitive individualism. African scholars have posited that communalism places a premium on sharing, mutual aid, caring for others, interdependence, solidarity, reciprocal obligation, and social harmony (e.g., Gyekye, 1996; Mbiti, 1970; Menkiti, 1984). This suggests an ethic of community similar to that described by Shweder et al. (1997) or an ethic of responsibility such as Gyekye (1996) discusses, both of which imply a moral obligation to be sensitive and responsive to the perceived or expressed needs of significant others.

Consistent with this view, Ward (1995) has posited that African-derived communal values prescribe a morality of care that has relevance for preventing black-on-black violence in urban communities. Some scholars contend that the racialized oppression experienced by African Americans dictates that communal sensibilities be extended beyond the traditional African boundaries of extended family and tribe to include all same-race others (e.g., Nobles, 1991; Kambon, 1992). Ward seems to agree, suggesting that a positive black racial identity is an important ingredient of a caring morality. Although this line of reasoning has some intuitive appeal, the links among communalism, a morality of care, and violence warrant further elaboration.

A morality of care can be informed by a communal-humanist identity. The humanist version of an African-American morality of care compels blacks to remain morally engaged – that is, to focus on the well-being of others as they conduct their daily affairs. Recent research supports this position. For example, a communal orientation among urban African-American youth was consistent with greater moral maturity (Humphries et al., 2000). In addition, such an orientation was positively associated with empathy (e.g., Jagers, Mock, Smith, and Dill, 1997) and forgiveness (Jagers and Mock, 1995). Empathy refers to psychological responses more closely aligned with another's situation than one's own and implies moral accountability (Hoffman, 1987). Forgiveness refers to a "giving up of resentment, hatred, and anger and taking up a stance of love and compassion" (Enright and the Human Development Group, 1991: 64). In turn, a communal orientation was associated with lower levels of violent behavior (Jagers, Mock, and Smith, in press). Other research studies seem consistent with these findings. Hart et al. (1995), for example, described an interconnected sense of self that distinguished inner-city adolescent exemplars of a caring morality from their peers. Astor (1994) reported that the nonviolent children in his sample, most of whom were African American, were more concerned than their violent counterparts with the harm done by hitting in retaliation to provocation.

Implied is a sense of ideal or cooperative reciprocity that emphasizes promotive interdependence (Piaget, 1965).

For the most part, social science research provides no explicit acknowledgment of the African origins of the humanist morality of care. Rather, in much of contemporary scholarship, this moral orientation is most closely linked to the Christian spiritual and religious traditions common among African Americans (Bocsak, 1995; Cone, 1997). Religions and spirituality introduce the notion of sacredness into relational life (Mattis and Jagers, in press; Pargament, 1997). They also provide believers with a moral system that includes notions about ultimate consequences of moral transgressions and strategies for triumphing over evil (Houf, 1945; Geertz, 1973). Among contemporary African-American youth in particular, spiritual and religious beliefs and practices have been found to engender a sense of well-being and interconnectedness with God and social others (Moore and Glei, 1995; Jagers and Smith, 1996; Mattis, 1997). Religious African-American youth have also been found to be less likely to engage in self-destructive behaviors such as substance abuse and suicide (Donahue and Benson, 1995). According to Stevenson (1997), African-American adolescent males who are more spiritual tend to exhibit greater anger control and engage in fewer acts of aggression. Jagers and Mock (1993) contend that more spiritual African-American youth report fewer delinquent acts and place greater emphasis on cooperation and empathy.

The spiritual grounding of communal humanists leads to a concern for others based on a shared spiritual essence. As such, the humanist version of a care morality calls for a transcendence of racial group membership and the challenging of the self-serving bourgeois morality embraced by acquisitive-assimilationist and acquisitive-oppressed blacks (King, 1958; Cone, 1986). However, it also stimulates a critique of European-American racial oppression. The critical use of religious tenets to interrogate the moral bankruptcy of oppressive social and political conditions offers African-American communal humanists an authoritative platform from which to challenge racist social arrangements. In this regard, these blacks have been inclined to participate in civil disobedience and nonviolent resistance to European-American exploitation and violence (Payne, 1995). Their principal assumption is that the use of such strategies will stimulate a sense of moral shame or guilt among the power elite that will open the way to forgiveness by the disenfranchised and movement toward meaningful reform of the existing social order (King, 1958; McCartney, 1992).

The Communal-Nationalist Identity. A substantial and diverse segment of the urban African-American community is attracted to a communal-nationalist identity (Bush, 1999). This identity type can derive from several overlapping sources: the ongoing desire of African Americans to frame and shape their own social reality, disenchantment with the integrationism associated with both the assimilationist and humanist social agendas, or the festering moral outrage at the continued interpersonal and systemic violence waged in and against the African-American community (Marable, 1991; Umoja, 1998). From the African-American communal-nationalist view, blacks comprise a distinct nation within the confines of the United States (Karenga, 1980; Marable, 1991; Ture and Hamilton, 1992). Self-definition and self-determination are the principal goals of the nationalist agenda that places a high priority on African Americans' pursuit of indigenous strategies and processes to effectively resist racist cultural oppression and move toward collective liberation and well-being. In this sense, communal nationalists extend the morality of care only to same-race others.

However, the communal-nationalist identity can manifest itself in two distinct but potentially intersecting forms: cultural or conservative nationalist identity and political or revolutionary nationalist identity (Bush, 1999; Cabral, 1979; Fanon, 1963; Karenga, 1980; X, 1964). The conservative nationalist identity is concerned primarily with the articulation and proliferation of an authentic national culture as the primary means for African-American liberation (Karenga, 1980). African-derived communal principles of compassion and mutual reciprocity guide the normative social functioning of conservative nationalists, along with a corresponding rejection of anti-humanist European-American cultural principles and practices (Myers, 1991; Ani, 1994). Conservative nationalists vary as to whether the cultural liberation process requires physical as well as psychological separation from European Americans. However, they draw on African-American cultural history to foster racial pride, personal responsibility, and collective creation of culturally grounded religious, economic, political, and aesthetic systems and institutions.

Some conservative nationalists contend that middle-income African Americans should commit "class suicide" – that is, eschew the privilege and isolation that confer with their socioeconomic status to lead the masses of African Americans in the cultural revitalization process (Karenga, 1990). This strategy positions middle-income African Americans as the leading arbiters of community culture and morality and suggests that conservative nationalism is not inconsistent with black capitalism. However, middle-income proponents of this view must guard against reducing African-American cultural revitalization to the commodification of black culture and the reproduction of American class-based exploitation within the desired African-American nation-state (Bush, 1999).

Despite the demonization of whites and their cultural agenda, most African-American conservative nationalists remain focused on individual and community morality and self-reliance. The apparent desire to participate in a plural capitalist society prompts conservative nationalists to avoid serious critiques and programmatic strategies for combating European-American exploitation and oppression. Rather, many adherents suggest that there will be divine retribution for European-American decadence and transgressions against African Americans. Thus, the conservative nationalist link to violence is more rhetorical and representational than otherwise. Subsequently, low-income urban members of the nationalist community often are left struggling to discern how the conservative nationalist agenda will bring them immediate relief from the violent social reality with which they are confronted.

By contrast, African-American political or revolutionary nationalists are decidedly opposed to the prevailing social order. They are concerned with achieving liberation through the expeditious transfer of material resources from the oppressor (whites) to the oppressed (nonwhites). Revolutionary nationalists view food, shelter, education, and land as essential ingredients for realizing cultural, sociopolitical, and economic self-determination for African Americans (Seale, 1970; Ture and Hamilton, 1992). They also tend to emphasize human rights as manifested by material conditions rather than by the civil rights associated with full participation in American society (McCartney, 1992). In this regard, African-American revolutionary nationalists construe their efforts as part of the anti-imperialist and anticapitalist movements throughout the world (Van Deburg, 1997). They further tend to believe that most members of the black middle class are too comfortable with their limited privilege in the existing U.S. social order to engage in critiques or activities that will bring about meaningful social change. The black oppressed classes, however, are seen as primed for revolutionary change "for they have nothing to lose and everything to gain" (Fanon, 1963: 61).

In order to engage in a sustained liberation struggle, African-American revolutionary nationalists contend that indigenous cultural resources must be used to inculcate a "revolutionary morality" (Santucho, 1982; Shanna, 1987). Consistent with a communal morality of care, this type of morality is believed to promote humility, sacrifice, generosity, patience, and love for fellow insurgents and members of the emerging African-American nation. These qualities, revolutionary nationalists contend, will guide the development and functioning of the new nation's infrastructure (e.g., education, health, politics) and thus imply the evolution of an egalitarian social order should the revolution be successful.

Revolutionary nationalists also maintain that violence may be an inevitable part of the liberation process. They reason that, since oppression is brought about and sustained by the oppressor's use of violence, revolutionary violence may be necessary to establish and defend the black nation-building project (Umoja, 1998; Bush, 1999). This restructuring has been framed alternately in terms of a socialist reshaping of the economic order and the pursuit of a divine social order associated with more zealous manifestations of religious nationalism (McCarthy, 1992; Van Deburg, 1997). The related moral disengagement processes involve construing revolutionary violence as a morally justifiable means to achieve justice and liberation. Within these processes, African Americans who are seen as contributing to African-American oppression are vilified.

The proliferation of a revolutionary morality actively redirects the horizontal, same-race violence occurring among the oppressed into vertical or revolutionary violence against agents of oppression. This transformation process can result in the emerging nationalist engaging in spontaneous mob violence or rebellions. Such reactions reflect an unfocused expression of collective anger at and frustration with an oppressive social system. However, the African-American revolutionary nationalist labors to evolve a system of "revolutionary justice" that features the disciplined and strategic use of instrumental violence (Bulhan, 1985; Cabral, 1979; Fanon, 1963). This type of violence can target same-race "auto-oppressors" (Bulhan, 1985) such as drug-dealers and agent provocateurs who compromise the black liberation effort (Williams, 1993; Umoja, 1998). Such action is a delicate matter, however, as imprudent or haste judgments can create fear and dissension among devotees and stimulate factionalization and internecine violence (Booker, 1998; Ngozi-Brown, 1997; Santucho, 1982).

The historical analysis of the revolutionary nationalists confirms for them the idea that moral appeals to one's oppressors do not result in the contrition and reconciliation that communal humanists seek. To the contrary, their reasoning suggests that such appeals tend to manifest in the levying of more intensive violence against African Americans and other oppressed groups (Memmi, 1965). The revolutionary nationalist concludes that revolutionary violence by the oppressed is the only mechanism by which oppressors can be forced into "reciprocal recognition" or full acknowledgment of the humanity and integrity of the oppressed (Fanon, 1963). The professed willingness to commit what Newton (1973) calls "revolutionary suicide" – to die fighting for liberation rather than to participate in one's own oppression – has made African-American revolutionary nationalists the targets of federal- and state-sponsored counterinsurgency efforts and repression. Such efforts have included covert programs of misinformation, infiltration, and cooption as well as imprisonment, torture, and assassination (Cabral, 1979; Churchill and Wall, 1990; Grady-Willis, 1998).

Future Directions. The framework proposed in this chapter is intended to catalyze and guide basic and applied psychological research on culture, morality, and African-American violence. Rather than being seen as rigid, static categories into which African Americans can be pigeonholed, the four racialized cultural identities offered herein should be viewed as rough anchor points for future scholarship. The first task is to document the existence and distribution of the proposed identities and to explore the putative moral implications for violence within these distinct but intersecting segments of the African American community. Priority should be given to the systematic study of communalism, an understudied cultural theme that may help promote collective well-being in the African-American community. Specifically, this research agenda should explore the ways in which communal-humanist and communal-nationalist communities have socialized African-American children and youth around issues of morality and violence. Recent work by Hughes and Chen (1997) has shown that child, parent, and contextual factors can inform the timing and content of cultural and race-related messages given to young people. The connections among socialization messages, parenting practices, and children's emerging moral sensibilities in family, peer, and community contexts also warrant close scrutiny.

Additionally, some attention should be given to spirituality and religion in future work. Through spiritual teachings and related activities, African-American religious institutions continue to help shape the moral life of African-American communities. The mainstream black Christian church has been central in militating against both community and structural violence. However, criticisms of the historical and contemporary role of Christianity in the African-American struggle for liberation also have been lodged (Azibo, 1994; Grier and Cobb, 1968; Karenga, 1980; Wilmore, 1989). A comparative analysis of traditional and Afrocentric forms of Christianity, Islam, and traditional African religions relative to their stances on morality and violence also might be a worthwhile undertaking.

Increasingly, psychologists, educators, and activists are promoting indigenous social change efforts within African-American communities. For example, Watts and Abdul-Adil (1997) have developed the Young Warriors program, which utilizes rap music videos to stimulate among young African-American men a critical consciousness of the ways in which they contribute to their own oppression and to promote among them a dialogue around the conflation of personal and community change. The *Nguzo Saba, or "Seven Principles of Blackness,"* has also emerged as a key feature in the ideological framings of the black independent school movement (Lee, 1994), and is being employed to provide a cultural basis for school- and community-based African-American social development and violence prevention programs. In a similar vein, Brookins and Robinson (1995) have offered a culturally specific rites of passage model that seeks to construct a set of roles and responsibilities for contemporary African-American adolescents and young adults by integrating traditional African social development beliefs with methods of coping in a racially oppressive environment. Efforts such as these are designed to promote and bring about culturally appropriate developmental outcomes for black youth while insulating them from the negative influences within American popular culture. Despite the growing popularity of such programs, there continues to be a need for efficacy and evaluative data documenting their implementation and impact. Of particular interest should be examination of the ways in which these programs accommodate the type of cultural and sociopolitical diversity suggested in the framework presented here and the related implications for morality and various forms of violence.[1]

[1] We would like to thank Drs. Jim Kelley and Darnell Hawkins for their comments on earlier versions of this manuscript. The editorial efforts of Kamili Anderson, Lisa Hill, and Erica Simpson are also greatly appreciated. The work reported herein was partially supported by a grant to the first author from the Office of Educational Research and Improvement, U.S. Department of Education. The findings and opinions expressed in this document do not reflect the position or policies of the National Institute on At-Risk Students, the Office of Educational Research and Improvement, or the U.S. Department of Education.

Racial Discrimination and Violence:
A Longitudinal Perspective

Joan McCord
Margaret E. Ensminger

A century ago, W. E. B. Du Bois wrote: "Crime is a phenomenon of organized social life, and is the open rebellion of an individual against his social environment" (1899/1996: 235). Explaining crime among blacks in Philadelphia between 1835 and 1895, Du Bois noted their overrepresentation in the courts as well as prisons and was acknowledging the damage to society done by racial discrimination both before and after the Civil War. Enumerations of prison populations in 1904, 1910, and 1923 showed serious overrepresentation of blacks both among resident prisoners and among those committed during the years of enumeration (Reuter, 1927). The fact that rates were higher for population counts than for intakes showed that blacks not only were convicted relatively more frequently but that, also, they were given longer sentences.

High crime rates among blacks are, of course, at least partly a function of the operation of the justice system and the way in which crimes and race are recorded. In many cases, white men have committed violence against blacks with impunity, thus not entering into any counts of violence. Although black recorded rates of violence exceeded the averages among whites, they did not rise to the levels of violence among Irish or Italian immigrants at particular times and places (Lane, 1997). Nevertheless, contemporary records indicate that violence among blacks, particularly among young black males, is an extremely serious phenomenon.

A plethora of social commentaries and theories have developed to identify conditions of the social environment that might account for crime among blacks. For example, some have suggested that there are pockets of people who approve the use of violence, referring to these groups as sharing a "subculture of Violence" (Wolfgang and Ferracuti, 1967/1982) or a "subculture of honor" (Butterfield, 1995; Nisbett and Cohen, 1996). These theories do not focus specifically on experiences of blacks but, rather, on the ease of transitions from civil exchange to aggressive actions among both blacks and whites. Although originating in the South, these subcultures are said to have been transported to inner cities along with the migration of freed blacks after the Civil War.

A variation on this theme suggests that social disorganization creates high tolerance for violence, although not necessarily approval of its use (Marable, 1996; Anderson, 1997; Sampson, 1997). William B. Harvey depicted the process by which social disorganization results in violence. Harvey described the Subculture of Exasperation as one in which "the dearth of opportunities that are available for black people to accrue reasonable incomes through socially sanctioned employment, to live in dignity and self-respect, and to realize the same benefits and pleasures as whites, inevitably results in displays of discontent and outward directed aggression" (1986: 155). Coupled with a constant bombardment of advertising that shows a form of life in which owning material goods constitute a "good life," the inability of many blacks to attain that life builds resentment. In a similar vein, Humphrey and Palmer suggest that "black interpersonal violence seems inextricably tied to the persistent difficulty black males have in obtaining a viable masculine identity" (1986: 65).

Despite the abundance of books and articles documenting high rates of violence among blacks, little empirical attention has been paid to identifying the source of violence among them. Exceptions can be found in studies showing effects of extreme poverty, unemployment, and family disruption (Blau and Blau, 1982; Fowles and Merva, 1996; Messner and Golden, 1992; Phillips, 1997; Sampson, 1985, 1987). Historical studies have indicated that rates of violence among blacks sometimes tend to increase during times of white prosperity – a tendency that has been taken by some to evidence effects of discrimination in employment (Henry and Short, 1954; Gurr, 1981; Lane, 1986).

In careful time-series analyses of crime rates between 1957 and 1988, LaFree, Drass, and O'Day found rates of crime declined – as expected – among whites during times of prosperity. To the contrary, however, they found that "for blacks, higher family income and educational attainment are generally associated with *higher* crime rates; conversely, increases in unemployment and percentage of female-headed families are associated with *declining* crime rates" (1992: 175). The authors suggested that education and prosperity might engender expectations that are conspicuously unfulfilled and that the consequent sense of injustice results in higher rates of crime.

American racism has created systematic biases that might influence rates of violence in a variety of ways. Katheryn K. Russell (1998) documented a litany of important issues in the criminal justice system that perpetuate racial stereotypes and feed into racial discrimination. Her historical summary covers slave codes and Black Codes of the nineteenth century as well as Jim Crow Laws of the twentieth. She discusses racial disproportionality, addressing the difficult task of trying to distinguish between discrimination in the system and differentiation in rates of crime. The issues link the past to the present, for as Russell noted, "Black distrust of the justice system is not new. It is historically rooted in the role police played in enforcing the slave codes, Black codes, Jim Crow segregation, the ultimate form of vigilante justice, lynching. . . . Today, police brutality hardly resembles its past forms. Many Blacks alive today, however, still remember the widespread, persistent, and inhumane abuse Blacks suffered at the hands of police" (1998: 35).

Racial biases among the police have frequently resulted in the arrest of black men who are innocent. Not only do such arrests inflate the crime figures reported to the FBI but, also, they undermine the legitimacy of law enforcement officers in their role as protectors. Therefore, police misconduct, too, contributes to the use of violence. If the police cannot be trusted, then citizens must control their own environments (McCord, 1997). Many, Anderson reports, "carry small handguns for protection" (1976: 185).

Burton Levy (1968) documented police abuses to show that deeply entrenched antiblack values, attitudes, and behavior permeate the police force. These values, attitudes, and actions contribute to distrust of and hostility toward police among the groups most in need of real protection. Darnell Hawkins (1986) suggests that the denigration of blacks by the police results in a lack of attention to those crimes that regularly can be used to foretell violence. In the absence of police control, some incidents that might have ended without violence escalate.

Hawkins (1986), like many others, considers the possibility that violence can be an attempt to gain some control in an environment over which young blacks appear to have no control. The use of violence to gain some control is a thesis developed more fully by Frantz Fanon. Fanon argued that the "colonized man" becomes so accustomed to violence that aggression seems "deposited in his bones" (1968: 52). At first, violence is used against those close to him, but later, violence becomes a threat to the colonizer. As the atmosphere fills with violence, the colonizer tries to defuse it. In taking responsibility for violence, the colonized man becomes integrated. Fanon suggests: "Violence is thus seen as comparable to a royal pardon" (1968: 86). Frederick Douglass (1845/1960), too, had deified violence. While still a slave, he finally fought his cruel and sadistic boss, Covey. Of this experience, he wrote: "It was a glorious resurrection, from the tomb of slavery, to the heaven of freedom. My long-crushed spirit rose, cowardice departed, bold defiance took its place; and I now resolved that, however long I might remain a slave in form, the day had passed forever when I could be a slave in fact (1845/1960: 105).

Nathan Irvin Huggins (1977/1990) places the experience of slavery at center stage for understanding the experience of being black in America.

Huggins believes that crime and other social ills can be attributed to failure to "bring slavery and the persistent oppression of race from the margins to the center" (1977/1990: lvi) in analyzing the American Dream. Because there was so much violence on plantations, those slaves willing to stand up to their bosses were typically seen as heroes for their toughness (Genovese, 1972). Links between violence and heroism have been perpetuated through some of the great black literatures, as well as through stories passed along by word of mouth (Takaki, 1993).

W. H. Grier and P. M. Cobbs introduce their book about what it means to be black in America by noting: "Black children from birth are exposed to heavily systematized hostility from the nation and for their own survival must reject the community's code of behavior, containing as it does the injunction that they themselves are to be the object of hatred" (1971: 1). The authors continue by remarking the series of degradations that can be expected in school. They note the anti-intellectualism foisted upon black males, and the constant pressures used by whites to keep blacks "in their place." The degradation, the lack of preparation for success, the clear signs of injustice surround young black males with reasons for violence.

Most discussions of black crime purport to explain why rates of violence are so high among blacks. It is clear, however, that only a minority of blacks commit violent crimes. Du Bois, for example, showed that a small proportion of Negroes committed the bulk of crimes. He suggested "that deep social causes underlie this prevalence of crime (and) . . . that to this criminal class and not to the great mass of Negroes the bulk of the serious crime perpetrated by this race should be charged" (1899/1996: 257).

The present study addresses the issue of why some blacks become violent and others do not. To do this, we will specifically consider perceived racial discrimination as a form of victimization contributing to violence. Recognizing that all blacks are at least potentially subjected to discrimination, we consider differences between those who have and those who have not been specifically deprived of their desired goals because – at least in their own opinions – they are black.

The present study tracks individuals from childhood to the age of thirty-two. These people were first studied in 1966, at the age of six. They were retraced twenty-six years later. To evaluate the effects of a variety of life experiences, criminal records were collected through the courts and the FBI.

Subjects, all of whom are African Americans, lived in a single urban community in the city of Chicago when they were in first grade. In 1966, Woodlawn was a black neighborhood on the south side of Chicago. From 1955 to 1966, the black proportion of the population in Woodlawn had risen from 40 percent to close to 100 percent. Overcrowded, run-down, and containing massive unemployment, in 1966, Woodlawn ranked among the four most impoverished neighborhoods (Kellam, Simon, and Ensminger, 1983).

At the height of the civil rights movement, Woodlawn community leaders agreed to cooperate with researchers to improve the lives of their children (Kellam, Branch, Agrawal, and Ensminger, 1975). Children in first grades throughout the community participated. The inclusiveness of the study permits analyses to compare blacks who became violent with those who did not.

The Setting

Not unlike other cities, Chicago has a long history of racial discrimination and white violence against blacks. Before the Civil War, free blacks were not permitted to vote and found widespread segregation in the schools, public transport, and the theaters of Chicago (Drake and Cayton, 1945/1962). Although blacks were hired as strikebreakers in the Chicago stockyards during 1904 and 1905, they were fired when the strikes ended (Spear, 1967; Trotter, 1993).

African Americans, who lived in a majority of the 431 census tracts of the city during the first decade of the twentieth century, were forced to leave their homes by white Chicagoans who did not want to have blacks in their neighborhoods. "In the spring of 1919," wrote Spear, "the bombing of Negro homes and assaults on Negroes in the streets and parks became almost everyday occurrences" (1967: 212). President Wilson, acknowledging the disappointment faced by Negro soldiers unable to find employment after defending their country, clearly held whites responsible as aggressors (Quarles, 1964: 193).

Between 1919 and 1948, restrictive covenants, described in a local newspaper as "a marvelous delicately woven chain of armor" against the infusion of blacks into neighborhoods designated for whites by whites (quoted in Drake and Cayton, 1945/1962: 79), kept blacks in segregated communities. Such restrictive covenants gained strong support from federal policies guaranteeing loans on the basis of nationally recognized standards of appraisal that used racial and ethnic characteristics of neighborhoods as criteria for assessments (Bartelt, 1993; Jackson, 1985; Quarles, 1964).

With their return from fighting in World War II, black soldiers expected to participate in the prosperity of their country as they had in its defense. Such was not the case. Again, promises for an open society were thwarted. Throughout Chicago, as black families attempted to move into newly purchased homes, white mobs destroyed their property and threatened their persons (Hirsch, 1983). Blacks experienced continued job and housing discrimination at every turn.

The civil rights movement of the 1960s brought renewed hope. The result, however, was almost a cruel joke. As government policies changed to force hiring of blacks, job opportunities for which they were qualified disappeared. Attractive loans for new construction and federal tax policies encouraged migration of industries from the cities. The federal Interstate Highway Act of 1956 assured funds for interstate highways, contributing to the exodus of industries from cities to suburbs (Sugrue, 1993). Tax breaks allowing accelerated depreciation for new constructions encouraged industries to build inexpensive single-story structures surrounded by parking lots, on inexpensive land, outside cities (Adams et al., 1991; Robinson, 1993). Shopping malls and other services followed industries to the suburbs, carrying with them many of the jobs suitable for unskilled workers.

Federal tax money from the sale of gasoline was dedicated to highway construction, rather than to public transportation. Therefore, not only had it become increasingly difficult for blacks to find work in the cities but also the lack of public transportation made it difficult for them to reach the suburbs where they might have found employment.

After studying interracial contacts in sixty large cities in 1970 and 1980, Massey and Denton concluded: "Blacks may have won political freedom, and may have made substantial progress in attaining their economic goals, but they have yet not achieved the freedom to live wherever they want" (1987: 823). Furthermore, the concentration of poverty was higher in Chicago than in the other major cities and the trend toward increasing isolation was most extreme there as well (Massey and Eggers, 1990).

The history of racial discrimination, we hypothesized, has contributed to high rates of black violence. We reasoned that those who were most exposed to discrimination would be most likely to become violent. Of course, we do not believe that only the exposure to discrimination accounts for violence. Our hypothesis was that early disruptiveness provided a risk factor for violence among blacks as it does among whites (Faretra, 1981; Farrington, 1992; Loeber, 1982; Magnusson, Klinteberg, and Stattin, 1992; McCord, 1983, 1994; Pulkkinen, 1983). We also believed that education might tend to mitigate effects of living in an environment that often required vigilance and introduced frustrations – or that, at a minimum, high school graduation represented a willingness to adapt to social conventions (see Hawkins and Lishner, 1987, and Maguin and Loeber, 1996, for reviews; and Crutchfield, 1995, for a discussion). We hypothesized that, among disruptive children, those with little education who experienced racial discrimination would be most likely to become violent criminals.

Method and Measurement

Subjects. In 1966, Woodlawn had a population of 78,182, with a median family income of $5,508 (Kellam et al., 1975). Subjects for the study were all of the 605 boys and 637 girls who attending first grade in the nine public or three Catholic schools in the area.

Between 1993 and 1994, attempts to locate these 1,242 children included going to their neighborhoods, telephone calls, record searches, and a variety of special techniques that depended on close cooperation between the Woodlawn community and the research staff. These efforts resulted in the successful tracing of 1,037 people, 83 percent of the total. Among them, forty-three had died, three were incapacitated, and thirty-nine refused to be interviewed. Those interviewed represented males and females almost equally. The 456 interviewed males constituted 75 percent of the boys in first grade and the 497 females constituted 78 percent of the girls who were in first grade at the time the study began in 1966.[1]

Those who were interviewed differed little from those who were not interviewed on the measures from first grade indicating early disruptiveness or intelligence of the participants. The group who were interviewed differed from those not interviewed, however, in terms of school attendance, juvenile records, and adult criminality as recorded officially. Those interviewed were more likely to attend school regularly in first grade ($X^2_{(1)} = 4.17$, $p = .041$) and less likely to have an official juvenile record ($X^2_{(1)} = 5.17$, $p = .023$). By contrast, the people interviewed were more likely to have been arrested for an index crime ($X^2_{(1)} = 4.98$, $p = .026$). For the following analyses, we focused on the 951 cases with complete data regarding early behavior and self-reported information at age thirty-two.

Measures. a. *Disruptiveness.*[2] During the first year of the study, teachers indicated which children in their class had problems in social adaptation related to failure to accept authority, fighting too much, lying, breaking rules, being destructive to others, or disobedience (Kellam, Brown, Rubin, and Ensminger, 1983). The scale had high test-retest reliability over a six-week period, $N = 282$ and Gamma $= .92$ (Kellam et al., 1983: 32). Furthermore, the scale has shown predictive validity measured against self-reported delinquency ten years later (Ensminger, Kellam, and Rubin, 1983). We considered subjects identified as having problems in social adjustment listed above as "disruptive" in terms of their social adaptation early in childhood. Among the 454 males with complete interview information, 172 (38 percent) had been rated as disruptive when they were six years old. Among the 497 females with complete interview information, 122 (25 percent) had been rated as disruptive when they were six years old.

b. *High School Graduation.* During the interview, respondents were asked to identify the highest grade in elementary or high school they had finished. They also were asked if they had ever received a high school diploma or a

---

[1] Seventy-nine percent of the men and 80 percent of the women who were still alive had been interviewed.

[2] In other publications, this scale has been referred to as aggression.

GED certificate. Those who received a high school diploma or GED certificate or completed at least one year of post–high school education were considered to have been high school graduates. Among the 454 males with complete interview information, 362 (80 percent) were high school graduates. Among the 497 females with complete interview information, 425 (86 percent) were high school graduates.

c. *Victim of Racial Prejudices.* Respondents were asked in the interview whether, because of being black, they have ever been denied a job, had a problem getting housing, had a problem walking in a neighborhood, gotten into trouble with teachers, had a problem going somewhere for entertainment, or been hassled by the police. Those who responded affirmatively to any of these were considered to have been victims of racial discrimination. Among the 454 males with complete interview information, 363 (80 percent) reported having been victims of racial discrimination. Among the 497 females with complete interview information, 290 (58 percent) reported having been victims of racial discrimination.

d. *Violence.* In 1993, names of each of the subjects was checked through the Chicago courts and the Federal Bureau of Investigation for records of their having been arrested for robbery, assault, battery, threat, weapons charges, kidnapping, manslaughter, domestic violence, rape, murder, and attempted murder. Those who had official records for having committed any of these offenses were considered violent criminals.

Granting that many violent people are never arrested – and that some people are arrested when they are not guilty – many studies have shown that criminal records identify roughly the same people as those who confess to frequent or very serious crimes (Elliott and Ageton, 1980; Farrington, 1989; Gold, 1966; Hindelang, Hirschi, and Weis, 1979). As have others, we found a higher prevalence of criminal violence among men than among women: among the 454 males and 497 females with completed interviews, 41 percent of the men and 11 percent of the women had been arrested for at least one of the listed violent crimes.

Our primary hypothesis, that the experience of unjust prejudice contributes to violence, would be tested by using information from three sources. The measure of disruptiveness depended on teachers' perceptions of the subjects when they were young children. The measures of educational achievement and unjust prejudice depended on the subjects' descriptions of their experiences. The measure of violence depended on police records.

Results

Measures of disruptiveness and of violence yielded information about those who had not been interviewed as well as those who had. As expected, males

Table 16.1. *Percent Arrested for a Violent Crime*

	Not disruptive	Disruptive
Female	($N = 480$) 7.1	($N = 157$) 15.9
Male	($N = 371$) 34.8	($N = 234$) 46.6

Table 16.2. *Percent Who Were Disruptive*

	Not exposed to discrimination	Exposed to discrimination
Female	($N = 207$) 23	($N = 290$) 26
Male	($N = 91$) 40	($N = 363$) 37

were more likely than females to have been rated as disruptive (39 percent versus 25 percent). Also as expected, a higher proportion of the males had been arrested for violent crimes (39 percent versus 9 percent).

Among both males and females, having been rated as disruptive at the age of six presaged subsequent arrest for violent crimes. Almost half (46.6 percent) of the disruptive males – compared with about a third (34.8 percent) of their nondisruptive counterparts – were arrested for violent crimes, $X^2_{(1)} = 8.387$, $p = .004$. Less than a fifth (15.9 percent) of the disruptive females – compared with less than a tenth (7.1 percent) of their nondisruptive classmates – were arrested for violent crimes, $X^2_{(1)} = 11.001$, $p = .001$ (see Table 16.1).

If being a victim of racial discrimination were a response to a disruptive orientation, one would expect disruptive children to report more victimization. Neither among males nor among females, however, were there indications that disruptive behavior presaged reporting being victims of racial prejudice (see Table 16.2).

We used logistic regression (CATMOD, SAS, 1985) to evaluate the hypothesis that exposure to racial discrimination contributes to violence. The model considered sex, whether the people had been disruptive when they were young children, whether they graduated from high school or received an equivalent degree, and whether they had been exposed to racial discrimination (see Table 16.3).

The Maximum-likelihood analysis of variance indicates that sex, disruptiveness in childhood, education, and exposure to racial discrimination contributed meaningfully to whether the children from Woodlawn became violent.

Table 16.3. *Maximum-likelihood Analysis of Variance*

Source	DF	Chi-Square	Prob
Intercept	1	81.80	0.0000
Sex	1	78.28	0.0000
Disruptiveness	1	10.34	0.0013
High school graduation	1	19.98	0.0000
Exposure to discrimination	1	10.39	0.0013
Likelihood Ratio	11	11.26	0.4220

Table 16.4. *Percent Arrested for a Violent Crime*

	Not exposed to discrimination	Exposed to discrimination
Female		
Not Disruptive		
High School Graduate	($N = 142$) 4	($N = 189$) 10
Not High School Graduate	($N = 18$) 17	($N = 26$) 12
Disruptive		
High School Graduate	($N = 36$) 14	($N = 58$) 16
Not High School Graduate	($N = 11$) 18	($N = 17$) 35
Male		
Not Disruptive		
High School Graduate	($N = 46$) 26	($N = 191$) 32
Not High School Graduate	($N = 9$) 56	($N = 36$) 67
Disruptive		
High School Graduate	($N = 22$) 27	($N = 103$) 50
Not High School Graduate	($N = 14$) 29	($N = 33$) 67

Table 16.4 shows the percent of those in each category of disruptiveness, education, and exposure to discrimination – separately for females and males – who were arrested for violent crimes.

In every category, males were more likely than females to become violent. In all eight comparisons, those with less education were more likely to become violent. The odds ratios for exposure to discrimination within sex, disruptiveness, and education categories range from 0.7 to 2.5 with a median of 1.55. The perception of having been exposed to racial discrimination failed to increase the probability of arrest for a violent crime only among females who had not been disruptive in first grade and who dropped out of school without receiving a high school diploma. In each of the other comparisons, exposure to racial discrimination increased the probability for violence.

Table 16.5. *Maximum-likelihood Analysis of Variance*

Source	DF	Chi-Square	Prob
Intercept	1	71.11	0.0000
Sex	1	77.52	0.0000
Disruptiveness	1	10.41	0.0013
High school graduation	1	20.48	0.0000
Crime victimization	1	0.88	0.3482
Exposure to discrimination	1	8.60	0.0034
Likelihood Ratio	26	23.99	0.5765

Summary and Discussion

This analysis has employed three types of measures, from three sources, to explore the hypothesis that, in addition to the more traditionally acknowledged sources of violence, exposure to racial discrimination is a risk factor.

Like others, we found that early signs of disruptiveness predicted violence. Like others, too, we found that lacking a high school education predicted violence. But, in addition, we found that exposure to racial discrimination increased the probability of violent crimes, particularly among black males.

It seemed plausible, however, that respondents reporting victimization in terms of racial discrimination were actually affected by a more general problem of victimization, one not specifically related to the prejudices of a powerful white society. To evaluate this possibility, we used a measure of crime victimization.

Respondents had been asked whether they had ever been purposely injured, had something stolen by threat or force, been swindled or conned, had something stolen from home or car, had a car stolen, or been forced to have sex. Affirmative answers to any of these questions resulted in classification as a crime victim.

The analysis indicates that being a victim of crimes could not account for the relation between being a victim of racial discrimination and violence (see Table 16.5).

We measured exposure to racial discrimination by noting whether respondents gave an affirmative answer to at least one of the questions about whether, because of being black, they have ever been denied a job, had a problem getting housing, had a problem walking in a neighborhood, gotten into trouble with teachers, had a problem going somewhere for entertainment, or been hassled by the police. Responses for both men and women ranged from 0 to 6. The mean for men, however, was 2.18 ($sd = 1.63$) affirmative answers as compared with a mean of 1.24 ($sd = 1.41$) for the women, $t_{(901.7)} = 9.473$, $p = .0001$.

It is unclear, of course, whether the recall of discrimination reflects differences in experience or differences in reporting. It is clear, however, that the perception of injustice is sometimes backed by solid evidence such as that produced by the careful examination of police deployment of dogs in Los Angeles (Campbell, Berk, and Fyfe, 1998).

This study provides reason to suppose that a risk factor to be addressed in serious attempts to reduce violence ought to include unjust discrimination. Indeed, the dismal history of justice for blacks in the criminal justice system led Russell to conclude: "American racism and criminal justice, which involved the systematic denial of basic human rights to Blacks for more than three hundred years, simply cannot be dismissed as irrelevant" (1998: 150).

The American dilemma of yesterday remains a serious problem for American society today. At least a part of that problem, as Gunnar Myrdal noted more than half a century ago, is "the opportunistic desire of the whites for ignorance. It is so much more comfortable to know as little as possible about Negroes, except that there are a lot of them in Harlem, the Black Belt, or whatever name is given to the segregated slum quarters where they live . . ." (1944: 48).

Echoing this theme, Darnell Hawkins suggested: "It may well be that reductions in levels of deprivation/inequality across ethnic/racial groups will not completely eliminate group differences in rates of involvement in crime. But public policies and programs aimed at such reductions are a social experiment worth pursuing" 1993: 114–15).

If we are to reduce violence, we would be wise to address the underlying problems that come from social policies. We ought to recognize that policies benefiting those who have political power may generate undesired responses by those who lack such power. As criminologists studying violence, we should expand our vision beyond individuals, families, and neighborhoods to take into account the laws, the habits, and the attitudes that form the fabric of out society.

Fair social policies are unlikely, by themselves, to eliminate violence. But absence of fair policies may make peace in a democracy impossible.

Honor, Class, and White Southern Violence: A Historical Perspective

Frankie Y. Bailey

Introduction

It is important for researchers of violence to remember that there are substantial intraracial differences in involvement in violence. In this chapter, I will explore the extent and determinants of those differences for Americans of European descent. Many of the past and contemporary explanations aimed at explaining racial and ethnic differences have tended to note the importance of culture and values (e.g., early work of Sellin on culture conflict). I focus here on white males in the South during the nineteenth century, examining the aspects of Southern culture that have been identified by various scholars as playing a role in the etiology of violence. My focus is specifically the nexus of honor, class, and violence. Interacting in a number of ways, these factors: (a) determined the circumstances in which a challenge to honor was perceived and how it was responded to; (b) determined how white males interacted not only with male peers, but with white women and African Americans; and (c) determined how white Southern males defined themselves as men.

As I will discuss, the historic existence of a "culture of honor" in the antebellum (pre–Civil War) South and in the postbellum (post–Civil War) South is generally accepted by historians. The question for modern social scientists is whether or not this culture of honor continues to play some role in creating a "subculture of violence" in the present-day South. Is the South more violent today than other regions of the country? Is honor somehow implicated in acts of violence between males in the South? Or is Southern violence today better explained by factors such as poverty or high rates of gun ownership?

I should note here that historically honor has never been strictly a white male prerogative. Honor, in its various guises, affected the self-definition and behavior of women (both white and black) and of black males.[1] This is relevant to this analysis of the South as an honor culture because, as I will discuss at the end of the chapter, one current debate among social scientists concerns the role of honor in the violence between inner-city black males.

Southern Violence

Hawley and Messner (1989) examine the "Southern violence construct" and what Hawley has described elsewhere (Hawley, 1987) as the "black legend" of the South. They argue that the South has been stigmatized not only in popular culture but also in elite social science as a region characterized by guns and violence. According to Hawley and Messner, this stigmatization came about because Southerners were the losers in the "stigma contest" that developed between the North and the South during the antebellum era and continues today. The argument these two scholars make concerning the stereotyping of Southerners is persuasive. However, stereotypes notwithstanding, there is both historical and contemporary evidence of a high rate of violence in the South.[2]

In his 1880 comparison of the Southern states to those in other regions, Redfield concluded that it was the "personal difficulties" with "deadly weapons, street fights, and affrays" that accounted for the higher Southern rate of violence. Over fifty years later, in a 1934 essay, the sociologist H. C. Brearley wrote:

> The South has been cynically and not inaccurately described as "that part of the United States lying below the Smith and Wesson line," a reference to the prevailing custom of carrying revolvers – and using them. . . . The southerner is, as a rule, "quick on the trigger." In contentions he is prone to resort to "fighting it out." (Brearley, 1934: 678)

Brearley found that the rate of homicide in the South between 1900 and 1924 had been "a little more than two and a half times greater than for the remainder of the United States" (1934: 681). In addition, he found that twelve Southern states accounted for "nearly 90 percent of the 1,886 lynchings that took place in the United States from 1900 through 1930" (1934: 679).

---

[1] For a discussion of honor and violence among African-American males in a Southern city in the years during and after the Civil War, see Tripp (1997) on race and class relations in Lynchburg, Virginia.

[2] Hawley and Messner (1989: 505) note the "rather confusing picture" to be derived from the quantitative research on the Southern violence construct. They see the need for greater precision in formulating the regional culture of violence thesis and more accurate measurement of variables. With regard to popular images of the violent South, after three school shootings in the South, CNN posted an article on its webpage with this headline: "School shootings cast shadow on Southern gun culture" (CNN Interactive, March 26, 1998).

More recently, the historians Courtwright (1996), describing the violence by young, single males in frontier conditions, and Lane (1997), in his history of murder in America, have each offered support for the depiction of the South as a region with a violent past. Bruce (1979: 3) notes that "fairly early in American history" the South had acquired a reputation for violence among those people acquainted with the region. He finds that statistics from the antebellum period support this reputation.

Currently, there is discussion among social scientists about whether the South as a region still has a higher rate of lethal violence than other regions of the United States. O'Carroll and Mercy (1989) and Kowalski and Petee (1991), in recent analyses of homicide rates in the South and West, have suggested that the South is no longer the most violent region in the country. Respectively, they suggest that homicide rates in the West may have exceeded or have converged with those of the South. However, Nelsen et al. (1994: 149), reanalyzing these data, suggest that the homicide rate for "non-Hispanic whites remains highest in the South."[3] They suggest the topic of violence in the South should remain on the agenda of researchers.

According to the FBI Uniform Crime Report, in 1998, 44 percent of the murders recorded in the United States occurred in the Southern states. In the other regions of the country, the Western and Midwestern states accounted for 22 percent and 21 percent, respectively, of the murders; the Northeastern states for 13 percent. Although the murder rate fell in all regions of the country from 1997 to 1998, in the South (and the Midwest) the decrease was 6 percent, compared to 10 percent and 9 percent, respectively, in the Northeast and the West.[4]

In discussions of Southern violence, particularly from a historical perspective, the concept of "honor" is often raised. Greenberg (1996) and Wyatt-Brown (1982) have posited the concept of honor as providing the historical framework for understanding relationships between white males and their perceived subordinates (women and blacks). More recently, Nisbett and

---

[3] Nelsen et al. (1994) recommend the disaggregation of homicides by race/ethnicity and type of residence. They find that the high homicide rates in the West reflect the high rates in the central cities (1994: 158) and overall homicide rates for the West are strongly affected by one state, California (1994: 156). The reader should note that in the West, large numbers of Mexican Americans and other Latinos are classified as whites, and that, especially in urban areas, Latinos have rates of homicide less than that of African Americans but higher than that of non-Hispanic whites. This is relevant in light of the racial/ethnic makeup of the South, which has historically been predominantly non-Hispanic white and African American. Nisbett and Cohen (1996: 17) argue that in analyzing "the relationship between southerness and homicide" it is important to be aware that the relationship will be distorted unless differential predictions are made for whites and blacks and for small and large cities. They find that the "[r]elationships between region and homicide rate for whites are stronger when only cities that are overwhelmingly white are examined."

[4] See "Murder and Nonnegligent Manslaughter," Crime in the United States – 1998. *FBI Uniform Crime Reports*. http://www.fbi.gov/ucr/98cius.htm. Section 1, page 2.

Cohen (1996) have again evoked the concept of honor – this time to explain the high rate of homicide among contemporary white Southern males. This focus on the South as an "honor culture" reflects the perception of scholars that the South shares in common with other historical and contemporary European and Asian societies the status of a culture in which much emphasis is placed on the defense of manhood and reputation against insult.

In the chapter that follows, I will examine violence and honor in the nineteenth-century South. How and when did white Southern males employ violence? How was honor related to their understanding of violence? Was honor relevant only to elite white males or did it also have relevance for lower-class white males? How was honor displayed? What were the societal expectations of a man of honor? How did these ideas shape the interactions that occurred between white males themselves and with the "others" (women, children, and nonwhite males) in their midst?

After discussing the concept of honor in the nineteenth-century South, I will briefly consider the argument that a contemporary "culture of honor" exists not only in the South but has migrated with native Southerners to other regions of the country.

Passion, Violence, and Self-Control

In his work on violence and culture in the antebellum South, Bruce (1979) argues that, during this period, white Southerners were deeply concerned about violence. Retaining a view of human nature that was both pessimistic and wary, many white Southerners believed that uncontrolled interactions in which emotions were freely expressed would inevitably lead to violence.[5] The elite sought rituals that would allow the structuring and control of social intercourse. The lower class – the "plain folk" – eschewed such rituals and prided themselves on their forthrightness.

However, for white Southern males from all walks of life, the matter of "honor" increased the likelihood that they would at one time or another find themselves in conflict with their fellows. The resolution of these conflicts sometimes took the form of what Donald Black has described as violent "self-help" (1993).[6] This self-help included duels, brawls, and feuds. It was

---

[5] Bruce (1979) argues that antebellum Southern culture reflected the concern with "passion" and human nature that was a major theme in Western thought during the eighteenth and early nineteenth centuries. This conception of passion focused on "irrational, selfish motivations" (1979: 8) in human nature. As other ideologies became dominant in the North, the South retained its "classical concerns about passion" (1979: 10) in both political life and social relations.

[6] In his theory of self-help, Black (1993: 6) addresses the "conditions under which people aggressively pursue their own grievances, such as unilaterally admonishing or injuring their antagonists or by entering bilaterally into a verbal or physical fight" rather than withdrawing "when conflict erupts."

directly related to how white Southern males perceived themselves in relation to other men. It often involved defense of reputation against insult or
the avenging of a perceived wrong. In this milieu, violence often served the
"social control" function that Black (1993) has described, in that it offered
one mechanism for dealing with the perceived defiance of or deviation from
social mores.

Honor and Its Meaning

The anthropologists Peristiany and Pitt-Rivers (1992: 5) write that "[i]t
is...an error to regard honor as a single constant concept rather than a
conceptual field within which people find the means to express their self-
esteem or their esteem for others." In any society, the exact meaning of
honor and how it should be interpreted is a matter of "[w]arring interpretations [that are] contended through their champions" (Peristiany and
Pitt-Rivers, 1992: 4). Historically, in the United States, the two regions North
and South diverged philosophically, developing mutually antagonistic ideas
about the individual and his relationship to others. By the mid-nineteenth
century, a "culture of dignity" had developed in the North, which rested
on "the conviction that each individual at birth possessed an intrinsic value
at least theoretically equal to that of the other person" (Ayers, 1984: 19).
Although this ideal was "qualified, violated, and undermined," it was also
antagonistic to the "culture of honor" that flourished in the South (Ayers,
1984: 19). Wyatt-Brown (1982: 20) states: "Honor in the antebellum North
became akin to respectability, a word that included freedom from licit vices
that once were signals of masculinity..."

As the two regions moved toward the eve of the Civil War, the North
showed both disdain and disrespect for the South's conception of "honor."
But in the South "honor" remained essential to the white male's sense of
manhood and self-esteem.

What did honor mean to the white Southern male? Williams (1980: 77)
states:

> To the Southern gentleman, honor had many facets. A gentleman paid his
> debts or made prompt arrangement about them. His word was always
> his bond, and no contracts were necessary in relationships with him. He
> was truthful, patriotic, courageous. Honor meant that a Southern gentleman
> was courtly and deferential in his association with women...

This ideal, too, was subject to qualification and violation. It was the perceived violation of the obligations of honor that brought Southern gentlemen to the "field of honor" to fight duels. But the concept of honor was
not restricted to Southern gentlemen. As some historians (e.g., Franklin

[1956], Bruce [1979], and Courtwright [1996]) have argued, honor was more democratic than elitist in its impact on white males.

Honor and Class in the South

Writing about Southern militancy in the antebellum era, Franklin (1956) asserts that no class of white Southern male had a "monopoly" on identification with the concept of honor:

> While the planters refined the notion of honor and set the pattern for adhering to certain rules of conduct in personal warfare, this concept and that of personal sovereignty descended to other groups as they assimilated the interests and points of view of the dominant elements of the community. The sense of personal insecurity in the absence of law and order was an important factor in the lives of all Southern whites, and violence to be found at every level. If there were distinctions, they were in the relative crudeness in the violence of the lower classes in contrast to the refinement in the upper. (Franklin: 36–7)

In the refined encounters of Southern gentlemen over matters of honor, the emphasis was on control rather than passion (i.e., emotional displays). Violence was ritualized and scripted in order to allow the gentleman to display his coolness in the face of threat to life and limb (Bruce, 1979). Gentlemen did not engage in bare-knuckle brawls with each other. Such behavior signified a lack of good breeding. However, when white lower-class males engaged in the brawls that the gentry looked down on, they were engaged in their own contests of status and reputation.

The question remains whether the notion of honor had, as Franklin suggested, somehow "trickled down" to lower-class males from those above them in the social hierarchy. Although agreeing with Franklin about the crudeness of the violence between lower-class males, several historians have argued that the notions of honor possessed by lower-class white males were the product of their "poor white" or "cracker" culture.

In American popular culture, the words "cracker" and "poor white" have come to be viewed as derogatory terms for the white lower class in the South. But Bolton (1994: 4) finds that white Southerners of the antebellum period did in fact make distinctions "between whites who were poor and 'poor whites' or, even more descriptively, 'poor white trash.'" These distinctions were made on "the basis of geography and culture" (Bolton, 1994: 4). They were also made based on an assessment of group character. As Boney (1984: 22) states: "Poor whites simply lacked economic resources . . . poor white trash lacked more than just money [and] were looked down upon by blacks and whites alike . . ."

However, McWhiney (1988), viewing white Southerners of all classes as a people with a shared heritage, describes a rich culture which he identifies without derision as "cracker culture." He asserts that this culture derived from the traditions of the Celtic immigrants who settled the frontier South and was the dominant culture of the Old South:

> To be sure, some residents of the Old South were not part of Cracker culture – specifically, a few planters, some townfolk and professional people, even some slaves – but the overwhelming majority of Southerners were, whether they acknowledged it or not. Some crackers were rich, others poor, and still others were neither; but they all more or less acted alike and shared the same values. And that is the point: Cracker culture does not signify an economic condition; rather it defines a culture. (McWhiney, 1988: xiv)

McWhiney (1988: 154) finds that in describing the violence of white Southerners, their antebellum contemporaries often "used the same terms employed in descriptions of other Celts and sometimes even compared Southerners to Celts." These Celts possessed codes of honor, and, in fact, the published *Irish Code of Honor* was the model for the South Carolina dueling code (McWhiney, 1988: 153). The less-refined Welsh sport of "purring" – grasping of shoulders and kicking – might have provided another model for Southern violence. McWhiney concludes:

> The types of combativeness and selective lawlessness found in the Old South were precisely those found in the premodern Celtic areas of the British Isles, and Antebellum Southerners were just as martial and prideful, just as combative and touchy about their honor as were their Celtic ancestors. (McWhiney, 1988: 167, 169)

In contrast, Boney (1984: 41) argues that calling white Southerners Celtic is "little more useful than describing Germans in the 1930s as principally 'Nordic' or 'Aryan.'" He argues that by the nineteenth century, whites "whether 'aristocrats' or 'rednecks,' lived in a bourgeois world far removed from any kind of an Old World seigneurialism or feudalism" (Boney, 1984: 3). Boney finds that the "get ahead" business spirit common in the North had already permeated and began to have an impact on Southern culture. However, other historians – although not necessarily sharing McWhiney's perspective – have described antebellum Southern society as distinctively more feudalistic than that of the North. For example, Williams (1980: 74) asserts that: "Faced with a social structure that included not only these rough whites [i.e., lower-class whites] but also free blacks and black slaves, the ruling class established something of a feudal regime, an Old World aristocracy in a New World wilderness." Ayers (1984: 21) describes the Southern gentry of the colonial period as adopting "the values of a proud and domineering English ruling class, a class whose power and authority they planned to replicate in the New World."

Regarding violence by both gentry and lower class, several other scholars join McWhiney in tracing its roots to the ancestral traditions of Southern colonists. Nisbett and Cohen (1996), who link the "herding culture" of Scotch-Irish immigrants to the Southern "culture of honor," share McWhiney's perspective on the antecedents of white Southerner combativeness. Fischer (1989) finds links between dueling in England and Virginia. He describes "the persistence of the family feud" in the southern highlands as flowing from "moral properties which belonged mainly to individuals in other English-speaking cultures. Chief among these were attributes of honor and shame" (Fischer, 1989: 668). In the same vein, Hatcher (1934: 392) attributes the blood feuds of the Appalachian South to "tradition [of Scotland] and isolation."

But, as noted above, these displays of violence in defense of honor by Southern gentlemen and by Southern lower-class males generally took different forms. Why did the Southern gentleman duel while Southern laborers brawled?

Gentility and the Southern Gentleman

Describing the "Celluloid South," Campbell (1981: 16) writes that in Hollywood films, the "code duello . . . figured prominently. The defense of one's honor became such a stock item that even the musical *Dixiana* (1930) had the required duel." Pistols at dawn were displayed in numerous other popular films about the South, including *Mississippi* (1935), a comedy featuring Bing Crosby and W. C. Fields. But whether the duel was played for laughs or presented as drama, it was Hollywood's tribute to one of the romantic myths of the antebellum South.

The reality was less romantic than the myth. The Southern gentleman who fought a duel engaged in a potentially lethal act. But although the duel might end in death, it was perceived by the gentry as clearly different from the violence of the lower-class brawler who responded to an insult with an eruption of fury. The ritual of the duel was a privilege reserved for gentlemen who met on the field of honor. A gentleman would duel only with a man who was his equal in social status.

But how exactly was this status defined? Was a man's status determined by birth, by wealth, or by both? Bowman (1990) notes the ambiguity inherent in the nineteenth-century conception of the gentleman in that "both honor and gentility (in the sense of that which is characteristic of a gentleman) could serve to denote either one's inner dignity and personal rectitude or one's external status and public repute" (Bowman, 1990: 22). Wyatt-Brown (1982) describes honor as applying to "all white classes" in the Old South, but he adds: "Gentility, on the other hand, was a more specialized, refined form of honor, in which moral uprightness was coupled with high social status" (Wyatt-Brown, 1982: 88). The gentleman was the master of those "quite subtle marks of status" having to do with dress, speech, and behavior that must be done according to "rules not easy to follow with aplomb" (Wyatt-Brown, 1982: 88).

By the eighteenth century, colonial Southerners were famed for their "easy sociability and generous hospitality" (Kierner, 1996: 449). Rituals of hospitality – both public and private – served both to establish their claim to gentility and to legitimate their claim to social dominance in relationship to those of the lower orders (Kierner, 1996: 449). By the nineteenth century, the duel – as did hospitality, gaming, and the exchange of gifts – provided the upper-class Southern male with the opportunity to affirm his status as a gentleman (Wyatt-Brown, 1982: 350; Greenberg, 1996). Each activity had to be performed with aplomb or the gentleman risked shame and dishonor. Greenberg (1996: xiii) asserts that white men of honor distinguished themselves from slaves (i.e., black males) in three ways: "[T]hey would never allow anyone to call them liars; they gave gifts; and they did not fear death." In meeting another gentleman in a duel, a man of honor might distinguish himself in all three ways. Often the cause of the duel was that one man perceived he had been called a liar by the other.[7] In challenging his accuser to a duel, the gentleman demonstrated that he would answer such an insult. He also demonstrated that he did not fear death. And he gave his opponent the "gift" of the opportunity to prove his own courage (Greenberg, 1996). Slaves could not duel because they by definition lacked honor. Lower-class white males were not worthy opponents because they were not gentlemen. Therefore, dueling was reserved as a form of violence to be practiced by members of the gentry. The duel became a form of "conflict management" employed by the elite (see Black, 1993: 74–92).

As Franklin (1956: 45) notes, gentlemen observed the "etiquette" of dueling with great care. In fact, the elaborate etiquette of the duel meant that some challenges never materialized in a meeting on the field of honor. As Greenberg (1996) and others have noted, there was ample opportunity for the gentlemen involved to gracefully extricate themselves from the affair as designated "seconds" (a close friend or associate of each man) met on their behalf and messages were exchanged. However, a gentleman could not withdraw in a manner that might lead his peers to suspect him of cowardice. A

---

[7] Greenberg (1996) argues for the central importance of "giving the lie" as a reason for Southern duels. Although the word "liar" was not always used in the verbal exchange that led to the duel, the idea of "giving the lie" was embodied in challenges to reputation or behavior. To "give the lie" was the equivalent of stripping away an opponent's public "mask." That is, "[i]t was to identify an image as falsely projected and to show contempt for it" (Greenberg, 1996: 8–9).

gentleman who wished to avoid a proposed duel had to courteously inform his opponent that there had been a misunderstanding – that his words or his actions had been misconstrued. He had to do this in such a way that both gentlemen could withdraw with honor – and hence reputation and status – intact. The seconds were crucial in this process that often allowed gentlemen to obtain "satisfaction" – that is, conflict resolution – without actually meeting in a duel (Bruce, 1979). A settlement negotiated by the seconds was a highly desirable outcome. If no settlement was reached, it was still possible to conduct a "bloodless duel" in which, after "an ineffectual exchange of shots," the seconds agreed that honor had been satisfied (Bruce, 1979: 36). These outcomes were practically speaking more desirable than an encounter that left one or both combatants injured or dead.

But as Wyatt-Brown (1982: 357) points out:

> Most duels were fought by young men. . . . Quite often their arrogance masked an uncertainty about their place in society and, indeed, about their manhood as well. The inexperienced youth was very likely to take his own measure from public opinion of himself, an inclination that forced a good number to fight – and die – when peers demanded it.

Aside from these young men who fought from a sense of false bravado, there were other men who fought because they were emotionally unstable. Some duelists were recognized by their contemporaries as being driven by "inner furies," by anxieties that brought them often to the field of honor but were not resolved there (Wyatt-Brown, 1982: 358). Still others found that the duel did more to harm their status and reputation than to enhance it. One such famous – or infamous – case was that of Aaron Burr, whose political career and personal standing was destroyed when he killed Alexander Hamilton in an 1804 duel.

But "as late as the early 1880s" (Bowman, 1990: 21), Southern gentlemen were still meeting (albeit more infrequently) to fight duels. They continued to meet even though opposition to dueling had begun in the antebellum period with both organized antidueling activity and state laws prohibiting dueling. As Ayers (1984: 28) observes, the Southern evangelicalism that flowered in the nineteenth century "defined itself in opposition to the culture of honor."

Even among "unchurched" Southerners, opposition to dueling was also burgeoning. Franklin (1956: 59–60) finds antidueling associations existed in Southern cities such as Savannah and Charleston. Antidueling laws had been enacted in North Carolina (1802), South Carolina (1812), Louisiana (1818), and "in all the other states below the Potomac" (Franklin, 1956: 58). Some states required public officials to take an oath promising not to participate in a duel (Franklin, 1956: 58). But as Greenberg states, the laws that reflected the clearest understanding of the nature of such encounters were those that "struck at the body of the duelist" (Greenberg, 1996: 15). Greenberg cites one such law that mandated that the slain duelist should be "buried without a coffin, with a stake drove through the body." His killer was to be first executed and then buried in the same fashion (Greenberg, 1996: 14–15). In life, these duelists would have considered the "tweaking" (pulling) of the nose a grave insult (Greenberg, 1996). How much more fearsome the prospect of such postmortem desecration of their bodies?

But the existence of such laws was not a completely effective deterrent. Laws did not bring an immediate cessation of dueling. As Franklin (1956: 61) points out, even those Southerners who opposed dueling in principle, "at times favored it in practice. To the Southern gentlemen, like slavery, it [dueling] was a necessary evil." These gentlemen did not see the courts as a viable option for the resolution of conflicts between them. This might be explained in part by the evolution of substantive and procedural law in cases of slander or libel that made the courts both less accessible and less attractive as an option for redress of personal (i.e., private, nonpolitical) grievances than they had been in the pre-revolutionary era (see Rosenberg, 1986; Hoffer, 1989; King, 1991; Eldridge, 1995; Spindel, 1995). However, this reliance on self rather than the courts also reflected the belief of Southern gentlemen that an insult or a wrong done to one required direct and immediate action by the victim. This was, of course, related to the idea that the possession of honor and manhood were proven by one's willingness to die in defense of them.

Moreover, like slavery, dueling exemplified the caste-class structure of Southern culture. The fighting of duels set the gentry apart from those of lower status. Lower-class white males were higher in status than African Americans, slave or free. But poor whites – like slaves – were perceived as the inferiors of the Southern gentry. Like the slaves, these white males needed to be controlled and kept in their place because of the potential threat they presented to the status quo.[8] Therefore, a gentleman insulted by his social inferior might well cane or horsewhip the offender, but he would not elevate him to his equal by meeting him on the dueling field.[9]

Yet, these lower-class white males – as white males – were also socialized into a culture of honor. They, too, felt called on to defend themselves against

---

[8] See for example, Morgan (1975) for his discussion of class conflict in colonial Virginia as the gentry responded to the perceived social and economic threats posed by the young white males who entered the colony as indentured servants but who obtained their freedom when their labor contracts were completed.

[9] Such was the case in May 1856 when Southern Congressman Preston Brooks, offended by comments made by Massachusetts Senator Charles Sumner, beat Sumner with a gold-headed walking stick on the floor of the Senate. Sumner was three years recovering from his wounds, and the incident deepened the divide between North and South. As Butterfield (1995: 17) points out, Brooks would have granted Sumner "respectability" if he had challenged him to a duel.

insult and to demand violent redress of grievances. In addition, for these males, unritualized, blatant violence also might serve as a mechanism for enhancing their status and prestige.

Violence and the Lower-Class White Male

Cooney (1997: 381) points to "the decline of elite homicide" among males in modern societies. In the twentieth century, homicide became "concentrated among low-status groups, such as the poor, the unemployed, the young, and cultural minorities." Although rates of homicide in the modern South are higher than those in other regions, this trend appears to hold true in the South as well. As Cooney argues, the decline of elite participation in homicide is in keeping with Donald Black's thesis concerning the use of violent self-help. In the post–Civil War era, the white Southern elite suffered a significant decline in the status that had put them "above the law." At the same time, the criminal justice system became a "stronger presence" and gained status. Reliance on the criminal justice system to resolve conflict became more acceptable to these elite (Cooney, 1997: 394–5).[10] However, for lower-class males, the law remained relatively unavailable in the sense that the criminal justice system could not be relied on either to render favorable treatment or to mediate disputes in a fashion that they deemed acceptable (Cooney, 1997: 395).

However, in the nineteenth-century South, both elite males and males of the lower class engaged in violence, including lethal violence. In the case of lower-class males, as Wyatt-Brown (1982: 353) asserts: "Just as lesser folk spoke ungrammatically, so too they fought ungrammatically, but their actions were expressions of the same desire for prestige." Gorn (1985) finds that these fights among lower-class white males were not just ungrammatical. In some areas of the Southern frontier, such fights involved eye-gouging and other attempts to permanently mutilate the body of an opponent. After reconstructing the nature of these brawls from oral tradition and travelers' accounts, Gorn reports that in the Southern backcountry, such encounters were an accepted way to respond to "slights, insults, and thoughtless gestures" (Gorn, 1985: 19). Around the beginning of the nineteenth century, this "brutal style of fighting" became known as "rough-and-tumble" or "gouging" (Gorn, 1985: 20). In such encounters, spectators formed a circle around the fighters to watch the two men go at each other. Each did his best

---

[10] Bailey (1986) has argued that, by the early twentieth century, in one upper South city, Danville, Virginia, economic interests also played a role in the willingness of the elites on both sides of the color line to engage in nonviolent "conflict management." These elites described the violence in their city as essentially lower-class violence by young men, white and black.

to kick, punch, pluck out the eyeball of the other, or bite off a lip or an ear. According to Gorn (1985: 21):

> The social base of rough-and-tumbling...shifted with the passage of time. Although brawling was always considered a vice of the "lower sort," eighteenth century Tidewater gentlemen sometimes found themselves in brutal fights. These combats grew out of challenges to men's honor...and were woven into the very fabric of daily life.

But as Kierner (1996: 461–2) notes with regard to Southern "sociability," by the final decades of the colonial era, "elites were adopting more pointedly exclusive sporting rituals, perhaps hoping to use such public displays of gentility to enhance a privileged status that appeared to be increasingly tenuous." Southern gentlemen of the planter class "now wanted to distinguish themselves from social inferiors more by genteel manners, gracious living, and material prestige than by patriarchal prowess" (Gorn, 1985: 22). Therefore, gentlemen turned from hand-to-hand combat to dueling. Poor white males continued to brawl. By the nineteenth century, rough-and-tumble fighting "had generated its own folklore" (Gorn, 1985: 27). This form of fighting acquired its "own unique rites of honor" that "allowed backcountry men to shout their equality to each other" (Gorn, 1985: 41).

Like their wealthier counterparts, backcountry folk felt the effects of antebellum evangelism. However, as with the gentry, "conversion was far from universal" (Gorn, 1985: 37). The colorful brawls that shocked travelers through the backcountry continued. But as the century advanced, new and improved weapons became available. Rough-and-tumble fighting was "circumscribed" as "a deadlier option" – "gunplay" – became available to lower-class males (Gorn, 1985: 43). Whether they were brawling or shooting, poor white males – as did the gentry – responded to "fighting words." Brearley (1934: 687) states: "According to folk belief, one who refuses to wipe out an insult with blood is a poltroon and a coward – he 'ain't no man.' "

Masculinity and the Southern Male

Historians have examined the differing conceptions of masculinity that evolved in the North and South during the nineteenth century. In an article about student misconduct in Southern antebellum colleges and universities, Drinkwater (1993: 323) notes that during that era, "frequent student unrest and periodic violence" occurred not only in the South but also throughout the country. Like those in the North, Southern universities were repressive. Strict discipline was enforced. But in the antebellum South, young males from "wealthy and influential families" rebelled more vigorously than did their Northern peers. White male college students in the South engaged in disruptive and destructive pranks, got drunk, gambled, fought, rioted, dueled – and sometimes attacked or on several occasions even killed faculty members. Drinkwater asserts such behavior was linked to the students' code of honor:

> Male children in the antebellum South were expected to demonstrate their virility early and often. Their honor – and that of their families – was linked to how well they fought, drank, rode horses, used weapons, and gambled. Even swearing and wenching were aspects of a boy's honor in some families. (Drinkwater, 1993: 328)

The mistreatment of faculty members and of servants who worked at the university by these male students also might be explained by their conception of honor. A young male of the gentry was expected to "exert himself and establish his superior position over his inferiors.... This later group often included teachers" (Drinkwater, 1993: 328).

This conception of honor as synonymous with virile manhood was a part of the Southern culture of honor. However, Bruce (1979: 62–4) argues that this display of violence by male college students reflected a violation of the expectation that passion (i.e., unruly emotions) would be contained by the exercise of self-control. It flew in the face of the childhood socialization that was intended to train young males in the appropriate uses of violence by gentlemen. It was, Bruce suggests, in part a letting off of steam by young males freed for the first time from parental control of their behavior. This violence contradicted the values of the adult gentry and was, in this respect, a caricature of adult masculinity.

During the nineteenth century, competing models of manhood and masculinity existed. Kimmel (1996: 7) states that the debate over the abolition of slavery "offers a fascinating window into the antebellum debate about masculinity." The Northern male abolitionists' opposition to slavery and support of women's rights "brought their manhood into question" by Southerners (Kimmel, 1996: 72). Differing ideas about manhood and honor and insult placed the North and South on a collision course as the debate over slavery and regional differences escalated. The Civil War was in some respects the South's response to the perceived insult given to its way of life by the North (Greenberg, 1996). The Civil War was, Kimmel argues, "the last stand of the Genteel Patriarch, now a Confederate cavalier" (1996: 76). He adds: "For Southern men, defeat meant a kind of gendered humiliation – the southern gentleman was discredited as a 'real man' " (Kimmel, 1996: 77). Dishonored "Southern manhood" in the postwar period and into the twentieth century "would continually attempt to assert itself against debilitating conditions..." (Kimmel, 1996: 78).

But for the lower-class whites who had been drawn often unwillingly into the conflict with the North, Ash (1991: 39) suggests: "The conquest of the South by Northern armies... begun the liberation of the region's poor whites as well as its enslaved blacks." It was a liberation that came as a mixed blessing. In the occupied South, poor whites were often as much in need of shelter, food, and clothing as were the former slaves. These lower-class whites were viewed as potential allies to the Union. But Yankee soldiers also shared the Southern gentry's disdain and distrust of poor whites (Ash, 1991: 42).

Lower-class whites saw new opportunities in the breakdown of the prewar Southern social structure. In this, they had something in common with the blacks. But there was little likelihood that poor whites and poor blacks would form the permanent alliances that the defeated Southern gentry feared. As Ash (1991: 59) observes: "Racism not only drove a wedge between the white and black lower classes... it also bound upper- and lower-class whites in a Procrustean unity." In the post–Civil War era, Southern whites were united in their perception of the social and economic threat from Southern blacks.

Southern Honor and Black Rapists

Bardaglio (1994: 755) asserts that, in the antebellum South, rape "brought dishonor not only upon the woman but also upon her entire household, and the male head of the household most of all." For the white Southern male, an assault on a female member of his household was like an assault on himself. When this assault was committed by a slave, it "challenged slavery and the racial order of southern society" (Bardaglio, 1994: 755). However, Bardaglio finds that procedural rights were sometimes extended to slaves in the courtroom. Doing so "protected property rights [of the master] as well as human lives" (Bardaglio, 1994: 765). Sommerville (1995: 484) analyzed over 250 cases of alleged sexual assault by black males of white females that occurred from 1800 to 1865. She suggests – based on the fact that nearly half of the black defendants escaped death – that antebellum white Southerners felt less compulsion to execute black males accused of the sexual assault of a white female than did postbellum white Southerners (Sommerville, 1995: 485).

In the postbellum period, control of a free black population who challenged the prewar status quo became of paramount importance for white Southerners. In the South, over time, a "cleavage" had developed "between honor and legality." Honor had originally grown "in the vacuum of justice" but eventually "[m]anhood came to be equated with the extralegal defense of one's honor." That honor was vested in part in "the control of one's woman" (Ayers, 1984: 234–5). After the Civil War, white Southern males manifested their fear of loss of status and control in the form of violence directed toward Southern blacks and their allies. White males acted out their fear of challenges to the racial caste hierarchy in their ritualized violence directed against the symbolic "black rapist" (see Myers, 1995).

Bederman (1995: 46) finds that by the 1890s, "most white Americans believed that African American men lusted uncontrollably after white women, and that lynchings occurred when white men were goaded beyond endurance by black men's savage, unmanly assaults on pure white womanhood." This "relatively new" myth (Bederman, 1995: 46) of "the Negro rapist" was used as one of the justifications for lynching. But, as Bederman notes, historians have found a variety of other factors "including Populism, economic depression, the uncertainty of a new market economy, and Southern politics" (Bederman, 1995: 47; see also Tolnay and Beck, 1995) that all played a role in white violence against black males. And women historians have asserted that white male violence also was "connected to white Southerners' interest in bolstering male power and authority" (Bederman, 1995: 47; see also Hall, 1993). The control of the newly freed black population was deemed essential to the maintenance of not only white male honor but also white male status.

Hodes (1993: 61) argues that in the Reconstruction South the assertion of black political rights became the equivalent of the assertion of black manhood and "political thought, now took on connotations in white minds, of black male sexual agency..." This concern on the part of white Southerners was "characterized by a language of sexual alarm." In the discourse that developed, white male violence became the "civilized" response to the "savagery" of the black man. Honor required a violent response to such attacks on all that white Southern males held dear.

A Contemporary Culture of Honor

Are white Southern males still ready to use violence in defense of what they hold dear? Does a culture of honor still exist in the South? Nisbett and Cohen (1996) assert that a culture of honor does still exist in the South and that it affects the homicide rate in this region of the country. Developing an argument similar to that made by McWhiney with regard to the forging of a "cracker culture" in the South, Nisbett and Cohen assert that the culture of honor of the Scotch-Irish immigrants who settled the South in the seventeenth century had a profound and long-term impact on the region. This was so because the frontier conditions encountered by the immigrants encouraged the continuation of the habits of herding and horticulture that they had brought with them from Britain (Nisbett and Cohen, 1996: 8). "Not until the invention of the cotton gin in the early nineteenth century would there be a viable economic competitor to herding" (Nisbett and Cohen, 1996: 9). By the nineteenth century, the culture of honor that was common to herding society had taken strong roots in the South.

With regard to the modern South, Nisbett and Cohen (1996: 3) note that four major explanations have been offered to explain high rates of violence. These four explanations are: (1) the climate; (2) the tradition of slavery; (3) Southern poverty; and (4) "the putative 'culture of honor' of the South." Nisbett and Cohen argue that "the role of 'honor' is independent of, and probably greater than, any role played by the other three [explanations]."

The other three major explanations have long been the subject of debate. Discussing the impact of climate on "Southern distinctiveness," Koeniger (1988) cites a letter written by Thomas Jefferson to the Marquis de Chastellux in 1785. In this letter, Jefferson compares the temperament of Southerners to that of Northerners. Jefferson concludes that those who live in the North are "cool; sober; laborious; independent; jealous of their own liberties, and just to those of others; interested; chicaning; superstitious and hypocritical in their religion." The residents of the South, on the other hand, are "fiery, voluptuary; indolent, unsteady; zealous for their own liberties, but trampling on those of others; generous; candid; without attachment or pretensions to any religion but that of the heart" (Jefferson, cited in Koeniger, 1988: 21).

These regional distinctions (with variations) that Jefferson related were also recognized by Americans of both regions and by foreign visitors. Over time, Koeniger finds that "the idea of a distinctive southern personality type has become well established in the literature of the American South." Koeniger acknowledges that there are many factors that may have helped to shape "the southern collective personality," including rural isolation, the frontier experience, and the South's history of slavery and racial conflicts (Koeniger, 1988: 21). However, he believes "climate has played a larger role in shaping southern distinctiveness than contemporary historians are prone to acknowledge" (Koeniger, 1988: 26). In support of his argument, Koeniger reviews the scientific research on the impact of climate on human behavior. He concludes: "Climate does not determine culture or other forms of human behavior, but historically it has influenced them, predisposing persons affected toward certain patterns" (Koeniger, 1988: 44).

If they have neglected serious attention to the possible role of climate in shaping Southern culture, historians have given much attention to the role of slavery. McLaurin (1991: xiii) writes:

> For many antebellum southerners, including the large majority who held no slaves, the moral dilemmas of slavery were hardly abstractions to be debated. They were instead among the inescapable realities of daily life, a significant aspect of the society. And as such southerners, slaveholders or not, were forced to cope with them in terms of the concrete rather than the theoretical...

This assertion of the central role of slavery in the lives of southerners from the colonial period to the first shots fired in the Civil War has been made by historians across the spectrum of intellectual and political opinion. In the antebellum era, the South was compelled to define itself and was defined by the North in large part by the presence of African Americans held in bondage. Their presence dictated the nature of economic, political, legal, religious, and social relationships in the region. Their presence not only brought whites of all classes together, it also created divisions between the gentry and the poor, slaveowners and nonslaveowners.

One of the arguments made by those Southerners who opposed slavery was that the presence of blacks as slaves restricted the economic opportunities available to Southern white men. In the postbellum period, Southerners, both black and white, struggled to survive in a region devastated by the war. In the present-day South, rates of poverty are still high. In its report on Hunger in America, the Physicians Task Force (1985: 28) found that a quarter of the population of the state of Mississippi lived below the poverty line. Conditions of abject poverty continue to exist in the foothills of Appalachia and elsewhere in the South (Mantsios, 1992: 97). Has this poverty contributed to the level of violence in the region? Or may high rates of homicide in the South be better attributed to a "subculture of violence" or to a contemporary "culture of honor"?

As Ellison (1991: 1223) states: "the literature on region and violence harbors considerable confusion over (1) what this southern subculture argument really implies, and (2) how to construct an appropriate empirical test of its core arguments." This chapter opened with a quote from H. C. Brearley (1934), who offered an early formulation of the argument linking Southern violence to culture. Later Hackney, in his essay on "Southern Violence" (1969: 925), concluded:

> Being southern, then, inevitably involves a feeling of persecution at times and a sense of being a passive, insignificant object of alien or impersonal forces. Such a historical experience has fostered a world view that supports the denial of responsibility and locates threats to the region and threats to the person outside the self. From the southern past arise the symbiosis of profuse hospitality and intense hostility toward strangers and the paradox that the southern heritage is at the same time one of grace and violence.

Support for such a culture of violence as an explanation of high homicide rates was offered by Gastil (1971). Loftin and Hill (1974) challenged this perspective, arguing that socioeconomic factors – poverty – might be a more salient explanation. In the aftermath of these studies, other researchers have examined and offered additional challenges to the Southern subculture of violence thesis. For example, Dixon and Lizotte (1987: 401) looked at gun ownership in the region. They conclude: "In our analysis, gun ownership, whether of pistol, rifle, or shotgun, is in no way related to either a regional or a nonregional subculture of violence."

However, Nisbett and Cohen, two cultural psychologists, have recently presented their argument for the existence of a culture of honor in the South. In their research, they attempt to compensate for what they describe as the "reliance on too narrow a range of methodologies" in the study of culture (1996: xvii).[11] Their broader approach to the study of culture and honor includes the use of attitudinal surveys administered in the rural South and Midwest in which respondents were presented with vignettes intended to gauge "responses to affronts." It also includes experimental (laboratory) research measuring the physiological and behavioral responses of subjects to affronts. In addition, Nisbett and Cohen analyze the social policy and laws ("collective expression") in different regions of the country on issues such as gun control, self-defense, domestic violence, and capital punishment. They conclude that white Southern males retain certain attitudes about violence and its use that distinguish them from males from other regions of the country. Nisbett and Cohen state:

> Southerners do not approve of violence in the abstract, nor do they approve of violence for any concrete purposes that we have been able to discover – except for the protection of self, family, and possessions, for responding to an insult, and for socializing children. (1996: 82)

They assert the Southerner's commitment to defense of self and others against perceived "affronts and threats to property or integrity of self" explains the more frequent types of homicide in the South that grow out of arguments, brawls, and lovers' triangles (Nisbett and Cohen, 1996: 82). Although acknowledging that the culture of honor "no longer has the strength it once had" in the South, Nisbett and Cohen (1996: 93) argue that this may well indicate a kind of "cultural lag" occurring in which public norms "lag behind private attitudes."

Chu, Rivera, and Loftin replicate the Nisbett-Reaves test of the herding-culture-of-honor hypothesis, which is the basis for the Nisbett and Cohen argument that the Southern culture of honor grew out of the economic conditions encountered by early Southern settlers who brought their herding culture with them from Europe. In their reanalysis of homicide data for 1976–83, Chu, Rivera, and Loftin find that contrary to the expectations of the herding-culture-of-honor hypothesis, rural counties in the South do not have especially high white non-Hispanic male homicide rates. They conclude, "when differences in white poverty are controlled, there is either no discernible contemporary (1976–83) relationship between white

---

[11] In a review of Nisbett and Cohen's *Culture of Honor*, Messner (1997: 1227) praises the authors' impressive use of diverse data sources and methods [which] . . . makes their overall case for a culture of honor in the South compelling."

male homicide rates and environmental regions, or a difference that is inconsistent with the predictions of the theory" (Chu, Rivera, and Loftin, 2000). However, they also note – significant for this discussion – that "[t]he origin of the culture of honor is logically independent of the mechanisms linking culture to violent behavior. It is quite possible for the argument that herding explains the origin of the culture of violence to be invalid while arguments about the consequences of the culture are valid" (Chu, Rivera, and Loftin, 2000).

One issue regarding the existence of a culture of honor in the South has been the possibility that – if such a culture does (did) exist – Southern migrants might have carried it with them into other regions, thereby increasing the rates of violence in those regions. In the face of high rates of violence in urban inner cities, some observers have posited a present-day culture of honor among young African-American males. But the question is whether this culture of honor, if it does exist, is indicative of the transportation and retention of a Southern cultural tradition or whether it is reflective of the social and economic conditions that historically have contributed to high rates of violence in some pockets of the country.

In 1995, the journalist Fox Butterfield published a provocative study of the notorious young New York felon Willie Bosket. Known as the most dangerous prisoner in the New York penal system, Bosket, a young, black male, was also highly intelligent and charming. In trying to understand Bosket's violent behavior, Butterfield began to examine his family history. In the end, he traced Bosket's family roots back to Edgefield County, South Carolina. In the eighteenth and nineteenth centuries, Southerners called the county "Bloody Edgefield," because of its extremely high rates of lethal violence. The settlers of this county were Scotch-Irish immigrants who came to America in the eighteenth century and made their way from Pennsylvania to South Carolina. Butterfield describes them as "poor but proud people who had left their homelands after centuries of incessant warfare. In temperament, they were tough, blunt, touchy, hard-drinking and pugnacious" (Butterfield, 1995: 3). Butterfield argues that beginning with Aaron Bosket, a former slave and Willie's great-great-grandfather, the Bosket males were influenced by this white Southern culture of honor of "Bloody Edgefield." Generation after generation, the Bosket males engaged in violent defense of honor against perceived insult. They defined their manhood in terms of violence. This violence continued to be played out in the twentieth century in a Northern urban setting. Butterfield concludes that in the case of Willie Bosket and other young African-American males, the old code of Southern honor "transmuted into the strictures of the streets" has become "a dangerous anachronism" (Butterfield, 1995: 328).

However, Courtwright (1996: 271) suggests the conditions of contemporary urban inner cities have much in common with those of bygone American frontiers. He writes:

> The social dynamics of a group of touchy, drunken bachelors in a backwoods tavern in seventeenth-century Virginia would not have been much different from those of a group of touchy, drunken bachelors in a bar in twentieth-century Harlem, and the color of the blood on the floor was surely the same.

Considering violence in urban ghettos from this perspective, it is not necessary to argue that Southern migrants have been carriers of violence to the urban ghetto. It would instead by possible to argue that similar circumstances produce similar responses by young males. Courtwright argues that American frontiers – lacking both sufficient law and the domesticating influence of women and children, but with much competition for resources and wealth as well as opportunities for drinking and gambling – were environments that spawned violence. He describes young urban males in inner-city areas – many of them single and unrestrained by families, influenced by the values of their peers, and unemployed or underemployed – as living in environments that are similarly conducive to violent interactions.

Ethnographer Elijah Anderson (1997: 1) has described the environment of the "poor inner-city black community" as one in which "two orientations – decent and street – socially organize the community." Anderson argues that these two competing orientations shape the lives of the residents, particularly the children, of inner-city community. Even those young black males who have "mainstream values" must learn the "code of the streets" in order to survive in this environment. According to Anderson (1997: 2):

> The rules prescribe both a proper comportment and the proper way to respond if challenged. They regulate the use of violence and so supply a rationale which allows those who are inclined to aggression to precipitate violent encounters in an approved way ... everybody knows that if the rules are violated, there are penalties. Knowledge of the rules is largely defensive, and it is literally necessary for operating in public ...

Based on the work of Elijah Anderson, William Julius Wilson, and others, Nisbett and Cohen (1996: 91) argue for the existence of a culture of honor in the urban inner city. They maintain that the roots of this violent culture, like those of the Southern culture of honor, are economic. They maintain that, as in the South, this urban culture of honor has appeared in a situation in which presentation of self as a man willing and able to use violence in defense of reputation and property is valued and rewarded by status and respect.

Adopting Black's thesis on social control, Cooney (1997) argues that elite male violence has decreased because of availability of other acceptable means of resolving conflict such as the law. In the case of young, African-American males in the inner city, the criminal justice system is often seen as neither available to them, favorably disposed toward them, or a desirable mechanism for resolving their conflicts.[12] In this setting, social control in the form of violent "self-help" (Black, 1993) may seem the only option and defense of honor may seem essential to survival.

Conclusions

It remains an intriguing question whether young black males in urban inner cities are indeed the direct heirs of a Southern tradition of honor-based violence (Butterfield, 1995) or whether what they instead have in common with nineteenth-century white Southerners are the social and economic conditions that give rise to cultures of honor (Nisbett and Cohen, 1996). The suggestion on the part of scholars that the urban inner city bears similarities to the nineteenth-century South or to the Western frontier and that young African-American males are engaging in rituals of manhood and violence similar to those played out by white males in other settings raises interesting questions about the complex nexus of race/ethnicity, gender, class, and culture. The concept of "manhood" is socially constructed, and it appears that, in various historical and modern settings, the use of violence and the rituals of honor play crucial roles in that construction. Moreover, the research of Nisbett and Cohen (1996) and the conclusions of O'Carroll and Mercy (1989) emphasize, respectively, the importance of applying a range of methodologies to the study of culture and of paying attention to the interactions of differences of race/ethnicity and rural/urban residence in discussing regional variations in violence.

Finally, returning to the primary focus of this chapter, what we can conclude is that historically – whatever their socioeconomic condition – white Southern males were concerned about how they were perceived by those with whom they had social interactions. They believed in – sometimes lived and died by – a conception of "honor" that emphasized the value of one's "reputation." For upper-class white males, this reputation was based on fulfilling the obligations and responsibilities of a gentleman. For lower-class white males, reputation was synonymous with "strength and toughness" (Nisbett and Cohen, 1996: xv) and the willingness to fight. The perception shared by white males of all classes of the necessity to defend honor and avenge insult contributed to the high rates of violence in the region. In the nineteenth century (and into the twentieth century in the case of lynchings), this "culture of honor" was a crucial factor in the race, gender,

---

[12] See Bailey and Green (1999) for their discussion of the perceptions of the criminal justice system held by African Americans.

and class relationships in the South. It affected the lives not only of white Southern males but also of those "others," white women and African Americans, who lived in their orbits. As we have seen, some scholars argue that this matter of honor and its defense continues to affect the lives of lower-class males, both white and black, and to contribute to the level of violence in our society.

References

Achenbach, T. M., and C. S. Edelbrock. 1983. *Manual of the Child Behavior Checklist and Revised Child Behavior Profile.* Burlington: University of Vermont Department of Psychiatry.

Adams, C., D. Bartelt, D. Elesh, I. Goldstein, N. Kleniewski, and W. Yancey. 1991. *Philadelphia: Neighborhoods, Division, and Conflict in a Postindustrial City.* Philadelphia: Temple University Press.

Agnew, R. 1992. "Foundation for General Strain Theory of Crime and Delinquency." *Criminology* 30: 47–87.

———. 1995. "Determinism, Indeterminism, and Crime." *Criminology* 33: 83–109.

Agresti, A. 1990. *Categorical Data Analysis.* New York: Wiley.

Aguirre, B. E., R. Saenz, and B. S. James. 1997. "Marielitos Ten Years Later: The Scarface Legacy." *Social Science Quarterly* 78 (June): 487–507.

Akbar, N. 1981. "Mental Disorder among African Americans." *Black Books Bulletin* 7: 18–25.

———. 1984. *Chains and Images of Psychological Slavery.* Jersey City, NJ: New Mind Productions.

———. 1991. "Mental Disorder among African Americans." In *Black Psychology (3rd edition),* ed. R. L. Jones, 339–52. Berkeley, CA: Cobb and Henry.

Alaniz, M. L., R. S. Cartmill, and R. N. Parker. 1998. "Immigrants and Violence: The Importance of Neighborhood Context." *Hispanic Journal of Behavioral Sciences* 20: 155–74.

Alba, R. D., J. R. Logan, and P. E. Bellair. 1994. "Living with Crime: The Implications of Racial/Ethnic Differences in Suburban Location." *Social Forces* 73, 2 (December): 395–434.

Alex-Assensoh, Y. 1995. "Myths about Race and the Underclass: Concentrated Poverty and 'Underclass Behaviors.'" *Urban Affairs Review* 31: 3–19.

Allard, M. A., M. E. Colten, R. Albelda, and C. Cozenza. 1997. *In Harm's Way? Domestic Violence, AFDC Receipt, and Welfare Reform in Massachusetts. Report (February).* Boston: University of Massachusetts.

Allard, S. A. 1991. "Rethinking BWS: A Black Feminist Perspective." *UCLA Women's Law Journal* 191, 1: 193–4.

Allport, G. 1979. *The Nature of Prejudice.* Reading, MA: Addison-Wesley.

Almgren, G., A. Guest, G. Immerwahr, and M. Spittel. 1998. "Joblessness, Family Disruption, and Violent Death in Chicago, 1970–1990." *Social Forces* 76, 4 (June): 1465–93.

Amdur, R. L. 1989. "Testing Causal Models of Delinquency: A Methodological Critique." *Criminal Justice and Behavior* 16: 35–62.

Ammons, L. L. 1995. "Mules, Madonnas, Babies, Bathwater. Racial Imagery and Stereotypes: The African-American Woman and the Battered Woman Syndrome." *Wisconsin Law Review* 5: 1003–80.

Anderson, E. 1978. *A Place on the Corner.* Chicago: University of Chicago Press.

———. 1990. *Streetwise: Race, Class, and Change in an Urban Community.* Chicago: University of Chicago Press.

———. 1994. "The Code of the Streets." *The Atlantic Monthly* 273, 5 (May): 80–3, 86–9, 92–4.

———. 1997. "Violence and the Inner-City Street Code." In *Violence and Childhood in the Inner City,* ed. J. McCord, 1–30. New York: Cambridge University Press.

———. 1999. *The Code of the Streets: Decency, Violence, and the Moral Life of the Inner City.* New York: W. W. Norton.

Anderson, L. P. 1991. "Acculturative Stress: A Theory of Relevance to Black Americans." *Clinical Psychology Review* 11: 685–702.

Ani, M. 1994. *Yurugu: An African-Centered Critique of European Cultural Thought and Behavior.* Trenton, NJ: Africa World Press.

Archer, M. 1994. *Culture and Agency.* New York: Cambridge University Press.

Armstrong, T., M. Guilfoyle, and A. P. Melton. 1996. "Native American Delinquency: An Overview of Prevalence, Causes, and Correlates." In *Native Americans, Crime, and Justice,* ed. M. Nielsen and R. Silverman, 75–88. Boulder, CO: Westview Press.

Asante, M. K. 1980. *Afrocentricity: The Theory of Social Change.* Buffalo, NY: Amulefi Publishing.

Asbury, J. 1987. "African-American Women in Violent Relationships: An Exploration of Cultural Differences." In *Violence in the Black Family: Correlates and Consequences,* ed. R. L. Hampton, 90–105. Lexington, MA: Heath.

Ash, S. V. 1991. "Poor Whites in the Occupied South, 1861–1865." *The Journal of Southern History* LVII, 1: 39–62.

Astor, R. A. 1994. "Children's Moral Reasoning about Family and Peer Violence: The Role of Provocation and Retribution." *Child Development* 65: 1054–67.

Atkinson, G. 1993. "Germany: Nationalism, Nazism and Violence." In *Racist Violence in Europe,* ed. T. Bjorgo and R. Witte. London: Macmillan.

Auletta, K. 1982. *The Underclass.* New York: Random House.

Aye Maung, N., and C. Mirrlees-Black. 1994. *Racially Motivated Crime: A British Crime Survey Analysis. Home Office Research and Planning Unit Paper 82.* London: Home Office.

Ayers, E. L. 1984. *Vengeance and Justice: Crime and Punishment in the 19th Century American South.* New York: Oxford University Press.

Azibo, D. A. 1994. "The Kindred Fields of Black Liberation Theology and Liberation Psychology: A Critical Essay on Their Conceptual Base and Destiny." *Journal of Black Psychology* 20: 334–56.

Bachman, R. 1992. *Death and Violence on the Reservation: Homicide, Family Violence, and Suicide in American Indian Populations.* New York: Auburn House.

———. 1994. *Violence Against Women: A National Crime Victimization Survey Report.* Washington, DC: U.S. Department of Justice, Bureau of Justice Statistics.

Bachman, R., and A. L. Coker. 1995. "Police Involvement in Domestic Violence: The Interactive Effects of Victim Injury, Offender's History of Violence and Race." *Violence and Victims* 10, 2: 91–106.

Bachman, R., and L. Salzman. 1995. *Violence Against Women: Estimates from the Redesigned Survey (NCJ #154348). Bureau of Justice Statistics Special Report.* Washington, DC: U.S. Department of Justice.

Bailey, F. Y. 1986. *Boundary Maintenance, Interest-Group Conflict, and Black Justice in Danville, Virginia, 1900–1930.* Ph.D. Dissertation for School of Criminal Justice, State University of New York at Albany.

Bailey, F. Y., and A. P. Green. 1999. *"Law Never Here": A Social History of African American Responses to Issues of Crime and Justice.* Westport, CT: Praeger.

Bailey, W. C. 1984. "Poverty, Inequality, and City Homicide Rates: Some Not So Unexpected Findings." *Criminology* 22: 531–50.

Baldwin, J. A. 1980. "The Psychology of Oppression." In *Contemporary Black Thought,* ed. M. Asante and A. Vandi, 95–110. Beverly Hills, CA: Sage Publications.

———. 1984. "African Self-Consciousness and the Mental Health of African Americans." *Journal of Black Studies* 15: 177–94.

Balkwell, J. W. 1990. "Ethnic Inequality and the Rate of Homicide." *Social Forces* 69: 53–70.

Bandura, A. 1991. "Social Cognitive Theory of Moral Thought and Action." In *Handbook of Moral Behavior and Development: Theory, Volume 1,* ed. W. M. Kurtines and J. S. Gewirtz, 45–103. Hillsdale, NJ: LEA.

Bandura, A., C. Barbaranelli, G. V. Capara, and C. Pastorelli. 1996. "Mechanisms of Moral Disengagement in the Exercise of Moral Agency." *Journal of Personality and Social Psychology* 71: 364–74.

Banfield, E. 1970. *The Unheavenly City: The Nature and the Future of Our Urban Crisis.* Boston: Little, Brown, and Company.

Bankston, C. L., III. 1998. "Youth Gangs and the New Second Generation: A Review Essay." *Aggression and Violent Behavior* 3, 1: 35–45.

Bardaglio, P. W. 1994. "Rape and the Law in the Old South: 'Calculated to Excite Indignation in Every Heart.'" *The Journal of Southern History* LX, 4: 749–72.

Baron, S. 1989. "Resistance and Its Consequences: The Street Culture of Punks." *Youth and Society* 21: 207–37.

Bartelt, D. W. 1993. "Housing the 'Underclass.'" In *The "Underclass" Debate,* ed. M. B. Katz, 118–60. Princeton, NJ: Princeton University Press.

Bathgate, M. 1988. *Housing Needs of the Maori Community.* Wellington: Housing Corporation of New Zealand.

Baumer, E. 1994. "Poverty, Crack, and Crime: A Cross-City Analysis." *Journal of Research in Crime and Delinquency* 31, 3 (August): 311–27.

Baumer, E., J. T. Lauritsen, R. Rosenfeld, and R. Wright. 1998. "The Influence of Crack Cocaine on Robbery, Burglary, and Homicide Rates: A Cross-City, Longitudinal Analysis." *Journal of Research in Crime and Delinquency* 35: 316–40.

Baumgartner, M. P. 1993. "Violent Networks: The Origins and Management of Domestic Conflict." In *Aggression and Violence: Social Interactionist Perspectives,* ed. R. B. Felson and J. T. Tedeschi, 209–31. Washington, DC: American Psychological Association.

Beasley, R. W., and G. Antunes. 1974. "The Etiology of Urban Crime: An Ecological Analysis." *Criminology* 11: 439–61.

Beauvais, F. 1996. "Trends in Indian Adolescent Drug and Alcohol Use." In *Native Americans, Crime, and Justice,* ed. M. Nielsen and R. Silverman, 89–95. Boulder, CO: Westview Press.

Beck, A. 1999. "Trends in U.S. Correctional Populations." In *The Dilemma of Corrections,* ed. K. C. Haas and G. Alpert. Prospect Heights, IL: Waveland Press.

Beck, E. M., and S. E. Tolnay. 1995. "Violence toward African Americans in the Era of the White Lynch Mob." In *Ethnicity, Race and Crime: Perspectives Across Time and Place,* ed. D. F. Hawkins, 121–44. Albany: State University of New York Press.

Becker, H. 1973 [1963]. *Outsiders: Studies in the Sociology of Deviance (2nd edition).* New York: Free Press of Glencoe.

Bederman, G. 1995. *Manliness and Civilization: A Cultural History of Gender and Race in the United States.* Chicago and London: University of Chicago Press.

Bell, C. C. 1987. "Preventive Strategies for Dealing with Violence among Blacks." *Community Mental Health Journal* 23: 217–28.

———. 1997. "Community Violence: Causes, Prevention, and Intervention." *Journal of the National Medical Association* 89: 657–62.

Bell, R. Q. 1954. "An Experimental Test of the Accelerated Longitudinal Approach." *Child Development* 25: 281–6.

Bellah, R. N., R. Madsen, W. M. Sullivan, A. Swidler, and S. M. Tipton. 1985. *Habits of the Heart: Individualism and Commitment in American Life.* Berkeley: University of California Press.

Benedict, R. 1959 [1940]. *Race: Science and Politics.* New York: Viking Press.

Ben-Jochannan, Y. 1991. *Cultural Genocide in Black and African Studies Curriculum.* New York: ESA Associates.

Benton, R. 1988. *Fairness in Maori Education: Royal Commission on Social Policy, The April Report, Vol. III, Part 2.* Wellington, New Zealand: Government Press.

Bernard, T. J. 1990. "Angry Aggression among the 'Truly Disadvantaged.' " *Criminology* 28: 173–94.

Betancourt, H., and S. R. Lopez. 1993. "The Study of Culture, Ethnicity, and Race in American Psychology." *American Psychologist* 28: 629–37.

Bingham, R., and J. Guinyard. 1982. "Counseling Black Women: Recognizing Societal Scripts." Paper presented at the Annual Convention of the American Psychological Association, Honolulu, Hawaii, August.

Birkbeck, C., and G. LaFree. 1993. "The Situational Analysis of Crime and Deviance." *Annual Review of Sociology* 19: 113–37.

Bjorgo, T. 1993. "Terrorist Violence Against Immigrants and Refugees in Scandinavia: Patterns and Motives." In *Racist Violence in Europe,* ed. T. Bjorgo and R. Witte, 29–45. London: Macmillan.

Bjorgo, T., and J. Kaplan, eds. 1998. *Nation and Race: The Developing Euro-American Racist Subculture.* Boston: Northeastern University Press.

Bjorgo, T., and R. Witte, eds. 1993. *Racist Violence in Europe.* London: Macmillan.

Black, D. 1993. *The Social Structure of Right and Wrong.* San Diego: Academic Press.

Blackman, J. 1989. *Intimate Violence: A Study of Injustice.* New York: Columbia University Press.

Blalock, H. M. 1967. *Toward a Theory of Minority Group Relations.* New York: John Wiley.

Blassingame, J. 1972. *The Slave Community.* New York: Oxford University Press.

Blau, J. R., and P. M. Blau. 1982. "The Cost of Inequality: Metropolitan Structure and Violent Crime." *American Sociological Review* 47: 114–29.

Blauner, R. 1972. *Racial Oppression in America.* New York: Grove Press.

Block, C. R. 1985. *Lethal Violence in Chicago over Seventeen Years: Homicides Known to the Police, 1965–1981.* Chicago: Illinois Criminal Justice Information Authority.

———. 1988. "Lethal Violence in the Chicago Latino Community, 1965 to 1981." In *Research Conference on Violence and Homicide in Hispanic Communities,* ed. J. F. Kraus, S. B. Sorenson, and P. D. Juarez, 31–65. Los Angeles, CA: UCLA Publication Services.

———. 1993. "Lethal Violence in the Chicago Latino Community." In *Homicide: The Victim/Offender Connection,* ed. A. V. Wilson, 267–342. Cincinnati: Anderson Publishing Company.

Block, C. R., and R. L. Block. 1980. *Patterns of Change in Chicago Homicide: The Twenties, the Sixties, and the Seventies.* Chicago: Illinois Criminal Justice Information Authority.

———. 1993. *Street Gang Crime in Chicago.* Washington, DC: National Institute of Justice.

Block C. R., R. L. Block, and the Illinois Criminal Justice Information Authority. 1994. *Homicides in Chicago, 1965–1990* [computer file]. ICPSR version. Chicago: Illinois Criminal Justice Information Authority [producer]. Ann Arbor, MI: Inter-University Consortium for Political and Social Research [distributor].

Block, R. 1979. "Community, Environment, and Violent Crime." *Criminology* 17: 46–57.

Block, R. L., and C. R. Block. 1992. "Homicide Syndromes and Vulnerability: Violence in Chicago Community Areas Over 25 Years." *Studies on Crime and Crime Prevention* 1: 61–87.

Blumstein, A. 1995. "Youth Violence, Guns, and the Illicit Drug Industry." *Journal of Criminal Law and Criminology* 86, 1: 10–36.

Blumstein, A., and D. Cork. 1996. "Linking Gun Availability to Youth Gun Violence." *Law and Contemporary Problems* 59, 1 (Winter): 5–24.

Blumstein, A., and R. Rosenfeld. 1998. "Explaining Recent Trends in U.S. Homicide Rates." *The Journal of Criminal Law and Criminology* 88, 4: 1175–213.

Bobo, L. D. 2000. "Reclaiming a DuBoisian Perspective on Racial Attitudes." *Annals of the American Academy of Political and Social Science* 568: 186–202.

Bobo, L. D., and D. Johnson. 2000. "Racial Attitudes in A Prismatic Metropolis: Mapping Identity, Stereotypes, Competition, and Views on Affirmative Action." In *Prismatic Metropolis: Inequality in Los Angeles*, ed. L. Bobo, M. L. Oliver, J. H. Johnson Jr., and A. Valenzuela Jr. New York: Russell Sage Foundation.

Bobo, L. D., and J. Kluegel. 1997. "The Color Line, the Dilemma, and the Dream: Racial Attitudes and Relations in America at the Close of the Twentieth Century." In *Civil Rights and Social Wrongs: Black-White Relations Since World War II*, ed. J. Higham, 31–5. University Park: Pennsylvania State University Press.

Boesak, W. 1995. *God's Wrathful Children: Political Oppression and Christian Ethics*. Grand Rapids, MI: William B. Eerdmans.

Bogle, D. 1973. *Toms, Coons, Mulattoes, Mammies, and Bucks – An Interpretive History of Blacks in American Films*. New York: Viking Press.

Bohannan, P., ed. 1960. *African Homicide and Suicide*. Princeton, NJ: Princeton University Press.

Bolton, C. C. 1994. *Poor Whites of the Antebellum South: Tenants and Laborers in Central North Carolina and Northeast Mississippi*. Durham, NC, and London: Duke University Press.

Bonacich, E. 1972. "The Theory of Elite Antagonism: The Split Labor Market." *American Sociological Review* 37: 547–59.

Bonczar, T., and A. Beck. 1997. *Lifetime Likelihood of Going to State or Federal Prison*. Washington, DC: U.S. Department of Justice, Bureau of Justice Statistics.

Boney, F. N. 1984. *Southerners All*. Macon, GA: Mercer University Press.

Bonger, W. 1916. *Criminality and Economic Conditions*. New York: Agathon Press.

Booker, C. 1998. "Lumpenization: A Critical Error of the Black Panther Party." In *The Black Panther Party Reconsidered*, ed. C. Jones, 337–62. Baltimore, MD: Black Classic Books.

Bourg, S., and H. V. Stock. 1994. "A Review of Domestic Violence Arrest Statistics in a Police Department Using a Pro-Arrest Policy: Are Pro-Arrest Policies Enough?" *Journal of Family Violence* 9, 2: 177–89.

Bourgois, P. 1995. *In Search of Respect, Selling Crack in El Barrio*. New York: Oxford University Press.

Bowler, A. C. 1931. "Recent Statistics on Crime and the Foreign Born." National Commission on Law Observance and Enforcement. *Report on Crime and the Foreign Born*, 83–196. Washington, DC: U.S. Government Printing Office.

Bowling, B. 1993. "Racial Harassment and the Process of Victimization: Conceptual and Methodological Implications for the Local Crime Survey." *British Journal of Criminology* 33, 1 (Spring): 231–50.

———. 1993. "Racial Harassment in East London." In *Hate Crime: International Perspectives on Causes and Control*, ed. M. S. Hamm. Academy of Criminal Justice Sciences/Anderson Publications.

———. 1998. *Violent Racism: Submission to the Stephen Lawrence Inquiry.* Cambridge: Cambridge Institute of Criminology.

———. 1999. *Violent Racism: Victimization, Policing, and Social Context (revised edition).* Oxford: Oxford University Press.

Bowling, B., and C. Phillips. 2000. *Racism, Crime and Justice.* Harlow: Pearson.

Bowling, B., and W. E. Saulsbury. 1993. "A Local Response to Racial Harassment." In *Racist Violence in Europe,* ed. T. Bjorgo and R. Witte, 221–35. London: Macmillan.

Bowman, S. D. 1990. "Honor and Materialism in the U.S. South and Prussian East Elbia during the Mid-Nineteenth Century." In *What Made the South Different?,* ed. K. Gispen, 19–40. Jackson and London: University Press of Mississippi.

Boykin, A. W. 1983. "The Academic Performance of Afro-American Children." In *Achievement and Achievement Motives,* ed. J. T. Spence, 321–71. San Francisco, CA: Freeman.

Boykin, A. W., R. J. Jagers, C. Ellison, and A. Albury. 1997. "The Communalism Scale: Conceptualization and Measurement of an Afrocultural Social Ethos." *Journal of Black Studies* 27: 409–18.

Bradshaw, B., D. R. Johnson, D. Cheatwood, and S. Blanchard. 1998. "A Historical Geographical Study of Lethal Violence in San Antonio." *Social Science Quarterly* 79: 863–78.

Braithwaite, J. 1979. *Inequality, Crime, and Public Policy.* London: Cambridge University Press.

———. 1989. *Crime, Shame, and Reintegration.* Cambridge: Cambridge University Press.

Brearley, H. C. 1934. "The Pattern of Violence." In *Culture in the South,* ed. W. T. Couch, 678–92. Chapel Hill: University of North Carolina Press.

Breines, W., and L. Gordon. 1983. "The New Scholarship on Family Violence." *Signs: Journal of Women and Culture in Society* 8, 3: 490–531.

Brisbane, F. L., and M. Womble. 1992. *Working with African Americans: The Professional's Handbook.* Chicago: HRDI International Press.

Brod, H., ed. 1987. *The Making of Masculinities – The New Men's Studies.* Boston: Allen and Unwin.

Brookins, C. C., and T. Robinson. 1995. "Rites-of-Passage as Resistance to Oppression." *Western Journal of Black Studies* 19: 172–80.

Brosnan, D. 1982. "Ethnic Origin and Income in New Zealand." *New Zealand Population Review* 8: 56–68.

Brown, C., and T. Boswell. 1995. "Strikebreaking or Solidarity in the Great Steel Strike of 1919: A Split Labor Market, Game-Theoretic, and QCA Analysis." *American Journal of Sociology* 100: 1479–519.

Browne, A. 1987. *Women Who Kill.* New York: Free Press.

———. 1992. "Violence against Women: Relevance for Medical Practitioners." *Journal of the American Medical Association* 267, 23: 3184–9.

———. 1997. "Violence in Marriage: Until Death Do Us Part." In *Violence between Intimate Partners: Patterns, Causes, and Effects,* ed. A. P. Cardarelli, 48–69. Boston: Allyn and Bacon.

Brownfield, D. 1986. "Social Class and Violent Behavior." *Criminology* 24: 421–38.

Bruce, D. D., Jr. 1979. *Violence and Culture in the Antebellum South.* Austin and London: University of Texas Press.

Bruce, M. A., V. J. Roscigno, and P. L. McCall. 1998. "Structure, Context, and Agency in the Reproduction of Black-on-Black Violence." *Theoretical Criminology* 2: 29–55.

Brunswick, A. 1988. "Young Black Males and Substance Use." In *Young, Black, and Male in America,* ed. J. T. Gibbs et al., 166–84. Dover, MA: Auburn House.

Bufford, B. 1990. *Among the Thugs.* London: Mandarin.

Bulhan, H. A. 1985. *Frantz Fanon and the Psychology of Oppression.* New York: Plenum.

Bullard, R. D. 1987. *Invisible Houston: The Black Experience in Boom and Bust.* College Station: Texas A&M University Press.

Bullock, H. A. 1955. "Urban Homicide in Theory and Fact." *Journal of Criminal Law, Criminology, and Political Science* 45: 565–76.

Burns, M. C., ed. 1986. *The Speaking Profits Us: Violence in the Cries of Women of Color.* Seattle, WA: Center for the Prevention of Sexual and Domestic Violence.

Burr, J. A., and J. E. Mutchler. 1993. "Ethnic Living Arrangements: Cultural Convergence or Cultural Manifestation." *Social Forces* 72: 169–79.

Bursik, R. J. 1988. "Social Disorganization and Theories of Crime and Delinquency." *Criminology* 26 (November): 519–51.

Bursik, R. J., and H. G. Grasmick. 1993. *Neighborhoods and Crime.* New York: Lexington Books.

Bush, R. 1999. *We Are Not What We Seem: Black Nationalism and Class Struggle in the American Century.* New York: New York University Press.

Buss, D. M. 1999. *The Dangerous Passion: Why Jealousy is as Necessary as Love and Sex.* New York: Free Press.

Butterfield, F. 1997 [1995]. *All God's Children: The Bosket Family and the American Tradition of Violence.* New York: Alfred A. Knopf.

Buzawa, E., and C. G. Buzawa. 1996. *Do Arrests and Restraining Orders Work?* Thousand Oaks, CA: Sage.

———. 1996. *Domestic Violence: The Criminal Justice Response.* Newbury Park, CA: Sage.

Buzawa, E., G. Hotaling, A. Klein, and J. Byrne. 1999. *Response to Domestic Violence in a Pro-Active Court: Final Report.* Lowell: University of Massachusetts.

Bynum, T., and R. Paternoster. 1984. "Discrimination Revisited: An Exploration of Frontstage and Backstage Criminal Justice Decision Making." *Sociology and Social Research* 69: 90–108.

Cabral, A. 1979. *Unity and Struggle: Speeches and Writings.* New York: Monthly Review Press.

Calmore, J. O. 1995. "Racialized Space and the Culture of Segregation: Hewing a Stone of Hope from a Mountain of Despair." *University of Pennsylvania Law Review* 143, 5: 1233–74.

Campbell, A. 1986. "Overview." In *Violent Transactions,* ed. A. Campbell and J. Gibbs. Oxford: Basil Blackwell.

Campbell, A., R. A. Berk, and J. J. Fyfe. 1998. "Deployment of Violence: The Los Angeles Department's Use of Dogs." *Evaluation Review* 22, 4: 535–61.

Campbell, A., and J. Gibbs, eds. 1986. *Violent Transactions*. Oxford: Basil Blackwell.

Campbell, D. W., B. Masaki, and S. Torres. 1997. " 'Water on Rock': Changing Domestic Violence Perceptions in the African American, Asian American and Latino Communities." In *Ending Domestic Violence*, ed. E. Klein, J. Campbell, E. Soler and M. Ghez, 64–87. Thousand Oaks, CA: Sage.

Campbell, E. D. C., Jr. 1981. *The Celluloid South: Hollywood and the Southern Myth*. Knoxville: University of Tennessee Press.

Canada, G. 1994. *Fist, Stick, Knife, Gun – A Personal History of Violence in America*. Boston: Beacon Press.

Canino, I., and G. Canino. 1980. "Impact of Stress on the Puerto Rican Family: Treatment Considerations." *American Journal of Orthopsychiatry* 50: 535–61.

Cannon, L. W., E. Higginbotham, and M. L. A. Leung. 1988. "Race and Class Bias in Qualitative Research on Women." *Gender and Society* 2, 4: 449–62.

Cao, L., A. Adams, and V. J. Jensen. 1997. "A Test of the Black Subculture of Violence Thesis: A Research Note." *Criminology* 35, 2: 367–79.

Carby, H. V. 1998. *Race Men*. Cambridge, MA: Harvard University Press.

Cardarelli, A. P., ed. 1997. *Violence between Intimate Partners: Patterns, Causes, and Effects*. Boston: Allyn and Bacon.

Carmichael, S., and C. Hamilton. 1967. *Black Power*. New York: Vintage Books.

Cathcart, B. 1999. *The Case of Stephen Lawrence*. London: Viking.

CazEnave, N. 1979. "Middle-Income Black Fathers: An Analysis of the Provider's Role." *Family Coordinator* 28: 583–93.

———. 1981. "Black Men in America: The Quest for Manhood." In *Black Families*, ed. H. P. McAdoo, 176–85. Beverly Hills, CA: Sage.

Cazanave, N., and M. Straus. 1979. "Race, Class Network Embeddedness, and Family Violence: A Search for Potent Support Systems." *Journal of Comparative Family Studies* 10 (Autumn): 281–300.

Centers for Disease Control. 1986. *Homicide Surveillance: High-Risk Racial and Ethnic Groups – Blacks and Hispanics, 1970–1983*. Atlanta, GA: Center for Environmental Health and Injury Control.

———. 1990. "Homicide among Young Black Males – United States, 1978–1987." *Morbidity and Mortality Weekly Report* 39: 1–5.

———. 1994. *Morbidity and Mortality Weekly Report* 43: 725.

Cernkovich, S. A., and P. C. Giordano. 1987. "Family Relationships and Delinquency." *Criminology* 25: 295–319.

Chahal, K. 1999. *"We Can't All Be White!" Racist Victimization in the UK*. York: Joseph Rowntree Foundation.

Chestang, L. W. 1972. "The Dilemma of Biracial Adoption." *Social Work* 17: 100–5.

Chicago Fact Book Consortium, eds. 1983, 1996. *Local Community Fact Book: Chicago Metropolitan Area: Based on the 1970 and 1980 Censuses*. Chicago: Chicago Review Press.

Chinchilla, N., N. Hamilton, and J. Loucky. 1993. "Central Americans in Los Angeles: An Immigrant Community in Transition." In *In the Barrios: Latinos and the Underclass Debate*, ed. J. Moore and R. Pinderhughes, 51–78. New York: Russell Sage Foundation.

Chu, R., C. Rivera, and C. Loftin. 2000. "Herding and Homicide: An Examination of the Nisbett-Reaves Hypothesis." *Social Forces* 78, 3: 971–89.

Churchill, W., and J. V. Wall. 1990. *Agents of Repression: The FBI's Secret War against the Black Panther Party and the American Indian Movement.* Boston, MA: South End Press.

Clark, K. B. 1965. *Dark Ghetto.* New York: Harper and Row.

Clark, K. B., and M. P. Clark. 1947. "Racial Identification and Preference in Negro Children." In *Readings in Social Psychology,* ed. T. M. Newcomb and E. L. Hartley. New York: Holt, Rinehart, and Winston.

Cleary, P. D., and R. Angel. 1984. "The Analysis of Relationships Involving Dichotomous Dependent Variables." *Journal of Health and Social Behavior* 25: 334–48.

Cloninger, D. O., and L. C. Sartorius. 1979. "Crime Rates, Clearance Rates, and Enforcement Effort: The Case of Houston, Texas." *American Journal of Economics and Sociology* 38, 4: 389–402.

Cloward, R., and L. Ohlin. 1960. *Delinquency and Opportunity: A Theory of Delinquent Gangs.* New York: Free Press.

CNN Interactive. 1998 (March 26). "School Shootings Cast Shadow on Southern Gun Culture." Retrieved online from: http://www.cnn.com/US/9803/26/rural.violence.

Cockerham, W., and M. Forslund. 1975. "Attitudes toward the Police among White and Native Indian Youth." *American Indian Law Review* 3: 193–8.

Cohen, J. 1983. "The Cost of Dichotomization." *Applied Psychological Measurement* 7: 249–53.

Cohen, J., D. Cork, J. Engberg, and G. Tita. 1999. "The Role of Drug Markets and Gangs in Local Homicide Rates." *Homicide Studies* 2: 241–62.

Cohen, L. E., and M. Felson. 1979. "Social Change and Crime Trends: A Routine Activity Approach." *American Sociological Review* 44: 588–608.

Coie, J. D., and K. A. Dodge. 1998. "Aggression and Antisocial Behavior." In *Handbook of Child Psychology (Volume 3),* ed. N. Eisenberg, 779–862. New York: John Wiley.

Coley, S. M., and J. O. Beckett. 1988. "Black Battered Women: Practice Issues." *Social Casework* 69, 8 (October): 483–90.

Comer, J. 1985. "Black Violence and Public Policy." In *American Violence and Public Policy,* ed. L. Curtis, 63–86. New Haven, CT: Yale University Press.

Cone, J. 1986. *Speaking the Truth.* Grand Rapids, MI: William B. Eerdmans.

———. 1997. *God of the Oppressed.* New York: Orbis Books.

Connell, R. W. 1987. *Gender and Power: Society, the Person and Sexual Politics.* Cambridge, UK: Polity Press.

Cooney, M. 1997. "The Decline of Elite Homicide." *Criminology* 35, 3: 381–407.

Cooper, C. R., and J. Denner. 1998. "Theories Linking Culture and Psychology: Universal and Community-Specific Processes." *Annual Review of Psychology* 49: 559–84.

Corzine, J., J. C. Creech, and L. Huff-Corzine. 1983. "Black Concentration and Lynching in the South: Testing Blalock's Power Threat Hypothesis." *Social Forces* 61: 774–809.

Corzine, J., L. Huff-Corzine, and J. C. Creech. 1988. "The Tenant Labor Market and Lynching in the South: A Test of Split Labor Market Theory." *Sociological Inquiry* 58: 261–78.

Cose, E. 1993. *The Rage of a Privileged Class*. New York: Harper-Collins.

Costello, E. J., and A. Angold. 1988. "Scales to Assess Child and Adolescent Depression: Checklists, Screens and Nets." *Journal of the American Academy of Child and Adolescent Psychiatry* 27: 726–37.

Costello, E. J., C. S. Edelbroch, and A. J. Costello. 1985. "The Validity of the NIMH Diagnostic Interview Schedule for Children (DISC): A Comparison between Pediatric and Psychiatric Referrals." *Journal of Abnormal Child Psychology* 13: 579–95.

Courtwright, D. T. 1996. *Violent Land: Single Men, Social Disorder from the Frontier to the Inner City*. Cambridge, MA: Harvard University Press.

Covington, J. 1995. "Racial Classification in Criminology." *Sociological Forum* 10, 4: 547–68.

———. 1997. "The Social Construction of the Minority Drug Problem." *Social Justice* 24, 4 (Winter): 117–47.

———. 1999. "African American Communities and Violent Crime: The Construction of Race Differences." *Sociological Focus* 32, 1: 7–23.

Covington, J., and R. Taylor. 1989. "Gentrification and Crime: Robbery and Larceny Changes in Appreciating Baltimore Neighborhoods." *Urban Affairs Quarterly* 25: 140–70.

Cox, O. 1940. "Sex Ratio and Marital Status among Negroes." *American Sociological Review* 5: 937–47.

Crenshaw, K. W. 1994. "Mapping the Margins: Intersectionality, Identity Politics, and Violence against Women of Color." In *The Public Nature of Private Violence*, ed. M. A. Fineman and R. Mykitiuk, 93–118. New York: Routledge.

Crowell, N. A., and A. W. Burgess. 1996. *Understanding Violence against Women*. National Research Council. Washington, DC: National Academy Press.

Crutchfield, R. D. 1989. "Labor Stratification and Violent Crime." *Social Forces* 68: 489–512.

———. 1995. "Ethnicity, Labor Markets, and Crime." In *Ethnicity, Race and Crime: Perspectives across Time and Place*, ed. D. F. Hawkins, 194–211. Albany: State University of New York Press.

Curtis, L. A. 1974. *Criminal Violence*. Lexington, MA: Lexington Books.

———. 1975. *Violence, Race, and Culture*. Lexington, MA: Lexington Books.

Dannefer, D. 1984. "Adult Development and Social Theory: A Paradigmatic Reappraisal." *American Sociological Review* 49: 100–16.

Davies, P. 1982. "Stratification and Class." In *New Zealand Society: A Sociological Perspective*, ed. P. Spoonley, D. Pearson, and I. Shirley. Palmerston, New Zealand: Dunmore Press.

Davis, A. Y. 1973. "Reflections on the Black Woman's Role in the Community of Slaves." In *Contemporary Black Thought, The Best from The Black Scholar*, ed. R. Chrisman and N. Ware, 138–49. New York: Bobbs Merrill.

———. 1998. *Blues Legacies and Black Feminism: Gertrude "Ma" Rainey, Bessie Smith, and Billie Holiday*. New York: Pantheon Books.

Davis, J. A. 1976. "Blacks, Crime, and American Culture." *Annals of the American Academy of Political and Social Science* 423: 89–98.

Davis, R., and B. Taylor. 1999. "Does Batterer Treatment Reduce Violence? A Synthesis of the Literature." In *Women and Domestic Violence: An Interdisciplinary Approach,* ed. L. Feder, 69–94. New York: Hayworth Press.

Deater-Deckard, K., K. A. Dodge, J. E. Bates, and G. S. Pettit. 1996. "Physical Discipline among African American and European American Mothers: Links to Children's Externalizing Behaviors." *Developmental Psychology* 32: 1065–72.

———. 1998. "Multiple Risk Factors in the Development of Externalizing Behavior Problems: Group and Individual Differences." *Development and Psychopathology* 10: 469–93.

Decker, S., and B. VanWinkle. 1996. *Life in the Gang.* Los Angeles: Roxbury Press.

Depew, R. 1992. "Policing Native Communities: Some Principles and Issues in Organizational Theory." *Canadian Journal of Criminology* 34: 461–78.

Derber, C. 1996. *The Wilding of America.* New York: St. Martin's Press.

Dixon, J., and A. J. Lizotte. 1987. "Gun Ownership and the Southern Subculture of Violence." *American Journal of Sociology* 93, 2: 383–405.

Dobash, R., and R. Dobash. 1979. *Violence against Wives.* New York: Free Press.

———. 1984. "The Nature and Antecedents of Violent Events." *British Journal of Criminology* 24: 269–88.

———. 1992. *Women, Violence, and Social Change.* London: Routledge.

Donahue, M., and P. Benson. 1995. "Religion and the Well-Being of Adolescents." *Journal of Social Issues* 51: 145–60.

Douglass, F. 1845/1960. *Narrative of the Life of Frederick Douglass, An American Slave, Written by Himself.* Cambridge, MA: Belknap Press.

Downs, D. 1996. *More Than Victims.* Chicago: University of Chicago Press.

Doyle, J. A. 1989. *The Male Experience.* Dubuque, IA: W. C. Brown.

Drake, S. C., and H. R. Cayton. 1945/1962. *Black Metropolis: A Study of Negro Life in a Northern City.* New York: Harper and Row.

Drinkwater, L. R. 1993. "Honor and Student Misconduct in Southern Antebellum Colleges." *Southern Humanities Review* XXVII, 4: 323–44.

Driscoll, A., and T. Henderson. 2001, March 31. "In Dade, Latin Percentage Highest in the Nation." *The Miami Herald,* p. 1a.

Du Bois, C. 1972. "Dominant Profile of American Culture." In *Culture and School,* ed. R. Shinn, 76–85. San Francisco, CA: Intext.

Du Bois, W. E. B. 1899. *The Philadelphia Negro: A Social Study.* New York: Benjamin Blom.

———. 1982. *The Souls of Black Folk.* New York: New American Library.

———. 1996. *The Philadelphia Negro: A Social Study.* Philadelphia: University of Pennsylvania Press.

Duff, A. 1993. *Maori: The Crisis and the Challenge.* Auckland: HarperCollins.

Dumont, J. 1993. "Justice and Aboriginal People." In *Aboriginal Peoples and the Justice System,* Royal Commission on Aboriginal Peoples. Ottawa: Ministry of Supply and Services.

Duncan, L. S. W. 1970. *Crime by Polynesians in Auckland: An Analysis of Charges Laid against Persons in 1966.* Unpublished M. A. Thesis, University of Auckland.

Dunn, M. 1997. *Black Miami in the Twentieth Century.* Gainesville: University Press of Florida.

Dutton, D. 1995. *The Domestic Assault of Women: Psychological and Criminal Justice Perspectives.* Vancouver, BC: UBC Press.

Dutton, D. G., K. Saunders, A. Starzomski, and K. Bartholomew. 1995. "Intimacy, Anger and Insecure Attachments as Precursors of Abuse in Intimate Relationships." *Journal of Applied Social Psychology* 24: 1367–86.

Earls, F., J. I. Escobar, and M. M. Spero. 1991. "Suicide in Minority Groups: Epidemiologic and Cultural Perspectives." In *Suicide Over the Life Cycle: Risk Factors, Assessment and Treatment of Suicidal Patients,* ed. S. J. Blumenthal and D. J. Kupfer, 571–98. Washington, DC: American Psychiatric Press.

Edelbroch, C. S., and T. M. Achenbach. 1984. "The Teacher Version of the Child Behavior Profile: Boys Aged Six through Eleven." *Journal of Consulting and Clinical Psychology* 52: 207–17.

Elder, G., Jr. 1994. "Time, Human Agency, and Social Change: Perspectives on the Life Course." *Social Psychology Quarterly* 57: 4–15.

Eldridge, L. D. 1995. "Before Zenger: Truth and Seditious Speech in Colonial America, 1607–1700." *The American Journal of Legal History* 39, 3 (July): 337–58.

Elkins, S. 1959. *Slavery.* New York: Grossett and Dunlap.

Elley, W. B., and J. C. Irving. 1976. "Revised Socio-Economic Index for New Zealand." *New Zealand Journal of Educational Studies* 11: 25–36.

Elliott, D. S. 1994. "Serious Violent Offenders: Onset, Developmental Course and Termination." *Criminology* 32: 1–21.

Elliott, D. S., and S. S. Ageton. 1980. "Reconciling Race and Class Differences in Self-Reported and Official Estimates of Delinquency." *American Sociological Review* 45: 95–110.

Elliott, D. S., S. S. Ageton, D. Huizinga, B. A. Knowles, and R. J. Canter. 1983. *The Prevalence and Incidence of Delinquent Behavior: 1976–1980.* Boulder, CO: Behavioral Research Institute.

Elliott, D. S., and D. Huizinga. 1989. "Improving Self-Reported Measures of Delinquency." In *Cross-National Research in Self-Reported Crime and Delinquency,* ed. M. W. Klein. Dordrecht: Kluwer Academic.

Elliott, D. S., D. Huizinga, and S. S. Ageton. 1985. *Explaining Delinquency and Drug Use.* Beverly Hills, CA: Sage.

Elliott, D. S., W. J. Wilson, D. Huizinga, R. J. Sampson, A. Elliot., and B. Rankin. 1996. "The Effects of Neighborhood Disadvantage on Adolescent Development." *Journal of Research in Crime and Delinquency* 33, 4: 389–426.

Ellis, L. 1990. "Introduction: The Nature of the Biosocial Perspective." In *Crime in Biological, Social and Moral Contexts,* ed. L. Ellis and H. Hoffman, 3–17. New York: Praeger.

Ellis, L., and A. Walsh. 1997. "Gene-Based Evolutionary Theories in Criminology." *Criminology* 35: 229–76.

Ellison, C. G. 1991. "An Eye for an Eye? A Note on the Southern Subculture of Violence Thesis." *Social Forces* 69, 4: 1223–39.

Ellison, C. 1992. "Are Religious People Nice People? Evidence from the National Survey on Black Americans." *Social Forces* 71: 411–30.

Enright, R. D., and the Human Development Study Group. 1991. "The Moral Development of Forgiveness." In *Handbook of Moral Behavior and Development: Theory (Volume 1)*, ed. W. M. Kurtines and J. S. Gewirtz. Hillsdale, NJ: LEA.

Ensminger, M. E., S. G. Kellan, and B. R. Rubin. 1983. "School and Family Origins of Delinquency: Comparisons by Sex." In *Prospective Studies of Crime and Delinquency*, ed. K. T. Van Dusen and S. A. Mednick, 73–97. Boston: Kluwer-Nijhoff.

Epstein, G., and R. Greene. 1993. "Dade's Crime Rate is Highest in U.S., Florida is 1st among States." *The Miami Herald*, October 3.

Esscok-Vitale, S. M., and M. T. McGuire. 1985. "Women's Lives Viewed from an Evolutionary Perspective, I: Sexual Histories, Reproductive Success, and Demographic Characteristics of a Random Sample of American Women." *Etiology and Sociobiology* 6: 137–54.

Etzioni, A. 1996. *The New Golden Rule: Community and Morality in a Democratic Society*. New York: Basic Books.

Fagan, J. 1996. *The Criminalization of Domestic Violence: Promises and Limits*. Research Report. Washington, DC: National Institute of Justice.

Fagan, J., and A. Browne. 1994. "Violence between Spouses and Intimates: Physical Aggression between Women and Men in Intimate Relationships." In *Understanding and Preventing Violence, Vol. 3*, National Research Council, 115–292. Washington, DC: National Academy Press.

Falk, W., and B. Rankin. 1992. "The Cost of Being Black in the Black Belt." *Social Problems* 39: 299–313.

Fanon, F. 1967. *Black Sin, White Masks*. New York: Grove Press.

———. 1968. *The Wretched of the Earth*. New York: Grove Press.

Faretra, G. 1981. "A Profile of Aggression from Adolescence to Adulthood: An 18-Year Follow-up of Psychiatrically Disturbed and Violent Adolescents." *American Journal of Orthopsychiatry* 51, 3 (July): 439–53.

Farley, R., and W. H. Frey. 1994. "Changes in the Segregation of Whites from Blacks during the 1980s: Small Steps toward a More Integrated Society." *American Sociological Review* 59: 23–45.

Farrington, D. P. 1986. "Stepping Stones to Adult Criminal Careers." In *Development of Antisocial and Prosocial Behavior*, ed. D. Olweus, J. Block, and M. Radke-Yarrow, 359–84. New York: Academic Press.

———. 1989. "Self-Reported and Official Offending from Adolescence to Adulthood." In *Cross-National Research in Self-Reported Crime and Delinquency*, ed. M. W. Klein, 399–423. Dordrecht, Netherlands: Kluwer.

———. 1991. "Longitudinal Research Strategies: Advantages, Problems and Prospects. *Journal of the American Academy of Child and Adolescent Psychiatry* 30: 369–74.

———. 1992. "Explaining the Beginning, Progress, and Ending of Antisocial Behavior from Birth to Adulthood." In *Facts, Frameworks, and Forecasts: Advances in Criminological Theory, Volume 3*, ed. J. McCord, 253–86. New Brunswick, NJ: Transaction Press.

———. 1998. "Predictors, Causes and Correlates of Male Youth Violence." In *Youth Violence*, ed. M. Tonry and M. H. Moore, 421–75. Chicago, University of Chicago Press.

Farrington, D. P., and R. Loeber. 1989. "Relative Improvement over Chance (RIOC) and Phi as Measures of Predictive Efficiency and Strength of Association in 2 × 2 Tables." *Journal of Quantitative Criminology* 5: 201–13.

———. 1999. "Transatlantic Replicability of Risk Factors in the Development of Delinquency." In *Historical and Geographical Influences on Psychopathology,* ed. P. Cohen, C. Slomkowski, and L. N. Robins, 299–329. Mahwah, NJ: Lawrence Erlbaum.

———. 2000. "Some Benefits of Dichotomization in Psychiatric and Criminological Research." *Criminal Behavior and Mental Health* 10: 102–24.

Farrington, D. P., R. Loeber, M. Stouthamer-Loeber, W. van Kammen, and L. Schmidt. 1996. "Self-Reported Delinquency and a Combined Delinquency Seriousness Scale Based on Boys, Mothers, and Teachers: Concurrent and Predictive Validity for African Americans and Caucasians." *Criminology* 34: 493–517.

Feagin, J. R., and M. P. Sikes. 1994. *Living with Racism: The Black Middle-Class Experience.* Boston: Beacon Press.

Feagin, J. R., and H. Vera. 1995. *White Racism.* New York: Routledge.

Federal Bureau of Investigation. 1995. *Crime in the United States.* Washington, DC: U.S. Department of Justice.

———. 1998. *Crime in the United States 1997.* Washington, DC: U.S. Government Printing Office.

———. 1998. "Murder and Nonnegligent Manslaughter." *Crime in the United States.* Retrieved online from: http://www.fbi.gov/ucr98cius.htm. Section 1, page 2.

———. Multiple Years. *Uniform Crime Reports.* Washington, DC: U.S. Government Printing Office.

Fekete, L. 1991. "The Far Right in Europe: A Guide." *Race and Class* 32/3, January–March.

Felson, R. B. 1993. "Predatory and Dispute-Related Violence: A Social Interactionist Approach." In *Routine Activity and Rational Choice, Volume 5,* ed. R. V. Clarke and M. Felson, 103–25. New Brunswick: Transaction Publishers.

Felson, R., W. Baccaglini, and G. Gmelch. 1986. "Bar-Room Brawls." In *Violent Transactions,* ed. A. Campbell and J. Gibbs, 153–66. Oxford: Basil Blackwell.

Fergusson, D. M., A. A. Donnell, and S. W. Slater. 1975. *The Effects of Race and Socio-Economic Status on Juvenile Offending Statistics.* Wellington, New Zealand: Government Printer.

Fergusson, D. M., J. E. Fergusson, L. J. Horwood, and N. G. Kinzett. 1988. "A Longitudinal Study of Dentine Lead Levels, Intelligence, School Performance and Behaviour. Part III. Dentine Lead Levels and Attention/Activity." *Journal of Child Psychology and Psychiatry* 29: 811–24.

Fergusson, D. M., J. Fleming, and D. P. O'Neill. 1972. *Child Abuse in New Zealand.* Wellington, New Zealand: Department of Social Welfare.

Fergusson, D. M., L. J. Horwood, and M. T. Lynskey. 1992. "Family Change, Parental Discord and Early Offending." *Journal of Child Psychology and Psychiatry* 33: 1059–75.

————. 1993. "Ethnicity and Bias in Police Contact Statistics." *Australian and New Zealand Journal of Criminology* 26: 193–206.

————. 1993. "Ethnicity, Social Background, and Young Offending: A 14-Year Longitudinal Study." *Australian and New Zealand Journal of Criminology* 26: 155–70.

————. 1994. "The Childhoods of Multiple Problem Adolescents: A 15-Year Longitudinal Study." *Journal of Child Psychology and Psychiatry* 35: 1077–92.

————. 1994. "Parental Separation, Adolescent Psychopathology, and Problem Behaviors." *Journal of the American Academy of Child and Adolescent Psychiatry* 33: 1122–33.

Fergusson, D. M., and M. Lloyd. 1991. "Smoking during Pregnancy and Effects on Child Cognitive Ability from the Ages of 8 to 12 Years." *Paediatric and Perinatal Epidemiology* 3: 278–301.

Fergusson, D. M., and M. T. Lynskey. 1997. "Physical Punishment/Maltreatment during Childhood and Adjustment in Young Adulthood." *Child Abuse and Neglect* 21: 789–803.

Field, S. 1990. *Trends in Crime and Their Interpretation.* Home Office Study No. 119. London: HMSO.

Fienberg, S. E. 1984. *The Analysis of Cross-Classified Categorical Data.* Cambridge, MA: MIT Press.

Fifield, J. K., and A. A. Donnell. 1980. *Socio-Economic Status, Race, and Offending in New Zealand. Research Report No. 6.* Wellington, New Zealand: Government Printer.

Fine, G., and S. Kleinman. 1979. "Rethinking Subculture: An Interactionist Analysis." *American Journal of Sociology* 85: 1–20.

Fingerhut, L. A., D. D. Ingram, and J. J. Feldman. 1992. "Firearm Homicide among Black Teenage Males in Metropolitan Counties." *Journal of the American Medical Association* 267: 3054–8.

Fischer, D. H. 1989. *Albion's Seed: Four British Folkways in America.* New York: Oxford University Press.

Fischer, J. 1976. "Homicide in Detroit." *Criminology* 14: 387–400.

Fitzgerald, M., and C. Hale. 1996. *Ethnic Minorities, Victimisation, and Racial Harassment: Findings from the 1988 and 1992 British Crime Surveys.* Home Office Research Study No. 154. London: HMSO.

Fitzpatrick, K. M., and J. P. Boldizar. 1993. "The Prevalence and Consequences of Exposure to Violence among African American Youth." *Journal of the American Academy of Child and Adolescent Psychiatry* 32: 424–30.

Fleiss, J. L. 1981. *Statistical Methods for Rates and Proportions (2nd edition).* New York: Wiley.

Fordham, S., and J. U. Ogbu. 1986. "Black Students' School Success: Coping with the Burden of Acting White." *Urban Review* 18: 176–206.

Fowles, R., and M. Merva. 1996. "Wage Inequality and Criminal Activity: An Extreme Bounds Analysis for the United States, 1975–1990." *Criminology* 34, 2: 163–82.

Fox, J. 1991. *Regression Diagnostics: An Introduction.* Newbury Park, CA: Sage.

Fox, J. A., and M. W. Zawitz. 1998. *Homicide Trends in the United States*. Washington, DC: U.S. Department of Justice.

Franklin, C. W. 1984. *The Changing Definition of Masculinity*. New York: Plenum.

———. 1987. "Surviving the Institutional Decimation of Black Males: Causes, Consequences, and Intervention." In *The Making of Masculinities*, ed. H. Brod, 155–69. Boston: Allen and Unwin.

Franklin, J. H. 1956. *The Militant South, 1800–1861*. Cambridge, MA: Belknap Press of Harvard University Press.

Franklin, J. H., and A. A. Moss. 1988. *From Slavery to Freedom: A History of Negro Americans (6th edition)*. New York: Alfred A. Knopf.

Frazier, E. F. 1939. *The Negro Family in the United States*. Chicago: University of Chicago Press.

Freeman, R. B. 1996. "Why Do So Many Young American Men Commit Crimes and What Might We Do About It?" *Journal of Economic Perspectives* 10: 25–42.

Fryer, P. 1984. *Staying Power: The History of Black People in Britain*. London: Pluto.

Gale, D. E. 1996. *Understanding Urban Unrest: From Reverend King to Rodney King*. Thousand Oaks, CA: Sage.

Gans, H. J. 1992. "Second Generation Decline: Scenarios for the Economic and Ethnic Futures of the Post-1965 American Immigrants." *Ethnic and Racial Studies* 15: 173–92.

———. 1995. *The War Against the Poor, the Underclass, and Antipoverty Policy*. New York: Basic Books.

Garrison, C. Z., R. E. McKeown, R. F. Valois, and M. L. Vincent. 1993. "Aggression, Substance Use and Suicidal Behaviors in High School Students." *American Journal of Public Health* 83, 2: 179–84.

Garvey, A. 1923. *The Philosophy and Opinions of Marcus Garvey*. New York: Atheneum.

Gary, L. 1986. "Drinking, Homicide, and the Black Male." *Journal of Black Studies* 17: 15–31.

Gastil, R. D. 1971. "Homicide and a Regional Culture of Violence." *American Sociological Review* 36: 412–27.

Gayford, J. J. 1975. "Wife Battering: A Preliminary Survey of 100 Cases." *British Medical Journal* 25: 194–7.

Geertz, C. 1973. *The Interpretations of Cultures*. New York: Basic Books.

Gelles, R. 1997. *Intimate Violence in Families (3rd edition)*. Thousand Oaks, CA: Sage.

Gelles, R. J., and M. Strauss. 1988. "Compassion or Control: Legal, Social, and Medical Services." In *Intimate Violence: The Definitive Study of the Causes and Consequences of Abuse in the American Family*, ed. R. J. Gelles and M. Strauss, 160–82. New York: Simon and Schuster.

———, eds. 1988. *Intimate Violence: The Definitive Study of the Causes and Consequences of Abuse in the American Family*. New York: Simon and Schuster.

Genn, J. 1988. "Multiple Victimisation." In *Victims of Crime: A New Deal?*, ed. M. Maguire and J. Pointing, 90–100. Milton Keynes: Open University Press.

Genovese, E. D. 1972. *Roll, Jordan, Roll: The World the Slaves Made*. New York: Vintage Press.

Georges-Abeyie, D. E. 1981. "Studying Black Crime: A Realistic Approach." In *Environmental Criminology*, ed. P. J. Brantingham and P. L. Brantingham, 97–109. Beverly Hills, CA: Sage Publications.

Gibbs, J. T. 1988. *Young, Black, and Male in America: An Endangered Species.* New York: Auburn House.

———. 1994. "Anger in Young Black Males: Victims or Victimizers?" In *The American Black Male*, ed. R. J. Majors and J. U. Gordon, 127–43. Chicago: Nelson-Hall.

Giddens, A. 1984. *The Constitution of Society.* Cambridge: Cambridge University Press.

Gilroy, P. 1993. *Small Acts: Thoughts on the Politics of Black Cultures.* London: Serpent's Tail.

Ginzburg, R. 1988. *100 Years of Lynchings.* Baltimore, MD: Black Classic Press.

Glasgow, D. G. 1980. *The Black Underclass.* New York: Vintage Books.

Glickman, N. J., M. Lahr, and E. Wyly. 1998. *The State of the Nation's Cities: Database and Machine-Readable File Documentation.* Center for Urban Policy Research. Rutgers: The State University of New Jersey.

Gold, M. 1966. "Undetected Delinquent Behavior." *Journal of Research in Crime and Delinquency* 12, 1: 27–46.

Goldberg, C. 1997, January 30. "Hispanic Households Struggle as Poorest of the Poor in U.S." *New York Times*, p. A1.

Golden, R. M., and S. F. Messner. 1987. "Dimensions of Racial Inequality and Rates of Violent Crime." *Criminology* 25: 525–41.

Goldhagen, D. J. 1996. *Hitler's Willing Executioners: Ordinary Germans and the Holocaust.* New York: Alfred A. Knopf.

Goldstein, P. 1989. "Drugs and Violent Crime." In *Pathways to Criminal Violence*, ed. N. Weiner and M. Wolfgang, 16–48. Newbury Park, CA: Sage Publications.

Goldstein, P. J., et al. 1989. "Crack and Homicide in New York City, 1988: A Conceptually Based Event Analysis." *Contemporary Drug Problems* 13: 651–87.

Gondolf, E., and E. Fisher. 1988. *Battered Women as Survivors: An Alternate to Treating Learned Helplessness.* Lexington, MA: Lexington Books.

Gondolf, E., E. Fisher, and J. R. McFerron. 1988. "Racial Differences among Shelter Residents: A Comparison of Anglo, Black and Hispanic Battered Women." *Journal of Family Violence* 30, 1: 39–51.

Gordon, L. 1988. *Heroes of Their Own Lives. The Politics and History of Family Violence.* New York: Viking.

Gordon, P. 1990. *Racial Violence and Harassment (2nd edition).* London: Runnymede Trust.

Gordon, R. A. 1968. "Issues in Multiple Regression." *American Journal of Sociology* 73: 592–616.

Gorn, E. J. 1985. " 'Gouge and Bite, Pull Hair and Scratch': The Social Significance of Fighting in the Southern Backcountry." *The American Historical Review* 90, 1: 18–43.

Gottdiener, M., and J. Feagin. 1988. "The Paradigm Shift in Urban Sociology." *Urban Affairs Quarterly* 24: 163–87.

Gottfredson, D. C., and C. S. Koper. 1996. "Race and Sex Differences in the Prediction of Drug Use." *Journal of Consulting and Clinical Psychology* 64: 305–13.

Gottfredson, D. C., R. J. McNeil, and G. D. Gottfredson. 1991. "Social Area Influences on Delinquency: A Multi-Level Analysis." *Journal of Research on Crime and Delinquency* 28: 197–226.

Gottfredson, M., and T. Hirschi. 1990. *A General Theory of Crime.* Stanford: Stanford University Press.

Gove, W. 1980. *The Labeling of Deviance: Evaluation of a Perspective (2nd edition).* Beverly Hills, CA: Sage Publications.

Grady-Willis, W. A. 1998. "The Black Panther Party: State Repression and Political Prisoners." In *The Black Panther Party Reconsidered,* ed. C. Jones, 363–89. Baltimore, MD: Black Classic Books.

Graef, R. 1989. *Talking Blues: The Police In Their Own Words.* London: Collins Harvill.

Graham, S., and C. Hudley. 1994. "Attributions of Aggressive and Nonaggressive African American Male Early Adolescents: A Study of Construct Accessibility." *Developmental Psychology* 30: 365–73.

Greenberg, K. S. 1996. *Honor and Slavery.* Princeton, NJ: Princeton University Press.

Greenfeld, L. A., M. Rand, D. Craven, et al. 1998. *Violence by Intimates: Analysis of Data on Crime by Current or Former Spouses, Boyfriends and Girlfriends.* Washington, DC: U.S. Department of Justice, Bureau of Justice Statistics.

Greenfeld, L. A., and S. K. Smith. 1999. *American Indians and Crime.* Washington, DC: U.S. Department of Justice, Bureau of Statistics.

Greenfield, P. M., and R. R. Cocking, eds. 1994. *Cross-Cultural Roots of Minority Child Development.* Hillsdale, NJ: LEA.

Grenier, G. J., and A. Stepick, III. 1992. "Introduction." In *Miami Now! Immigration, Ethnicity and Social Change,* ed. G. J. Grenier and A. Stepick, III. Gainesville: University Press of Florida.

Grier, W. H., and P. M. Cobbs. 1968/1992. *Black Rage.* New York: Basic Books.

———. 1971. *The Jesus Bag.* New York: McGraw-Hill.

Griffiths, C., and S. Verdun-Jones. 1994. *Canadian Criminal Justice (2nd edition).* Toronto: Harcourt Brace.

Gurr, T. R. 1977. "Contemporary Crime in Historical Perspective: A Comparative Study of London, Stockholm, and Sydney." *Annals of the American Academy of Political and Social Science* 434: 114–36.

———. 1981. "Historical Trends in Violent Crimes: A Critical Review of the Evidence." In *Crime and Justice, Volume 3,* ed. M. Tonry and N. Morris, 295–353. Chicago: University of Chicago Press.

———. 1989. *Violence in America.* Newbury Park, CA: Sage Publications.

Gyekye, K. 1996. *African Cultural Values: An Introduction.* Philadelphia, PA: Sankofa Publishing.

Hackney, S. 1969. "Southern Violence." *American Historical Review* LXXIV (February): 906–25.

Hagan, J. 1974. "Criminal Justice and Native People: A Study of Incarceration in a Canadian Province." *Canadian Review of Sociology and Anthropology.* Special Issue: 220–36.

———. 1975. "Locking Up the Indians: A Case for Law Reform." *Canadian Forum* 55: 16–18.

———. 1985. "Toward a Structural Theory of Crime, Race, and Gender: The Canadian Case." *Crime and Delinquency* 31: 129–46.

———. 1992. "The Poverty of a Classless Criminology – The American Society of Criminology 1991 Presidential Address." *Criminology* 30: 1–19.

Hagan, J., A. R. Gillis, and J. Chan. 1978. "Explaining Official Delinquency: A Spatial Study of Class, Conflict, and Control." *The Sociological Quarterly* 19: 386–98.

Hagan, J., and B. McCarthy. 1997. "Intergenerational Sanction Sequences and Trajectories of Street Crime Amplification." In *Stress and Adversity Over the Life Course: Trajectories and Turning Points,* ed. I. Gotlib and B. Wheaton, 73–90. New York: Cambridge University Press.

———. 1997. *Mean Streets: Youth Crime and Homelessness.* New York: Cambridge University Press.

Hagan, J., and A. Palloni. 1988. "Crimes as Social Events in the Life Course: Reconceiving a Criminological Controversy." *Criminology* 26: 87–100.

———. 1990. "The Social Reproduction of a Criminal Class in Working-Class London, Circa 1950–1980." *American Journal of Sociology* 96: 265–99.

———. 1998. "Immigration and Crime in the United States." In *The Immigration Debate,* ed. J. P. Smith and B. Edmonston, 367–87. Washington, DC: National Academy Press.

———. 1999. "Sociological Criminology and the Mythology of Hispanic Immigration and Crime." *Social Problems* 46: 617–32.

Hagan, J., and R. D. Peterson. 1995. "Criminal Inequality in America: Patterns and Consequences." In *Crime and Inequality,* ed. J. Hagan and R. D. Peterson, 14–36. Stanford, CA: Stanford University Press.

Hagedorn, J. M. 1994. "Homeboys, Dope Fiends, Legits and New Jacks." *Criminology* 32: 197–219.

———. 1997. "Homeboys, New Jacks, and Anomie." *Journal of African American Men* 3: 7–28.

———. 1998. *People and Folks: Gangs, Crime and the Underclass in a Rustbelt City (2nd edition).* Chicago: Lakeview Press.

Hall, J. D. 1993. *Revolt Against Chivalry: Jesse Daniel Ames and the Women's Campaign Against Lynching.* New York: Columbia University Press.

Hall, P., I. Tessero, and J. Earp. 1995. "Women's Experiences with Battering: A Conceptualization from Qualitative Research." *Women's Health Issues* 5, 4: 173–92.

Hamberger, L. K., J. M. Lohr, D. Bonge, and D. F. Tolin. 1997. "An Empirical Classification of Motivations for Domestic Violence." *Violence Against Women* 3, 4: 401–23.

Hamilton, R. F. 1972. *Class and Politics in the United States.* New York: John Wilcy and Sons.

Hamm, M. S. 1993. *American Skinheads: The Criminology and Control of Hate Crime.* Westport, CT: Praeger.

———, ed. 1993. *Hate Crime: International Perspectives on Causes and Control.* Academy of Criminal Justice Sciences: Anderson Publications.

Hammond, W. R., and B. Yung. 1993. "Psychology's Role in the Public Health

Response to Assaultive Violence among Young African American Men." *American Psychologist* 48: 142–54.

Hampton, R. 1974. *The Social Construction of Statistics: Labelling Theory Applied to the Police Decision to Prosecute Juveniles.* Paper presented to the 4th National Conference of the New Zealand Sociological Association. Auckland University.

———. 1987. "Family Violence and Homicides in the Black Community: Are They Linked?" In *Violence in the Black Family: Correlates and Consequences,* ed. R. L. Hampton, 90–105. Lexington, MA: DC Heath.

Hampton, R. L., and R. J. Gelles. 1994. "Violence toward Black Women in a Nationally Representative Sample of Black Families." *Journal of Comparative Family Studies* 25, 1: 105–19.

Hampton, R. L., R. J. Gelles, and J. W. Harrop. 1989. "Is Violence in Black Families Increasing? A Comparison of 1975 and 1985 National Survey Rates." *Journal of Marriage and the Family* 51: 969–80.

Hampton, R. L., and B. T. Yung. 1996. "Violence in Communities of Color. Where We Were, Where We Are and Where We Need To Be." In *Preventing Violence in America,* ed. R. L. Hampton, P. Jenkins, and T. P. Gullotta, 53–86. Thousand Oaks, CA: Sage.

Hannerz, U. 1969. *Soulside: Inquiries into Ghetto Culture.* New York: Columbia University Press.

Hare, N. 1964. "The Frustrated Masculinity of the Negro Male." *Negro Digest* 13: 5–9.

Harer, M. D., and D. Steffensmeier. 1992. "The Differing Effects of Economic Inequality on Black and White Rates of Violence." *Social Forces* 70: 1035–54.

Hargreaves, D. H. 1967. *Social Relations in Secondary School.* London: Tinling.

Harper, F. 1976. "Alcohol and Crime in Black America." In *Alcohol Abuse and Black America,* ed. F. Harper, 129–40. Alexandria, VA: Douglass Publishers.

Harper, P. B. 1996. *Are We Not Men? Masculine Anxiety and the Problem of African American Identity.* New York: Oxford University Press.

Harries, K., and A. Powell. 1994. "Juvenile Gun Crime and Social Stress: Baltimore, 1980–1990." *Urban Geography* 15, 1: 45–63.

Harris, A., and J. Shaw. 2000. "Looking for Patterns: Race, Class, and Crime." In *Criminology: A Contemporary Handbook,* ed. J. Sheley, 128–63. Belmont, CA: Wadsworth.

Harris, D. B. 1998. "The Logic of Black Urban Rebellions." *Journal of Black Studies* 28: 368–85.

Hart, D., M. Yates, S. Fegley, and G. Wilson. 1995. "Moral Commitment in Inner-City Adolescents." In *Morality in Everyday Life: Developmental Perspectives,* ed. M. Killen and D. Hart, 317–41. New York: Cambridge University Press.

Harvey, W. B. 1986. "Homicide among Young Black Adults: Life in the Subculture of Exasperation." In *Homicide Among Black Americans,* ed. D. F. Hawkins, 153–71. Lanham, MD: University Press of America.

Harway, M., and J. M. O'Neill, eds. 1999. *What Causes Men's Violence against Women?* Thousand Oaks, CA: Sage.

Hatcher, J. W. 1934. "Appalachian America." In *Culture in the South,* ed. W. T. Couch, 374–402. New York: Columbia University Press.

Hawkins, D. F. 1983. "Black and White Homicide Differentials: Alternatives to an Inadequate Theory." *Criminal Justice and Behavior* 10: 407–40.

———. 1986. "Black and White Homicide Differentials: Alternatives to an Inadequate Theory." In *Homicide Among Black Americans,* ed. D. F. Hawkins, 109–35. New York: University Press of America.

———, ed. 1986. *Homicide among Black Americans.* Lanham, MD: University Press of America.

———. 1987. "Beyond Anomalies: Rethinking the Conflict Perspective on Race and Criminal Punishment." *Social Forces* 65: 719–66.

———. 1987. "Devalued Lives and Racial Stereotypes: Ideological Barriers to the Prevention of Family Violence among Blacks." In *Violence in the Black Family,* ed. R. L. Hampton, 189–207. Lexington, MA: Lexington Books.

———. 1991. "Explaining the Black Homicide Rate." *Journal of Interpersonal Violence* 5 (June): 151–65.

———. 1993. "Crime and Ethnicity." In *The Socioeconomics of Crime and Justice,* ed. B. Forst, 89–120. Armonk, NY: M. E. Sharpe.

———. 1994. "Ethnicity: The Forgotten Dimension of American Social Control." In *Inequality, Crime, and Social Control,* ed. G. S. Bridges and M. A. Myers, 99–116. Boulder, CO: Westview.

———, ed. 1995a. *Ethnicity, Race and Crime: Perspectives across Time and Place.* Albany: State University of New York Press.

———. 1995b. "Ethnicity, Race and Crime: A Review of Selected Studies." In *Ethnicity, Race and Crime: Perspectives across Time and Place,* ed. D. F. Hawkins, 11–45. Albany: State University of New York Press.

———. 1997. "Building Peace in the Inner Cities." In *Violence: from Biology to Society,* ed. J. S. Grisolia et al., 161–70. Amsterdam: Elsevier.

———. 1999. "African Americans and Homicide." In *Studying and Preventing Homicide: Issues and Challenges,* ed. M. Smith and M. A. Zahn, 143–58. Thousand Oaks, CA: Sage Publications.

———. 1999. "What Can We Learn from Data Disaggregation? The Case of Homicide and African Americans." In *Homicide – A Sourcebook of Social Research,* ed. M. D. Smith and M. A. Zahn, 195–210. Thousand Oaks, CA: Sage Publications.

Hawkins, D. F., J. H. Laub, and J. L. Lauritsen. 1998. "Race, Ethnicity, and Serious Juvenile Offending." In *Serious and Violent Juvenile Offenders: Risk Factors and Successful Interventions,* ed. R. Loeber and D. P. Farrington, 30–46. Thousand Oaks, CA: Sage.

Hawkins, J. D., T. Herrenkohl, D. P. Farrington, D. Brewer, R. F. Catalano, and T. W. Harachi. 1998. "A Review of Predictors of Youth Violence." In *Serious and Violent Juvenile Offenders: Risk Factors and Successful Interventions,* ed. R. Loeber and D. P. Farrington, 106–46. Thousand Oaks, CA: Sage.

Hawkins, J. D., and D. M. Lishner. 1987. "Schooling and Delinquency." In *Handbook on Crime and Delinquency Prevention,* ed. E. H. Johnson, 179–221. Westport, CT: Greenwood Press.

Hawley, F. F. 1987. "The Black Legend in Southern Studies: Violence, Ideology, and Academe." *North American Culture* 3, 1: 29–52.

Hawley, F. F., and S. F. Messner. 1989. "The Southern Violence Construct: A Review of Arguments, Evidence, and the Normative Context." *Justice Quarterly* 6, 4 (December): 481–511.

Haymes, S. N. 1995. *Race, Culture, and the City, A Pedagogy for the Black Urban Struggle.* Albany: State University of New York Press.

Heimer, K. 1997. "Socioeconomic Status, Subcultural Definitions, and Violent Delinquency." *Social Forces* 75, 3: 799–833.

Henry, A. F., and J. F. Short, Jr. 1954. *Suicide and Homicide: Some Economic, Sociological, and Psychological Aspects of Aggression.* Glencoe, IL: Free Press.

Herman, J. L. 1992. *Trauma and Recovery.* New York: Basic Books.

Hernton, C. 1965. *Sex and Racism in America.* Garden City, NY: Doubleday.

Herrnstein, R. J., and C. Murray. 1994. *The Bell Curve.* New York: Free Press.

Hesse, B., C. D. K. Rai, C. Bennett, and P. McGilchrist. 1992. *Beneath the Surface: Racial Harassment.* Aldershot: Avebury.

Hill, C., and D. Brosnan. 1984. "The Occupational Distribution of the Major Ethnic Groups in New Zealand." *New Zealand Population Review* 10: 33–42.

Hill, P. 1992. *Coming of Age: African-American Rites of Passage.* Chicago: African American Images.

Hindelang, M. 1978. "Race and Involvement in Common Law Personal Crimes." *American Sociological Review* 46: 93–109.

Hindelang, M., M. R. Gottfredson, and J. Garofalo. 1978. *Criminal Victimization in Eight American Cities: A Descriptive Analysis of Common Theft and Assault.* Cambridge, MA: Ballinger Publishing.

———. 1978. *Victims of Personal Crime: An Empirical Foundation for a Theory of Victimization.* Cambridge, MA: Ballinger Publishing.

Hindelang, M., T. Hirschi, and J. Weis. 1979. "Correlates of Delinquency: The Illusion of Discrepancy between Self-Report and Official Measures." *American Sociological Review* 44: 995–1014.

———. 1981. *Measuring Delinquency.* Beverly Hills, CA: Sage Publications.

Hine, D. C. 1989. "Rape and the Inner Lives of Black Women in the Middle West." *Signs* 14: 912–20.

Hirsch, A. R. 1983. *Making the Second Ghetto: Race and Housing in Chicago, 1940–1960.* Cambridge: Cambridge University Press.

Hirschi, T. 1969. *Causes of Delinquency.* Berkeley: University of California Press.

Hirschi, T., and M. Hindelang. 1977. "Intelligence and Delinquency: A Revisionist Review." *American Sociological Review* 42: 471–586.

Hoberman, J. 1997. *Darwin's Athletes: How Sport Has Damaged Black America and Preserved the Myth of Race.* New York: Houghton Mifflin.

Hodes, M. 1993. "The Sexualization of Reconstruction Politics: White Women and Black Men in the South after the Civil War." In *American Sexual Politics: Sex, Gender, and Race since the Civil War,* ed. J. C. Fout and M. S. Tantillo, 59–74. Chicago and London: University of Chicago Press.

Hoffer, P. C. 1989. "Honor and the Roots of American Litigiousness." *The American Journal of Legal History* 33, 4 (October): 295–319.

Hoffman, M. L. 1987. "The Contribution of Empathy to Justice and Moral Judgment." In *Empathy and Its Development,* ed. N. Eisenberg and J. Strayer, 47–80. New York: Cambridge University Press.

Hoffman, M. S., ed. 1991. *The World Almanac and Book of Facts, 1992.* New York: Pharos.

Hollingshead, A. B. 1975. *Four Factor Index of Social Status.* Unpublished Manuscript.

Holmes, S. 1996, October 13. "For Hispanic Poor, No Silver Lining." *New York Times,* p. E5.

Home Office. 1981. *Racial Attacks.* London: Home Office.

———. 1996. *Taking Steps: Multi-Agency Responses to Racial Attacks and Harassment: The Third Report of the Inter-Departmental Racial Attacks Group.* London: Home Office.

———. 1999. *Action Plan: Response to the Stephen Lawrence Inquiry.* London: HMSO.

hooks, bell. 1989. *Talking Back: Thinking Feminist, Thinking Black.* Boston: South End Press.

———. 1992. *Black Looks: Race and Representation.* Boston: South End Press.

Horowitz, R. 1983. *Honor and the American Dream: Culture and Identity in a Chicano Community.* New Brunswick, NJ: Rutgers University Press.

Horton, J. 1972. "Time and Cool People." In *Rappin' and Stylin' Out,* ed. T. Kochman, 19–31. Urbana: University of Illinois Press.

Hotaling, G. T., and D. B. Sugarman. 1990. "A Risk Marker Analysis of Assaulted Wives." *Journal of Family Violence* 5, 1: 1–13.

Houf, H. 1945. *What Religion Is and Does: An Introduction to the Study of Its Problems and Values.* New York: Guilford Press.

Houston Chronicle. (Electronic database.) Houston, TX: Author (Producer and Distributor).

Houston Police Department. 1996. *Houston Homicides, 1984–1994.* Houston, TX: Homicide Division.

Hsieh, C., and M. D. Pugh. 1993. "Poverty, Income Inequality, and Violent Crime: A Meta-Analysis of Recent Aggregate Data Studies." *Criminal Justice Review* 18: 182–202.

Hudson, J. 1972. "The Hustling Ethic." In *Rappin' and Stylin' Out,* ed. T. Kochman, 410–24. Urbana: University of Illinois Press.

Huggins, N. I. 1977/1990. *Black Odyssey: The African American Ordeal in Slavery.* New York: Random House.

Hughes, D., and L. Chen. 1997. "When and What Parents Tell Children about Race: An Examination of Race-Related Socialization among African American Families." *Applied Developmental Science* 1: 200–14.

Huisinga, D., and D. S. Elliott. 1986. "Reassessing the Reliability and Validity of Self-Report Measures." *Journal of Quantitative Criminology* 2: 293–327.

Huizinga, D., F. Esbensen, and A. W. Weiher. 1991. "Are There Multiple Paths to Delinquency?" *Journal of Criminal Law and Criminology* 82: 83–118.

Human Rights Watch. 1997. *Racist Violence in the United Kingdom.* London: Human Rights Watch Helsinki.

Humphrey, J. A., and S. Palmer. 1986. "Race, Sex, and Criminal Homicide: Offender-Victim Relationships." In *Homicide among Black Americans,* ed. D. F. Hawkins, 57–67. New York: University Press of America.

Humphries, M., B. Parker, and R. J. Jagers. 2000. "Predictors of Moral Maturity among African American Children." *Journal of Black Psychology* 26, 1: 51–64.

Hunter, A., and J. E. Davis. 1994. "Hidden Voices of Black Men: The Meaning, Structures, and Complexity of Manhood." *Journal of Black Studies* 25: 20–40.

Husbands, C. 1983. *Racial Exclusionism and the City: The Urban Support for the National Front.* London: Allen and Unwin.

Institute of Race Relations. 1987. *Policing against Black People.* London: IRR.

Jackson, J. 1973. "But Where Are the Men?" In *Contemporary Black Thought, The Best from The Black Scholar,* ed. R. Chrisman and N. Hare, 158–167. New York: Bobbs-Merrill.

Jackson, K. T. 1985. *Crabgrass Frontier: The Suburbanization of the United States.* New York: Oxford University Press.

Jackson, M. 1988. *The Maori and the Criminal Justice System, A New Perspective: He Whaipaanga Hou, Part 1.* Wellington, New Zealand: Department of Justice.

———. 1988. *The Maori and the Criminal Justice System, A New Perspective: He Whaipaanga Hou, Part 2.* Wellington, New Zealand: Department of Justice.

Jacobs, J., and K. Potter. 1998. *Hate Crimes: Criminal Law and Identity Politics.* New York: Oxford University Press.

Jaffe, P. G., D. A. Wolfe, and S. K. Wilson. 1990. *Children of Battered Women.* Newbury Park, CA: Sage.

Jagers, R. J. 1996. "Culture and Problem Behaviors among Inner-City African American Youth: Further Explorations." *Journal of Adolescence* 19: 371–81.

———. 1997. "Afrocultural Integrity and the Social Development of African American Children: Some Conceptual, Empirical, and Practical Considerations." *Journal of Prevention and Intervention in the Community* 16: 7–34.

Jagers, R. J., and L. O. Mock. 1993. "Culture and Social Outcomes among Inner-City African American Children: An Afrographic Exploration." *Journal of Black Psychology* 19: 391–405.

———. 1995. "The Communalism Scale and Collectivistic-Individualistic Tendencies: Some Preliminary Findings." *Journal of Black Psychology* 21: 153–67.

Jagers, R. J., L. O. Mock, and P. Smith. In Preparation. "Cultural and Race-Related Factors Associated with Youth Violence."

Jagers, R. J., and P. Smith. 1996. "Further Examination of the Spirituality Scale." *Journal of Black Psychology* 22: 429–42.

Jagers, R. J., P. Smith, L. O. Mock, and E. Dill. 1997. "An Afrocultural Social Ethos: Component Orientations and Some Social Implications." *Journal of Black Psychology* 23: 328–43.

Jah, Y., and S. Shah' Keyah. 1995. *Uprising.* New York: Scribner.

Jargowsky, P. A. 1996. "Beyond the Street Corner: The Hidden Diversity of High Poverty Neighborhoods." *Urban Geography* 17, 7: 579–603.

Jargowsky, P. A., and M. J. Bane. 1991. "Ghetto Poverty in the United States." In *The Urban Underclass,* ed. C. Jencks and P. E. Peterson, 235–73. Washington, DC: The Brookings Institution.

Jaynes, G. D., and R. M. Williams. 1989. *A Common Destiny: Blacks and American Society.* Washington, DC: National Academy Press.

Jencks, C. 1994. *Rethinking Social Policy.* Cambridge, MA: Harvard University Press.

Jenkins, E., and C. C. Bell. 1997. "Exposure and Response to Community Violence among Children and Adolescents." In *Children in a Violent Society,* ed. J. Osofsky, 9–31. New York: Guilford Press.

Jenkinson, J. 1996. "The 1919 Riots." In *Racial Violence in Britain (2nd edition),* ed. P. Panayi. London: Leicester University Press/Printer.

Jenness, V., and K. Broad. 1997. *Hate Crimes: New Social Movements and the Politics of Violence.* New York: Aldine de Gruyter.

Jensen, E. 1993. "International Nazi Cooperation: A Terrorist-Oriented Network." In *Racist Violence in Europe,* ed. T. Bjorgo and R. Witte, 80–96. London: Macmillan.

Joe, T., and P. Yu. 1984. *The Flip-Side of Black Families Headed by Women: The Economic Status of Black Men.* Washington, DC: Center for the Study of Social and Budget Priorities.

Johnson, C. 1993. "Wounded Killers." *Focus* (February): 3–5.

Johnson, C. J. 1997. *The Structural Determinants of Homicide: Chicago 1970, 1980, and 1990.* University of Maryland, College Park. Doctoral Dissertation.

Johnson, G. 1941. "The Negro and Crime." *Annals of the American Academy of Political and Social Science* 27: 93–104.

Johnson, R., and P. S. Leighton. 1995. "Black Genocide? Preliminary Thoughts on the Plight of Americana's Poor Black Men." *Journal of African American Men* 1: 3–21.

Jones, A. 1994. *Next Time, She'll Be Dead. Battering and How to Stop It.* New York: Beacon Press.

Jones, A., and S. Schecter. 1992. *When Love Goes Wrong.* New York: HarperCollins.

Jones, J. M. 1972. *Prejudice and Racism.* Reading, MA: Addison-Wesley.

Jones, T., B. D. Maclean, and J. Young. 1986. *The Islington Crime Survey: Crime, Victimisation and Policing in Inner City London.* Aldershot: Gower.

Jourard, S. 1971. "Some Lethal Aspects of the Male Role." In *Self-Disclosure: An Experimental Analysis of the Transparent Self,* ed. S. Jourard, 34–41. New York: Wiley.

Kambon, K. K. K. 1992. *The African Personality in America: An African-Centered Framework.* Tallahassee, FL: Nubian Nation Publications.

Kantor, G. K., J. L. Jasinki, and E. Aldarondo. 1994. "Sociocultural Status and Incidence of Marital Violence in Hispanic Families." *Violence and Victims* 9, 3: 207–22.

Kanuha, V. 1997. "Domestic Violence, Racism, and the Battered Women's Movement in the U.S." In *Future Interventions with Battered Women and Their Families,* ed. J. Edelson and Z. Eisikovitz. Thousand Oaks, CA: Sage Publications.

Kardiner, A., and L. Ovesey. 1962. *The Mark of Oppression: Explorations in the Personality of the American Negro.* Cleveland: World Publishing Company.

Karenga, M. 1980. *Kawaida Theory: An Introductory Outline.* Inglewood, CA: Kawaida Publications.

———. 1988. *The African American Holiday of Kwanzaa.* Los Angeles: University of Sankore Press.

———. 1988. "Black Studies and the Problematic of Paradigm – The Philosophical Dimension." *Journal of Black Studies* 18: 395–414.

———. 1990. "The African Intellectual and the Problem of Class Suicide: Ideological and Political Dimensions." In *African Culture: Rhythms of Unity,* ed. M. Asante and K. Asante, 91–106. Trenton, NJ: Africa World Press.

Kasarda, J. D. 1989. "Urban Industrial Transition and the Underclass." *Annals of the American Academy of Political and Social Sciences* 501: 26–47.

———. 1993. "Inner-City Concentrated Poverty and Neighborhood Distress: 1970 to 1990." *Housing Policy Debate* 24: 215–41.

Kasarda, J. D., and M. Janowitz. 1974. "Community Attachment in Mass Society." *American Sociological Review* 39: 328–39.

———. 1993. "Urban Industrial Transition and the Underclass." In *The Ghetto Underclass,* ed. W. J. Wilson, 43–64. Newbury Park, CA: Sage Publications.

Katz, J. 1988. *Seductions of Crime.* New York: Basic Books.

Katz, M. R. 1995. *Improving Poor People, the Welfare State, the "Underclass," and Urban Schools as History.* Princeton, NJ: Princeton University Press.

Kaufman, J., and E. Zigler. 1987. "Do Abused Children Become Abused Parents?" *American Journal of Orthopsychiatry* 57, 2: 186–93.

Keiser, R. L. 1979. *The Vice Lords: Warriors of the Streets.* New York: Holt, Rinehart, and Winston.

Kellam, S. G., J. D. Branch, K. C. Agrawal, and M. E. Ensminger. 1975. *Mental Health and Going to School: The Woodlawn Program of Assessment, Early Intervention and Evaluation.* Chicago: University of Chicago Press.

Kellam, S. G., C. H. Brown, B. R. Rubin, and M. E. Ensminger. 1983. "Paths Leading to Teenage Psychiatric Symptoms and Substance Use: Developmental Epidemiological Studies in Woodlawn." In *Childhood Psychopathology and Development,* ed. S. B. Guze, F. J. Earls, and J. E. Barrett, 17–51. New York: Raven Press.

Kellam, S. G., M. B. Simon, and M. E. Ensminger. 1983. "Antecedents in First Grade of Teenage Substance Use and Psychological Well-Being: A Ten-Year Community-Wide Prospective Study." In *Origins of Psychopathology,* ed. D. F. Ricks and B. S. Dohrenwend, 17–42. Cambridge: Cambridge University Press.

Kelley, M. L., T. G. Power, and D. D. Wimbush. 1992. "Determinants of Disciplinary Practices in Low-Income Black Mothers." *Child Development* 63: 573–82.

Kelley, R. D. G. 1994. *Race Rebels. Culture, Politics and the Black Working Class.* New York: Free Press.

Kelly, L. 1987. "The Continuum of Sexual Violence." In *Women, Violence and Social Control,* ed. J. Hamner and M. Maynard. London: Macmillan.

Kelman, H. C., and V. L. Hamilton. 1989. *Crimes of Obedience: Toward a Social Psychology of Authority and Responsibility.* New Haven, CT: Yale University Press.

Kelsey, J. 1984. "Legal Imperialism and the Colonization of Aotearoa." In *Tauiwi: Racism and Ethnicity in New Zealand,* ed. P. Spoonley, C. MacPhearson, D. Pearson, and C. Sedgewick, 15–43. Palmerston North, New Zealand: Dunmore Press.

Kennedy, D. M. 1996. "Can We Still Afford to be a Nation of Immigrants?" *The Atlantic Monthly* 278 (November): 52–4, 56, 58, 61, 64, 65–8.

Kierner, C. A. 1996. "Hospitality, Sociability, and Gender in the Southern Colonies." *The Journal of Southern History* LXII, 3: 449–80.

Kimmel, M. 1996. *Manhood in America: A Cultural History.* New York: Free Press.

King, A. J. 1991. "The Law of Slander in Early Antebellum America." *The American Journal of Legal History* 35, 1 (January): 1–43.

King, M. L., Jr. 1958. *Stride Toward Freedom: The Montgomery Story.* New York: Harper and Row.

———. 1968. *Where Do We Go from Here: Chaos or Community?* Boston: Beacon Books.

Kirshenman, J., and K. M. Neckerman. 1991. " 'We'd love to hire them, but . . .' The Meaning of Race to Employers." In *The Ghetto Underclass,* ed. C. Jencks and P. E. Peterson, 203–32. Washington, DC: The Brookings Institution.

Klaus, P. A., and M. R. Rand. 1984. *Family Violence.* Washington, DC: Bureau of Justice Statistics.

Klein, M., C. T. Maxson, and L. C. Cunningham. 1991. "Crack, Street Gangs, and Violence." *Criminology* 29, 4: 623–49.

Klein, M. W., C. T. Maxson, and J. Miller, eds. 1995. *The Modern Gang Reader.* Los Angeles: Roxbury Publishing.

Klier, J. D. 1993. "The Pogrom Tradition in Eastern Europe." In *Racist Violence in Europe,* ed. T. Bjorgo and R. Witte, 128–38. London: Macmillan.

Knowles, L. L., and K. Prewitt. 1968. *Institutional Racism in America.* Englewood Cliffs, NJ: Prentice Hall.

Koeniger, A. C. 1988. "Climate and Southern Distinctiveness." *The Journal of Southern History* LIV, 1: 21–44.

Kornhauser, R. R. 1977. *Social Sources of Delinquency: An Appraisal of Analytic Models.* Chicago: University of Chicago Press.

Koss, M. P., et al. 1994. *No Safe Haven: Male Violence against Women at Home, at Work and in the Community.* Washington, DC: American Psychological Association.

Kotch, J. B., D. J. Chalmers, J. L. Fanslow, S. Marshall, and J. D. Langley. 1993. "Morbidity and Death Due to Child Abuse in New Zealand." *Child Abuse and Neglect* 17: 233–47.

Kowalski, G. S., and T. A. Petee. 1991. "Sunbelt Effects on Homicide Rates." *Sociology and Social Research* 75: 73–9.

Krisberg, B., et al. 1986. *The Incarceration of Minority Youth.* Minneapolis: H. H. Humphrey Institute of Public Affairs, University of Minnesota.

Krivo, L. J., and R. D. Peterson. 1996. "Extremely Disadvantaged Neighborhoods and Urban Crime." *Social Forces* 75, 2 (December): 619–48.

Kugler, K. E., and W. H. Jones. 1992. "On Conceptualizing and Assessing Guilt." *Journal of Personality and Social Psychology* 62: 318–27.

LaFree, G. 1995. "Race and Crime Trends in the United States, 1946–1900." In *Ethnicity, Race, and Crime: Perspectives Across Time and Place* ed. D. F. Hawkins, 169–93. Albany: State University of New York Press.

LaFree, G., K. A. Drass, and P. O'Day. 1992. "Race and Crime in Postwar America: Determinants of African-American and White Rates, 1957–1988." *Criminology* 30, 2: 157–85.

Lamm, R. D., and G. Imhoff. 1985. *The Immigration Time Bomb: The Fragmenting of America.* New York: Truman Talley.

Lamont, M. 1999. "Introduction: Beyond Taking Culture Seriously." In *The Cultural Territories of Race: Black and White Boundaries,* ed. M. Lamont, ix–xx. Chicago: University of Chicago Press.

Land, K., P. L. McCall, and L. E. Cohen. 1990. "Structural Covariates of Homicide Rates: Are There Any Invariances Across Time and Social Space?" *American Journal of Sociology* 95: 922–63.

Lane, R. 1979. *Violent Death in the City: Suicide, Accident and Murder in Nineteenth Century Philadelphia.* Cambridge, MA: Harvard University Press.

———. 1986. *Roots of Violence in Black Philadelphia 1860–1900.* Cambridge, MA: Harvard University Press.

———. 1997. *Murder in America: A History.* Columbus: Ohio State University Press.

LaPrairie, C. 1994. *Seen But Not Heard: Native People in the Inner City. Reports #1–3, Aboriginal Justice Directorate.* Ottawa: Department of Justice.

Larzelere, R. E., and G. R. Patterson. 1990. "Parental Management: Mediator of the Effect of Socio-Economic Status on Early Delinquency." *Criminology* 28: 301–24.

Lattimore, P. K., J. Trudeau, J. K. Riley, J. Leiter, and S. Edwards. 1997. *Homicide in Eight U.S. Cities: Trends, Context, and Policy Implications* (NCJ 167262). Washington, DC: U.S. Department of Justice.

Le Blanc, M., and R. Leber. 1998. "Developmental Criminology Updated." In *Crime and Justice: A Review of Research, Volume 23,* ed. M. Tonry, 115–98. Chicago: University of Chicago Press.

Lee, C. D. 1994. "African-Centered Pedagogy: Complexities and Possibilities." In *Too Much Schooling, Too Little Education: A Paradox of Black Life in White Societies,* ed. M. J. Shujaa, 295–318. Trenton, NJ: African World Press.

Lee, M. T., R. Martinez, Jr., and R. Rosenfeld. 2001. "Does Immigration Increase Homicide Rates? Negative Evidence from Three Border Cities." *The Sociological Quarterly* 42, 4: 559–80.

Lee, M. T., R. Martinez, Jr., and S. F. Rodriguez. 2000. "Contrasting Latinos in Homicide Research: The Victim and Offender Relationship in El Paso and Miami." *Social Science Quarterly* 81: 375–88.

Lentzer, H. R., and M. DeBerry. 1980. *Intimate Victims: A Study of Violence among Friends and Relatives.* Washington, DC: U.S. Department of Justice, Bureau of Justice Statistics.

Leonard, K. E., and H. T. Blane. 1992. "Alcohol and Marital Aggression in a National Sample of Young Men." *Journal of Interpersonal Violence* 7, 1: 19–30.

Levine, F. J., and K. J. Rosich. 1996. *Social Causes of Violence: Crafting a Science Agenda.* Washington, DC: American Sociological Association.

Levinger, G. 1965. "Sources of Marital Dissatisfaction among Applicants for Divorce (1965)." *American Journal of Orthopsychiatry* 36, 5: 803–7.

Levy, B. 1968. "Cops in the Ghetto: A Problem of the Police System." In *Riots and Rebellion: Civil Violence in the Urban Community,* ed. L. H. Masotti and D. K. Bowen, 347–58. Beverly Hills, CA: Sage Publications.

Leyba, C. 1988. "Homicides in Bernalillo County 1978–1982." In *Research Conference on Violence and Homicide in Hispanic Communities,* ed. J. Kraus, S. B. Sorenson, and P. D. Juarez, 101–19. Los Angeles: UCLA Publication Services.

Lichter, D. 1989. "Race, Employment, Hardship, and Inequality in the American Nonmetropolitan South." *American Sociological Review* 54: 436–46.

Lieberson, S. 1980. *A Piece of the Pie: Black and White Immigrants Since 1980.* Berkeley: University of California Press.

Liebow, E. 1967. *Tally's Corner.* Boston: Little, Brown, and Company.

Liska, A. E., and M. D. Reed. 1985. "Ties to Conventional Institutions and Delinquency: Estimating Reciprocal Effects." *American Sociological Review* 50 (August): 547–60.

Lockhart, L. 1985. "Methodological Issues in Comparative Racial Analysis: The Case of Wife Abuse." *Social Work Research and Abstracts* 21: 35–41.

———. 1987. "A Reexamination of the Effects of Race and Social Class on the Incidence of Marital Violence: A Search for Reliable Differences." *Journal of Marriage and the Family* 49, 3: 603–10.

Lockhart, L., and B. W. White. 1989. "Understanding Marital Violence in the Black Community." *Journal of Interpersonal Violence* 49: 421–36.

Loeber, R. 1982. "The Stability of Antisocial and Delinquent Child Behavior: A Review." *Child Development* 53: 1431–46.

Loeber, R., D. P. Farrington, M. Stouthamer-Loeber, and W. B. van Kammen. 1998. *Antisocial Behavior and Mental Health Problems: Explanatory Factors in Childhood and Adolescence.* Mahwah, NJ: Lawrence Erlbaum.

Loeber, R., and K. Keenan. 1994. "Interaction between Conduct Disorder and Its Comorbid Conditions: Effects of Age and Gender." *Clinical Psychology Review* 14: 497–523.

Loeber, R., and M. LeBlanc. 1990. "Toward a Developmental Criminology." In *Crime and Justice: A Review of Research, Volume 12,* ed. M. Tonry and N. Morris, 375–437. Chicago: University of Chicago Press.

Loeber, R., M. Stouthamer-Loeber, W. B. van Kammen, and D. P. Farrington. 1989. "Development of a New Measure of Self-Reported Antisocial Behavior for Young Children: Prevalence and Reliability." In *Cross-National Research in Self-Reported Crime and Delinquency,* ed. M. W. Klein, 203–25. Dordrecht, Netherlands: Kluwer.

Loftin, C., and R. Hill. 1974. "Regional Subculture and Homicide: An Examination of the Gastil-Hackney Thesis. *American Sociological Review* 39: 714–24.

Loftin, C., and R. N. Parker. 1985. "An Errors-in-Variable Model of the Effect of Poverty on Urban Homicide Rates." *Criminology* 23: 269–87.

Logan, J. R., and S. F. Messner. 1987. "Racial Residential Segregation and Suburban Violent Crime." *Social Science Quarterly* 68: 510–27.

Logan, J., and H. Molotch. 1987. *Urban Fortunes: The Political Economy of Place.* Berkeley: University of California Press.

Lombroso, C. 1876. *L'Uomo Delinquente (The Criminal Man).* Milan: Hoepli.

Long, J. S. 1997. *Regression Models for Categorical and Limited Dependent Variables.* Thousand Oaks, CA: Sage.

Loow, H. 1993. "The Cult of Violence: The Swedish Racist Counterculture." In *Racist Violence in Europe,* ed. T. Bjorgo and R. Witte, 62–79. London: Macmillan.

Loseke, D. 1992. *The Battered Woman and Shelters.* Rutgers: State University of New Jersey Press.

Lovell, R., and M. Norris. 1990. *One in Four: Offending from Age Ten to Twenty-four in a Cohort of New Zealand Males.* Wellington, New Zealand: Department of Social Welfare.

Luckenbill, D. F. 1977. "Criminal Homicide as a Situated Transaction." *Social Problems* 25: 176–86.

Luckenbill, D., and D. Doyle. 1989. "Structural Position and Violence." *Criminology* 27, 3: 419–36.

Lujan, C., L. DeBruyn, P. May, and M. Bird. 1989. "Profile of Abused and Neglected American Indian Children in the Southwest." *Child Abuse and Neglect* 13: 449–61.

Lundsgaarde, H. P. 1977. *Murder in Space City: A Cultural Analysis of Houston Homicide Patterns.* New York: Oxford University Press.

McAdoo, H. 1979. "Black Kinship." *Psychology Today* 12 (May): 67–70.

McCarthy, B., and J. Hagan. 1992. "Mean Streets: The Theoretical Significance of Situational Delinquency among Homeless Youths." *American Journal of Sociology* 98: 597–627.

McCartney, J. T. 1992. *Black Power Ideologies: An Essay on African American Political Thought.* Philadelphia, PA: Temple University Press.

McClain, P. 1981. "Social and Environmental Characteristics of Black Female Homicide Offenders." *The Western Journal of Black Studies* 5: 224–30.

McCord, J. 1983. "A Longitudinal Study of Aggression and Antisocial Behavior." In *Prospective Studies of Crime and Delinquency,* ed. K. T. Van Dusen and S. A. Mednick, 269–75. Boston: Kluwer-Nijhoff.

———. 1994. "Family Socialization and Antisocial Behavior: Searching for Causal Relationships in Longitudinal Research." In *Cross-National Longitudinal Research on Human Development and Criminal Behavior,* ed. G. M. Weitekamp and H. J. Kerner, 217–27. Dordrecht, Netherlands: Kluwer.

———. 1997. "Placing American Urban Violence in Context." In *Violence and Childhood in the Inner City,* ed. J. McCord, 78–115. New York: Cambridge University Press.

———. 1997. *Violence and Childhood in the Inner City (edited volume).* New York: Cambridge University Press.

McLaurin, M. A. 1993 [1991]. *Celia, A Slave.* New York: Avon Books.

McLeer, S. V., and R. Anwar. 1989. "A Study of Women Presenting in an Emergency Department." *American Journal of Public Health* 79: 65–7.

MacLeod, J. *Ain't No Making It.* Boulder, CO: Westview Press.

McLeod, J. D., C. Kruttschnitt, and M. Dornfeld. 1994. "Does Parenting Explain the Effects of Structural Conditions on Children's Antisocial Behavior? A Comparison of Blacks and Whites." *Social Forces* 73: 575–604.

MacPherson, W. (advised by T. Cook, S. Wells, and J. Sentamu). 1998. *The Stephen Lawrence Inquiry.* London: HMSO.

McWhiney, G. 1988. *Cracker Culture: Celtic Ways in the Old South.* Tuscaloosa and London: The University of Alabama Press.

Madhubuti, J. 1990. *Black Men – Single, Dangerous, and Obsolete.* Chicago: Third World Press.

Magnet, M. 1993. *The Dream and the Nightmare, the Sixties Legacy to the Underclass.* New York: William Morrow.

Magnusson, D., B. Klinteberg, and H. Stattin. 1992. "Autonomic Activity/Reactivity, Behavior, and Crime in a Longitudinal Perspective." In *Facts, Frameworks, and Forecasts: Advances in Criminological Theory, Volume 3,* ed. J. McCord, 287–318. New Brunswick, NJ: Transaction Press.

Maguin, E., and R. Loeber. 1996. "Academic Performance and Delinquency." In *Crime and Justice: A Review of Research, Volume 20,* ed. M. Tonry, 145–264. Chicago: University of Chicago Press.

Maguire, K., and A. L. Pastore, eds. 1997. *Sourcebook of Criminal Justice Statistics.* [Online].

Majors, R., and J. Mancini-Billson. 1992. *Cool Pose: The Dilemmas of Black Manhood in America.* New York: Touchstone.

Malik, M. 1999. "Racist Crime: Racially Aggravated Offences in the Crime and Disorder Act, 1998, Part II." *Modern Law Review* 62: 409–24.

Malveaux, J. 1988. "The Economic Status of Black Families." *Black Families (2nd edition),* ed. H. P. McAdoo, 133–47. Thousand Oaks, CA: Sage Publications.

Mann, C. R. 1996. *When Women Kill.* Albany: State University of New York Press.

Mantsios, G. 1992. "Rewards and Opportunities: The Politics and Economics of Class in the U.S." In *Race, Class, and Gender in the United States: An Integrated Study (2nd edition),* ed. P. S. Rothenberg, 96–110. New York: St. Martin's Press.

Marable, M. 1991. *Race, Reform, and Rebellion: The Second Reconstruction of Black America, 1945–1990.* Jackson: University Press of Mississippi.

———. 1996. *Speaking Truth to Power: Essays on Race, Resistance, and Radicalism.* Boulder, CO: Westview Press.

Marshall, I. H., ed. 1997. *Minorities, Migrants, and Crime: Diversity and Similarity Across Europe and the United States.* Thousand Oaks, CA: Sage Publications.

Martin, D. 1976. *Battered Wives.* San Francisco: Glide Publications.

Martinez, R. A., Jr. 1996. *Examining Ethnicity in Victim-Offender Homicides: The Case of Miami in the 1990s.* Paper presented at the Annual Conference of the Homicide Research Working Group. Santa Monica, CA, June.

———. 1996. "Latinos and Lethal Violence: The Impact of Poverty and Inequality." *Social Problems* 43, 2 (May): 131–46.

———. 1997. "Homicide among Miami's Ethnic Groups: Anglos, Blacks, and Latinos in the 1990s." *Homicide Studies* 1, 1 (February): 17–34.

———. 1997. "Homicide among the 1980 Mariel Refugees in Miami: Victims and Offenders." *Hispanic Journal of Behavioral Sciences* 19 (May): 107–22.

Martinez, R., Jr., and M. T. Lee. 1998. "Immigration and the Ethnic Distribution of Homicide in Miami, 1985–1995." *Homicide Studies* 2 (August): 291–304.

———. 1999. "Extending Ethnicity in Homicide Research: The Case of Latinos." In *Homicide: A Sourcebook of Social Research,* ed. M. D. Smith and M. A. Zahn, 211–20. Thousand Oaks, CA: Sage Publications.

———. 2000a. "On Immigration and Crime." In *Criminal Justice 2000: The Changing Nature of Crime, Vol. 1.* Washington, DC: National Institute of Justice.

———. 2000b. "Comparing the Context of Immigrant Homicides in Miami: Haitians, Jamaicans, and Mariels." *International Migration Review* 3: 793–811.

Martinez, R., Jr., M. T. Lee, and A. L. Nielsen. 2001. "Revisiting the Scarface Legacy: The Victim/Offender Relationship and Mariel Homicides in Miami." *Hispanic Journal of Behavioral Sciences* 23: 37–56.

Martinez-Garcia, A. T. 1988. "Culture and Wife-Battering among Hispanics in New Mexico." In *Research Conference on Violence and Homicide in Hispanic Communities,* ed. J. F. Kraus, S. B. Sorenson, and P. D. Juarez, 205–14. Los Angeles: UCLA Publication Services.

Massey, D. 1990. "American Apartheid: Segregation and the Making of the Underclass." *American Journal of Sociology* 96: 329–57.

———. 1995. "Getting Away with Murder: Segregation and Violent Crime in Urban America." *University of Pennsylvania Law Review* 143, 5 (May): 1203–32.

Massey, D. S., and N. A. Denton. 1987. "Trends in the Residential Segregation of Blacks, Hispanics, and Asians: 1970–1980." *American Sociological Review* 52 (December): 802–25.

———. 1993. *American Apartheid: Segregation and the Making of the Underclass.* Cambridge, MA: Harvard University Press.

Massey, D. S., and M. Eggers. 1990. "The Ecology of Inequality: Minorities and the Concentration of Poverty, 1970–1980." *American Journal of Sociology* 95, 5: 1153–88.

Massey, D. S., A. B. Gross, and K. Shibuya. 1994. "Migration, Segregation, and the Spatial Concentration of Poverty." *American Sociological Review* 95: 425–45.

Matsueda, R. L., and K. Heimer. 1987. "Race, Family Structure and Delinquency: A Test of Differential Association and Social Control Theories." *American Sociological Review* 52: 826–40.

Mattis, J. 1997. "The Spiritual Well-Being of African Americans: A Preliminary Analysis." *Journal of Prevention and Intervention in the Community* 16: 103–20.

———. 2000. "Religion and African American Political Life." *Political Psychology,* Special Issue: "Psychology as Politics," 22, 2: 263–78.

Mattis, J., and R. J. Jagers. In press. "Toward a Relational Framework for the Study of Religiosity and Spirituality in the Lives of African Americans." *Journal of Community Psychology.*

Maxson, C. L., and M. W. Klein. 1995. "Street Gang Violence: Twice as Great, or Half as Great." In *The Modern Gang Reader,* ed. M. W. Klein, C. L. Maxson, and J. Miller, 24–32. Los Angeles: Roxbury Publishing.

May, R., and R. Cohen. 1974. "The Interaction between Race and Colonialism: A Case Study of the Liverpool Race Riots of 1919." *Race and Class* 16, 2: 111–26.

Mayhew, P., D. Elliott, and L. Dowds. 1989. *The British Crime Survey: Home Office Research Study No. 111.* London: HMSO.

Maynard, W., and T. Read. 1997. *Policing Racially Motivated Incidents: Police Research Group Crime Detection and Prevention Series, No. 59.* London: Home Office.

Mbiti, J. S. 1970. *African Religions and Philosophy.* New York: Doubleday.

McBride, D. C., C. Burgman-Habermehl, J. Alpert, and D. D. Chitwood. 1986. "Drugs and Homicide." *Bulletin of the New York Academy of Medicine* 62: 497–508.

Memmi, A. 1965. *The Colonizer and the Colonized.* Boston: Orien Press.

Menjivar, C. 2000. *Fragmented Ties: Salvadoran Immigrant Networks in America.* Berkeley: University of California Press.

Menkiti, I. A. 1984. "Person and Community in African Traditional Thought." In *African Philosophy: An Introduction (3rd edition),* ed. R. A. Wright, 171–81. Lanham, MD: University of American Press.

Mercy, J., and L. Salzman. 1989. "Fatal Violence among Spouses in the U.S., 1976–1985." *American Journal of Public Health* 79, 5: 595–9.

Merton, R. K. 1938. "Social Structure and Anomie." *American Sociological Review* 3: 672–82.

———. 1968. *Social Theory and Social Structure.* New York: Free Press.

Messerschmidt, J. W. 1993. *Masculinities and Crime.* Lanham, MD: Roman and Littlefield.

Messner, S. F. 1982. "Poverty, Inequality, and the Urban Homicide Rate: Some Unexpected Findings." *Criminology* 29: 329–44.

———. 1983. "Regional and Racial Effects on the Urban Homicide Rate: The Subculture of Violence Revisited." *American Journal of Sociology* 88: 997–1007.

———. 1997. "A Review Essay of 'Culture of Honor: The Psychology of Violence in the South' by R. E. Nisbett and D. Cohen." *American Journal of Sociology* 102, 4: 1225–7.

Messner, S. F., and R. M. Golden. 1992. "Racial Inequality and Racially Disaggregated Homicide Rates: An Assessment of Alternative Theoretical Explanations." *Criminology* 30: 421–47.

Messner, S. F., and R. Rosenfeld. 1997. *Crime and the American Dream (2nd edition).* Albany, NY: Wadsworth Publishing.

———. 1999. "Social Structure and Homicide – Theory and Research." In *Homicide – A Sourcebook of Social Research,* ed. M. D. Smith and M. A. Zahn, 27–41. Thousand Oaks, CA: Sage Publications.

Messner, S. F., and K. Tardiff. 1986. "Economic Inequality and Levels of Homicide: An Analysis of Urban Neighborhoods." *Criminology* 24: 297–317.

Miler, T. R., M. A. Cohen, and B. Wiersema. 1996. *Victim Costs and Consequences.* Washington, DC: National Institute of Justice.

Miller, J. G. 1997. *Search and Destroy: African-American Males in the Criminal Justice System*. New York: Cambridge University Press.

Miller, W. 1958. "Lower Class Culture as a Generating Milieu of Gang Delinquency." *Journal of Social Issues* 14: 5–19.

Mills, C. W. 1959. *The Sociological Imagination*. New York: Oxford University Press.

———. 1963. "Two Styles of Social Science Research." In *Power, Politics, and People: The Collected Essays of C. Wright Mills*, ed. I. L. Horowitz, 553–67. New York: Ballantine.

Milner, C., and R. Milner. 1972. *Black Players – The Secret World of Black Pimps*. New York: Little, Brown, and Co.

Mladenka, K., and K. Hill. 1976. "A Reexamination of the Etiology of Urban Crime." *Criminology* 13: 491–506.

Moffit, T. R. 1990. "The Neuropsychology of Juvenile Delinquency: A Critical Review." In *Crime and Justice: A Review of Research, Volume 12*, ed. M. Tonry and N. Morris, 99–169. Chicago: University of Chicago Press.

Molotch, H. 1988. "Strategies and Constraints of Growth Elites." In *Business Elites and Urban Development*, ed. S. Cummings, 25–48. Albany: State University of New York Press.

Monk, D. H. 1981. "Toward a Multilevel Perspective on the Allocation of Educational Resources." *Review of Educational Research* 51: 215–36.

Monkkonnen, E. 1995. "Racial Factors in New York City Homicides." In *Ethnicity, Race, and Crime: Perspectives across Time and Place*, ed. D. F. Hawkins, 99–120. Albany: State University of New York Press.

Montagu, A. 1997. *Man's Most Dangerous Myth: The Fallacy of Race (6th edition)*. Walnut Creek, CA: AltaMira Press.

Moore, J., and R. Pinderhughes, eds. 1993. *In the Barrios: Latinos and the Underclass Debate*. New York: Russell Sage Foundation.

Moore, J., and J. D. Vigil. 1993. "Barrios in Transition." In *In the Barrios: Latinos and the Underclass Debate*, ed. J. Moore and R. Pinderhughes, 27–49. New York: Russell Sage Foundation.

Moore, K. A., and D. Glei. 1995. "Taking the Plunge: An Examination of Positive Youth Development." *Journal of Adolescent Research* 10: 15–40.

Morenhoff, J. D., and R. J. Sampson. 1997. "Violent Crime and the Spatial Dynamics of Neighborhood Transition: Chicago." *Social Forces* 76, 1: 31–64.

Morenoff, J. D., R. J. Sampson, and S. W. Raudenbush. 2001. "Neighborhood Inequality, Collective Efficacy, and the Spatial Dynamics of Urban Violence." *Criminology*, 39: 517–60.

Morgan, E. S. 1975. *American Slavery, American Freedom: The Ordeal of Colonial Virginia*. New York: W. W. Norton.

Morrison, T. 1996. *Paradise*. New York: Knopf.

Moynihan, D. P. 1965. *The Negro Family: The Case for National Action*. Washington, DC: U.S. Department of Labor.

Murray, C. A. 1984. *Losing Ground: American Social Policy*. New York: Basic Books.

Myers, L. J. 1991. "Expanding the Psychology of Knowledge Optimally: The Importance of World View Revisited." In *Black Psychology (3rd edition)*, ed. R. L. Jones, 15–28. Berkeley, CA: Cobb and Henry.

Myers, M. A. 1995. "The New South's 'New' Black Criminal: Rape and Punishment in Georgia, 1870–1940." In *Ethnicity, Race, and Crime: Perspectives across Time and Place,* ed. D. F. Hawkins, 145–66. Albany: State University of New York Press.

Myrdal, G. 1944. *An American Dilemma: The Negro Problem and Modern Democracy, Volume 1.* New York: Harper and Row.

Naison, M. 1992. "Outlaw Culture and Black Neighborhoods." *Reconstruction* 1: 128–31.

National Center for Health Statistics. 1998. *Health, United States, 1998.* Rockville, MD: U.S. Department of Health and Human Services.

Neff, J. A., B. Holamon, and T. D. Schluter. 1995. "Spousal Violence among Anglos, Blacks and Mexican Americans: The Role of Demographical? Variables, Psychosocial Predictors and Alcohol Consumption." *Journal of Marriage and the Family* 10, 1: 1–21.

Nelsen, C., J. Corzine, and L. Huff-Corzine. 1994. "The Violent West Reexamined: A Research Note on Regional Homicide Rates." *Criminology* 32, 1 (February): 149–61.

Neugebauer-Visano, R. 1996. "Kids, Cops, and Colour: The Social Organization of Police-Minority Youth Relations." In *Not a Kid Anymore: Canadian Youth, Crime, and Subcultures,* ed. G. O'Bireck, 283–308. Toronto: Nelson.

Neville, H., and A. Pugh. 1997. "General and Culture Specific Factors Influencing African American Women's Reporting Patterns and Perceived Social Support Following Sexual Assault." *Violence Against Victims* 3, 4 (August): 361–81.

Newbold, G. 1992. *Crime and Deviance.* Auckland, New Zealand: Oxford University Press.

Newham Monitoring Project. 1991. *Forging a Black Community: Asian and Afro-Caribbean Struggles in Newham.* London: Newham Monitoring Project/ Campaign Against Racism and Fascism.

New Haven Register. December 19, 1996. "Crimes against Women Are on the Rise." Page A9.

Newton, H. P. 1973. *Revolutionary Suicide.* New York: Harcourt Brace Jovanovich.

New Zealand Council for Educational Research. 1988. "How Fair is New Zealand Education?" *Royal Commission on Social Policy, The April Report, Vol. III, Part 2.* Wellington, New Zealand: Government Press.

Nielsen, M. 1992. "Introduction." In *Aboriginal Peoples and Canadian Criminal Justice,* ed. R. Silverman and M. Nielsen, 3–10. Toronto: Butterworths.

———. 1996. "Contextualization for Native American Crime and Criminal Justice Involvement." In *Native Americans, Crime, and Justice,* ed. M. Nielsen and R. Silverman, 10–19. Boulder, CO: Westview Press.

Nielsen, M., and R. Silverman, eds. 1996. *Native Americans, Crime, and Justice.* Boulder, CO: Westview Press.

Nightingale, C. H. 1993. *On the Edge, A History of Poor Black Children and Their American Dreams.* New York: Basic Books.

Nisbett, R. E., and D. Cohen. 1996. *Culture of Honor: The Psychology of Violence in the South.* Boulder, CO: Westview Press.

Nobles, W. W. 1991. "African Philosophy: Foundations of African Psychology." In *Black Psychology (3rd edition)*, ed. R. L. Jones, 47–64. Berkeley, CA: Cobb and Henry.

Norton-Taylor, R., ed. 1999. *Colour of Justice*. London: Theatre Communication Group.

O'Brien, P. H. 1995. *Impact of a Stay in a Battered Woman's Shelter on the Self-Perceptions of Women of Color*. Ph.D. Dissertation in Sociology, University of Illinois at Chicago.

O'Carroll, P. W., and J. A. Mercy. 1989. "Regional Variation in Homicide Rates: Why is the *West* So Violent?" *Violence and Victims* 4, 1: 17–25.

Ogbu, J. 1985. "A Cultural Ecology of Competence among Inner City Blacks." In *Beginnings: The Social and Affective Development of Black Children*, ed. M. Spencer, G. Brookins, and W. Allen, 45–66. Hillsdale, NJ: LEA.

Okun, Lewis. 1986. *Woman Abuse: Facts Replacing Myths*. Albany: State University of New York Press.

O'Leary, K. D. 1993. "Through a Psychological Lens: Personality Traits, Personality Disorders, and Levels of Violence." In *Current Controversies on Family Violence*, ed. R. J. Gelles and D. R. Loseke, 7–30. Newbury Park, CA: Sage.

Oliver, W. 1984. "Black Males and the Tough Guy Image: A Dysfunctional Compensatory Adaptation." *Western Journal of Black Studies* 8: 199–203.

———. 1989. "Black Males and Social Problems: Prevention through Afrocentric Socialization." *Journal of Black Studies* 20: 15–39.

———. 1994. *The Violent Social World of Black Men*. New York: Lexington Books.

———. 1998. *The Violent Social World of Black Men*. San Francisco: Jossey-Bass.

Olzak, S. 1992. *The Dynamics of Ethnic Competition and Conflict*. Stanford, CA: Stanford University Press.

Osgood, W. 2000. "Poisson-Based Regression Analysis of Aggregate Crime Rates." *Journal of Quantitative Criminology* 16: 21–43.

Osofsky, J. D. 1995. "The Effects of Exposure to Violence on Young Children." *American Psychologist* 50: 782–8.

Ousey, G. C. 1999. "Homicide, Structural Factors, and the Racial Invariance Assumption." *Criminology* 37, 2: 405–25.

Panayi, P. 1996. *Racial Violence in Britain (2nd edition)*. London: Leicester University Press/Printer.

Pargament, K. 1997. *The Psychology of Religion and Coping: Theory, Research, Practice*. New York: Guilford Press.

Parker, G., H. Tupling, and L. B. Brown. 1979. "A Parental Bonding Instrument." *British Journal of Medical Psychology* 52: 1–10.

Parker, K. F., and P. L. McCall. 1999. "Structural Conditions and Racial Homicide Patterns: A Look at the Multiple Disadvantages in Urban Areas." *Criminology* 37: 447–77.

Parker, R. N. 1989. "Poverty, Subculture of Violence, and Type of Homicide." *Social Forces* 67: 983–1007.

Parnas, R. 1967. "The Police Response to the Domestic Disturbance." *Wisconsin Law Review* 914, 2 (Fall): 914–60.

Paschall, M. J., S. T. Ennett, and R. L. Flewelling. 1996. "Relationships among Family Characteristics and Violent Behavior by Black and White Male Adolescents." *Journal of Youth and Adolescence* 25: 177–97.

Paschall, M. J., R. L. Flewelling, and S. T. Ennett. 1998. "Racial Differences in Violent Behavior among Young Adults: Moderating and Confounding Effects." *Journal of Research in Crime and Delinquency* 35: 148–65.

Paternoster, R., and L. Iovanni. 1989. "The Labeling Perspective and Delinquency: An Elaboration of the Theory and Assessment of the Evidence." *Justice Quarterly* 6: 359–94.

Pattillo-McCoy, M. 1999. *Black Picket Fences: Privilege and Peril among the Black Middle Class.* Chicago: University of Chicago Press.

Payne, C. 1995. *I've Got the Light of Freedom: The Organizing Tradition and the Mississippi Freedom Struggle.* Berkeley: University of California Press.

Pearson, G., A. Sampson, H. Blagg, P. Stubbs, and D. J. Smith. 1989. "Policing Racism." In *Coming to Terms with Policing: Perspectives on Policy.* London: Routledge.

Peoples, F., and R. Loeber. 1994. "Do Individual Factors and Neighborhood Context Explain Ethnic Differences in Juvenile Delinquency?" *Journal of Quantitative Criminology* 10, 2 (June): 141–57.

Percy, A. 1998. "Ethnicity and Victimisation: Findings from the 1996 British Crime Survey." *Home Office Statistical Bulletin,* 6/98, 3 April. London: Home Office.

Peristiany, J. G., and J. Pitt-Rivers, eds. 1992. *Honor and Grace in Anthropology.* Cambridge and New York: Cambridge University Press.

Perkins, C., and P. Klaus. 1996. *Criminal Victimization, 1994: National Crime Victimization Survey (NCJ #158022).* Washington, DC: U.S. Department of Justice.

Perkins, U. E. 1975. *Home is a Dirty Street: The Social Oppression of Black Children.* Chicago: Third World Press.

———. 1986. *Harvesting New Generations – The Positive Development of Black Youth.* Chicago: Third World Press.

Peterson, R. D., and L. J. Krivo. 1993. "Racial Segregation and Black Urban Homicide." *Social Forces* 71, 4 (June): 1001–26.

Peterson, R. D., L. J. Krivo, and M. A. Harris. 2000. "Disadvantage and Neighborhood Violent Crime: Do Local Institutions Matter?" *Journal of Research in Crime and Delinquency* 37: 31–63.

Phillips, C. D. 1987. "Exploring Relations among Forms of Social Control: The Lynching and Execution of Blacks in North Carolina." *Law and Society Review* 21: 361–74.

Phillips, C., and A. Sampson. 1998. "Preventing Repeated Victimisation: An Action Research Project." *British Journal of Criminology* 38, 1 (Winter): 124–44.

Phillips, J. A. 1997. "Variation in African-American Homicide Rates: An Assessment of Potential Explanations." *Criminology* 35, 4: 527–59.

Physicians Task Force on Hunger in America. 1986 [1985]. *Hunger in America: The Growing Epidemic.* New York: Harper and Row.

Piaget, J. 1965. *The Moral Judgment of the Child.* Trans. Marjorie Gabain. New York: Free Press.

Pierce, C. M. 1974. "Psychiatry Problems of the Black Minority." In *American Handbook of Psychiatry, Volume 3*, ed. S. Arieti and G. Kaplan. New York: Basic Books.

Pinkney, A. 1994. *White Hate Crimes: Howard Beach and Other Racial Atrocities*. Chicago: Third World Press.

Pitts, J. 1993. "Stereotyping: Anti-racism, Criminology and Black Young People." In *Racism and Criminology*, ed. D. Cook and B. Hudson. London: Sage.

Pizzey, E. 1974. *Scream Quietly or the Neighbors Will Hear*. London: Penguin.

Platt, A. M. 1995. "Crime Rave." *Monthly Review* (June): 35–46.

Pleck, J. H. 1987. *The Myth of Masculinity*. Cambridge, MA: M.I.T. Press.

Pokorny, A. D. 1965. "A Comparison of Homicides in Two Cities." *Journal of Criminal Law, Criminology, and Police Science* 56: 479–87.

Polk, K. 1994. *When Men Kill – Scenarios of Masculine Violence*. New York: Cambridge University Press.

Pomare, E. W., and G. M. de Boer. 1988. *Hauora: Maori Standards of Health: A Study of the Years 1970–1984*. Wellington, New Zealand: Department of Health.

Pomare, E. W., V. Keefe-Ormsby, C. Ormsby, et al. 1995. *Hauora: Maori Standards of Health III: A Study of the Years 1970–1991*. Wellington, New Zealand: Te Ropu Rangahau Hauora Eru Pomare.

Portes, A. 1996. *The New Second Generation*. New York: Russell Sage Foundation.

Portes, A., and A. Stepick. 1993. *City on the Edge: The Transformation of Miami*. Berkeley: University of California Press.

Poussaint, A. F. 1972. *Why Blacks Kill Blacks*. New York: Emerson Hall.

———. 1983. "Black-on-Black Homicide: A Psycho-Political Perspective." *Victimology* 8: 161–9.

Pratt, J. 1990. "Crime and Deviance." In *New Zealand Society: A Sociological Perspective*, ed. P. Spoonley, D. Pearson, and I. Shirley. Palmerston North, New Zealand: Dunmore Press.

Pressman, B. 1994. "Violence Against Women: Ramifications of Gender, Class and Race Inequality." In *Women in Context: Towards a Feminist Reconstruction of Psychotherapy*, ed. M. P. Merkin, 352–89. New York: Guilford.

Pulkkinen, L. 1983. "Search for Alternatives to Aggression in Finland." In *Aggression in Global Perspective*, ed. A. P. Goldstein and M. H. Segall, 104–44. Elmsford, NY: Pergamon Press.

Quarles, N. 1964. *The Negro in the Making of America*. New York: Collier Books.

Quinney, R. 1970. *The Social Reality of Crime*. Boston: Little, Brown, and Company.

Rainwater, L. 1970. *Behind Ghetto Walls: Black Families in a Federal Slum*. Chicago: Aldine.

Randolph, M. K., and L. K. Conkle. 1993. "Behavioral and Emotional Characteristics of Children Who Witness Parental Violence." *Family Violence and Sexual Assault Bulletin* 9, 2: 23–6.

Raphael, J. 1996. "Domestic Violence and Welfare Receipt: Towards a New Feminist Theory on Welfare Dependency." *Harvard Women's Law Journal* 201: 19.

Raudenbush, S., and R. Sampson. 1999. "Ecometrics: Toward a Science of Assessing Ecological Settings, with Application to the Systematic Social Observation of Neighborhoods." *Sociological Methodology* 29: 141.

Redfield, H. V. 1880. *Homicide, North and South*. Philadelphia: Lippincott.

Reich, M. 1981. *Racial Inequality: A Political Economic Analysis*. Princeton, NJ: Princeton University Press.

Reiman, J. H. 1984. *The Rich Get Richer and the Poor Get Prison: Ideology, Class, and Criminal Justice (2nd edition)*. New York: John Wiley and Sons.

Rein, M. 1983. *From Policy to Practice*. London: Macmillan.

Reiss, A. J., and J. A. Roth, eds. 1993. *Understanding and Preventing Violence*. Washington, DC: National Academy Press.

———. 1994. *Understanding and Preventing Violence, Volume 3: Social Influences*. Washington, DC: National Academy Press.

Reuter, E. B. 1927. *The American Race Problem: A Study of the Negro*. New York: Thomas Y. Crowell.

Richie, B. 1996. *Compelled to Crime: The Gender Entrapment of Battered Black Women*. New York: Routledge.

———. 2000. "A Black Feminist Reflection on the Antiviolence Movement." *Signs: Journal of Women in Culture and Society* 25, 4: 1133–7.

Ricks, J. L., C. J. Vaughan, and S. F. Dziegielewski. 2002. "Domestic Violence among Lesbian Couples." In *Handbook of Domestic Violence Intervention Strategies*, ed. A. L. Roberts, 451–63. New York: Oxford University Press.

Riedel, M. 1989. *Murder, Race, and Gender: A Test of the Hagan Hypotheses*. Paper presented at the American Society of Criminology, Reno, Nevada, November.

Riedel, M., and J. Best. 1998. "Patterns in Intimate Partner Homicide: California, 1987–1996." *Homicide Studies* 2: 305–20.

Roberts, J., and A. Doob. 1997. "Race, Ethnicity, and Criminal Justice in Canada." In *Crime and Justice: A Review of Research, Volume 19*, ed. M. Tonry, 469–522. Chicago: University of Chicago Press.

Roberts, W., and J. Strayer. 1996. "Empathy, Emotional Expressiveness, and Prosocial Behavior." *Child Development* 67: 449–70.

Robinson, L. N. 1933. "History of Criminal Statistics." *Journal of Criminal Law and Criminology* 24: 125–39.

Rodriquez, O. 1988. "Hispanics and Homicide in New York City. In *Research Conference on Violence and Homicide in Hispanic Communities*, ed. J. F. Kraus, S. B. Sorenson, and P. D. Juarez, 67–84. Los Angeles: UCLA Publication Services.

Rolleston, S. 1989. *He Kohikohinga: A Maori Health Knowledge Base*. Wellington, New Zealand: Department of Health.

Roncek, D. 1981. "Dangerous Places: Crime and Residential Environment." *Social Forces* 60: 74–96.

Roncek, D., and D. Faggiani. 1985. "High Schools and Crime." *The Sociological Quarterly* 26, 4: 491–505.

Roncek, D., and P. Maier. 1991. "Bars, Blocks, and Crimes Revisited: Linking the Theory of Routine Activities to the Empiricism of 'Hot Spots.'" *Criminology* 29, 4: 725–53.

Root, M. P. P. 1996. "Women of Color and Traumatic Stress in 'Domestic Captivity': Gender and Race as Disempowering Statuses." In *Ethnocultural Aspects of Posttraumatic Stress Disorder: Issues, Research and Clinical Applications*, ed. A. J. Marsella et al., 363–88. Washington, DC: American Psychological Association.

Roscigno, V. J. 1995. "The Social Embeddedness of Racial Educational Inequality: The Black-White Gap and the Impact of Racial and Local Political-Economic Contexts." *Research in Social Stratification and Mobility* 14: 137–68.

Roscigno, V. J., and M. A. Bruce. 1995. "Racial Inequality and Social Control: Historical and Contemporary Patterns in the U.S. South." *Sociological Spectrum* 15: 323–49.

Roscigno, V. J., and D. Tomaskovic-Devey. 1994. "Racial Politics in the Contemporary South: Toward a More Critical Understanding." *Social Problems* 41: 585–607.

Rose, D. 1996. *In the Name of the Law: The Collapse of Criminal Justice.* London: Vintage.

Rose, D. R., and T. R. Clear. 1998. "Incarceration, Social Capital, and Crime: Implications for Social Disorganization Theory." *Criminology* 36: 441–80.

Rose, H. M., and P. D. McClain. 1990. *Race, Place, and Risk: Black Homicide in Urban America.* Albany: State University of New York Press.

———. 1998. "Race, Place and Risk Revisited, A Perspective on the Emergence of a New Structural Paradigm." *Homicide Studies* 2 (May): 101–29.

Rose, P. 1994. *Black Noise: Rap Music and Black Culture in Contemporary America.* Hanover, NH: Wesleyan University Press.

Rosenberg, N. L. 1986. *Protecting the Best Men: An Interpretive History of the Law of Libel.* Chapel Hill and London: University of North Carolina Press.

Rosenthal, R., and D. B. Rubin. 1982. "A Simple, General Purpose Display of Magnitude of Experimental Effect." *Journal of Educational Psychology* 74: 166–9.

Rosenwaike, I., and K. Hempstead. 1990. "Mortality among Three Puerto Rican Populations: Residents of Puerto Rico and Migrants in New York City and in the Balance of the United States, 1979–81." *International Migration Review* 24: 684–702.

Rowe, D. C., and W. Osgood. 1984. "Heredity and Sociological Theories of Delinquency: A Reconsideration." *American Sociological Review* 49: 526–40.

Rowe, D. C., A. T. Vazsonyi, and D. J. Flannery. 1994. "No More Skin Deep: Ethnic and Racial Similarity in Developmental Process." *Psychological Review* 101: 396–413.

Rushton, J. P. 1999 [1995]. *Race, Evolution and Behavior. Special Abridged Edition.* New Brunswick, NJ: Transaction Publishers.

Russell, K. K. 1998. *The Color of Crime: Racial Hoaxes, White Fear, Black Protectionism, Police Harassment, and Other Macroaggressions.* New York: New York University Press.

Rutter, M. 1981. "The City and the Child." *American Journal of Orthopsychiatry* 51: 10–62.

———. 1989. "Pathways from Childhood to Adult Life." *Journal of Child Psychology and Psychiatry and Allied Disciplines* 30: 23–51.

Salovey, P. 1991. "Social Comparison Processes in Envy and Jealousy." In *Social Comparison: Contemporary Theory and Research,* ed. J. Suls and T. A. Willis, 261–85. Hillsdale, NJ: LEA.

Sampson, A., and C. Phillips. 1992. *Multiple Victimisation: Racial Attacks on an East London Estate. Police Research Group Crime Prevention Unit Series Paper 36.* London: Home Office.

———. 1996. *Reducing Repeat Victimisation on an East London Estate. Police Research Group Prevention Unit Crime Prevention and Detection Paper 67.* London: Home Office.

Sampson, E. E. 1988. "The Debate on Individualism: Indigenous Psychologies of the Individual and Their Role in Personal and Societal Functioning." *American Psychologist* 43: 15–22.

Sampson, R. J. 1985. "Race and Criminal Violence: A Demographically Disaggregated Analysis of Urban Homicide." *Crime and Delinquency* 31: 47–82.

———. 1985. "Structural Sources of Variation in Race-Age–Specific Rates of Offending across Major U.S. Cities." *Criminology* 23, 4: 647–73.

———. 1987. "Urban Black Violence: The Effect of Male Joblessness and Family Disruption." *American Journal of Sociology* 93, 2: 348–82.

———. 1988. "Local Friendship Ties and Community Attachment in Mass Society: A Multi-Level Systemic Model." *American Sociological Review* 53: 766–79.

———. 1997. "The Embeddedness of Child and Adolescent Development: A Community-Level Perspective on Urban Violence." In *Violence and Childhood in the Inner City,* ed. J. McCord, 31–77. New York: Cambridge University Press.

Sampson, R. J., and W. B. Groves. 1989. "Community Structure and Crime: Testing Social-Disorganization Theory." *American Journal of Sociology* 94: 774–802.

Sampson, R. J., and J. Laub. 1993. *Crime in the Making: Pathways and Turning Points through Life.* Cambridge, MA: Harvard University Press.

———. 1995. "A Life-Course Theory of Cumulative Disadvantage and the Stability of Delinquency." In *Advances in Criminological Theory, Volume 7: Developmental Theories of Crime and Delinquency,* ed. T. Thornberry, 133–61. New Brunswick, NJ: Transaction Press.

Sampson, R. J., and J. L. Lauritsen. 1994. "Violent Victimization and Offending: Individual-, Situational-, and Community-Level Risk Factors." In *Understanding and Preventing Violence, Volume 3: Social Influences,* ed. A. J. Reiss, Jr. and J. A. Roth, 1–114. Washington, DC: National Academy Press.

———. 1997. "Racial and Ethnic Disparities in Crime and Criminal Justice in the United States." In *Crime and Justice: A Review of Research, Volume 19,* ed. M. Tonry, 311–74. Chicago: University of Chicago Press.

Sampson, R. J., J. D. Morenoff, and F. J. Earls. 1999. "Beyond Social Capital: Spatial Dynamics of Collective Efficacy for Children." *American Sociological Review* 64: 633–60.

Sampson, R. J., S. W. Raudenbush, and F. Earls. 1997. "Neighborhoods and Violent Crime: A Multilevel Study of Collective Efficacy." *Science* 277 (August 15): 918–24.

Sampson, R. J., and W. J. Wilson. 1995. "Toward a Theory of Race, Crime and Urban Inequality." In *Crime and Inequality,* eds. J. Hagan and R. D. Peterson, 37–54. Stanford, CA: Stanford University.

Sanchez-Hucles, J., and M. A. Dutton. 1999. "The Interaction between Societal Violence and Domestic Violence: Racial and Cultural Factors." In *What Causes Men's Violence against Women,* ed. M. Harway and J. M. O'Neil, 183–205. Thousand Oaks, CA: Sage.

Sanders, W. B. 1994. *Gangbangs and Drive-Bys: Grounded Culture and Juvenile Gang Violence.* New York: Aldine de Gruyter.

Sanders-Phillips, K. 1997. "Assaultive Violence in the Community: Psychological Responses of Adolescent Victims and Their Parents." *Journal of Adolescent Health* 21: 356–65.

Santucho, M. R. 1982. *Notes on Revolutionary Morals.* Puerto Rico: Movimiento de Liberacion Nacional.

Saulsbury, W. E., and B. Bowling. 1991. *The Multi-Agency Approach in Practice: the North Plaistow Racial Harassment Project. Home Office Research Study No. 64.* London: Home Office.

Schaefer, R. J. 1993. *Racial and Ethnic Groups.* New York: Harper Collins.

Schechter, S. 1982. *Women and Male Violence: The Visions and Struggles of the Battered Women's Movement.* Boston: South End Press.

Scheff, T. 1988. "Shame and Conformity: The Difference-Emotion System." *American Sociological Review* 53: 395–406.

Scheff, T., and S. Retzinger. 1991. *Emotions and Violence: Shame and Rage in Destructive Conflicts.* Lexington, MA: Lexington Books.

Scheler, M. 1994. *Ressentiment.* Milwaukee, WI: Marquette University Press.

Schlesselman, J. J. 1982. *Case-Control Studies.* New York: Oxford University Press.

Schmidt, J. D., and L. W. Sherman. 1996. "Does Arrest Deter Domestic Violence?" In *Do Arrests and Restraining Orders Work?* ed. E. Buzawa and C. Buzawa, 43–53. Thousand Oaks, CA: Sage.

Schulman, M. A. 1979. *Survey of Spousal Violence against Women in Kentucky. Harris Study #7092701.* Washington, DC: U.S. Government Printing Office.

Schultz, D. A. 1969. *Coming Up Black: Patterns of Ghetto Socialization.* Englewood Cliffs, NJ: Prentice Hall.

Seale, B. 1970. *Seize the Time: The Story of the Black Panther Party and Huey P. Newton.* Baltimore, MD: Black Classic Books.

Sellers, R. M., M. Smith, J. N. Shelton, S. A. J. Rowley, and T. M. Chavous. 1998. "Multidimensional Model of Racial Identity: A Conceptualization of African American Racial Identity." *Personality and Social Psychology Review* 2: 18–39.

Sellin, T. 1938. *Culture, Conflict, and Crime.* New York: Social Science Research Council.

Semyonov, M., and Y. Cohen. 1990. "Ethnic Discrimination and the Income of Majority-Group Workers." *American Sociological Review* 55: 107–14.

Shai, D., and I. Rosenwaike. 1988. "Violent Death Among Mexican, Puerto Rican, and Cuban-Born Migrants in the United States." *Social Science and Medicine* 36, 2: 269–76.

Shakoor, B. H., and D. Chalmers. 1991. "Co-Victimization of African American Children Who Witness Violence and the Theoretical Implications of Its Effects on Their Cognitive, Emotional and Behavioral Development." *Journal of the National Medical Association* 83: 233–38.

Shanna, A. 1987. "Revolutionary Morality: An Overview." In *Vita Wa Watu (Book 10)*, 29–36. Chicago, IL: Spear and Shield Publications.

Shaw, C. R., and H. D. McKay. 1931. *Social Factors in Juvenile Delinquency.* (Volume II of Report on the Causes of Crime. National Commission on Law Observance and Enforcement, Report No. 13.) Washington, DC: U.S. Government Printing Office.

Shaw, C. R., and H. D. McKay. 1942. *Juvenile Delinquency in Urban Areas.* Chicago: University of Chicago Press.

Sherman, L. 1993. "Defiance, Deterrence, and Irrelevance: A Theory of the Criminal Sanction." *Journal of Research in Crime and Delinquency* 30: 445–73.

Sherman, L. W., and R. A. Berk. 1984. "The Specific Deterrent Effects of Arrest for Domestic Assaults." *American Sociological Review* 49: 261–72.

Shihadeh, E. S., and N. Flynn. 1996. "Black Residential Segregation and Crime." *Social Forces* 74, 4 (June): 1325–52.

Shihadeh, E. S., and D. J. Steffensmeier. 1994. "Economic Inequality, Family Disruption, and Urban Black Violence: Cities as Units of Stratification and Social Control." *Social Forces* 73: 729–51.

Shoemaker, D. 1984. *Theories of Delinquency: An Examination of Explanations of Delinquent Behavior.* New York: Oxford University Press.

Short, J., Jr. 1997. *Poverty, Ethnicity, and Violent Crime.* Crime and Society Series. Boulder, CO: Westview Press.

Shweder, R. A. 1991. *Thinking through Cultures: Expeditions in Cultural Psychology.* Cambridge, MA: Harvard University Press.

Shweder, R. A., N. C. Much, M. Mahaptrah, and L. Park. 1997. "The 'Big Three' of Morality (Autonomy, Community and Divinity) and the 'Big Three' Explanations of Suffering." In *Morality and Health*, ed. A. Brandt and P. Rozin, 119–69. Stanford, CA: Stanford University Press.

Sibbitt, R. 1997. *The Perpetrators of Racial Harassment and Racial Violence: Home Office Research Study No. 176.* London: Home Office.

Silverman, R. 1996. "Patterns of Native American Crime." In *Native Americans, Crime, and Justice*, ed. M. Nielsen and R. Silverman, 58–74. Boulder, CO: Westview Press.

Simcha-Fagan, O., and J. E. Schwartz. 1986. "Neighborhood and Delinquency: An Assessment of Contextual Effects." *Criminology* 24: 667–703.

Smith, D. A., and G. R. Jarjoura. 1988. "Social Structure and Criminal Victimization." *Journal of Research in Crime and Delinquency* 25: 27–52.

Smith, R. H., W. G. Parrott, D. Ozer, and A. Moniz. 1994. "Subjective Injustice and Inferiority as Predictors of Hostile and Depressive Feelings in Envy." *Personality and Social Psychology Bulletin* 20: 705–11.

Smith, S. J. 1989. *The Politics of 'Race' and Residence: Citizenship, Segregation and White Supremacy in Britain.* Cambridge, MA: Polity.

Sniderman, P., and E. Carmines, eds. 1997. *Reaching Beyond Race.* Cambridge, MA: Harvard University Press.

Snyder, H., and M. Sickmund. 1995. *Juvenile Offenders and Victims: A Focus on Violence.* Washington, DC: Office of Juvenile Justice and Delinquency Prevention, U.S. Department of Justice.

———. 1999. *Juvenile Offenders and Victims: 1999 National Report.* Washington, DC: Office of Juvenile Justice and Delinquency Prevention, U.S. Department of Justice.

Snyder, H. N., M. Sickmund, and E. Poe-Yamagata. 1997. *Juvenile Offenders and Victims: 1996 Update on Violence.* Washington, DC: Office of Juvenile Justice and Delinquency Prevention, U.S. Department of Justice.

Snyder-Joy Z. 1995. "Self-Determination and American Indian Justice: Tribal Versus Federal Jurisdiction on Indian Lands." In *Ethnicity, Race, and Crime: Perspectives across Time and Place,* ed. D. Hawkins, 310–22. Albany: State University of New York Press.

Soja, E. 1987. "Economic Restructuring and the Internationalization of the Los Angeles Region." In *The Capitalist City,* ed. M. P. Smith and J. R. Feagan, 178–98. New York: Basil Blackwell.

Solomos, J. 1993. *Race and Racism in Contemporary Britain.* London: Macmillan.

Sommerville, D. M. 1995. "The Rape Myth in the Old South Reconsidered." *The Journal of Southern History* LXI, 3: 481–518.

Sorenson, S. B., et al. 1987. "The Prevalence of Adult Sexual Assault: The Los Angeles Epidemiologic Catchment Area Project." *American Journal of Epidemiology* 126: 1154–64.

Sparks, E. 1994. "Human Rights Violations in the Inner City: Implications for Moral Educators." *Journal of Moral Education* 23: 315–32.

Spear, A. H. 1967. *Black Chicago: The Making of a Negro Ghetto 1890–1920.* Chicago: University of Chicago Press.

Spector, M., and J. I. Kitsuse. 1987. *Constructing Social Problems.* New York: Aldine de Gruyter.

Spence, J. T. 1985. "Achievement American Style: The Rewards and Costs of Individualism." *American Psychologist* 40: 1285–95.

Spergel, I. A. 1992. "Youth Gangs: An Essay Review." *Social Service Review* (March).

Spindel, D. J. 1995. "The Law of Words: Verbal Abuse in North Carolina to 1730." *The American Journal of Legal History* 39, 1 (January): 25–42.

Spoonley, P. 1990. "Racism and Ethnicity." In *New Zealand Society: A Sociological Introduction,* ed. P. Spoonley, D. Pearson, and I. Shirley. Palmerston North, New Zealand: Dunmore Press.

Squires, G., R. DeWolfe, and A. S. DeWolfe. 1979. "Urban Decline or Disinvestment: Uneven Development, Redlining and the Role of the Insurance Industry." *Social Problems* 27: 79–95.

Squires, G., W. Valez, and K. E. Taeuber. 1991. "Insurance Redlining, Agency Location, and the Process of Urban Disinvestment." *Urban Affairs Quarterly* 26: 567–88.

Stampp, K. M. 1956. *The Peculiar Institution.* New York: Vintage Books.

Stanko, E. 1988. "Hidden Violence against Women." In *Victims of Crime a New Deal?,* ed. M. Maguire and J. Pointing. Milton Keynes: Open University Press.

Staples, R. 1974. "Violence and Black America: The Political Implications." *Black World* 23: 16–34.

―――. 1982. *Black Masculinity: The Black Male's Role in American Society.* San Francisco: Black Scholar Press.

―――. 1986. "The Masculine Way of Violence." In *Homicide among Black Americans,* ed. D. F. Hawkins, 137–53. New York: University Press of America.

Stark, E. 1990. "Rethinking Homicide: Violence, Race and the Politics of Gender." *International Journal of Health Services* 20, 1: 3–27.

―――. 1993. "The Myth of Black Violence." *Social Work* 38, 4 (July): 485–91.

―――. 1996. "Re-presenting Woman Battering: From Battered Woman Syndrome to Coercive Control." *Albany Law Review* 58: 101–56.

Stark, E., and A. Flitcraft. 1984. "Domestic Violence, Child Abuse and Social Heredity: What Is the Relationship?" In *Marital Violence, Sociological Review Monographs,* ed. N. K. Johnson, 147–92. London: Routledge, Kegan, and Paul.

―――. 1988. "Women and Children at Risk: A Feminist Perspective on Child Abuse." *International Journal of Health Services* 18, 1: 97–118.

―――. 1995. "Killing the Beast Within: Domestic Violence and Female Suicide Attempts." *International Journal of Health Services* 25, 1: 43–64.

―――. 1996. *Women at Risk: Domestic Violence and Women's Health.* Thousand Oaks, CA: Sage.

State of California. 1998. *County Population Projections with Race/Ethnic Detail.* Sacramento, CA: Department of Finance, Demographic Research Unit.

Statistics Canada. 1992. *Age, Sex and Marital Status: 1991 Census of Canada.* Ottawa: Industry, Science, and Technology.

―――. 1993. *Age and Sex, Aboriginal Data.* Ottawa: Industry, Science, and Technology.

―――. 1999. *Crime Statistics.* Ottawa: Statistics Canada Daily Report.

―――. 1999. *Prison Population and Costs.* Ottawa: Statistics Canada Daily Report.

Steinberg, S. 1989 [1981]. *The Ethnic Myth: Race, Ethnicity and Class in America.* Boston: Beacon Press.

Stepick, A. 1992. "The Refugees Nobody Wants: Haitians in Miami." In *Miami Now!,* ed. G. Grenier and A. Stepick III. Baltimore, MD: Johns Hopkins University Press.

Stepick, A. 1998. *Pride Against Prejudice: Haitians in the United States.* Boston: Allyn and Bacon.

Stevenson, H. C. 1997. "Managing Anger: Protective, Proactive, or Adaptive Racial Socialization Identity Profiles and African American Manhood Development." *Journal of Prevention and Intervention in the Community* 16: 35–61.

Stokes, R., and J. P. Hewitt. 1976. "Aligning Actions." *American Sociological Review* 41: 838–49.

Straus, M. A. 1988. "Violence in Hispanic Families in the United States: Some Preliminary Findings on Incidence and Etiology." In *Research Conference on Violence and Homicide in Hispanic Communities,* ed. J. F. Kraus, S. B. Sorenson, and P. D. Juarez, 171–92. Los Angeles: UCLA Publication Services.

―――. 1996. "Identifying Offenders in Criminal Justice Research on Domestic Violence." In *Do Arrests and Restraining Orders Work?* ed. E. S. Buzawa and C. Buzawa, 14–29. Thousand Oaks, CA: Sage.

Straus, M. A., and R. Gelles. 1986. "Societal Change and Change in Family

Violence from 1975 to 1985 as Revealed by Two National Surveys." *Journal of Marriage and the Family* 48: 465–70.

Straus, M., R. Gelles, and S. Steinmetz. 1980. *Behind Closed Doors: A Survey of Family Violence in America.* New York: Doubleday.

Sudarkasa, N. 1997. "African American Families and Family Values." In *Black Families (3rd edition),* ed. H. P. McAdoo, 9–40. Thousand Oaks, CA; Sage Publications.

Sugrue, T. J. 1993. "The Structures of Urban Poverty: The Reorganization of Space and Work in Three Periods of American History." In *The "Underclass" Debate,* ed. M. B. Katz, 85–117. Princeton, NJ: Princeton University Press.

Sullivan, C. M. 1994. "Adjustment and Needs of African-American Women Who Utilized a Domestic Violence Shelter." *Violence Against Women* 9, 3: 275–86.

Sullivan, M. 1989. *"Getting Paid": Youth Crime and Work in the Inner City.* Ithaca, NY: Cornell University.

Sutherland, E. H. 1934. *Principles of Criminology.* Chicago: Lippincott.

Sutherland, E. H., and D. R. Cressy. 1978. *Criminology.* Philadelphia: Lippincott.

Sutherland, O. R. W., J. T. Hippolite, A. M. Smith, and R. A. Galbreath. 1973. *Justice and Race: A Monocultural System in a Multicultural Society.* Paper presented to the New Zealand Race Relations Council Annual Conference.

Swidler, A. 1986. "Culture in Action: Symbols and Strategies." *American Sociological Review* 51: 273–86.

Szymanski, A. 1976. "Racial Discrimination and White Gain." *American Sociological Review* 41: 403–14.

Takaki, R. T. 1972. *Violence in the Black Imagination.* New York: J. P. Putnam and Sons.

———. 1993. *Violence in the Black Imagination.* New York: Oxford University Press.

Tangney, J. P., P. E. Wagner, D. Hill-Barlow, D. E. Marschall, and R. Gramzow. 1996. "Relation of Shame and Guilt to Constructive and Destructive Responses to Anger across the Lifespan." *Journal of Personality and Social Psychology* 70: 797–809.

Tanton, J., and W. Lutton. 1993. "Immigration and Criminality in the U.S.A." *Journal of Social, Political and Economic Studies* 18: 217–34.

Tardiff, K., et al. 1995. "A Profile of Homicides on the Streets and in the Homes of New York City." *Public Health Reports, January–February* 70, 1: 13–17.

Task Force on Violence and the Family. 1996. *Violence and the Family. Report.* Washington, DC: American Psychological Association.

Taylor, I., P. Walton, and J. Young. 1973. *The New Criminology: For a Social Theory of Deviance.* New York: Harper and Row.

Taylor, P. S. 1931. "Crime and the Foreign Born: The Problem of the Mexican." *National Commission on Law Observance and Enforcement: Report on Crime and the Foreign Born.* Washington, DC: U.S. Government Printing Office.

Taylor, R. and J. Covington. 1988. "Neighborhood Changes in Ecology and Violence." *Criminology* 26: 553–90.

Taylor, R. J., B. R. Leashore, and S. Toliver. 1988. "An Assessment of the Provider Role as Perceived by Black Males." *Family Relations* 37: 426–31.

Taylor, R. L. 1979. "Black Ethnicity and the Persistence of Ethnogenesis." *American Journal of Sociology* 84: 1401–23.

———. 1991. "Poverty and Adolescent Black Males: The Subculture of Disengagement." In *Adolescence and Poverty: Challenges for the 1990s*, ed. P. B. Edelman and J. Ladner, 139–61. Washington, DC: Center for Policy Studies.

Texeira, M. T. 1995. "Policing the Internally Colonized: Slavery, Rodney King, Mark Furman and Beyond." *Western Journal of Black Studies* 19: 235–43.

Thomas, W. I., and F. Znaniecki. 1920. *The Polish Peasant in Europe and America: Volume 4, Disorganization and Reorganization in Poland*. Boston: Gorham Press.

———. 1984. *The Polish Peasant in Europe and America: Edited and Abridged*. Chicago: University of Illinois Press.

Thompson, M. S., and W. Peebles-Wilkins. 1992. "The Impact of Formal, Informal and Societal Support Networks on the Psychological Well-Being of Black Adolescent Mothers." *Social Work* 37, 4: 322–8.

Thornberry, T. 1987. "Toward an Interactional Theory of Delinquency." *Criminology* 25: 863–91.

Thornberry, T. P., A. J. Lizotte, M. D. Krohn, M. Farnworth, and S. J. Jang. 1991. "Testing Interactional Theory: An Examination of Reciprocal Causal Relationships among Family, School and Delinquency." *Journal of Criminal Law and Criminology* 82: 3–35.

Thornberry, T. W., and M. Farnworth. 1982. "Social Correlates of Criminal Involvement: Further Evidence on the Relationship between Social Status and Criminal Behavior." *American Sociological Review* 47: 505–18.

Thrasher, F. 1927. *The Gang*. Chicago: University of Chicago Press.

Tienda, M., and D. Lii. 1987. "Minority Concentration and Earnings Inequality: Blacks, Hispanics and Asians Compared." *American Journal of Sociology* 93: 141–65.

Toch, H. 1969. *Violent Men*. Chicago: Aldine.

Tolnay, S. E., and E. M. Beck. 1995. *A Festival of Violence: An Analysis of Southern Lynchings, 1882–1930*. Urbana and Chicago: University of Illinois Press.

Tomaskovic-Devey, B., and D. Tomaskovic-Devey. 1988. "The Social Structural Determinants of Ethnic Group Behavior: Single Ancestry Rates among Four White American Ethnic Groups." *American Sociological Review* 53: 650–9.

Tomaskovic-Devey, D. 1993. *Gender and Racial Inequality at Work: The Sources and Consequences of Job Segregation*. Ithaca, NY: ILR Press.

Tomaskovic-Devey, D., and V. J. Roscigno. 1996. "Racial Economic Subordination and White Gain in the U.S. South." *American Sociological Review* 61: 565–89.

———. 1997. "Uneven Development and Local Inequality in the U.S. South: The Role of Dependency, Elite Agendas, and Racial Competition." *Sociological Forum* 12: 565–97.

Tompson, K. 1988. *Under Siege: Racial Violence in Britain Today*. Harmondsworth: Penguin.

Tonry, M. 1997. "Ethnicity, Crime, and Immigration." In *Ethnicity, Crime and Immigration: Comparative and Cross-National Perspectives*, a Special Edition of *Crime and Justice: A Review of Research, Volume 19*, ed. M. Tonry, 469–522. Chicago: University of Chicago Press.

————, ed. 1997. *Ethnicity, Crime and Immigration: Comparative and Cross-National Perspectives*, a Special Edition of *Crime and Justice: A Review of Research, Volume 19*. Chicago: University of Chicago Press.

————. 1997. *Malign Neglect – Race, Crime and Punishment in America*. New York: Oxford University Press.

Tripp, S. E. 1997. *Yankee Town, Southern City: Race and Class Relations in Civil War Lynchburg*. New York and London: New York University Press.

Tuck, M. 1989. *Drinking and Disorder: A Study of Non-Metropolitan Violence. Home Office Research Study No. 108*. London: Home Office.

Ture, K., and C. V. Hamilton. 1992. *Black Power: The Politics of Liberation*. New York: Vintage Books.

Turiel, E. 1998. "The Development of Morality." In *Handbook of Child Psychology, Volume 3: Social, Emotional, and Personality Development (5th edition)*, ed. W. Damon (Series Ed.) and N. Eisenberg (Volume Ed.), 863–932. New York: Wiley and Sons.

Turk, A. 1982. "Social Control and Social Conflict." In *Social Control: Views from the Social Sciences*, ed. J. Gibbs, 249–64. Beverly Hills, CA: Sage.

Umoja, A. O. 1998. "Set Our Warriors Free: The Legacy of the Black Panther Party and Political Prisoners." In *The Black Panther Party Reconsidered*, ed. C. Jones, 417–41. Baltimore, MD: Black Classic Books.

————. 1999. "The Ballot and the Bullet: A Comparative Analysis of Armed Resistance in the Civil Rights Movement." *Journal of Black Studies* 29: 558–78.

U.S. Bureau of the Census. 1992. *Statistical Abstract of the U.S.: 1992 (112th edition)*. Washington, DC: U.S. Government Printing Office.

————. 1993. *Census of the United States, 1990*. Washington, DC: U.S. Government Printing Office.

————. 1996. *Statistical Abstract of the United States – 1996*. Washington, DC: U.S. Government Printing Office.

————. 1998. *Statistical Abstract of the United States – 1998*. Washington, DC: U.S. Government Printing Office.

U.S. Bureau of Justice Statistics. 1994. *Survey of State Prison Inmates: Women in Prisons*. National Institute of Justice. Washington, DC: U.S. Department of Justice.

————. 1996/1997a. *Changes in Criminal Victimization, 1994–1995*. National Institute of Justice. Washington, DC: U.S. Department of Justice.

————. 1998. *Prevalence, Incidence and Consequences of Violence against Women: Findings from the National Violence against Women Survey*. National Institute of Justice. Washington, DC: U.S. Department of Justice.

————. 1999. *Criminal Victimization in the United States, 1998*. Washington, DC: U.S. Department of Justice.

————. Multiple Years. *Sourcebook of Criminal Justice Statistics*. Washington, DC: U.S. Government Printing Office.

U.S. Department of Justice. 1986. *Criminal Victimization in the United States*. Washington, DC: U.S. Government Printing Office.

————. 1988. *Criminal Victimization in the United States*. Washington, DC: U.S. Government Printing Office.

————. 1997. *Violence Related Injuries Treated in Hospital Emergency Departments.* Washington, DC: U.S. Government Printing Office.

————. 1998. *Crime in the United States.* Washington, DC: U.S. Government Printing Office.

U.S. General Accounting Office. 1996. *Sex Offender Treatment: Research Results Inconclusive about What Works to Reduce Recidivism.* GGD96–137. Washington, DC: U.S. General Accounting Office.

Valdez, A. 1993. "Persistent Poverty, Crime, and Drugs: U.S.-Mexican Border Region." In *In the Barrios: Latinos and The Underclass Debate,* ed. J. Moore and R. Pinderhughes. New York: Russell Sage Foundation.

Valdez, R. B., and P. Nourjah. 1988. "Homicide in Southern California 1966–1985: An Examination Based on Vital Statistics Data." In *Research Conference on Violence and Homicide in Hispanic Communities,* ed. J. F. Kraus, S. B. Sorenson, and P. D. Juarez, 85–100. Los Angeles: UCLA Publication Services.

Valente, R. 1995. "Addressing Domestic Violence: the Role of the Family Law Practitioner." *Family Law Quarterly* 29, 2: 187–96.

Valentine, C. A. 1971. "Deficit, Difference, and Bicultural Models of Afro-American Behavior." *Harvard Educational Review* 41: 137–57.

Van Deburg, W. L. 1997. *Modern Black Nationalism: From Marcus Garvey to Louis Farrakhan (edited volume).* New York: New York University Press.

Van Dussen, K. T., S. A. Mednick, W. F. Gabrielli, and B. Hutchings. 1983. "Social Class and Crime in an Adoption Cohort." *Journal of Criminal Law and Criminology* 74: 249–69.

Van Haitsma, M. 1989. "A Contextual Definition of the Underclass." *Focus* 12: 27–31.

Vazsonyi, A. T., and D. J. Flannery. 1997. "Early Adolescent Delinquent Behaviors: Associations with Family and School Domains." *Journal of Early Adolescence* 17: 271–93.

Vigil, J. D. 1988. "Barrio Gangs: Street Life and Identity in Southern California." In *The Modern Gang Reader,* ed. M. W. Klein, C. L. Maxson, and J. Miller, 125–31. Los Angeles: Roxbury Publishing.

Virdee, S. 1995. *Racial Violence and Harassment.* London: Policy Studies Institute.

Wacquant, L. J. D. 1996. "The Rise of Advanced Marginality: Notes on Its Nature and Implications." *Acta Sociologica* 39: 121–39.

Wacquant, L. J. D., and W. J. Wilson. 1989. "The Cost of Racial and Class Exclusion in the Inner City." *Annals of the American Academy of Political and Social Sciences* 501 (January): 8–25.

Wadsworth, M. 1979. *Roots of Delinquency.* London: Martin Robertson.

Waits, W. 1985. "The Criminal Justice System's Response to Battering: Understanding the Problem, Forging the Solution." *Washington Law Review* 60: 267–329.

Walker, L. 1977–8. "Battered Women and Learned Helplessness." *Victimology: An International Journal* 2, 3–4: 525–34.

————. 1979. *The Battered Woman.* New York: Harper and Row.

————. 1989. *Terrifying Love: Why Battered Women Kill and How Society Responds.* New York: Harper and Row.

Walker, R. 1996. *Nga Pepa a Ranginui: The Walker Papers.* Auckland: Penguin.

Ward, J. V. 1988. "Urban Adolescents' Conceptions of Violence." In *Mapping the Moral Domain*, ed. C. Gilligan, J. Ward, and J. Taylor, 175–200. Cambridge, MA: Harvard University Press.

———. 1995. "Cultivating a Morality of Care in African American Adolescents: A Culture-Based Model of Violence Prevention." *Harvard Educational Review* 65: 175–88.

Wardell, M., and A. M. Zajicek. 1995. "Social Problems: Pathways for Transcending Exclusive Sociology." *Social Problems* 42: 301–17.

Warshaw, C. 1997. "Intimate Partner Abuse: Developing a Framework for Change in Medical Education." *Academic Medicine* 72 (1 suppl.): S26–S37.

Waters, M. C. 1999. "Sociology and the Study of Immigration." *American Behavioral Scientist* 42: 1264–7.

Waters, T. 1999. *Crime and Immigrant Youth*. Thousand Oaks, CA: Sage Publications.

Watts, R. J., and J. K. Abdul-Adil. 1997. "Promoting Critical Consciousness in Young, African American Men." *Journal of Prevention and Intervention in the Community* 16: 63–86.

Weatheritt, M. 1986. *Innovations in Policing*. London: Croom Helm.

Webster, C. 1997. *Local Heroes: Racial Violence among Asian and White Young People*. Leicester: Leicester University.

Weis, J. G. 1986. "Issues in the Measurement of Criminal Careers." In *Criminal Careers and "Career Criminals," Volume 2*, ed. A. Blumstein, J. Cohen, J. A. Roth, and C. A. Visher, 1–51. Washington, DC: National Academy Press.

Welsing, F. C. 1978. "Mental Health: Etiology and Process." In *Mental Health: A Challenge in the Black Community*, ed. L. Gary, 48–72. Philadelphia: Dorrance.

———. 1991. *The Isis Papers – Keys to the Colors*. Chicago: Third World Press.

West, C. 1994. *Race Matters*. New York: Vintage.

West, C. M. 1995. *Courtship Violence among African-Americans*. Ph.D. Dissertation in Sociology, University of Missouri.

West, D. J., and D. P. Farrington. 1973. *Who Becomes Delinquent?* London: Heinemann.

———. 1977. *The Delinquent Way of Life*. London: Heinemann.

Whitehead, T. L., J. Peterson, and L. Kaljee. 1994. "The Hustle: Socioeconomic Deprivation, Drug-Trafficking, and Low-Income African American Male Gender Identity." *Pediatrics* 93: 1050–4.

Whitson, M. H. 1997. "Sexism and Sexual Harassment Concerns of African American Women of the Christian Methodist Episcopal Church." *Violence against Women* 3, 4: 382–400.

Wiggins, W. H., Jr. 1973. "Jack Johnson as Bad Nigger: The Folklore of His Life." In *Contemporary Black Thought, the Best from The Black Scholar*, ed R. Ware and N. Ware, 53–70. New York: Bobbs-Merrill.

Wilbanks, W. 1984. *Murder in Miami: An Analysis of Homicide Patterns and Trends in Dade County (Miami) Florida 1917–1983*. Lanham, MD: University Press of America.

Wilkinson, D. L., and J. Fagan. 1996. "The Role of Firearms in Violence 'Scripts': The Dynamics of Gun Events among Adolescent Males." *Law and Contemporary Problems* 59: 55–89.

Williams, E. 1993. *Inadmissible Evidence.* New York: Lawrence Hill.

Williams, J. K. 1980. *Dueling in the Old South (Vignettes of Social History).* College Station: Texas A & M University Press.

Williams, K. R. 1984. "Economic Sources of Homicide: Reestimating the Effects of Poverty and Inequality. *American Sociological Review* 49: 283–9.

Williams, O. J. 1994. "Group Work with African-American Men Who Batter: Toward More Ethically Sensitive Practice." *Journal of Comparative Family Studies* 25, 1: 91–103.

Willis, P. 1981. *Learning to Labor.* New York: Columbia University Press.

Wilmore, G. S. 1989. *Black Religion and Black Radicalism: An Interpretation of the Religious History of Afro-American People (2nd edition).* Maryknoll, MD: Orbis Books.

Wilson, C. A. 1992. "Restructuring and the Growth of Concentrated Poverty in Detroit." *Urban Affairs Quarterly* 28: 187–205.

Wilson, J. Q., and R. J. Herrnstein. 1985. *Crime and Human Nature.* New York: Simon and Schuster.

Wilson, M., and M. Daly. 1993. "A Lifespan Perspective on Homicidal Violence: The Young Male Syndrome." In *Questions and Answers in Lethal and Non-Lethal Violence. Second Annual Workshop of the Homicide Research Working Group.* Washington, DC: National Institute of Justice.

Wilson, W. J. 1978. *The Declining Significance of Race.* Chicago: University of Chicago Press.

———. 1987. *The Truly Disadvantaged: The Inner City, the Underclass, and Public Policy.* Chicago: University of Chicago Press.

———. 1996. *When Work Disappears: The World of the New Urban Poor.* New York: Alfred P. Knopf.

Wise, A. E., and T. Gendler. 1989. "Rich Schools, Poor Schools: The Persistence of Unequal Education." *College Board Review* 151: 12–17.

Witte, R. 1996. *Racist Violence and the State.* London: Longman.

Wolfgang, M. E. 1958. *Patterns in Criminal Homicide.* Philadelphia: University of Pennsylvania Press.

Wolfgang, M. E., and F. Ferracuti. 1967. *The Subculture of Violence: Towards an Integrated Theory in Criminology.* London: Tavistock Publications.

Wright, J. D., J. F. Sheley, and M. D. Smith. 1992. "Kids, Guns, and Killing Fields." *Society* 30, 1 (Nov./Dec.): 84–9.

Wright, R. T., and S. H. Decker. 1997. *Armed Robbers in Action – Stickups and Street Culture.* Boston: Northeastern University Press.

Wuthnow, R. 1987. *Meaning and Moral Order.* Berkeley: University of California Press.

Wyatt, G. E. 1992. "The Sociocultural Context of African American and White American Women's Rape." *Journal of Social Issues* 48: 77–91.

Wyatt-Brown, B. 1982. *Southern Honor: Ethics and Behavior in the Old South.* New York: Oxford University Press.

X, Malcolm. 1965. *Malcolm X Speaks.* New York: Grove Press.

Yancey, W. L., E. P. Ericksen, and R. N. Juliani. 1976. "Emergent Ethnicity: A Review and Reformulation." *American Sociological Review* 41: 391–403.

Yllo, K., and M. Bograd. 1988. "Political and Methodological Debates in

Wife Abuse Research." In *Feminist Perspectives on Wife Abuse,* ed. K. Yllo and M. Bograd. Newbury Park: Sage.

Yung, B. R., and W. R. Hammond. 1994. "Native Americans." In *Reason to Hope: A Psychosocial Perspective on Violence and Youth,* ed. L. D. Eron, J. H. Gentry, and P. Schlegel, 133–44. Washington, DC: American Psychological Association.

Zahn, M. A. 1987. "Homicide in Nine American Cities: The Hispanic Case." In *Research Conference on Violence and Homicide in Hispanic Communities,* ed. J. Kraus, S. Sorenson, and P. Juarez, 13–30. Office of Minority Health, U.S. Department of Health and Human Services. Washington, DC: U.S. Government Printing Office.

Zahn, M. A., and P. C. Sagi. 1987. "Stranger Homicides in Nine American Cities." *Journal of Criminal Law and Criminology* 78: 377–97.

Zierler, W. E., W. E. Cunningham, R. Andersen, et al. 2000. "Violence Victimization after HIV Infection in a U.S. Probability Sample of Adult Patients in Primary Care." *American Journal of Public Health* 90, 2: 208–15.

Zimring, F. E. 1996. "Kids, Guns, and Homicide: Policy Notes on an Age-Specific Epidemic." *Law and Contemporary Problems* 59, 1 (Winter): 25–37.

Author Index

Moffit, T. R., 240
Molotch, H., 246
Monkkonnen, E., xxiii
Montagu, A., xxiii–xiv, xvi
Moore, J., 46, 47, 48, 49, 64
Moore, K. A., 313
Morenoff, J. D., 3, 20, 23, 31
Morgan, E. S., 341n8
Morrison, T., 175, 193, 196
Moss, A. A., 292
Moynihan, D. P., 189, 241
Much, N. C., 305, 307
Murray, C., xviii, xxii, 239, 240
Murray, C. A., 3
Mutchler, J. E., 249
Myers, L. J., 314
Myers, M. A., 346
Myrdal, G., 330

Naison, M., 304
National Center for Health Statistics, 282, 283
National Family Violence Survey, 177, 199
National Institute of Justice, 68
Neckerman, K. M., 245, 287, 294, 301
Neff, J. A., 186
Nelsen, C., 333, 333n3
Neugebauer-Visano, R., 124
Neville, H., 176n7, 183n16, 184
Newbold, G., 139, 140
Newham Monitoring Project, 159, 165
Newton, H. P., 316
New Zealand Council for Educational Research, 140
Ngozi-Brown, 316
Nielsen, A. L., 29
Nielsen, M., 117, 118, 119, 124
Nightingale, C. H., 16, 309
Nisbett, R. E., 319, 333, 333n3, 338, 346, 347, 349, 349n11, 351, 352

Nobles, W. W., 306
Norris, M., 139
Norton-Taylor, R., 155n1
Nourjah, P., 51, 52

O'Brien, P. H., 187
O'Carroll, P. W., 333, 352
O'Day, P., 320
Ogbu, J., 248, 249, 304
Ohlin, L., 257, 286
Okun, Lewis, 173n6
O'Leary, K. D., 188
Oliver, W., 255, 263–6, 269, 271, 274, 294, 295, 296, 297, 298, 300, 304
Olzak, S., 244, 245
O'Neil, J. M., 188
O'Neill, D. P., 139
Ormsby, C., 153
Osgood, W., 32, 240
Osofsky, J. D., 311
Ousey, G. C., 8, 20, 25
Ovesey, L., 189, 190, 255

Palloni, A., 28
Palmer, S., 320
Panayi, P., 156
Pargament, K., 313
Park, L., 305, 307
Parker, B., 304
Parker, G., 144
Parker, K. F., 91
Parker, R. N., 24, 26, 72
Parnas, R., 173
Paschall, M. J., 217, 218, 236
Pastore, A. L., 121, 122, 123
Pastorelli, C., 305
Patterson, G. R., 227
Pattillo-McCoy, M., 308
Payne, C., 313
Pearson, G. A., 159, 163
Peebles-Wilkins, W., 185
Peeples, F., 11, 236
Percy, A., 158, 159

Subject Index